THE ORIGINS OF YOGA

Yoga, Tantra and other forms of Asian meditation are practised in modernised forms throughout the world today, but most introductions to Hinduism or Buddhism tell only part of the story of how they developed. This book is an interpretation of the history of Indic religions up to around 1200 CE, with particular focus on the development of yogic and Tantric traditions. It assesses how much we really know about this period, and asks what sense we can make of the evolution of yogic and Tantric practices, which were to become such central and important features of the Indic religious scene. Its originality lies in seeking to understand these traditions in terms of the total social and religious context of South Asian society during this period, including the religious practices of the general population with their close engagement with family, gender, economic life and other pragmatic concerns.

GEOFFREY SAMUEL is Professorial Fellow at the School of Religious and Theological Studies at Cardiff University. His publications include *Mind, Body and Culture: Anthropology and the Biological Interface* (2006).

THE ORIGINS OF YOGA AND TANTRA

Indic Religions to the Thirteenth Century

GEOFFREY SAMUEL

CAMBRIDGE
UNIVERSITY PRESS

CAMBRIDGE
UNIVERSITY PRESS

University Printing House, Cambridge CB2 8BS, United Kingdom

One Liberty Plaza, 20th Floor, New York, NY 10006, USA

477 Williamstown Road, Port Melbourne, VIC 3207, Australia

4843/24, 2nd Floor, Ansari Road, Daryaganj, Delhi - 110002, India

79 Anson Road, #06-04/06, Singapore 079906

Cambridge University Press is part of the University of Cambridge.

It furthers the University's mission by disseminating knowledge in the pursuit of education, learning and research at the highest international levels of excellence.

www.cambridge.org
Information on this title: www.cambridge.org/9780521695343

First published 2008
4th printing 2013
First paperback edition 2017

A catalogue record for this publication is available from the British Library

Library of Congress Cataloging in Publication data
Samuel, Geoffrey.
The origins of yoga and tantra: Indic religions to the thirteenth century / Geoffrey Samuel.
p. cm.
Includes bibliographical references and index.
ISBN 978-0-521-87351-2 (hardback) – ISBN 978-0-521-69534-3 (pbk.)
1. India–Religion. 2. Yoga–History. 3. Tantrism–History. I. Title.
BL2005.S26 2008
294.09'01–dc22 2007046053

ISBN 978-0-521-87351-2 Hardback
ISBN 978-0-521-69534-3 Paperback

Contents

Figures

To my wife and fellow-scholar

Santi Rozario

who inspired this book and without whose help and support it would never have been written

Preface

This book is based on the Wilde Lectures in Natural and Comparative Religion, which I delivered at the University of Oxford in November and December 2002 under the title 'Indic religions to 1200 AD: a critical and anthropological approach'. Those who were present at the lectures will realise that this book differs from the lectures in other respects besides the title. Most of the text of the lectures is here, in one form or another, but I have taken the opportunity to rethink and extend the argument in many places. Unfortunately, the extensive visual material presented in the lectures has had for practical reasons mostly to be excluded from the book.

This is a relatively short book, however, on a very large subject, and there has been no attempt to be comprehensive. The book focuses on the development of the yogic and Tantric tradition in Indic societies, and while I have discussed the wider context in which these events happened in considerable detail, I have not attempted to provide a comprehensive history of Indian religion.

It is difficult to deal with language transcription consistently and systematically in a book that ranges over several bodies of scholarly literatures with different conventions. The omission of diacritics is nevertheless a major irritant and often deprives the reader of vital information, quite apart from rendering it impossible to know how words might be pronounced. My general strategy has been to give only modern place names and words that are thoroughly Anglicised without diacritics. I have generally given Sanskrit forms in preference to Pali or other Prakrits, though have employed the latter in contexts where it would seem clumsy or inappropriate to do otherwise (e.g. when I am citing the Pali Canon). I beg the reader's indulgence for remaining errors and inconsistencies; I am not a Sanskritist.

I wish to express my appreciation to the Electors of the Wilde Lectures for allowing me to give the lectures, and in particular to Richard Gombrich, who was a most kind and gracious host during my stay in Oxford, as indeed during my previous stay in 1999, and who helped me in very many respects in relation to this book. I would also wish to thank those who attended the lectures and provided valuable discussion and insight, and to many others with whom I have discussed some or all of these issues in recent years. The list is a long one, but I wish to mention at least Naman Ahuja, Nick Allen, Robert Beer, Jim Benson, Marieke Clarke, Lance Cousins, Max Deeg, Gill Farrer-Halls, Gavin Flood, Will Tuladhar-Douglas, David Gellner, Sanjukta Gupta, Adam Hardy, James Hegarty, Saunaka Rishi Das, Will Johnson, Klemens Karlsson, Kim Chong-Ho, Elizabeth de Michelis, Mogg and Kym Morgan, Ruth Rickard, Rob Mayer, Cathy Cantwell, Brian Bocking, Kate Crosby, Brenda McGregor, Ted Proferes, Robert Pryde, Julia Shaw, Andrew Skilton and Michael Willis. I apologise to others whom I have undoubtedly omitted. I particularly thank Thomas J. Hopkins for his graciousness in allowing me to read and refer to his unpublished work on the early history of Indian religions, Gunnar Haaland for allowing me to use a photograph of a thang-ka in his possession for the cover, and Rob Linrothe, Theresa McCullough, Mark Nichter, Asko Parpola, Sylvia Sax and Anne Vergati for providing photographs and for assistance in obtaining permission to use photographs. I also thank the National Museum of India, the Department of Archaeology and Museums, Government of Pakistan, for permission to use images and Peshawar Museum, Vidisha Museum, and the Indian Museum, Calcutta for permission to photograph objects in their collections. I thank Kate Brett, Gillian Dadd, Jodie Barnes and Sarah Barnes, of Cambridge University Press, for their friendly, helpful and efficient assistance with producing the book.

I also thank the University of Newcastle, New South Wales for allowing me to undertake two periods of study leave during which much of the research for the book was undertaken, the Leverhulme Trust and Brian Bocking for a visiting professorship at the School of Oriental and African Studies in 2003–4 which gave time for valuable further work on this project, and Cardiff University for appointing me to the Professorial Fellowship which has allowed its completion. I also wish to acknowledge the participants in the May 2004 workshop at SOAS on the politics of Asian religions, among them Saunaka Rishi Das, Madhu Kishwar, Rajiv Malhotra, Hiroko Kawanami, Chakraborty Ram Prasad and Ursula King, who helped greatly in formulating some of the ideas in Chapter 1 and elsewhere in the book. I do not think that at this point in time there is any fully satisfactory answer to the questions raised on that occasion, but I hope that this book will be in its way a positive contribution to the ends towards which that workshop was directed.

CHAPTER I

Introduction

The 'Indic Religions' of my subtitle are early forms of what we now know as Hinduism, Buddhism and Jainism. Their development, even with an arbitrary end-date of 1200 CE,[1] is a large topic, and only some aspects are covered in this book. I am particularly concerned with the growth of one of their central and most characteristic features, the group of traditions of mental and physical cultivation that developed into what we now know as 'yoga', 'Tantra', and 'meditation'. The indigenous terms vary, and do not correspond neatly to modern Western uses of these terms, but practices involving mental and physical cultivation, mostly directed towards the achievement of some kind of liberating insight,[2] are found in all the major religions originating in the Indian sub-continent.

The main body of the book consists of five chapters (3 to 7) focusing on the early growth of Buddhism, Jainism and the renunciate traditions within Brahmanical religion, roughly from the fourth to second centuries BCE, and three chapters (10 to 12) discussing the period from the fifth to twelfth centuries. The first of these periods corresponds, as far as we can tell, to the initial development of yogic and meditational techniques; the second period covers the growth of Tantric practices and the relationship between yoga and Tantra. The remaining chapters provide introduction and commentary, and sketch developments before, between and after these two key periods.

At the beginning of the twentieth century, these practices were scarcely known outside of South Asia and the Buddhist societies of Southeast and East Asia, a few specialist scholars and esoteric practitioners aside. By the beginning of the twenty-first century, millions, if not tens of millions, of

[1] I use BCE (before the common or Christian era) and use CE (common or Christian era) in place of the specifically Christian terms BC and AD, as is the general convention in religious studies.

[2] 'Liberating insight' is a generic term that I use in this book, following Johannes Bronkhorst (1993), for the various goals of the renunciate traditions of India (*nirvāṇa*, *mokṣa*, *bodhi*, *kevala*/*kaivalya*, etc.).

people around the world were practising Hindu yoga, Buddhist meditation and related traditions, and ideas, concepts and practices deriving from yogic and Tantric contexts had become a familiar part of global society. Although this massive social development is not dealt with in detail in these pages, it helps to explain why it is worth understanding these practices and their origins. Like many other people, I have lived through aspects of these developments in my own life, as a scholar of Tibetan and Indian religions and of social and cultural anthropology, as a friend and acquaintance of numerous people involved with the global spread of yogic and Tantric practices, and as an intermittent practitioner myself of several varieties of these traditions.

The impetus behind this book is the desire to understand what these developments mean, and what yoga, meditation and Tantra have become and might still become within their new global context. Part of the answer to that question has to come from a study of contemporary developments in their own terms. There have been quite a few studies of Western adoptions of Asian spiritual techniques and approaches, including some of my own, and there is plenty more to be done along these lines. Another part of the answer, though, involves re-examining the history of these practices within the Indic religions from which they originated. That is the focus of the present work.

Yoga, meditation and Tantra are complex and problematic labels, and rather than attempting to define them in detail at this point, I shall leave the scope and meaning of our investigation to emerge in the course of the book. Perhaps it is enough at this point to say that we are concerned with disciplined and systematic techniques for the training and control of the human mind-body complex, which are also understood as techniques for the reshaping of human consciousness towards some kind of higher goal.[3] In an earlier work, I have made some suggestions about the anthropological analysis of mind-body processes in human life (Samuel 1990). This book only occasionally ventures into such areas; it is primarily an attempt at the historical understanding of the development of a particular set of techniques and practices within Indic religions.

The most usual starting point for a history of Indic religions is the religion of the Indus Valley cultural tradition in what is now Pakistan and

[3] For any readers who are familiar with yoga primarily as a physical exercise, as one often encounters it today, it is important to appreciate that the physical aspects of yoga were historically a secondary part of a set of techniques that was aimed at training mind and body as a whole, and that (given some quibbles about exactly what is meant by 'religion') had a specifically religious orientation. See e.g. Alter 2005; de Michelis 2004.

North-West India, best known from the extensive remains of the early urban societies at Mohenjo-Daro, Harappa and elsewhere. These cities correspond to what is now known as the 'Integration Era' of the Indus Valley cultural tradition, and dated to around 2600 to 1900 BCE. The large body of imagery found on the seals at these urban sites has been particularly significant for scholars seeking to understand the religious life of the Indus Valley peoples. In particular, ever since Sir John Marshall's suggestion in the 1930s that one of the Indus Valley seals represented an early version of the god Śiva in a specifically yogic posture, it has been common to trace the origins of yoga and of various other aspects of Indian religion back to the Indus Valley cultural tradition (Marshall 1931: vol. I, 7).

I begin my account of the history of Indic religions by discussing some of these interpretations, but I should make it clear from the start that I do not feel that we can learn very much from this early material. Given what we now know about cultural continuities in the archaeological record between the Indus Valley cultural tradition and succeeding populations in the region, it is certainly possible that there was some continuity in the area of religion. The difficulty is that the early evidence is far from unambiguous, and that it is almost always interpreted by reading later religious forms into it.

Consider the well-known image (Fig. 1.1) that Marshall regarded as depicting a three-headed god, seated in a yogic posture, and saw as a prototype of Rudra or Śiva as Lord of the Beasts (Paśupati). This story has been widely accepted and the presence of a 'proto-Śiva' figure in the Indus Valley is perhaps the most frequent assertion made about religion in that period. However, on closer examination, the case for a 'proto-Śiva' interpretation of this image is far from conclusive. To begin with, Śiva is not shown in this posture in later iconography.[4] Nor is he ever shown with a horned headdress in later times. Nor is it clear that the image has three heads. Nor is it self-evident that the animals are to be read in terms of the main figure being a 'Lord of the Beasts'.

In fact, this image has been read in a variety of other ways. Alf Hiltebeitel has suggested that the head represents a buffalo (others have preferred a bull), and that the four surrounding animals correspond to the Vedic gods of the four directions (Hiltebeitel 1978). For Bridget and Raymond Allchin the image is ithyphallic (1982: 214). Herbert Sullivan and Shubhangana Atre have both argued that it does not depict a god at all, but a female deity (Sullivan 1964; Atre 1998).[5] As for the posture of the figure on this and similar

[4] For early Śiva iconography, see N. Joshi 1984 and Srinivasan 1984.
[5] For further interpretations, see Dhyansky 1987: 90–1.

Figure 1.1. 'Proto-Śiva' Seal (M-304)

seals, for Yan Dhyansky (1987: 94–9) and Thomas McEvilley (2002: 104), it is clearly the yogic posture *mūlābandhāsana*, and has to be understood in terms of proto-Tantric techniques aimed at driving 'the sperm-marrow-soul fluid up the spinal channel' (McEvilley 2002: 110; cf. Dhyansky 1987: 100). Sullivan notes that the posture 'seems to us a natural enough one and need not be a yogic posture at all' (1964: 120), while Asko Parpola suggests that this 'so-called "yoga" posture may simply imitate the Proto-Elamite way of representing seated bulls' (1994: 250, caption to fig. 14.16)! The only reasonable conclusion is that we do not actually *know* how to interpret the figure, nor do we know what he or she represents.

Another possibly more explicit piece of imagery is the famous ritual scene shown on the Mohenjo-daro seal M-1186.

It seems reasonably safe to interpret this as a ritual scene, since a simpler version of the same scene is shown on several other seals, such as Harappa H-177 (illustrated in Parpola 1994: 110, fig. 7.13) and Mohenjo-Daro M-488 (illustrated in Farmer, Sproat and Witzel 2004). All three of these seals show a divine or human figure standing in a tree-frame of some kind (Parpola

Figure 1.2. Seal Mohenjo-Daro (M-1186)

reads this as a fig-tree (1994: 256–61), another human figure kneeling or sitting before him/her, and an animal with long wavy horns. One might read the figure in the tree as a standing version of the 'proto-Śiva', and the kneeling or seated figure as a priest or priestess who is worshipping him/her, though it may be noted that in the two Mohenjo Daro seals both wear the horned headdresses (if that is what they are), and in the Harappan seal neither do.

For Parpola, the worshipper on M-1186 is 'probably the chief priest of the deity who possessed this seal' and the animal is a human-faced markhor goat. In front of the priest is a low table 'on which is placed a human head, identifiable as that of a warrior from its "double-bun" hairstyle which recurs elsewhere in fighting scenes and is of Mesopotamian origin' (Parpola 1999b: 249). The seven figures at the bottom are apparently female, since they wear their hair in a plait, so the rest of the interpretation is straightforward:

The tree is probably the banyan fig, and the deity inside it a predecessor of Durgā, the goddess of victory and love, to whom a human sacrifice of a brave warrior has been made. The decapitated victim is likely to have been the groom in a 'sacred marriage' performed at the new year festival, and to have personified the predecessor of Rudra/Skanda/Rohita/Agni. [. . .] The seven females at the bottom probably represent the 'Seven Mothers' of this war-god, the stars of the Pleiades, which became the constellation of the new year when the nakṣatra calendar was compiled around the 23rd century BC. The markhor goat (*śarabha* in Sanskrit) is a symbol of Agni in Vedic texts; according to the Kālikā-Purāṇa, the Goddess most appreciates man as a sacrificial victim, but next to a human victim she likes best the *śarabha*. The human face of this beast in the seal may indicate that a ritual of head exchange was practised [. . .]. (Parpola 1999b: 249–50; see also 1994: 259–61)

Now, I must admit that all this *could* be true. What is happening here, however, is that Parpola, like other interpreters of these seals, is straining to interpret objects that are far from clear, and is reading them in terms of his knowledge of a wide range of texts and practices dating from a much later period. If we did not have these parallels in mind, it is unlikely that we would read the figure in the tree-frame as Durgā or Kālī, let alone see the scene as implying a human sacrifice of a god impersonating Rudra/Skanda etc.[6] It is hardly obvious that the object on the table is a human head, for one thing, though Farmer, Sproat and Witzel are apparently convinced, since they read the equivalent object on Mohenjo Daro M-488 as another human head (2004: 46, Fig. 13). It should also be noted that the *Kālikā Purāṇa* is generally dated to the eleventh or twelfth century CE (Urban 2001), so that Parpola is assuming that the Goddess's tastes in sacrificial meat remained unchanged for around three thousand years.[7]

However, as with the 'proto-Śiva' figure, a variety of other interpretations are possible. Jayakar, looking at the same seal (M-1186), reads the figure in the tree as a *yakṣī*, and the seven figures at the bottom as *apsarās* or virgins rather than the Seven Mothers. The kneeling figure is an alchemist-priest, and the trunk of the tree is 'shaped like the *garbha yantra*, the womb vessel, wherein the ultimate secrets of alchemy were revealed' (Jayakar 1989: 73). In her interpretation, the object that Parpola reads as the head of a decapitated warrior has been transformed into the Śrī Cakra, the 'mark and altar of the goddess' (1989: 73). Shubhangana Atre reads the kneeling figure as a 'High Priestess', noting that this 'is obvious from her attire which exactly resembles that of the deity' (Atre 1998: 168), and the seven figures, rather as in Jayakar's version, as 'vestal virgins'; she neglects to mention the alleged warrior's head, but interprets the scene as part of a sequence illustrating the

6 Note that Parpola needs to conflate Rudra and Skanda, because Rudra (Śiva) is the goddess's consort in later Brahmanical mythology, but it is Skanda who is associated with the 'Seven Mothers'.

7 For a more detailed presentation of Parpola's overall perspective on the origins of 'Śākta Tantrism', see Parpola 2002a.

retirement of an older High Priestess and the consecration of a replacement from among the seven vestal virgins (1998: 167–8).

We note that both Parpola and Jayakar read 'Tantric' themes into the material (the sacred marriage and human sacrifice for Parpola, the priest-alchemist and Śrī Cakra for Jayakar), but the Tantric themes are completely different from each other and have nothing in common. Atre's interpretation is not 'Tantric' at all. Clearly, these seals are not self-explanatory. In all three cases, the reading of the seal depends on a whole set of assumptions about the nature of Indus Valley religion.[8]

I find similar difficulties with other readings of the seal-images, such as Jayakar's interpretation of what she regards as a series of seals depicting a goddess and a tree (Jayakar 1989: 71–3 and pls. 5–8). Here, again, the possibility of onward continuity of tree and goddess cults is quite tempting, but completely unproven. One has to strain quite hard to find continuities, and there is ample scope for fantasy.

In any case, we have little or no idea what these so-called 'seals' were used for, which makes it difficult to be sure that the images represent scenes of religious significance. They are too fragile for use for labelling consignments of goods, which seems to have been the function of apparently similar seals in the Mesopotamian context. Farmer, Sproat and Witzel apparently assume that they have a ritual function, and that the 'inscriptions' (which for them are non-linguistic) are collections of symbols of deities or celestial forces. Again they could be right, but there is little to inspire any degree of certainty in this or any other interpretation (Farmer, Sproat and Witzel 2004: 41–3).

Parpola's reading of a 'sacred marriage' theme into M-1186 (Fig. 1.2) is premised on his assumption of a linkage with sacred marriages in Mesopotamian religion (1994: 256), a suggestion also made by the late Prof. D. D. Kosambi. Kosambi suggested that the Great Bath at Mohenjo Daro served as an artificial 'lotus pond' constructed for ritual purposes, and was surrounded by rooms in which visiting men took part in ritual sexual union with 'female attendant representatives of the mother goddess to whom the citadel complex belonged'. 'This is not far-fetched', Kosambi continues.

[8] One could easily provide further possible interpretations. If the kneeling figure is seen as female and a high priestess, for example, as argued by Atre, the standing animal could represent her consort and Sacred King, giving another variant of Parpola's (Frazer-style) sacred marriage. This would link with the well-known seal from Chanhujo-daro which may (or may not) represent a 'bison bull about to have intercourse with a priestess lying on the ground' (Parpola 1994: 256, fig. 14.32), not to say with Biardeau's work on goddesses and buffalo-gods in modern South India (Biardeau 1989). One could then interpret the numerous representations of individual bulls and other animals on seals as representing Sacred Kings of particular communities. But the real point is that all these interpretations, Parpola's, Jayakar's, Atre's and my own, have to be regarded as speculative and unproven.

'The temples of Ishtar in Sumer and Babylon had similar practices in which girls of the leading families had also to participate'. These priestesses were the origin of the later Indic mythology of the *apsaras*, 'irresistibly beautiful women who would entice men to consort with them and eventually lead the heroes to destruction' (Kosambi 1965: 68).

Kosambi was often a sensitive and insightful scholar, and such an interpretation might, like some of the other interpretations we have been considering here, enable us to take back the origins of sexual yoga in India by another 2000 years, but it does, like the work of Parpola, Jayakar and others, seem to go rather a long way beyond the evidence.

Other attempts to make positive assertions about Indus Valley religion strike me as equally conjectural (e.g. Jairazbhoy 1994). I am in no position to say that any of these interpretations are incorrect, but they certainly cannot all be right. Since there is no obvious way to choose between them, they do not actually take us very far. At the end of the day, we know quite a lot about the daily life of the people of the Indus Valley urban civilisation, but little or nothing for certain about their religious practices. In particular, it seems to me that the evidence for the yogic or 'Tantric' practices is so dependent on reading later practices into the material that it is of little or no use for constructing any kind of history of practices. I am therefore taking a more cautious view in the present work, and assume that we do not have conclusive evidence for yogic or 'Tantric' practices in the Indus Valley cultural tradition.

I find myself equally unpersuaded by attempts to see yogic or 'Tantric' practices in their developed forms in the Ṛgveda or Atharvaveda. There are certainly indications both of magical ritual for pragmatic purposes, and of ecstatic religious practices, 'shamanic' if the reader wishes to use the term. I shall discuss some of these in later chapters (7 and 9). There is also conceptual material, such as the role of 'breath' (*prāṇa*) within the body, which is taken up and reworked by later yogic and 'Tantric' theory.

There is nothing, however, to imply yogic practice, in the sense of a developed set of techniques for operating with the mind-body complex. Our best evidence to date suggests that such practices developed in the same ascetic circles as the early *śramaṇa* movements (Buddhists, Jainas and Ājīvikas), probably in around the sixth and fifth centuries BCE.

It is for these reasons that Part One of my book is focused in this period, which follows on what has been called the 'Second Urbanisation' of South Asia (the first being the growth of the Indus Valley cities in the third millennium BCE). The growth of cities and early states in the sixth and fifth centuries BCE was the context for the early *śramaṇa* movements, and this is where, as far as we can tell, the new techniques of spiritual development were first developed and propagated.

As for 'Tantra', much depends on what we mean by that much-contested term, which has a wide variety of meanings within the Indic traditions themselves. The central issue with which I deal in Part Two, however, is the development of the relatively coherent set of techniques and practices which appears in a more or less complete form in Buddhist and Śaiva texts in the ninth and tenth centuries CE. This comprises a number of elements: elaborate deity visualisations, in which the practitioner identifies with a divine figure at the centre of a *maṇḍala* or geometrical array of deities; fierce male and particularly female deities; the use of transgressive 'Kāpālika'-style practices associated with cremation-grounds and polluting substances linked to sex and death, and internal yogic practices, including sexual techniques, which are intended to achieve health and long life as well as liberating insight.

The various components of this set of spiritual techniques appear to come from different sources. I attempt to trace their growth, and to make sense of their adoption within relatively mainstream Buddhist, Jaina and Brahmanical contexts.

Thus my main narrative runs approximately from about 500 BCE to about 1200 CE. These limits are somewhat arbitrary, particularly given the uncertainties of dating for the early part of this period. 'About 500 BCE', however, represents a point at which I assume that an early form of 'Brahmanical' culture using an Indo-Aryan language had been firmly established in parts of Northern India (present day Punjab, Haryana and Western UP), but had not yet reached dominance over the North-Eastern areas (including present-day Bihar, West Bengal and Bangladesh), or over the remainder of South Asia. The year 1200 CE represents a point at which Muslim rule had been established over most of North and Northeast India, and the main remaining centres of Buddhist culture in these regions had been destroyed. This was far from the end-point of Indic religious developments, but it forms a convenient point at which to close a narrative that is already seeking to encompass a very large range of cultural time and space.

Islam, of course, had an impact on India and other areas of Indic culture well before 1200 CE. The story of the early stages of its incorporation within Indic societies is an important and significant one, but it goes well beyond my personal competence, and I have not attempted to tell it here. As for Buddhism, it continued to develop both within and beyond South

Asia after 1200 CE, but that development entered a new phase, and took place in very different conditions. Part of that story, the part that involved the people of Tibet, was the subject of one of my earlier books, *Civilized Shamans* (Samuel 1993), and in some ways the present work is a kind of prequel to that book.[9]

The study of Indic religious traditions has to be approached today with some sensitivity and care. During the main period discussed in this book, Buddhism, Jainism and forms of Brahmanical religion ancestral to modern Hinduism were all vital parts of the South Asian religious scene, alongside a basic level of folk and village religious practice that still exists today in various forms throughout South Asia and is best regarded as neither Buddhist, Jaina nor Brahmanical.[10] Today's Hindus, Buddhists and Jains have their own traditions of scholarship and study, and their own ways of understanding themselves and their religions. Much of this may be a modern development, a reaction to the unequal dialogue with Christianity and other Western forms of knowledge during colonial times (cf. Lopez 1995; King 1999; Viswanathan 2003). The modernist self-understandings that have resulted from this dialogue, however, are a reality in the lives of thousands of millions of people in Asia and the Asian diasporas. These people have a legitimate concern with how their religions are portrayed. At times, however, this can lead to problematic attempts by pressure groups to control what is said about Indic religions and eliminate features that do not fit neatly into a spiritually sanitised and benign picture. This is unfortunate, since attempts at excessive purity in the religious field generally backfire.

At the same time, Western societies have developed their own modes of understanding Asian religions, both popular and academic, and these undoubtedly have their own flaws and limitations. Critics of Western academia often fail to appreciate the deep and positive engagement with Indic religions that underlies much 'Orientalist' and more recent scholarship. This aside, I would hardly want to suggest that all of this work is beyond criticism.[11]

9 Three substantial chapters (Twenty to Twenty-Two) of *Civilized Shamans* discussed the history of Buddhism in India up to around 1200 CE. I realised at the time that an adequate treatment of the material in those chapters was a much larger project than I could then undertake. In subsequent years, I have become increasingly involved with the early history of Indic religions, particularly of Tantric Buddhism. The present book is to some degree an attempt to take stock of my work in this area.

10 We can see these, for example, in the women's rituals of marriage (*strī-ācār*) practiced by Hindus, Muslims and followers of other religions in West Bengal and Bangladesh today and in similar rituals elsewhere in South Asia (Fruzzetti 1990; Good 1991).

11 Much of this discussion in its modern form goes back to the late Edward Said's *Orientalism* (1978). Said's argument developed primarily in relation to the Arab context. The Indian and various

The story of Indic religions is nevertheless an important one, and part of the world's heritage. It would be unfortunate if scholars, Asian or Western, were to feel that it has become too politically sensitive to give as honest as possible an account of that story.

The central concern of this book is to sketch the development of the techniques of mental and physical cultivation that came to form a key element of the religious traditions of the Indic world. This is, however, part of the wider story of the growth of Indic civilisation and of societies in South and Southeast Asia, and this story, like that of other civilisations and societies, contains its fair share of warfare, destruction, human exploitation and suffering. The lotus of spiritual enlightenment, as Indian traditions themselves so often remind us, grows out of the mud of everyday life. I have tried to include both sides of this picture, the sophisticated spiritual culture and the solid ground of ordinary life out of which it grows. A prettified and unrealistic picture of a religious tradition is of little use to anyone.

Thus I hope that this book will be found useful by Westerners interested in Asian religions (including scholars working in this and related areas) and also by Asian members of the religious traditions that I am discussing. I hope too that it will be found of value by a third group of people: Westerners and other non-Asians who have become personally involved in the practice of one or another of these religious traditions. It is particularly difficult to get a clear view of a religious tradition when one encounters it in a cultural setting very different from its own, mediated perhaps through English or another Western language, and without the social and cultural context that gives sense to many of its practices. Indeed, that context has changed radically in the societies where these religions grew up as well. I feel that there are many important things that the world can learn from Asian religious traditions, but that our ability to integrate their knowledge into the evolving body of understandings on which our now global civilisation conducts its affairs will be greatly aided by knowing more about the origins of these traditions. That is one of the principal aims of this book.

It is important in approaching subject-matter as large and complex as that considered here to recognise the limits of our knowledge. A striking feature of the last few decades of Indological research has been not only the growth of new knowledge but also the gradual realisation that much of what scholars thought that they already knew was far less secure than

Southeast Asian contexts have both similarities and differences, reflecting in part different schools of colonial scholarship (British, French, Dutch, German) and different periods. Cf. Inden 1992; Mackenzie 1995; King 1999; Viswanathan 2003; D. Smith 2003.

had been assumed. This is perhaps most striking in the area of chronology, where a series of conjectural datings adopted as working hypotheses by the great nineteenth-century Indologists and Buddhologists had become a kind of received doctrine. It is now clear that many of the details were wrong and that the scheme as a whole is quite shaky and problematic (see Chapter 2). This is hardly a surprise, given the scanty evidence on which our chronological understandings were initially constructed, but certainly for someone approaching the field from the outside it is striking how unsure we are about the dating of many crucial events, people or texts.

Our knowledge of the texts is also less secure than might appear at first sight in a world where works like the Vedas, the Upaniṣads and large parts of the Pali canon have been translated repeatedly into European languages. The Vedas were not written down until a fairly late stage, and I do not believe myself that they can be taken as a literal and accurate witness for any specific stage of early Indic religion. It is far from clear exactly what the established text of the Pali Canon amounts to in terms of its relation to early Buddhism (see e.g. Collins 1990), or when to date any particular Upaniṣad or section of an Upaniṣad. Similar problems attend texts such as the *Rāmāyaṇa* or the *Mahābhārata*, the Purāṇas, or the Jaina canon, though the precise ways in which our previous certainties have been eroded varies.

As a totality, this uncertainty is part of the corrosive effect of a pluralistic intellectual universe on the established assumptions of a field, a phenomenon that can be observed in many parts of today's intellectual universe. In the case of Asia, there is also the specific issue of post-colonialist critiques, and the complex ways in which Westerners and Asians position themselves in relation to the many tense and difficult political issues which have affected the study of Asia in the Western academy in recent years.

I will say a little more about what might be called the 'standard view' of Indian religions and their history in Chapter 2, but I do not intend to rehearse its problems here at length. This is a job that has been done with commendable enthusiasm – some people clearly think a little too much enthusiasm – by a variety of scholars in recent years under the impact of post-modernist and post-colonialist thought.[12]

On the whole, I feel that there is a good deal to be said for these critiques. My job in this book, however, is somewhat different: it is to ask what we could put in the place of the problematic conceptions which have come to dominate this field of study. After all, terms such as 'Hinduism',

12 See King 1999 for a good summary; also Viswanathan 2003 and D. Smith 2003 for two contrasting recent perspectives.

'Buddhism', and the like, and definitions of those religions in ways ultimately derivative from Christian theology, for all of their questionable origins, have now become very real parts of contemporary discourse, and central to the self-definition of present-day Asian nations. Is there some way in which we can move beyond these damaging and limiting perspectives?

To an anthropologist like myself, at least, it comes fairly naturally to argue for a wider and more inclusive understanding of religion, and to see Brahmanical Hinduism, Buddhism and Jainism as variant developments from a shared basis of relationship to the problems of everyday life. That is essentially the view from which I work in this book. However, I would not want my approach to be read as 'anthropological' in a narrow sense, and it should be plain to most readers that it is not. As far as I am concerned, no point of view – textual, anthropological, internal or external – can be taken as absolute or primary. All may have truth-content (using those words in a general rather than a technical philosophical sense). We are almost always better off integrating as many different perspectives as possible into our understanding. Encounters between disciplines can be bruising at times, with a sense on each side that the other's presuppositions, if accepted, will undermine one's own position. However, there are usually ways of going forward which lead us to greater understanding by integrating the key points of both perspectives.

In arguing for the fundamental commonality of the Indic religious background (a very different position, it should be added, from seeing Buddhism merely as a development from or reaction to 'Hinduism', which is a position that by now has hopefully lost any scholarly respectability it may once have had), I am aware of the political dimensions of what I am saying. In any case, one can scarcely speak of investigating the history of Indic religions today without being aware of the contemporary political implications of any such inquiry. As the conflict over the site of the former mosque of Babur at Ayodhyā – now claimed as the birth-site of Lord Rāma – has demonstrated, religion nowadays can be an immensely divisive and destructive force within Indian society. The Ayodhyā conflict, which led to several hundred deaths in Gujarat in 2002, is only one of a number of such conflicts of varying degrees of intensity. Elsewhere in India, Hindus and Sikhs, and Hindus and Kashmiri Muslims have been embroiled in bitter and long-standing conflicts in which religion plays a major role. Nor are things much better in other parts of South Asia: Sinhalese religious nationalism has been a major contributor to the Sri Lankan conflict, while both Pakistan and Bangladesh have seen violence against religious minorities in recent times.

Yet this religious nationalism, or 'communalism', as it is known in India, is in many ways a modern imposition. It has to be understood in terms of the colonial and post-colonial social transformations of the sub-continent, and the globalising forces to which South Asia, like the rest of the world, is now subject. The similarities between the religious nationalisms of South Asia and those of West Asia, the Philippines, Indonesia or the Balkans – or even Northern Ireland – are scarcely coincidental, though I will not argue the point further here (cf. Fox 1996; Castells 1997: 1–67). What it is more important to appreciate is that the societies of South Asia before, say, the mid-nineteenth century, while not entirely free from religious conflicts, had much more fluid and less categorical conceptualisations of religious identity than we now see.

Thus the creation of a Sikh religion and identity distinct from 'Hinduism' is a fairly recent and still-contested development (e.g. Oberoi 1994). As for Hindus and Muslims, in many parts of India they regularly took part in each other's festivals and visited each other's temples and shrines, while some communities were quite difficult to categorise as either 'Hindu' or 'Muslim'. There has been pressure from both sides for clearer definition and more puristic forms of observance, but even nowadays the boundary between 'Hindu' and 'Muslim' is often hazier and more complex than one might think at first sight (see e.g. Salomon 1991; Openshaw 1997; Saheb 1998; Mayaram 2000; Gottschalk 2000). I do not intend to idealise the past here, but the changes have been real, and not for the better, and interpretations of the Asian past have gained a new salience as justifications for contemporary political positions.

Thus it is that a study of the past, even of the relatively distant period discussed in this book, is far from irrelevant to the present. We are, I think, at a point in time when stressing the commonalities and the deep mutual implications of the religious traditions of South and Southeast Asia, from a perspective sympathetic to, but by no means identified with, any of them, may be a useful exercise for reasons that go beyond the purely scholarly. If this book can, in any way, help to point to ways of going beyond some of the entrenched hostilities between Asian communities, then the exercise will have been well worthwhile.

CHAPTER 2

Stories and sources

The standard story of the development of Indic religions was developed in the mid to late nineteenth century, in a collaboration between Western scholars on the one side, and Hindu and Buddhist scholars and intellectuals on the other. This story was essentially that of the development of a number of separate religions, principally Hinduism, Buddhism and Jainism, with Hinduism being seen as the earliest and Buddhism and Jainism as reactions against it. The narrative began with the hymns of the Ṛgveda, thought to be the oldest existing texts in an Indian language. The Ṛgveda was seen as representing the earliest stage of Hinduism and subsequent stages as a series of developments from it. The Ṛgveda was treated as, in effect, a foundational text with a somewhat similar role to that of the Five Books of the Jewish Torah in relation to traditional accounts of Judaism, Christianity and Islam.

The story continued through the remaining texts of the Vedic corpus, down to such 'late Vedic' texts as the Upaniṣads, Śrauta Sūtras, Gṛhya Sūtras and Dharma Sūtras. All these texts were placed in a historical sequence, and seen as defining an early Hinduism, composed of sacrificial rituals, legal prescriptions and philosophical speculations, against which the *śramaṇa* movements (Jainism and Buddhism) reacted.

The great epics (*Mahābharata* and *Rāmāyaṇa*) formed the defining texts of the next period on the Hindu side, and the Purāṇas, along with the writings of the Vedānta philosophers and the *bhakti* poets, of the next, with the Tantras as a rather uncomfortable parallel development. Buddhist and Jain histories, after the initial break with Hinduism, were presented as largely separate stories. The Buddhist story focused on the preservation of a rational and philosophical 'early' Buddhism by the Theravādins, and the development of new philosophical schools by the Mahāyānists. Jainism, like Theravāda Buddhism, was seen primarily in terms of the preservation of rational and philosophical early traditions. Tantra again formed a somewhat unwelcome parallel development on both sides, though the influence of

Tibetan lamas on Buddhist scholarship in recent years has meant that Vajrayāna Buddhism has gained a new respectability.

The above story may be something of a parody, and most contemporary scholars give a more nuanced and tentative version, but it is still recognisable behind modern accounts of the development of Indic religions prior to the arrival of Islam in the subcontinent. Yet, as has been repeatedly pointed out by numerous scholars, most parts of this story are problematic, and the story as a whole is largely untenable.

Many of the problems here derive from the tendency of past Western scholars, whether or not themselves Protestant Christians, to see religion in terms of Protestant Christianity, a religion that defined itself against its rivals in terms of a return to the 'authentic' texts of the Bible. The Protestant polemic against Catholicism was largely carried out in terms of accusations of deviation from the 'original' teachings of Jesus as seen in the New Testament. These deviations consisted in the growth of magical and superstitious practices, unnecessary theological complexities, and a subordination of religion to political and economic purposes. Religions in this model were founded by an inspired teacher who created a body of texts that were then systematically misinterpreted and distorted through succeeding generations. There was little point in studying what people actually did, since it was only valid if it reflected the texts.[1]

This Protestant model formed a template that was repeatedly applied by Western scholars to Asian religious traditions. At the same time, it provided a model in terms of which nineteenth and twentieth century Hindu and Buddhist reformers, from the Brahmo and Arya Samaj down to the Mahabodhi Society, attempted to reshape their own religious traditions. Buddhism, which had its own narrative of teaching and decay, fitted the model particularly neatly. The Buddha could be seen as a humane religious reformer on the model of Jesus, teaching through parables and other simple and straightforward means. In this perspective the Buddha became a kind of Christ figure reacting against a legalistic and caste-bound Brahmanical priesthood, the Hindu equivalent of the Sadducees and Pharisees of the New Testament account.

Theravāda Buddhism, with its claims to be a pure, uncorrupted tradition, fitted neatly into this view of religion. The Pali Canon was seen by both Sinhalese and many Western scholars as the original version of a body of scriptures later expanded and corrupted by later Mahāyāna or, worse,

[1] There was also an interest on the part of Catholic scholars, especially Jesuit and other missionary orders working in Asia, with local traditions of ritual practice. This led to some important early studies of Asian ritual life, though it arguably had little effect on a dominant view of religion as based around 'belief', at least in the English-speaking world.

Tantric clerics. Sinhalese Buddhist reformers in the late nineteenth and early twentieth century emphasised the rational and 'scientific' nature of Theravāda Buddhism, so that seeing the Buddha in this light also provided a useful weapon against the Christian dominance of European society. This also had the advantage that the Asian Buddhism actually being practised by most Asian Buddhists (including most Buddhists in Sri Lanka and Southeast Asia) could be dismissed as a superstitious and degenerate development of the real teachings of the Buddha. This left a scholarly elite as the true interpreters of the teachings of the Buddha, as well as opening the way to racist interpretations of Buddhism as an 'Aryan' teaching corrupted by its Asian environment (cf. Deeg 2006). Such interpretations are out of fashion, but the idea of a 'real' Buddhism that can be found in the Pali Canon rather than the practice of historical or contemporary Buddhists remains alive and well.

The model worked rather less well on the Hindu side, since the Vedic hymns are not much like the Pentateuch either in content or in the way in which they were used by later Indian religious traditions. Hindu religious reformers did not necessarily use the early Vedic texts as their primary 'scriptural' basis, since these were poorly adapted to such a function; Rām Mohan Roy looked rather to the Upaniṣads and the *Brahma Sūtra*.

Increasingly, scholars have seen 'Hinduism' as a problematic term for the pre-modern period, at least before the mid-first millennium CE, when a religious tradition with recognisable similarities to modern Brahmanical Hinduism took shape under the patronage of the Guptas and subsequent dynasties. The terms 'Buddhism' and 'Jainism' are still widely used for the early period, but they too tend to carry questionable Western assumptions about the nature of religion along with them.[2]

In particular, for Christianity, exclusivity has always been a critical issue. One cannot be a Christian and a member of another religion at the same time.[3] Yet virtually all Buddhists in Southeast Asia have also been involved in the cult of local gods and spirits, just as most East Asian Buddhists have

[2] Both 'Jaina' and 'Hindu' as terms used to designate religions date from the second millennium CE (see Flügel 2005 for 'Jaina'), though terms relating to 'Buddha' were used as self designations by Buddhists from relatively early times.

[3] In part this is linked to the misleading and confusing Western identification of religion with 'beliefs' (in the sense of 'statements held to be true'). 'Belief' and the related word 'faith' in religious statements ('I believe in/have faith in Jesus Christ' etc.) have shifted historically from meaning something like 'I have trust in, I have made a personal commitment to the Christian deity' to meaning 'I affirm that the Christian deity exists and that some version of Christian theology is a correct account of the nature of the universe'. If religion is identified with theology and belief statements, then being involved in two religions at the same time implies being committed to two irreconciliable sets of statements about the nature of the universe. This, however, is a problem for philosophers and theologians, not for most ordinary human beings. See e.g. Southwold 1979, 1983.

also been involved in Confucian, Taoist, Shinto or shamanic cults. We will see more of this relationship in later chapters. As for Jainism, the question of whether it is a part of 'Hinduism' or a separate 'religion' is far from resolved even for many contemporary Jains. The terms 'Buddhism' and 'Jainism' also tend to suggest that these 'religions' are primarily modes of understanding the universe (the first question for a naïve Western student even today tends to be 'What do they believe in?') rather than ways of living in relation to the universe (including one's fellow human beings).

The implicit (and occasionally explicit) parallels with the development of Western religions in the 'standard story' are dated historical baggage, but they still have a real presence in and beyond the Western academy. At the same time, the kind of multi-dimensional approach that I undertake here, where textual, epigraphic, iconographic and archaeological material are seen as mutually-illuminating bodies of evidence, is widely accepted in theory, if not always in practice, and there are plenty of studies that have explored such combined approaches for particular periods or topics (cf. Schopen 1997a; Kosambi 2002a).

Yet there are still problems. The histories of the Buddhist and Jain traditions remain far from adequately integrated into the general history of Indic religions, and the development of specialist fields of Buddhist, Hindu and Jaina studies, dealing with distinct bodies of texts, has meant that this division has become increasingly entrenched in academic approaches. Even to write a general history of Indic religions is at this point in time an undertaking that is somewhat against the grain of academic work.

A recurrent issue is in effect a derivation from the Protestant model and the primarily textual approach to religion that it encourages. This is the question of how much of the ongoing development of Indic religions can be traced back to the texts of the Vedas, meaning both the hymns of the Ṛgveda and the extensive body of early material that grew around them, down to the Brāhmaṇas, Āraṇyakas, Upaniṣads and the ritual and legal manuals (Śrauta Sūtras, Gṛhya Sūtras, Dharma Sūtras), and how much needs to be assigned to 'external' influences. Approaches that emphasise continuity are sometimes called 'orthogenetic' (as opposed to 'heterogenetic'). Such approaches can be found among Buddhist scholars as well as scholars of Tantra and of Brahmanical Hinduism.

By necessity, most serious nineteenth-century approaches to Hinduism and Buddhism were in effect orthogenetic. Western scholars of this period were working primarily with texts and their primary tools were philological. A significant part of their task was to arrange the texts in a presumed historical sequence of development. The hymns of the Ṛgveda were clearly the most archaic texts around in terms of their linguistic features and were therefore assumed to be the oldest, especially in view of their evident affinity with the early texts of Iranian religion.

Much of this changed in the course of the twentieth century, and for a variety of reasons, both political and academic. On the political side, 'racial' theories of Aryan origins become popular among a variety of groups: racially-motivated Western scholars, Indian groups for whom the myth of 'Aryan' racial identity provided a positive self-image, Tamil nationalists who developed the mythic corollary of an indigenous 'Dravidian' racial identity. The racial foundations of such ideas were largely discredited by the mid-twentieth century. The assumed linkage between culture and genetics is now evident nonsense, and in any case recent developments in genetic research have made it clear that, as with most or all modern human populations, the genetic variety and complexity of the population of South Asia today is far too great to be encompassed in such simplistic models.

Other, more academic reasons, included the discovery of the early urban cultural tradition of the Indus Valley. This provided evidence for an indigenous cultural tradition that appeared both distinct from the Vedic material and to have some continuities with later Indian religion, as with Sir John Marshall's identification of a 'proto-Śiva' image on an Indus Valley seal (Chapter 1). Initially, these discoveries fed into the racially-based models of 'Aryan' invasions and conquest of 'Dravidian' indigenes and the like, but they also raised intellectual issues that could not be dealt with so crudely, and are still far from resolved today. More generally, the gradual uncovering of the archaeological record, for all of its inadequacies by modern scientific standards, made it clear that South Asia had a complex and varied prehistory, and that this involved a number of cultural complexes that could not be mapped at all easily onto a simple model of an expansionist Vedic civilisation.

The growth of social scientific approaches to culture also began to bring about more awareness of the many aspects of culture that are not transmitted textually. Social and cultural anthropology in particular mostly developed in the context of studies of non-literate societies and so developed approaches that emphasised actual cultural and ritual practices and their variations and transformations rather than elite textual models. In the Indian context, this meant that a large body of material was progressively revealed with often only a remote relationship to the Vedic texts.

Indologists in the late twentieth and early twenty-first century are still divided on these issues. In part, this is a methodological question. Textual scholars are at home working with texts, and are not necessarily at ease dealing with other kinds of material. The revival of 'orthogenetic' approaches provides a way to bypass the problem. Textual studies are far more sophisticated today, if only because we have a far greater body of textual material at our disposal and the substantial body of work creates a background in relation to which today's scholars must operate.

It is tempting to comment here, as Olivelle has done, that it is time 'to move beyond this sterile debate and artificial dichotomy' and to reject 'the untenable conviction that we can isolate Aryan and non-Aryan strands in the Indian culture a millennium or more removed from the original and putative Aryan migrations' (Olivelle 2003: 273). His own suggested focus on 'social, economic, political and geographical factors' is also very much in tune with my own sympathies. Yet the dispute is not so easy to dismiss, in part because there is undoubtedly a political edge to many of the arguments involved. The texts, some of them at least, are part of the way in which modernist versions of Hinduism, Islam and Jainism see themselves, and both Asian and Western adherents to these modernist versions of Asian religions clearly prefer to present their traditions in ways that emphasise 'orthogenetic' textual elements and downplay both 'external' influences and folk and popular 'deviations'.

In practice, the orthogenetic approach, combined with a central emphasis on the textual tradition, leaves a number of problems unanswered, particularly for the earlier part of the period covered in this book (the second half of the first millennium BCE):

- It is clear that large parts of later Indic religions do not derive in any simple way from the Ṛgveda or other early Vedic texts. But how does one fit the non-Vedic components of Indic religions into the picture? What kind of historical, cultural or social location did they have?
- Given the late date at which much of the textual material was committed to writing, and the even later date of most of our surviving texts, how representative are the texts we have of religion in any particular area or period?
- Our texts undoubtedly reflect urban elite and court religious practices much more than those of villages and of non-elite strata of society. What kind of relationships do we assume between urban religion and village religion, between elite and non-elite religious practices?
- The geography of early Indic religions is only beginning to be charted. When we are talking about early Indic religions, where and when specifically are we talking about? At what stage were various parts of South and Southeast Asia drawn into the orbit of Brahmanical and Sanskritic culture (to the extent that one can talk of such a thing as a unity at all)?

Similar uncertainties surround the major religious developments of the second half of the period. The growth of the cults of Brahmanical, Buddhist and Jain deities (including the deified Buddhas, bodhisattvas and tirthankaras) is far from fully understood. The same can be said for the growth of the cult of fierce deities, male and female, of the origins of Tantric religion and its effects on the Indic religious field, issues that will be of considerable prominence in our account. Another major development, that of the *bhakti* cults, will be treated in much less detail, but is of equal significance.

I do not intend to be over-dismissive of work based on 'orthogenetic' assumptions. Much of the research carried out by scholars working in this way has been of very high quality, and all scholars of Indic religions are indebted to it. Conceptually and intellectually, however, a strictly orthogenetic and textual view of Indic religions seems to me to be fundamentally flawed. A religious tradition is not just a body of texts. It is, above all, something that lives and is maintained through the lives of human beings. A text, unless we assume that certain texts are indeed divinely inspired and so beyond academic analysis or criticism, can only be the product of one or more human beings and has to make sense in terms of their lives and their understandings of their situation (which may of course include concepts of divine revelation through dreams or other visionary processes). The onward transmission of a text, often complex in the South Asian context where our written versions can be quite recent and can reflect a long textual history, similarly has to make sense in the same terms.

In reality, then, even textual scholarship cannot be divorced from a reconstruction of the intellectual, emotional, social and political context of the people who produced those texts, however difficult that might be to achieve. I would go further and state that it is that intellectual, emotional, social and political context which is the real object of study of scholars of Indian religion. Ultimately, it is people and their specific life-worlds that we are attempting to understand.

Viewed from within this perspective, it is not surprising that much Indian textual material can be represented in orthogenetic form, in terms of the continual reworking of intellectual frameworks laid down in the early years of the Brahmanical tradition. This material was, after all, almost all written by scholars who were trained in the Brahmanical tradition of scholarship or in the closely related Buddhist and Jaina variants of that tradition. In the case of specifically Brahmanical scholars, demonstrating continuity with Vedic texts was, as it were, part of their job description. For the Buddhists and Jainas this was less true, but they were still working within the same intellectual universe, with common intellectual tools, and shared many of the same basic assumptions. In such a world it is to be expected that, for example, the Brahmanical and Buddhist scholars who wrote down the early Tantras would do so in terms that replicated Vedic models and presented the material in terms of familiar intellectual categories.

Yet to assume that this is all that was going on would be to neglect that we all live in several intersecting cultural contexts. These same scholars were involved in folk and domestic ritual, or its monastic equivalents. If living in urban contexts, as most of them were, they had access, if they chose, to people and ideas from a wide range of intellectual traditions. They were almost certainly deeply involved in Tantric practice at an experiential level. They might, as the great Nāgārjuna was said to have been, be specialists in ritual magic, erotics and medicine as well as in Tantric philosophy and practice. Above all, whatever they wrote had to make sense in terms of their everyday lives, including the court and elite cultures of which they might be a part, as well as in terms of the textual tradition to which they belonged. These assumptions underlie much of what I write in this book.

Thus I proceed, where possible, by trying to reconstruct what we can about the life-world within which a particular religious development took place, including its social, cultural and political aspects, as an essential background to what we can see in the surviving texts and other material (iconography, archaeology). Such an approach tends to militate against orthogenetic explanations, and indeed I try where possible to highlight the complex and multidirectional influences that may underlie particular development. This often makes for a more conjectural and provisional result than some writers on these topics, but perhaps also for a more realistic one. After all, our evidence for many of the developments I shall be considering in this book is fragmentary and partial, and much of what scholars can say is necessarily guesswork and conjecture.

THE NATURE OF THE EVIDENCE: ARCHAEOLOGY, NUMISMATICS, ICONOGRAPHY

In the following sections, I look at the nature of the evidence on which our account is built. I begin with the archaeological evidence. While the 'standard story' was essentially constructed from texts, and archaeology was called on, if at all, to support the texts, scholarship is increasingly moving in the direction of taking the archaeology as primary and reading the texts in relation to that account. This, it seems to me, is an essential move, though it should be noted that it would scarcely have been possible for nineteenth- or early twentieth-century scholars, since it is really the development of modern scientific approaches to archaeology (e.g. radiocarbon dating) that has begun to give us a moderately reliable chronological sequence for the prehistory and history of South and Southeast Asian societies. A large part of the surviving textual material cannot be located at all securely in time and space through textual criteria alone, and any attempt to derive a historical sequence primarily on the basis of texts seems to me to be doomed to failure, particularly for the pre-Gupta period (up to early fourth century CE).

At the same time, it is worth retaining some caution in relation to the archaeological record. Relatively few sites in the geographically extensive territories of South and Southeast Asia have as yet been subjected to modern scientific archaeological techniques. Many major sites were excavated before the development of such techniques, while many others have not been excavated at all.

In addition, there are massive issues of interpretation with the archaeological material, particularly when it is attempted to bring it into relation with information from textual and other sources. For example, the recent move from seeing a radical break between the Indus Valley urban cultures and subsequent developments towards stressing continuities between them is undoubtedly significant, but it is far from clear precisely what it may mean in relation to cultures on the ground (e.g. Kenoyer 1995). Cultural complexes defined in terms of pottery and other artefacts do not necessarily bear a simple and straightforward relationship to actual social, cultural or linguistic groups. There is thus always a risk of over-interpreting the evidence.

As far as radiocarbon dating is concerned, there are also both general and specific problems. Dates can be over-interpreted and taken too literally; more specifically, the C14 calibration curve is more or less flat for a substantial and critical part of the first millennium BCE (c. 750–450 BCE; cf. Magee 2004: 38), making it impossible to arrive at C14 datings for this period with any degree of precision. The archaeological record, however, combined with radiocarbon and other modern dating methods, is the nearest we have to solid ground in understanding the social and cultural developments of which Indic religions formed part, and it needs to be primary in our understanding of the situation.

Epigraphic and numismatic evidence also adds to our basis of information from the third and second century BCE onwards. Inscriptions are important but unfortunately scanty and not always easy to date clearly. There are nevertheless some very important bodies of inscriptions (for example, land grants to Brahmins in Bengal, Orissa and South India are all vital clues to the expansion of Brahmanical culture (e.g. Morrison 1970;

Singh 1993). Numismatic evidence is also valuable, as with the early religious iconography on Indo-Greek and Kuṣāṇa coinage (e.g. Srinivasan 1997: pls. 16.6, 16.7, 16.9; Cribb 1997).

Iconographical evidence is also important and again provides a fairly continuous record from around the third century BCE onwards. There have been some impressive recent studies on the basis of iconographical material: instances include Doris Meth Srinivasan's *Many Heads, Arms and Eyes* (1997) and Rob Linrothe's recent book, *Ruthless Compassion* (1999), both impressive examples of what can be done by combining iconographical and textual material, though there are certainly outstanding issues in either case (cf. Bakker 1999 on Srinivasan). But iconographical evidence has its problems too. The dates for iconographical material are often uncertain, since relatively few images are unambiguously dated. Also, many things may be missing from the iconographical record, either because they were created in perishable materials (images of wood, clay, cowdung, etc., which may have been deliberately destroyed after the ritual as is still frequently done) or simply because they have disappeared in the vagaries of history.

THE NATURE OF THE EVIDENCE: TEXTS

In relation to texts, we undoubtedly have a very large body of texts relating to the subject-matter of this book, Indic religions up to 1200 CE. In comparison, however, with European or for that matter Chinese history of the same period, there is a great deal of uncertainty attached to the origins and chronology of much of this material. The lack of early manuscripts and the general fluidity of the textual tradition means that it is often difficult to know exactly when large parts of many of these texts were written. In the following section, I examine some of these issues, since they form an important background to much of what follows.

Vedic and Brahmanical material

I start by looking at textual sources associated with the Brahmanical traditions (i.e. modern 'Hinduism').[4] Our oldest substantial texts are undoubtedly, in some sense, the Vedas, both the hymns of the Ṛgveda itself, and the associated material, including the Atharvaveda, Yajurveda, Brāhmaṇas and Āraṇyakas. The Ṛgveda Saṃhitā (Saṃhitā = textual collection) consists

[4] For concise introductions, see Olivelle 1998: xxiv–xxxiii; Jamison and Witzel 2002; Kulke and Rothermund 1990.

of a body of 1028 ritual texts or hymns[5] in the form of invocation to various deities, attributed to various inspired sages (*ṛṣis*) who are associated with several identified priestly families. It is generally, no doubt correctly, assumed by modern scholars to have been written over a period of several hundred years, although its precise textual history is far from clear. The Sāmaveda Saṃhitā and Yajurveda Saṃhitā are rearrangements of parts of the Ṛgvedic hymns in the context of specific sacrificial rituals, including additional ritual and explanatory material in the case of the Yajurveda, while the Atharvaveda Saṃhitā consists of a largely similar but mostly separate body of ritual hymns, many of them intended for healing and other pragmatic purposes.

A further large body of Vedic material (the Brāhmaṇas and Āraṇyakas) indicate how the Vedic hymns were employed in ritual, how they were performed, and how they were understood. This material, along with the later hymns of the Ṛgveda itself and the Atharvaveda, is often interpreted by modern scholars as deriving from a reconstruction of an original body of Vedic religious practices, associated with a primarily pastoral and tribal way of life, in the context of a new, settled agricultural, context (e.g. Heesterman 1985, 1993; Witzel 1995a, 1995b, 1997, 2003). It is possible that some of the hymns of the Ṛgveda Saṃhitā itself go back to the earlier period. In the view of Witzel and others, these would reflect ritual practices of the Indo-Aryan-speaking peoples before and in the earliest stages of their arrival in the Indian subcontinent.

The Brāhmaṇas and Āraṇyakas were again clearly written over a long period of time, and merge into another body of texts, the Upaniṣads, which include further speculation on the meaning of the sacrificial ritual as well as independent philosophical and metaphysical speculation. While some of the material in the earliest Upaniṣads evidently predates the earliest Buddhist texts, works which described themselves as Upaniṣads were written over a very long period, perhaps as late as the sixteenth century CE (Olivelle 1996: xxxiii).

A further body of 'Vedic' texts are the Śrauta Sūtras, Gṛhya Sūtras, and Dharma Sūtras, ritual and legal manuals that were probably written in the second half of the first millennium BCE and are attributed to specific Brahmanical authors. As we will see, these are often interpreted by modern scholars as part of a second reconstruction of Vedic religion, parallel to the development of the *śramaṇa* traditions of the Buddhists, Jainas and

[5] The term 'hymn' in this context is a Christian borrowing and while it has become widely accepted it has misleading connotations. These texts were and still are used as ritual invocations, not occasions for congregational singing.

Ājivikas. All of this material can be referred to as 'Vedic', which leads to a certain blurriness as to how the term is used by some modern writers. The term is, however, significant, among other reasons because modern Hinduism is often defined through its reference back to the Vedic texts (e.g. B. Smith 1989: 13–20).

The hymns of the Ṛgveda Saṃhitā have been given a wide variety of dates, with a group of mostly Indian revisionist scholars nowadays arguing for an extremely early dating (e.g. 4000 BCE; cf. Rajaram and Frawley 1995: 142–3). The Western scholarly consensus would probably place them somewhere between 1200 BCE and 1000 BCE. While the oldest parts of this body of 'Vedic' material undoubtedly go back in some form to before my notional starting point of 500 BCE (the striking similarities between the Ṛgveda and the parallel body of early textual material from Iran, written in a closely related language, make this clear), it is important to be aware that our actual textual evidence for the Vedas, and for everything else, is relatively late. The oldest surviving manuscripts for *any* of the Brahmanical textual corpus, including the epics and the Purāṇas, date from around the eighth century CE, and many of the texts we are using are much later.

The oldest layer of the parallel Iranian material consists of the seventeen hymns or *gāthās* attributed to the semi-legendary figure of Zarathustra, along with a short liturgy, the *Yasna Haptanghāiti*, from around the same period or slightly later, both in the Old Avestan language. Both this and later material in the Avestan language appears to have been written in Eastern Iran (Boyce 1997; Skjærvø 1995).

Zarathustra's historicity was generally taken for granted in Avestan scholarship until fairly recently, but it is by no means certain that he was the author of the *gāthās* or the *Yasna Haptanghāiti*, or that he was a historical figure at all. The Old Avestan texts, which were not written down until the Sasanian period (third to seventh century CE), are nevertheless in a language close to Vedic Sanskrit, and the *gāthās* are ritual hymns similar to those of the Ṛgveda (Boyce 1997; Skjaervø 1997).

The state religion of the Achaemenid empire (sixth to fourth century BCE), based in western Iran, was evidently closely related to the early Zoroastrian texts, though it is not known to what extent, if at all, they would have considered themselves as followers of Zarathustra. This religion is represented by a body of inscriptional material from the sixth century onwards. This provides evidence for a state ideology based on Zoroastrian principles, including the idea of the king as a maintainer of justice and divine order (Skjaervø 2005).

The dating of the Old Avestan texts is as controversial and unsettled as that for the Vedas, with figures for the lifetime of Zarathustra (and/or the composition of the *gāthās*) ranging between 1400 BCE and 500 BCE. The earlier dates are largely based on parallels with the Vedic material, the dating of which as we have seen is also uncertain, but seem more plausible than the later figure, based on the 'traditional' date for Zarathustra.

The one secure early date for something recognisably 'Vedic' comes from West Asia, where the Mitanni archives preserve some names of recognisable Vedic deities and other terms in a language identifiable as an early form of Vedic Sanskrit in texts dating from around 1360–80 BCE (Thieme 1960). Exactly what this early proto-Vedic group was doing in the region is a puzzle to which a variety of speculative answers has been proposed (Parpola 1994: 126, 145–8, 1995, 1999a; Witzel 1995a, 2005). In fact the whole question of the early history of the Indo-Aryan and Indo-Iranian speaking peoples is both heavily contested and, at least at this point in time, largely undecidable (see Erdosy 1995a; Bryant and Patton 2005). I discuss the Mitanni evidence further in Chapter 5.

Returning to the Vedic material itself, the absence of early textual material is worth underlining, since there is still a tendency to assume that the Vedas represent early Indian religion in a relatively unproblematic manner.[6] Many of the texts of European religious history are of course equally based on quite late manuscripts, but the European textual tradition does have many early texts from Egypt and Mesopotamia, with relatively secure dates, and significant parts of the Greek and Latin corpus survive in manuscript sources from Roman and Hellenistic times. It also seems that there was considerably more textual stability in Europe than in South Asia, so that we are not generally in serious doubt, except with very early or primarily legendary figures such as Homer, as to how much dates back to the original author or compiler. The conditions of textual transmission in India, however, are such that we rarely know with certainty which parts of a text date from which period. This is not only true for the Vedic corpus, but also for later texts such as the *Ramāyaṇa*, the *Mahābharata* or the Purāṇas, or the works attributed to well-known authors such as Nāgārjuna or Śaṅkara.

It is possible to work on internal evidence in such matters, as Max Müller and more recently Michael Witzel have for the Vedas, or John Brockington for the Ramāyaṇa. As Arvind Sharma pointed out some years ago, however, we could be completely wrong about some of our basic

[6] It would be more correct to say, as Olivelle does, that '[t]hese texts [. . .] offer us only a tiny window into this period, and that too only throws light on what their priestly authors thought it important to record' (2003: 273).

assumptions, including the periodisation of the major components of the Vedic corpus, which after all were clearly edited and arranged in their present form well after the time when many of the component items were first composed (A. Sharma 1995).

In fact, dating is a major issue throughout a project such as this and I will say more about it in a little while. An even more critical issue, and it is one that I shall attempt to say something about later, is the question of who used the Vedas. Our evidence increasingly suggests that the context for the hymns of the Ṛgveda and other presumably 'early' stages of the Vedic corpus was geographically localised in North-West India (roughly present-day Punjab, Haryana and Western Uttar Pradesh, as well as adjoining parts of modern Pakistan). This raises the obvious question of what was going on elsewhere in South (and Southeast) Asia at the time, and how Vedic culture related to this wider context. Here it is important, as Parpola and others have noted, to separate the question of the specifically Vedic culture associated with the Ṛgveda from that of the usage of Indo-Aryan languages, which may have been much more widespread. The worship of Vedic deities may also have been present elsewhere in forms other than those of the Ṛgvedic tradition.

Michael Witzel and others have suggested that the highly sophisticated techniques used for memorising and transmitting Vedic texts, which have a great deal of internal redundancy, have ensured that we have an extremely accurate representation of the original – '[w]e can actually regard present-day Ṛgveda-recitation as a *tape recording* of what was first composed and recited some 3000 years ago' (Witzel 1995a: 91). While I do not have any personal expertise with Vedic texts, there seem to me to be some problems here.[7] The elaborate mnemonic devices used, in which syllables are repeated and permutated repetitively in complex formal patterns, doubtless did lead to a high degree of textual stability, but since we have no independent evidence as to how far back these techniques go, this does not necessarily help us in determining the antiquity of any particular part of the textual corpus, or for that matter in knowing how representative the surviving material is of what might have been around at an earlier period. To me, some at least of the Vedic hymns themselves look as if they originated in a society considerably earlier than that which produced the mnemonic system; they might have been passed on and transformed through many generations of oral transmission before the mnemonic techniques were elaborated to their

[7] Witzel is undoubtedly right that the Ṛgveda itself, and the early Vedic material in general, contains numerous traces of its complex history, regional origins, substrate languages and the like. As a non-specialist, I am unsure how precise a reconstruction can be made on the basis of these traces.

present degree of complexity. Certainly other authors have taken a much less sanguine position than Witzel regarding the antiquity of these texts, with a number of authors arguing for the eighth century BCE or later (e.g. Wright 1966; Pirart 1998).[8] In any case, we need to be aware that the early Vedic texts represent at best a narrow and selective window into a restricted part of north Indian society in the first millennium BCE.

Apart from the various texts in the Vedic corpus, three texts associated with named authors have been used as significant witnesses for early Indian religion and religious history: the grammatical texts attributed to Pāṇini and Patañjali, and the *Arthaśāstra* or treatise on statesmanship attributed to Kauṭilya. Unfortunately, yet again, none of these can be dated with much reliability. I shall discuss the case of Pāṇini and Patañjali below, as an example of the kinds of uncertainties prevalent within Indological scholarship. As for Kauṭilya, he is traditionally associated with the court of Candragupta I (c. 300 BCE) but the linkage is far from certain and the *Arthaśāstra* as we know it today is almost certainly a compilation from somewhere between the mid-second and fourth century CE (Willis 2004: 25 n. 114).

Other very important sources include the two major Indian Epics (*Mahābhārata* and *Rāmāyaṇa*, to which may be added the *Mahābhārata*'s appendix, the *Harivaṃśa*) and the Purāṇas. In all these cases, we again have to bear in mind the existence of a complex and uncertain textual history. Current scholarship includes respected authorities arguing that the *Rāmāyaṇa* and the *Mahābhārata* were each written over a period of three to four centuries (e.g. Brockington 1985 for the *Rāmāyaṇa*), and other equally respected authorities arguing for authorship by a single person or group of people over a few years (e.g. Hiltebeitel 2004). To some degree this is a question of exactly what is meant by the authorship of the text, since in either case the existence of prior oral versions is highly probable, but there are also genuine disagreements. In any case, there is wide variation between the existing manuscripts, particularly in relation to the *Mahābhārata*, suggesting that the texts as we know them developed over a long period of time and represent material from a variety of periods and places. While there

[8] 'La Ṛgvedasaṃhitā n'est pas aussi ancienne qu'on le dit. Les Perses, qui séparait les Mèdes des Indiens et qui ont pu causer le déplacement de ces derniers d'Iran vers l'Inde, sont nommés. D'autre part, le contenu des hymnes suppose la renaissance du mouvement urbain en Inde, si bien que la date à retenir doit se situer après la première mention des Perses dans les documents assyriens et la réapparition des villes en Inde: le VIIIe siècle?' (Pirart 1998: 521). Witzel on the contrary regards the Ṛgveda as composed up to c.1200 BCE and redacted in the 'Brāhmaṇa period', perhaps around 700 BCE. The redaction involved selecting texts from existing collections; apart from minor details of pronunciation, the text remained the same (Witzel 1995a: 91 n.13).

has been a lot of very interesting and creative scholarship on both epics in recent years, we are far from being able to give a precise historical location to any individual section of either text (cf. Fitzgerald 2004; Hiltebeitel 2001, 2004; Brockington 1985, 1998, 2003a).

The Purāṇas raise similar issues, more acute because they have received less detailed attention. As far as I know, the oldest Purāṇic manuscript we have is the early *Skanda Purāṇa* MS on which Hans Bakker, Harunaga Isaacson and others have been working. This manuscript dates from around the eighth century, and the original text may go back to the sixth. This version of the *Skanda Purāṇa* is quite different in textual content from the modern text of that name, although it was later incorporated as a component of it under a different name (Adriaensen, Bakker and Isaacson 1994, 1998).

Overall, the dating of Purāṇic texts seems to be an extremely conjectural area, which is hardly surprising since many of the Purāṇas were being added to and revised until quite recent times. Some of these variations can be quite striking: does the *Devīmāhātmya*, a relatively short section of one of the Purāṇas which is the classic early textual basis for the worship of a fierce warrior goddess, date from the third or fourth century (M. Joshi 2002: 47) or the eighth (Yokochi 1999: 89–90)? What are the implications for the development of the cult of the fierce warrior goddesses in India if one makes one choice or the other?

Other important bodies of texts (e.g. the Śaiva Tantric texts) raise similar issues, with the dating, localisation and authorship both of surviving texts as a whole and of individual parts of texts being still largely conjectural.

By the middle of the first millennium CE, many texts are attributed to known authors, but this does not necessarily resolve issues of dating. The dates of authors may be far from certain, and the attribution of texts to authors is often equally problematic. Even as late and central a figure as Śaṅkara raises major problems in this respect: his dates are far from certain and many of the texts attributed to him are probably apocryphal.

All in all, we have a lot of material for the Brahmanical and associated traditions but it often tends to be heavily rewritten and edited in the forms we have, we do not know for certain when it dates from and we are not always too sure what it means.

Buddhist and Jaina material

When we turn to Buddhist texts, the situation is in some ways considerably better. The earliest Buddhist texts consist mostly of *sūtras* (Pali *suttas*), which are held to be accounts of the actual words of the historical Buddha Śākyamuni, inserted in a short narrative describing the place and occasion of their first delivery and those present at their delivery. These texts were held to have been recited immediately after the death of the Buddha, which is now dated by the majority of scholars (see below) to around 400 BCE. The texts were eventually compiled into a number of collections: long *sūtras* (the *Dīrghāgama*, Pali *Dīghanikāya*), medium-length *sūtras* (*Madhyamāgama*, *Majjhimanikāya*), two collections of shorter *sūtras*, and in some traditions a group of miscellaneous texts (*Kṣudrakāgama*, *Khuddakanikāya*). All this made up the Sūtra Piṭaka. Two further groups of texts, the Vinaya Piṭaka and Abhidharma Piṭaka, contained the Vinaya or monastic disciplinary code and the Abhidharma texts, presenting an early school of Buddhist philosophical analysis.

The Buddhist tradition divided into a variety of schools over the next few centuries, and what we actually have are versions of these collections of texts as transmitted by particular schools, notably the Theravādins (in Pali) and the Sarvāstivādin and Dharmaguptaka (in Chinese), along with some mostly fragmentary texts in Sanskrit and Prakrit, again probably from either the Dharmaguptaka or the Sarvāstivādin school. The collections as transmitted by different schools do not correspond precisely to each other, with different *sūtras* being included in some cases, and the texts of individual *sūtras* also do not correspond precisely to each other, but changes are for the most part relatively minor (e.g. Choong 2005).[9]

The existence of Chinese translations means that we have fairly reliable early datable versions of parts of the textual corpus from around this period, though this refers mostly to the Mahāyāna sūtras (eg. Harrison 1987a, 1993); the Chinese versions of the *āgamas* date from around the fourth century CE onwards.[10] In some cases, in fact we have a series of dated translations representing different Sanskrit texts from different periods. The Pali textual tradition also seems to have been relatively stable from about the first century CE onwards, and some of the Sanskrit and Prakrit fragments contain manuscript material from about the same period. We also have far more in the way of historical writing from Sinhalese, Tibetan and Chinese authors than from the subcontinent itself. However, as Stephen Collins pointed out in his 'On the Very Idea of the Pali Canon', there are still unanswered questions about exactly how and when the texts came to be written down

9 The recent discovery of a Sanskrit text of the *Dīrghāgama* is likely to throw considerable light on early textual history (Cousins 2005).

10 Max Deeg (personal communication, February 2007). For translations of Tantric texts, see Matsunaga 1977a.

and how they came to be assembled into the relatively closed textual canons we know today (Collins 1990). The Gandhārī material suggests that there was a substantial period when there were short anthologies of *sūtras* rather than the larger and more systematic collections we know today, which may not have taken shape until well into the first millennium CE.

Altogether, even if we accept the new chronologies for the life of the historical Buddha, which would reduce the period in which versions of the *sūtras* were being transmitted orally to perhaps only two or three centuries, we do not know and cannot know what the historical Buddha might really have said in more than a very approximate way. It also seems likely, as Richard Gombrich has pointed out, that people may have lost touch quite soon with much of the necessary interpretive background of the texts (Gombrich 1990, 1992, 1996). If Gombrich is right that we should read a fair amount of humour and irony into the voice of the Buddha as represented in the early *sūtras* (the suggestion seems to me both attractive and plausible), then this makes it even more difficult to interpret these texts as literal accounts of the social and religious life of their times.

Jaina textual material has often received less attention than Brahmanical or Buddhist texts, since relatively few scholars have worked on Jaina material, but it is of considerable importance. Early Jaina scriptural material survived only in the Śvetāmbara tradition, and it is not clear when the surviving texts were first written down; the existing manuscripts date back only to the eleventh century CE. The standard version of the canon today contains 45 texts, some of which undoubtedly go back in some form to quite early times (Dundas 2002: 73–5). Thus the situation here is more like that of the Brahmanical tradition than the Buddhist, in that the texts contain quite early material but the surviving texts are all late.

The various issues with the textual material, much of which falls generally into the category that we could refer to as scriptural, demonstrate why a viable history of Indic religions has to look elsewhere for much of its evidence, particularly for the first millennium BCE. The texts are vital, but they are not self-explanatory.

CHRONOLOGICAL ISSUES

It is worth looking briefly at what the textual material provides us with on the chronological front. As noted above, our one secure textual date for the second millennium BCE is provided by the Mitanni archives, and this is essentially an isolated item of information which has not yet been brought into any meaningful relationship with South Asian history. For the whole of the first millennium BCE there is only one reliable fixed point, the invasion of Alexander in 329 to 325 BCE, which coincided with the rise to power of Candragupta, the founder of the Mauryan empire. Everything else – the datings for Aśoka (including the dates of the Aśokan inscriptions), the Buddha, Mahāvīra, the Upaniṣads and the guesstimates for the Vedic texts – is inference and guesswork on the basis of this one figure.

The earlier Persian presence in Northwest India (Gandhāra) in the sixth century BCE left little that can be linked directly to later developments, but there is some room here for speculation about the possible impact on state-formation and concepts of the state in the sub-continent (see Chapters 3 and 4). The relationship between earlier Iranian and early Indian ('Vedic') material has received relatively little attention, despite the obvious connections, though there has been some work in this area of late, particularly in relation to the vexed question of Vedic *soma*/Iranian *haoma* (cf. Parpola 1995; Houben 2003a, 2003b; Thompson 2003).

The general social and political chronology of South Asia becomes more secure after the start of the common era, particularly once we reach the Guptas (c. 320 CE onwards).[11] The datings of many of the major religious texts and figures of the first millennium CE however still remain less than certain.

Given this overall situation, it is not entirely surprising that there is some circularity to much Indological argument, particularly in relation to dates. To quote Patrick Olivelle on the dating of the early Upaniṣads, 'in reality, any dating of these documents that attempts a precision closer than that of a few centuries is as stable as a house of cards' (Olivelle 1998: xxxvi). This is one of the reasons why radical revisionist authors such as David Frawley, N.S. Rajaram, Subhash Kak and others can advance alternative chronologies in which, for example, the hymns of the Ṛgveda date back to 4000 BCE (e.g. Rajaram and Frawley 1995: 142–3) rather than the 1200–1000 BCE suggested by Max Müller and broadly accepted by most modern scholars, at least for the older hymns.

I do not find the contentions of the radical revisionists persuasive. The astronomical datings that provide their most significant support are unconvincing, and such early dates would require a radical and implausible rethinking of our understanding of both global history and of human cultural processes. However, the fact that it is possible to advance such contentions and for them to be taken seriously by many people, at least

[11] The chronology of events in the preceding centuries is still somewhat unclear, although the dating of the Kuṣāṇas has now probably been placed on a reasonably secure basis (see Sims-Williams and Cribb 1996).

outside the academy, stands as something of a warning of the weakness of the conceptual edifice that has been built up over the last couple of centuries of Indological and Orientalist research.

In any case, while the redating of the Ṛgveda to 4000 BCE may not be a real issue, there have been less dramatic but still quite substantial upheavals in other areas. One of the most significant of these is the recent controversy over the date of the historical Buddha. The traditional Theravādin date for the Buddha's death or *parinirvāṇa* of 543 BCE had already been generally brought forward by sixty years or so, to c. 486 BCE. In a series of conferences and associated publications in the early 1990s, it became clear that the scholarly consensus had moved considerably further forward again. Many scholars now support a date for the Buddha's death of c. 400 BCE or somewhat later (Bechert 1991–1997; Cousins 1996a).

This is a move that has considerable implications not only for our understanding of the origins of the Buddhist tradition but also for the Jain and Brahmanical traditions, since much of their early chronology too was determined in relation to the date of the historical Buddha. What has happened here, though, as in many parallel cases, is not so much that the scholarly community now knows that the Buddha lived 150 years longer than it had originally thought. It is more that an accepted date has been replaced by a question mark; we now know that what appeared to be solid knowledge was in fact conjecture.

A case study of the chronological problem: Pāṇini

One has only to look at the uncertainties surrounding the dating of major figures such as Pāṇini or Nāgārjuna, and the indirect nature of much of the evidence on which our datings depend, to see that similar rethinkings might well be likely in a variety of areas. It is worth giving an illustration of the kind of situation we are in. Consider the evidence for the dating of Pāṇini, the semi-legendary figure associated with the first surviving grammar, as summarised some years ago by George Cardona (Cardona 1976: 260–8).[12]

To begin with, there is no direct evidence at all for the date of Pāṇini. However, Cardona notes, Pāṇini has to be dated substantially before the grammarian Kātyāyana, since Kātyāyana both commented on Pāṇini's work and had predecessors who had also commented on Pāṇini. Cardona suggests that a period of one or two centuries would be appropriate.

[12] I omit a whole series of arguments advanced by other scholars that Cardona found irrelevant or inconclusive.

Unfortunately, we have no substantial evidence for the date of Kātyāyana either. Cardona cites a couple of arguments for his being in the mid-third century, but clearly regards these as quite weak. However, Kātyāyana in his turn has to be substantially before Patañjali (another one or two centuries) for similar reasons. This Patañjali is the grammarian Patañjali, who may or may not be the same person as the Patañjali who wrote the *Yogasūtra*.

Consequently, everything depends on the dating of the grammarian Patañjali. Unfortunately, Patañjali is also not easy to date reliably. However, he provides in his grammar, as a grammatical example illustrating the present tense, the sentence *iha puṣyamitraṃ yājayāmaḥ*, 'We are officiating here at Puṣyamitra's sacrifice'. This *may* mean that he was writing during the reign of Puṣyamitra, the first Śuṅga king (c. 178–c. 142 BCE), though it is also possible that he is talking about a different Puṣyamitra or that the sentence should be seen as merely a grammatical example. Patañjali also gives grammatical examples suggesting that a *yavana* (Indo-Greek) king attacked the towns of Sāketa and Madhyamikā during his lifetime. This *might* be a reference to the Indo-Greek king Menander, between 140 and 120 BCE, though other dates are possible.

Cardona considers various arguments for later dates for Patañjali, which he also finds inconclusive, and concludes 'The evidence is thus not absolutely probative but sufficient to warrant considering seriously that Patañjali lived in the second century B.C.' (Cardona 1976: 266).

At this point we can return to Pāṇini, but now everything turns on how long an interval needs to be assumed between Pāṇini and Kātyāyana, and between Kātyāyana and Patañjali. Cardona outlines two possibilities:

(1) If Patañjali dates from the mid-second century BCE, and we allow two centuries between him and Kātyāyana and two centuries between Kātyāyana and Pāṇini, then Kātyāyana would be mid-fourth century BCE and Pāṇini would be mid-sixth century BCE.

(2) If we accept the mid-second century BCE dating for Patañjali, but allow only one century between Patañjali and Kātyāyana and between Kātyāyana and Pāṇini, then Kātyāyana would be mid-third century BCE and Pāṇini would be mid-fourth century BCE. This would fit with the other (very weak) evidence for Kātyāyana being mid third century BCE.

Cardona's overall conclusion is:

> The evidence for dating Pāṇini, Kātyāyana, and Patañjali is not absolutely probative and depends on interpretation. However, I think there is one certainty, namely that the evidence available hardly allows one to date Pāṇini later than the early to mid fourth century B.C. (Cardona 1976: 268)

But is this really the case? Cardona admits that Patañjali might be using stock grammatical examples from an earlier period, so that he might not actually have been a contemporary of either the *yavana* attack or Puṣyamitra's sacrifice. Even if he was, the reference might also have been to another *yavana* attack or to another Puṣyamitra, since there were several of each. It hardly seems beyond question that further evidence might lead to significant further movement. In addition, the whole of this discussion assumes that the present text of Pāṇini (or of Patañjali) was in origin the unified work of a single author and was not substantially modified at a later period. In reality, we do not have anything like a solid date for Pāṇini or even for Patañjali.[13]

Now, I could have chosen any out of quite a long list of the significant dates of South Asian history and gone through a similar exercise. I chose this one primarily because Cardona lays out his arguments with such exemplary clarity. It is also significant for another reason, however. The dates of Pāṇini and Patañjali are themselves one of the most important sources for dating many other developments – for example, references in Pāṇini and Patañjali are important evidence for the growth of the Bhagāvata cult and early Vaiṣṇavism. It makes quite a lot of difference to our understanding of early Indian religion whether Pāṇini lived in the fourth or the sixth century BCE – to stay within the range that Cardona suggests. But a high proportion of the dates we deal with, including many of those I give in this book, have to be treated as equally uncertain.

It is striking how far Cardona's arguments, and for that matter those he cites and dismisses, are textual in nature. In this he is not unusual. Indologists have tended to take the texts first – and often a fairly small selection of texts – often treating what they said rather literally, and have tried to fit everything else into the framework this produces.

CONCLUSION

Thus any coherent account of the first millennium BCE has to depend heavily also on the archaeological evidence. The archaeological record for South Asia has its own problems, with many major sites either excavated at a period before the development of modern scientific techniques in archaeology, or still unexcavated, but with the advent of modern dating techniques

[13] Sheldon Pollock recently noted that '[a]rguments placing [Patañjali] as late as the middle of the second century CE are entirely credible' (2007: 80). This would allow for a considerably later dating for Pāṇini than those suggested by Cardona; Pollock places him in the third or fourth century BCE (2007: 45).

it is at last becoming possible to construct a sensible account of the development of Indic civilisation on the basis of the archaeological record, and to bring the various textual sources into some kind of relationship to it. It seems to me that this is the only way in which to place the earlier stages of the historical record on a reasonably firm basis, and to get a real sense of what we know and what we do not know.

I do not want to be too discouraging here, because in some respects this openness of the evidence seems to me to represent an opportunity as well as a limitation. We have room now in a way that we did not perhaps have fifty years ago to look for models considerably different from those we have previously accepted. But I think that the situation requires a certain tentativeness about our approach, and a willingness to accept that any one kind of evidence is unlikely to be decisive. Instead, we need to work towards a mutual coherence of our different kinds of evidence. The aim should be to work gradually towards something which fits as well as possible all round but which does not privilege any particular material – particularly textual material, which is the most tempting, but in some ways the least reliable in the South and Southeast Asian context.

PART ONE

Meditation and yoga

In spite of a life devoted to meditation, prayer and books, Brahmagupta was like many other monks I have come to know and admire who are perpetually cheerful, who laugh easily and loudly, the laughter not springing from a sense of humour but from an evolved spirit of mischief and playfulness. Sometimes, watching the frequent and obvious merriment of these monks, I have wondered whether the Buddha's message is indeed about the world being full of pain and sorrow; or perhaps, the Enlightened One has left a secret message for his monks, a cosmic joke which never palls with any number of re-tellings, which makes them laugh so much.

Sudhir Kakar, *The Ascetic of Desire* (Kakar 1998: 157)

CHAPTER 3

The Second Urbanisation of South Asia

The term 'Second Urbanisation' in the title of this chapter refers to the growth of cities in South Asia during the first millennium BCE. The process is described as a 'Second Urbanisation' because of the existence of a 'First Urbanisation', that which was associated with the Indus Valley cultural tradition. The major cities of the Indus Valley, including Mohenjo-Daro and Harappa, are now generally dated to the period from c. 2500 to c. 1900 BCE, the so-called 'Integration Era' of the Indus Valley cultural tradition, which followed on a long period of more localised, small-scale settlement in the Indus Valley region (e.g. Shaffer 1992; Shaffer and Lichtenstein 1995; Kenoyer 1995). 'Integration' here is used in a cultural sense, since the evidence does not at present suggest a high degree of political integration for the region (Possehl 1998; Samuel 2000). In around 1900 BCE, the major Indus Valley cities ceased to exist, and settlement size became much smaller. This may be linked with the drying up of the Ghaggar-Hakra river system, generally identified with the River Sarasvatī mentioned in the Ṛgveda, and the gradual desertification of much of the area which this river used to irrigate. Around 75 per cent of the Indus Valley settlements from the Integration Era are in fact along the banks or close to this river system.

Substantial urban settlements did not appear again until about 500 BCE. It is clear from the archaeological record however that there was considerable cultural continuity after the end of the Integration Era, with localised versions of the Indus Valley tradition continuing to exist in the Punjab and elsewhere until about 1200 BCE.

It is I think important to establish as detailed a picture as possible of the social and cultural aspects of the period of the Second Urbanisation as a background to the development of religion in South Asia. An important starting point is an understanding of the regional differences in North and Northeast India at the period when the Second Urbanisation got under way.

This will then give us a context within which we can place the dramatic religious developments of this period.

Here there is evidence from a variety of sources, of three main kinds. In the first place, there is the *archaeological* evidence, which is by now quite extensive and detailed, and provides the basis for a reasonably secure chronology through carbon-12 datings and other modern techniques. However, many important sites have still not been excavated in detail, and there are technical issues with carbon dating, in particular the flat C14 calibration curve for the period from c. 750 to c. 450 BCE, that mean that radiocarbon dates give only very approximate dates for some critical periods (e.g. Erdosy 1995c: 100; Magee 2004: 38).

None of our *textual* material dates from as early as the start of the Second Urbanisation, but some of it probably represents traditions that go back close to this period, so that there is information here which needs to be reconciled with the archaeological evidence. In particular, traditions regarding the early Indian states or *mahājanapadas*, while legendary rather than historical for this early period, still convey useful information, and I will look at some of this material in Chapter 4. Another kind of textual evidence comes from close textual analysis of the early Vedic corpus, as with the work of Michael Witzel. Witzel's material bears in part on underlying language patterns in the surviving texts, including indications of 'substrate languages', that is traces of languages that were spoken before the adoption of Indo-Aryan languages in various parts of north and east India. *Language* in general, both from early textual material and from the modern linguistic record, provides a third body of material that needs to be reconciled with archaeology and textual sources. Other sources of evidence, for example iconography and numismatics, also provide useful clues at later stages in our enquiry.

THE SECOND URBANISATION IN SOUTH AND SOUTHEAST ASIA AS A WHOLE

First, however, it is useful to look at the whole question of the Second Urbanisation in a slightly wider context than that of North India alone.

At the beginning of this period, both South and Southeast Asia were very different from today, with a very much lower population density and large areas still covered with forest. There were, however, agricultural communities throughout the region, with most of the major crops used today already being grown. These were wheat and barley in the northwestern areas, rice in the Central Gangetic and Bengal Delta regions, South India and Southeast Asia,[1] and various millets throughout the region. While iron did not form part of the Indus Valley civilisation or, apparently, of early Vedic society, its use was also becoming fairly common by this period.

What did not yet exist in either South or Southeast Asia at this time is anything that could be called a medium-sized town, or a medium to large-scale state organisation. It is unclear in fact how far the First Urbanisation in South Asia, the Indus Valley civilization involved a centralised state organisation. Kenoyer, Shaffer, Possehl and others have suggested in recent years that the Indus Valley societies were not in fact centralised states as we know them today (e.g. Possehl 1998). Given the extensive trading networks associated with the Indus Valley towns, we might think of them more as trading communities with localised governmental structures, such as existed in large parts of West Africa in quite recent times. We do not really know very much about the social and political structures, though Possehl points to the lack of evidence for war or militarism of any kind (Possehl 1998: 269, see also Samuel 2000). However, there is no doubt that the Indus Valley civilisation supported relatively large communities: Mohenjo-Daro and Harappa appear to have covered over 200 and around 150 hectares respectively (Chakrabarti 1995: 61, 83) with populations of perhaps around twenty or thirty thousand.

By comparison, the largest settlement sizes in the post-Harappan period are around 10 hectares. It was from this basis that the so-called Second Urbanisation began. Chakrabarti places the early growth of substantial fortified urban settlements, initially at Ujjayinī, Kauśāmbī, Vārāṇasī, Rājagṛha and Campā, in around 600 BCE, though we need to remember that the flatness of the C14 calibration curve for this period makes precise dating impossible (Chakrabarti 1995: 247).

Why did it happen at this time? As usual, a complex development like this probably had multiple causes, but one component may well have been a significant rise in agricultural production resulting from the introduction of multi-cropping techniques. This meant that the old combination of agriculture and pastoralism typical of the Indus Valley cultures and their successor states was shifted decisively in the direction of agriculture. This could have provided the surplus in production that could support a centralised state. It could also have set off the progressive clearing of forests, with consequent further rises in production and in population

[1] Pejros and Shnirelman 1998 cite 7500–5450 BCE as the earliest date for Oryza indica in the Central Gangetic valley, 4600 BCE for South China, 3250 BCE for Thailand (1998: 384, fig. 16.1). They also note that 'the Dravidians had borrowed rice-growing technology from a Sino-Tibetan group by the end of the third millennium BC' (1998: 385).

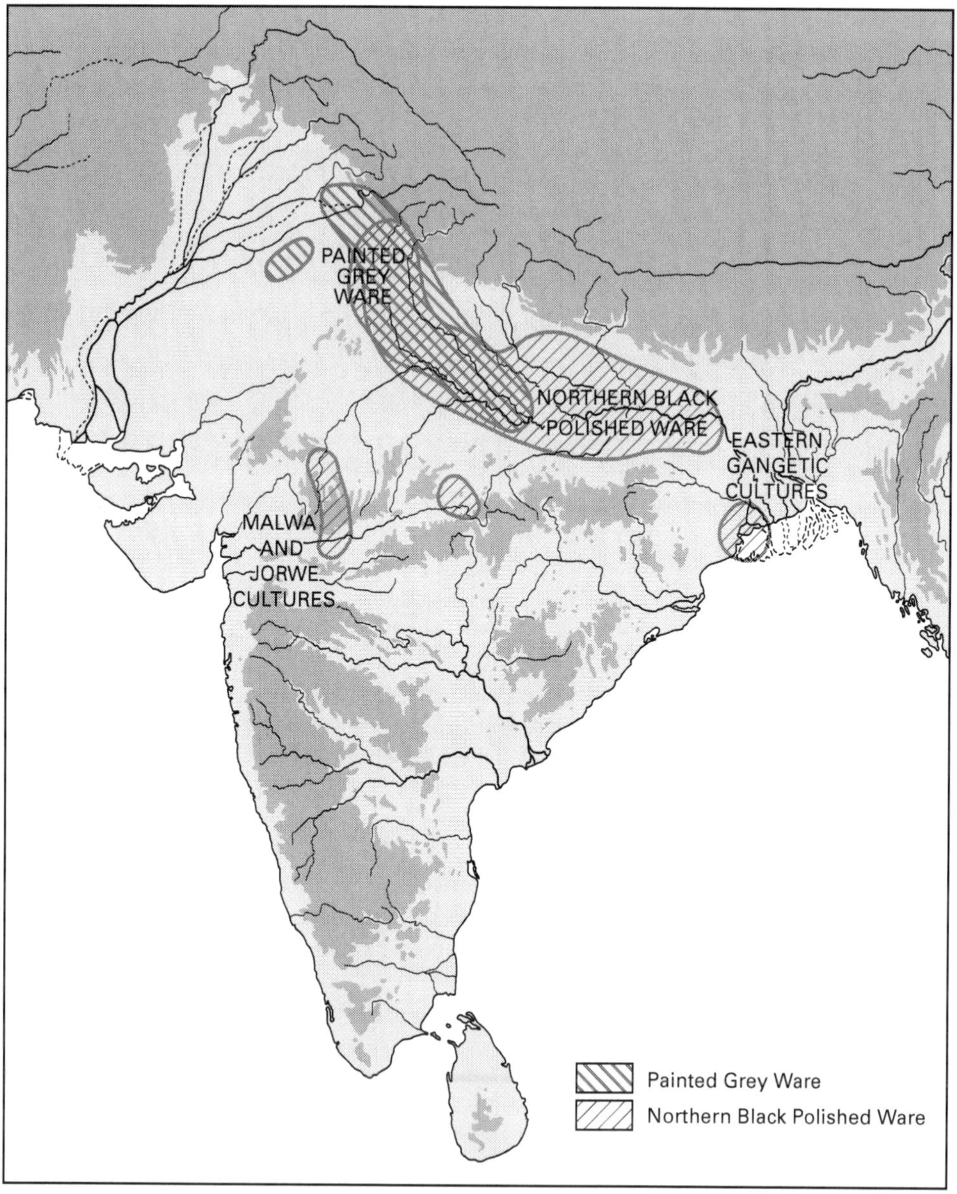

Figure 3.1. Map: Painted Grey Ware and Northern Black Polished Ware

(cf. e.g. Erdosy 1995c: 119–22). The introduction of iron has been suggested as a major factor in the growth of cities, but Chakrabarti argues against this, noting that

> the village-life and the crop patterns of the entire subcontinent were laid down in the earlier chalcolithic stage and that not a single major crop was added to the list after iron was introduced [. . .] Given the firm-rooted agricultural base all over the country, especially in the fertile alluvium of the Gangetic valley, the catalytic factor in the early historic urban growth in the region is more likely the formation of clear and powerful regional kingdoms which confront us right in the first phase of our documented political history. (1995: 169)

A critical marker for early urbanisation has generally been taken to be the advent of a new pottery style, known as Northern Black Polished Ware (NBPW) and associated with the early urban settlements, initially in the Central Gangetic region (Kauśāmbī, Sāketa etc.) and later elsewhere (see Fig. 3.1). Dates for the beginning of NBPW again run up against the flat C14 calibration curve problem: the majority of the radiocarbon dates appear to cluster around 400–450 BCE and a plausible starting point for this period might be around 550 BCE (e.g. Erdosy 1995c: 102–5; see also Possehl and Rissman 1992), but Chakrabarti and others have suggested earlier dates (Chakrabarti 1995: 169, 170; Magee 2004: 43). There are preceding pre-NBPW phases at some of these sites, going back perhaps to around 1000 BCE.

These earlier phases are characterised by Painted Gray Ware (PGW), which has been associated, in the Indo-Gangetic divide and the Doab, and by Black Slipped Ware (BSW) further east. PGW, which appears from around 1100 BCE in the Kuru-Pañcāla Region, has generally been linked with the early Vedic-Brahmanical culture of that area. One should perhaps not put too much reliance on pottery styles. Erdosy suggests that the emphasis on PGW in relation to the early Vedic material is a result of the general poverty of material culture in the archaeological record; there is little else to go by. He nevertheless comments

> While it may be a mistake to equate the distribution of this ware [i.e. PGW] with an effective social group, the coincidence of the territory of *madhyadeśa*, representing the heartland of *ārya* orthodoxy, with it is striking. (Erdosy 1995b: 95, referring to Witzel 1989: 243)

Dates for the early use of iron in the subcontinent are again contested, though dates of around 700 BCE have been suggested for the north-eastern region, with earlier occurrences (around 1000 BCE) in the south of India (Chakrabarti 1995: 167–9). It has been plausibly argued that iron-smelting may have been an indigenous development within the Indian subcontinent (cf. Erdosy 1995b: 83–4).

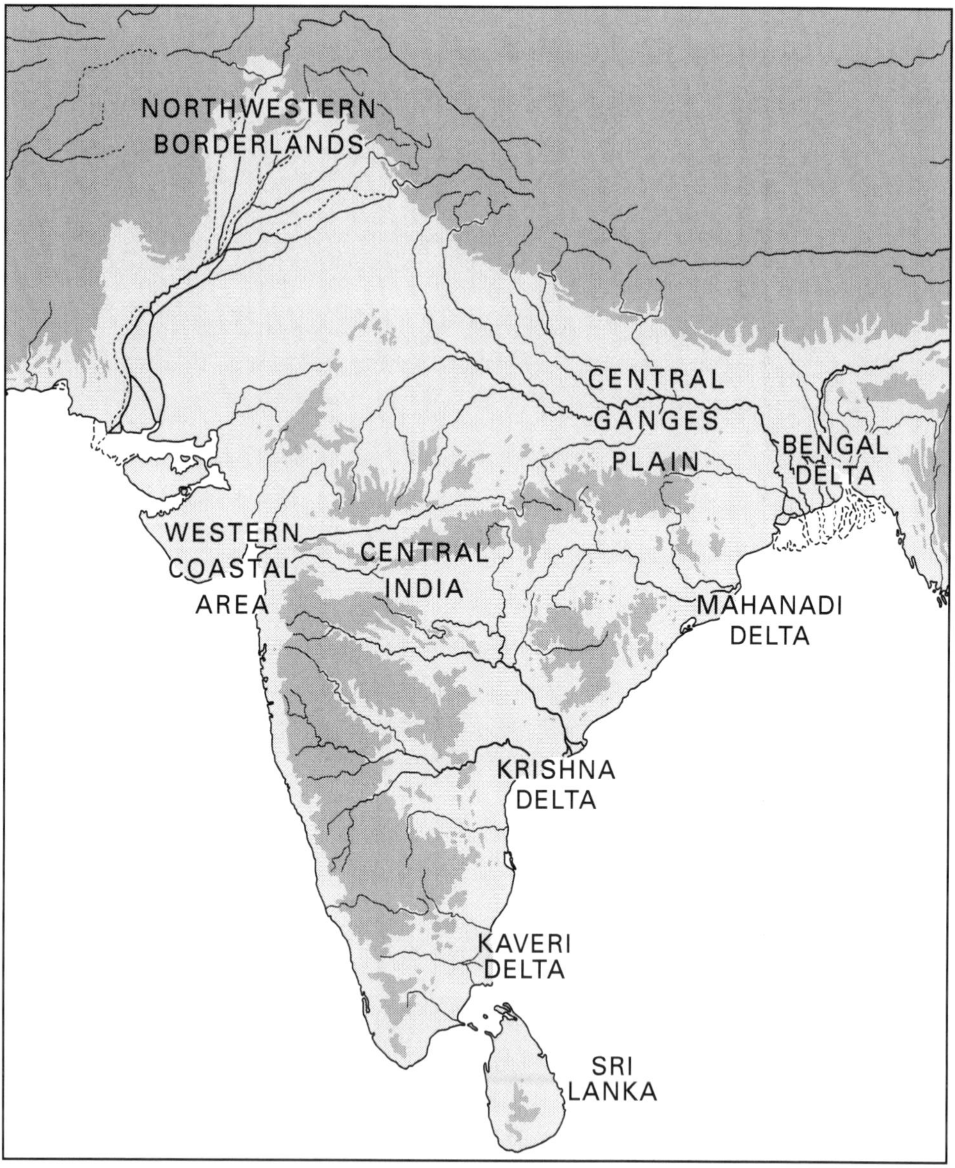

Figure 3.2. Map: Areas of Early Urbanisation

While the Second Urbanisation attained its first major development in the central Ganges plain, it was not confined to this region. Bridget Allchin notes that the new cities were located in a 'a wide range of different regions' (B. Allchin 1995: 13). Figure 3.2 shows the principal areas of early urbanisation in South Asia. Similar developments in Southeast Asia took place somewhat later. The use of iron became common in the northern parts of Southeast Asia from around 500 BCE onwards, and there is growth in settlement size and some indications of political centralisation in areas such as northern Vietnam, which was the centre of the Dong-son culture (Bellwood 1999: 94), from this period. The first real Southeast Asian polities, however, seem to date from around the second to fourth centuries CE.[2] These states were closely linked to the developing maritime trade with India and China, and some of them became early centres of Indic culture.

To return to South Asia, the early political units in the northern part of the subcontinent are the so-called *mahājanapadas*. The term derives from an earlier Vedic term *janapada* for the territory of a Vedic tribe. There are classical lists of sixteen *mahājanapadas* (see below and Fig. 3.3), and they are described as having a variety of different political structures.[3] Further to the south, the river deltas and coastal plains of South India and Sri Lanka were also early centres of urbanisation and political centralisation.

It is useful to have this larger picture in mind. While the Ganges plain was the location of the majority of the *mahājanapadas*, and later became the centre of the first large Indian state, Magadha, and the first Indian empire, that of the Mauryas, India's Second Urbanisation in India took place over a number of different regions during more or less the same period. These were not independent of each other or separate from the outside world. Thus, for example, the question of Iranian influences on political and religious developments in the Gangetic plain, which has been raised on and off over the years (Wright 1966; Boyce 1997), is by no means implausible, especially given the Achaemenid control over the North-Western region from around 520 BCE onwards.[4]

2 McGee 1967: 29–41; Wheatley 1979, 1983; Bronson and White 1992; Hall 1999: 192; K. Taylor 1999. There again a critical feature seems to be agricultural productivity. ('The area around Oc-eo is the only place near the coast west of the Mekong where a particular kind of topography and soil enabled its people to grow significant amounts of rice with the existing pre-canal irrigation wet-rice methods of cultivation', Hall 1999: 192). The capital of the Oc Eo state, a few miles inland, was known as Vyadhapura.

3 As Thapar points out, the original meaning was something like 'the place where the tribe places its foot'. The *janapada* was normally named for the ruling clan within the tribe (Thapar 2003: 121).

4 The suggestion surfaced again in early November 2002 on the INDOLOGY e-list: see contributions by Michael Witzel and others (http://listserv.liv.ac.uk/cgi-bin/wa?A1=ind0211&L=indology).

The Central Gangetic plain was one of the two most significant regions in relation to early religious movements. This was where the early ascetic movements, including the Buddhists and Jains, took shape, and it was also a very important area for the Upaniṣads and developments in Brahmanical traditions. The other significant region in relation to early religion was the area to the immediate west and north-west, including present-day Western UP, Haryana and Punjab. This was the region associated with the early Vedic texts and was clearly the heartland of the early development of the Vedic and Brahmanical tradition in India. By contrast, this region initially took a much more marginal role in relation to the Second Urbanisation.

The population (or at least the ruling elite) in this region, which I refer to, following Witzel, as the Kuru-Pañcāla Region, after the names of the two classical political units (*mahājanapadas*) most closely associated with it, saw itself as 'Aryan' (*ārya*) by contrast with surrounding peoples and used Vedic Sanskrit for ritual purposes. We do not have any meaningful information about the ethnic composition of the region at this stage, but 'Aryan' here is best interpreted as a cultural rather than an ethnic or linguistic label (cf. Deshpande 1995). As for language, it seems likely that by 500–400 BCE the population of the fertile lowland areas of most of present-day North India and Pakistan were already speaking Indo-Aryan languages, so that the contrast between the Aryan heartland and the areas to its south and east was not primarily language-based (Deshpande 1995; Parpola 1988).

TWO DIFFERENT WORLDS: KURU-PAÑCĀLA AND THE CENTRAL GANGETIC REGION

In a recent unpublished work (Hopkins 1999), the American Indologist Thomas Hopkins has emphasised the cultural differences between these regions. Rather than seeing Vedic-Brahmanical culture as expanding outwards into areas which were culturally and technologically at a much lower level, he develops a picture in which the Kuru-Pañcāla region in around 500–400 BCE was surrounded to the east and south by a group of related cultures with a complex and sophisticated cultural adaptation as well as probable links to the Iranian world via Gandhāra. A detailed presentation of Hopkins' arguments would be inappropriate here, and in any case I hope that Hopkins will publish his own work in this area in the near future.[5]

[5] Hopkins was in Oxford in 1999 as director of the Oxford Centre for Vaishnava and Hindu Studies. He was kind enough to lend me a copy of his unpublished manuscript at that time, and we have had further discussions regarding this material (Hopkins, personal communication, 2006).

However I will sketch some of the main features of his model, since it brings together much of the archaeological and textual material in a useful synthesis. In addition, as we will see, there is further material in support of several parts of his picture.

In agreement with most recent authorities, Hopkins regards the PGW pottery, beginning in around 1100 BCE, as associated with the Vedic-Brahmanical complex in the Kuru-Pañcāla region, and as overlapping in some areas at least with late settlements of the Indus Valley Cultural Tradition. He notes however that if the PGW culture 'defines the region of Aryan control and primary influence, it also marks its limits' (1999:14). More specifically, it indicates that this culture did not expand past the Ganga-Yamuna Doab, stopping before the 'heavily forested eastern tip where the Ganges and Yamuna converge' (1999: 33).

What then was happening in other parts of north and central India? Looking first at the northern and western Deccan areas, to the south of the Ganga-Yamuna valleys and the PGW region, Hopkins stresses the different ecological conditions here from that in the 'western and northern alluvial plains' (1999: 17). A variety of subsistence strategies developed in these upland areas during the period of the Indus Valley traditions, coalescing into the so-called Malwa and Jorwe Cultures (beginning around 1700 BCE and 1400 BCE respectively) in the northern and western Deccan (cf. Figure 3.1, and Possehl and Rissman 1992: I, 486–7). These peoples grew barley and millet, lentils, rice, and a variety of fruits, and the archaeological material from these sites shows no traces of influence from the 'Aryan' areas to the north. The region remained important (as the kingdom of Avanti) in the time of the Buddha, and its major cities, including Vidiśā and Ujjayinī, were significant centres during the following centuries.

The Central Gangetic region was characterised by a distinct but related cultural complex. This was the area of the earliest known cultivation of rice in South Asia and by 1800 BCE was the location of an advanced Neolithic population associated with the sites of Chirand and Chechar who appear from their subsistence repertoire to be associated with the Malwa culture and the Deccan. Hopkins notes that this culture 'had reached the Chalcolithic stage by the time the Aryans came into northwest India [. . .] and entered the Iron Age at least as early as any known sites in the Doab – i.e. by around 700 BCE' (Hopkins 1999: 32–33).

Thus, Hopkins argues, we should revise our model from one of an Aryan-dominated expansion into the Central Gangetic region, bringing with it Iron Age culture and urbanisation, to a model of two cultural processes moving more or less concurrently toward the use of iron and urbanization from two separate sources: one in the eastern Punjab, Rajasthan, the Doab, and northward to the Himalayas west of 81° longitude, identified with the Painted Grey Ware culture and the Aryans; the other – based on the Eastern Gangetic culture with its apparent initial connection to the Malwa-type cultural complex – in the region of Patna, in the valleys of the Ghagara and Gandak rivers northwest of Patna, and westward to the region around the lower Doab. (Hopkins 1999: 34)[6]

Hopkins goes on to note specifically that the urban sites of Śrāvastī and Sāketa (Ayodhyā) were outside the PGW region 'and had only marginal contact with PGW culture before their inclusion in the iron-using Northern Black Polished Ware culture around 700/600 BCE' (Hopkins 1999: 36).[7] This later (NBPW) culture was associated with the expanding urban culture of the Central Gangetic region and the early states of Kosala and Magadha. Hopkins notes the association of this region with the story of the *Rāmāyaṇa*, a theme to which I shall return later. He also points to the contacts from the early stages between the NBPW culture and the Achaemenid-ruled territories in the Northwest (1999: 48–52). These are probably associated with the early adoption of coinage in the Central Gangetic region and with trade routes between the Central Gangetic region to the Deccan and via Mathurā to Gandhāra and the Northwest.[8] Hopkins stresses the difference between the 'new political-economic culture' being created in these regions, a culture within which the Buddhists and Jains played an active role, and the Vedic-Brahmanical culture of the Kuru-Pañcāla region:

To say that there was tension between these two worlds – the non-Aryan/Buddhist/Jain world on the one hand, and the Aryan/Brahmanical/Vedic world on the other – is to understate the case. In the sixth century BCE they were really two different worlds, at least as perceived by their main representatives, or perhaps – as seen especially by the Brahmans – two opposite worlds. (1999: 53–4)

If the Kuru-Pañcāla region was dominated in religious terms by the progressive reworking of Vedic material represented by the Brāhmaṇas, the

[6] Hopkins refers to the 'Eastern Gangetic' culture in the following quote and elsewhere; I have preferred to speak of the 'Central Gangetic region' throughout this book, partly for consistency with other authors, and partly to distinguish it from the Bengal Delta region further to the east. We are however referring to the same area.

[7] Unfortunately, this is the period for which radiocarbon dating is least precise (see e.g. Magee 2004).

[8] Hopkins does not regard the new model of kingship itself as a borrowing because he is still using the 'old' dating of the life of the Buddha and consequently dates the growth of Magadha to around 540 BCE. If we move this forward to 420–400 BCE (cf. Bechert 1991–7; Cousins 1996a) direct influence on adminstrative structures becomes more plausible, though as Kulke and Rothermund note this still does not explain the success of Magadha in relation to its rivals (Kulke and Rothermund 1990: 57).

Central Gangetic region and the northern Deccan was by contrast a 'world of female powers, natural transformation, sacred earth and sacred places, blood sacrifices, and ritualists who accept pollution on behalf of their community' (Hopkins 1999: 55). Here Hopkins' evidence derives in part from the mythology and legends associated with the Central Gangetic region, above all the *Rāmāyaṇa*, and in part perhaps on later ritual patterns that would not appear to derive from Vedic sources. We can also point here to extensive iconographical evidence for a religion of fertility and auspiciousness throughout this region (Central Gangetic, Mathurā, Gandhāra) from the Mauryan period onwards. I shall discuss both this material, and the evidence of the *Rāmāyaṇa* and the *Mahābhārata*, which developed out of the corresponding Kuru-Pañcāla legends, in subsequent chapters.

THE VEDIC MATERIAL: THE VIEW FROM KURU-PAÑCĀLA

Working from a very different body of material, the Vedic texts themselves, Michael Witzel, Jan Gonda, Jan Heesterman, Harry Falk, Patrick Olivelle and others have produced a picture of the growth and expansion of the Kuru-Pañcāla cultural complex. Some of this will be best considered in subsequent chapters, but an introductory sketch will be given here, with particular reference to Witzel's work.

Witzel's argument about the Kuru-Pañcāla region and its relationship to the 'Vedic' element within Indian society has several components. Basic to them is a revised periodisation of the so-called Vedic literature, the body of literature which includes the hymns of the Ṛgveda and Atharvaveda and a substantial body of ritual commentaries, philosophical texts, and ritual and legal manuals and treatises, which are generally regarded as the oldest layer of surviving Indian literature.

Witzel divides the language in these texts into five sub-periods, which fall within three main periods, Old Vedic, Middle Vedic and Late Vedic (e.g. Witzel 1989, 1995a, 1995b, 1995c, 1997; Jamison and Witzel 2003). The most important contrast from our point of view is between Old Vedic, which corresponds to the hymns of the Ṛgveda, and Late Vedic, represented by the later Brāhmanas, Āraṇyakas, early Upaniṣads and most of the Sūtras. So far, this may seem relatively conventional, but Witzel's intention is to give this material a historical placing in the social and political developments of the time.

Specifically, Witzel argues that the geographical context of the Old Vedic material is Afghanistan, the Punjab and the surrounding areas up to the Yamunā. In other words, this material goes back to the period of and immediately before the arrival of the Vedic peoples in North India. The society of that time, in Witzel's view, consisted of around fifty small tribes in constant conflict with each other and with other peoples, whom he refers to as 'aborigines' (Witzel 1995c: 4–5). 'Aborigines' is a problematic term in this context; Witzel uses it as equivalent to 'servant/slave (*dāsa*, *dasyu*, *puruṣa*)' and evidently assumes a model in which an invading elite has enslaved an indigenous population (1995c: 5).[9]

The leading role in the tribes was taken by chieftains (*rājan*), belonging to an aristocratic group (the *rājanya* or *kṣatriya*) who dominated the *viś* or mass of the people. In Witzel's account, it is under the leadership of one of these tribes, the Pūru subtribe of the Bharata tribe, that the Kuru tribal federation in the Haryana-West UP region was formed. Witzel dates the coming of the Kuru to power during the period from c. 1200 to c. 900 BCE. In the subsequent period, from c. 900 to c. 500 BCE, leadership in the region shifted to their allies, the Pañcāla, and expansion continued to the south and west.

The period of dominance of the Kuru and then of the Pañcāla corresponds to Witzel's Middle Vedic period and the establishment of the four Vedas in more or less the form we know them today. Witzel sees this latter process as closely linked to the evolving structure of the Kuru state. It is in this period, too, that we would need to place the transformation of the Vedic sacrifice from a competitive performance by tribal chieftains to the royal ritual of the Kuru kings (cf. Heesterman 1985, 1993; Smith 1989: 36–45).

Witzel's Late Vedic period corresponds to the somewhat tentative '500 BCE' that forms the starting point for my own narrative. The compass of the Late Vedic texts is all of Northern India from Gandhāra to Bengal, and south to what is now Northeast Maharashtra and Andhra. I think that we need to bear in mind however that this region would have been far from evenly 'Āryanised' at this time. This issue will be explored in later chapters in relation to the role of Brahmins in Kuru-Pañcāla and elsewhere in north India.

The Kuru state according to Witzel was actually a dual state made up of the Kuru and Pañcāla tribes. He regards it as the first large state in the post-Indus Valley period (1995c: 9), with its origins going back to the immediately post-Ṛgvedic period.[10] The Kuru people regarded Kurukṣetra as the sacred centre of their realm. As Kuru-Pañcāla power increased to

9 'Aborigines' implies a population that is in some sense indigenous. The local population is likely to have included Indo-Aryan-speaking elements, if we assume a two- or multi-wave migration model (e.g. Parpola 1988), and Dravidian speakers may also be relatively recent immigrants (McAlpin 1981). For Parpola's later thoughts on the multi-wave model, see Parpola 2002a.

10 See the Kuntāpa rituals, carried out at the winter solstice on the *mahavrāta* day at the end of the one-year rite. This occasion was a fertility ritual as well as a ritual to help bring back the sun and some of the hymns are also about royal fame and power (1995c: 7).

absorb Ṛgvedic tribes in the eastern Punjab, Haryana and Western UP, Kurukṣetra became the 'center of the newly emerging Vedic orthopraxy and "orthodoxy"' (1995c: 8). The Kuru-Pañcāla state undertook a well-planned process of Sanskritisation[11] (1995c: 9), including the creation of the new complex Śrauta ritual, which allowed various ranks of society to claim status through appropriate levels of ritual performance, and which also included some major new royal and 'national' rituals (1995c: 18). Another result of this process was that non-Aryans,[12] who had previously been able to follow Aryan religion, were now only admitted to Vedic society as Śūdras, unable to perform ritual (and so unable to enter heaven). 'The effect was the creation of a permanent . . . artificial boundary between Aryans and non-Aryans' (1995c: 10).

The Kuru-Pañcāla state was also responsible for the collection of the old ritual hymns of the Ṛgveda, until then still associated with individual Brahmin families, and their compilation into a standard anthology that forms the basis of the Ṛgveda as we know it today. They also produced the original forms of the other three Vedic collections. All of these were edited and compiled, according to Witzel, in forms that suited the new Kuru political programme (1995c: 14–15).

The Kuru idealogues developed a new mythology for the Kurukṣetra region (1995c: 15–16), in which the Sarasvatī river, equated with the goddess Sarasvatī and the Milky Way, flowed down from heaven in Kurukṣetra at the time of the winter solstice. Kurukṣetra was conceived of as the centre of the world. Essentially, the Kuru state created the Aryan sense of ritual and cultural superiority to surrounding peoples that was to become a central component of later Brahmanical culture.

LINGUISTICS

Apart from the limited information that can be derived from possible traces of 'substrate languages', the history of the replacement of indigenous languages by Indo-Aryan languages in North India has left little by which

[11] It should be noted that Witzel is using the term 'Sanskritisation' here in a very different sense from that well-established in the anthropological literature, which refers to a voluntary adoption of high-status cultural practices by low-status groups in an attempt to raise their status. This anthropological usage goes back to MN Srinivas (Srinivas 1952). Witzel appears to be referring instead to an imposition of a cultural pattern from above. Witzel also uses the term to refer to the expansion of Brahmanical culture to other regions; I discuss this usage in Chapter 4.

[12] I should stress again that this did not necessarily mean 'indigenous' people as opposed to Indo-European speaking populations. If we accept something like the Parpola model of several waves of Indo-European-speaking migration (Parpola 1988), and assume that this was followed by a gradual replacement of non-IE languages by IE languages, then non-Aryans by this period could be IE or non-IE speaking, and of 'indigenous', 'immigrant' or (most likely) mixed origins.

it can be traced (Deshpande 1995).[13] What is striking about the Upaniṣadic, Buddhist and Jaina texts is that there is little or no suggestion of non-Indo-Aryan languages being spoken in the Eastern Indian regions where much of these narratives are placed.[14] Arguments from silence are always risky, but one would imagine that if Munda, Dravidian or other non-Indo-Aryan languages were still being widely spoken in the major centres of population at the time of the Buddha or Mahāvīra (say c. 425–400 BCE), they would have left more significant traces. Languages do not disappear overnight, and it seems likely that the shift to Indo-Aryan languages had got going several centuries before the time of these texts.[15]

There is little real evidence in support of the suggestions that the Indo-Aryan languages originated in India, and strong arguments against the idea (see Bryant and Patton 2005 for a presentation of arguments on both sides). Thus, if one assumes that the Indo-Aryan languages were brought into South Asia from the outside, as linguistic and other evidence strongly suggests, then this process was presumably well underway by 1200 BCE, and had been largely completed by the time that the Second Urbanisation got under way. I would have to agree, however, that we do not have any very precise knowledge of how and when the population of large parts of the Indian sub-continent became speakers of Indo-Aryan languages. The most plausible scenario would have Indo-Aryan-speaking groups moving into South Asia from the Iran-Afghanistan region from around 1500 BCE.

13 To the extent that we can trace pre-Indo-Aryan substrate languages in North and North-East India, they do not seem to be Dravidian. They either show Austroasiatic features, as do many of the surviving tribal languages, or in a few cases relate to no currently known language group.

14 As opposed to occasional suggestions of mispronunciation of Indo-Aryan languages.

15 Whether the population of the main Indus Valley cities spoke an Indo-Aryan language during the Integration Era has not been decided conclusively and is unlikely to be resolved without a convincing decipherment of the Indus Valley seal inscriptions. Probably the most scholarly attempt to decipher the inscriptions is that of Asko Parpola, who assumes a Dravidian basis for the language, but it can hardly be regarded as decisive (Parpola 1994). Steve Farmer has produced arguments recently for the seal-inscriptions being non-linguistic (Farmer, Sproat and Witzel 2004). It is also entirely possible that the Indus Valley tradition encompassed groups speaking a variety of languages. Given the presence of a Dravidian language (Brahui) in the region, a Dravidian-speaking population would nevertheless seem plausible. David McAlpin's Proto-Elamo-Dravidian hypothesis, which assumes a common ancestor for the Elamite languages of Western Iran and the Dravidian languages would make this more likely, but this hypothesis is again far from universally accepted (McAlpin 1981; Parpola 1994: 128). An interesting aspect of McAlpin's argument is that he argues on lexical grounds that Dravidian and Elamite separated from each other at a relatively late period (perhaps in the fifth millennium BCE) and that this took place in West Asia. This would suggest that Dravidian speakers were not indigenous to the Indian sub-continent, and may indeed have arrived there not very long before Indo-Aryan speaking populations. McAlpin suggests that the reason why Sinhalese is an Indo-Aryan language rather than a Dravidian one is that Indo-Aryan speakers, moving down the east coast, in fact got to Sri Lanka *before* the Dravidians, moving down the west coast (McAlpin 1981).

This would seem to have been a gradual process over several hundred years in which various tribal groups progressively trickled in. The starting point for the process is less clear, though there are arguments for identifying sites in Swat towards the end of the Indus Valley Localisation period with Indo-Aryan speaking populations (Stacul 1992; also see Erdosy 1995b).

By the time of the Second Urbanisation, however, the general distribution of Indo-Aryan languages in North India and Pakistan was perhaps not all that different from the distribution in modern times. There was also considerable differentiation among the Indo-Aryan-speaking population. While there may have been some presence of Brahmins and of Vedic deities throughout the region, the specific body of ritual hymns and practices associated with the Ṛgveda grew up among a self-consciously distinctive group in the Punjab-Himachal Pradesh-Western Gangetic region, in the region which was at a later stage the location of the Kuru and Pañcāla peoples. This community saw itself as '*ārya*' and as distinct from surrounding peoples, especially those to the east, whom it regarded as outside the 'Aryan' fold. These were areas where Brahmins from the Kuru-Pañcāla region should not venture. If they did, they had to be purified upon return.

There are a number of ways in which one can read this evidence, assuming that it is accepted that Indo-Aryan languages did not begin to reach South Asia until the end of the Indus Valley urban period and the succeeding centuries. The principal alternatives are to assume that a number of already distinct waves of immigrants arrived in South Asia, so that the distinction between 'Aryans' and others reflects pre-existing divisions, or to suppose a relatively homogenous Indo-Aryan population moving into South Asia and subsequently differentiating into 'Aryan' and 'non-Aryan' components. The former position has been taken by Asko Parpola, who has produced a series of studies postulating increasingly complex migratory patterns to make sense of the archaeological and textual material (Parpola 1988, 1995, 1999a; Parpola and Carpelan 2005).[16] F. R. Allchin has argued for a more homogenous population, subsequently differentiating in South Asia, while suggesting that the difference between the models is not all that significant (F. R. Allchin 1995b: 50–1; cf. also Erdosy 1995b).

As far as our present purposes are concerned, we can agree with Allchin that the difference between the models is not critical. The difference between the self-consciously 'Aryan' region and the surrounding populations is however of considerable importance. On an Allchin-type model, this may reflect differing relationships between Indo-Aryan speaking

[16] According to Michael Witzel 1995b, the Inner and Outer Wave idea goes back to Hoernle in 1880.

immigrants and local populations, with a higher proportion of Indo-Aryan speakers in what was to become the Kuru-Pañcāla region and lower proportions elsewhere. It doubtless also reflects specific local and regional histories. In the period described by the early Buddhist texts, as we will see, certain fundamental assumptions were shared by the Aryans and the populations to the south, east and west. Elite groups in both regions saw themselves as *kṣatriyas* and traced their descent to a common body of early mythic figures. Brahmins of some kind were present throughout both regions, and were providing priestly services to ruling groups. Indra and Brahmā were recognised deities throughout the region. Yet there were also notable differences, and the Brahmins had clearly achieved or maintained a much higher status in the Kuru-Pañcāla region than in surrounding areas.

THE *MAHĀJANAPADAS*

The political map of this period according to the textual material consists of the so-called *mahājanapadas*. The political situation is described in texts of slightly later periods from Brahmanical, Jain and Buddhist traditions (see Fig. 3.3). The *mahājanapadas* were medium size political units, mostly consisting of one or two major towns and a rural hinterland. Traditionally there were sixteen of them, though somewhat different lists survive in various Buddhist, Jain and Brahmanical texts, perhaps reflecting different times or the perspectives from various parts of the subcontinent. In the time of the historical Buddha, these had been absorbed into a small number of expansionist states, which were to be incorporated shortly after into the first large-scale empire in Indian history, that of the Mauryas. Thus by the time that the Buddhist *sūtras* were committed to writing in the second and first centuries BCE, the *mahājanapadas* had long disappeared into history. Much the same is true in regard to Jaina references to this period.

The Upaniṣads say little directly about the *mahājanapadas*, reflecting their historical mise-en-scène in a largely legendary period of early Vedic sages, though the earliest texts in this corpus do refer to a couple of kings, Janaka of Mithilā and Ajātaśatru of Kāśī. Pāṇini's grammar also contains a considerable amount of geographical information, including references to many of the *mahājanapadas*. As I noted in Chapter 2, Pāṇini's dating is very uncertain, but his references are generally treated as describing a somewhat earlier situation than the Buddhist material.

Erdosy refers to the *mahājanapadas* as 'city states' (Erdosy 1995c), and like the Greek city-states they exhibited a variety of political structures, though

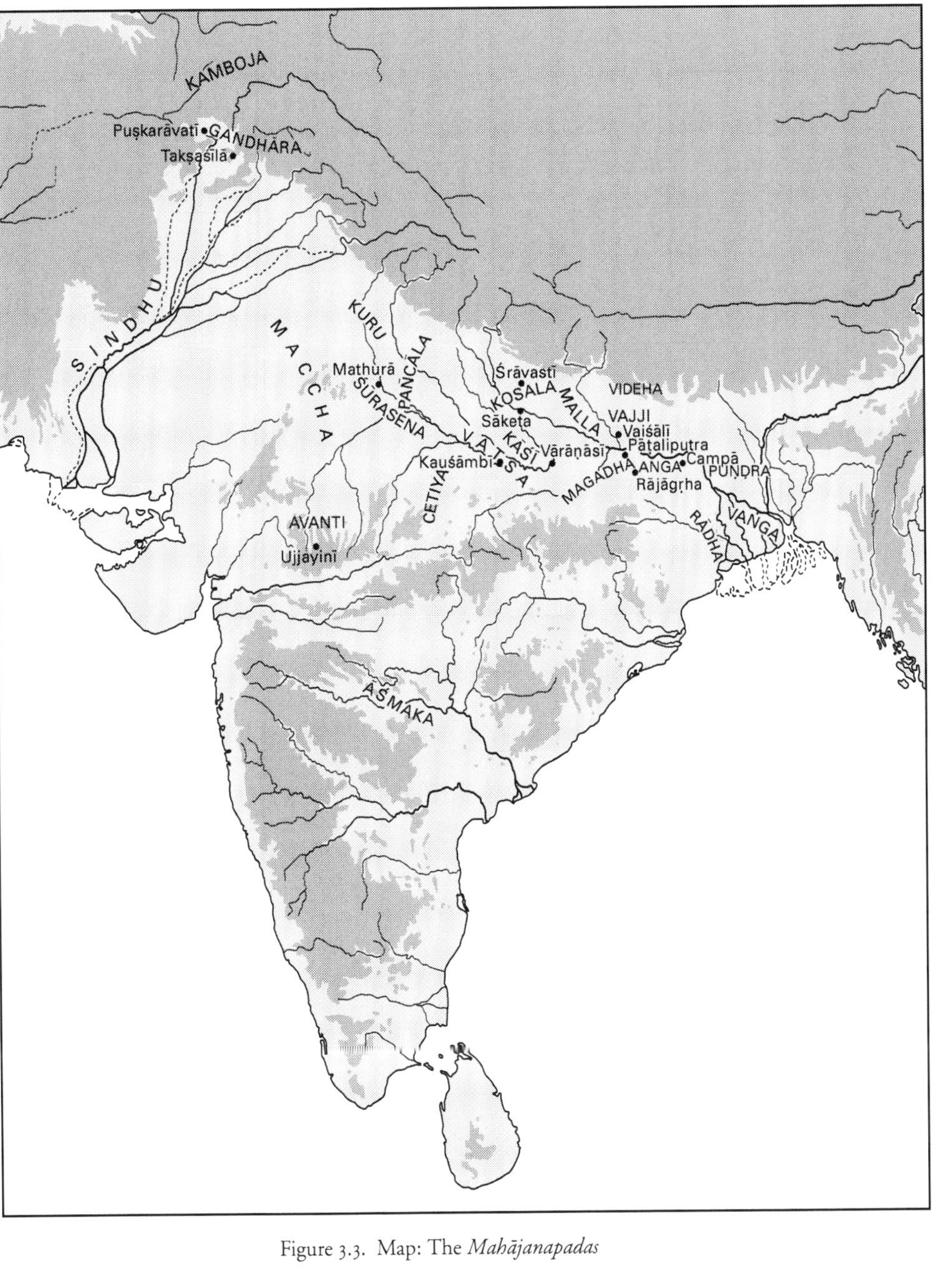

Figure 3.3. Map: The *Mahājanapadas*

the analogy with the city states of classical Greece at around the same time may be misleading. Certainly they were quite varied in political structure and economy. In the Buddha's time, they included four substantial kingdoms (Magadha, Kosala, Vatsa and Avanti), though all of these were incorporated into Magadha during or shortly after his lifetime. So were a variety of smaller states that employed a system known as *gāṇa-saṅgha*, generally referred to in English as 'oligarchies' or 'republics'. These were governed by a council of clan heads or members of leading families (J. Sharma 1968; Thapar 2002: 146–50). The largest of these, the Vajjian confederacy, was actually a league of several such units and its capital, Vaiśālī, was one of the main cities of the Central Gangetic region in the Buddha's time. The Buddha is described as commending the *gāṇa-saṅgha* system and it was evidently a significant influence on the early development of the Buddhist and Jaina orders.

A brief survey of the individual *mahājanapadas* may be useful. **Kuru** and **Pañcāla** together made up the core region of the self-consciously 'Aryan' region associated with the compilation of the Ṛgveda and other early Vedic texts (Brāhmaṇas, etc.). For Witzel, the Kuru state was the original focus for the creation of the Vedic Aryan model of society, in the early part of the first millennium BCE. By 500 BCE, this area seems to have been something of a backwater politically and economically, though it may have continued to be an important centre of Brahmanical influence.

Kosala and **Magadha** were the major kingdoms in the Central Gangetic region in the time of the Buddha. Kosala's main towns were Śrāvastī and Sāketa (the later Ayodhyā), Magadha's were Rājagṛha and later Pāṭaliputra (modern Patna). Kosala had recently conquered and absorbed the kingdom of **Kāśī**, previously an important kingdom with its capital at the city of Kāśī (Vārāṇasī). During the lifetime of the Buddha, the neighbouring state of **Aṅga** (capital Campā) and Kosala itself were absorbed into Magadha. A number of smaller states in the region were ruled by assemblies of local *rājas* or other notables. The largest of these was the Vajjian confederacy, with its capital at the large town of Vaiśālī. This confederacy, which included the Buddha's own home territory of the Śākyas and the old kingdom of Videha, was absorbed into Magadha shortly after the Buddha's death, as was the nearby Malla territory.

To the south of the Kuru-Pañcāla region were a number of other early states. These included **Vatsa** (Vaṃsa), with its main city of Kauśāmbī to the southwest of Kāśī, **Śūrasena** to its west with its capital at Mathurā, **Maccha** (Matsya) and **Cetiya** (Cedi). Further south, on the *dakśiṇāpatha* or southern route, were the important early kingdom of **Avanti**, with its

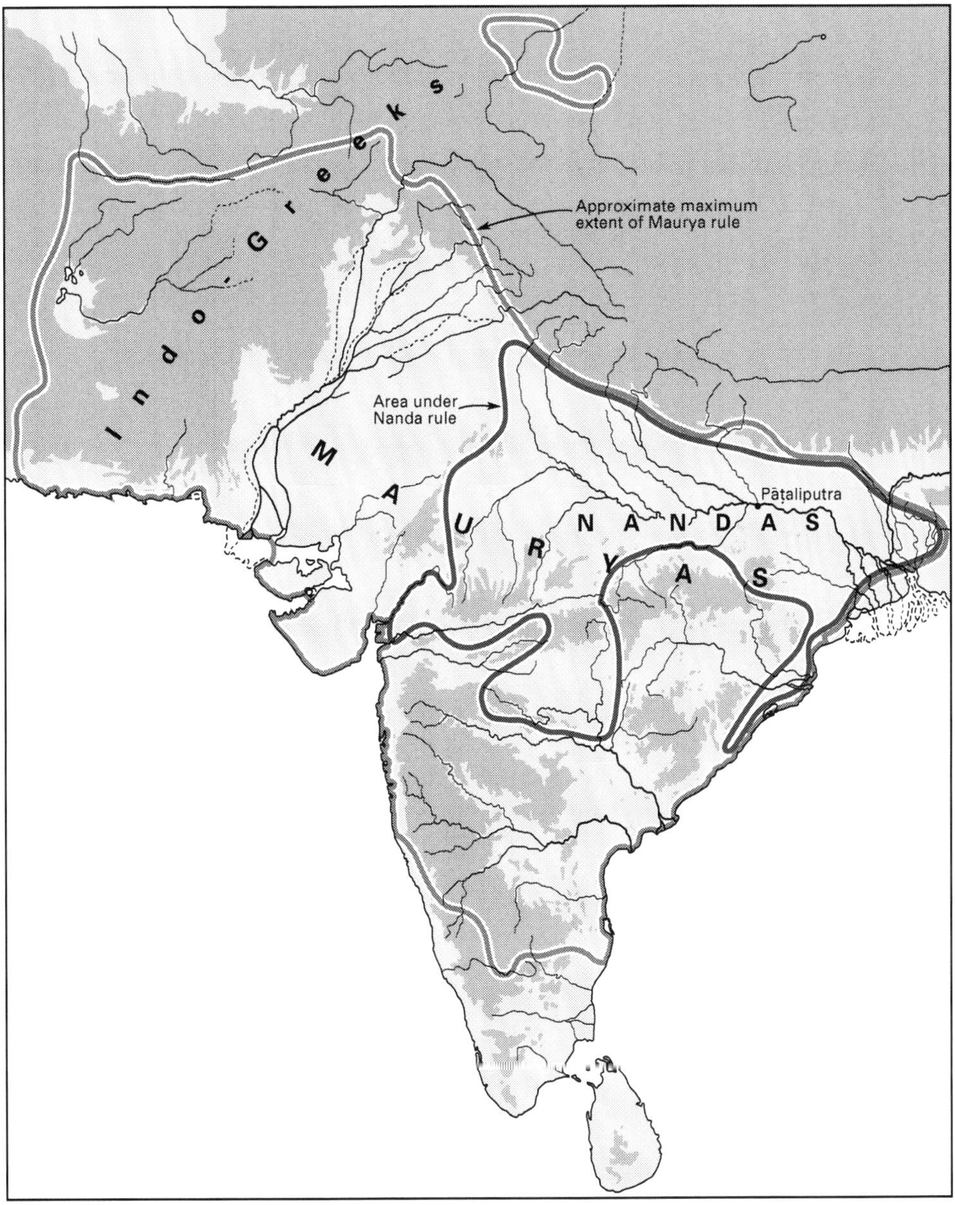

Figure 3.4. Map: Nanda and Mauryan states

capital at Ujjayinī, and **Āśmaka** (Assaka). This whole region, stretching down to the northern part of the Deccan plateau, included important early centres of commercial activity and of support for the *śramaṇa* movements (the Buddhists, Jainas and Ājīvikas).

Further to the east, in the Ganges Delta, the regions of **Puṇḍra**, **Vaṅga** and **Rādha** were not listed among the sixteen *mahājanapadas*, but included significant commercial centres, certainly by Mauryan times (Jahan 2004).

In the northwest, along the *uttarapatha* or northern route, lay the *mahājanapadas* of **Gandhāra** and **Kamboja**. The major cities in this area were Takṣaśīlā (Taxila) and Puṣkarāvatī. Gandhāra and Kamboja, along with the Indus valley (Sindhu), had been incorporated into the Achaemenid empire and provided an important channel through to Iran and the West. Takṣaśīlā itself was both the location of the first major academic centre of the subcontinent, and an important early centre of Buddhism.

The conquests of Anga, Kosala and the Vajiian confederacy by Magadha, which took place towards the end of the fifth century BCE,[17] made Magadha much the largest and strongest state in North India. The dynasty of Bimbisāra and his son Ajātaśatru, the kings of Magadha during the Buddha's life, was followed by that of Śiśunāga and that of the usurper Mahāpadma Nanda, founder of the Nanda dynasty. Mahāpadma Nanda was of *śūdra* background, not *kṣatriya*, as were many subsequent dynasties; his dynasty was replaced by that of another usurper, Candragupta Maurya, in around 321 BCE, shortly after Alexander's invasion of India (Thapar 2002: 154–6, 175–6). The Mauryas established the first large-scale Indian empire (see map, Fig. 3.4).

The *varṇa* status of the Mauryas was contested (Thapar 2002: 176), with Buddhist writers according them *kṣatriya* status and Brahmanical writers describing them as *śūdra*, but in any case they became supporters of the *śramaṇa* traditions. Candragupta is said to have been a convert to Jainism, and his grandson Aśoka was a strong supporter of Buddhism. The Mauryans were also on friendly terms with the Seleucid (Indo-Greek) successor states to Alexander's empire in the north-west (Thapar 2002: 177). Thus India at this stage was relatively open to outside influences. In this and other respects, the Mauryan state was to be a successor to the Central Gangetic world much more than to that of Kuru-Pañcāla.

In Chapter 4, however, we return to the fifth century BCE, and look more closely at the two contrasting worlds which Hopkins suggests existed at that time.

17 On the basis of the 'new' chronology for the Buddha's life.

CHAPTER 4

Two worlds and their interactions

Chapter 3 introduced the wider context within which early developments in Indian religion and society were taking place at around 500 to 400 BCE. In it I mentioned Tom Hopkins' suggestion that Northern India at that time contained two contrasting and in some ways opposed worlds, the Brahmanical and Vedic-derived world associated with the Kuru and Pañcāla kingdoms, and the non-Vedic world of the Central Ganges and northern Deccan (Fig. 4.1).

While these worlds were in many ways opposed, it is important to remember that they also had some important things in common. These included a shared Indo-Aryan language. They also shared at least some other elements of Indo-Aryan cultural heritage, including the presence of Brahmins and of the basic social divisions of Indo-Aryan society, as well as the worship of some Indo-Aryan deities such as Indra. This is not an 'Aryan invasion' model; I assume that populations in both regions were mixtures of earlier Indo-Aryan and non-Indo-Aryan speaking populations. The distinctiveness of the Kuru-Pañcāla region was cultural, not racial.

In addition, we should be aware that the two worlds were not in any way sealed from each other; the early Upaniṣads describe Kuru-Pañcāla Brahmins travelling to Kāśi and Mithilā, and Buddhism and Jainism rapidly made inroads into areas like Śūrasena with close links to the Kuru-Pañcāla region. In fact Mathurā, the capital of Śūrasena and an important early urban centre with trading connections to the Northwest, Deccan and Central Gangetic regions, was a major point of intersection of the two worlds, and would become an important location for all of the newly developing religious traditions (Srinivasan 1989).

Yet the two worlds were different, and saw themselves as different. In this chapter, I look at the bodies of myths and legends through which two main regions (Kuru-Pañcāla and Kosala-Videha) saw themselves, with a view to gaining some insight into the social and political orientations of these societies. I will also look more briefly at two other areas of significance

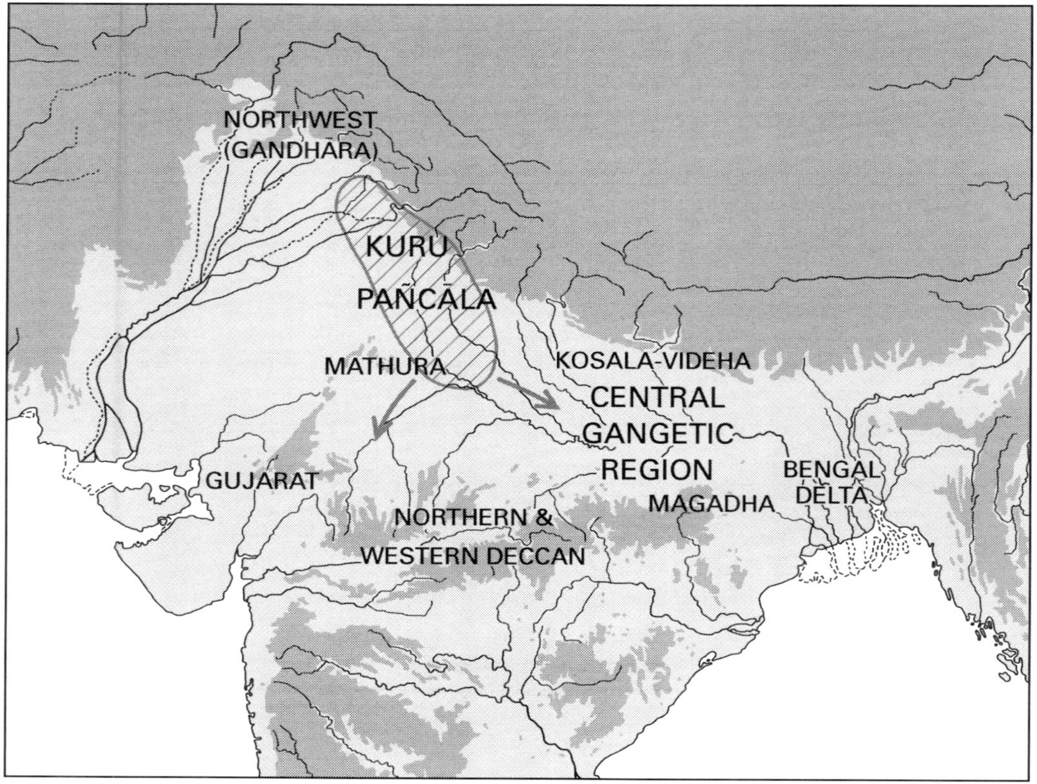

Figure 4.1. Map: The Two Worlds (c. 500 BCE)

in the cultural and religious history of this period. These are the Bengal Delta region, and the Northwest Region (Gandhāra and Kamboja), which formed part of the Achaemenid empire through the sixth, fifth and early fourth centuries BCE, and then became incorporated into the Indo-Greek states that resulted from the conquests of Alexander the Great. Finally, I look at South India, an area which probably did not come into direct contact with North India until a considerably later period, but which may have some important clues about the nature of early Indic society and religion.

LUNAR AND SOLAR DYNASTIES

An important clue to the self-understanding of the Kuru-Pañcāla and Kosala-Videha regions is provided by the body of legends and myths surrounding their origins and the origins of their ruling dynasties. The Kuru kings of the Kuru-Pañcāla belonged, at least according to later Indian sources, to the Lunar Dynasty (Candravaṃśa), ultimately tracing their descent to the Moon (Candra) through a complicated series of mythological events that was set in motion by a sexual relationship between the Moon and the goddess Tārā, wife of Bṛhaspati (the planet Jupiter). The son of the Moon and Tārā was Budha (the planet Mercury). His son, a king named Purūravas, formed a liaison with the *apsaras* (celestial nymph) Urvaśī.[1] Their descendant, King Yayāti, had five sons of whom the youngest was Pūru, originator of the Paurava clan in which the great king Bharata was born.

Bharata is the eponymous ancestor of the Bhārata tribal group and the figure from whom the modern name of India (Bhārat) derives.[2] Witzel reads the Ṛgveda as providing evidence for a struggle between the main body of the Pūrus and the Bhāratas, who originally formed part of the same tribal federation.[3] This is the point of the 'Battle of the Ten Kings'

[1] The story is the subject of a presumably late Ṛgvedic hymn in the form of a dialogue between Purūravas and Urvaśī (10.95; see O'Flaherty 1981: 252–6).

[2] While the *Mahābhārata* account of Bharata's birth, as represented in Figure 4.2, makes Bharata the son of King Duḥṣanta and Śakuntalā, who was the daughter of the sage Viśvāmitra and another *apsaras*, Menakā, he was a sufficiently important figure to be the subject of competing genealogies. There is a particularly interesting Jaina version, which was later incorporated into the *Bhāgavata Purāṇa*, in which Bharata is the son of the first Jain *tīrthaṅkara* (enlightened teacher) of the present time cycle, Ṛṣabha, by Ṛṣabha's twin sister Sumaṅgalā (see Jaini 1977). Bharata's struggle for world domination leads to a fight with his brother Bāhubali. Bāhubali wins but chooses to become a renunciate rather than accept the kingdom.

[3] Note that Witzel includes the Yadu-Turvaśa and Anu-Druhyu groupings as part of the peoples who produced the Ṛgveda. The descendants of Ayu (i.e. the Bharatas) are latecomers who defeat them and take control.

in which the Bhārata king Sudas defeats all the other groups and gains supremacy (Witzel 1995b: 329, 331).

The subject matter of one of the two great Indian epics, the *Mahābhārata*, is the war between the Pāṇḍavas and the Kauravas, two groups of descendants of Bharata, in which the Pāṇḍavas, aided by Kṛṣṇa, were victorious, but virtually the entire *kṣatriya* population was destroyed. The central battle of the war took place at Kurukṣetra, at the heart of the Kuru-Pañcāla realm. As we saw in Chapter 3, Kurukṣetra, according to Witzel, was the central point in the state mythology devised for the Kuru realm in the early Vedic period.

The Kuru kings claimed descent from one of the great heroes of the *Mahābhārata*, Arjuna, via his son Abhimanyu, whose mother was Kṛṣṇa's sister Subhadrā. Abhimanyu was killed at Kurukṣetra, but his posthumous son Parikṣit continued the Pāṇḍava lineage; it is Parikṣit's son, Janamejaya, who held the snake sacrifice that provides an outer frame story for the narration of the *Mahābhārata*. It seems likely that the basic text of the *Mahābhārata* as we know it today was assembled at a relatively late date, probably in response to the Sanskrit *Rāmāyaṇa* and to a period of Buddhist and Jaina dominance over North India (e.g. Hiltebeitel 2001, 2004; Fitzgerald 2004) although the period is still open to dispute (whether the time of the Guptas or a couple of centuries earlier). However, the core of the epic presumably derives in large part from pre-Mauryan stories about the Lunar Dynasty and the mythology of the Kuru-Pañcāla region. Figure 4.2 shows the basic Lunar Dynasty genealogy in diagrammatic form.

The legends and mythology of the Central Gangetic region are based around a separate series of legends and myths, those of the Solar Dynasty (Sūryavaṃśa). The central figure here is Rāma, King of Ayodhyā, and the other major Indian epic, the *Rāmāyana*, is built around his marriage to Sītā, adopted daughter of the King of Mithilā. The dynasty is represented as originating from a figure named Ikṣvāku, who is a son of Vaivasvata Manu, the sun of Vivasvat (Sūrya, the Sun) and the first human being in this world-age. The name Ikṣvāku is mentioned in the Ṛgveda (10.60.4) and the Atharvaveda (19.40.9) but neither reference is particularly informative. Michael Witzel has suggested that the Ikṣvāku may have been a sub-tribe of the Pūru people, but there is little evidence either way.[4] Figure 4.3 presents the principal relationships here.

[4] See Witzel 1995b: 319, 329, 339. Ikṣvāku's position in the genealogy is that of common ancestor, not of founder of a Pūru sub-tribe. If he were the latter, one would expect to find him presented as a descendant of Pūru.

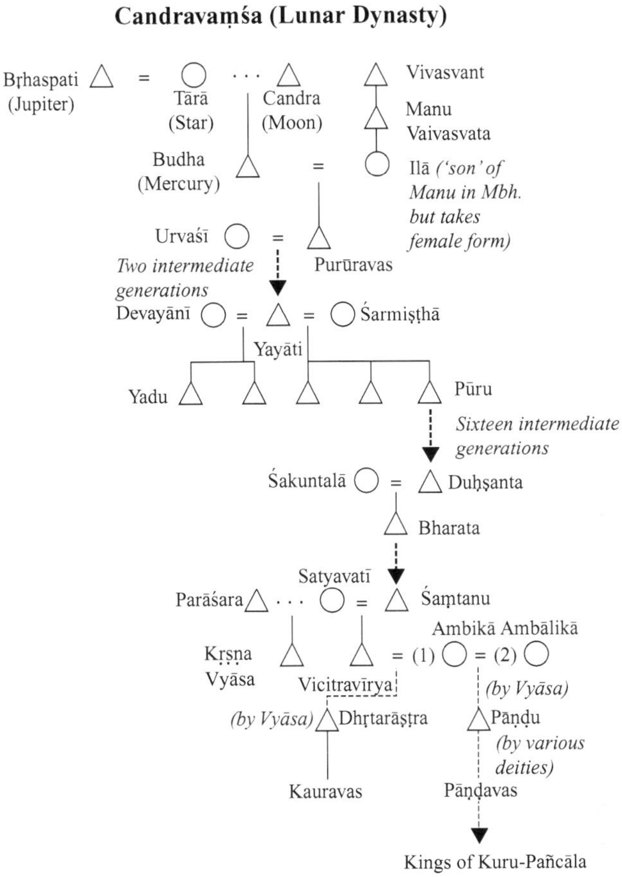

Figure 4.2. The Candravaṃśa (Lunar Dynasty): Outline Diagram

These dynastic lists and traditions are preserved in a variety of sources, none of them particularly early, although fragments of the stories on which they are based occur in the Ṛgveda and the Brāhmaṇas. The earliest complete versions are those in the *Mahābhārata* and *Rāmāyaṇa*, while the Purāṇas include a series of later reworkings. All this is much later than the period of which we are speaking here (500–400 BCE), but it has generally been assumed that these stories preserve early traditions, and there is sufficient consistency between the accounts, allowing for different viewpoints, to support such an assumption.

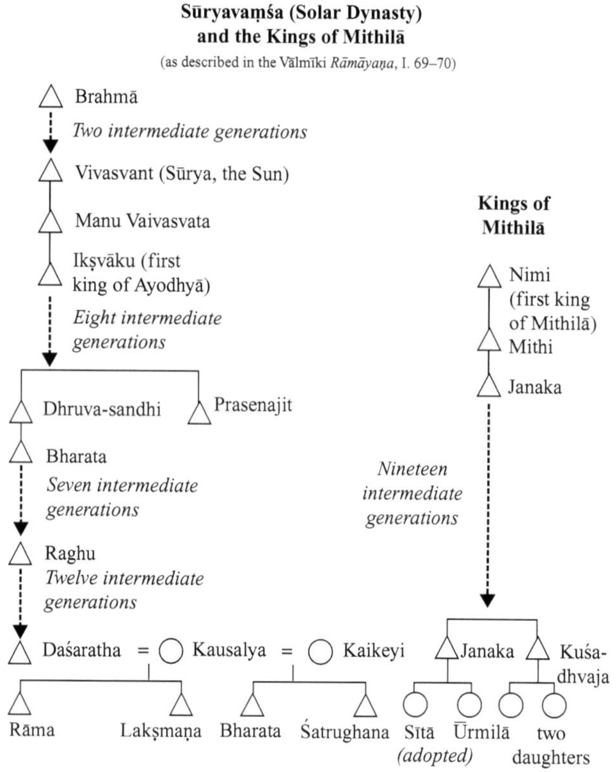

Figure 4.3. The Sūryavaṃśa (Solar Dynasty) and the Kings of Mithilā: Outline Diagram

At the same time, with the exception of some of the most recent figures in the Purāṇic king lists, these accounts are clearly not literal history. There have been attempts to interpret them as such, but for the most part they need to be read in other ways.

As was classically demonstrated in British social anthropology through the work of Sir Edward Evans-Pritchard and his colleagues on the Nuer and other lineage-based societies in East and West Africa, such genealogical accounts are generally, at one level of meaning at least, narratives of the political relationships between the groups that claim descent from the figures described (cf. Evans-Pritchard 1940). These myths also have a considerable amount to say about the nature of kingship and polity within the realms they refer to. What is striking is the extent to which these stories, particularly the Lunar group as a whole when contrasted with the Solar group as a whole, represent several quite distinct mythologies, which have been only very loosely fitted together by later tradition, and which encode different concepts of kingship and ideas about the nature of the state.

The Lunar Dynasty stories, as I noted, are primarily focused around the Kuru-Pañcāla region, but also involve other groups to their south and west that evidently played an important part in the early period. Most conspicuous are the Yādavas, who are descended in the genealogy from Yadu, an elder half-brother of Pūru and so are a Bhārata clan closely related to the Kauravas and Pāṇḍavas. The Yādavas are the people associated with Kṛṣṇa.

Kṛṣṇa, as is well known, reveals himself in a key episode of the *Mahābhārata*, the *Bhagavadgītā*, to be a divine emanation, but this is unlikely to be an early feature of the mythology, and the *Bhagavadgītā* itself has often been regarded as a late addition to the Sanskrit *Mahābhārata*. Kṛṣṇa as a heroic rather than divine figure may go back further, as an early mythological leader of the Yādava people who were allied to the Kuru-Pañcāla rulers. The *Mahābhārata* does not include the well-known legends of Kṛṣṇa's childhood, although a version of these forms part of an early 'appendix' to the *Mahābhārata*, known as the *Harivaṃśa*.

By the time that the Sanskrit text of the *Mahābhārata* was compiled there clearly was very little left of these 'Lunar Dynasty' *kṣatriya* descent groups, and the ruling dynasties in North India were no longer claimants to *kṣatriya* descent.[5] A dominant role in the story, and presumably also in the society in which it was written, had been taken over by a particular group of Brahmins, the Bhārgava (i.e. descendants of Bhṛgu). The stories specifically associated with the Bhārgavas are centred around warrior-type Brahmins such as Rāma Jāmadagnya (Paraśurāma) and represent them as rightfully taking over dominance from the *kṣatriya* (Sukthankar 1936; Goldman 1977; Hein 1986a; Fitzgerald 2002). Thus the 'Lunar Dynasty' myths in the Sanskrit *Mahābhārata* were no longer functioning as legitimation charters for specific dynasties.[6] However it is reasonable to assume that the basic mythological material from which it is compiled goes back considerably earlier, and represents, in effect, the mythological charter of the Kuru-Pañcāla region.

The Solar and Lunar Dynasty stories are connected together somewhat arbitrarily through the figure of Ilā, wife of Budha (Mercury), who is

[5] The Śuṅgas were not *kṣatriyas* and neither were the Guptas, although the Guptas married into the Licchavi royalty, who claimed descent from the Solar Dynasty.

[6] A number of later dynasties in the first millennium CE claimed Solar Dynasty ancestry, including the Ikṣvāku kings of Central India and several Rajput clans. Other Rajput clans claimed Lunar Dynasty affiliation or descent from Agni.

described as the daughter of Manu Vaivasvata and so sister of Ikṣvāku.[7] In some accounts, Ilā's identity shifted between female and male, so s/he is also credited with a series of descendants in his/her male identity of Sudyumna.[8]

THE SOLAR DYNASTY AND THE *RĀMĀYAṆA*

I turn now to look at the Solar Dynasty in more detail. If the *Mahābhārata* is centred around the mythology of the Lunar Dynasty kings, the *Rāmāyaṇa* represents the story of the Solar Dynasty kings. This is the dynasty to which Rāma, ruler of the city of Ayodhyā and king of Kosala, belongs.

These Solar Dynasty kings are also important in Buddhist and Jain history. The Śākyas, the family of the historical Buddha, claimed descent from the Solar Dynasty founded by Ikṣvāku (Pali Okkāka[9]). The Ikṣvākus are also the lineage from which Mahāvīra, the twenty-fourth and last Jain *tīrthaṅkara* or enlightened teacher of the present age, and all but two of his twenty-three predecessors are held to derive. While the Solar Dynasty kings are represented as Aryan by descent there are, as we shall see, notable and characteristic differences between the two bodies of stories that suggest a separate political history and cultural identity.

As I mentioned earlier, the name Ikṣvāku is mentioned in the Ṛgveda and Atharvaveda, but this does not really establish whether the Central Gangetic people associated with Solar Dynasty mythology had or claimed a common origin with the Kuru-Pañcāla group (for example, as a continuation of the Ikṣvāku sub-tribe which Witzel postulates as part of the Pūru group who were defeated by the Bharatas at the Battle of the Ten Kings). They could equally well be a separate group who found Ikṣvāku a convenient ancestral figure. The genealogy of Ikṣvāku in the *Rāmāyaṇa* is not particularly elaborated, particularly in contrast with the complex Lunar Dynasty genealogies in the *Mahābhārata*, and this may suggest that it is a later invention, though it may also reflect the different style of the two texts and the different context of narration (Brockington 1985, 1998). In either case, it would seem that the group claiming descent from Ikṣvāku were recognised as Aryan, but were distinct from the Aryans of the Kuru-Pañcāla region.

7 Ilā is a complex figure who appears in the middle vedic *Śatapatha Brāhmaṇa* as the goddess Iḍā, a personification of the domestic fire-offering ritual or *iḍā*, one of whose purposes is to bring about progeny (e.g. Gonzalez-Reimann 2006: 222; B. Smith 1989: 162–6). See also Hartzell 1987: 114–15, which discusses the possible relationship between Ilā/ *iḍā* and the Tantric channel *iḍā*.

8 In the Skt. *Mahābhārata* 1.70 s/he is described as a son of Manu and as both father and mother of Purūravas (van Buitenen 1983: 174).

9 *Dīghanikāya* 3 (*Ambaṭṭha Sutta*), 1.15–16.

MITHILĀ AND THE WISDOM KING MODEL

The contrast between the Lunar and Solar Dynasty mythologies emerges most clearly when we look at one of the key figures in the Solar Dynasty mythology, King Janaka of Videha. Videha is generally placed by modern scholars in northern Bihar and its capital city, Mithilā or Janakpur, is identified with the modern city of Janakpur in southern Nepal. This location was not identified with the city of king Janaka, however, until the eighteenth century, when the town was taken over by the Ramanandi order (Burghart 1978; cf. Fuller 1992: 166–9). It seems likely that the original Mithilā was a legendary location as much as a real one, as indeed was Rāma's own city of Ayodhyā (see below).

The most familiar item in the mythology of Videha is undoubtedly the marriage of Sītā, adopted daughter of Janaka, King of Videha, with Rāma, a central episode in the *Rāmāyaṇa*. Thus the *Rāmāyaṇa* is not just the account of the Aryan descendants of Ikṣvāku; it is also centrally about an alliance between these kings and the Kings of Mithilā, which is sealed by a marriage – four marriages, in fact, in the Sanskrit *Rāmāyaṇa* of Vālmīki, since Rāma's three brothers are also married to daughters of Janaka and Janaka's brother.

The kings of Mithilā are occasionally presented with an Aryan genealogy but they seem to contrast strongly with the Aryan kings of the Kuru-Pañcāla region, and to represent a significantly different pattern of kingship. In brief, this is a model of the wisdom king rather than the warrior king; its ideal figure is a sage, not a warrior, and he shows strong renunciate tendencies. Vālmīki's *Rāmāyaṇa* can in fact also be seen as about the relationship between these two kinds of kingship, a theme to which we will return in Chapter 9. Rāma is a warrior, but it is no accident that he spends an extended period of renunciation in the forest. Before considering Vālmīki's *Rāmāyaṇa* in more detail, however, it is worth looking at some of the other contexts in which the kings of Videha appear.

The most striking element of this kingdom is the strong association between this dynasty and the idea of the ruler who is a figure of wisdom and/or renunciation. Wiltshire discusses various wise or just kings of Videha in Brahmanical sources, some of them called Nami or Nimi and others by other names, including 'Janaka', the name of Rāma's father-in-law and also of the patron of Yājñavalkya in the *Bṛhadāraṇyaka Upaniṣad* and the *Śatapatha Brāhmaṇa*. Wiltshire traces a range of references to these renouncer or quasi-renouncer kings of Videha, including a number of *Jātaka* stories, and four distinct episodes in the *Mahābhārata* (Wiltshire 1990).

Nami or Nimi is the type of the renunciate king in early Indian religious literature, and is described as a royal renouncer in Brahmanical, Buddhist and Jain sources. In Buddhist and Jain sources he is one, and much the most significant, of a set of four renunciate kings who became *pratyekabuddhas*, a type of enlightened being who is regarded by the later Buddhist and Jain tradition as somewhat less in stature than that of a fully enlightened Buddha or *tīrthaṅkara*. This set occurs in both Buddhist and Jain sources, an indication of its early date. In Wiltshire's book, *Ascetic Figures before and in Early Buddhism* (1990) he analyses and discusses these sources.[10] The names of the kings are essentially the same in both Buddhist and Jain versions, although the brief accounts of how they came to renounce their kingdoms for the life of a *śramaṇa* are slightly different. The four kings are King Nimi or Nami of Videha, King Dummukha or Dummuha of Pañcāla, King Karaṇḍu (or Kakaraṇḍu) of Kālinga and King Naggaji (or Naggai) of Gandhāra (Wiltshire 1990: 120).[11]

Three of these kings are known essentially only from this list of four kings, but King Nimi or Nami of Videha is a more substantial figure who occurs in a variety of other sources, Buddhist and Jain. He is in fact included by the Jains as one of the twenty-four *tīrthaṅkaras* (No. 21 – not to be confused with No. 22, Nemi).

Returning to the central myth of the *Rāmāyaṇa*, this tells the story of the marriage between a prince of Kosala, Rāma, and a princess of Videha, Sītā, whose name means 'furrow', is born of the earth and, Hopkins has suggested, can be considered as a personification of the earth goddess. By implication at least, Janaka could be regarded as married to the earth, so that both Rāma and Janaka are kings who are seen to rule as consorts of the earth goddess.

When Sītā's father Janaka recites his lineage, as Sītā's adoptive father, in the 'Bālakāṇḍa', Book I of Vālmīki's Sanskrit *Rāmāyaṇa*, he begins it with Nimi, describing Nimi's son Mithi, the founder of the city of Mithila, as the first Janaka, and himself as a distant descendant. Janaka describes three of his ancestors as royal sages (*rājarṣi*) and describes how his father renounced the kingdom and went to the forest (I, 70, vv.1–16 = Goldman

[10] The Buddhist version occurs in the *Kumbhakāra Jātaka*, and the Jain version in the Uttarādhyāyana Sūtra. Wiltshire also cites a later Jain commentary on this sūtra. Nimi is also mentioned in the *Majjhimanikāya*, *Sutta* 83 (*Makhādeva Sutta* = Ñāṇamoli and Bodhi 1995: 692–7). In this sūtra, he is described as the last of a long series of 84,000 kings of Mithilā, all of whom became renunciates when their first grey hairs appeared, passing on their kingdoms to their sons. The first of the series, Makhādeva, is described as a previous rebirth of the Buddha.

[11] At 1990: 120, Wiltshire makes both Nami and Dummuha into kings of Pañcāla in the Jain sources but this seems to be an error, see 1990: 139 where Nami is king of Videha.

2005: 360–3). The lineage seems intended to contrast significantly with that which had been recited immediately before by Vasiṣṭha at the request of Rāma's father Daśaratha. This contains far more in the way of warlike deeds and not a single *rājarṣi* (I, 69, vv.19–36 = Goldman 2005: 358–61).[12] The Bālakāṇḍa of the *Rāmāyaṇa* is a relatively late source, but it is clear that there was still a distinct image of the Videhan kings even at this stage.

WARRIOR KINGS AND WISDOM KINGS IN THE EPICS

The Sanskrit *Rāmāyaṇa* and *Mahābhārata* as we know them today are complex texts from a considerably later period, and each has clearly undergone a considerable amount of internal evolution and reworking. The original locations of the story are perhaps mythical rather than actual places. As Hans Bakker has pointed out, the city now known as Ayodhyā, originally known as Sāketa, only became gradually identified as Rāma's capital, probably not until well into the Gupta period (Bakker 1986: 11–12). Bakker noted in 1986, some time before the site of Rama's birthplace became a major issue in modern Indian politics, that 'Ayodhyā, like Laṅkā was most probably a creation of the poet's imagination' (Bakker 1986: 10). Laṅkā, too, is almost certainly an imaginative creation, which only much later became identified with the island of Sri Lanka (Bakker 1986: 10; Brockington 1985: 109–20), while the small town of Janakpur in Southern Nepal that is now regarded as the capital of King Janaka was, as we have seen, not identified as such until the eighteenth century. The capital of Kosala in the Buddhist and Jain texts, and in Pāṇini, was not in fact at Ayodhyā-Sāketa but at Śrāvastī. However, there seems no reason not to accept that the epic belongs to the Central Gangetic region, or that its basic core derives from oral legends of that region.

The Sanskrit *Mahābhārata* is a longer and more complex text than the Vālmīki *Rāmāyaṇa*, but again the body of myths that underlie it presumably derives from oral legends of the Kuru-Pañcāla region and centres around the history of the Lunar Dynasty. The original story may well be modelled, as Witzel suggests, on early battles between chieftains of which we can still see traces in the Ṛgveda. However, while the epic eventually expanded to incorporate peoples from virtually the entire subcontinent on one side or the other of the war, its central events are for the most part clearly located in the old Aryan heartland around Kurukṣetra, with links to Witzel's postulated Kurukṣetra-centred state ideology (Witzel 1995b, 1995c).

[12] Except perhaps for Daśaratha himself, who has explicitly been described as a *rājarṣi* in I, 6, v.4.

I have already referred to V. S. Sukthankar's study of the so-called Bhārgava element in the *Mahābhārata*, displayed in characters such as Rāma Jāmadagnya (Paraśurāma) or Droṇa. The emphasis here is on Brahmins who are aggressive, often warriors, and on the necessary destruction of *kṣatriya* rule. Sukthankar attributed this to a period in which Bhārgava Brahmins had taken over custodianship and performance of the epic from the *sūtas*, the bards who were its original performers. At the same time, the *Mahābhārata* shows signs, most visibly in the figure of Yudhiṣṭhira, of a different emphasis, and one that introduces elements of the Central Gangetic wisdom-king pattern. In an article from 1986, Norvin Hein identified an 'irenic' or peaceful element in the *Mahābhārata* (Hein 1986a). This, Hein argued, is associated with a distinct group of editors or compilers from the 'Bhārgava editors' responsible for the warrior Brahman emphases. These people are associated particularly with the recurring phrase *sarvabhūtahite rataḥ* ('delighting in the welfare of all beings'). This phrase occurs in some sections of the *Mahābhārata*, but is on the whole absent from the major episodes. It is used frequently throughout the *Rāmāyaṇa*. In both epics, it occurs particularly as a description of how a king should feel and behave.

James Fitzgerald has suggested that Yudhiṣṭhira 'was designed as a refutation, or at least a rebuttal, of the emperor Aśoka' (2001: 64). He argues

> that the figure of Yudhiṣṭhira at the beginning of the *Śānti Parvan*, in his attempt to renounce the kingship and go to the forest, was deliberately scripted by the authors of the epic to represent what they saw to be wrong with the Mauryan emperor Aśoka, to purge and refute whose rule was, I believe, the principle [*sic*] purpose for the creation of the first generation of our written Sanskrit *Mahābhārata*. Yudhiṣṭhira's attempted renunciation of the Bhārata kingship was made to allow the epic poets to show him being corrected and refuted by his family, by the Brahmins led by Vyāsa, and ultimately by Kṛṣṇa Vāsudeva. (Fitzgerald 2001: 64–5)

It may be noted that Yudhiṣṭhira himself is a son of the god Dharma, and acts as the exemplar of righteous conduct within the epic.[13]

Thus the Sanskrit texts of the *Rāmāyaṇa* and the *Mahābhārata* are both evidently advancing a compromise of some kind between the irenic and warrior models of kingship. I return to this theme in Chapter 9. For the present, it is enough to note that we already seem to have two different models of kingship in the sources from which the Sanskrit *Rāmāyaṇa* and

[13] Thus Fitzgerald reads this episode as a rejection of the idea of the renunciate king. On Yayāti, the most conspicuous example in the *Mahābhārata* of a king who actually succeeds in renouncing his kingship, see Chapter 9 n. 14.

the *Mahābhārata* are drawn. The *Rāmāyaṇa* myth also suggests that the king is expected to be in harmony with the local powers, as represented by Rāma's marriage (and Janaka's implicit marriage) to an earth-goddess figure (Hopkins 1999). I shall speak of these in general as the wisdom king and warrior king models; in Indic terms we might speak of them as the *dharmarāja* and *cakravartin* models.

Despite the relatively late date of the epics, the stories on which they are based probably go back to earlier sources, and they seem to be part of a wider body of narratives about kings and their subjects. As I have elsewhere suggested in relation to the Tibetan Epic of Gesar, and as in fact seems the case for many epic stories in different cultures, these stories were doubtless from the beginning, to a significant degree, stories about power and how it should be properly used (Samuel 1992, 2002a).

I think all this is enough to make it very likely that there was a widespread stereotype of the wisdom king or proto-*dharmarāja* model of kingship in India in the period from 500 BCE onwards, and that it was particularly associated with the kings of Videha, a principal power in the region before the rise to dominance of Magadha. A variety of stories describe these kings as having tendencies towards the *śramaṇa* or renunciate lifestyle, or as actually becoming *śramaṇas* or renunciates. It also seems likely that this model of kingship was seen at the time to contrast markedly with the warrior king or *cakravartin* model of kingship associated with the Brahmanical reforms in the Kuru-Pañcāla Region.

The warrior king model was based on the concept of the king as an exponent of military prowess who had the military force to ensure compliance from the surrounding chiefs or kings. In ritual terms, this is expressed by the famous *aśvamedha* or horse-sacrifice. Before the horse-sacrifice can be performed, a horse is allowed to roam at will for a year and the king's warriors have to defend and guard it in whichever territory it may wander (P. Dumont 1927; Bhawe 1939). Part of what is happening in the Bālakāṇḍa of the *Rāmāyaṇa*, and in the final book (Uttarakāṇḍa), is perhaps about an attempt to combine or reconcile these two models, with Rāma seen as a synthesis between the two. The first involves an *aśvamedha* performed for his father, the *rājarṣi* Daśaratha, while the last involves an *aśvamedha* performed for Rāma himself.

It is tempting to go a step further, and ask whether the Kuru-Pañcāla (Vedic) warrior king variant can be more closely associated with an Indo-Aryan or Indo-European structure, and the Videha (Central Gangetic) wisdom king model with something more indigenous. I am not sure that we have enough information to justify such a step. By 500 BCE, the Central

Gangetic region would have had several centuries of history during which a mixed population of Indo-Aryan immigrants and hypothetical indigenes had arrived at a common cultural tradition. The warrior king model does, though, look like the kind of model of kingship associated with a mobile and originally horse-riding pastoralist population. The horse-sacrifice model seems much more about the control over grazing territory appropriate for a low-density pastoralist society than about the relationship between a king and a settled population of agricultural communities. The wisdom king model, particularly if we accept the 'marriage to the land' idea as one of its components, seems more the kind of model one might expect in a settled agricultural society.[14]

However, we could also perhaps identify different models of kingship within the 'Indo-Aryan' material itself. Varuṇa, although viewed in an increasingly negative way in later Brahmanical material, retains some of this sense of a just king (Sutherland 1991: 76–83); originally, Stanley Insler has suggested, Varuṇa corresponded to the role of the tribal ruler or chieftain in time of peace and Indra, prototype of the warrior king, to the war-leader elected to take over in time of conflict (Insler 2004). If this is so, then one could comment further that the Iranian and Indian branches of the Indo-Aryan peoples took different choices in relation to this dichotomy. In Iran, the *asura* Varuṇa seems to have been the basis of Zarathustra's new supreme deity of Ahura Mazdā, and Indra was in effect demonised in Iran as one of the rejected *daevas* (see Chapter 5). In India, especially in the Kuru-Pañcāla region where the 'Vedic' model was developed, Indra took over dominance, and Varuṇa faded into the background as a *yakṣa* deity (Sutherland 1991: 77–83). Thus the prime identity of the king in this region was that of war-leader. The Achaemenid kingship, by contrast, picked up on the 'Varuṇic'

[14] As J. Clifford Wright has pointed out, stories of marriages between rulers and *yakṣiṇīs*, chthonic female deities, are a staple of the early literature of the period, whether Buddhist, Jain, or Brahmanical. He instances a Jain text, the *Miyāvutta Sutta*; a Buddhist *jātaka* story, the *Kinnarī Jātaka* (in fact there seem to be a number of *jātaka* stories involving marriages or relationships between kings or princes and *yakṣiṇīs*). and, doubtless the best known, Kālidāsa's stage play about such an encounter, the *Vikramorvaśī* (Wright 1966: 20). The *Vikramorvaśī* is based on the story of the marriage between the Lunar Dynasty ancestor Purūravas and the *apsaras* Urvaśī, a legend which occurs in embryonic form in the Ṛgveda and the *Śatapatha Brāhmaṇa*. These stories have widespread parallels in other cultures; one might think of the European story of Melusine (also the foundation legend of a dynasty through marriage between a ruler and a chthonic goddess), or the Javanese myth of the marriage between the Sultans of Jogjakarta (Jogja = Ayodhyā) and the Goddess of the South Seas, Ratu Kidul. It has been suggested that Kālidāsa's *Vikramorvaśī* may itself have been written on the occasion of the installation of the son of one of the Gupta kings as crown prince or *yuvarāja* (Michael Willis, personal communication, April 2004). The critical point about the *Rāmāyaṇa* variant, if one wishes to accept this argument, is that Sītā was born out of the earth; in the case of the Lunar Dynasty story of Purūravas, the relationship is with a celestial spirit.

theme of divine righteousness and cosmic order as refigured in the shape of Ahura Mazdā.[15]

For my purposes, I think it is best to leave the issue of Indo-Aryan versus indigenous origins as undecided and probably undecidable. What is important is that we have a contrast in political style and mythology between the two regions that helps considerably to explain the religious and political developments that took place.

The Buddhist texts describe the *mahājanapadas* in the Central Gangetic region as mostly operating in the Buddha's lifetime according to the *gāṇa-saṅgha* system of rule by a council of community leaders (Thapar 1984; J. Sharma 1968). The term *saṅgha* was of course to become the term for the Buddha's own community, and the practices of these *gāṇa-saṅgha* are clearly regarded in the early Buddhist texts as an important model for the Buddhist *saṅgha*. According to the Buddhist texts, however, these city-states were being absorbed during the lifetime of the historical Buddha into new, larger kingdoms, with the two expansionist kingdoms of Kosala and Magadha gradually absorbing the others. As mentioned in Chapter 2, the traditionally-accepted dates for the historical Buddha are now generally regarded as too late and these events might now be best placed in around 450–400 BCE, a dating which fits reasonably well with the growth of sizeable, elaborately fortified towns in the region.

What all these accounts make clear is the systematic differences between the Central Gangetic Region and the Kuru-Pañcāla Region (Fig. 4.1). The region centring around Kurukṣetra in what is now Northern UP and Haryana was as mentioned earlier regarded in the Vedic texts as the original *āryavarta* or homeland of the people who identified their culture as *ārya* ('Aryan'). It too was divided into *mahājanapadas*, with the twin kingdoms of Kuru-Pañcāla at its centre. The *gāṇa-saṅgha* system was not found in the Kuru-Pañcāla Region or neighbouring areas, and urbanisation seems to have lagged significantly behind the north-east. While the north-east was the area of the growth of the ascetic orders, among both non-Brahmins (Jains, Buddhists, Ājīvikas) and Brahmins, the Kuru-Pañcāla Region is associated with conservative forms of Brahmanical culture, though here as at other points in Indian history 'conservative' should perhaps be read more in terms of self-image than in terms of actual continuity with the past. As we shall see, it is arguable that Kuru-Pañcāla was the location where a major

[15] There is a possibility that Achaemenid kingship was itself a significant influence on the new Central Gangetic kingdoms (see below). As far as I know, however, the theme of renunciation of kingship does not form part of the 'Varuṇic' or Achaemenid pattern.

reconstruction of Vedic-Brahmanical culture took place, one which in fact led to the Vedic texts in the form we know them today.

BRAHMANIC EXPANSION AND INTERACTION BETWEEN THE TWO REGIONS

As I noted above, the Central Gangetic region and the Kuru-Pañcāla region shared a considerable amount of cultural material in the time of the Buddha. I have suggested above that some of this derived from a shared Indo-Aryan background. There was also an ongoing interaction. Thus, for example, we already find in the early Buddhist texts that dynasties are presented as having Vedic ancestry, elite groups are defining themselves as *kṣatriya*, and Brahmins are common figures within the society. These texts were not as far as we know written down until the first century BCE, and their picture of social realities may in some respects reflect this period rather than the time to which they refer, which is now best dated to the second half of the fifth century and late fourth centuries BCE, but it would nevertheless seem likely that these aspects date back close to the lifetime of the Buddha. Early Jain texts also appear to reflect a similar ambience.

It is worth looking at the modes by which Vedic and Brahmanical influences might have spread to these regions.

Certainly, there is substantial textual evidence for the outward expansion of Vedic-Brahmanical culture. Early texts describe the areas to the east as impure and as unsuitable for Brahmins to live in. The boundary gradually shifts. In a well-known passage, the *Śatapatha Brāhmaṇa* I.4,1,14–16 describes the conquest of the Kosala-Videha region through an early prince, accompanied by Agni, the god of fire (Kulke and Rothermund 1990: 50). By the *Śatapatha Brāhmaṇa*'s time, perhaps the sixth or seventh century BCE, this region is regarded as having been acceptable for Brahmin residence. Areas further to the east, such as Magadha and present-day Bengal, remained problematic. However, this referred specifically to where it was acceptable for Brahmins to settle. It did not imply that Brahmanical religion had become the dominant or universal religion in these regions. Here we have to be wary of reading the present into the past.

Certainly this process would seem to have been only to a limited degree a question of the extension of political control. According to Witzel, the Kuru-Pañcāla realm expanded towards the South and to the East, incorporating the kingdom of Kāśī.[16] It was eventually overcome by the Śālvas,

[16] Witzel speaks of the 'materially little progressed, chalcolithic cultures of the east' (1995c: 21).

a probably non-Vedic group who subsequently coalesced with the Kurus. Following this, the Pañcāla tribe took over as the centre of Vedic culture and influence.

There is little or nothing to suggest the existence of a large-scale state including all of these regions for any length of time. It would seem that the Kuru-Pañcāla region at this stage did not have the economic resources to support a large-scale state structure. It is possible that temporary military conquest was followed by the expanded area thus controlled breaking up into a number of separate territories controlled by brothers or sons (a common enough theme in Sanskrit literature). However, the states with rulers belonging to or affiliated with the Lunar Dynasty rulers would seem to mark the limits for this mechanism.

Instead or in addition, we should consider a range of other mechanisms:

(1) the settlement of isolated families or clans of cultivators in areas which were previously uncleared. Such settlement may have involved obtaining permission from a local ruler, where there was one. In some areas it may have led to the creation of a new local political entity that might be 'Aryan' in style.

(2) Brahmin families might also settle on an isolated basis, as part of 'Aryan' settlements of the above kind, or in non-Aryanised regions, in agricultural settlements or in nearby forest areas, relying in whole or part on their ability to provide ritual services to the local population for support.

(3) Brahmin families may also have been granted land on the basis of their providing priestly services to non-Aryan rulers. There is no evidence for substantial land grants in the early period and in fact it is unclear how far Kuru-Pañcāla kings would have been seen as entitled to alienate and redistribute land (see Thapar 1984). The first evidence for land grants refers to the Magadhan period (see Thapar 1984: 110). For this time, the Buddhist *sūtras* describe what was in later periods a standard mechanism for the expansion of Vedic-Brahmanical culture: the settlement of Brahmins on land granted by local rulers (Tsuchida 1991).[17] Generally, these would have been to Brahmins who were serving as court ritualists or performing other functions for the kings.

[17] A typical account is given in the *Kūṭadanta Sutta* of the *Dīghanikāya*: 'Once the Lord was traveling through Magadha with a large company of some five hundred monks, and he arrived at a Brahmin village called Khānumata. [. . .] Now at that time the Brahmin Kūṭadanta was living at Khānumata, a populous place, full of grass, timber, water and corn, which had been given to him by King Seniya Bimbisāra of Magadha as a royal gift and with royal powers' (Walshe 1995: 133).

The Kuru-Pañcāla state was, on Witzel's account, a joint Brahmin-*kṣatriya* project, and its achievement involved creating an important new role for Brahmins where they increasingly formed part of the ideology and practices of kingship. If this ideology spread to the East, the need for court Brahmins would have arisen, but it is not really clear why or how this might have happened. There are, however, references to the sponsorship of Brahmins by kings and to grants of cattle being given to them in the early Upaniṣads. This suggests that the initial spread may have been on a much more individualistic pattern.

Witzel has used the term 'Sanskritisation' in relation to the expansion of Vedic-Brahmanical culture, though I am not clear how far he intends this term to carry the theoretical weight that it has in the contemporary anthropology of India.[18] 'Sanskritisation' was initially introduced by the anthropologist M. N. Srinivas in the context of a so-called 'tribal' population, the Coorgs of South India, to describe a process by which the group gradually adopted characteristics of surrounding 'Sanskritic' culture in order to raise its status in relation to those cultures (Srinivas 1952).

There are some possible analogies with this process. Contemporary 'tribal' populations in South India, however, have been in a process of constant relations and cultural interchange with surrounding Hindu and Brahmanical cultures for up to fifteen hundred years or more.[19] There were obvious gains for the Coorgs in adopting Sanskritic cultural markers of various kinds. It is not as clear why populations outside the Vedic-Brahmanical orbit in the first millennium BCE would gain by adopting the Brahmanical cultural patterns developed in the Kuru-Pañcāla region, since these patterns would not initially have been associated with a dominant ruling elite or have provided access to material resources. In fact the process was not a straightforward or unidirectional one, since, as the Upaniṣads and the Jain and Buddhist texts indicate, the Central Gangetic region rapidly became locations of major cultural innovation in its own right.

There remains the possibility, particularly if one assumes that there had been previous waves of Indo-Aryan-speaking migrants, that some idea of Vedic-style ritual was already accepted in many of these regions, whether performed primarily by householders or by local priestly lineages. In this

[18] In his discussion of the 'Sanskritisation' of the Kuru-Pañcāla region it clearly does not, since 'Sanskritisation' there is imposed from above (see Chapter 3).

[19] I use quote marks around 'tribal' to indicate that this is a colloquial term in contemporary Indian society (and a legal term, in the form of 'Scheduled Tribes') rather than a coherent anthropological category. It covers a very wide variety of peoples speaking many different languages and with varying degrees of incorporation into mainstream Indic social and religious life.

case, the Kuru-Pañcāla Brahmins might have been seen as specialists in ritual performance, and invited by local rulers and elite families primarily as ritual performers. This might help to make sense of the ambivalent orientations towards the Brahmins that we see in the Upaniṣads and the Jain and Buddhist texts.

THE NORTHWEST REGION AND THE BENGAL DELTA

Were there other regions that presented important alternative social, political and religious models? There are at least two that are worth considering for this period, the North-West, with its links to the Achaemenids, and the Bengal Delta. A third, South India, is probably more significant at a later period, but will also be discussed here.

The Northwest Region

As I mentioned in Chapter 3, the Northwest Region of Gandhāra and Kamboja came under the control of the Achaemenid dynasty of Iran from around 520 BCE onwards. Gandhāra and Kamboja are two of the classic *mahājanapadas*. The capital city of Gandhāra was at Takṣaśīlā, a major early centre of urbanisation and trade and a channel through which influences from the West might, hypothetically, enter into the Punjab and North India. The region was included in a single large satrapy that stretched from the Beas to the Hindu Kush. There is very little information regarding this area during the period of Achaemenid rule. There is little direct archaeological evidence and little indication that the region was tightly integrated into the Achaemenid system. If, as has been suggested by Kosambi and others, the King Porus and his people who were Alexander's chief opponents in the region represent the Vedic people of the Pūru, then it would seem that Indo-Aryan political institutions in the region, probably tribal federations of some kind, maintained a presence throughout the period, and that there was by that time a presence of Brahmanical and *śramaṇa* institutions (Kosambi 2002b: 78).

However it is clear that Takṣaśīlā was the main city in the region from early in the period and that it was a major trading city with connections through to the west (Fussman 1993: 84–6). If nothing else, this region must have represented a channel through which influences from the Achaemenid state could flow.

Can we in fact trace influences from the Mesopotamian region and elsewhere on the new states of the Central Gangetic and Bengal Delta regions and the northern Deccan? Cyrus, the founder of the Achaemenid state (559–530 BCE), appears to have originated from a culturally Elamite rather than Iranian area (Potts 2005: 16–17). His son Cambyses was installed during Cyrus's lifetime as ruler in Mesopotamia in 538 BCE in the 'traditional Babylonian manner', in a ritual involving Cambyses' approval and adoption by the Babylonian god Marduk, and later went through a similar ritual in Egypt in relation to an Egyptian deity (Hinnells 1985: 99).

By the time of Darius (522–486 BCE), the Achaemenids clearly had a developed idea of divinely sanctioned kingship, derived from Avestan (Zoroastrian) sources, and linked to the idea of the king as being engaged in a cosmic struggle for the forces of good against those of evil (Skjærvø 2005: 52–81; Hinnells 1985: 98–109, note seal on p. 100). Whether or not the Achaemenid rulers could be described as wisdom kings in the sense of Janaka, they clearly saw themselves as kings who ruled by the authority of Ahura Mazdā and who were responsible for securing peace and well-being on earth in his name, for combatting the forces of the 'Lie', and for educating their people in the ways of wisdom (Skjærvø 2005: 61–5; Lincoln 2003).

In passing, it seems at least possible that the Vedic *devas* were regarded for the most part as belonging to the forces of the Lie in Achaemenid terms. How far this was an issue for Achaemenid rulers encountering Vedic Indians it is hard to say. They were probably still conscious of their Indian subjects as being 'Aryan' (see Grenet 2005 on the famous list of Aryan peoples in the *Videvdad*), and in any case the Cambyses episode suggests that the Achaemenids were relatively pragmatic about such matters.

It is conceivable though that the Achaemenid model may itself have been a significant influence on the evolution of the wisdom king model in the Central Gangetic region, especially if, as Wright suggests, there was a kind of polarisation taking place between Brahmanical and counter-Brahmanical models in the region (Wright 1966: 16–17). If the local rulers were looking for alternative models for a state to those offered by the Brahmins, they might well have looked to the Achaemenids.[20] Yet one might expect contacts with the Achaemenid state to have left deeper traces. There have been suggestions that writing (the Kharoṣṭhī script, which may have served as a model for the Brāhmī script, the ancestor of all modern Indian scripts) came through Iran, and also the Aśokan practice of public stone inscriptions (Thapar 2003). Punch-marked coinage, the first known form of Indian currency, may also have come from the Achaemenids, though the evidence seems to

[20] Cf. e.g. Kulke and Rothermund 1990: 57. At a later stage, the Indo-Greek kingdoms might have offered a similar resource.

point to the Indo-Greek period (Bailey and Mabbett 2003: 57 n.2, referring to Cribb 1985).

The Northwest was also a channel to Greek knowledge: we know that there were substantial transfers of knowledge along this route, for example in the case of Indian astrology, which derives from the Greek system. The influence of Greek sculpture on Indian sculpture is also obvious and has long been recognised. We will see some further examples of this kind later, some relatively secure, others more speculative.[21]

Magadha and the Bengal Delta

Moving east from the Central Gangetic region, we come to Magadha and then to the Bengal Delta. Magadha has already been mentioned as one of the *mahājanapadas*. It was in the end the most successful of them as an expansionist state, becoming the basis of the first major north Indian empire, that of the Nandas. The kings of Magadha in the Buddha's time seem to have no real claims to Vedic connections, and in fact the then ruling dynasty does not seem to have gone back very far, though Magadha was included in the *Mahābharata* under the rule of a doubtless fictional earlier dynasty. Magadha probably owed much of its initial significance to its natural resources; this was an early area for iron mining (Kosambi 1965: 123). From the Vedic perspective, however, this was a transition region, only partially Brahminised and still of suspect nature.

The areas further to the east were presumably even more so. Yet there are mentions of these regions in fairly early Vedic material and the coastal trading states that evolved in the nearby Ganges-Brahmaputra delta, along with other coastal settlements such as the Mahanadi delta in Orissa, may have been of importance from quite early times. The unstable nature of the Ganges-Brahmaputra delta means that many early port sites may have disappeared, but Tamluk, the ancient port of Tamralipti, on the western edge of the delta, has been excavated and dates at least as far back as the second century BCE, while Chandraketugarh, in the 24 Parganas district, has an occupational sequence going back to a period before the Northern Black Polished Ware (NBPW) which is generally associated with the developed kingdoms of the Central Gangetic region (Chakrabarti 1995: 218). We

[21] I should note that I have no interest here in trying to claim that everything valuable in South Asia came from outside. However it is pointless to exclude the possibility of external borrowings on *a priori* grounds and as noted there will be further examples in later chapters. I do not see that it lessens the achievements of the people of South Asia throughout history to recognise that there was sharing and interaction between cultures.

know from Greek and Roman sources that there were important trading communities here at a somewhat later stage.

The extent to which the Bengal delta area shared a cultural identity with present day Eastern UP and Bihar at the start of the period is unclear; I would tend to assume that as trading settlements grew in the small towns of the Eastern UP-Bihar area, there was increasing cultural importation by these urban centres along the trade routes from the delta. The Bengal region in more recent times developed a caste system with distinct differences from that of most of North India, with little or no *kṣatriya* presence, and a basic division between Brahmin landowners, lower castes and untouchables, but given that substantial Brahmin settlement in the region probably did not get underway until well into the first millennium CE this can probably not be read back very far.

As elsewhere, for example in pre-colonial West Africa or with the cities of the Hanseatic League in northern Europe, one might expect a coastal community based on trade to have political models based on the maintenance of the law of the market and of peace between the various trading communities. It is uncertain how strong a contrast would have existed at this period between the social and political style of the delta towns and inland settlements, but there were clearly connections between them, and a trading state might provide a natural environment in which a wisdom king ideology might develop. Traders would have had little interest in war, since their urban bases were natural victims in times of military conquest, and they would have preferred to see their kings as relaxed and somewhat hands-off administrators of justice rather than as aggressive conquerors.

It may be worth noting the significance of cult-associations in the West African region in recent times. Such associations, centred around initiation into the cult of the various spirits of the local pantheon, have offered in recent times some of the same advantages that early ascetic Buddhist, Jain or Ājīvika ascetic orders may have offered to the growing merchant community: a trans-local association based on ethical principles, with a network of cult-centres and fellow practitioners scattered throughout the cities and settlements of the trading region.[22] The initiatory cults of the Hellenistic world (Demeter at Eleusis, Isis, Mithras) may have offered somewhat similar advantages to their members. I shall suggest in Chapter 6 that

[22] For example the *ekpe* or *ngbe* societies of the Cross River region of south-eastern Nigeria, which 'were instrumental in the transformation of an aggregate of agnatically organized fishing communities [. . .] into the hub of a vast transethnic exchange system based on the circulation not just of slaves, palm oil and European commodities, but of sacred knowledge as well' (Palmié 2006: 100), or the Poro and Sande societies in Liberia, Sierra Leone and neighbouring regions (Little 1965, 1966; Fulton 1972; Leopold 1983).

cult-associations of this kind may have been significant predecessors to the Buddhist and Jain orders.

SOUTH INDIA AND THE CASTE SYSTEM

As I mentioned, South India probably did not come into direct contact with North India until a considerably later period. As a consequence, we have information about South Indian society which arguably predates extensive influence from the 'Indo-Aryan-speaking' component in the North, and this may provide some important clues about the nature of Indian society before the arrival of these elements. In particular, the southern material introduces a theme which will be significant throughout this book; the low-caste or outcaste group with an important spiritual or ritual function. Indeed, George Hart has argued that this non-Indo-European theme is at least as important for the development of the caste system as the Indo-European structure represented by the familiar *varṇa*-system, with its fourfold division into Brahmin, *kṣatriya*, *vaiśya* and *śūdra*.

The population of the four southern states of modern India, as is well known, mostly speak Dravidian languages, unrelated to the Indo-Aryan languages dominant in the north. These areas were only slowly and progressively incorporated into the new order developing in the north, and they retained their linguistic distinctiveness and a considerable degree of cultural distinctiveness as well. This is particularly true of the regions that make up what are now the two southernmost states, Tamilnadu and Kerala. The two states to the north, Karnataka and Andhra Pradesh, were substantially incorporated into the Sātavāhana and Meghavāhana states from the first century BCE or so, and presumably came under significant Indic and Brahmanical influences at this time. The Meghavāhanas also made a substantial incursion into Tamilnadu in the first century BCE, but on the whole the politics of the south centred around conflicts between relatively small locally-based regimes, and even when larger-scale states such as the Pallavas developed, they were themselves southern in origin and reflected southern emphases.

As these larger states developed, South Indian kings increasingly looked to the north and to the import of Indic models of religion and of kingship. These were, however, not the only influences at hand. The Malabar coast, in what is now Kerala, had strong trading connections to Egypt and the Mediterranean, as the *Periplus of the Erythrean Sea*, a guide to the sea-trade to India written in Egypt in the early second century CE, demonstrates (Huntingford 1980). Richard Fynes demonstrated a few years ago that the cult of the Goddess Pattinī, important today in Sri Lanka and earlier also significant in much of South India, is probably derived from the Hellenistic cult of Isis in Egypt, and was transmitted along this sea route (Fynes 1991, 1993). So, no doubt, was much else. There was a Roman settlement with a Temple of Augustus at Mouziris on the Malabar coast (Huntingford 1980: 116), so there was at least some presence of European ideas of divine kings as well as Brahmanical ones.[23]

Indic influences in the south included not only Brahmanical religion, but also Buddhism and Jainism. According to Jain tradition, there was a strong Jain presence in the south from the third century BCE onwards, and Śravaṇa Beḷgoḷa in Karnataka remains one of the most important of Jain pilgrimage sites. Sri Lanka was traditionally converted to Buddhism at the time of Aśoka and there was a Buddhist presence in the Andhra region by around the same time. However, substantial evidence for Buddhism in Tamil-speaking regions only dates from the fourth century CE, with Brahmanism and Jainism perhaps a couple of centuries earlier (Schalk 1994).

Here, however, we are interested in what might have preceded the arrival of Brahmanism, Buddhism and Jainism. Our main source is early Tamil literature. Some of this is very informative but unfortunately, the dating of early Tamil literature is subject to the usual controversies.[24] In addition, much of what we have has clearly been formalised for literary purposes. However the Tamil Sangam literature, generally regarded as the earliest layer of the Tamil literary heritage, can perhaps be dated to the third to sixth centuries CE onwards.[25]

George Hart, who works primarily on early Tamil poetry, has developed an interesting account of Tamil ritual kingship, which he suggests was an important source for the Indian caste system as we know it today (Hart 1987). Essentially, he argues that the indigenous South Indian political model was based around the ritual power of the king, supported by a group of ritual and magical specialists of low social status. Hart has also suggested that this provides an indigenous model for the caste system, and that we

[23] A recent novel by the Indological scholar Kamil Zvelebil gives a fictional, though historically based, account of the Roman trade with India (Zvelebil 2001).

[24] All this is today rather political. Given the anti-Brahmanical and anti-Sanskritic tendency of much Tamil politics in the twentieth century, there is a tendency for some modern Tamil historical writing to play down Brahmanical influences at the expense of Buddhist and indigenous material, just as there is a tendency among North Indian writers influenced by Hindu nationalism to emphasise Vedic and Brahmanical material and push it back into earlier periods.

[25] Datings for this literature vary but the scholarly consensus seems to be settling on this period (e.g. Zvelebil 1992).

should look here rather than to the Indo-Aryan *varṇa* model for central aspects of the Indian caste system as it later developed.

The question of the origins of caste (here referring to what in Sanskrit and North Indian vernaculars is referred to as *jāti*, not *varṇa*, see below) is a large and important one, and any substantial treatment of it would take me well beyond the scope of this book. Controversies over caste in recent years have centred around a number of related issues: how far one can talk about a single caste system for India; how far back we can trace caste as we know it in modern times into earlier Indian society; how dominant the values associated with caste were in Indian society; how far caste represents an autonomous domain of hierarchy which can, conceptually at least, be seen as distinct from the authority of the king.

On all these issues, Louis Dumont's classic work on the caste system, *Homo Hierarchicus*, took a clear position: he held that there was an underlying caste system, of which local caste hierarchies are individual expressions; that this was the basic structure of pre-modern Brahmanical society; that its values totally dominated all levels of Indian society; and that the Brahmanical domain of caste hierarchy should, conceptually at least, be kept separate from the power of the king (L. Dumont 1972).

There has been a great deal of rethinking and further study since the time of Dumont, and all of these contentions have been variously contested. Dumont's work was a major contribution, if only in the clarity with which it stated the Brahmanical perspective on Indian society (Berreman 1971; Mencher 1974). More recent re-analyses, however, have surely been right to emphasise the extent to which the caste system is always about power, politics and practical success. Caste cannot be treated as primarily derivative from a hierarchy of relative purity, with other factors as a simple add-on (Quigley 1993; Searle-Chatterjee and Sharma 1994). If only because of its close relation to the political domain, caste is constantly open to change and transformation, and it is hard to believe that Dumont's idealised picture of the caste system was ever an empirical reality anywhere, though it has undoubtedly been a powerful ideological conception in many places and times.

Susan Bayly's recent demonstration of the relative modernity of much of what we now recognise as the caste system, in her recent book *Caste, Society and Politics in India*, may itself be open to criticism in details, but the general picture it paints is persuasive (Bayly 2001). As for values, I have argued elsewhere that at the very least caste needs to be supplemented within the value-systems of everyday Indian life by additional systems of values more oriented around the practicalities of everyday life (Samuel 1997).

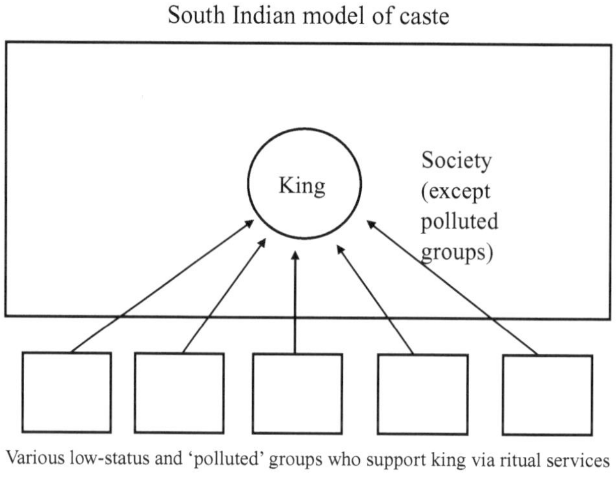

Figure 4.4. The Early South Indian Caste System according to George Hart

The relevance of Hart's work on early South India to all this is that he argues that those aspects of caste which are about polluted and low status can be traced back to a period of Tamil society which, arguably, had not yet been substantially restructured in accordance with Brahmanical norms. The ritual kingship of the early Tamil king was dependent on a variety of court ritualists, including drummers and other musicians, who were essential to the maintenance of the king's power, but who were themselves regarded as of low and 'polluted' status, like the so-called untouchables or *dalit* groups of modern Indian society (Hart 1987).[26]

In other words, the major division in society was between a majority without internal caste-like divisions and a minority consisting of a number of small occupationally-polluted groups (Fig. 4.4).

This is a completely different structure from that familiar to us from early Vedic sources. Here, by contrast, we find the well-known division into four groups, the three upper *varṇas* (Brahmin, *kṣatriyas* and *vaiśyas*), and the remainder, the *śūdras* (Fig. 4.5).

Within this system, we have a series of distinctions, between the *kṣatriya* and the Brahmins, between these two and the *vaiśyas*, and between these three 'twice-born' castes and the *śūdras*. The first three categories here

[26] *Dalit* and low-status groups have continued to have an important ritual role in Indian society into modern times, particularly in the South, and there is an extensive body of anthropological material bearing on this theme. See for example Brubaker 1979.

Brahmanical Model of Caste (*varṇa*)

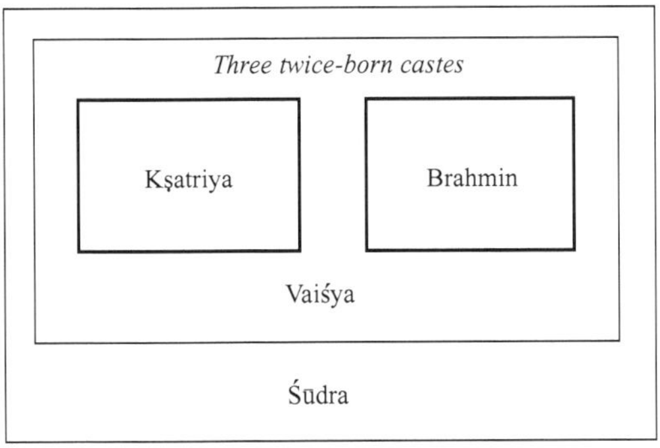

Figure 4.5. The Brahmanical *Varṇa* System

probably derive, like the parallel formulations which Georges Dumézil pointed out in other Indo-European societies such as Rome, Greece or Scandinavia, from a common Indo-European basis, while its extension to a fourfold structure through the addition of the *śūdras* is presumably a Brahmanical formulation from North India.[27] If Witzel is right, in fact, we can locate this development in the early ideological restructuring of the Kuru state, which also insisted on the dominant position of the Brahmins as the most pure of the *varṇas*.[28]

However, as is well-known, this does not constitute the caste system in any of the various forms in which we find it in present-day South Asia. As has been shown by a wide variety of anthropological studies, the most 'typical' form of the South Asian caste system actually consists of a large number of in-marrying sub-groups (*jāti*) (e.g. L. Dumont 1972). Typically some of these groups are generally accepted by members of the community as being at the pure end of a spectrum of purity and pollution, others at being the impure end. Disagreements about status are however endemic, often phrased in terms of competing claims to Brahmin, *kṣatriya* or *vaiśya* status, and expressed through refusal to accept various kinds of food or drink

[27] A convenient introduction to Dumézil's theories is provided by Littleton 1982. Discussion in recent years has focused on the question of whether a 'fourth function' is implied in the general Indo-European context, see e.g. N. Allen 1987, 1996.

[28] It may be noted that this Brahmanical dominance was contested outside the Kuru region. We know from Buddhist texts that the priority of the Brahmins was not accepted by the compilers of the Pali Canon, who repeatedly represent Śākyamuni as informing Brahmins that they are inferior by caste status to *kṣatriyas*. Thus it would seem that while the people of the Central Gangetic region accepted the general idea of the division into Brahmin, *kṣatriyas*, and *vaiśyas*, they rejected the primacy of the Brahmins that was a key feature of the Kuru-Pañcāla system.

from other groups (implying that the members of the other groups are less pure). It is also clear that the ultimate authority in terms of determining status lay in the local ruler. Many agricultural communities also include a large majority of a single caste, usually peasant farmers, with so-called untouchable groups owning little or no land and providing agricultural labour for this 'dominant' caste.

This is a very different picture from the *varṇa* system. At most the *varṇa* system provides one component of the caste system, the idea of a hierarchy of status in which the Brahmins occupy the highest position and claims to membership of other twice-born *varṇa* provide the basis for status competition. The other major component of the caste system is provided, Hart suggests, by the ritual kingship of South India, with its low-status polluted ritual practitioners.

These low-status polluted ritual groups are an important issue in relation to the development of the ascetic orders, and later of Tantra, and I will return to them in Chapter 6 in this connection. For the present, I want to note, however, that there are indications that this scheme was not just a local South Indian issue but may have had a wider distribution. It may well be that the kind of situation described by Hart, in which the ruler was surrounded by a number of groups of occupational specialists with ritual functions, but low or compromised social status, was more widespread in early times.[29] We still find something very much like it today among Tibetan communities in Ladakh, Nepal and elsewhere in the Himalayas, where low-status drummers (usually referred to as Mon), blacksmiths and other specialists retain a significant religious role (e.g. Jest 1976; Kaplanian 1981: 176–89; Dollfus 1989).

In fact, the North Indian system of social stratification itself, in social reality rather than Brahmanical theory, may have been more like this even before the encounter with the south got under way. A common pattern in many areas in recent times, including large parts of Bengal and even the Punjab, is one where the majority of the population belonged to a single cultivator-type caste, with small numbers of attached low-caste ritual specialists of various kinds. This again seems to hark back more to the kind of model suggested by Hart, especially when it is borne in mind that many priests, whether or not they claim Brahmin identity, are in various ways still regarded as being of low or compromised status. The preoccupation with Brahmanical texts such as the *Manusmṛti* ('Laws of Manu') with explaining

[29] For an example in a pastoralist society, see Galaty 1979. It is interesting though that of the five low-caste occupations regularly mentioned in the Pali Canon (*caṇḍāla, nesāda, veṇa, rathakāra, pukkusa*, e.g. Masefield 1986: 148) none appears to have a ritual role.

how low-status and outcaste groups originated from improper marriages of various kinds may be an early attempt to give an acceptable ideological spin to this situation (cf. Tambiah 1973).

GENDER ATTITUDES ACROSS SOUTH AND SOUTHEAST ASIA

A further issue needs to be introduced at this point; the variations in gender attitudes and specifically in the status of women across the entire region of South and Southeast Asia. Southeast Asia as a region is characterised by a relatively high status for women and by relatively equal gender relations, and it seems clear that this pattern has a considerable history in the region:

> Relations between the sexes are one of the areas in which a distinctive Southeast Asian pattern exists. Even the gradual strengthening of the influence of Islam, Christianity, Buddhism and Confucianism in their respective spheres over the last four centuries has by no means eliminated this common pattern of relatively high female autonomy and economic importance. In the sixteenth and seventeenth centuries the region probably represented one extreme of human experience on these issues. It could not be said that women were *equal* to men, since there were very few areas in which they competed directly. Women had different functions from men, but these included transplanting and harvesting rice, weaving and marketing. Their reproductive role gave them magical and ritual powers which it was difficult for men to match. These factors may explain why the value of daughters was never questioned in Southeast Asia as it was in China, India, and the Middle East; on the contrary, 'the more daughters a man has, the richer he is'.[30]

All this could certainly not be said of contemporary South Asia. Despite the significance of female forms of divinity in modern Hinduism, and a marked role of women in ritual, particularly at the domestic and village level, the status of women in most of South Asia is undoubtedly lower than that of men (cf. Samuel 1997). As for the value of daughters, the economic costs associated with daughters, specifically in relation to dowry payments, is now so high that the South Asian population has a large deficit of women, much of it undoubtedly resulting from abortion, infanticide and selective directing of health and food resources to male children. While the inflation of dowry in recent years and the vulnerability of the poorer sections of the South Asian population to international market forces have made this situation much worse, it also reflects a preference for sons over daughters that goes back for many centuries.

[30] Reid 1988: 629; the quote at the end is from the sixteenth-century Portuguese author Antonio Galvão (Galvão 1971: 89).

A widespread North Indian, Pakistani and Bangladeshi village marriage pattern exacerbates women's low status. Women typically move at marriage into their in-law's household, generally in another village at some distance from their natal household. This creates a structural vulnerability for young married women, who are isolated in a household where they have no close ties except to their husband, who is himself typically in a junior position in an extended family household.

Ideas of female bodily functions, above all menstruation and childbirth, as intrinsically polluting appear to be deeply rooted in much of South Asian culture, and clearly provide at least one level of ideological justification for women being viewed as inferior (Rozario and Samuel 2002a). Southeast Asia is again different in this respect, and the differences are evident in terms of the attitudes to and treatment of childbirth practitioners in South and Southeast Asia. In much of village India, Pakistan and Bangladesh, childbirth practitioners (*daī*) are of low status, barely remunerated for their services and mostly from *dalit* ('untouchable') caste backgrounds. Educated women are reluctant to take on this work, and even where doctors and trained nurses or midwives are present they are frequently unwilling to come into physical contact with women in childbirth. The consequences for the mortality of mothers and children in childbirth are appalling, and there is little sign of the situation changing (cf Rozario and Samuel 2002b).

At the same time, South Asia is not uniform in this respect. South India and Sri Lanka have a markedly more positive attitude to female bodily functions. There is a widespread practice of ritual celebration of a girl's first menstruation in these regions. Traditional childbirth practitioners also appear to be more respected, and childbirth practices more focused on the welfare of mother and child, and less on issues of pollution (Samuel 2002b: 10). It has generally been argued by anthropologists that this is linked to the South Indian marriage and kinship system, which encourages marriage between related families, so that brides are rarely moving into a completely isolated situation in their new household, and also operates so as to maintain status equality between households.[31]

Any attempt to deal with such complex matters in such a limited compass is inevitably somewhat of a caricature, and I am aware of the limitations of the above account. It nevertheless reflects something real about the nature of South and Southeast Asian societies in recent times, and it raises the question of the historical dimension of these differences.

[31] It has been suggested that the kinship system in the Central Gangetic region may have been more 'Dravidian' in form at the time of the Buddha. The evidence for this is weak, see Trautmann 1979.

Here there are a number of points to be made in brief, some of which I shall return to in later chapters. An initial point is that the negative valuation of female biological functions is closely tied up with aspects of Vedic-Brahmanical religion. Elsewhere I have cited Julia Leslie's discussion of the widespread myth of Indra's guilt, and its transfer to women, where it takes the form of menstruation. The myth occurs as early as the *Taittirīyasaṃhitā*; other versions are found in the *Mahābhārata, Rāmāyaṇa* and the *Skanda* and *Bhāgavata Purāṇas* (Leslie 1996a). The earth is also a frequent recipient of Indra's guilt, and its seasonal changes are treated as a form of menstruation.

> Menstruation is thus the sign of a woman's participation in Brahmin-murder. It marks her innate impurity, her cyclical fecundity, her uncontrollable sexuality, and, by extension, the inescapable wickedness of her female nature. (Leslie 1996a: 91)

What is clear, though, is that the Brahmanical set of values, with its basically soteriological orientation centred around concepts of purity and caste-duty, is not the only set of values found within Hindu villages today. A countervailing set of values, generally referred to by anthropologists as 'auspiciousness', and centred around fertility, productivity, and this-worldly success, is also very much present. Auspiciousness has a close linkage both with women and with goddesses (Samuel 1997).

I discuss the relationship between these two value systems further in Chapter 7. There is, I think, a historical as well as a logical relationship between the two sets of values.

The presence of significant festivals which celebrate the menstruation of a female deity in parts of East India (Orissa, Bengal and Assam, cf. Marglin 1994, 1995; Samanta 1992: 59–60; Chawla 2006) is one significant indication of an earlier situation which gave more positive recognition to female values. So also perhaps is the presence of more gender equality and a more positive orientation to sexuality in various Indian 'tribal' populations, though I think we need to approach this material with considerable caution. Contemporary 'tribal' populations in India and South Asia cannot reliably be treated as a relic of earlier times. While there may be and probably are cultural features which derive from earlier patterns, these cannot be easily disentangled from more recent developments.

Here it is important to appreciate that 'tribal' populations in South and Southeast Asia today cover a variety of different situations. Those in much of South Asia have been involved over more than two millennia with mainstream forms of Indian society. Thus there is also a long-term relationship of mutual influence and of systematic mutual differentiation. The tribes are what they are today in large part because of their dialectical relationship with the 'mainstream' population (cf. e.g. Gell 1982). In addition, there is a tendency to see the tribes from the mainstream Hindu perspective precisely in terms of stereotypes of sexual freedom. At the same time, there are indications of preserved values that are indeed more gender-positive and more celebratory of female sexuality and fertility (e.g. Elwin 1947; Archer 1974; Zvelebil 1988).

The highland tribal populations of areas such as Arunachal Pradesh, Assam, Mizoram, Tripura, and Manipur are in a rather different situation, and one can class these in general terms along with many of the Southeast Asian highland populations. Here, there is also a recognisable highland-lowland dialectic, but tribal populations have generally had more autonomy and more ability to conduct life on their own terms, at least until relatively recent times. There is an interesting body of literature focusing on these tribal populations and their relationship to mainland Southeast Asian populations. Durrenberger and Tannenbaum have noted the lack of penetration of mainstream (i.e. Buddhist) religious discourse into highland populations, which continue to emphasise values of fertility, productivity and success values over the soteriological goals of mainstream religious traditions (Durrenberger and Tannenbaum 1989). All this raises a number of interesting and important issues (cf. Kirsch 1973; Russell 1989; Kammerer and Tannenbaum 1996), but they are not ones that I can deal with in detail in this book, which is essentially concerned with lowland and 'mainstream' populations.

One question that should perhaps be considered is the possible historical impact of the Muslim invasions on gender relations in South Asia. There undoubtedly was an impact here: one can see it, for example, in the dramatic shift in modes of dress in South Asia around the time of the Muslim conquests (Fabri 1994). However, the issue is less one of Islam as such than of the specific Muslim populations that were involved in the conquest, and the general feudalisation and militarisation of Indian society on a patriarchal lineage model that took place before and during the Muslim invasions.[32] Elsewhere, as in Southeast Asia (Malaysia and Indonesia), Islam itself has proved quite capable of coexisting with relatively gender-equal societies.

More specifically, the Afghan and similar Central Asian Muslim populations that took a leading role in the Muslim conquests were themselves based around a patrilineal clan system with strong patriarchal elements, and the general militarisation of Indian society over the seventh to twelfth

[32] This is the process which Davidson 2002a refers to as *sāmantization*, and which I shall discuss in more detail in relation to the growth of Tantra and the fierce goddess cults in Chapter 12.

centuries tended to reinforce the hierarchical and patriarchal elements of the Indian value system as against the feminine and auspiciousness elements. All this coincided with the initial impact of Islamic cultures in northwest India and with the eventual Muslim conquest of most of India, but it was as much an outgrowth of endogenous factors as of external ones. This issue will be considered further in Chapter 12.

This concludes our survey of the various social contexts within which Indic religions were developing in around 500–400 BCE, or which may have influenced those developments. Much of the evidence I have presented is sketchy or indirect, or pertains more to the realm of ideology than of solid empirical fact, but there is perhaps enough to point to some of the variety of resources available to the developing religious cults of North India at this time. In the following chapter we turn to look at these cults and practices.

CHAPTER 5

Religion in the early states

I begin this chapter with an overview of evidence about South Asian religion before 500 BCE. This discusses both archaeological evidence, mainly relating to the Indus Valley urban tradition and textual sources relating to the early religion of Indo-Aryan speaking peoples. In subsequent sections, I look at the development of Vedic-Brahmanical religion in the Kuru-Pañcāla region, and at other aspects of early Indian religion, particularly the religion of local gods and spirits

ARCHAEOLOGICAL SOURCES FOR EARLY INDIC RELIGION

I have already provided some discussion of religion in the Indus Valley cultural tradition in Chapter 1. I suggested there that while there are certainly features of the Indus Valley material that might be interpreted in terms of continuities with later periods, we know very little for certain. The evidence is capable of many interpretations, and analyses are so heavily dependent on reading later practices and concepts into the material that they are of little help in evaluating whether there really were continuities.

One intriguing indication of possible continuities in religious practices is provided by a striking group of terracotta figurines from Mehrgarh, dated to about 2800–2600 BCE, so two or three centuries before the Indus Valley Integration era. Some of the female figurines from Mehrgarh have a hair-parting with a streak of red pigment, and it has been suggested that this can be related to the modern Hindu practice of women placing *sindhur* in their hair-parting as a sign of their married status (e.g. Kenoyer 1998: 44–5). In fact, it is not clear whether the red pigment on these figurines is confined to the hair-parting, or found all over the bodies, and it appears that some at least of the figurines are modern fakes,[1] so it may be unwise to put too much emphasis on the similarity to the modern use of *sindhur*. The use of

[1] Theresa McCullough (personal communication, September 2006).

red ochre in sacred contexts remains common, however, in modern Indian religious practice more generally. Deity images, especially rocks or natural features held to represent female deities, are often coated in red pigment, and the association of red with fertility is also fairly explicit in many folk ritual contexts. Here again, though, we have nothing at all specific about how these figurines were used or regarded by the people who made them.

As far as the Indus Valley seal images are concerned, we can perhaps accept the likelihood of the cult of some kind of goddess, and of sacrificial offerings to her, on the basis of the 'fig tree deity' seals discussed in Chapter 1 (e.g. Fig. 1.2). The existence of theriomorphic deities (gods in animal form) in the Indus Valley Integration Era also seems fairly likely, on the basis of the many seals that show animals, most often cattle of some kind, with what may be offerings in front of them. This might link with the cult of wild yaks, rams and other animals in Tibet, and I have suggested elsewhere that there may be some linkages between the Indus Valley culture and early Tibetan religion (Samuel 2000). But it would be unwise to build too much on such connections. The linkages between any Indus Valley cult of goddesses or theriomorphic deities and the Vedic religion, or any other subsequent Indic religion, are far from obvious. Nor do the horned headdresses visible in the Indus Valley seals (cf. Figs. 1.1, 1.2) link up with anything obvious in later Indic cultures.[2] The Indo-Aryan immigrants clearly had their own cattle-centred culture, as is evident both from the Ṛgveda and from the comparable Avestan materials, so we hardly need an Indus valley bull cult to explain the significance of cattle in later times.

My comments in Chapter 1 referred primarily to the so-called 'Integration Era' of the Indus Valley cultural tradition, in other words the period of the large-scale urban society that we know from Mohenjo-daro and Harappa in particular. This period is now generally dated from approximately 2600 to 1900 BCE. In relation to the period from the end of the Integration Era up to around 500 BCE (in fact, until the start of the Mauryan state) there is again little direct archaeological evidence relating to religion.[3] A number of figurines dating from this period have been regarded by some authors as representing goddesses. These include, for example, some small nude figurines from early farming settlements in Maharashtra, which appear

2 The only parallel known to me is with the bison-horn headdresses used by some Gond tribes, but again the connection is highly speculative.

3 One study from well outside the Indus region is worth mentioning: F. R. Allchin's work on prehistoric ash-mounds from around 2000 to 750 BCE in Mysore and Andhra Pradesh. Allchin has suggested that these mounds may result from annual festivals involving fire and the worship of cattle, similar to the modern festivals of Holī, Dīvalī and Pongal (Allchin 1963; Sullivan 1971).

to have been associated with storage jars or grain silos (Poster 1986, cat. Nos. 8–10, pp. 80–2; see also M. Joshi 2002: 40). These figurines may date from 1300 to 1200 BCE. A group of somewhat later terracotta figures from the Swat valley in Pakistan have also been interpreted as mother goddess figures (Poster 1986, cat. No.12, p. 84). There is need for caution when it comes to identifying female figurines as representing a goddess cult (see Haaland and Haaland 1995; Goodison and Morris 1998), but there may be some justification for these interpretations. A much more substantial iconography of figures representing female deities can be found from the Mauryan period onwards, so it would not be surprising if there were earlier examples.

It is interesting in any case to note that while the Vedic tradition seems not to have employed images of deities until late Mauryan or Śuṅga times (third to second century BCE) at the earliest, sculptural images of deities may go back much further in these folk contexts. Given the fragile nature of the evidence, and the fact that many images may have been made of substances that would not leave any trace in the archaeological record (e.g. cow-dung, regularly used for images of deities in the folk tradition in South Asia in modern times, cf. Samuel 2005a: 259, 280 n.3), such practices could have been quite common and widely distributed. The same is true of ritual wall-painting and floor-painting (*kolam, alpana, aripan, muggu*, etc.), again very widespread in modern times but unlikely to survive in the archaeological record (E. Gupta 1983; Nagarajan 1997; Thakur n.d.: 36–50; Kilambi 1985; Jayakar 1989: 118–19).

TEXTUAL SOURCES FOR THE EARLY RELIGION OF THE INDO-ARYAN-SPEAKING PEOPLES

The oldest datable evidence for the early religion of the Indo-Aryan-speaking peoples is the Mitanni inscription, a peace treaty between the Hurrian kingdom of the Mitanni and the Hittites, and it dates from about 1360–1380 BCE (Thieme 1960). Five male deities are called as witnesses and keepers of the treaty, and their names are recognisable Vedic Sanskrit for Mitra, Varuṇa, Indra and the twin divine horsemen or Nāsatyas (Aśvins). All these are well-known Vedic deities, though only Indra is a central figure in the Vedas, suggesting that the cult of the other deities (who belong to a group known as the Ādityas) had become less significant in the meantime.[4]

[4] Cf. Brereton on the Ādityas (Brereton 1981). Insler notes that the predominance of Indra is primarily in books Three, Four, Six and Eight of the Ṛgveda; in books Five and Seven, there are almost as many hymns to Varuṇa and the Ādityas as to Indra (Insler 2003).

The early Iranian material, as noted in Chapter 2, is linguistically and stylistically close to the hymns of the Ṛgveda. However, it post-dates the reconstruction of Iranian religion associated with the figure of Zarathustra and incorporates his rejection of the cult of the *daevas* (corresponding to the Vedic *devas* or gods) so that the Vedic deities do not appear directly (Insler 2003).[5]

Stanley Insler suggests that the Vedic and Iranian material together points to a primarily pastoralist culture, living in small villages and settlements under chieftains or minor sovereigns who were expected to protect their subjects and also to judge in disputes. The deities Mitra and Varuṇa are associated with the role of these minor sovereigns. There was also a warlord chosen temporarily in time of attack, and associated with the deity Indra. These people seem to have called themselves *ārya* (perhaps originally meaning 'hospitable', 'cultivated').

Their primary ritual was a sacrifice or offering performed outdoors under an open sky and involving the delimitation of a sacred space, its covering with grass to provide a comfortable seat for the deities, and the lighting of a fire to provide warmth and represent truth. Food was then offered to the deities; on big occasions, animals were sacrificed and *soma* juice[6] prepared. It was important to have a priest (Skt. *hotṛ*, Avestan *haotar*) present to formulate the praises that accompanied the sacred meal, and which correspond to the Ṛgvedic hymns or the Avestan *gāthās*.

THE VEDIC RELIGION AND THE WIDER RELIGIOUS SCENE

If Insler's reconstruction is a reasonable picture of Indo-Aryan religion at around the middle of the second millennium BCE, before the Indo-Aryan speakers arrived in North India, then the religion of the Ṛgveda, the Brāhmaṇas and associated texts already represent a substantial reformulation. While a relatively simple set of domestic or *gṛhya* rituals centred

[5] Of the five Vedic deities in the Mitanni treaty, only Mitra appears unambiguously in the early Iranian material, though Stanley Insler has suggested that Ahura Mazda, the new deity associated with the reforms of Zarathustra, takes over many features of Varuṇa, and that indications of Indra, the Nāsatyas and another Vedic deity, Aryaman, can also be found in Zarathustra's hymns (the Gāthās). Indra, Saurva and Nanhaithya, corresponding to Vedic Indra, Sarva and the Nāsatyas, occur in the later Avesta as members of the rejected *daeva* category (Insler 2003). Parpola has developed a complex argument according to which the presence of Mitra-Varuṇa alongside Indra in the Mitanni material indicates a temporary compromise reached in Bactria between *asura* and *deva* worshippers (Parpola 1999a). See also Parpola 2005.

[6] The precise nature of *soma* is still uncertain, though an extract of Ephedra seems the most plausible current opinion (cf. Houben 2003a, 2003b). See also Spess 2000, who argues for species of Nymphaea and Nelumbo.

around the domestic sacred fire, which is set up at marriage, was practised at the household level, and is in fact central to the Vedic ideology of marriage and the household (B. Smith 1989: 146–68), a much more elaborate series of rituals performed by the *brahmin* on behalf of others had developed alongside it. This *śrauta* ritual is a 'highly complex and very expensive set of sacrifices requiring the services of an array of ritual specialists' (Olivelle 1998: xli). It involves several ritual fires and a number of priests. Several major rituals are explicitly linked to kingship (the *rājasūya* or royal consecration and the *aśvamedha* or horse sacrifice) and the whole body of material suggests a development and reconstruction in the context of a much-expanded royal role. It seems clear that much of this would have taken place some time before the Second Urbanisation got properly under way. This process can doubtless be associated with the transformation of the arriving Indo-Aryans, along with elements of the existing local populations, into an increasingly settled and largely agricultural society, although one that was still largely committed to pastoralist values at an ideological level.[7] The *soma* ritual continued as a key part of the complex, but it appears that actual knowledge of the *soma* plant was lost at an early stage, perhaps before the settlement in Northwest India, so that *soma* became a focus for symbolic elaboration rather than the ingestion of a pharmocologically-active substance.[8]

I have already referred to Witzel's arguments regarding this process of reformulation, which he associates with the development of the Kuru state, initially a 'super-tribe' or tribal federation, and will return to them again later. At this point, it is important to remind ourselves that these developments were, initially at least, regional developments, confined to the Kuru state and its immediate neighbours.

As I noted earlier, the development of Indian religions is most often presented in 'orthogenetic' style, as something that grows out of the Vedic material, with other influences coming in as external influences if at all. This reflects the Brahmanical textual tradition's view of itself, but it does not necessarily represent the way things happened at the time. The Brahmanical

7 In this it might resemble a range of East and Southern African populations in more recent times, which combined a mostly agricultural economy with ritual and ideological complexes that were still largely based around pastoralism. The Ndembu, studied by Victor Turner, and related Lunda populations, are classic examples (cf. Turner 1957, 1968, 1970).

8 A brief description of the *soma* sacrifice is provided by Olivelle (1998: xlv). One of the problems with identifying *soma* with ephedra (see above) is that ephedra has little in the way of psychoactive effect. However, it is by no means certain that the original *soma* was psychoactive. The extensive use of cannabis by modern Hindu and Muslim ascetics in India is nevertheless suggestive of a long-standing tradition of employment of psychoactive substances (cf. Movik 2000).

texts are written from within the Vedic-Brahmanical setting, and often at a much later date than the events to which they refer. The earliest layers of Buddhist and Jaina material, to the extent that we can reconstruct them, depict a rather different model, but they too tend to have been read through assumptions of the kind of Brahmanical presence characteristic of modern India (see Chapter 6).

The material presented in Chapter 4 suggests a more complex picture. To make sense of it we need to keep a number of issues distinct that can easily be confused and have often been conflated in the past. The first distinction that needs to be held clear is between the immigrant Indo-Aryan-speaking populations which (presumably) entered South Asia in the course of the second millennium BCE (possibly continuing up to about 800 BCE or later in some parts on Witzel's model), and the settled Indo-Aryan-speaking populations of the mid to late first millennium BCE. We can assume that the latter were all by this time mixed populations of immigrants and earlier residents, though the proportions of the mix doubtless differed from place to place, with the ratio of immigrants to prior population probably highest in the Northwest and decreasing eastwards towards Bihar and Bengal and southwards towards the Deccan plateau.

These groups were all speaking Indo-Aryan languages by 500 BCE or so, and we can presume that they had all accepted some aspects of the cultural heritage that came with the immigrant Indo-Aryan speakers. These would have included the tripartite Indo-European distinction between a ruling warrior group (*kṣatriya*), a priesthood carrying out sacrificial ritual (Brahmins) and a wider population, now largely farmers (*vaiśya*). We can probably also assume some presence of Indo-Aryan deities and rituals, including the deities Indra and Brahmā, both prominent in the Buddhist texts, and perhaps some of the widespread seasonal rituals. I refer to this kind of material for convenience as the ***generic Indo-Aryan cultural tradition***, though we should not assume that it was entirely uniform or equally strong throughout this whole large area.

A second important distinction is between this generic Indo-Aryan cultural tradition and the specific body of rituals and practices which were developing in the Kuru state and the Kuru-Pañcāla region. I refer to the latter as the ***early Vedic-Brahmanical*** ritual complex or early Vedic-Brahmanical religion. The use of 'early' is meant to distinguish it from the modified and transformed version of this complex which was actively propagated throughout the wider Indo-Aryan-speaking region, perhaps from around 400 BCE onwards. We will consider this development later in this chapter.

There appears to be evidence of shared material, and also evidence of the formation of a distinctive self-conscious group in the Kurukṣetra region which saw itself as 'Aryan' as contrasted with other Indo-Aryan-speaking populations. Aryan in the Iranian context appears to be a term applied to Indo-Aryan populations as a whole (Shahbazi 2005) so this is presumably a development in the Indian context. I assume that it was consequent upon the differentiation of the Indo-Aryan-speaking population in India, whether before or after their arrival, and perhaps also on differing degrees of accommodation to and adoption of practices of previous populations in South Asia. At the same time the Kuru-Pañcāla state was associated with an evident 'drive to the East', a desire or need to convert the populations of the Central Gangetic region to the new Brahmanical orthodoxy (Heesterman 1962).

It would seem that by the time of the historical Buddha and of the Jaina teacher Mahāvīra, the generic Indo-Aryan cultural tradition was an accepted part of society through much of the Central Gangetic region. There were also Brahmins and a degree of movement between the Brahmins of this region and those of Kuru-Pañcāla. It seems clear, however, that the nature of Vedic and Brahmanical religion in this region was different and considerably less dominant than in the Kuru-Pañcāla region. Even in texts such as the Upaniṣads, which appear to originate in some cases from the North, in others from the Central Gangetic region, we appear to have an ongoing dialogue between models of what Brahmins are or should be doing, about whether Brahmanical knowledge represents the ultimate truth, etc. (Olivelle 1998: xxxvii–xl). This is even more obviously true, of course, in relation to the Buddhist and Jaina material.

As for the suggestion, still prevalent in popular literature, that Buddhism represented a protest against the pre-existing Brahmanical caste system, there seems little truth in this. The Buddha's comments on Brahmin claims of high caste suggest less an opposition to an already imposed caste system than a refusal by a spiritual leader belonging to an established group of high status to accept a new imported Vedic-Brahmanical model in which the Brahmins are supreme.[9] References to Vedic material in the earliest Buddhist literature are limited although there is evident knowledge of the existence of the Ṛg, Sāma and Yajur Vedas and suggestions of detailed engagement with Vedic ideas (e.g. Jurewicz 2000). There are also fairly clear references to material that is found in the Upaniṣads (Gombrich

[9] See *Dīghanikāya* 3 (Ambaṭṭha Sutta), *Dīghanikāya* 27 (*Aggañña Sutta*), *Majjhimanikāya* 93 (*Assalāyana Sutta*) etc.

1990, 1992), indicating that this material was in circulation in some form or another, if not necessarily that of even the oldest Upaniṣads as we know them today. I return to some of these issues in the next chapter, in relation to the origins of the ascetic tradition.

There are indications, however, as we have seen, of royal patronage for Kuru-Pañcāla Brahmins in the evolving states and we may suppose that one of the main things which they could offer was the body of ritual practices regarding state power which had been developed in the Kuru-Pañcāla context. The model of kingship that developed in South and much of Southeast Asia, in other words, largely adopted a Vedic-Brahmanical ritual idiom, as indeed is the case in Buddhist states in modern times. As we will see, there were extensive efforts on the point of the Buddhist tradition in later times to provide its own rituals for royalty, but it seems that the Vedic-Brahmanical tradition established itself as the prevailing model in this area quite early on.[10]

The Buddhist and Jaina texts also provide evidence of more local and specific levels of religious practice, of cults of what were called the *laukika* or 'worldly' deities.[11] They included the cults of guardian deities (*yakṣas, nāgas*, etc.) linked to various early states, as well as no doubt more local cults at the village level such as are found in modern India. In origins, this seems to have been essentially separate from both the generic Indo-Aryan cultural tradition and the specific Vedic-Brahmanical traditions from the Kuru-Pañcāla region. We might also consider here the cults of warrior deities (Balarāma/ Saṃkarṣaṇa, Vāsudeva, Skanda, etc.) and the other early religious forms out of which Vaiṣṇava and Śaiva cults later developed. These were eventually incorporated into the developing Vedic-Brahmanical corpus, but may have started out quite separately.

By the first century BCE it is clear that there are cults of protective deities of towns, states and families,[12] often associated with shrines in groves or on hills outside the city proper, and frequently centred around a tree where the deity lived. There seems no reason to assume that these do not go back to before the time of the historical Buddha, especially given their strong presence in the *sutra* narratives. Cults of deities associated with rivers and lakes are probably also early.

[10] See Klimburg-Salter 1989 and Walter 2000 for Buddhist developments. Also Chapter 12, below.

[11] The term is used by Brahmanical (Patañjali), Buddhist and Jain authors with approximately the same meaning, in each case opposed to higher levels of deities who include the Vedic deities Indra, Brahma etc. (deCaroli 2004: 13 for Brahmanical and Jain authors).

[12] E.g. the Buddha's clan (deCaroli 2004: 15).

These deities have most usually been referred to in modern times, following Coomaraswamy (1928–31), as *yakṣas*, and I shall follow this terminology here for convenience, while recognising that I am using *yakṣa* and *yakṣi* as generic terms for deities which would have been referred to in a variety of ways at the time, including some that would have been called by other terms, such as *nāgas* and *devas*.[13] In later times, the *yakṣas* along with the *nāgas* dwindled to beings of minor importance, guardians of treasures, or tree-dwelling spirits that may frighten an unwary traveller, a status they retained into modern times in parts of rural South Asia.

In the late first millennium BCE, and for many subsequent centuries, *yakṣas*, male and female, were an important part of the religious landscape. Male deities of this kind were gods of prosperity and protection (Fig. 5.1). While they have a kind of warrior role as generals over lesser *yakṣas* – we will see some of this below, and more in Chapter 12 – they are not portrayed in a particularly militaristic fashion. Female deities are generally associated with prosperity and fertility, both human and agricultural, and are often associated with tree or plant imagery. It is clear from the Purāṇas and other later sources that these deities were worshipped all over North India, including the Kuru-Pañcāla region; even Kurukṣetra had a set of four *yakṣa* deities who acted as *dvārapālas* for the sacred territory (Bharadwaj 1989).[14]

While representations of some of the major figures, such as Śrī, Kubera and Sūrya, are found in many different locations, for the most part *yakṣas* and *nāgas* were associated with specific regions and localities. This is clear in the later discussion of these deities in the Epics and Purāṇas, as well as in Buddhist and Jain material. The *yakṣas* we know of were generally linked to sizeable towns or regions, though one can imagine that there was another layer of more local deities again who have left little or no trace in the literature.

A list of major regional *yakṣa* deities from a somewhat later period is included in a Tantric ritual text, the *Mahāmāyūrī*, where a long series of *yakṣas* is invoked by name and location, alongside a whole series of other deities. The *Mahāmāyūrī* list, which might date from around the fourth or fifth century CE,[15] was studied and translated by Sylvain Lévi (1915), and again by D. C. Sircar (1971–72).

[13] DeCaroli suggests 'spirit-deities' as a generic term (deCaroli 2004). Other recent treatments include Sutherland 1991 and Misra 1981.

[14] On other local *Yakṣa* cults see Agrawala and Motichandra 1960; von Mitterwallner 1989.

[15] It is not included in the two early Chinese translations of the text, made in the early fourth century, but forms part of a translation made in 516 CE (Sircar 1971–72: 262). I am indebted to Will Tuladhar-Douglas for bringing the *Mahāmāyūrī yakṣa* list to my attention.

Figure 5.1. Unidentified Yakṣa. Vidisha Museum

Krakucchanda stays at Pāṭalīputra, Aparājita at Sthūṇā, the Yakṣa Śaila at Bhadrapura and Mānava in the northern quarter.

Vajrapāṇi stays at Rājagṛha; he has his abode at Gṛdhrakūṭa; three times he traverses the earth as far as the ocean; he has great strength and great might and his valour spreads over (or, step covers) a hundred *yojanas.*

The Yakṣa Garuḍa stays at Vipula, Citragupta at Sthitimukha and the Yakṣa Vakula possessing a great army and great strength stays at Rājagṛha.

The two Yakṣas, Kāla and Upakālaka, live at Kapilavāstu where the sage Buddha called Śākyaketu and Mahāmuni was born. (Sircar 1971: 265–8)

These are the first few verses, which deal with the area around Pāṭalīputra and the earlier Magadhan capital of Rājagṛha. The next verses deal with other towns in the Central Gangetic region associated with the life of the Buddha, before gradually moving out into the surrounding regions. The text understandably emphasises those deities who are important for the Buddhists, such as Vajrapāṇi (Fig. 5.2). Vajrapāṇi, who appears to have begun life as the guardian deity of Rājagṛha, was to become a very important figure in the evolution of Tantric Buddhism. He was regarded as having become a devotee of the Buddha and already appears in this role in the early sutras.

By the first and second centuries CE, Vajrapāṇi is frequently depicted in Buddhist iconography, as in this Gandhāran image, where he is standing behind the Buddha and holding his *vajra*, as always. The set of the Four Great Kings, consisting of Vaiśravaṇa (Kubera, the king of the *yakṣas*), Dhṛtarāṣṭra, Virūḍhaka and, Virūpākṣa, also developed an important role as guardian deities, and are still often painted on the walls of Buddhist temples in the Tibetan and East Asian traditions (Fig. 5.3). Other important *yakṣa* deities include Maṇibhadra, who seems to have become a guardian deity for merchants and travellers (Thapan 1997) and Pūrṇabhadra, who are both included among Kubera's eight attendant *yakṣas* in Buddhist material.

One can perhaps get some of the character of these deities, if in a literary mode, from the account of Vaiśravaṇa and Pāñcika helping out prince Sudhana in the *Divyāvadāna*:

At that very time, the great king Vaiśravaṇa, attended by many *yakṣas*, many hundreds, many thousands, many hundreds of thousands of *yakṣas*, was travelling that way to a meeting of *yakṣas*. [. . .] [H]e caught sight of Prince Sudhana and it occurred to him, 'This is the Bodhisattva of the present Auspicious Aeon; he is headed for disaster, setting out for battle! I should help him out. That hill-tribe chieftain must be made to submit, but without harm being inflicted on any living being.' Knowing this, he summoned Pāñcika, the great field marshal of the *yakṣas*:

Figure 5.2. Indra disguised as a woodcutter offers grass to Śākyamuni (accompanied by Vajrapāṇi), Gandhara, 1st cent CE, Peshawar Museum

'Come, Pāñcika! Make the hill-tribe chieftain submit to Prince Sudhana without a fight and without harm being inflicted on any living being!

'Very well,' Pāñcika, the great field marshal of the *yakṣas*, replied to the great king Vaiśravaṇa, and he created the four divisions of a divine army: men as tall as palm trees, elephants the size of mountains and horses the size of elephants. Then, using both all manner of weapons, such as swords, clubs, lances, javelins, discuses, pikes and axes, and the cacophony of massed musical instruments to inspire great fear, Pāñcika and that mighty host reached the hill-tribe village. (Tatelman 2005: 261)

Needless to say, the hill-tribe village decide that resistance is pointless and submit without a fight.

The female *yakṣa* (*yakṣi*, sometimes *yakṣiṇī*) imagery raises the wider question of the role of female deities in popular religion. I have already alluded to the presence of what appears to be goddess imagery from the

Figure 5.3. Vaiśravaṇa. Modern Tibetan wall-painting, Tongsa Gompa, Kalimpong

late second millennium BCE onwards. The early material is difficult to interpret conclusively, but a body of archaeological material from Mauryan times onwards is strongly suggestive of a goddess cult of some kind and/or a religious attitude to sexuality in the first millennium BCE.

In the first place, we could point to a substantial number of images of figurines from North and Northeast India, mostly dated to the Maurya period.[16] These appear to develop towards later figures whose iconography is best known from West Bengal, where the type-site is Chandraketugarh (see below), but which have evident links to similar figures over much of North and East India, including present-day Pakistan.[17] As noted earlier, one should not jump to conclusions about goddess cults whenever one finds a female figure, but in these cases the continuity with later iconography that can be securely identified with goddesses of fertility and auspiciousness would seem to justify such an assumption. The so-called 'ring stones', also from the Mauryan period, ornamented with what have been plausibly interpreted as goddess figures, point in a similar direction, as do a number of other small pieces from the same period and general context.[18] The prominence of vegetation imagery in the terracotta figures and plaques from Bengal and elsewhere, and to a lesser extent on the ring stones, is striking, and make it clear that this is a body of imagery which is associated with a primarily agricultural society.

In fact, the extent to which early Buddhist *stūpas* and temples were also ornamented with imagery concerning fertility and auspiciousness is quite striking. This varies from the largely floral and animal imagery at the oldest Sāñcī *stūpa* (No.2; Karlsson 1999: 88–94) to the so-called *Gajalakṣmī* imagery (two elephants asperging a goddess, e.g. Fig. 5.4, Karlsson 1999: 92 fig.11; in later iconography at any rate the goddess is identified as Lakṣmī) and the male-female couples (the so-called *mithuna* motif, cf. Agrawala 1983) found extensively on early *stūpa* and temple railings such as those

16 For reproductions, see e.g. Poster 1986, cat. nos. 18–19 (Mathura, UP), 20 (UP); Klimburg-Salter 1995, cat. nos. 10 (near Peshawar), 11–12, 18, 20 (Mathura, UP), 15–17, 19, 21–22 (UP). It is tempting to identify other figures, such as the headless female figurines from Maharashtra (Poster 1986, cat. nos. 8, 10) as goddess figures, but perhaps safer to be cautious.

17 See Poster 1986: cat. nos. 23–24 (Kausambi, UP; Poster identifies these as 'Shri Lakshmi'), 25–26 (Mathura, UP); nos. 33–34 ('north or eastern India'); also note the couple from Mathura, no. 29.23 (Mathura, UP); Harle and Topsfield 1987, cat. No. 6 (Northwest Province in Pakistan), No. 9 (a small bronze, Northwest India or Pakistan c.100 CE).

18 For ring stones, see e.g. Klimburg-Salter 1995, cat. no. 3 (Taxila, 3rd to 2nd century BCE), Joshi 2002 (fig. 2, Bihar, 3rd century BCE; fig. 3, Punjab. 3rd century BCE); Allchin 1995c, 263–9 and fig. 11.31 (Taxila and Bihar). For other related material, see Allchin 1995c, figs. 11.32–11.34.

Figure 5.4. Gajalakṣmī on Stūpa 2, Bharhut Stūpa, Indian Museum, Calcutta

at Bharhut and Bodhgaya and as a recurrent motif at Nāgārjunakoṇḍa.[19] These issues will however be discussed later in the book. A third body of significant imagery from a somewhat later period is also worth mentioning (the earliest examples are dated to the first century CE, Desai 1990). These are the so-called Lajjāgaurī figures, representing nude female figures with their legs apart, often with a lotus instead of a head.[20]

[19] Much the same is true of the Jaina imagery on the so-called votive tablets or *āyāgapaṭa* (Quintanilla 2000).

[20] Desai 1990: 268–9 and fig. 48.3 (Bhita); Poster cat. no. 55 (Jhusi, UP, 2nd century CE); Agrawala 1983, figs. 6 (Karnataka, c.700 CE) and 9 (Nagarjunakonda, 3rd century CE). Also Brown 1990; Bolon 1992; Agrawala 1983: pls.6 and 9.

All this iconographic material points to a religion of fertility and auspiciousness that gives full recognition to the female aspect of the procreative process and which finds its full expression in the early Buddhist sites that I have just mentioned.[21] This religion is often described as the religion of the *yakṣas* (fem.) and regarded as forming a single complex with the cults of local guardian deities mentioned above. I shall discuss it further in the following chapters in the specific context of its relationship with the developing *śramaṇa* (Buddhist, Jain etc.) and Vedic-Brahmanical traditions.

In relation to goddess imagery, it is also worth noting the very substantial iconography from Gandhāra and Mathurā, depicting a female figure, often with one or more children or other signs of fertility and auspiciousness, sometimes with a male consort. The female figure has traditionally been referred to as Hāritī and the male figure as her consort Pāñcika but these are maybe just labels of convenience; in reality there is as far as I know no solid evidence to link these figures with the Buddhist *yakṣas* of those names in Buddhist textual sources, although the Buddhist Hāritī is associated with children and the seventh-century Chinese pilgrim, Yijing, reports a *stūpa* linked to her legend in the Gandhāra region (cf. Samuel 2002b). Here as elsewhere a group of plausible conjectures has become received opinion.[22] What is undoubtedly true however is that this goddess of fertility and prosperity was an important figure at both Gandhāra and Mathurā, since hundreds of statues and images of all sizes have been found in both locations. An interesting question here is the possible linkage with the very similar Iranian iconography associated with the goddess Ardoxsho (who is depicted with her consort Pharro).[23]

In the Buddhist legend of Hāritī, she is a dangerous *yakṣiṇī* who is responsible for the deaths of many children before the Buddha 'converts'

[21] The well-known erotic imagery on later Hindu temples is doubtless to a large degree an outgrowth of this early imagery of sexuality and fertility, as will be discussed in later chapters.

[22] While a few of these images bear inscriptions, none as far as I know mention Hāritī. The one apparent exception I have come across, an inscription mentioned in Mathur 1998: 59 (referring to an image now in the Central Museum, Lahore) is a false trail, since the part of the inscription that might have mentioned the name is unreadable (see *Archaeological Survey of India Annual Report 1903–4*, Calcutta 1906, p. 255). It is possible that the inscription mentions smallpox, but this too is uncertain. Lerner notes that the identification of the Gandhāran-Mathurān goddess with Hāritī relies primarily on the report by Yijing (Lerner 1984: 145).

[23] Ardoxsho occurs frequently on Kuṣāṇa coinage. John Huntington comments on a couple of Ardoxsho images from Gandhāra, 'While I believe that Ardoxsho is conflated with Hārītī in symbolic function, I feel that her identification on the coins (Hārītī does not occur on Kushan coins that I am aware of) and the iconographic component of the Cornucopia as seen in the coins and the two sculptures mentioned above is enough to keep Ardoxsho as a discrete entity' (H-Buddhism list, www.h-net.org/~buddhism/, 24 Feb. 2005).

her and establishes a monastic cult to her (Samuel 2002b; Strong 1992; de Caroli 2004). This raises the question of whether these deities were in fact seen only as benevolent and positive figures. In fact, demonic female spirits seem often to be seen as responsible for childhood illness in later sources, including the medical treatises and the Purāṇas (Wujastyk 1997, 1999). The principal Hindu goddess of childbirth, Ṣaṣṭhī, seems to have had similar associations (Gadon 1997). One could provisionally imagine a cult of local deities, many of them female, who are responsible for illness if offended. I will return to this theme in Chapter 10, since it is closely connected with the origins of some parts of the religious complex referred to as 'Tantra'.

Thus in both regions, the dominant religious tradition of the emerging state had to reach some kind of accommodation with the local cults of the settled agricultural population, what I am calling the *yakṣa* religion in this chapter. The *yakṣas* and *yakṣīs* were mostly benevolent local gods and goddesses associated with agriculture, fertility and protection. A number of deities who were important in the historic development of Indian religion but have no real connection with the Vedic-Brahmanical pantheon seem to originate in this general stratum: perhaps the best-known cases are Gaṇeśa and Lakṣmī. Gaṇeśa seems to have come to prominence at a fairly late stage, perhaps around the fifth to sixth centuries CE,[24] but Lakṣmī, or very similar goddesses, are clearly present in the iconographical record at a much earlier time.

One of the most consistent and impressive bodies of *yakṣa*-type imagery comes from the Ganges Delta, an area that lay outside the penetration of Vedic-Brahmanical culture until quite a late stage. Certainly there is little or no sign of the Vedic deities in the imagery of the Chandraketugarh terracottas, a wide range of which has been made available in Enamul Haque's splendid recent book (Haque 2001).

The first of these images to become known in the West, the well-known Ashmolean *yakṣī* relief, was found at Tamluk, the site of the ancient Bengali port city of Tāmralipti, in 1883 (Harle and Topsfield 1987: 6–7). It was only much more recently that a large number of similar figures were uncovered in the Calcutta area, in particular at the site of Chandraketugarh, with which they have become associated. It is not certain what the ancient identity

[24] Though there are some intriguing elephant figures from Chandraketugarh (e.g. Haque 2001, nos. C673–677, C681), and elephants, apparently as symbols of prosperity and auspiciousness, are also common at Sāñcī.

of this city was, but from the richness of the material it was evidently an important place: Dilip Chakrabarti has suggested that it may have been the capital of the ancient state of Vaṅga (Chakrabarti n.d.). The date is also somewhat uncertain, though it is generally assumed that the onset of urbanisation in this area was about 300 BCE, so that the terracottas must date from after that. This is obviously a sophisticated urban art. Similar terracottas have been found in other parts of North India, with a similar general iconography.

I wrote at the beginning of this chapter about the difficulties of interpreting iconography, and suggested that we cannot establish anything very definite on the basis of the Indus Valley seals. I think that when we come to the Chandraketugarh terracottas we are in a different situation. The iconography here is detailed and consistent over a wide range of material. This is particularly true for the large class of female figures depicted frontally, often with an elaborate and characteristic headdress involving a number of large hairpins. While many of the Chandraketugarh images appear to be representations of ordinary human beings, it is clear in the case of these images that the figure represented is intended to be divine (Bautze 1995; Haque 2001). Versions of this goddess with the elaborate headdress are found all over North India, and several hundred have been found at Chandraketugarh and nearby sites.

In one of the most striking of these images (Bautze Fig. XIII; Haque no. 501), flowers fall from the sky around the goddess and merge into a shower of coins from a bag in her hand. The resemblance to the common modern iconography of Lakṣmī as showering money on devotees is remarkable. Perhaps it is not accidental that we find this imagery at what would presumably have been a major trading centre. In any case, it seems entirely plausible to identify this figure as a version or more exactly a local equivalent of Lakṣmī. Another striking group of presumably divine females consists of figures represented with wings, often against a background of vegetation that seems to make an interpretation in terms fertility and prosperity difficult to deny (e.g. Haque 2001, C344).

We should be careful about assimilating all goddesses of this kind into Lakṣmī, since as I shall later argue this process of assimilation, which is a characteristic feature of how Brahmanical religion came to work in later times, is actually part of what we should be studying rather than something to be taken for granted. At any rate, at a somewhat later period we find a variety of female deities of prosperity and fertility in different regions and contexts, including the Brahmanical Śrī-devī, the mother-goddess

Aṃbikā, who becomes quite important in Jain contexts, the goddess Hāritī, whom we discussed above, and the snake-goddesses Padmāvatī and Manasā (cf. Cort 1987; Sen 1953).

Despite the large number of terracottas that have been found at Chandraketugarh, there are relatively few male figures that might be deities. A few are winged, which makes their identity as deities reasonably certain (e.g. Haque 2001: C319, C321, C328). These and some other figures bear some resemblance to the *yakṣa* figures at Bhārhut. A number of male figurines (mostly small rattles) have been tentatively identified as versions of the important *yakṣa* deity Kubera, a classic *yakṣa* figure. Kubera is also portrayed as a young man, and the winged figures might tentatively be connected with him. There are also some elephant figures which might be seen as early versions of Gaṇeśa (e.g. Haque 2002: C673). Nothing in this pantheon, however, can be unambiguously identified with the Vedic-Brahmanical pantheon, as distinct from the *yakṣa*-type deities that later became associated with it. If anything, the winged figures suggest West Asian influences, though there are also examples of winged figures from Bhārhut and Sāñcī (Haque 2001: 98).

Certainly the emphasis in the terracotta iconography is on well-being and prosperity. Apart from the goddess plaques, which I think can clearly be regarded as items for religious devotion in one form or another, and a few conjectural male deity plaques, much of the other iconography seems playful and perhaps decorative. It includes a great deal of erotic art, including many representations of *mithuna* or amorous couples, often in sexually explicit poses. There has of course been an extensive literature on the symbolism of erotic sculpture in Indic religions and I do not intend to get involved in it at length here, but I think it is striking that here and at other relatively early sites such as Mathurā, Bodhgayā, Nāgārjunakoṇḍa and elsewhere the theme is treated naturalistically and seems most easily interpretable as a generalised representation of good fortune and prosperity. The Tantric treatment of sexuality is a quite different matter, and its real development lay several centuries in the future.

While issues of fertility and good fortune are clearly important in the Ṛgveda and early Vedic-Brahmanical material, and there are some indications in both of the presence of female deities, the general Vedic-Brahmanical picture is quite different. The dominant Vedic deities are male and this tradition also appears to have been largely aniconic in its earlier period, in other words there were no images of deities as such. This was also the case with early Buddhist sites, where the Buddha himself is not portrayed directly (Karlsson 1999; Rabe 1999). I turn now to examine the early Vedic-Brahmanical material in a little more detail.

THE DEVELOPMENT OF VEDIC-BRAHMANICAL RELIGION

I have already alluded to the chronological difficulties regarding the dating of Vedic material (Chapter 2). The current consensus among Western scholars tends to accept the basic sequencing of the Vedic material developed by nineteenth-century scholars but it is very difficult to reach any precision with relation to absolute chronology. Witzel's datings provide a working basis but one should clearly be wary of taking any of these figures too literally.

A lot has been written about Vedic religion on the basis of the Vedas themselves and the various Brāhmaṇas, ritual manuals and so on. There is little point in presenting this material at length since I have little original to add. However, it is worth summarising some main points:

There is a ***basic level*** of material with close relation to the Indo-Iranian texts, which can be seen in many of the Ṛgvedic hymns. This corresponds to what I have referred to above as a generic Indo-Aryan cultural tradition. It includes aspects of the cults of the 'imported' Indo-Aryan gods such as Indra, Agni, Varuṇa, Mitra and Soma. The 'shamanic' and 'ecstatic' aspects of Vedic ritual probably also go back to this layer, including the *soma*-fuelled visionary state in which the Vedic *ṛṣis* were supposed to have composed their hymns (Gonda 1963; Houben 2003b; Thompson 2003), and the famous description of the *keśin* or long-haired sage (*muni*) in Book 10, hymn 136 of the Ṛgveda (Werner 1989; Deeg 1993). These aspects of the Indo-Aryan cultural material are significant in terms of the ways in which they may have contributed to the later role of the Indic ascetic, and I shall return to them in this context in Chapter 8. The complex figure known as the *vrātya* perhaps also goes back to this layer, but will be discussed separately.

A ***second phase*** includes the reformulation of the Ṛgvedic hymns in the Samaveda and Yajurveda. This is Witzel's middle period and he associates it with the creation of the Kuru state ritual and mythology. This formed the ritual basis (the *rājasūya, aśvamedha*, etc.) for the warrior king model discussed in Chapter 4, evidently one of the more successful Kuru-Pañcāla exports. The *aśvamedha* or horse-sacrifice, already mentioned in Chapter 4, makes the point most clearly; it can only be performed when the king has established his military authority over the region through which the horse travels. Also in this phase we begin to see an expanded role for a number of deities who take only a minor part in the Ṛgvedic hymns. Among the most significant of these are Viṣṇu and Rudra (Śiva).

Viṣṇu (along with his various avatars) and Śiva were of course to become in time the two most significant male deities in the Hindu pantheon, each the focus of a major devotional cult. Both deities were in particular to become strongly associated with kingship, a process perhaps prefigured in Viṣṇu's case by his close relationship with the sacrifice in the Brāhmaṇas, and moving much further on in the *Mahābhārata* and *Rāmāyaṇa*.[25] Śiva himself, along with subsidiary forms of Śiva such as Bhairava, was also to become a major deity associated with yogic and Tantric practice. This development took many centuries, however, and was preceded by a phase in which we can see a variety of gods taking on the role of patron deity of kingship and battle, including Skanda, Sūrya and the Vṛṣni deities (Saṃkarṣaṇa, Vāsudeva, etc.) among others (see Chapter 9).

The first major text associated with Śiva is the *Śatarudrīya*, a liturgy which forms part of the *Taittirīyasaṃhitā*, part of Witzel's second phase. Śiva here is invoked mainly under the name Rudra, although the text includes the first known occurrence of Śiva's mantra *(oṃ) namaḥ śivāya*. Śiva's role in this text is as a potential source of disorder, chaos and misfortune who is invoked to protect and help, though there are also indications of a more soteriological role (e.g. Sivaramamurti 1976: 24–5).

This combination of a position outside the ordered world of civilised society and a soteriological role is an important one, which we will find recurring in a number of forms later in this book. As I have noted above, there is probably not very much to be gained by seeing Śiva as an inheritance from the Indus Valley. This may or may not be the case, and his 'outsider' role may or may not derive from his earlier non-Vedic history. What is undoubtedly true, however, is that he became the first and supreme example of a fundamental principle of Indian religious life; the power of disorder, destruction and transgression, the positive results to be gained from breaking through the patterns of normal behaviour. Seen in a somewhat different light, one could express this as the need to come to terms and worship the things that can go wrong and create misfortune.

This is not as alien a pattern as it might seem. In some ways, it is the basis of the religious orientation of many small-scale preliterate peoples

[25] The story of Viṣṇu's three steps occurs in the *Śatapatha Brāhmaṇa*. Viṣṇu plays only a minor role in the Upanisads, perhaps reflecting their ascetic ambience as much as their date: he occurs in the *Bṛhadāraṇyaka Upaniṣad* 6.4.21 as part of a ritual to have a child; he occurs in the opening invocation of the *Taittirīya Upaniṣad* (and its recapitulation at end of Chapter 1); the highest step of Viṣṇu is mentioned in the *Kaṭha Upaniṣad* 3.7, 8–9.

and of village communities within pre-modern states in many parts of the world.[26] Misfortune is seen as the action of the spirits and as a consequence of their being offended or provoked. It can be countered, if one is lucky, by reconciling oneself with the offended powers.

Western religion, while accepting the idea of divine punishment, has tended to associate it with ideas of divine love and divine justice. This goes with the tendency, strongest in Christianity and marked in Islam as well, to dichotomise good and evil. Indic religions rarely do this as systematically or completely as do Western religions. In psychoanalytic terms, Indic deities encompass the bad father or mother as well as the good father or mother. Śiva and Kālī are supreme examples of this principle.

This question of the positive value attached to the forces of disorder and transgression also seems to be a key issue in relation to a group of people in Vedic society who have often referred to in relation to the growth of yogic and Tantric practice, the *vrātyas*. They will turn up in a couple of later chapters, so I introduce them in some detail here.

There has been a lot of speculation about the *vrātyas*, much of it perhaps bordering on the realms of fantasy.[27] One reason for confusion is that (as with a number of Vedic terms) the term *vrātya* appears to have shifted its meaning considerably over time.[28] A reasonably consistent picture has however emerged in recent years through the work of Falk, Witzel and others (Heesterman 1962; Bollée 1981; Falk 1986; White 1991; Witzel 1995c). At the time of the Kuru-Pañcāla state or its historical equivalent, they seem to have been associations of young men who have not yet married and achieved full adult status. These groups of young men went out on raiding expeditions into neighbouring territories, these expeditions perhaps acting as a way of canalising the 'traditional aggression resulting in cattle rustling, fighting and small scale warfare existing with one's neighbours' (Witzel 1995c: 18). They also had a specific ritual function, which Witzel regards as preserving elements of the old Vedic ritual before the Kuru reformation. It particularly involved the performance of extended midwinter sacrificial rituals out in the forest, away from the village community, on behalf of the community as a whole (White 1991; 95ff). The *vrātyas* have been linked to

[26] One should really say, it is one basis of their religious orientation. Other idioms of misfortune, such as witchcraft, sorcery and soul loss, work in different ways. Most small-scale pre-modern societies seem to give primary emphasis to one or another of these.

[27] The *vrātyas* have also regularly been read as proto-shamans, linked to the supposed Vedic shamans of the *Ṛgveda*.

[28] Thus by the time of the *Laws of Manu*, perhaps around the first or second century CE, the *vrātyas* (2.39; 10.20) are sons of 'twice-born' groups who fail to undergo the sacred thread ceremony, and their children in turn become the origin of various non-Aryan or other disvalued groups (10.21–23).

evidence for sodalities or associations of young men in Iranian and other Indo-European material, and Falk and Witzel appear to imagine them rather after the model of the age-set system of organisation, known in particular from the studies of Oxford anthropologists, among others, in East Africa.

If this is a plausible model, we might suppose that all men probably went through a period as members of the *vrātyas*, and that they originally at least formed the basis of the fighting force of the tribal group in times of war. From Falk's material, it seems that some men who for one reason or another were not able to proceed to the subsequent stage of adult householders may have remained as *vrātyas* and become the leaders of the *vrātya* groups. Some of these may have been younger sons of families where the oldest son had taken over as head of the household. As time went on, the shift from a pastoralist to an increasingly agricultural economy may have meant that the standard solution to inheritance in a pastoralist society, of redistributing the herds through marriage or other mechanisms so that each family has enough to live on, was breaking down. Such *vrātyas* may have played a part in the outward expansion of Vedic-Brahmanical culture from the Kuru-Pañcāla region (see below). We have little direct evidence, but the association of various eastern groups with *vrātyas* in Manu is perhaps suggestive that they may have been involved in settlement in this area, or at least that there were groups out to the east that could be compared with them.

As for the ritual function of the *vrātyas*, Falk regards their midwinter twelve-day sacrifices as related to such Indo-European phenomena as the Roman Lupercalia and the twelve nights of Christmas. This was the time when the wild hunter Odin rode through the forests of northern Europe. Odin's equivalent in the Vedic context was Rudra, the Vedic prototype of Śiva. As Rudra's 'dogs' or 'wolves' (White 1991: 101) they slay the sacrificial cow in the food shortages and drought of mid-winter and so help to bring about the return of prosperity in the following year. The most notorious *vrātya* ritual was the *mahāvrata* or 'great observance', which involved ritual sex between a *brahmacārin* (presumably, in this context, meaning a young man otherwise vowed to celibacy) and a prostitute (Gonda 1961).

I would assume that if the kind of picture sketched by Falk and Witzel has some plausibility, these midwinter rituals might be seen as gradually disappearing during the second phase of the development of Vedic religion, to be replaced by the seasonal sacrifices and rituals described in the Brahmanas and later texts.[29] If so, the *vrātyas* might have ceased to exist in

[29] See for example the *Śatapatha Brāhmaṇa* (2.5.1).

the sense described here some time before the time of the historical Buddha, with the term itself coming to be used as a label for various low-caste and devalued populations, including peoples geographically outside of the areas of proper Aryan society, which by that time comprised the Middle Ganges valley as well as the Kuru-Pañcāla region. The *vrātyas* in the earlier period though represent an important prototype for the situation of an 'unorthodox' group whose activities, though dark and associated with death and transgression, are nevertheless somehow essential to the wellbeing of society. As we will see in the following chapter, this has led to their being seen, perhaps surprisingly, as predecessors of the *śramaṇa* movements.[30]

We have seen two examples above of the presumably 'transgressive' use of sexuality, in the *mahāvrata* rituals of the *vrātyas* and also in the *aśvamedha* which includes a notorious sequence where the chief queen simulates intercourse with the sacrificed horse. It would be wrong to give the impression that such practices are characteristic of Vedic ritual as a whole; they are not. They are however significant as indicative of an attitude towards the ritual power of 'transgressive' sexuality; there would be no point in performing these rather bizarre sequences if they were not felt to be ritually very powerful (one can hardly imagine that the chief queen enjoyed the experience). Mainstream Vedic texts are however surprisingly explicit about sexuality in its proper marital context: in the Upaniṣads, sex is homologised to the sacrifice, and ritual formulae are provided to influence conception.[31] The idea of the *brahmacārin*, the young celibate male as a source of spiritual power, is present, but it has not taken on the sense it has in later Brahmanical religion, as a specific stage in the life-cycle.[32]

Various processes have been suggested for the development and transformation of Vedic religion and it seems to me that most or all of these have some explanatory content. For the early phases, these include Heesterman's model of the move from the agonistic model of the sacrifice to a ritual concerned primarily with status-affirmation, a development which can be correlated with the move to permanent settlement (Heesterman 1985, 1993) and Witzel's argument about the needs of the Kuru state (Witzel 1995c). Later phases are driven perhaps by the growth of the model of the Brahmanical

[30] Heesterman regards the *vrātya* practices as representing an earlier stage of Indo-Aryan ritual, before the Vedic reforms, and as being characterised by violent and conflictual themes that had been cleaned out of the orthodox forms of the ritual (Heesterman 1962). I am not entirely convinced by Heesterman's picture of the early form of the sacrifice (see Heesterman 1985, 1993; B. Smith 1989: 40–6), but would in any case suggest that it is useful to see the *vrātyas* structurally, in relation to the mainstream and orthodox ritual of their time, rather than in terms of presumed origins.

[31] E.g. *Bṛhadāraṇyaka Upaniṣad* 6.4 (= Olivelle 1998: 88–93).

[32] On the early role of the *brahmacārin* see Crangle 1994; N. Bhattacharyya 1996: 137–9.

ascetic, which will be discussed in Chapters 6 and 7, and by the development of forms of Vedic ritual suitable for widespread domestic adoption in the new urban culture. I shall return to the later development of Vedic religion in Chapter 7. Chapter 6, however, is primarily concerned with the non-Vedic *śramaṇa* renunciate orders, particularly the early Buddhists and Jains, and I now turn to consider these orders.

CHAPTER 6

The origins of Buddhist and Jaina orders

The origin of the renunciate orders in India, and particularly of monasticism, is one of the most intriguing and significant questions that arises in the study of Indic religions. The idea of asceticism leading to magical power is not uncommon in religions of tribal and pre-literate peoples. One might think here of the idea of vision quests among the Plains Indians, and of the ascetic practices associated with initiation into spirit-cults in many parts of the world. We might imagine, though we do not know for certain, that similar practices were common among preliterate societies in earlier periods. However, the idea of someone permanently committed to an ascetic state is much less common, and indeed since religious specialists in most preliterate societies are only part-time practitioners, it would scarcely be practicable. While there are plenty of examples in the ethnographic record of individuals who are regarded as having special powers and who may be set somewhat aside from the community as a whole and regarded with some suspicion as a consequence, these people normally make a living through hunting and gathering, pastoralism or farming like other members of their society.

As for monasticism, we know nothing much like the Buddhist and Jaina monastic traditions from elsewhere in the world before this date. Monasticism was in time to become an extremely important and influential institution within world culture, particularly in the Buddhist version, which spread through most of South, Southeast, Central and East Asia, and in the later Christian version. Thus the question of how the ascetic orders got going is well worth some attention.

The renunciate traditions of North India in the fifth and fourth centuries BCE appear to mark the appearance of a new kind of goal or purpose for ascetic practice, variously known by terms such as *mokṣa, nirvāṇa, kaivalya* or *bodhi* (below I shall generally speak of 'liberation from rebirth', since the subtle distinctions of later traditions presumably developed a good deal later on). In the Vedic world, asceticism is for this-worldly purposes or for a good afterlife (rebirth in heaven) rather than for the attainment of some radically other state. The new goals appear to be premised on the idea of a self-conscious individual who finds his or her everyday life as a member of society radically unsatisfactory. In their mature forms at any rate, they came to terms to some degree with the everyday world, since those who were striving to attain them were also seen as acquiring skills and powers that could be used in the service of the community, but ideologically they are committed to withdrawal from not only everyday society but the entire cycle of rebirth (*saṃsāra*). This too is, as far as we know, a new development, and we may ask how and why it arose.

Thus we have several related questions: how the goal of liberation from rebirth came about among the Jainas, Buddhists and other *śramaṇa* (non-Brahmanical ascetics), how it came about among the Brahmanical ascetics, and how the idea of collective and organised practice in the context of celibate communities arose. This chapter deals primarily with the Buddhists and Jainas. In addition to discussing the development of the renunciate traditions themselves, I will also examine the ways in which Buddhist and Jaina renunciates engaged with the religious life of the larger communities who provided the material support for their activities. My discussion will necessarily also deal to some degree with issues relating to Brahmanical ascetics, but the full development of the Brahmanical model, and the different mode of engagement of the emergent Brahmanism with the larger community, is the subject of Chapter 7. Chapter 8 considers how we might explain and understand all these developments.

THE CONTEXT OF THE EARLY *ŚRAMAṆA* ORDERS

The Sanskrit term *śramaṇa* is a generic term that was used by members of several ascetic orders, including the Jainas, Buddhists and Ājīvikas. We assume that these orders came into existence in the time of the historical Buddha (i.e. fifth century BCE on current datings). Each of these renunciate orders had a named founder, Mahāvīra (also known as Nirgrantha Nātaputta or Vardhamāna) for the Jainas, the Buddha Śākyamuni (Siddhārtha or Gautama) for the Buddhists, Makkhali Gosala for the Ājīvikas.[1] Each order, however, had a tradition of previous teachers, and it seems clear that these founders of renunciate orders operated in a context in which a variety of such teachers were active.[2] Although the

[1] Our information on the Ājīvikas derives from Jaina and Buddhist sources, since their own texts have not survived (see Basham 1951, Bronkhorst 2000).

[2] In fact the term Ājīvikas may have been used as a general term, especially for naked ascetics. Bronkhorst has recently raised the possibility that the followers of Mahāvīra may have been referred to as Ājīvikas in the Pali scriptures, and the followers of Nirgrantha Nātaputta in the Pali scriptures, who are

Figure 6.1. Śākyamuni prior to his enlightenment (accompanied by Vajrapāṇi) consults a *jaṭila* Brahmin. Gandhara, late first century CE, Peshawar Museum

Jaina and Buddhist accounts are from several centuries later, and contain a large admixture of legendary material, it has generally been accepted that Mahāvīra, Śākyamuni, and the other main characters mentioned in these texts were real historical characters, and that the narratives contain a core of genuine historical events. While I assume myself that this is the case, it is important to be aware of the distance in time between the sources and the events being described. There is still a strong tendency in Buddhist studies to say 'the Buddha said so-and-so' when what is meant is that 'such-and-such a *sutta* in the Pali Canon describes the Buddha as saying so-and-so'.[3]

These three founding figures, Mahāvīra, Śākyamuni and Makkhali Gosāla, are described as more or less contemporary, with Mahāvīra probably the earliest. As noted in an earlier chapter, the dating of the historical

generally identified with the Jainas, may have been primarily the followers of Mahāvīra's predecessor Pārśva (Bronkhorst 2000).

[3] There is nevertheless reason to assume that the *sūtras*, once compiled, were passed through some generations with reasonable accuracy – at least enough accuracy to preserve jokes and references that the Pali commentators no longer understood (Gombrich 1990, 1996).

Buddha is uncertain, but if we accept the present consensus which places his death in around 400 BCE or a little earlier (see Chapter 2), Mahāvīra's death might have taken place in around 425 BCE or a little after (Dundas 2002: 24).

The emergence of Brahmanical ascetics and renunciates is a separate phenomenon that also needs some explanation. The existence of ascetic semi-renunciate Brahmins is evident in the Buddhist and Jaina sources (see e.g. Tsuchida 1991). This is also confirmed from Brahmanical sources, in particular the Dharma Sūtras, where we find a number of terms, particularly *vānaprastha* and *vaikhānasa*, for these people (Bronkhorst 1998a: 18–26). These refer to unmarried or married practitioners who live in the forest, subsist on forest produce, maintain a ritual fire (like a normal Vedic household) and pursue ascetic practices. The men are sometimes described as having matted hair (e.g. Bronkhorst 1998a: 33, citing the *Mahābhārata*). These seem to be the same people as the *jaṭila* or matted-hair Brahmins described in the Buddhist texts as being relatively highly regarded by the Buddha (Fig. 6.1), especially by comparison with other, wealthy Brahmins who are normal householders (*gṛhastha*) and had been given land and wealth by local rulers in exchange for their services as Vedic teachers and ritualists (Tsuchida 1991: 54–7). The stated aim of the way of life of these ascetic Brahmins is to attain rebirth in heaven. These Brahmins co-exist with other, fully renunciate practitioners who by contrast to them are seeking liberation from rebirth, either through withdrawal from action or through the pursuit of wisdom.[4] Presumably these renunciates would have included the *śramaṇas* as well as Brahmanical renunciates pursuing similar goals.

For the early Dharma Sūtras, which presumably originated in circles close to the urban Brahmins with their royal endowments, being a *gṛhastha* or householder is the only proper way of life, and the alternatives (which also include being a *brahmacārin* or unmarried man living at one's teacher's household and after his death with his son) are all to be rejected. The *Chāndogya Upaniṣad*, evidently closer to the ascetic circles, presents the reverse picture (Bronkhorst 1998a: 17–18). What is clear, though, is that both existed at this time, the *vānaprastha* brahmins and other ascetics aimed at liberation from rebirth. It is only at a considerably later point (in the *Manusmṛti* or 'Laws of Manu', perhaps first century CE) that

[4] E.g. in the *Āpastamba Dharmasūtra* which has two varieties of these, one again called *vānaprastha*, the other *parivrāja*. Bronkhorst describes these as 'non-Vedic' in contrast to the married *vānaprastha* with a domestic fire (1998a: 13–20). They do not have a sacred fire. Bronkhorst assumes that the standard pattern for a Hindu *saṃnyāsin* in modern times, where the sacred fire is 'internalised' within the *saṃnyāsin*'s body, is a somewhat later development.

the Brahmanical list of *āśramas* developed into the now-familiar series of four (*brahmacārin, gṛhastha, vānaprastha* and *saṃnyāsin*), seen as successive stages rather than as alternatives (see also Olivelle 1993).

In the later tradition of the sequence of four *āśramas*, becoming a forest-dwelling or *vānaprastha* Brahmin tends to be seen as something done late in life, as a precursor to the *saṃnyāsin* stage, but this is not necessarily what is at issue here. These early forest-dwelling Brahmins represent part of the growth of an ascetic tradition among the Brahmins, a tradition that was in time justified through the development of a body of stories regarding the sages (*ṛṣi*) who wrote the Ṛgveda, who are themselves generally portrayed as living the life of a *vānaprastha*. Thus the Buddhist texts give a standard list of ten *ṛṣi* or Brahmin sages, making a point of their ascetic lifestyle.[5] By the time of the *Mahābhārata*, it is taken for granted that the Vedic *ṛṣis* lived austere lives in forest hermitages.[6]

Thus the evidence here points to two types of ascetics, a 'Vedic' semi-renunciate type maintaining a ritual fire and aiming at rebirth in heaven and a 'non-Vedic' renunciate type, without a fire, who is aiming at liberation from rebirth.[7] If, as Bronkhorst suggests, the other types of ascetics, the renunciates who sought liberation from rebirth, were initially distinct from the *vānaprastha* Brahmins, there was evidently interchange between the two. The early Upaniṣads, such as the *Chāndogya* and *Bṛhadāraṇyaka*, which can be taken as compilations of materials produced by and for these various ascetic Brahmin groups, indicate that the goal of liberation from rebirth, and the idea of achieving it through the pursuit of wisdom, became widely distributed. The early Buddhist *sūtras* suggest knowledge of this early Upaniṣadic material (Gombrich 1990), though not necessarily of the texts as later compiled,[8] suggesting that the sayings that they knew were part of a floating body of wisdom sayings, circulated primarily in oral form.

5 Most of these are figures listed in the Ṛgveda Saṃhitā as authors of Vedic hymns, and many of them are important in later Brahmanical legend: Aṭṭhaka, Vāmaka, Vāmadeva, Vessāmitta, Yamataggi, Angirasa, Bhāradvāja, Vāseṭṭha, Bhagu (Tsuchida 1991 and Walshe 1995: 121).

6 Here, as always, 'forest' refers more to wild and uncultivated regions than to any particular kind of vegetation.

7 This discussion is in part suggested by Olivelle, who makes the important distinction here between the 'hermit' or 'anchorite' who has physically withdrawn from society (i.e. the *vānaprastha*), and the 'renouncer' who 'lives in proximity to civilized society and in close interaction with it' as a 'religious beggar'. The former type became obsolete early on, although it remained as a literary ideal (Olivelle 2003: 272).

8 Other authors (e.g. Horsch 1968) have argued that the Buddhist *sūtras* do not show clear evidence of familiarity with any of the Upaniṣads as complete texts. This is perhaps not surprising. The *Bṛhadāraṇyaka* and *Chāndogya Upaniṣads* have passages in common, and are evidently compilations of shorter texts which circulated independently before being assembled in the forms we now know (cf. Olivelle 1998: 95).

There are other indications of such a generally-shared body of wisdom sayings and stories, such as that remarkable Jaina text, the *Isibhāsāiyam* (Schubring 1942–52). Certainly this text provides a view of early Indian spirituality that is markedly at contrast with any assumptions about discrete and opposed traditions. The title of the *Isibhāsāiyam*, which was included in the Śvetāmbara Jaina canon, means the *Sayings of the* Ṛṣis, and the book consists of a series of verses attributed to particular named *ṛṣis*. These verses are mostly of the nature of moral maxims, and have short commentaries. What is most striking is the identity of the *ṛṣis* who are included in this text, for while they include Pārśva, Mahāvīra (here called Vaddhamāṇa) and other Jaina figures, they also include Vedic and Brahmanical sages such as Nārada, Yājñavalkya and others, as well as well-known Buddhist figures such as Śāriputra and Mahākāśyapa, and Makkhali Gosāla, the founder of the Ājīvikas. We seem here to be in a pluralist society of ascetic practitioners whose members are quite willing to regard members of the other semi-renunciate and renunciate religious traditions as 'sages' of a standing comparable to their own.

Similarly, we have seen how the narratives of the renouncer-king Nami or Nimi appear to have been common property between Buddhist, Jaina and Brahmanical writers, for all of whom he served as an early model of the renunciate life (Chapter 4). Another intriguing indication of the extent to which narratives were shared between traditions is the story of the encounter between the materialist king Paesi or Pāyāsi and a *śramaṇa* teacher. This occurs both in a Jaina version, where the *śramaṇa* teacher is a Jaina monk, and in a Buddhist version (*Dîghanikāya*, no. 23), where he is a Buddhist (Bollée 2002; Balcerowicz 2005; Walshe 1995: 351–68). The verbal details of the dialogue vary somewhat, but the story is recognisably the same. Yet another example of the same kind is given by a dialogue between a son who wishes to become an ascetic and rejects the arguments of his father who tells him first to study the Veda, establish a sacred fire, and have children. This appears in Jaina, Buddhist and Brahmanical versions (Olivelle 2003: 279–80).

Such cases suggest the development of a shared 'wisdom' type literature, doubtless mostly circulated orally in the first place as the tradition suggests, and focusing on the attainment of liberation from rebirth. Some of this would have been the preserve of particular Brahmin groups, other parts of the various emerging *śramaṇa* orders, Buddhist, Jaina and Ājīvikas. There is nevertheless clearly a considerable body of shared intellectual content among all of this material, with ideas such as the understanding of *karma* and the analysis of perceived experience being issues for all participants. The Buddhist and Jaina[9] orders then can be seen to have emerged from the circles in which material such as this was circulating.

While the stories regarding Buddha's predecessors are generally treated as legendary, those regarding Mahāvīra's immediate predecessor, whose name was Pārśva, have often been considered to have some historical content, in part because some traditions have been preserved regarding the difference between his teachings and those of Mahāvīra.[10] The traditional period of 250 years between Pārśva and Mahāvīra is as insecure as the 218 years between the Buddha's death or *parinirvāṇa* and the accession of Aśoka on which the older Buddhist chronology was dated, so if we want to give Pārśva a historical date we could probably imagine him as active at any time up to say the late sixth or early fifth century BCE.[11]

The stories of Pārśva, and for that matter of his predecessors and of the previous Buddhas, give some support to an idea that religious orders or traditions of the *śramaṇa* kind might predate the time of the Buddha and Mahāvīra (I shall refer to these as 'proto-*śramaṇa*' movements). Perhaps significantly, there is some ambiguity about whether Pārśva and his predecessors required celibacy of their followers, and these pre-Mahāvīra 'Jaina' movements appear to have been more open to the participation of women than Jainas in later times (cf. Williams 1966). This suggests that Pārśva's movement, if we accept it as historical, may not have been a fully renunciate movement. At the same time, it seems to have been an organised movement of some kind, and the Jaina scriptures describe its followers as still around in the time of Mahāvīra.[12] Thus we seem to be dealing here with an organised urban movement rather than with an isolated forest householder-ascetic model such as that of the *jaṭila* Brahmins. It has been

[9] Strictly speaking, the term Jaina is anachronistic at this period. As Peter Fluegel has recently noted, the earliest known usage of the term dates from the seventeenth and eighteenth centuries CE; its use as a self-designation may not be much earlier (Fluegel 2005). The issue is not entirely trivial, since the relationship between the *nigganthas* referred to in early Buddhist sources and the modern Jainas is not clear (see main text, and Bronkhorst 2000). However, I shall continue to use the term for convenience; where not otherwise explicit, it refers to the followers of Mahāvīra.

[10] Possibly, as Williams has suggested (R. Williams 1966), Pārśva's predecessor Nemi also has some historical reality. This is a different person from the Nimi or Nami of Videha whom I discussed in Chapter 4; he is placed in Gujarat and Williams speculates on the possibility of a pre-Pārśva tradition from Gujarat.

[11] See also Dundas 2002: 32.

[12] The *Uttarādhyayana Sūtra*, Chapter 23, consists of a dialogue between Keśi, a follower of Pārśva, and Gautama, a follower of Vardhamāna (Mahāvīra), which results in Keśi adopting the teachings of Mahāvīra (Jacobi 1895: 119–29). See also Dundas 2002: 30–3.

suggested recently that early Buddhist references to *nigaṇṭhas*, which have generally been taken to refer to followers of Mahāvīra, may in fact have been primarily to members of Pārśva's movement (Bronkhorst 2000).

It is evident that the early Jaina and Buddhist materials had a great deal in common, including much of their terminology. The traditional temporal sequence, in which the Jaina order or orders took form somewhat earlier than the Buddhist *saṅgha*, makes some sense. In areas such as its attitude to asceticism, or its modes of meditation, the Buddhist teachings give the impression of a modified and developed version of the Jaina tradition. Thus early Jaina yoga seems primarily to consist of extreme ascetic practices on the Brahmanical model, while the Buddhists added to this both what was a novel systematisation of the *dhyāna* practices, and the new *vipaśyanā* or insight practices (see below).[13] At the same time, the Buddhist suggestion that extreme asceticism is inappropriate can be seen as a criticism of the Jainas as well as of Brahmanical ascetics.

All this suggests, in terms of the new chronology, that we might be looking at a developing semi-renunciate householder movement in the sixth and fifth centuries BCE, culminating in the establishment of a full-scale renunciate movement in the mid to late fifth century. As noted in Chapter 3, the dating of the Second Urbanisation in North India is uncertain because of the C14 calibration problem for this period. It would seem, however, that the emergence of fortified cities at places such as Rājagṛha, Campā, Ujjayinī and Vārāṇasī, the capitals of four of the major states described in the Pali canon and Jaina sources, would have taken place by around 550 BCE at the latest, perhaps one or two centuries earlier (the city of Śrāvastī is somewhat later) (Erdosy 1995c: 109–10; Chakrabarti 1995). Thus, as has often been suggested, we are probably dealing with a movement that got going either around or shortly after the time of the initial growth of these cities.

While the historical Buddha and Mahāvīra can probably be dated at least a couple of centuries after the establishment of urban settlements (cf. Bailey and Mabbett 2003), 'proto-*śramaṇa*' movements such as those represented by the stories of Pārśva and his predecessors may have been closer to the initial process of the Second Urbanisation. If the cult-association model discussed in Chapter 4 has any value, there may have been a connection between these movements and the growth of trading networks and market centres that led to the early urban centres. In other words, membership in a cult-association with branches in various urban trading centres would have been helpful for merchants travelling from one centre to another, since it

[13] Bronkhorst 1993; Cousins (personal communication, 2002).

would have provided them with a network of fellow cult-members in these places who could be trusted and who shared their values.

I return to this suggestion again in Chapter 8. Here, however, I move to another proposed influence on the early ascetic orders: the *vrātyas*.

THE *VRĀTYAS* AS PREDECESSORS?

Dundas suggested some years ago that the *vrātyas*, the somewhat mysterious Vedic ritualists mentioned in Chapter 5, might have been a significant precedent for the *śramaṇa* traditions (Dundas 1991, 2002). Dundas in fact did not refer directly to the *vrātyas* but to 'ancient Indo-European warrior brotherhoods' (1991: 174; 2002: 17). W. B. Bollée, whom he cited as his source, however, was concerned primarily with the *vrātyas*, whom he traced back to earlier Indo-European groups of male warriors (Bollée 1981).

At first sight, it is hard to see what the *vrātyas* might have to do with the notoriously pacifist Jainas, or for that matter the Buddhists. The *vrātyas* were after all, on the Falk-Witzel model at any rate, gangs of aggressive young men who went out raiding cattle from neighbouring tribes when they were not involved in transgressive rituals out in the forests.

There is more however to the argument than perhaps appears at first sight. Dundas noted the prevalence of martial imagery in Jaina sources – Jina, after all, means 'conqueror', so that, as Dundas put it 'martial conquest is the central image and metaphor of Jainism, giving the religion its very name' (Dundas 1991: 173). In fact military imagery is quite widespread in both Jaina and Buddhist traditions. Of course, both the Jainas and the Buddhists had founders from the *kṣatriya* or warrior caste. Dundas noted that Jainism has in fact historically been ambivalent about war, and Jaina communities have certainly been supported by violent and aggressive rulers.

The same would have to be said about Buddhists, for all of the splendid example of the Emperor Aśoka's conversion to Buddhism as a result of his revulsion at the slaughter involved in the war against Kaliṅga. The Sinhalese Buddhist willingness to justify King Duṭṭhagāmaṇi's slaughter of the Tamils on religious grounds is only one well-known example, if one that has become particularly notorious because of its lethal consequences in modern times.

In fact, ascetics have often been linked with militarism in Indian history and have frequently even served as warriors.[14] Dundas's real point though

[14] One can think of the armed and militaristic *saṃnyāsins* known as the *nāgas*, or of the *saṃnyāsin*-led revolt against the British immortalised in Bankim Chandra Chatterji's novel *Anandamath* (Chatterji

was about formal structural models.[15] How did the idea come about of having a formal organisation of ascetics living together and pursuing a common religious goal?

> Terms employed in Jainism and Buddhism to employ groups of ascetics such as *gaṇa*, 'troop,' and *saṅgha*, 'assembly,' are used in early Vedic texts to refer to the warrior brotherhoods, the young men's bands which were a feature of Āryan nomadic life, and the stress found in the old codes of monastic law on requirements of youth, physical fitness and good birth for Jain and Buddhist monks, along with the frequent martial imagery of Jainism and its repeated stress on the crushing of spiritual enemies, may point to a degree of continuity with these earlier types of warrior. (Dundas 2002: 17)

Certainly this warrior-brotherhood emphasis might help to explain the ambivalence that these movements have shown to women members (Sponberg 1992). However, while Dundas's point about martial imagery is true enough, it is also true that the central emphasis of the early Buddhist and Jaina teachings are anything but martial. The *vrātyas* may have provided an organisational model and some imagery, but it is hard to see them as the major predecessor of the *śramaṇa* orders.[16]

THE *ŚRAMAṆAS* AND THE DEAD

In another sense, however, the *vrātyas* may have more to offer us. Bollée suggests that the *śramaṇa* orders may have derived their close association with the cult of the dead from the *vrātyas*. Bollée suggests that an association with the cult of dead was a significant theme for the early *śramaṇa* communities. They frequently settled at sites associated with the dead and seem to have taken over a significant role in relation to the spirits of the dead. Here, I think, Bollée was onto something important, and often neglected, though again it is unclear how much weight to give to the *vrātya* connection.

1992). (See also Boullier 1993). One can also consider such 'export versions' of Indian asceticism as the military cult in early Korea, linked to the future Buddha Maitreya (Mohan 2001), or, at a later date, the Samurai in Japan (Victoria 2005). It is also a matter of some interest that the Iranian branch of the Indo-Aryan tradition seems to have led to a cult-organisation with an explicitly militaristic orientation, that of Mithras, at around the same time or somewhat later, though the extent of the connection is admittedly problematic (Sick 2004).

15 Witzel has argued similarly, apparently independently of Dundas: 'the Buddhist *saṅgha* has, unobserved so far, some *vrātya* features as well: a single leader of a larger group of equals who wander about in the countryside and live on extortion (or by begging), stay away from settlements, have special dress and speech, etc.' (Witzel 2003: 90).

16 At the same time, the early use of the term *yoga* in the context of the warrior's transfer to heaven (see White 2006, and Chapters 9 and 14) may provide some support for this connection. This also connects with the issue I discuss below of the relationship between the *śramaṇa* orders and the cult of the dead.

To begin with, it is worth noting that the most salient linkage between Buddhist monks and lay communities in modern times in both Southeast Asian and East Asian Buddhist societies has been their role in relation to death. That Buddhist monks are specialists in death is something of a cliché of modern ethnography on Buddhist societies (e.g. Tambiah 1970), and it seems to be a theme that goes back a very long way in Buddhist history (see deCaroli 2004; White 1986).

As we will see below, this appears to have been part of how the early *śramaṇa* communities, at any rate the Buddhists, built up links with local communities. They settled at places associated with the cult of the dead, and they took over responsibility for dealing with the process of dying and of looking after the spirits of the dead. That they were prepared and able to do this is doubtless connected to the idea that they were in a sense already part of that world. The world of the *śramaṇa*s and the Brahmanical renunciates seeking liberation from rebirth, in other words, like that of the dead, was opposed to that of the everyday community of the living. In some ways, it was even more radically opposed than that of the dead themselves, since these ascetics were structurally outside the cycle of rebirth itself.

This brings something else along with it. The world of death is also a world of misfortune and of potential threat. To become a specialist in this area through renouncing secular life is to step into an unsavoury world of dangerous and problematical supernatural powers that most people are in fact doing their best to stay away from. Given the high prestige of monasticism in modern Buddhist societies, the splendour of many Buddhist and Jaina monasteries and temples and, for that matter, the relatively comfortable and worldly lifestyle of many ordinary members of these orders in modern times, this aspect of the *śramaṇa* traditions is not always conspicuous. There are reasons why we should take it seriously, however, since it brings us back to a central theme of the book, the ongoing dialogue between the everyday world and the world of misfortune, with its associations of death, transgression and the unsavoury.[17]

We might start with the very deliberate structural stepping outside of secular society that is involved in becoming a Buddhist or Jaina *śramaṇa* or a Brahmanical *saṃnyāsin*. In the case of the *saṃnyāsin*, the developed form of this transition involves the actual performance of one's own funeral ceremony and the 'internalisation' of the sacred fire that is a critical part of the everyday life of the householder. In all cases, including that of the

[17] I would like to acknowledge the work of my former student Kim Chongho in helping me to think through these questions (cf. Kim 2003).

Buddhist and Jaina *śramaṇa*, it involves a thorough rejection of secular identity, including one's previous name. The life of the *bhikṣu* or beggar-ascetic, living off food-offerings which are, again ideally, being made to the monk as representative of the community rather than as individual, points in the same direction (see below). Of course, in practice, family connections and caste identity may remain important for Buddhist monks or other ascetic practitioners, who are not necessarily outside the world of power and politics, and individual monks may become significant actors in the secular world in their own right, but ideologically the transition is a significant one.

We might also note the 'extreme' behaviour associated with many renunciate ascetics. In the Buddhist tradition we could point to practitioners such as the Tibetan *chödpa* (*gcod pa*) who, ideally at least, spend their lives wandering from place to place, practising in places associated with frightening and dangerous spirits, where they visualise the offering of their bodies to the Buddhist deities, local gods, ghosts and demons. Most Tibetan families would have some ambivalence about a son or daughter becoming a wandering *chödpa*, but *chödpa* are also believed to be among the most powerful of ritual performers and are the people who are expected to deal with the dead in cases of epidemic disease and generally to cope with serious episodes of misfortune (Tucci 1980: 92, Samuel 1993: 211–12). They are expected also to have a certain invulnerability to epidemic diseases and other supernatural hazards, which is not really surprising when one considers that they are already themselves living within this world of evil and misfortune to a significant degree.

Much the same is true of the *aghori* renunciates in later Hindu tradition (Parry 1994; Svoboda 1986, 1993). The detailed practices of these ascetics come out of the 'Tantric' traditions which I discuss in later chapters, but the idea that at least one form of ascetic involves a radical rejection of conventional lifestyle, associated with such unsavoury practices as living naked with one's body covered with ashes, eating out of a human skull-bowl, and the like, is as we will see an old one. Again, there is very considerable ambivalence about this lifestyle in modern Indian society, as to other more 'extreme' forms of *yogin*, *faqir*, etc., but the idea that they are such people and that they may have real powers has by no means disappeared even from modern secularised South Asia. Nakedness itself was one of the key indicators of early ascetics, being both standard Ājīvika practice and part of the rule taught by Mahāvīra (e.g. Bronkhorst 2000). Symbolically, it is another very clear rejection of secular identity.

The Buddhist tradition aimed at a 'middle way' which opposed more extreme forms of asceticism, though in practice it was engaged in a constant dialectic with them, as with the disputes over the so-called *dhutanga* practices, a set of 'extreme' ascetic practices that were eventually judged to be allowable but not required of Buddhist monks (e.g. Gombrich 1988: 94–5; Tambiah 1984). Buddhist monks wore robes, though in principle these were made of salvaged rags, and although they are described in the early *sūtras* as spending most of the year wandering from place to place it is clear that from an early stage most of the monastic population lived in settled communities. Various other accommodations to secular life have been part of the history of the Jaina and Brahmanical ascetic traditions though in each case the 'extreme' options have retained a presence. However, the idea of the Buddhist monk as being protected against and as offering protection against the malevolent attacks of the spirit world and the realm of misfortune is a key one in the Buddhist tradition as well from relatively early times, in the form of the *paritta suttas*, texts which are recited for protection and the generation of 'auspiciousness' and which generally derive from narratives in which the Buddha states that those of his disciples who recite these texts will be protected against supernatural powers of various kinds and other afflictions (Tambiah 1970; Gombrich 1971: 201–9; de Silva 1981). They are also used in other contexts that for pre-modern South Asians were heavily associated with supernatural danger, such as childbirth.[18]

The point I am making here is that there is a structural opposition between the realm of happiness, prosperity, good fortune and worldly life, on the one hand, and that of the ascetic world-renouncer, whether a Buddhist or Jaina *śramaṇa* or a Brahmanical ascetic, on the other. This opposition does not imply a lack of contact: the inhabitants of the worldly realm need access to the powers of the world-renouncer, above all when things are not going as they should. In addition, the opposition is not equally strong or equally significant at all times and in all places within the sphere of Indic religions. However, we will see it recurring in virtually all times and places in one form or another, and it will be one of the basic building blocks of our analysis.[19]

THE *VRATA* OR VOW

The concept of the *vrata* or vow (not, apparently, related to that of the *vrātya*) is also worth some discussion. This term has a long history in Indic

[18] The *Aṅgulimāla Sutta* is recited for protection in childbirth, which is conceived of in South Asia as a time of very high susceptibility to spirit attack (de Silva 1981: 13; cf. Rozario and Samuel 2002b).

[19] Again, Louis Dumont offers a classic treatment (1960, cf. Madan 1988), but I would prefer to provide a greater degree of historicisation and to treat the question of renunciation less as a given and more as a variable over time.

religions, and in its modern meaning it consists essentially of a vow or ritual observance addressed to a particular deity and aimed at influencing that deity to help oneself or to help another on one's behalf.

In modern times, *vrata* are most often performed by women for the benefit of their families (husbands and children) and typically involve fasting along with the recitation of a story associated with the *vrata* (Wadley 1980; S. Robinson 1985; McGee 1992; Gupta 1999). The concept in the Ṛgveda and early Brahmanical texts is somewhat different and has been discussed recently by Lubin (2001). Lubin, following Joel Brereton, interprets the *vrata* as initially having the meaning of a kind of commandment expressing the nature of a particular deity and so constitutive of the order of the world as we know it. 'Each deity's *vratá* defines its nature and role in the world' (Lubin 2001: 568). These commandments set up a moral obligation on human beings who have relationships with the gods to adhere to the divine patterns and so to act in ways that follow them. In some places in the Ṛgveda and in later texts however the term *vrata* is used to designate 'rule[s] of ritual actions' or of 'specific, initiatory regimens required for worship and Vedic study' (Lubin 2001: 566). The *vrata* of *brahmacarya* is of this kind (*Atharvaveda* 11.5, *Śatapatha Brāhmaṇa* 11.5.4). Dundas suggests that the term in its earlier meaning 'conveyed the notion of a "calling" in the sense of a solemn dedication of oneself on a permanent basis to one single purpose' (Dundas 2002: 157–8). Certainly it is this sense that appears to be intended when the five vows of the Jaina follower are referred to as the *mahāvrata* ('great *vrata*').[20] These five Jaina Great Vows are abstention from killing and violence of any kind, not lying, not taking what has not been given, the renunciation of sexual activity, and the renunciation of attachment (Dundas 2002: 158–9).[21]

These are very similar to the five lay precepts of the Buddhist tradition, which are against killing, stealing, sexual misconduct, false speech and the taking of intoxicants. The term *vrata* is not used in the same way in the Buddhist context, perhaps reflecting the early Buddhist critique of Jaina 'extremism', but the idea of the various levels of monastic initiation as involving a set of vows or commitments that define a pattern of life with a

[20] The same term is used for the major ritual of the *vrātyas*, referred to in Chapter 5, where it clearly has a very different meaning.

[21] The Jaina *mahāvrata* is also very close to the *mahāvrata* described in Patañjali's *Yogasūtra* ii.30–1, which consists of the practice in all circumstances of non-injury, truthfulness, non-theft, *brahmacarya* and *aparigraha* (not accepting more than is necessary for bodily subsistence). Lorenzen regards this as the *mahāvrata* of the Kālāmukha ascetics (Lorenzen 1991: 81). The close similarity of the two sets of vows is unlikely to be coincidence, but perhaps results less from borrowing in one direction or the other than from both going back to a shared ascetic background.

particular expected outcome in terms of divine favour or spiritual success remains.

But what was this expected outcome? What were the teachings of the Buddha, Mahāvīra and their contemporaries about?

THE CONTENT OF THE *ŚRAMAṆA* TEACHINGS

There are two main ways in which one can approach this question. One is to take one or another modern form of the tradition as providing an authoritative view of the tradition as it existed twenty-five centuries ago, in the mid-first millennium BCE. In this case the self-understandings of one or another presentation of the modern Jaina tradition or of one or another representative of the often substantially different Buddhist schools becomes primary. The other is to concentrate on the historical and textual evidence, such as it is, and come up with our own guesses regarding 'the original teachings'. Many people have walked along this road with variable and contradictory results (e.g. Ling 1973; Vetter 1990; Gombrich 1990, 1992, 1996, 1997, 2003; Bronkhorst 1993, 1998a, 1998b, 2000; Lindtner 1991–93, 1999).

What I write here necessarily falls into the second category, and I have no real confidence of coming up with anything more secure or final than my predecessors, many of them scholars with competences far greater than mine in relation to the textual material. Nor does what follows have any real claim to originality. Something, however, does need to be said at this point in the book.

I think it helps to begin, at least provisionally, with one key element from the traditional approaches. This is the awareness that whatever it was that was involved in the *śramaṇa* teachings required a radical reshaping of the individual and his or her relationship to everyday life, that transforms the initiate in such a way that the ordinary, everyday life of the householder is either left behind or transvalued, so that if one continues to live it, it is in a radically altered form, as a stage on a progress towards a goal that lies beyond or behind the appearances and assumptions of everyday life. The *śramaṇa* traditions in their modern form of the organised religious traditions of Buddhism and Jainism continue to hold that what they are transmitting is not a simple set of moral or ethical teachings, or merely a new intellectual understanding, but something that is intended to transform the individual at a profound level. This might arise from or be supported by moral and ethical teachings, or new intellectual understandings, but it is the transformation itself that is at the centre of the process. I assume that this at least goes back to early times. If it does not, then the whole business becomes of much less interest.

Johannes Bronkhorst's *Two Traditions of Meditation in Ancient India* (1993) is a useful starting point for a discussion of the texts themselves. Bronkhorst re-examined the Buddhist and Jaina texts, along with the early Brahmanical sources, in some detail to see what they had to say about early meditation techniques. He concludes that both early Jaina and Brahmanical practices were essentially attempts to bring the body and/or mind to a halt through ascetic practice. 'Among the non-Buddhists (Jainas), meditation was a forceful effort to restrain the mind and bring it to a standstill' (1993: 22). In a more 'advanced' form of the process, one also attempts to bring breathing to a stop. Here Bronkhorst is referring to descriptions in Buddhist sources, but the Jaina sources themselves are essentially in agreement (1993: 31–44), and much the same is true of early Brahmanical sources. In addition, the idea of fasting to death is also found in both contexts. Bronkhorst comments in relation to the Jainas that '[e]arly Jaina meditation was only one aspect of a more general attempt to stop all activities of body and mind, including even breathing' (1993: 44).

If all this is correct, we might wonder how far we really should be speaking of 'meditation techniques' in the ordinary sense at all in this context. What seems to be at issue is more a way of dying which leads to escape from the cycle of rebirth, as opposed to the normal way that ties one back into the cycle.[22] This has remained an important Jaina theme up to modern times, and the religious ideal of fasting to death has been maintained to the present day, though not often practised (Dundas 2002: 179–81). Dundas notes that in this process (*sallekhanā*) 'the central austerity of cutting down the consumption of food is taken to its logical conclusion so that the body is "scoured out" (*sallikhita*) of its negative factors and the mind can focus solely upon spiritual matters as death approaches' (179).

However, while a 'holy death' may be the eventual goal of early Jaina and Brahmanical practice, these practices are not described in these terms, either by themselves or by the Buddhists, nor does Bronkhorst imply that they necessarily should be. In any case, I would rather read this material in a slightly different sense, which is that the goal of 'liberation from rebirth' existed, and was linked to a 'stopping' in some sense of the activities of body and mind, but that a developed technology of how to attain that goal

[22] It may be significant that the theme of fasting to death occurs also in the early South Indian material as a way in which a defeated king might die (Hart 1975: 88–91).

did not exist. In other words, it was largely up to individual practitioners how they might pursue that goal.

In fact, other sets of practices existed that are closer to what we might refer to as meditation, including the four Brahmic States (*brahmavihāra*). This well-known set of practices involves the cultivation of *maitrī* (P. *mettā*, love/friendliness towards other beings), *karuṇā* (compassion), *muditā* (sympathy towards the joy of others), and *upekṣā* (equanimity). They are described in the early Buddhist texts as having been practised by both Buddhists and by some non-Buddhists, although the Buddha is reported as saying that his followers take them further (Bronkhorst 1993: 93–4), and they are presumably an old component of the shared culture of ascetic practitioners I referred to earlier in this chapter.[23] Bronkhorst suggests that members of this culture were working on the basic assumption that action leads to misery and rebirth. 'In this tradition some attempted to abstain from action, literally, while others tried to obtain an insight that their real self, their soul, never partakes of any action anyhow' (1993: 128).

Thus the key process within this 'mainstream' tradition, which for Bronkhorst includes both Jaina and Brahmanical practitioners, was aimed at stopping activities of the body and mind. The Buddhists, by comparison, describe their own practice as that of attaining equanimity towards the senses, rather than making the senses cease to function (Bronkhorst 1993: 30). The key to doing this for the early Buddhist textual tradition is through the four *dhyāna*, a standard series of meditative states. The classical account of this is given in a number of places in the early *sūtras*, including the *Mahāsaccaka Sutta*, where it follows on a description of the Buddha's initial attempts at Bodhgayā to practise the forceful stopping of breathing and other such meditations. These practices are here associated with three Ājīvika teachers rather than with the Jainas, but this is probably, as Bronkhorst suggests, because Saccaka, the Buddha's interlocutor on this occasion is himself a Jaina (Bronkhorst 1993: 22–5; cf. Ñāṇamoli and Bodhi 1995: 332–43).[24]

> I considered: 'I recall that when my father the Sakyan was occupied, while I was sitting in the cool shade of a rose-apple tree, quite secluded from sensual pleasures, secluded from unwholesome states, I entered upon and abided in the first jhāna, which is accompanied by applied and sustained thought, with rapture and pleasure born of seclusion. Could that be the path to enlightenment?' Then, following on

[23] On *maitrī*/*mettā*, see also Schmithausen 1997.

[24] Note that Bronkhorst regards parts of the *Mahāsaccaka Sutta* as later additions to an original core (1993: 15–18).

that memory, came the realisation: 'That is the path to enlightenment.' (Ñāṇamoli and Bodhi 1995: 340)

The four *jhāna* (Skt *dhyāna*) are meditative states characterised by the presence of various components (applied thought, rapture, etc.). The Buddha explains how he then decided to end his extreme ascetic practices, ate some food and regained his strength. He then entered the four *jhānas* in succession in order to purify his mind, and was then able to attain to the liberating insight that leads to liberation from rebirth (and, in his case, Buddhahood). In the present text of the *Mahāsaccaka Sutta*, this consists of three stages, (1) the Buddha recollected his own previous lives, (2) he understood the passing away and rebirth of beings according to their actions (*karma*), and finally (3) he knew directly the Four Noble Truths and the way leading to the cessation of the *āsava* (Skt. *āsrava*, taints or intoxicants).

This is a standard passage, repeated in many places in the early suttas:

When my concentrated mind was thus purified, bright, unblemished, rid of imperfection, malleable, wieldy, steady, and attained to imperturbability, I directed it to knowledge of the destruction of the taints. I directly knew as it actually is: 'This is suffering';... 'This is the origin of suffering';... 'This is the cessation of suffering';... 'This is the way leading to the cessation of suffering';... 'These are the taints';... 'This is the origin of the taints';... 'This is the cessation of the taints';... 'This is the way leading to the cessation of the taints.' (Ñāṇamoli and Bodhi 1995: 341–2)

Bronkhorst suggests that neither the Four Noble Truths (suffering, the origin of suffering, the cessation of suffering, the way to the cessation of suffering), nor the account of the recognition, origin etc. of the taints or *āsavas*, which is clearly modelled on the Four Noble Truths, originally belonged in this context. The Four Noble Truths, after all, describe the knowledge needed to set out on the path to liberation from rebirth, but the Buddha is now near the end of this path, and he has already recognised the path to liberation in the earlier passage about his youthful experience of the first *jhāna* under the rose-apple tree. Instead, the earliest accounts of the Buddha's liberation from rebirth probably did not specify the nature of the 'liberating insight' (Skt *prajñā*, Pali *paññā*) beyond saying that it consisted in the destruction of the *āsrava* (Pali *āsava*), the 'taints' or 'intoxicants'. This is an inner psychic process, Bronkhorst notes, and one that could hardly be formulated discursively in a general way. Instead, the Buddha's teaching to his advanced disciples was likely to have consisted of personal advice appropriate for the specific needs of each person (1993: 108–9). The Four Noble Truths were, Bronkhorst suggests, incorporated into the account of the Buddha's liberation from rebirth at a later stage, in response to pressure from the ascetic community generally to provide a discursive account of the nature of the Buddha's liberating insight (1993: 110–11).[25]

Thus what was seen as original and new in the Buddhist tradition may have been not so much the discursive content as the practical method, which consisted in the application of the *dhyāna* or meditational states as a way of bringing about the elimination of what we would see in modern language as subliminal or subconscious impressions in the mind or body-mind. These are described in a variety of ways in early Buddhist texts (*āsrava, vāsanā, saṃskāra*). Both the use of the *dhyāna* and the formulation in terms of the elimination of subconscious impressions were eventually taken over within the Brahmanical tradition, where they form an important part of the *Yogasūtra*[26] (Bronkhorst 1993: 68–77). Within the Buddhist tradition, the *dhyāna*-techniques (*śamatha* in Skt, *samatha* in Pali) were progressively developed alongside practices that involved direct achievement of liberating insight (*vipaśyanā* in SKt, *vipassanā* in Pali).[27] The question of the relationship between these approaches and their relative importance has continued to be a central issue for the Buddhist tradition through to modern times (cf. Griffiths 1981; Cousins 1996b).

Bronkhorst's account seems to me to have considerable plausibility, given the historical distance between even the earliest sources as we have them and the lifetime of the Buddha. The rose-apple tree episode also strikes me as a significant element, since it suggests the kind of spontaneous 'visionary experience' that occurs quite often in childhood and early adolescence (cf. Hoffman 1992; E. Robinson 1996; Maxwell and Tschudin 1996). If we accept this as historical, then Bronkhorst's conclusion seems reasonable: 'There seems little reason to doubt that Buddhist meditation was introduced by the founder of Buddhism, i.e. by the historical Buddha' (1993: 123).

Bronkhorst's suggestion that the nature of the Buddha's liberating insight (*prajñā*, Pali *paññā*) was not initially specified fits in some respects with another intriguing study of early Buddhism, Peter Masefield's *Divine Revelation in Early Buddhism* (Masefield 1986; cf. also Harrison 1987). Masefield points to evidence in the Pali *nikayas*, generally assumed to be the earliest layer of texts in the Pali Canon, that the important division for its compilers

25 There is some evidence that the first two *dhyāna* meditations were also practised by Jainas, but this Jaina meditation tradition seems to have died out at a fairly early stage (Ferreira-Jardim 2005, 2006).

26 This is the classic text on yoga attributed to Patañjali. This Patañjali is generally regarded as a different person to the grammarian Patañjali discussed in Chapter 2, and the dating of the *Yogasūtra* remains controversial. See Chapter 9.

27 On Buddhist *dhyāna/jhāna*, see also Cousins 1973, 1992.

was not between the monk and the layman, but between the *ariyasāvaka*, the noble (*ariya* = Skt. *ārya*) person who has heard the teachings, acquired the 'right view' and so is on the path to *nibbāna* (Skt. *nirvāṇa*), and the *puthujjana* who has not yet understood the impermanence of the phenomenal world. This division cross-cuts that between laymen and monks. Laymen (and also the *devas* or gods) might be *ariyasāvaka*, and monks might be *puthujjana* (Masefield 1986: xvii-xviii). What is also significant is that becoming a member of the *ariyasāvaka* (also described in terms of *paññā*, insight, or attaining the *dhammacakkhu* or *dharma*-vision) is almost always described as taking place through the actual teaching of the Buddha (in a few unclear cases, it may be a result of the teaching of one of his disciples). As a result of this encounter with the Buddha, a person attains the *dhammacakkhu* and is on the path to a specific level of attainment. Without it, it would seem, no amount of practice will bring about the transition to *ariyasāvaka* status and the path to liberation.

This is, as Harrison notes, in accordance with the way that many contemporary Buddhists, in Theravāda Buddhism in particular, see the situation. It is often held that nobody has been able to attain *nibbāna* or any of the other exalted spiritual goals laid down in the texts since shortly after the time of the Buddha, and that the best that one can hope for today is to accumulate enough good *karma* over successive rebirths to be born in the time of the next Buddha, Maitreya, and become a member of the *ariyasāvaka* in his presence. This is by no means the only understanding of the situation in modern Buddhist societies, however, even those where Theravāda Buddhism is practised; as Harrison again notes, it is widely believed that exceptional individuals do continue to attain these high levels of spiritual realisation and in fact can act as conduits of magical power for ordinary people, empowering amulets and other ritually-powerful devices (cf. Tambiah 1984).

One response to Masefield's argument is to regard the Buddha and his contemporaries as 'charismatic spiritual leaders' or something of the kind. In a sense, this is no doubt true. The tradition makes the personal impact of the Buddha and Mahāvīra on their followers clear. However, it fails to explain very much about what was going on at the time, and about why it was that these men were able to have the impact that they did on the society of their time. I think that the kind of arguments advanced by Bronkhorst take us considerably further, and they present a view of the Buddha as someone who had attained, in contemporary terms, deep psychological insight into the workings of his own body-mind complex, and so was able to understand how to bring about transformations in the body-mind complexes of the people whom he encountered. This image of the Buddha as someone who had achieved a deep level of insight into his own body-mind complex was central to the early Buddhist tradition, and it was associated with a crucial innovation: the idea of a programme of specific practices through which others might replicate his achievement.[28]

I suggested many years ago that the Buddha's teaching was a reformulation of a kind of shamanic training (Samuel 1993: 370–3), and while I would be wary of using the term 'shamanic' now, after having to deal with the multiple misunderstandings which it has led to in the context of that book (cf. Samuel 2005a: 8–13), I would still suggest that the historical core of the Buddha's teachings was likely to have been a set of practical and experiential techniques rather than a body of discursive knowledge.

This is in line too with some other recent approaches to the Buddha's teaching, for example Sue Hamilton's emphasis on the role of experience in the Buddhist analysis of the *khandhas* (Hamilton 1996, 2000). Hamilton argues that the *khandhas* (Skt. *khandhas*), the five constituents which are presented in the early teachings, are 'not a comprehensive analysis of what a human being is comprised of [. . .] Rather, they are the factors of human experience [. . .] that one needs to understand in order to achieve the goal of Buddhist teachings, which is liberation from the cycle of lives' (Hamilton 2000: 8). In other words, the *khandhas* began less as a body of discursive knowledge than an aid to practice, which was gradually transformed over time into a set of philosophical assertions.

It is easy enough to imagine how the discursive knowledge arose, and how the hints and suggestions in the discourses attributed to the Buddha became gradually expanded into a body of doctrine and theory. As for methodology, the instruction imparted by the Buddha himself seems to have been both personal and closely tailored to the needs of the individual student. The Buddhist *sūtras* themselves preserve suggestions of this, and their formal structure ('Thus have I heard at one time . . .') with its enumeration of place, audience and situation retains a sense that the teachings need to be understood in relation to their specific recipients. Yet in the longer term there was perhaps no alternative but to produce a series of discursive accounts of methodology, based on texts such as those we saw, in which the Buddha describes what he had done himself. As we will see, this was not an

[28] Precisely what was in the original programme is difficult to recover, since this depends on how one dates various parts of the early material. However, some kind of mindfulness of breathing would seem a strong contender as the basic technique for entering the *dhyāna* states. Cf. *Satipaṭṭhāna Sutta* (*Dīghanikāya* 22, *Majjhimanikāya* 10; cf. also Nyanaponika Thera 1969); *Ānāpānasati Sutta* (*Majjhima Nikāya* 118; cf. also Ñāṇamoli Thera 1964); Cousins 1996b.

entirely satisfactory situation, and the need to produce new methods that might be effective in achieving the Buddha's original insight continued over the succeeding centuries and has indeed continued up to modern times.

How this process of the gradual accumulation of discursive material regarding both insight and methods worked in relation to the development of the Buddhist schools as we know them from their literature is a complex question which we are only beginning to be able to trace in detail (e.g. Cousins 1992, 1996b; Lindtner 1991–93, 1999; Choong 2005; Kuan 2005; Ferreira-Jordim 2005), but the overall process is not too hard to imagine. Since, in time, the *sūtras* presenting the teaching of the Buddha came to be seen as authoritative texts, reformulations of theory and of method (including monastic discipline) could only be achieved by the ongoing revision of existing *sūtras* or the production of new *sūtras*.

Having said this, we need to recall that all discursive formulations of the insights achieved by the Buddha, Mahāvīra, or the Upaniṣadic sages are just that: attempts to put things down into words. The temptation for scholars is to provide a rational and discursive model, but the material we are talking about may simply not be amenable to such approaches.

In the remainder of this chapter I turn to look at an important aspect of the accommodation which Buddhism and Jainism made to the pre-existing cultural context they encountered, their relationship to the local gods of the folk and civic religion.

LOCAL DEITIES AND EVERYDAY CONCERNS: THE BUDDHIST AND JAINA PATTERN

A presentation of the *śramaṇa* orders which focuses on their internal organisation and on their meditational practices leaves out significant dimensions of their place in society and religion of the time. The question of the relationship between these traditions and the presumably pre-existing cults of gods and spirits provides an important additional perspective.

It is well-known that the Buddhist and Jaina *sūtras* contain many accounts of encounters with gods and spirits of various kinds, including the major Brahmanical gods, Sakka (Indra) and Brahmā, and a host of lesser deities, male and female.[29] These figures appear in the narrative on the same level

[29] For the Buddhists, see Jootla 1997; DeCaroli 2004; for parallel early Jaina examples, see e.g. the *Uttarādhyayana Sūtra* ch. 9 (Jacobi 1895: 35–41, Indra appears to King Nami in the form of a Brahmin), ch. 12 (Jacobi 1895: 50–4, a *yakṣa* in a tree), ch. 23 (Jacobi 1895:121–2, various deities assembling to hear Jaina teachings). Padmanabh Jaini suggests however that Jaina *sutta* do not advocate offerings to *yakṣa* deities and that the Jaina *yakṣa* cult (on which see e.g. J. Sharma 1989; Zydenbos 1992; Pal 1994; Cort 1987) was a later development (Jaini 1991: 193).

Figure 6.2. *Stūpa* as depicted on Bharhut Stūpa, Indian Museum, Calcutta

and in much the same terms as the other, human characters; they speak to the Buddha, ask for and are given teachings, etc. (Jootla 1997).[30] Spirits of the dead also play a significant part in the story. The gods are also portrayed at early Buddhist *stūpa* sites such as Bhārhut and Sāñcī (Fig. 6.2).

It is also reasonably well known that many sites of significance for early Buddhism are also sites with important associations with local and regional deities. The term *caitya*, nowadays synonymous with *stūpa* as indicating the relic-mounds which are primary sites of Buddhist worship and which enclose the relics of Buddhist saints, including those of the Buddha himself, originally appears to have meant a spirit-shrine (cf. Trainor 1997; DeCaroli 2004). The trees which were so strongly associated with the *yakṣas* became

[30] All of which again suggests that we would be better off being careful about taking anything in these accounts too literally, however accurately they may have been preserved.

associated with the Buddha as well; the tree under which Śākyamuni achieved Buddhahood was the central location for Buddhist devotional activities, and earlier Buddhas were associated with specific trees under which they had achieved Buddhahood.

In a recent book (DeCaroli 2004), Robert DeCaroli has analysed the relationship between Buddhism and the 'spirit-deities' (to use his term) in detail, arguing that it needs to be taken more seriously than has generally been the case in the past.[31] Specifically, he suggests, following in part from the work of Gregory Schopen about the association between early Buddhist sites and places of the cult of the dead (Schopen 1996), that a major initial function of the monks was to deal with the spirit-world in general and the spirits of the dead in particular (e.g. DeCaroli 2004: 87–103).[32] I have referred earlier in this chapter to this question of the association with the dead, in particular in relation to the *vrātyas*.[33]

As I noted, DeCaroli uses the term 'spirit-deity' as a general term for both the spirits of the dead and the local and regional deities. More customarily, the local and regional deities have been referred to by the generic term *yakṣa*, a term which seems to have had a variety of applications in the period, being used both generically (e.g. in the *Āṭānāṭiya Sutta*, see below) and more specifically to refer to a sub-category of such beings associated with nature, fertility etc. Neither terminology is entirely appropriate, but deities of these kinds were clearly significant for the Buddhists and for the general population of the time. We have already seen something of them in Chapter 5.

YAKSA RELIGION AT THE BHĀRHUT STŪPA

The well-known remains of the Bhārhut *stūpa*[34] that today form a highlight of the Indian Museum in Calcutta provide the single most substantial body of sculptural material regarding these regional deities and the relationship

[31] Richard Cohen has argued a similar case for a later period in an important article on Ajanta, where he also emphasises the political dimensions of the spirit-deity cults (Cohen 1998).

[32] DeCaroli also notes that the offerings to monks echo the offerings made to the dead. He suggests that a relationship between the two is strongly implied by the Buddhist narratives of the food offered to Śākyamuni immediately before his enlightenment, which takes place close to Gayā, closely associated with Brahmanical rites for the dead (DeCaroli 2004: 106–14).

[33] Note that the Wheel of Rebirth incorporates everyone into the family – non-relatives, gods, demons, spirits of the dead, even animals.

[34] A *stūpa* contains relics of the Buddha or of someone who has attained a high level of Buddhist realisation. In later Buddhist thought the *stūpa* became a key symbolic representation of the central goals of Buddhism.

Figure 6.3. Two Deities. Bharhut Stūpa, Indian Museum, Calcutta

that developed between them and Buddhism. The remains consist primarily of parts of a stone railing that encircled the *stūpa*.

Much of the railing consists of decorative motifs or scenes from *Jātaka* stories, but at intervals there are large figures carved in relief from the stone. Most of these have inscriptions, which identify them as *yakṣas*, *nāgas* or *devas*. Similar individual figures are known from other sites, but Bhārhut is the only place where we have a large number of them from a single context, or where they are systematically identified. Clearly, their positioning presents them as in some sense accessory to or attendant upon the central message of Buddhism as figured by the shrine. Since a *stūpa* such as that at Bhārhut is a large state edifice, the *yakṣas* could also have a political message.

Unfortunately, we only have part of the Bhārhut railing, and perhaps one-third of the total number of *yakṣa* figures. It is not really possible to reconstruct the complete set of deities on the railings. In addition, the railing appears to have been rebuilt at some point, and the surviving figures belong to at least two different phases, so what we now have does not necessarily derive from an original and consistent scheme.[35] However, it

[35] See Barua 1934–37; Kala 1951; Coomaraswamy 1956.

appears that the scheme included the four Great Kings or Lokapālas, a set of *yakṣa*-type deities, already mentioned in Chapter 5, who have the role of protectors of the four directions within Buddhism. Two of these figures survive (Virūḍhaka, the deity of the South, and Kubera, the deity of the North). The scheme may also have included a set of four images of Lakṣmī, or rather Sirima (Śrī-ma) *devatā*, as the goddess is called in the railing inscriptions. Kubera is depicted as a young man, rather than the corpulent middle-aged figure more familiar from later iconography. Sirima has an upright posture and is rather more formal in style than the remaining deities, male and female, who are variously identified as *yakṣas*, *devas* or *nāgas*.

Lakṣmī is incidentally also depicted in several other places on the railing in one of her classic iconographical forms, that in which she is asperged by two elephants to right and left, a form that has continued in use right up to the present day (see the Sāñcī image, Fig. 5.4). These can perhaps be interpreted as generalised symbols of prosperity and good fortune. The large figures however are clearly something rather more than that, both because of their size, but also because they are carefully identified by inscriptions and individualised in their portrayals.

We do not really have anything comparable to the Bhārhut iconographical scheme from any other site of the period, though we have quite a few individual figures from elsewhere. However Benimadhab Barua, who published the most detailed study of the *stūpa* in the 1930s, compares the iconographical scheme to the description of the construction of the Great Stūpa in Chapters 29 and 30 of the *Mahāvaṃsa*, the Sinhalese religious chronicle. This *stūpa* included images of the Four Great Kings, the Thirty-Three Gods, Thirty-Two Celestial Maidens and Twenty-Eight Chiefs of the Yakṣas, raising their folded hands.[36]

At Chandraketugarh we saw the *yakṣa*-type deities in isolation. Here they have been brought into connection with a new sacred order, that of the Buddha. As we learn from the Buddhist *sūtras*, some of these deities are thought of as obedient to the Buddha, others as disliking or resisting his teachings. Chief among those who are followers of the Buddha are the Four Great Kings of the four directions, and it is their leader, Kubera,

[36] 'At the four quarters of the heaven stood the (figures of) the four Great kings, and the thirty-three gods and the thirty-two (celestial) maidens and the twenty-eight chiefs of the yakkhas; but above these devas raising their folded hands, vases filled with flowers likewise, dancing devatas and devatas playing instruments of music, devas with mirrors in their hands, and devas also bearing flowers and branches, devas with lotus-blossoms and so forth in their hands and other devas of many kinds, rows of arches made of gems and (rows) of dhammacakkas; rows of sword-bearing devas and also devas bearing pitchers.' (Geiger 1964: 207).

who comes to the Buddha in the *Āṭānāṭiya Sutta* to provide him (or rather his followers) with spells that can be used to keep the other *yakṣas* under control should they cause trouble for the Buddha's followers. The Four Kings became major figures in Buddhist iconography in Tibet and East Asia.[37]

In general, though, the *yakṣa* deities can be incorporated into the Buddhist scheme as lesser beings that rule over the everyday or *laukika* world. This, I think, is the message conveyed by the Bhārhut images. The contrast with the Buddha, who rules over the higher, *lokottara*, realms, is explicit not only in the folded hands and respectful postures of the Bhārhut *yakṣa* deities but also in the fact that they are represented at all. The Buddha at Bhārhut is not depicted directly in iconographic form, except in the sense that the central *stūpa* itself is a representation of him.

As I noted above, we should see a construction like the Bhārhut *stūpa* as a political statement as much as a religious one. In signalling his support for the universal order of the Buddha, and portraying the various regional spirit-deities as submitting respectfully to that order, the ruler who sponsored the *stūpa* construction was surely making an implicit claim to a similar status. The moral and ethical dimension of the Buddhist teachings were also, as the Aśokan inscriptions suggest, an intrinsic part of the package.

Note that we do not see anything in either body of material, or in other comparable material, to suggest the presence of fierce or aggressive goddesses. There have been suggestions that they can be found in the Vedas, but our evidence for them is really from a later period altogether, and I will leave it to a subsequent chapter (Chapter 10).

The evidence from these early sites and from the early textual material suggests that Buddhism from its initial stages took on a significant role in relation to the existing local and regional spirit-cults. Much the same was doubtless true of the Jaina tradition in the areas where it became established. These spirit-cults, rather as in countries such as Thailand today, would have existed at many different levels, from protective spirits of households to protective spirits of wider communities, probably (from later evidence) mainly at trees or sacred groves outside towns (*caityas*), to regional cults associated with emergent states. There would also have been concern with the potentially malevolent role both of these spirits and of the spirits of the dead.

37 The Bhārhut Stupa, and the description in the *Mahāvaṃsa*, are also reminiscent of the description in *Mahāsamaya Sutta*, where a huge array of deities comes to attend on the Buddha (*Dīghanikāya*, 20 = Walshe 1995: 315–20).

The role of the *śramaṇa* traditions as far as the lay population was concerned was to bring the spirits under control, to civilise them and incorporate them within the community, and to provide an overall ideological framework within which their cult could be maintained on an ongoing basis. The cult itself, as again in Southeast Asia today, would probably have been mostly carried out by lay priests, not by monks, though the monastery provided a centre of spiritual power and expertise that could be called upon in cases of emergency.

BUDDHIST AND JAINA ATTITUDES TO THE YAKṢAS

Thus in regions where Buddhism had become a state or official religion, the *yakṣas* were subordinated to Buddhism but their cult was allowed to continue. They were expected to be polite and respectful to the Dharma and its representatives, and could be threatened by ritual means if they caused trouble, but the relationship was one of a harmonious coexistence, in which the *yakṣa* deities represented the *laukika* (this-worldly) values while the Buddha, and in later times the developing cult of bodhisattvas and other Buddhist deities, represented the *lokottara* or trans-worldly values of rebirth and enlightenment. A number of the *yakṣa* deities were regarded as particularly close to the Buddhist teachings and as acting as their protectors. We have seen examples in the case of Vajrapāṇi and the Four Great Kings. Much the same is true in the Jaina tradition, where the *tīrthaṅkaras* are portrayed with attendant *yakṣa* and *yakṣī* deities, who can be appealed to to serve the mundane needs of their followers (Cort 1987; J. Sharma 1989).

This is a picture that is familiar from the modern ethnography of the Theravāda societies of Southeast Asia. While there are obviously local variations and issues in each of the major Southeast Asian cultures, we can, I think, see in the relationship between Buddhism and the spirit cults in places such as rural Thailand or Burma, as it was in fairly recent times, a demonstration of how this kind of situation worked. For an example of a major regional centre, we could look at the city of Chiang Mai in Northern Thailand, formerly the capital of the state of Lan Na, which goes back to the thirteenth century and was through much of its history more or less independent of the Thai state at Sukhothai or Ayutthaya (Wijeyewardene 1986; Davis 1984; Rhum 1987; Aasen 1998: 65–7).

Chiang Mai is a walled city with a series of important monasteries, one of them containing a crystal Buddha which had much the same state-protective function for the Lan Na state as the well-known Emerald Buddha at Bangkok (Aasen 1998: 85–6). Close to the city is the sacred hill of Doi

Suthep, with a famous Buddhist *stūpa* containing a relic of the Buddha and supposedly visited by him in his historical lifetime (Swearer 1976; Wijeyewardene 1986; Rhum 1987; Samuel 2001a: 399–400).

There is no doubt that at one level this is a prototypically Theravāda Buddhist community. Yet the equivalent of the *yakṣa* cult is still very much alive. As at Bangkok, there is a City Pillar shrine that is the place where the guardian spirit of the city is worshipped. The hill of Doi Suthep also has guardian spirits, who receive annual buffalo sacrifice and possess local spirit-mediums. The myth of these guardian spirits regards them as the parents of a local Buddhist *ṛṣi*, Vāsudeva (the origin of the name Suthep, in fact) whose story is part of the origin myth of the first Buddhist kingdom of the region, the Mon kingdom of Haripuñjaya.[38]

Chiang Mai was a sophisticated urban centre, as of course Bhārhut must have been. Folk and village religion leaves little direct trace in the archaeological record but we can imagine that it existed and that it dealt with smaller-scale deities of a basically similar type, as we can again see in the village ethnography of contemporary Thailand and Burma. In the religious life of the Northeast Thai village studied by Stanley Tambiah, for example, the village's annual ritual cycle is a complex interweaving of Buddhist festivals linked to the universal Theravada Buddhist festival cycle (and to the Thai state) with local celebrations tied in with the village's agricultural cycle and directed towards the founding ancestor spirits of the village and the regional protector spirit residing in the local marsh. This marsh-dwelling deity is identified, as is apparently quite common in rural Thailand, with the Buddha's miracle-working disciple Upagupta (Tambiah 1970; Strong 1992; cf. also Samuel 2001a).

The spirit-cult is about this-worldly success and prosperity, while the values of Buddhism are directed towards *karma*, rebirth, and, if only indirectly, the attainment of *nirvāṇā*. Yet the two are closely interwoven. The young men of the village spend a period as monks in the monastery, but this is not expected to be the beginning of a monastic career, and only a tiny minority remain as monks. For the majority, this temporary ordination is in fact a rite of passage to adulthood and marriage. The central transactions between villagers and monks relate to the making of merit, or positive karma leading to a good rebirth, by donations of food, clothing and other items to the monks, and through the temporary ordination of young men

[38] I have written elsewhere about the role of *ṛṣis* and sages in both Brahmanical and Buddhist contexts as providing local associations and connections for religious concepts and traditions that in fact originated outside a particular region (Samuel 2001a).

as monks. Both of these are meritorious actions helping to ensure a good life in one's next rebirth.

In his 1970 book, Tambiah summarised the relationships between rituals, concepts and values in the following diagram. The diagram belongs in some respects to an era of structuralist over-tidiness which Tambiah himself moved away from in his later work, but gives a useful sense of the range of

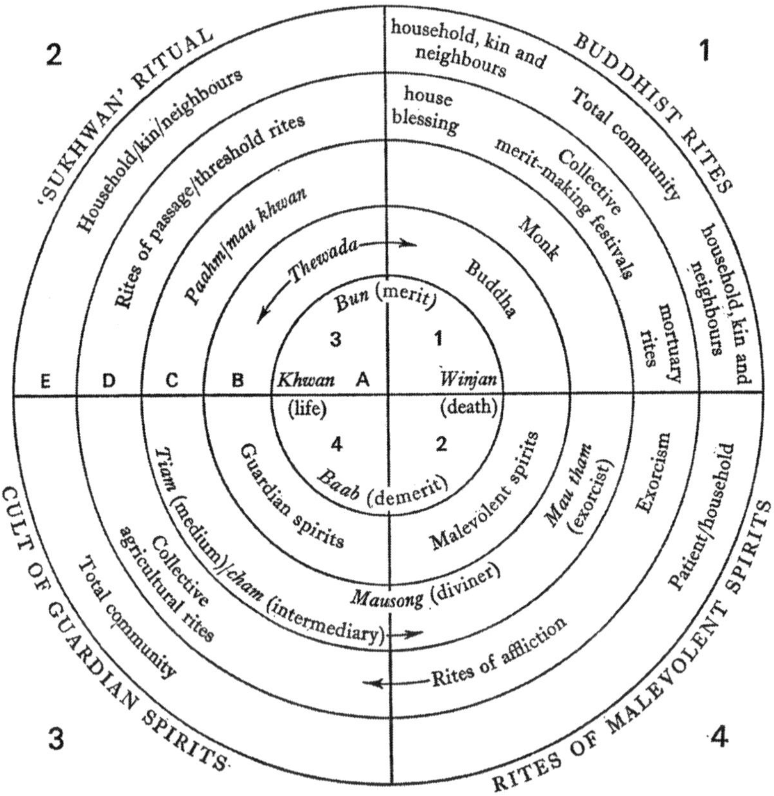

A. Primary religious concepts and fields of socio-religious interest
B. Supernatural personifications relating to A
C. Ritual specialists associated with B
D. Rites conducted by C
E. Scale of social participation in D

Figure 6.4. S.J. Tambiah's Diagram of the Value System of Northeast Thai Village Society

concerns of village religion, and of the relatively limited place of Buddhism within it:

Here the *sukhwan* rituals are rituals relating to the idea of a life-force, soul or inner vitality (*khwan*) which can be lost from the body and which is summoned back at times of danger and also of rites of passage; marriage in the village is a *sukhwan* rite, not a Buddhist ritual. The cult of guardian spirits and rites of malevolent spirits refer to positive and negative relationships with local spirits, as guardians and as causes of illness. The relationship of Buddhist monks to these three spheres is tangential, although some Buddhist monks serve as exorcists, and *paritta* rituals (the recitation of specific Buddhist *sutta* with magical-protective functions) may be integrated with spirit-cult practices. Overall, however, in this village, as in other village ethnographies from Thailand, Burma and Sri Lanka (Brohm 1963; Ames 1964; Spiro 1967, 1971; Davis 1985; Rhum 1994), the opposition between 'worldly' and Buddhist religion (*laukika* and *lokottara*) is ideologically quite clear. They are both seen as legitimate, and there is a structural relationship between their underlying values (as Tambiah's diagram is intended to show), but they occupy separate spheres.

In fact, some analysts of village Buddhism in Southeast Asia have spoken of separate religions (e.g. Spiro 1967). This, I think, is to go too far. Buddhism and the spirit cults, *sukhwan* rituals, etc., are clearly related in all kinds of ways in village thought and practice. The idea, however, of a separate set of village concerns dealt with by a separate body of people, who are specifically *not* Buddhist monks, is clearly present. The Buddhist monk does not interfere in rituals of everyday life, except to be present as a way of generating merit or auspiciousness. Major village festivals may be Buddhist dominated or lay-dominated or involve elements from both, but the two spheres remain conceptually separate, and the monastic-lay opposition (which corresponds clearly to celibate versus non-celibate, to other-worldly versus this-worldly) runs throughout the society.

The details vary in other Theravādin countries (temporary ordination is a characteristically Thai and Burmese feature, and is not found in Sri Lanka, for example) but we find much the same overall pattern. Western observers often used to interpret this as a situation in which Buddhism is a superficial veneer over the spirit-cults, but the anthropological studies of the 1960s onwards made it clear that it is a much more complex situation in which both are an integral part of the society. Buddhism provides a specific ethical dimension to village life, linked to the Buddhist teachings on virtuous and non-virtuous action and their consequences. People's respect for Buddhist values may be real, and may be a real part of their understanding of the world, even if they have no expectation or intention of seriously pursuing the Buddhist goal of *nirvāṇa* in their own lifetime. At the same time, those values come, in a sense, from outside the village community, and are aligned with the official values of the wider state of which the village forms part. Buddhism, in other words, is a state ideology as well as an integral part of village religion.

Both Buddhists and Jainas were prepared to include the Brahmanical deities in their scheme on essentially the same basis as the *yakṣas*, as lesser spirits who could be invoked for this-worldly and pragmatic purposes as long as they accepted their inferior position. There are no specifically Brahmanical figures included at Bhārhut, but we can find them elsewhere, for example in the early Buddha images from Mathurā, Gandhāra and elsewhere in which Indra and Brahmā are shown as smaller figures on either side of the Buddha, often asking him to teach (e.g. Klimburg-Salter 1995: 188 no.168, 189 no.169). The *Mahāmāyūrī* list mentioned in Chapter 5 includes many of the well-known Brahmanical deities, each treated as a *yakṣa* with a specific location. Unfortunately, not all of these locations are identifiable, but they include Viṣṇu at Dvārakā, Śiva at Śivapur (Shorkot in the Punjab), Siva's son Kārttikeya at Rohitaka or Rohtak, Indra at Indrapura (Indore in Bulandshahr Distt., UP or Indore in MP) and so on (Sircar 1971–2: 270, 279, 275, 280). I imagine the Buddhist compiler of this text taking a certain ironic pleasure in treating what were undoubtedly by this period major all-India deities as, in effect, local protective spirits. Similarly, the *Aṭānāṭiya Sutta* closes with a list of *yakṣas* (this is what the text calls them) who may be invoked as protection against those disobedient even to the Four Great Kings. The first members of the list are Brahmanical deities or sages: Inda, Soma, Varuṇa, Bhāradvāja, Pajāpati (Dīgha Nikāya 32.10 = Walshe 1995: 477).

This inclusion of the early Brahmanical deities, again, is a feature of modern Theravādin communities: the city pillar shrine in Chiang Mai is linked to Indra as well as to the city's protective spirit, and rituals are still performed there to ensure the rains, a traditional Vedic function of Indra. The most popular shrine in downtown Bangkok, outside the Hotel Erevan, is a shrine to Brahmā, regularly invoked for this-worldly and pragmatic purposes (Majupuria 1993). In Sri Lanka, Indra, or Sakka as he is usually called in Pali, is regarded the protector of the island under Buddhist auspices, with a set of four gods (the list varies somewhat) as his immediate assistants, including Viṣṇu, Pattinī, and Kārttikeya (Ames 1964, 1966; Seneviratne 1978; Holt 2004). The specific cult of the deities here reflects the close historical relationships between the Kandyan state and South India.

The general conceptual structure, however, including the dominance of Indra, a deity who has been largely marginalised in India proper, is very much the same as in other Theravādin countries.

There is much more that could be said about this general situation, in which the developing Buddhist and Jaina traditions constructed a harmonious if hierarchical relationship between themselves and the cults of local *yakṣa*-type deities. For example, many of the sites associated with both the teachings of the historical Mahāvīra and Śākyamuni, and with their early religious centres, seem to have had previous *yakṣa* associations. I have said enough here for my purposes, however, except that I want to emphasise the contrast with the pattern we find generally in modern Hindu communities. Here the local deities, even where they clearly have strong local identities, are (officially at least) regarded not as a separate sphere of worldly gods, but as local transforms of an all-India or regional deity such as Śiva or Pārvatī. This is so even in major temples – we can think, for example, of the great goddess temples of South India, such as Mīnākṣī at Madurai, which I will discuss briefly in Chapter 7, of Kāmākṣī at Kanchi, or of Kumārī at Kanyakumari, all goddesses who have a very strong local identity and individuality, but are officially regarded as transforms of Pārvatī or Durgā. In the north, the myth of the Śākta pīṭhas similarly links many local and regional religious sites to the Śiva-Pārvatī story. Other myths interpret local shrines in terms of Kṛṣṇa, Viṣṇu and other all-India deities – Jagannāth at Puri would be a classic example (Eschmann et al. 1986).

This – to anticipate my later argument – can be seen as typical of 'Tantric' religion, using 'Tantric' in a fairly wide sense. A key issue here will be the nature of the *maṇḍala* as a spiritual and political model (see Chapter 9). For the present, though, we might look at the *Matsya Purāṇa*'s story of the *yakṣa* Harikeśa, son of the great *yakṣa* king Pūrṇabhadra. Harikeśa was a devotee of Śiva, and after quarrelling with his father went to Vārāṇasī and engaged in a thousand years of austerities 'with his mind intent on Śiva'. Eventually Śiva, pleased with his devotion, allowed him to stay permanently in Vārāṇasī and appointed him as the *kṣetrapāla* or guardian of the city, with four other *yakṣas* as his subordinates (Agrawala and Motichandra 1960).

Today, though, the spiritual guardianship of Vārāṇasī is not in the hands of *yakṣas*, whether Buddhist or Śaivite, but those of a set of Bhairava deities, regarded as fierce transforms of Śiva. This was perhaps already under way when the *Mahāmāyūrī*'s catalogue was written, since it refers to the *yakṣa* of Vārāṇasī as Mahākāla, which in Buddhist contexts generally denotes a fierce transform of Śiva who is acting as a protective deity. The nature of this transition will be one of the key themes of Part 2 (Chapters 9 to 13) of this book.[39] First I turn, in Chapter 7, to the developments in the Brahmanical tradition from the fifth century BCE onwards that paralleled those that we have considered in the present chapter among the Buddhists and Jains.

[39] Tibet, by the way, offers a mixture between the two models, early Buddhist coexistence and Tantric incorporation. In this respect, as in others, Tibet represents a much more radical transformation of Tantric religion, Śaiva or Buddhist, in the South Asian context than we find among the Newars or in Bali (Samuel 1982, 1993). Some major mountain deities (Kailash, Tsari) were incorporated via the Cakrasaṃvara mythos (Macdonald 1990; Huber 1999). Possibly Panden Lhamo, the protective deity of Lhasa and of the Gelugpa order, and apparently related to a pre-Buddhist deity of Tibet, is a similar case. The Bhairava or Mahākāla pattern of protector is also important in monastic ritual contexts. For the most part, though, Tibetan local deities are treated as a separate and lower order of beings, not as transforms of Buddhist deities. There can be some overlap and confusion here, and the notorious Shugden controversy, which divided the Tibetan refugee community in recent years, was in part about whether this deity should be regarded as a (possibly malevolent) worldly spirit-deity or an enlightened Tantric protector and transform of Mañjuśrī (cf. Dreyfus 1998).

CHAPTER 7

The Brahmanical alternative

I referred in Chapter 6 to Brahmanical asceticism, but did not go into much detail about how it was practised and understood, and how it related to the 'Vedic' pattern of religion developing in the Kuru-Pañcāla region. In this chapter I explore the development of asceticism on the Brahmanical side in more detail, and discuss how Brahmanical thinkers and priests responded to the challenge of the *śramaṇa* traditions which we considered in Chapter 6. At the end of this chapter, I look at the way in which the Brahmanical alternative related to regional and local deities and cults, contrasting its approach to the Buddhist and Jain approach sketched in Chapter 6.

VARIETIES OF BRAHMINS

I referred in Chapter 6 to the indications of a variety of different Brahmin roles in the fifth and fourth centuries BCE or thereabouts, and mentioned Patrick Olivelle's demonstration in his book *The Āśrama System* that the so-called *āśramas* originally represented alternative ways of life rather than a sequence of stages through which all men of the Vedic elite groups (Brahmin, *kṣatriya*, *vaiśya*) should progress (Olivelle 1993). Olivelle notes that there 'appear to have been tensions and rivalries between the traditional Brahmins of the villages, who were the heirs and guardians of the vedic world, and the newly-urbanized Brahmins' (1993: 59). Elsewhere in *The Āśrama System*, Olivelle points to the references in Buddhist and Brahmanical sources to married semi-renunciate Brahmins, characterised by their matted or braided hair (*jaṭila*) hairstyle, living in uninhabited areas outside towns with their wives and children. We have already met these *jaṭila* Brahmins in Chapter 6. They maintained a sacred fire, and their life 'centered around the maintenance of and the offering of oblations in the sacred fire' (1993: 24). Their residences were described as *āśrama*; Olivelle argues that this is the original meaning of *āśrama*, preceding the later usage to refer to a particular period or stage of life. They also performed *tapas* or austerity and were part way at least to an ascetic lifestyle.

Interestingly, these *jaṭila* Brahmins were viewed with respect by the early Buddhists. Olivelle notes, for example, that the Vinaya code exempts them from the four months probationary period normally required before admission to the *saṅgha* (1993: 21). Buddhist sources often describe Śākyamuni as pointing out that this was how Brahmins used to live and ought to live, by contrast with the village-dwelling Brahmins. However, the Buddha argues that they need to abandon the sacred fire and go beyond the life of a householder.

As we saw in Chapter 6, we seem to have a variety of Brahmins at this period: traditional village-dwelling Brahmins, urban Brahmins who were perhaps taking on the role of spiritual teachers of the new Brahmanical ritual practices for householders (and so were in competition for patronage with the Buddhists and Jains), semi-renunciate Brahmins who had retreated to settlements outside the town or village, and, apparently a later development, fully-fledged Brahmanical renunciates who had abandoned their householder lifestyle and also abandoned (or rather internalised) their sacred fires. The unpopulated areas with which these last two groups were associated were also of importance to the non-Brahmanical ascetic traditions. As I pointed out in Chapter 6, these Brahmanical ascetics seem to have been part of a common ascetic culture with a tradition of wisdom practices, teachings and sayings that were at least partly shared. They also shared with them a liking for the 'forest', in other words for uncleared and unpopulated areas outside the cities and their agricultural hinterland.

BRAHMANICAL ASCETICISM

What, though, were the sources within the Brahmanical tradition that might lead to such a development? I referred in Chapter 1 to the 'shamanic' and 'ecstatic' elements of the early Vedic material. I am somewhat wary about using the word 'shaman' these days (see Samuel 2005a: 9–13), but if one takes the contrast between shaman and priest to be, at least in part, that the shaman deals with the gods or spirit as an equal, while the priest treats them from a position of inferiority, then it is clear that the Ṛgveda at least looks back towards a shamanic kind of relationship with the gods. The *ṛṣis* to whom the Vedic hymns are attributed, whether or not they actually existed as historical figures, were seen as having power to compel the gods and so compel the natural order (Gonda 1963; see also Crangle 1994). So, one assumes, were the ritualists who claimed descent from them, at least initially. Different groups of these shamanic-type *ṛṣis* were employed by various chieftains and warriors to further their own interests, and they might invoke the spirits against each other and try to interfere with each other's rituals.

At some point, however, no doubt gradually over time, things changed, and the Brahmins of a later period, though still tracing their ancestries to clans or *gotra* founded by one or another of the original seven *ṛṣis* took on a much more priestly role, as sacrificial performers. The Vedic hymns were gradually transformed into ritual formulae to be recited at various stages of the Brahmanical ritual, which was elaborated into a set of formalised procedures and the conflictual elements played down.[1] Falk, Heesterman and others have written about this development, as has Witzel, who as we have seen associated it particularly with the Kuru-Pañcāla state. I assume that he has the general place and period more or less right, and that this development can be linked in particular with the shift from a primarily pastoral-nomadic economy to a situation where the Vedic population was living among and increasingly merging with agricultural populations in North India, many of them probably already Indo-Aryan speaking. The stories of the seven *ṛṣis*, and of the conflicts between the *ṛṣi* or their associated tribes, such as that between Vāsiṣṭha and Viśvāmitra, gradually became mythic material that was reworked in a variety of contexts (see Chapter 9, where I discuss the role of these two *ṛṣis* in Book One of the *Rāmāyaṇa*).

To the extent that the sacrificial rituals became about the assertion of status, they also perhaps increasingly lost their explicitly instrumental character. If Witzel and Falk are correct, however, the process of regularisation of Vedic ritual left some important functions to be dealt with by other kinds of ritual specialists. In Chapter 5, we considered the special case of the *vrātyas*, but there are other examples. The hymns of the Atharvaveda, including many pragmatically-oriented rituals, were the preserve of a separate group of Brahmins from those associated with the first three Vedas. Thus the Vedic material retained the possibility of providing a body of magical techniques for pragmatic purposes, and the idioms that it provided for doing this are of significance for later developments. It is worth looking briefly at two complexes of ideas, one relating to the terms *tapas* and *śrama* and the second relating to the term *vrata*.

The term *tapas*, which is often translated as 'austerity', in the sense of carrying out demanding or extreme ascetic practices, derives from the root

[1] While the high status of the Brahmins in Kuru-Pañcāla is evident, it is probably also worth bearing in mind Richard Lariviere's point that our view is biased in their favour by the Brahmanical nature of most of our sources. The king, even in Kuru-Pañcāla, retained the real power (Lariviere 1997).

tap, to give heat, to make hot, to be hot. Walter Kaelber's *Tapta Marga* (1989) traces the associations of this root in Vedic literature with the fire and with the sun which provides the heat needed to ripen the fields and which also generates rain. *Tapas* is a basic creative force, with close links also to sexual desire and excitation, intercourse and orgasm.

Hints of these associations can already be found in the Ṛgveda. Their full development, however, takes place in the Brāhmaṇas and especially in the Śrauta Sūtras, where ascetic practice has become a key part of the conception of the sacrificer's role (Kaelber 1989: 23). *Tapas* thus becomes something which can be built up within one's self, so generating power:

> Crucially, man may develop or generate such 'magical heat' within himself through the performance of various self-imposed austerities, such as fasting or chastity. [. . .] In that such austerities generate heat within man, they too are regarded as a form of *tapas*. *Tapas* refers therefore not only to heated power but also to the heated effort which produces it. [. . .] The accumulated *tapas* of asceticism 'saturates' the devotee, making him a reservoir of heated potency. This power may manifest itself as a sexual and fecundating energy which when released generates rainfall, fertile fields, and biological offspring. Through an asceticism that 'overcomes' nature, man is able to control nature. (Kaelber 1989: 144)

This generates another series of images; the heated sweat of the sacrificer corresponds to the heated milk in the cauldron of the *pravargya*, a hot milk sacrifice to the Aśvins, and the overflowing of the cauldron corresponds to ejaculation.

> [T]he heat assumed by the devotee in the presence of the sacred fire makes him susceptible to visions and divine revelation. Agni, himself a seer, provides the devotee with 'head-heat,' turning him into a seer as well. Relatedly, the heated effort of ascetic practice kindles an 'inner fire' of illumination, yielding ecstatic insight. Like the paradigmatic *ṛṣis*, the earthly ascetic is able to 'see' or behold through his *tapas*, through his self-imposed austerity. In this context his *tapas* takes the form of 'cognitive brooding' or 'intense meditation'.[. . .] Once again, however, we see a clear transparency to that natural heat generated by a hen as she broods over her eggs. Relatedly, visions mature in the heated mind just as crops mature and ripen upon a gently heated earth. (Kaelber 1989: 145–6)

Closely related to *tapas* is another term; *śrāma*, a Vedic root meaning 'to strive', 'toil' or 'to exert oneself'. Here again this can refer to the accumulation of creative power, or its sexual expression: the creator god Prajāpati's creative intercourse with the earth, for example, is referred to as *śrāma* (Olivelle 1993: 9). One can exert oneself through sexual intercourse, so creating new life, or one can exert oneself in ascetic practice (*tapas*). A well-known dialogue hymn from Book One of the Ṛgveda, in which the speakers are identified as Lopāmudrā, the wife of the *ṛṣi* Agastya, the *ṛṣi* himself, and the commenting Vedic poet, seems to counterpose the two meanings of 'toil', with Lopāmudrā succeeding in distracting her husband from ascetic 'toil' to sexual 'toil':

1. [*Lopāmudrā*:] 'For many autumns past I have toiled, night and day, and each dawn has brought old age closer, age that distorts the glory of bodies. Virile men should go to their wives.
2. 'For even the men of the past, who acted according to the Law and talked about the Law with the gods, broke off when they did not find the end. Women should unite with virile men.'
3. [*Agastya*:] 'Not in vain is all this toil, which the gods encourage. We two must always strive against each other, and by this we will win the race that is won by a hundred means, when we merge together as a couple.'
4. [*Lopāmudrā*:] 'Desire has come upon me for the bull who roars and is held back, desire engulfing me from this side, that side, all sides.'
   [*The poet:*] Lopāmudrā draws out the virile bull: the foolish woman sucks dry the panting wise man.
5. [*Agastya*:] 'By this Soma which I have drunk, in my innermost heart I say: Let him forgive us if we have sinned, for a mortal is full of many desires.'
6. Agastya, digging with spades, wishing for children, progeny, and strength, nourished both ways, for he was a powerful sage. He found fulfilment of his real hopes among the gods. (O'Flaherty 1981: 250–51 = *Ṛgveda* 1.179)

This hymn is one of a number of dialogue hymns, in all of which one character attempts to persuade the other to sexual activity (O'Flaherty 1981: 245). While we can only guess at the original ritual context, it seems fairly clear that the central theme here is the diversion of the ascetic energy of the *tapasvin*, the person who is generating *tapas*, to productive ends. However, *śrām* is the root of *śramaṇa*, the word for renunciate ascetic that at a later period becomes clearly opposed to the Brahmanical priest, being typified by the Buddhist and Jaina *śramaṇas* (Olivelle 1993: 9).

Not all *śrāmaṇas*, however, were outside the Vedic fold. Even in the Ṛgveda, there seems to have been a range of different kinds of practitioners besides the sacrificial priests. These include the long-haired (*keśin*) sage or *muni* described in *Ṛgveda* 10.136, a text that has often been interpreted as describing a kind of shamanic practice (cf. Werner 1989; Deeg 1993). This is a translation of the first four verses:

1. Long-hair holds fire, holds the drug, holds sky and earth. Long-hair reveals everything, so that everyone can see the sun. Long-hair declares the light.
2. These ascetics, swathed in wind, put dirty red rags on. When gods enter them, they ride with the rush of the wind.

3. 'Crazy with asceticism, we have mounted the wind. Our bodies are all you mere mortals can see.'
4. He sails through the air, looking down on all shapes below. The ascetic is friend to this god and that god, devoted to what is well done. (O'Flaherty 1981: 137–8)

In the final verse, the long-haired sage 'drinks from the cup, sharing the drug with Rudra' (O'Flaherty 1981: 138). He seems to be a naked sage ('swathed in wind') and there are suggestions of control over sexual power (Olivelle 1993: 12–14). The association with Rudra, the god who provides the prototype for the later Śiva, and who in the Vedas is an ambivalent figure who is not fully incorporated into the Vedic pantheon, is intriguing in view of the later linkage between Śiva and ascetics. But there are other possible ascetic figures too in the Vedas, including the *vrātyas*, who have been discussed in Chapters 5 and 6, and the *brahmacārin*, a figure who we will examine briefly below.

For the early Vedic context, Kaelber appears willing to follow Eliade, Oldenburg and others in comparing the 'heated passage' leading to insight to the heated passage of 'classical' shamanic initiation, though these are of course homologies rather than suggestions of historical linkages (Kaelber 1989: 125–41). Whether or not we use the term 'shaman' for the long-haired *muni*, the *vrātya* or for that matter for the *ṛṣis* themselves, it is clear that we have a tradition of figures who communicate with the gods while in ecstatic states, and who have visionary powers as a result of their divine contact. These figures exercise *tapas* in some sense, and this is seen in terms of the accumulation of sexual or quasi-sexual 'heat'. They are also, in some cases at least, expected to put their power to the service of the community (e.g. Kaelber 1989: 17–22).

The sexual dimension to Vedic asceticism helps to explain why the *brahmacārin*, who is defined by his abstinence from sexual intercourse, is a central figure (Kaelber 1989: 17–22). The logic here is that sexual 'energy' is either expended in family life for the production of children or for pleasure, or directed towards the attainment of ascetic power. In later tradition, the primary reference of the term *brahmacārin* is to the stage of being a Vedic student in the four-*āśrama* scheme, but this scheme is itself a later development. What is clear in the earlier material is that the *brahmacārin* is a repository of power built up through his *tapas* (in this sense meaning 'ascetic practice') and this *tapas* can be put to the use of the community. For Kaelber, a key example is the well-known *mahavrāta* ritual of the *vrātyas*, described in the *Jaiminīya Brāhmaṇa* and the Śrauta Sūtras, which appears to have involved ritual intercourse between a *brahmacārin* and a prostitute (see Chapter 5, and Gonda 1961). Here both *brahmacārin* and prostitute are sources of power. The creative ritual role of the *brahmacārin* is already stated in the Atharvaveda (11, 5):

> 1. Stirring both worlds the Brahmacārī moveth: in him the deities are all one-minded, He hath established firmly earth and heaven: he satisfies his Master with his Fervour [=tapas]
> 2. After the Brahmacārī go the Fathers, the heavenly hosts, all Gods in separate order, After him too have the Gandharvas followed, thirty and three, three hundred, and six thousand. He satisfies all Gods with his devotion . . .
> 6. Lighted by fuel goes the Brahmacārī, clad in blackbuck skin, consecrate, long-bearded. Swiftly he goes from east to northern ocean, grasping the worlds, oft bringing them anear him . . .
> 12. Thundering, shouting, ruddy-hued, and pallid, he bears along the earth great manly vigour.
> Down on the ridge of earth the Brahmacārī pours seed, and this gives life to heaven's four regions . . . (Griffith 1916, vol. 2: 68–70 = vv.1, 2, 6, 12; cf Kaelber 1989: 17)

In the Vedic material, the point of the exercise is to put the power of *tapas* at the service of the community, to generate fertility and productivity, in a word what contemporary anthropologists of India call 'auspiciousness' (V. Das 1987; Marglin 1985a; Madan 1985; cf. Samuel 1997). This is what the post-Vedic tradition referred to as the *karma-kāṇḍa*. But the forest ascetic tradition, as witnessed in the early Upaniṣads, moves in another direction. Here *tapas* is used to drive the search for knowledge (*jñāna*) and liberation (*mokṣa*), a search which involves the rejection of ordinary social identity and of obligation to the community through identification with the Absolute. This *jñāna-kāṇḍa* is a direct assault on the traditional view that ascetic practice is for the good of the community:

> The tradition and spirit of the *karma-kāṇḍa* was at first challenged by the innovations of the *jñāna-kāṇḍa*. This took place on many fronts. Traditional ritual and its rewards were challenged by a saving knowledge. The prestige of priest and sacrificer was challenged by ascetics of the forest. [. . .] The value of worldly goals was challenged by a pessimism regarding *saṃsāra*. [. . .] The value of *karma* was challenged by a salvation beyond action and the value of *dharma* was challenged by a salvation beyond conventional morality.
>
> In time, however, the orthodoxy and orthopraxis of the *karma-kāṇḍa* met these challenges. The result has been termed the Brāhmaṇic(al) synthesis. In point of fact, however, it was not so much a synthesis of the two trends as it was the absorption of one tradition by the other. The orthodoxy of the *karma-kāṇḍa* found room for the innovations of the *jñāna-kāṇḍa* and brought them into its fold. [. . .]

> Although *mokṣa* is cited as the culmination of Vedic values, *dharma* invariably remains primary in the law books. Although knowledge is lauded, ritual action remains paramount in the Śrauta Sūtras. Despite the elitist goal of *mokṣa*, the priesthood and its constituency still sought rainfall, fertility, pleasure, success, and a repertoire of worldly ends. (Kaelber 1989: 79)

What was at stake here was the incorporation of the Vedic version of the *śramaṇa* option within the Brahmanical fold, and the defusing of the challenge that it posed to the priestly families. As Kaelber notes, one can go for an 'orthogenetic' model here, following Biardeau and Heesterman among others, and stress the continuity of these developments with the original Vedic material, or, following writers such as Eliade, Dumont or Olivelle, one can see a process of 'challenge and assimilation' in which new models and approaches, not necessarily emerging from within the Vedic context, are confronted and incorporated more or less successfully. Kaelber prefers the latter approach, though as he rightly notes, neither can provide a complete model of processes of such complexity (1989: 107–9). I would agree, and suggest that this is generally a more productive way to approach these complex processes than purely in terms of the internal dynamics of Brahmanical thought. The 'orthogenetic' approach offers elegance and closure, but it lacks a certain degree of realism, especially given that the logic of Vedic thought and practice is such that new developments are regularly incorporated through the use of resources already present within the tradition.

The actual assimilation, in Kaelber's view, took place through the adaptation of the *brahmacārin* model to include the rival forms of ascetic practice. These became included within the Brahmanical model through the four *āśrama* model (*brahmacārin, gṛhastha, vānaprastha, saṃnyāsin*) that was to become normative in later times. Originally, though, as we saw in Chapter 6, these four stages (*brahmacārin*, householder, forest-dwelling semi-renunciate ascetic and fully renunciate ascetic) were alternatives rather than sequential. In the new model, *brahmacārin* gradually became a kind of period of studentship before married life, while the forest-dweller and renunciate options were effectively tamed and incorporated. Renunciation, rather than being a rejection of *dharma* and Brahmanical regulation, became progressively regulated by Dharmic codes. It now became conceptualised as a period of penance, purification and preparation for death at the end of one's life (1989: 121). In reality, many, probably the majority, of *saṃnyāsins* even today renounce earlier in their lives, and their ascetic career is really an alternative to that of the householder rather than a concluding winding-down after secular obligations have been fulfilled. At the ideological level, though, the Brahmanical solution achieved total dominance within texts such as the Laws of Manu.

We also note that these terms connect up with a view of the *brahmacārin* or celibate young man as a reservoir of sexual and magical potency. If we can judge from the pervasive imagery of beautiful young women, male and female couples, motherhood and vegetative fertility, the *yakṣa* religion tended to celebrate adult sexuality, both male and female. By contrast, it seems, the Vedic culture preferred to celebrate the unmarried male, a choice that makes some sense in its earlier incarnation as a pastoralist culture with a strong emphasis on conflict, raiding and fighting. If so, we can perhaps see here the origins of the specifically Indic tension over sexuality. While post-Christian Europe was concerned about whether sex was sinful, the Indic problem was whether it represented a loss of power. I consider these issues further in Chapter 8, which forms an interlude before Part 2 of the book.

In relation to asceticism, the term *vrata*, which has already received some discussion in Chapter 6, is also of significance. I noted in Chapter 6 Timothy Lubin's suggestion, developing ideas from Paul Hacker and Joel Brereton, that the original meaning of *vrata* was something like 'rule' in the sense of 'fixed, characteristic mode of behaviour that manifest one's will' (Lubin 2001: 568). Thus one can speak of the *vrata* of a particular deity, as defining that deity's 'nature and role in the world' (2001: 568). Collectively, these 'pattern[s] of divine agency and authority' can be seen as 'defin[ing] a cosmic and social order that calls for a human response' (2001: 575). Lubin suggests that

> what the early Veda contributes to the later-attested ascetical rules is the basic idea that observing a rule (*vrata*) of ritual service can put a human worshipper in accordance with divine laws (*vrata*) and thereby confer divine blessings. The *Atharva Veda* and the various *brāhmaṇa* texts combine this premise with the notion that the observance of such rules requires sustained exertion (*śrama*) and fervid dedication to fasting and celibacy (i.e. *tapas*). (Lubin 2001: 578–9)

Asceticism is of course very important in later Indic religion, and the idea that through *tapas* or austerity one can compel the gods to behave in certain ways is a basic trope that runs not only throughout Brahmanical asceticism but also later Tantric practice. There is a striking similarity between Lubin's early Vedic version of *vrata* and the mature Śaiva or Buddhist Tantric idea that by doing *sādhana* of a particular deity one, in effect, compels that deity to act according to the deity's own prior promise or will and so brings about the desired result. An important additional element, however, is that in many forms of Tantric ritual one also identifies with the deity. We will explore the development of this idea in later chapters.

Whatever the initial origins of the idea of asceticism as generating magical power,[2] this concept of the *vrata* as a pattern of behaviour that can compel divine blessings would seem to be an important early contribution to it. We have evidence from the Brāhmaṇas, from early Buddhist *sūtras* and other sources of people who follow *vrata* modelled on the behaviour of various animals, such as a ox-*vrata* or dog-*vrata*.[3] Daniel Ingalls, commenting on the Pāśupatas, an early group of ascetics who were worshippers of Śiva as Pāśupati, the Lord of the Beasts, suggests that '[t]he aspirant hoped to transform himself first into the Lord's beast and finally into the Lord of Beasts himself' (Ingalls 1962: 295). We will see more of the Pāśupatas in Chapter 10.

The Buddha is famously described as being dismissive of this kind of thing, though the Buddhist account also accepts implicitly at least that such *vrata* are meant as a serious spiritual path. In the *Kukkuravatika Sutta*, the Buddha tells Puṇṇa and Seniya, an ascetic who is pursuing the ox-*vrata* and a naked ascetic who has long pursued the dog-*vrata*, that their vows will at best lead them to rebirth in the company of oxen and dogs, not the company of gods. However, when Seniya, the naked dog-*vrata* ascetic, asks to join the Buddhist order, he is offered full admission after the usual probation,[4] and soon attains the state of *arhat* (*Majjhima Nikāya* 67, e.g. Ñāṇamoli and Bodhi 1995: 493–7). As I noted in Chapter 6, it is not so difficult to see the rules for order of the Buddhist *saṅgha* as themselves constituting a kind of *vrata* intended to lead to a certain kind of result.

It is worth taking a brief look at the speculative and philosophical dimensions of the Vedic material, since these present another dimension of the ideological movement which is taking place here. Some of the late Ṛgvedic hymns, such as the well-known 'creation hymns,' 10.121 and 10.129, already have a strong speculative element (e.g. O'Flaherty 1981: 25–9). In fact, the term, 'already' is probably not appropriate, since it would seem to suggest that nobody ever speculated about the nature of reality in the tribal-shamanic and pastoral context we are supposing for the early Indo-Aryan

[2] Nick Allen has suggested that it goes back to shared Indo-European narrative structures (N. Allen 1998).

[3] For references from Brahmanical sources, see Olivelle 1992: 109–11, which cites the *Mahābhārata* (5.97.14) and the *Bhāgavata Purāṇa* (5.5.32); Olivelle also gives further Buddhist references.

[4] Seniya responds by suggesting that he should undertake a four-year probation rather than a four-month probation (Ñāṇamoli and Bodhi 1995: 497). This might be a way to indicate the disfavour with which these practices are held, but it seems more likely to be simply an expression of Seniya's level of commitment, which is clearly depicted as being higher than that of his ox-*vrata* companion.

peoples. There is plenty of ethnographic evidence to demonstrate that sophisticated philosophical thought can be found among preliterate pastoralist peoples.[5] For such peoples to put their reflections into verse and hand them on to succeeding generations is perhaps less frequent, and these speculative hymns are generally regarded as a late addition to the Ṛgvedic collection.

These hymns nevertheless suggest a move to the detailed exploration of abstract philosophical notions. Such exploration is characteristic of the next phase of the Vedic material and has been explored by a variety of authors (e.g. Miller 1985; B. Smith 1989, 1994). The Vedas were used by later Brahmanical tradition as a foundational text, and later developments were constantly referred back to precedents in the Vedas, so there is a systemic tendency in Brahmanical scholarship to read the Vedic material as more philosophical and less ritually-oriented than it perhaps was. For all this, there is little doubt that the Kuru-Pañcāla theorists had a sophisticated set of understandings regarding the divine order and the system of correspondences within experienced reality. Central to this was the multivalent concept of *bráhman* (B. Smith 1989: 69–72; Witzel 2003: 70–1).[6] Witzel, following Thieme and others, suggests that the original Vedic sense of *bráhman* is something like 'the "formulation" or capturing in words of a significant and non-self-evident truth', and notes that '[t]he formulator (*brahmán*) of such truths has special powers, effecting this world and the cosmos' (Witzel 2003: 70). Later the term develops a wider and more cosmological meaning, with *bráhman* as 'the source and foundation of all that exists – the nexus of all cosmic connections – and the connective force itself lying behind all knowledge and action that constructs ontologically viable forms' (B. Smith 1989: 72), eventually personified as a creator-deity.

Brahmins clearly have a special relationship with *bráhman*, but since this relationship is founded in the ability of the original Brahmin *ṛṣis* to 'capture' reality in their inspired verses, the question of whether Brahmins in later times were valid representatives of the original *ṛṣis* could always be raised. The Buddhists, as we saw, argued that the Brahmins employed as court ritualists by the new rulers (the *karma-kaṇḍa* Brahmins, in Kaelber's terms) had lost any valid connection with the original Brahmanical tradition. The

[5] Evans-Pritchard's *Nuer Religion* is a classic demonstration (Evans-Pritchard 1956). As for Indo-Iranian and Indo-Aryan pastoralists, the similarity has long been noted between the Vedic concept of *ṛta* (divine order, etc.; Witzel prefers 'active realization of truth') and the Avestan (Iranian) concept of *aṣa* (e.g. Witzel 2003: 70). If this implies a common origin, then the concept would go back to the pastoralist context.

[6] I have generally omitted Vedic accents but in this case they resolve an important ambiguity.

ascetic forest-dwelling Brahmins (the *jñāna-kāṇḍa* Brahmins, in Kaelber's terms) were closer, but the true 'Brahmins', the true knowers of the 'nexus of all cosmic connections', were the Buddhists themselves.

The *jñāna-kāṇḍa* Brahmins would presumably have rejected such an assertion, however close they might be in practice to the Buddhist and Jaina monks. However, they accepted the idea of knowledge of *bráhman* as liberating insight. This is the basis of the position taken in the early Upaniṣads, the body of texts associated with this group.

The status of the *karma-kāṇḍa* Brahmins was not based on their personal attainment to knowledge of *bráhman*, but on their possession of the lineages of transmission of the Vedic hymns, which gave them the right to recite these ritually-powerful verses. However, they too needed to respond to the Buddhist and Jaina critique, and in practice, as Kaelber notes in the passages discussed above, they sought to adopt some of the ascetic developments into their own practices. This led to the semi-ascetic style that became characteristic of later Brahmanical culture. How far this was a simple need to counter the rhetoric of the Buddhists and other *śramaṇa* groups, and how far it derived from a desire to incorporate what were seen as important and valid elements of the ascetic approach, it is hard to say. I imagine that both factors were operative. The specific intellectual resources of the Vedic tradition, however, led to a particular construction of asceticism which, as we have already noted, tended to focus on the 'taming' and directing of human sexuality, specifically adolescent male sexuality, for ascetic ends.

Certainly, the transformations in Brahmanical ritual and practice during this period were by no means purely defensive. They also laid the foundations for the future integration of the Brahmins within the wider context of Indic society. The recent work of Timothy Lubin provides a useful analysis of this process (Lubin 2005). Lubin has suggested that in the Gṛhya Sūtras (texts on household ritual) and elsewhere we can see a deliberate simplification of the complex *śrauta* sacrifices to provide rituals that could be performed by the householder under the instruction and direction of Brahmin priests.

> In the Gṛhyasūtras, the claim is first made that study of the Veda is not merely available to but incumbent on kṣatriyas and vaiśyas as well as brahmins, with the corollary that initiation and the daily use of Vedic mantras become the defining mark of elite, Ārya status in a religiously and ethnically diverse society. The trend toward identifying initiation and brahmacarya (rather than marriage) as the starting point for constructing a framework for an orthoprax life of piety, and the multiplication of similar vratas as a framework for personal piety,were developments

parallel with the rise of ascetical (Śramaṇa) movements such as Buddhism. (Lubin 2005: 88)

Elsewhere in the same article he suggests that the effect of this development may have been to 'divide the territory' between the Brahmins and the *śramaṇa* movements. Thus Lubin suggests that

> Buddhism initially won out in the urban zones, where traditional social and cultural structures were fragmentary and diluted. Meanwhile, Brahmanism reinvented itself in a form that simultaneously provided a model of domestic piety and personal sanctification (in a range of degrees of ascetic rigor) that had, especially in rural society, much of the appeal that Buddhist piety had in the cities and along trade routes: namely, a code of self-discipline and direct personal access to the presumed power of sacred mantras. (Lubin 2005: 91–2)

The success of the Brahminical strategy can be seen in the increase in the use of Sanskrit and the increasing evidence of royal patronage for Brahmins in the post-Mauryan period. Here an important role was played by foreign rulers (Scythians and Kuṣānas) for whom the use of Sanskrit and the patronage of Brahmins helped to legitimise their position. The pattern was then adopted and further popularised by the imperial Guptas (Lubin 2005: 92–7).

LOCAL DEITIES AND EVERYDAY CONCERNS: THE BRAHMANICAL PATTERN

Lubin points to the way in which this model meant that the Brahmins remained relatively decentralised, with a firm base at the village level. They never developed the degree of centralisation in large monasteries in or near cities that was characteristic of the Buddhist and Jaina pattern, and which was eventually to lead to the vulnerability of those traditions to loss of state support. Brahmins became court ritualists, often associated with spectacular and wealthy temples, and they became royal administrators and bureaucrats, but they also built up a solid base of family land-holdings within South Asian villages that enabled them to survive the loss of power and support at the centre during the long periods of Muslim and British domination. Above all, this was a question of property gifted to specific Brahmin families and handed down to their descendants.

The downside, if that is the correct term, to the semi-ascetic Brahmin model was the linkage between Brahmins and purity that became the basic ideological underpinning of the Hindu caste system (L. Dumont 1972). Here I am speaking not so much of the cost to the Brahmins themselves as to the wider society. If Brahmins responded to the *śramaṇa* challenge by asserting their own purity through a semi-ascetic lifestyle, the necessary corollary was that others must be less pure, and that there had to be an opposite ideological pole to the pure Brahmin. As Dumont put it, 'The whole is founded on the necessary and hierarchical coexistence of the two opposites' (L. Dumont 1972: 81). This other pole was formed by the various *dalit* ('untouchable') groups, the low-caste groups who were associated with occupations seen as intrinsically impure.

Thus the caste structure of Indian village society, from the Brahmin point of view at any rate, became based on a hierarchical opposition between the pure Brahmin and the impure untouchable. Texts such as the Ṛgveda's well-known 'Puruṣa-Sūkta' (Hymn 10.90, see e.g. O'Flaherty 1981: 29–32), in which the four *varṇa* originate from the dismemberment of the primaeval cosmic giant, with the Brahmin arising from his mouth, the *kṣatriya* from his arms, the *vaiśya* from his thighs and the *śūdra* from his feet, are frequently referred to in this connection.

As I described in Chapter 4, however, the caste hierarchy as it developed in later times was in fact a very different business from the *varṇa* classificatory scheme, and could encompass a large number of separate hereditary groups (*jāti*), with varying claims to one or another *varṇa* status, as well as others which were seen as outside the *varṇa* system altogether (cf. L. Dumont 1972; Quigley 1995; Searle-Chatterjee and Sharma 1994; Bayly 2001). Here the South Indian (and perhaps originally more widespread) conception of the necessity of low-caste polluted groups to handle the dangerous magical power of the king (see Chapter 4) may have made an important contribution.

Purity here seems originally to have been a question of the ritual purity necessary for the proper performance of Vedic sacrifices, a theme which doubtless goes back to the Indo-Aryan-speaking immigrant population, since it is also a key issue for the Zoroastrian tradition. In the new Brahmanical social and religious order, however, it became a more generalised and intrinsic question, with the lower groups in the caste hierarchy defined as intrinsically impure, and women defined by their bodily functions as periodically impure. In both cases, the human consequences were to be severe, and are still very much active today.

In the 1980s, a number of authors developed a critique of Dumont's analysis through pointing to, in effect, the existence of a religion of fertility and everyday life as a counterpoint to Brahmanical religion in the modern Hindu context. This is the religious complex that has generally been referred to by anthropologists as 'auspiciousness'. The writers who raised the question of auspiciousness, such as Triloki Nath Madan (1985,

1987), Frédérique Marglin (1982, 1985a, 1985b) and Veena Das (1987), were involved in a sympathetic critique and extension of Dumont's work rather than a radical rejection. These writers agreed with Dumont in taking the question of values in South Asian societies seriously, but they felt that Dumont's account was over-simple and inadequate. Purity was important in Indian society, but it was not the only central value. So 'auspiciousness' was seen as being an independent value, as delimiting a separate sphere, or (at least with Veena Das and T. N. Madan) as defining a second axis around which the structural analysis of Indian society might be based. 'Auspiciousness' became a general label for concerns with attaining health, success and prosperity and avoiding death, disease, poverty and misfortune.

There seems to be a close relationship between auspiciousness and gender. Women's ritual is largely about generating auspiciousness.[7] The converse is also true: much ritual concerned with auspiciousness is in fact ritual performed by women, as with the auspicious diagrams (*kolam*, etc.) drawn on or in front of the threshold of houses by women each morning in parts of India (Nagarajan 1997), or with the *vrat* rituals performed by Hindu women for the welfare of their husbands and children (S. Robinson 1985; S. Gupta 1999). In addition, the deities invoked (for example, Ṣaṣṭhī or Lakṣmī) are frequently female, and women act as key signifiers of auspiciousness and inauspiciousness (as in the concept of a married woman as *sumaṅgalī* or intrinsically auspicious, or of a widow as inauspicious). This new focus on auspiciousness therefore provided a context in which the role of women in ritual and religious life received considerably more attention from anthropologists than had previously been the case.

A convenient starting point for a discussion of this literature on auspiciousness might be Veena Das's diagrammatic representation (V. Das 1987: 143; also reproduced in Marglin 1985a: 294), in which the idea of the two axes of purity-pollution and auspiciousness appears particularly clearly. Das's diagram was modelled on the diagram from Tambiah's 1970 book that I reproduced in Chapter 6 (Fig. 6.4). Das's diagram, like Tambiah's, reflects the tendency for abstract formulism of the anthropology of the time, but, again like Tambiah's, it presents a useful perspective on village values.[8] However, the similarities between the two diagrams are more apparent than real.

[7] See, for example, the *strī ācār* associated with marriage in rural West Bengal and Bangladesh (Fruzzetti 1990). See also Samuel 1997. A related issue here is whether one interprets such rituals in terms of what they mean to their performers or to male ritual experts within the society. See Brown on the meanings of Mithilā art (C. Brown 1996).

[8] It should also be noted that Tambiah's diagram is intended to represent the constellation of values within a particular Thai (more accurately Lao or Isan) village, whereas Das's is a generalisation across Indian society as a whole.

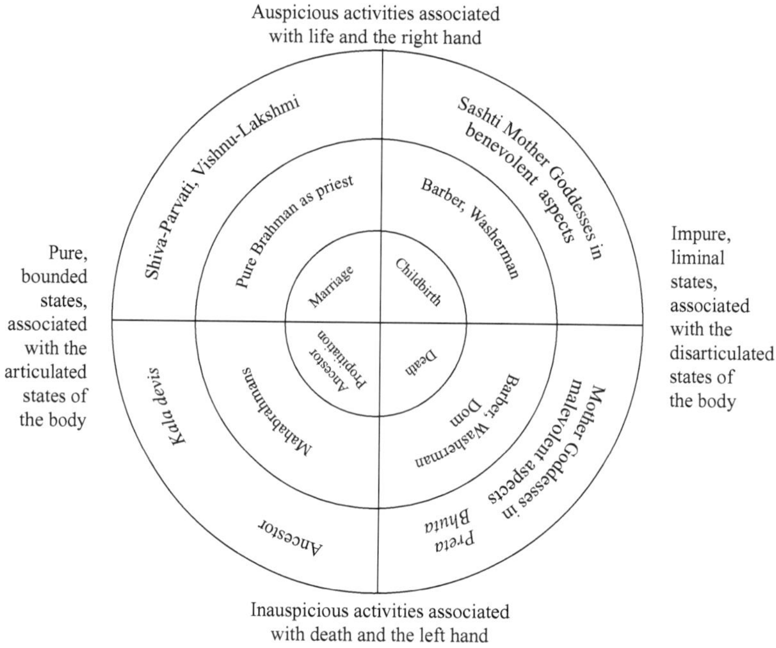

Figure 7.1. Veena Das's Diagram of the Value System of Indian Society

There are a number of things which might be noted about this diagram, but I will limit myself here to one major point: unlike those in the Buddhist diagram, the two sets of values are closely entangled with each other. In fact, an ongoing problem with 'auspiciousness' is that it does not correspond to a clear indigenous category; Das, Marglin (1985a) and Madan (1985, 1987) refer to a variety of indigenous terms (notably *śubha* and *mangala*) and, as Parry (1991) eventually noted, it does not seem possible to derive a single coherent category of non-Brahmanical concerns here. There is virtually no village ritual that cannot ideally be done according to Brahmanical prescriptions, which is not to say that all roles will necessarily be taken by Brahmins, since some of them may involve inappropriate involvement with impurity. Brahmanical values of purity pervade the whole field and, in effect, claim dominance over the world of everyday life.

This is most notable in relation to women's bodily functions, which have a close linkage in Brahmanical thought to the whole question of fertility in nature more generally. In Chapter 4, I discussed Julia Leslie's analysis of a widespread myth of menstruation, which sees its origin in a process by which the god Indra transfers his guilt at an unavoidable act of Brahmin-killing to women, to nature and to the earth. Women's fertility, and the earth's fertility, are somehow intrinsically linked to their polluted and devalued nature.

Of course, there is a kind of built-in irony or contradiction here, since the birth of children is necessary for the existence of society, and the birth of male children at least is a highly desired event. The relationship between auspiciousness and purity is complex and often contradictory. Groups that are impure may well also be auspicious, as with the *hijra* (eunuchs) who have an important role in much of India as bearers of auspiciousness in the context of marriage and the birth of male children (e.g. Nanda 1990: 1–6).

It is, however, perhaps not surprising that the contradictions are most conspicuous in relation to women and their role in village society (Samuel 1997). Brahmanical thought, as mentioned above, centres around the ideal of the celibate young male. Women's bodily functions, particularly menstruation and childbirth, are seen as polluting and problematic within this set of values. The 'auspiciousness' principle, by contrast, tends to focus around questions of prosperity, good health, and human and animal fertility. The imagery of the goddess Lakṣmī, with its close affiliations to the non-Brahmanical *yakṣa* religion, is a key representation of 'auspiciousness', and a young fertile married woman is the most immediate human representative of Lakṣmī. Yet, for the Brahmanical scheme of things, childbirth is seen as the most polluting of bodily processes, and traditional childbirth attendants generally belong to the lowest of social categories and are viewed with little or no respect.

In Chapter 4, I alluded briefly to the problematic consequences of this entangled relationship between what is desired and what is pure for childbirth in contemporary South Asia (see also Rozario and Samuel 2002a). Here it is perhaps enough to note that this mutual entanglement creates a very different relationship to the everyday religion of the village than that found in the Buddhist context in Southeast Asia (see Chapter 6), or than that which seems to have been characteristic of Jaina and Buddhist contexts in South Asia in the past.[9]

Women clearly have a 'lesser' status in some respects in Southeast Asian Buddhist societies as well, most conspicuously in relation to their

[9] To a considerable degree, modern Jains have preserved this relationship in modern India, although there has been some degree of assimilation to Brahmanical values. Jain communities include hereditary Brahmins who carry out Brahmanical ritual functions for the community, but they are not regarded as ideologically dominant in the way that Brahmins in Hindu communities are. Cf. Carrithers and Humphrey 1991; Cort 2001.

participation in monastic Buddhism (cf. Keyes 1984, 1986; Kirsch 1985). This negative valuation of women as Buddhist practitioners does not seem, however, to imply the same devaluation and loss of autonomy characteristic of women's situation in many modern Hindu communities. Some authors (e.g. Reid 1988) have seen this greater autonomy of women in Southeast Asian societies as a specifically Southeast Asian characteristic, and certainly it was true in the pre-modern period for Muslims in Malaya and Indonesia, and Christians in the Philippines, and tribal populations in many areas, as much as for Buddhists. My point here though is not to construct causal relationships, and it would be simplistic, to say the least, to claim that 'Hinduism' led to less freedom for women, and 'Buddhism' to more. The situation in the pre-modern period was the result of a complex series of historical developments in which the role of developing religious traditions to other aspects of society is best seen in terms of what Weber would have called 'elective affinities' (*Wahlverwandschaften*).

Thus one might suggest that, historically, restrictive forms of Hinduism and Islam made sense in relation to the specific forms of patrilineal kinship and marriage found in most South Asian village societies, particularly as the process of 'sāmantisation' in the course of the first millennium CE led to an accentuation of the patriarchal features of these societies. They made less sense in Southeast Asia, where matrilineal and bilateral kinship practices are more common. To the extent that one or another religious tradition was adopted, the inner logic of each tradition allowed for and encouraged a further intensification of the particular pattern that became associated with it. Thus, for example, restriction of women (*parda*, etc.) became a sign of high status in Hindu societies throughout much of North India, including present-day Bangladesh and Pakistan, and was adopted where possible by groups that wished to claim higher status.[10] All this, however, is only part of the story, and clearly there was also a great deal of historical contingency at work.

The (pre-Tantric) Buddhist and Jaina construction of things saw everyday life, including its ritual aspects, as a separate (*laukika*, worldly) sphere which co-existed with the teachings and practices of Buddhist and Jaina monastics but was not properly their concern. As in countries such as Thailand and Burma in recent times, there would presumably have been a range of priests and minor ritual practitioners at the village level, as well as rituals performed by householders and lay ritual specialists, but none of these had

[10] South India, which has a quite different ('Dravidian') system of kinship and marriage, had a somewhat different history, and women's status today is in some respects significantly better in these regions (Samuel 2002b: 9–11).

the kind of ideological dominance claimed by the Brahmins in the Brahmanical model. Thus weddings in Buddhist Southeast Asia, Sri Lanka or Tibet were not Buddhist ceremonies, although in some cases monks might be invited to generate auspiciousness and merit (good karma) in association with them through recitation of Budhist *sūtras* or other auspicious acts.

By contrast, the Brahmins as village-level ritual practitioners saw their role as setting the authoritative mode of performance of all of the rituals of everyday life (the *saṃskāras*, see e.g. Pandey 1969). In reality, this 'Sanskritisation' (perhaps one should rather say 'Brahminisation') of village life is far from complete, even today, with the performance of the *saṃskāras* by Brahmin priests often confined to the wealthier (and so usually higher) castes who are in a position to employ them, but the ideological dominance of the Brahmanical perspective in the wider society is well-established, with village rituals often seen as faulty and incorrect due to a lack of knowledge of the proper Brahmanical way to do things. This is however part of an ongoing dialectic between lay people and religious experts, village level and urban centre which would seem to go back to the early period we are here discussing (e.g. Marriott 1969b).

If we were to look for a Brahmanical equivalent to Chiang Mai, the Thai city which I cited as an example of the Buddhist relationship between power and the state, we might select Madurai in Tamil Nadu, a city of similar size and like Chiang Mai the capital of a medium-sized kingdom for hundreds of years, initially during the Pāṇḍya period (seventh to thirteenth centuries) and more recently under the Nayaka kings (sixteenth to eighteenth centuries). Little survives from the Pāṇḍya period; the city in its present form dates mostly from the seventeenth century, and is centred not, like Chiang Mai, on a modest city pillar shrine where Indra and the city guardian spirits are worshipped, but on the famous and splendid temple of the goddess Mīnākṣī (Hudson 1993; Harman 1989; Mitchell 1989: 449–52; Volwahsen 1969: 80–6, 88).

Mīnākṣī was almost certainly a local deity in origin, but is now regarded as a transform of Pārvatī and married to Śiva, who under his local name of Sundareśvara has a shrine next to hers at the centre of the temple.[11] She is also regarded as sister of Viṣṇu, and the ritual cycle of the temple

[11] Historically, it seems that early Brahmanical temples in South India were mostly dedicated to Śiva or other male deities. It was only from the thirteenth century onwards that shrines to the local goddesses, generally treated as consorts of a male Brahmanical deity, were incorporated within them (Stein 1994: 237, 465). By the time of construction of the Madurai temples as we know it today, this development had taken place. The temple today contains dual shrines to both Mīnākṣī and Śiva, but it is evident that Mīnākṣī is the dominant partner.

focuses on her the three deities of Mīnākṣī, Śiva and Viṣṇu (Harman 1992: 64–99). What might originally have been a shrine of a local deity has been transformed into a temple integrally tied into all-India Brahmanical cults and focusing on Śiva, here functioning as a deity of kingship, and on his marriage to the local goddess.

The nearby hill-shrine of Tirupparaṅkunram, once a Jain sanctuary, and now one of the six famous shrines of the Tamil deity Murugan, has likewise been integrated into the Brahmanical structure through Murugan's assimilation to Skanda, son of Śiva; the mythology of the site now centres around Murugan-Skanda's marriage to Devasenā (Clothey 1978: 124–7; cf. also Zvelebil 1991). The deities from this shrine, along with Mīnākṣī's brother Viṣṇu and his entourage from the important local Vaiṣṇava temple of Alakarkovil are also invited to the annual wedding ceremony of Mīnākṣī at Madurai (Harman 1989: 98).

Thus we see contrasting orientations towards the local deities and the religions of everyday life in the Brahmanical and Buddhist contexts; Brahmanical incorporation and mutual entanglement in the one case, parallel but distinct spheres in the other. Some further discussion of some of these issues is provided in the following Interlude (Chapter 8), which brings the first major part of the book to an end. The second major part commences with the subsequent chapter (Chapter 9), and will focus on the development of the various religious practices that are generally now labelled as 'Tantra'.

CHAPTER 8

Interlude: Asceticism and celibacy in Indic religions

Chapters 3 to 7 have presented a survey of the evidence relating to the first stages of the history of Indic religions from the Second Urbanisation onwards. Key issues here have included the growth of the ascetic orders and of Brahmanical asceticism and the development of a series of new techniques of mind-body cultivation in the context of these ascetic groups. We have also seen something of the wider context of these ascetic traditions in the religious life of North Indian communities (particularly in relation to the so-called *yakṣa* religion) and looked forward to a glimpse of the 'mature' relationship between Buddhism or Jainism and village religion on the one hand, and Brahmanical religion on the other. In this Interlude, I step back a little to look at some further issues relating to these developments.

I start by asking why the ascetic orders and the new goal of liberation from rebirth developed at the time when it did. Who and what were the Buddha, Pārśva, Mahāvīra, Makkhali Gosāla and the other spiritual leaders of the *śramaṇa* tradition, to the extent that we can take them as historical figures?

Each generation notoriously remakes major historical figures such as the Buddha or Mahāvīra in its own image and we can hardly expect our own time to be exempt from such a rule. However, looking at the evidence presented in the previous two chapters, it would seem that the key component of the message of these teachers, at least as understood by its early transmitters, was not primarily a rational theory of the nature of the universe. It was rather the ideal of the renunciation of ordinary life and of the emotions, feelings, impulses that tied one to it, a renunciation that also included a rejection of family, descendants and rebirth. At the centre was a conversion experience brought about through contact with a charismatic leader, and an ideal of a heroic struggle against the emotional entanglements and deep-seated volitional impulses of ordinary life, aimed at the achievement of a state of power, self-control and equanimity which is contrasted with the suffering and confusion of everyday life.

The relationship to a specifically renunciate lifestyle is a complex one. All these teachers had lay followers. If Masefield (1986) is right, lay followers were as capable of the conversion experience as renunciates, and they might or might not subsequently proceed to *bhikṣu* or wandering mendicant status. The key element was a reversal of everyday life such that the goal of liberation from rebirth came to be the centre around which their lives was now constructed. Following this reversal, the emotional entanglements of everyday life came to be seen as traps and obstacles to the achievement of that goal. Each tradition had its own specific set of techniques for how one then proceeded to actualise this vision, with the Jains and Ājīvikas, along with the Brahmanical renunciates who developed at around the same time, emphasising ascetic practice, with simple contemplative exercises (the *brahmavihāras*, perhaps some simple *dhyāna* practices), while the Buddhists emphasised the development of the full range of *dhyāna* practices as a technique for calming and purifying the mind.

The relationship between practice and insight (*prajñā*, *vipaśyanā*) was an ongoing issue within these traditions, with some later Buddhist meditation traditions developing a variety of *dhyāna* or *samādhi* practices and others treating *dhyāna* essentially as a prelude to insight, though arguably the reduction of *dhyāna* to a brief preliminary found in modern Theravādin meditation is a recent development (Cousins 1996b). In the modern Southeast Asian context, the *dhyāna* (*samatha*) practices are closely linked to the 'pragmatic' exercise of magical power (e.g. Houtman 1996, 1999). It seems likely that such magical practices were always part of the stock in trade of those *śramaṇas* who were dependent on individual lay support, though they might become less important in contexts where large monasteries were supported by the state or by urban or rural communities.

The development of monasticism, in the sense of substantial communities of renunciates living together, seems to have taken place relatively quickly, and they were certainly well established by the time when the *sūtras* and *vinaya* texts were written down in the second and first centuries BCE. The state support for Buddhism and the *śramaṇa* traditions at the time of Aśoka would doubtless have provided the necessary conditions, even if this did not exist already.

EXPLAINING THE GROWTH OF THE NEW ASCETIC TRADITIONS

What, however, were the social and cultural traditions that led to these developments? Strictly speaking, we do not have any evidence that the goal of liberation from rebirth itself was new, only that it is not present in the Vedic material. It might have had an earlier presence outside the

Vedic region, and the tradition of wisdom kings of Mithilā and other early renunciate rulers might point in this direction. It is hard, though, to think of it as developing in a small-scale village society. The idea of liberation from rebirth presupposes that one can see the structure of society 'from outside', in the form of the cycle of rebirth. One cannot rule out that such an idea and goal might occur to isolated individuals in a small-scale village society, but it seems unlikely that it would come to be shared by enough individuals to constitute a movement.[1]

Yet this is implied by the coming into being of organisations such as the Buddhist and Jain orders. We have here groups of people who felt it appropriate and meaningful to get together so as to pursue this goal as a group, along with further larger communities of people for whom this project somehow meant enough that they were willing to provide it with material support. This could surely only happen in a context where people's experience led them to start to see their own particular cultural form of human life in society from the outside. That in turn probably implies that they had several such examples of different forms of human society to think with.

In other words, the renunciate orders are unlikely to have developed until there were urban centres and trade between people from different localities. In these circumstances, an understanding could come into being that the way things were in one's own village or community was not simply the way things always had been and must be, but one of a number of possible options, and not necessarily, therefore, the best of those options.

That all of this is tied up with the new urban civilisation growing up at this time in the Central Gangetic region in North India has been widely assumed. Indeed, it seems to be almost inescapable, though it is less clear how long the cities had been in existence when the new ascetic orders got going or precisely how one might explain the relationship between the new movements and the urban milieu. On current datings, Greg Bailey and Ian Mabbett are probably correct in arguing in their recent *Sociology of Early Buddhism* that the rise of the ascetic orders followed the initial growth of cities: 'early Buddhism developed as a consequence of *a changed situation*, rather than of a rapidly changing one' (Bailey and Mabbett 2003: 260).[2]

[1] I suggested in Samuel 1990 that such an experience may be a necessary part of how shamanic practitioners operate, although the viewing from outside here may also take place, and more typically does take place, in a mythological language in which social life is constituted through the action of the spirits. In the case of the early ascetic groups, however, we need to assume a context in which such an understanding might come to be widely shared.

[2] Their account is not directly concerned with Jainism, but the same comment would apply in the Jaina case. The 'proto-*śramaṇa*' movements discussed in Chapter 6, if they had historical reality, might have been closer to the time when cities began to develop, and might indeed have been involved with their initial growth (see below).

The connection is again best seen in terms of what Weber would have called an 'elective affinity' rather than a process of causation. Something about the new form of life which was emerging meant that the Buddhist and Jain communities made sense, to all the parties concerned, whether those who became fully-committed ascetic members of the new orders, those who were lay followers and providers of food and material support, or the rulers and elite groups who minimally had to be prepared to tolerate this new development and who, if the Buddhist and Jain accounts are reliable, in fact often became active supporters of the new teachings. I think it is partly this multiplicity of actors, and the fact that we are looking at an 'elective affinity' rather than a causal relationship, that leads to the multiplicity and (real or apparent) inconsistency of explanations noted by Bailey and Mabbett's (Bailey and Mabbett 2003: 13–36).[3]

It is clear in any case that the new communities were from the beginning engaged with patrons and supporters in the cities, and were typically located close to them though not within them, in locations that were easily accessible to their populations. At this stage, I return to the question I posed at the start of this chapter. Why did the ascetic movements and the institution of celibate monasticism develop in India at this time?

In anthropological terms, what was happening could best be described as a revitalisation movement, a restructuring of modes of thinking and feeling, often through visionary processes, such as we see in many times of abrupt and radical change in human history and society. There was certainly enough change going on at this time, with the growth of new urban communities and a new lifestyle associated with them, and, presumably, the move to these new centres of a population which had previously lived in a much smaller-scale and culturally-enclosed context. However, demonstrating a closer relationship between these changes and the new movements is complex.

It has of course long been observed that the new traditions had an ethical component. From the point of view of practice as a renunciate, the ethical component is in a sense secondary, since it is primarily an aid to reducing one's involvement in the affairs of the everyday world. However, from the point of view of the lay life, the ethical version is more central. Thus it is clearly quite possible to see a need for ethical guidelines being met by the

[3] Attempts to find linear causal relationships are in fact not particularly useful in social analysis, since even when there is an event which has a massive impact on a community (war, famine, earthquake), the response is socially and culturally mediated, and may take any of a variety of forms. For similar reasons, the classical Popperian vocabulary of falsification has limited applicability to the social sciences, including their historical applications.

new religions, in a situation where choices have become much wider and indeed the idea of the individual as having choices to make has become much more salient. One can also see the new traditions as providing rational arguments to legitimise and explain the gradual abandonment of ritual practices that made sense in the village context but had less meaning in the city. Meanwhile, the Brahmins were reformulating their own practices for performance by householders under Brahmanical guidance, to some extent in competition with this new development (cf. Lubin 2005, and Chapter 7). Doubtless this is one reason why the new *śramaṇa* movements were more comfortable with the semi-ascetic wilderness-dwelling *jaṭila* Brahmins, who were potential allies, than with the new class of urban Brahmans who were their competitors for support and sponsorship.

One can also see ways in which the rulers of these new states could find the *śramaṇa* traditions, with their universal ethical principles and also perhaps their *kṣatriya* sympathies, a useful ideology for their new states. As Olivelle has noted, the early Upaniṣads also suggest a need to accommodate to the needs of kings (1998: xxxv), and if the Central Gangetic region already had, as I have suggested, a tradition of wisdom-kings with renunciate tendencies, there would be a natural synergy between the two developments, even if there were no direct influence from the wisdom-king traditions upon the evolving *śramaṇa* movement itself.[4]

The Buddhist tradition's classic emphasis on *dukkha*, on the suffering or unsatisfactory nature of everyday life, and on meditation as an important aspect of how one deals with it, is also worth taking seriously as a clue to what people might have been looking for when they turned to the Buddhists and the other new movements. Suffering in the old village context – the 'ancient matrix', as Stan Mumford once called it, quoting Bakhtin (Mumford 1989: 16ff, cf. Samuel 1993: 6) – was at least part of an ongoing cycle of life in which the individual was deeply connected with the wider community. The city was a context in which this connectedness was no longer there. The urban individual had to deal with a world in which he or she had to make his or her own way, with little guidance from the past (cf. Gombrich 1988: 72–81). The early Buddhists and the other groupings within the *śramaṇa* movement provided a guide to the path, techniques to calm and understand the suffering of the newly self-conscious individual, and a group of like-minded people with whom one could construct a new kind of kinship and community based upon a common goal.

[4] In fact Olivelle does not take the wisdom-king traditions seriously, and implies that the Brahmins presented their new doctrines as being taught by kings as a deliberate device to encourage acceptance by their royal patrons. This may be a little too cynical (Olivelle 1998: xxxv).

Was there actually more *dukkha* around in the new urban environment? There have been various attempts to link the growth of the ascetic orders to the negative impact of social change and the new urban way of life. There is probably at least some truth in these suggestions. Richard Gombrich, for example, suggests that the new cities provided an environment in which disease would flourish, so that illness and death were widespread. 'It is quite possible that in the Buddha's environment disease and sudden death had actually become more frequent. Maybe it is no accident that the early Buddhists were fond of medical metaphors, describing the Buddha as the great physician, etc.' (Gombrich 1988: 57).

There is perhaps a further issue here, which relates to my earlier point about viewing society from the 'outside'. The new social environment had the potential to create a new kind of self-awareness, particularly among people such as merchants, entrepreneurs, government officials and other people who were living in an unpredictable and high risk environment in which individual choices were difficult to make and might have a dramatic impact on their future prospects. The village, by contrast, was an environment in which people's lives were more or less pre-given; for most people, their life-prospects, illness or accident aside, would be much the same as their father's or mother's. Harvests could vary from year to year with the weather, floods and other natural disasters were always a possibility, but farmers tend to have tried and true techniques for dealing with them. In such a situation, there is only a limited scope needed for individual judgement.

All this would have been very much less true in the new urban environment. There would be many examples of different life-choices around, and for some people at least a constant need to make one's own choices about the course of one's own life. At the same time, individuals were still part of a complex web of obligations and commitments to spouses, children and other relatives, with little certainty as to whether they could meet them. It is not unreasonable to see this as a situation in which people might start to question the value and meaningfulness of any of the choices they are making within the 'round of rebirth'.

If life was risky and unpredictable, with outcomes that no longer seemed clearly linked to one's immediate actions, one can see some of the attraction of the choice of withdrawal from society. To become a renunciate was to accept one's own death, in both the physical and (more immediately) social sense. The renunciate's previous social personality and role has been abandoned and has gone for ever. He or she was, in theory at least, no longer indebted to anyone in lay society, and no longer obliged to undertake anything. The renunciate was free, except for the limited rules structuring the life of the monastic community, and the even more circumscribed rules regarding support from the laity.

In reality, of course, Buddhist or Jain monks or nuns, or Brahmanical *saṃnyāsins*, were not necessarily totally free from the entanglements of their previous social connections, but the attraction of the ideal state is perhaps understandable, especially now that it had been linked to the new goal of liberation from rebirth and offered the company of a community oriented towards the same goal.

Why though did the new ascetic orders appeal to the individuals who became lay followers and supporters? Much of the argument about the new kind of awareness associated with the urban lifestyle might apply to lay followers as well, particularly for the relatively prosperous, wealthy and powerful individuals who made up much of the following of the new orders. One might also consider some of the practical aspects of involvement with the Buddhist order. The connection between Buddhism and trade has long been noticed. As Bailey and Mabbett note, 'It is possible that trade was mentioned ubiquitously in Buddhist literature not just because it was conspicuous in the society reflected in the texts, but because the actual development and expansion of Buddhism was so closely connected with it. Buddhist monks often travelled with caravans of merchants [. . .]. It is likely the extension of Buddhist culture into the Deccan was closely associated with trade' (2003: 62; see also Heitzman 1984; O'Connor 1989; Lewis 2000: 49–88).

Weber's argument for the 'elective affinity' between the mercantile culture of north-western Europe in the later Middle Ages and the rise of Protestantism cannot be transferred as a whole to the different situation of fifth and fourth century BCE North India, but one wonders if some of the same elements might hold. Certainly the restrained, moderate lifestyle of the lay Buddhist would go well with the trading ethos of that time as of the Netherlands, Germany or Switzerland in the sixteenth and seventeenth centuries (cf. Gombrich 1988: 76–81).

One can also point to the practical utility for people engaged in long-distance trade, or in travel to distant places on administrative or other missions, of having a community of people with whom they could claim fellowship, whom they had some reason to trust, and from whom they could expect support in distant cities and locations. Trading communities such as the Buddhist Newars of the Kathmandu Valley are perhaps a good modern example of this kind of situation, with Newar communities scattered as far as Lhasa, Kalimpong and Kashmir (Lewis 2000: 53–4). So of course are the modern Jains. There are parallels here with the mystery cults of the classical and Hellenistic world (Eleusis, Isis, etc.), with the Sufi brotherhoods that provided fellowship and a home away from home for Islamic travellers throughout the long trade routes across Europe, Asia and North Africa, or with the cult groups (Ekpe, Poro, Sande etc.) that existed into modern times through the trading states of West Africa, providing linkages between people over vast areas which were politically various and often, for someone without local connections, quite dangerous. As I suggested in Chapter 6, the early proto-*śramaṇa* communities, such as the followers of Pārśva, if they had historical reality, might be seen as local equivalents of such cult groups, and as providing a similar mixture of spiritual insight and practical assistance.

In asking why the new ascetic orders appealed to rulers of the time, it is of course true that rulers were also human beings dealing with a new and challenging situation. Some of the arguments about new forms of self-awareness might apply as strongly to them as others, especially given the risks and unpredictability of being a ruler of a North Indian state at that time. But kings also had practical concerns and one can see ways in which Buddhism and Jainism might be of use to them. Here the ethical component of the new traditions has already been mentioned. Bailey and Mabbett have also advanced an interesting argument about the role of the *śramaṇas* as intermediaries between the expanding centres of urban power and the various populations they encountered:

> [*Ś*]*ramaṇa* teachers were not just rustic medicine men from the wilderness. They were active everywhere. They could therefore be co-opted to stand for the solidarity of the kingdom, a solidarity that was cemented by a new message that insisted upon the universality of values, and subverted the privileged authority of Vedic rituals and myths which were controlled by a special group. This sort of message was just what rulers needed when they were trying to bring beneath their dominion communities too diverse in culture and origins to be accommodated within a ready-made Sanskrit-brāhmanical image. (Bailey and Mabbett 2003: 175)

I assume that some such arguments give us a reasonable grasp on how and why the ascetic traditions developed at the time that they did. In the remainder of this interlude I move to consider the wider question of the two different kinds of accommodation we have seen between religion and society, the Buddhist and/or Jaina pattern and the Brahmanical pattern. I begin with the question of celibacy.

THE LOGIC OF MALE CELIBACY

I have already pointed to the central relationship in Brahmanical thought between celibacy, religion and male identity.[5] The logic behind this centrality is quite explicit in modern Hindu contexts, and undoubtedly goes back a very long way; we can see it in the work by Kaelber on Vedic texts which I discussed in Chapter 7 (Kaelber 1989). The general Indic notions regarding seminal continence and loss are well known in both textual and popular sources, and have been highlighted in recent years by a number of authors, perhaps most notably by Joseph Alter in his studies of contemporary North Indian wrestlers (Alter 1997; see also Khandelwal 2001). These notions imply that personal power and authority arise from abstention from and/or control over male ejaculation.

This theme links up closely to that of the renouncer (e.g. L. Dumont 1960). Indic religions, including Buddhists and Jainas as well as modern Brahmanical thinkers, have seen and still today see the ascetic as someone who renounces and rejects, above all, the claims and appeal of family life and of sexuality, and so of the society that is built upon the foundation of the life of the householder. Here the renouncer is implicitly figured as male, while women routinely serve as representations of the family life to be renounced.

Thus spiritual power, which is expressible through various this-worldly results, is derived from asceticism, while the normative mode of asceticism is carried out by males, and involves the rejection of, or at least conscious control over, sexuality. Correlatively, as we learn from the Purāṇas and other sources of Hindu legend, if an ascetic was becoming so powerful that the gods felt threatened and the order of nature was being interfered with, the standard solution was to send along an *apsarās* or celestial dancing-girl to seduce him and so destroy his power.

It is worth stressing that none of this necessarily has anything to do with morality. When the ascetic succumbs to the *apsarās*'s wiles, this is not a moral fall, but a loss of self-control, leading to a loss of spiritual power. This is only a moral or ethical issue in so far as self-control is seen as morally good. In the Buddhist or Jain traditions, one can argue more convincingly that some degree of positive moral value has become attached to celibacy, but here again the key issue would appear to be self-control as part of a process of discipline. The discipline is justified not for its own sake but

[5] By celibacy here, I imply the rejection of (hetero-)sexual relations, since the term is also sometimes used to refer to the rejection of marriage. See Bell and Sobo 2001.

because it is held to lead to a state of enlightenment or liberation.[6] Here there is an explicit contrast with the idea in mainstream Christian traditions that celibacy is a morally superior state in its own right, as opposed to any end-result that is supposed to arise from its practice.

In reality, things are more complex. Celibacy is associated with purity, and purity is undoubtedly seen as a valued state in Indian society.[7] Sexuality, women and family life are all in various ways associated with impurity and pollution.[8] There undoubtedly are senses in which the normative Brahmanical tradition regards purity as morally superior, and the Brahman as morally superior to the untouchable, though even here it is difficult to be too categorical. As always in India, it is easy to find support for both a statement and its opposite. When Mahatma Gandhi proclaimed that in an ideal Hindu society, Brahmans and street-sweepers would go on being Brahmans and street-sweepers, but each would be regarded as of equal value as a human being, he was speaking out of a valid strain within the Indian tradition, but it was one that had little correspondence to the social reality of his time.

Ascetics are prototypically male, and the role of female ascetics in Indic societies has been and is today marginal and problematic. The goddess Pārvatī's ascetic practice is only superficially an exception, since it was aimed at acquiring a husband, in her case the god Śiva. In fact, as is well known, women's religious practice regularly involves fasting and asceticism of various kinds, but its proper aims are generally held to be the establishment and welfare of her family (S. Robinson 1985; M. McGee 1992). This introduces a certain blurriness into the logic. If spiritual power derives in some sense from control over the ejaculation of semen, it requires a male physiology. Women, though, clearly are seen as able to accumulate power through ascetic practice, even if its utilisation is ideally confined to the welfare of husband and household.

One solution here, and it is followed in later traditions such as Vajrayāna (Tantric) Buddhism, is to see both male and female essences as present in both men and women, so that the internal energy processes are more or less the same despite the physiological differences between them. But in practice there is a strong strain of thought that implies that ascetic celibacy

[6] In the Tibetan context, it is not unusual to have a married, non-celibate lama presiding over a monastery of celibate practitioners. There is really no contradiction in this situation, since the normative assumption is that the non-celibate lama has transcended the need for celibacy, and is capable of sexual relations without attachment.

[7] Here again Louis Dumont gives the classic account (L. Dumont 1972).

[8] Cf. Leslie 1996a; Rozario and Samuel 2002a.

is essentially a male business. It is clear that Hindu, Buddhist and Jain traditions are all uncomfortable with female ascetic practitioners, and none treats them as fully equal to men. This reflects the complex relationship between household and this-worldly-centred ritual and religious life, which is seen as a proper concern of women, and ritual and religious life that is aimed at more transcendental and other-worldly goals, which is not so seen.

In any case, the equation between celibacy and male spiritual power is quite familiar, and it is expressed in various ways across Brahmanical Hinduism, and across the Jain and Buddhist traditions. No doubt it gains some of its familiarity and obviousness from the idea of celibacy in the context of Christian monasticism. Buddhist and Christian monasticism in particular have spread over vast areas of the planet and acquired a very substantial presence in many societies. Yet, perhaps as a result, we may be failing to look closely enough at what is going on when Indic religions take as perhaps their single most culturally-valued goal the pursuit of spiritual power by male ascetics.

WARRIOR BROTHERHOODS AND WISDOM TRADITIONS

One approach is to ask how this pattern developed historically. One origin has been identified, perhaps somewhat speculatively, in the social and religious role of young men in Indo-European pastoralist society. In Chapter 6 I mentioned the suggestion made by the British scholar of Jainism, Paul Dundas, which in its turn derived in part from work by Willem Bollée, that the early Buddhist and Jain monastic orders were a kind of transformation of Indo-European male warrior brotherhoods, and that a transitional stage could be seen in that shadowy and mysterious group in late Vedic and early Brahmanical texts, the *vrātyas* (Bollée 1981; Dundas 1991).

This suggestion has its problems, but it seems clear enough in any case that a major strain of early Indic religious life valorised male celibacy and purity. One can, I think, see an early version of this strain as being located in the Kuru-Pañcāla region, and as linked in many ways to the values of a pastoralist society, or at least of a pastoralist elite.

As for the *vrātyas*, scholarship since Bollée's time seems to support the idea that they were, in the earlier Vedic material at least, something like a warrior age-set, a phase through which the young men of the tribe go prior to marriage (see Chapter 5, and Falk 1986). The *vrātyas* were unmarried young men, active as cattle-raiders and warriors, and they also had a significant ritual role, which was tied up to the ongoing fertility and productivity of the land. All this came to an end when they married and become incorporated into ordinary society as householders, though a small minority, unable or unwilling for one reason or another to move to the householder stage, remained as permanent *vrātyas* and acted as leaders of the *vrātya* troops. The important point, though, is that we see here an initial context in which an early Indic society makes use of and valorises the specific age group of young unmarried men.

As I suggested in Chapter 5, iconographical sources from the Central Gangetic and Bengal Delta regions, such as the Chandraketugarh terracottas, suggest a religion focusing on something quite different: the cult of a goddess of fertility and prosperity. This material can be seen as an early instance of another pervasive theme in Indian thought and imagery, most familiar in the *mithuna* (male and female couple) images which run through Indian sacred architecture from the early Buddhist *stūpas* to the spectacular erotic sculpture of Khajuraho and Konarak. I will have some comments on these later temples and their imagery in Chapter 12, but here I would point to the more restrained but much more widespread imagery that we find throughout Buddhist, Hindu and Jaina architecture.

We could consider here, for example, the male and female couples who separate the narrative scenes from the Buddha's previous lives on the Buddhist stupa at Nagarjunakonda, dating from around the third century CE (Agrawala 1983; figs. 79–83), although there are thousands of similar scenes that could be chosen. I would suggest that in this imagery we can see an alternative conception of both kingship and human society to that which centres around the celibate young man. If the celibate young man as hero had his natural home in the pastoralist ideology of the north, then the agricultural societies of the north-east, the homeland of Buddhism and the ascetic traditions, tended instead to celebrate agricultural prosperity and fertility.

ASCETIC PRACTICES

It is also to this Central Gangetic region that our early evidence of asceticism and yogic practices aimed at liberation or enlightenment refers. I would suggest that it is in the interaction between these two regions that we can see the origins of Brahmanical asceticism, and of the growth of the idea of the Brahmin as in part an ascetic. I think that there may well be some truth in Bollée's suggestion that the *vrātya* and similar Vedic social institutions were reshaped in the process as something rather different, forming the basic structure of the new ascetic orders, though we can hardly exclude that, as the Buddhist and Jain traditions both assert, there were earlier teachers of a path to enlightenment. While these figures seem largely legendary or mythical, with the possible exception of Pārśva, the twenty-third Jain *tīrthaṅkara*, they are mostly also located in the Northeast Indian region.[9]

Given that the idea of permanent ascetic withdrawal seems itself not to have been a feature of the earliest Vedic context, this perhaps suggests that the key stage as far as celibate power is concerned in the Vedic context was the *brahmacārin* himself, particularly the *brahmacārin* who, like the *vrātya* leaders, remains in the celibate role rather than marrying. In particular, the *brahmacārin* who moved directly into a renunciate lifestyle may be regarded as the prototypical generator of ascetic power.

In later Indian religious history, we might think here of figures such as Śankara, who are described as adopting the ascetic lifestyle from youth without ever becoming a householder. The iconography of Śankara depicts him as a young man, and his biographies describe him as a child prodigy who died at the age of thirty-two. We might think too of the iconography of young ascetic deities such as Ayyappan at Śabarimala, the ascetic form of Murugan (Skanda) who is worshipped at the great Tamil shrine of Palani, or Dakṣiṇāmūrti, the ascetic teacher form of Śiva. It may be no accident that these are all celibate forms of deities who elsewhere are strongly associated both with male sexuality and with warriorship.

Is it reasonable then to see the *brahmacārin* as a kind of 'civilised' and 'spiritualised' version of the original role of the *vrātya* as young male warrior? If so, we can perhaps begin to sense how the cultural and psychic valorisation of young men that we already saw in the *vrātya* role was transformed into something rather different, as a key symbolisation of the value of purity that was at the peak of the Brahmanical scale of values.

CELIBACY AND MALE IDENTITY IN CONTEMPORARY BUDDHISM

Here it is useful to move to more contemporary material, while remaining cautious about the extent to which the present can be read into the past. The question of celibacy and male identity in contemporary Buddhism nevertheless has some interesting continuities with the material considered above. I shall look specifically at material from Northern Thailand, although there are comparable features in other parts of Thailand and in other Southeast Asian societies. As mentioned in Chapter Six, ordination is usually treated by Thais and other Southeast Asian Buddhists as a temporary

[9] If Williams is correct in taking Nemi, the twenty-second *tīrthaṅkara*, as historical (R. Williams 1966), we would need to include Gujarat as well. Gujarat would have been part of the 'non-Āryan' world at that time, and like the Central Gangetic region and Bengal Delta had strong early links to trade.

period of transition to the marriageable state (Tambiah 1970; Spiro 1971; Davis 1984; Rhum 1994). Thus what we actually have in relation to most of the male population is a period when young men withdraw from society and live in an exclusively male group, followed by their return to society, marriage and incorporation as male householders. Structurally at least, we can see here a considerable similarity to the old *vrātya* pattern. If we recall the suggestions in Northern and Northeast Thai ethnography that the celibacy of the ordinands is, in some respect, tied up with the coming of the rains, the fertility and productivity of the land (e.g. Tambiah 1970), the similarity is even stronger.

What is different in the Buddhist pattern, presumably, is the absence of the warrior role, and the stress on the ethical dimension of Buddhism, particularly on moral restraint, represented here above all by the sexual purity (i.e. celibacy) that is a central element of the definition of a Buddhist monk in contemporary Southeast Asian states. As Charles Keyes notes, the high status of monastic celibacy creates certain paradoxes for male identity in Northern Thai society (Keyes 1986). The ideal male is a Buddhist monk, a *bhikkhu*, so where does this leave the male householder?

Keyes sees the practice of temporary ordination as a way in which the ambiguities of the male Buddhist householder role are partially resolved. Temporary ordination is a rite of passage to adult male status. It involves a reformulation of man's link to his mother in the course of the ordination ritual, and it is normally followed by marriage after a short interval.

Some features of Keyes' analysis are specific to Northern Thailand. This is a society with matrilocal residence, meaning that girls remain in the same household at marriage, and men move to their future wife's household. This is associated with a sense of women and women-centred households as the stable elements in society, and men as mobile and unrooted, which is quite different from, for example, the standard North Indian pattern, where women move to the husband's household and have a marginal status within it for many years. However the idea of the 'morally tempered male householder' as a compromise between renunciation (the *bhikkhu*) and over-indulgence (the tough aggressive male personality) would seem to have wider applicability. So does the sense that a woman's role is defined by the domestic context (Keyes 1984; Kirsch 1985; Kawanami 2001).[10]

I would emphasise that this is not just a question of Buddhist monasticism in Thailand serving as a rite of passage for young men and providing a certain degree of moral tempering. One can also see this in slightly different

[10] On the female role in Theravāda Buddhist societies see also Andaya 1994.

terms, in terms of what one might call the psychic economy of Thai peasant life. The energy and psychic orientation of young men is being directed in a particular direction through the practice of temporary ordination. Looking at the situation in this way makes it considerably clearer why the monastic role is largely seen as irrelevant and inappropriate for women. It may also help to explain the continuing relevance of imagery of warfare, warriorship and conquest within Buddhism, in relation to the conquest of the ordinary self and its motivations.

In relation to everyday life (and to women in so far as they are seen as located in the domain of everyday life), this pattern constructs a separation between the two domains: *laukika* and *lokottara*, worldly and beyond the world. Although, in doctrinal terms, the Buddhist teachings can seem dismissive of the concerns of everyday life, the characteristic orientation towards everyday life in Buddhist societies is rather to treat it as a separate domain with its own integrity and logic and its own largely autonomous ritual life (see Chapters 6 and 7). Thus, as previously noted, marriage in Buddhist societies was generally not a Buddhist ritual or sacrament, but a secular contract whose ritual dimensions were linked to the creation of auspiciousness and good fortune, matters essentially disconnected with the Buddhist goal of enlightenment. The critical point of intersection between the two domains, everyday and transcendental, was death, the one point in the life cycle where Buddhist clergy played a critical and central role.

In many ways, this is all very Indic, if not particularly 'Indian' in the sense of resembling the situation in modern India. The Thais themselves seem to have arrived in Thailand fairly late, from the tenth century onwards. Theravāda Buddhism, however, was already well established in the region at that time and the general pattern of male identity here seems similar enough to that in other parts of Buddhist Southeast Asia to allow one to assume that it is to a substantial degree of Indic origins.

CELIBACY AND MALE IDENTITY IN BRAHMANICAL SOCIETY

Thus, if temporary ordination can be seen as a process that should ideally result in all men having a kind of spiritually-tempered male identity, somewhere between the extremes of ascetic and warrior, what we could call the mature Brahmanical model moves in a quite different direction. Here, it is assumed that different social groups within the village community take on different roles, with the Brahmins towards the ascetic pole, the *kṣatriyas* towards the warrior pole. Of course, the *varṇa* scheme has only a tenuous relationship to the social reality of Indian villages in modern times, but it retains an important ideological role.

Purity in the Brahmanical structure of ideas is seen as something which varies up and down the social hierarchy, again an idea that has a strong presence in South Asian communities, if increasingly contested by groups who find themselves defined as impure or polluted. From the Brahmanical point of view at least, spirituality is associated less with a stage in the life-cycle than with an elite group within society. Yet in other ways, what we have seen in Thailand contrasts with what we could call the typical Brahmanical construction of things.

Thus where the dominant Southeast Asian solution was to see male purity as a phase in the life-cycle, the mature Brahmanical mode of thinking saw it as the function or role of a particular social group. Here purity and spirituality become part of a hierarchical construction of society, in which the purity of the Brahmin was counterposed to the impurity and this-worldly orientation of lower orders of society. At the same time, everyday life was systematically structured through a series of sacramental rituals, the *saṃskāra*, performed by Brahmin priests.

This is a more complex pattern, and in fact it involves two ascetic roles: the ideally semi-ascetic (but married) role of the Brahman within caste society, and the fully-ascetic role of the *saṃnyāsin* outside caste society proper. It took quite a while to get to this point, historically, and even longer for village ritual life to be fully incorporated into the Brahmanical system, a process that in most parts of India had not been fully achieved even in modern times. However, the pattern proved to be a durable one. Its greatest strength was perhaps its ability to survive in the absence of state patronage. The inability of monastic Buddhism to do the same proved to be a crucial weakness after the Islamic takeover and the collapse, in all but a few marginal parts of South Asia, notably Sri Lanka and the Nepal Valley, of the state regimes which had traditionally supported Buddhism.

At the same time, the incorporation of women, the lower castes, and everyday life into the Brahmanical structure came at a price, which was the dominance of the ideology of purity, and the definition of female biology as intrinsically impure. The Brahmanical societies of South Asia put much more work, culturally, into an ongoing struggle to maintain purity than did the Buddhist societies of Southeast Asia, and this cultural concern or obsession had destructive consequences for women in particular, as I noted in Chapters 4 and 7.

Thus it seems that the role of the renunciate, preserved in a relatively early form in the role of the *bhikkhu* among the Buddhist societies of modern

Southeast Asia, has in a sense bifurcated in the Brahmanical context. On the one hand, we have the semi-renunciate village Brahman, who at least in theory plays a central role in the ritual life of the village.[11] On the other, there is the fully-renunciate *saṃnyāsin*. Each has acquired some of the psychic and symbolic value of the *brahmacārin*. Put otherwise, the *brahmacārin* acts as a kind of bridge between the two, with the possibility of movement in either direction. Both patterns, Buddhist and Brahmanical, nevertheless, have in-built tensions and complexities: and in both cases, women have an ambivalent and difficult relationship to a social and ideological order constructed around the supremacy of certain kinds of men.

CONCLUSION

I have tried to suggest here the two major directions in which the Indic religions were to develop, the Brahmanical and that represented by the *śrāmaṇa* movements, both Buddhist and Jain. I have also sketched something of the contrasting orientations towards pragmatic and everyday religion, and towards women and their religious and biological functions, which we find today associated with them.

Both patterns, I suggest, originated in various ways in the complex interaction between Vedic culture and the wisdom-oriented traditions and earth-centred rituals of fertility and prosperity of Northeast India. They constituted different mixtures of these elements, and we can see these in transformed versions in the later developments of Brahmanical Hinduism within India, and of Theravāda Buddhism in particular outside it.

It is important to appreciate here that the role of asceticism and celibacy within Buddhism and other Indic traditions can only make sense in relation to the wider assumptions and practices within the society where they are practised, particularly the assumptions regarding gender and sexuality. It is worth seeing this issue in the context of the psychic or cultural balance within society as a whole. Aggression, violence and competitiveness are clearly modes of human social behaviour which have appeared in one form or another in most of all human societies, and particularly perhaps among young men. The formation of groups of young men, whether neighbourhood gangs, football teams, or *vrātya* bands raiding the neighbouring tribe's cattle, provide ways of channelling such behavioural modes in more or less destructive directions. The idea of young men undergoing a temporary period as a Buddhist monk or in some other semi-ascetic role could be

[11] I say 'in theory', because most men from Brahmin families are not priests and perhaps never were.

seen as a way of taking that aggression and competitiveness and directing it inwards, into the quest of self-mastery. It is perhaps not surprising that the imagery of warriorship and victory that remain significant within Buddhism has occasionally expressed itself in real-life violence and war (e.g. Mohan 2001; Victoria 2005). The problem is nevertheless one that every society has to deal with, our own included, and the 'temporary ascetic' approach may well be judged, in relation to the historical record, one of the more successful.

PART TWO

Tantra

The Tantras – there is hardly any other kind of literature that has met with so much abuse, particularly by those who never read or seriously studied a single line of it; or that has so much fascinated those who on the testimony of misinformed and uninformed people thought the Tantras to be a most powerful, and hence strictly guarded means for the gratification of purely biological urges. Only very few people tried to form an opinion of the Tantras by their own. It is true the Tantras are nothing for those who are so pure in mind and, alas! so poor-minded that they are unable to see that actual life is different from the fantastic and mutually contradictory theories and ideas they have about it; nor are the Tantras meant for those who consider life to be nothing else but a *chronique scandaleuse*. But since it is easier to follow extremes than to weigh the evidence and to decide upon a middle path, there can be no doubt that these extremists have done great harm to the study and understanding of what the Tantras have to tell. For it is by their verdict – unjustified abuse based upon wilful ignorance and misconceptions about the aim of the Tantras engendered by this ignorance – that the Tantras are nowadays held in contempt and considered to be something depraved and mean. Yet the fact is that the Tantras contain a very sound and healthy view of life.

Herbert Guenther, *Yuganaddha: The Tantric View of Life*
(Guenther 1969: 3)

CHAPTER 9

The classical synthesis

Part Two of the book is focused on the period from the fourth to twelfth centuries CE, essentially from the foundation of the Gupta Empire in around 320 CE to the final establishment of Muslim rule over North and Northeast India. I shall be particularly concerned with the growth of 'Tantric' forms of religion. To begin with, some discussion is necessary regarding the years between Part One and Part Two. This is the period in which what might be regarded as the classical synthesis of Indian culture took shape, a synthesis that is most familiar through the great artistic and literary achievements of the Gupta period in North India.

Part One closed with the initial development of what were to become the two alternative and parallel cultural patterns that would shape the history of Indic religions over the centuries to follow. These were the Buddhist/Jain pattern and the Brahmanical pattern. The Buddhist/Jain pattern worked in terms of large monastic religious centres and treated the world of popular and civic religion and of the rituals of everyday life as a parallel sphere that was largely beyond the concern of Buddhist and Jain religious specialists. It appears to have been closely linked to urban centres and the trading and administrative groups within these centres, and initially received a high level of state support. Buddhism and Jainism also developed pilgrimage and cult centres where there was a major monastic presence, including those at the sites associated with the events of the life of the Buddha and the *tīrthaṅkaras*.

It is not really clear how far Buddhism and Jainism penetrated to the village level in areas away from big cities.[1] In later years, in Sri Lanka,

[1] The only substantial regional study of Buddhist temples in South Asia known to me is Julia Shaw's work from the Vidiśā region. The monasteries in this study were distributed over a fairly large area, but they are all quite close to a major administrative centre of the period (Vidiśā /Besnagar), and may not be representative of more remote areas (J. Shaw 2000; J. Shaw and Sutcliffe 2001). Most of the monastery sites uncovered or located in Bangladesh are also close to major administrative centres (Dhaka-Vikrampur, Mainamati-Comilla, Mahasthan) (Chakrabarti 2001; Samuel 2002c).

Southeast Asia and Tibet and in parts of East Asia, Buddhism became a religion of the countryside and the village as well as of the urban centres, though it has mostly coexisted with other religious complexes which have dealt with the affairs of this world: the spirit-cults of Burma, Thailand and Sri Lanka, and with Confucianism, Taoism, shamanism and Shinto in East Asia. Here Buddhism and Jainism were following the inner logic of their ascetic, renunciate and world-transcending origins. The power of the Buddha in these countries became an important source of magical ritual technology, which was harnessed for this-worldly purposes (Tambiah 1984; Spiro 1971; Tannenbaum 1987, 1989) but Buddhism maintained some ideological distance from the affairs of the world and of the gods and spirits of this world. Only in those countries where Vajrayāna (Tantric) Buddhism became dominant (Nepal, Bali, Tibet, Mongolia) did Buddhism itself become so integrally involved in worldly and pragmatic issues that one can speak of a single religion rather than the co-existence of two or three distinct religious complexes (Samuel 1982; Samuel 1993).[2] We will see something later of the developments that allowed this integral relationship to take form.

The Brahmanical pattern, by contrast, saw itself from the beginning as integrally involved in worldly affairs, and established itself so successfully in this regard that, even in the modern Buddhist countries of Southeast Asia and Sri Lanka, some kind of Brahmanical presence exists in both urban and rural settings.[3] Brahmins, as hereditary priestly families, became a presence at the rural level throughout India, often with substantial land-holdings. This did not mean that all village ritual was performed by Brahmins, or that all (or even most) Brahmins were employed primarily as ritual performers, but it established the ideological supremacy of Brahmanical ritual as the 'correct' way in which all kinds of ritual, including the most humble domestic practice, should be performed. At the other extreme, Brahmins largely came to monopolise the ritual of state and kingship. Buddhist state rituals were developed (Klimburg-Salter 1989; Walter 2000), but even in the modern Buddhist kingdom of Thailand, the king is installed by court Brahmin priests.

Keyes suggests that the situation was similar in Southeast Asia prior to the missionising activities of the thirteenth to sixteenth centuries, in other words there were relatively small numbers of Buddhist monks living 'in temple-monasteries in or near the major political centres' (Keyes 1987: 133).

[2] The Bon religion of Tibet in recent centuries is best regarded as a variant form of Tibetan Vajrayāna Buddhism. In any case Buddhism and Bon are competitors for the same territory, rather than religions which operate in parallel but separate spheres.

[3] For rural Brahmins in Thailand and Burma see Brohm 1963, Tambiah 1970 (*paahm*), etc.

The establishment of Brahmanical Hinduism as a state religion can be associated above all with the Gupta dynasty in North and Central India (c. 320–c. 510 CE). I use the term 'Brahmanical Hinduism' here, because I think that if we want to use the term Hinduism at all before the nineteenth century then this is the point at which we can reasonably start using it. By around 500 CE, we have state religions focused on the theistic cult of deities, Śiva and Viṣṇu, who are still central figures of modern Hinduism, we have most of the major schools of Hindu philosophy at least in embryonic form, we have temples and temple rituals which are recognisably continuous with the versions we know today, and we have much of the social regulation of later Hindu society. In addition, this religion was the dominant religion of much of the population of South Asia. At the same time, much of the development of the caste system lay ahead, and the degree of penetration of this new Brahmanical culture at the village level was probably considerably more limited than in modern times.

Some account is needed here of how these developments came about. I start with a brief summary of political developments over the period. There are the usual provisos for dates and details, though in comparison with the periods we have looked at in Chapters 3 to 7, by this period we begin to get substantial amounts of epigraphic material, and the Chinese translations and early manuscript material also give us some hold on dating for the Buddhist material specifically. There are still a lot of open questions, but at the level at which I am dealing with the material they are for the most part perhaps not too critical.

After the collapse of the Mauryan empire (c. 185 BCE) there followed a long period during which a variety of large-scale regional powers existed. These included ruling dynasties originating from within the limits of present-day South Asia (Śuṅga, Sātavāhana, Meghavāhana, Khāravela, Ikṣvāku, Vākāṭaka, Gupta) and others originating from outside (Indo-Greek/Bactrian, Śaka, Indo-Parthian, Kuṣāṇa).

It is difficult in retrospect to know how stable social life was, or appeared to be, for those who lived in South Asia at this time. Looking from a vantage-point two thousand years further on, this looks like a period of political instability for much of the sub-continent, with many areas moving back and forth between the control of one or another regional power. The situation is complicated by historical uncertainties, such as the still not entirely resolved question of the dating of the Kuṣāṇa dynasty (cf. Sims-Williams and Cribb 1996). Some of these dynasties, however, lasted for considerable periods, at least in their core regions. This is particularly true for the two most important powers, the Sātavāhana and the Kuṣāṇa states. The Sātavāhanas lasted

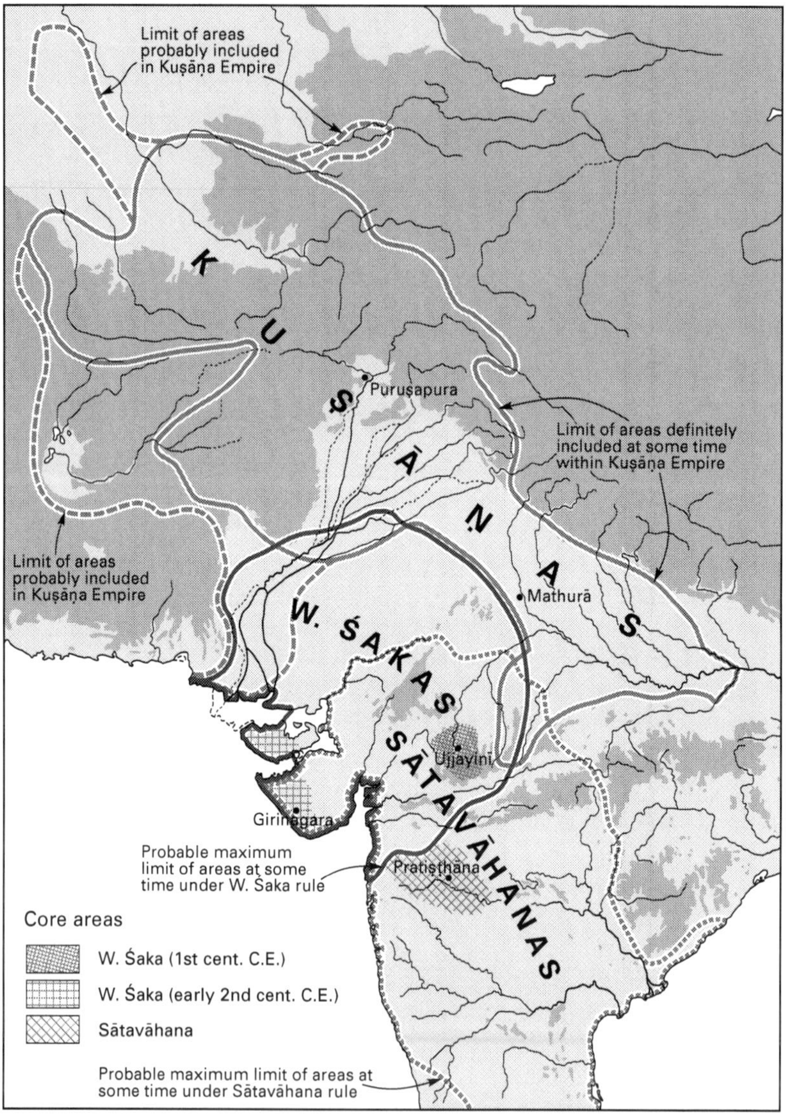

Figure 9.1. Map of Kuṣāṇa and Sātavāhana States, first to third centuries CE

for about two and a half centuries (50 BCE to 200 CE), the Kuṣāṇas for perhaps two centuries (50–250 CE). For much of the first to third centuries, large parts of South Asia were divided between these two major powers. It may have seemed like a period of prosperity and relative peace, especially for many of the inhabitants of the Sātavāhana and Kuṣāṇa states.

The Kuṣāṇa realm extended into Central Asia and this was also a period of extensive trade through to the Parthian and Roman empires to the West and increasingly into Southeast Asia and China to the East. Buddhism was spreading along these trade channels to Central Asia and to China, and other cultural influences were doubtless coming in the reverse direction. Some of India's greatest creative thinkers and artists lived in this period, if we accept the most likely chronologies: these included, for example, the great philosopher Nāgārjuna and the poet Aśvaghoṣa. It was during this period too that the great stūpas at Amarāvatī and Nāgārjunakoṇḍa were erected, and their fragmentary remains bear witness to the immense sophistication of South Asian art and life at this period. We are accustomed to think of Gupta rule as the 'golden age' of Indian artistic and cultural achievement, perhaps because of a later prejudice against the 'foreign' rule of the Indo-Greek, Kuṣāṇa and Śaka dynasties and their patronage of Buddhism, but the achievements of the Gupta period would not have been possible without the foundations, and the cultural hybridisation, of the preceding centuries.

A period of dynastic transition followed in the late third and early fourth centuries, with the situation stabilising again in the fourth century CE, with Gupta control over most of North India, Vākāṭaka rule in Central India and Kuṣāṇa rule continuing for a while in the Northwest. The Guptas and Vākāṭakas[4] were both primarily pro-Brahmanical in their religious preferences, although Buddhism continued to flourish during this period. We can assume a pluralist religious situation, much in fact as has existed in India in more recent times, with individual families, occupational and caste groups affiliated by and large to one or another local version of Brahmanical, Buddhist, or Jaina religion.[5] The Buddhists and other *śramaṇa* groups were probably strongest in the urban areas, among trading and artisan communities, while the Brahmanical lineages gradually gained strength in the countryside as more and more land was gifted to Brahmin families. Buddhist and Jaina shrines and monasteries and Brahmanical temples were

[4] The Vākāṭakas should probably be considered as comprising two separate states, the Eastern Vākāṭakas with their capital at Nandivardana and the Western Vākāṭakas with their capital at Vatsagulma (Kulke 2004). For the Vākāṭakas in general, see Bakker 2004.

[5] Also Ājīvika, though they never seem to have received a high level of state patronage (Basham 1951).

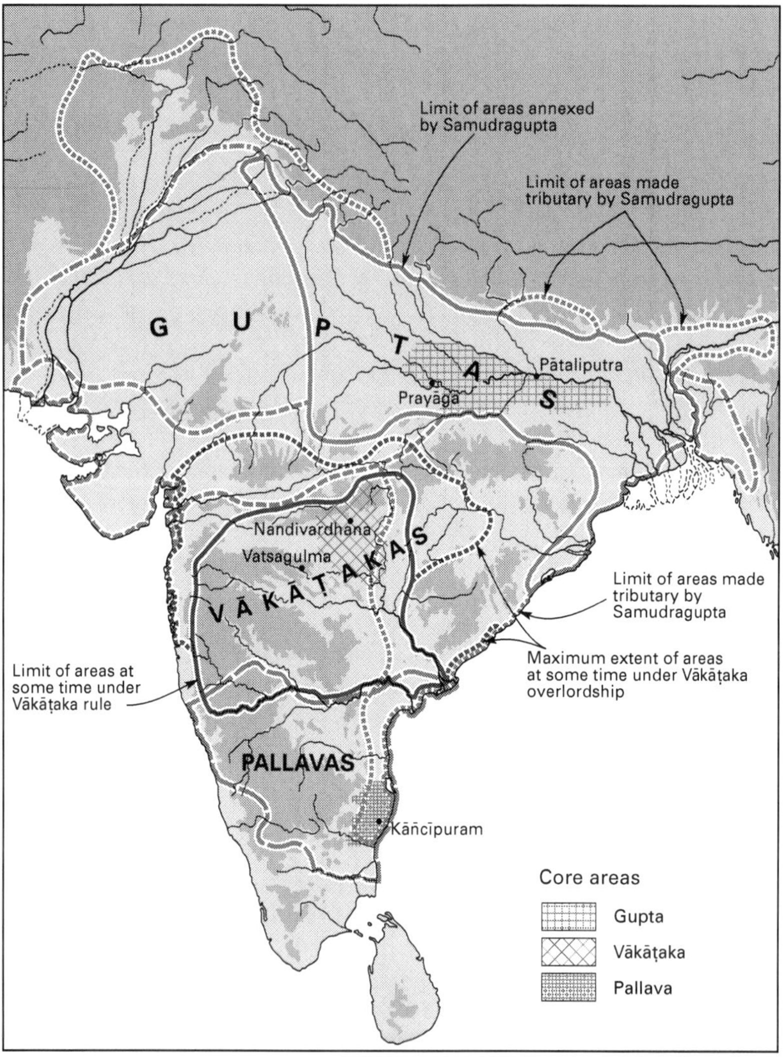

Figure 9.2. Map of Gupta, Vākāṭaka and Pallava States, fourth to sixth centuries CE

scattered throughout the countryside, as no doubt were places of power linked to the various local deities of the *yakṣa* class. The ruling families probably felt some need to patronise all the major traditions, though over time the balance shifted increasingly towards the Brahmins and what was eventually to become Hinduism.

These dynasties ruled over much the same regions that we have been considering in Chapters 4 to 7, and over which the Mauryan empire had ruled, but another important feature of this period is that the newly-established Indic cultural patterns were by now expanding into new regions: Central Asia, South India and Southeast Asia.

Central Asia has already been mentioned: Kuṣāṇa rule, like Indo-Greek rule before it, led to regions such as Bactria and modern Afghanistan being confluences of Indic and Central Asian cultural patterns, with explicitly Buddhist kingdoms being created at locations such as Bāmiyān (Klimburg-Salter 1989). Over the succeeding centuries, the Buddhist regions of Central Asia would arguably make a major contribution to the development of the Mahāyāna and early Vajrayāna. The importance of Gandhāra, the gateway to Central Asia and the location of the great early centre of scholarship at Taxila (Takṣaśīlā), has already been noted in Chapters 3 and 4. Asaṅga and Vasubandhu, two of the greatest of Mahāyāna Buddhist scholars, came from this region (Davidson 2002b: 159–60). The regions beyond Gandhāra were however also significant. It has been plausibly argued that the cult of Maitreya derives in part at least from Iran (Nattier 1988: 45 n.51); the *Avataṃsaka Sūtra* may have been compiled and partly authored 'within the Indic cultural sphere of Central Asia' (P. Williams 1989: 121), while the cult of Mañjuśrī also has strong associations with Inner Asia (Gibson 1997: 43–5). There were also non-Buddhist influences, particularly in the Kuṣāṇa period, and a significant cult of Śiva developed in Bactria (Scott 1993).

By the first and second centuries CE, the Dravidian-speaking regions of the south were also increasingly being incorporated into the general North and Central Indian cultural pattern, as were parts at least of Southeast Asia. The Pallava kingdom in South India was largely Brahmanical in orientation although it included a substantial Jain and Buddhist population, while Indic states were also beginning to develop in Southeast Asia. Tamilnadu was however to remain an important centre for Buddhism for many centuries, with connections to the Buddhists in Sri Lanka.

In South India and Southeast Asia, Indic models of the state were to have a massive impact, and the same can perhaps also be said for areas of Eastern India such as East Bengal and Assam which had arguably been marginal to the previous North Indian cultural complexes. In South India, as in East India, the records of Brahmin settlement, witnessed by land-grant inscriptions, are an important indication of the process of 'Indianisation'. I avoid the term 'Sanskritisation' in this context, since what is involved is the borrowing by a state of a whole model of social organisation, rather than the attempt of a group to raise its own status *vis-à-vis* other groups.

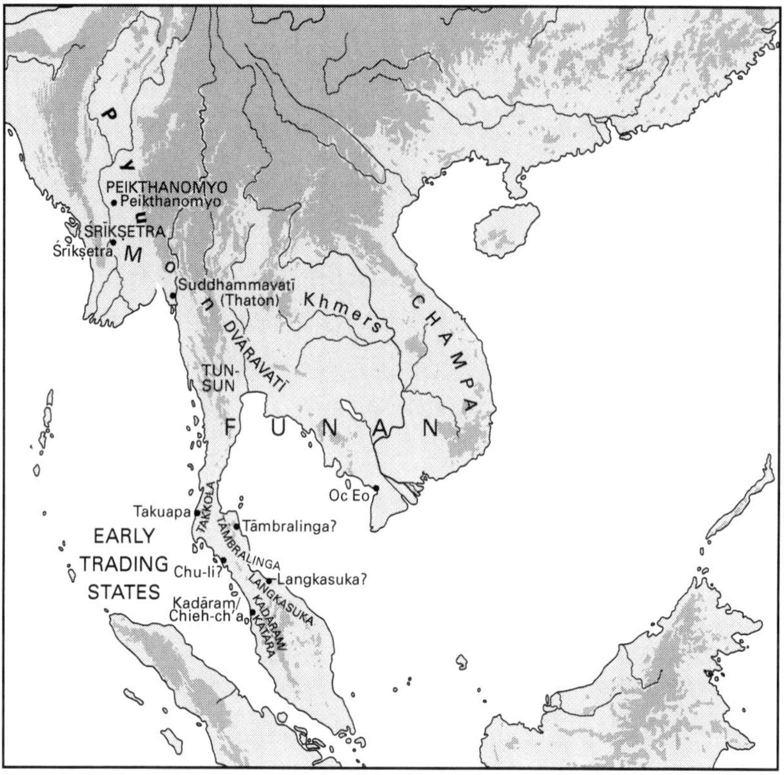

Figure 9.3. Early states in SE Asia to c. 650 CE

However this undoubtedly was a culture closely associated with the Sanskrit language.

While there are differences between South India and Southeast Asia, there is also much to be said for seeing these as parallel developments. The spread of Indian influence through Southeast Asia is a complex process and only partly understood (Coedès 1975; Mabbett 1977a, 1977b; Wheatley 1983; Bentley 1986). Rice cultivation in Southeast Asia would seem to go back at least to the later third millennium BCE, bronze to some date after 1500 BCE, and iron to around 500 BCE. By this stage, Southeast Asia was becoming 'a vital component of an exchange network which linked the Roman and Chinese empires' (Higham 1999: 82).

A number of states developed in the region from around 200 CE onwards, initially at Oc Eo ('Funan') in the lower Mekong delta, later at Dvāravatī in central Thailand, at Angkor in Cambodia, and Champa in present-day coastal Vietnam, among others. In Burma, a group of Pyu city-states belong to the later third century CE onwards, and were linked to the Bengal region through further coastal Mon and Arakanese kingdoms (Stargardt 2000). These states gradually came under Indic cultural influences, incorporating aspects of both Buddhist and Brahmanical religion. As Mabbett rightly notes, 'Indianisation' here was not necessarily a radically different process from similar processes in South Asia proper, particularly in non-Indo-Aryan speaking areas or those without significant local populations claiming Brahmin or *kṣatriya* status:

> India is not an integrated social and cultural unit in which a particular system of ideas controls a system of social behaviour. It is an arena of vastly different groups jostling together, with their several ethnic affinities, languages and cultures, and Sanskrit lore is like a great stain that has spread unevenly throughout the whole, changing its colour repeatedly as it came into contact with different elements. Southeast Asia is the same, and the differences within the two zones are as great as those between. There is no reason in principle why the stain of Sanskrit lore should not spread across into Southeast Asia by the same social processes that advance it in India, growing fainter or more mutable as it recedes further from its original source. There need be no reason why there should be a difference in kind. And the record of 'Indianized' kingdoms is testimony that this is what happened. (Mabbett 1977b: 160)

As the existence of Chinese translations of Buddhist scriptures from the first century CE onwards indicates, Buddhism was also being exported to East Asia. Here, however, there were already well-developed local models of state organisation and Indic models of society and the state had much less impact. Buddhism was regarded as a foreign religion in China and its situation was always vulnerable to nationalist attacks, such as the major persecutions of Buddhists during the later T'ang period (Weinstein 1987, and see Chapter 12 below).

EARLY THEISM: BHĀGAVATA AND ŚAIVA CULTS

A major religious development during this period was the growth of a new kind of conception of the deity. Whatever the differences between Vedic deities and *yakṣa* cults, there is no real evidence that either class of deity was conceived of as a transcendental and all-embracing presence, in the way that Śiva and Viṣṇu were later to be imagined.[6]

[6] Here I am not particularly using 'transcendental' by contrast with 'immanent', but simply to indicate that the deity has taken on a universal and cosmic role. As is well known, Indian philosophical

One can certainly see signs of a movement in this direction in some of the later Brāhmaṇa speculations and the earlier Upaniṣads. Thus, references such as that to the deity Skanda in the *Chāndogya Upaniṣad* (7.26, cf. Olivelle 1998: 166) suggest that the author or authors are constructing a relationship with an independent cult of Skanda.[7] It becomes explicit in texts such as the *Śvetāśvara Upaniṣad* (perhaps second or first century BCE), in which the universal deity is Śiva, or the *Bhagavadgītā* (perhaps first or second century CE), where he is Viṣṇu as revealed through Kṛṣṇa. These texts suggest a coming together of the philosophical and metaphysical tendencies of the Upaniṣads with a commitment to a specific universal deity that derives from other sources. Similarly, I would assume that the authors of the *Śvetāśvara Upaniṣad* and the *Bhagavadgītā* were providing, as it were, a sophisticated metaphysical understanding for deities who had already assumed a considerable importance in the external world.

For all this, our evidence for the cult of these deities from non-textual sources is initially limited. The first sculptural representations of any of the new deities dates from around the first century BCE, either at around the same time as the earliest *yakṣa* imagery or a little later. These early deity images include representations of the Bhāgavata deities, who represent the earliest sculptural phase of the Vaiṣṇava cults. A little later (first and second centuries CE) we also have representations of some of these deities on Indo-Greek coinage.

The origins of the Bhāgavata deities are connected with the Vṛṣṇi people of North India, an initially fairly marginal group who were coming to dominance during the period of the composition of the *Mahābhārata*. The cult of Kṛṣṇa as Vāsudeva seems to have risen to prominence along with them.[8] The main figures are two male warrior deities, Vāsudeva (Kṛṣṇa) and Saṃkarṣaṇa (Balarāma), sometimes expanded through the addition of a goddess, their sister or consort Ekānaṃśa/Nidrā to make the so-called Vṛṣṇi Triad (cf. Couture and Schmid 2001; Yokochi 2004).[9] We have early

traditions developed a variety of ways of conceptualising the relationship between universal deity and devotee in later centuries, including monist, dualist and more complex options.

7 The *Chāndogya Upaniṣad* is generally regarded as one of the earliest Upaniṣads (fifth to fourth centuries BCE, if one accepts the 'late' dating for the Buddha), but this looks like a later addition. Skanda is identified in this text with Sanatkumāra ('Ever-Young'), elsewhere regarded as a form of or a son of Brahmā and apparently a deity associated with the ascetic tradition. Sanatkumāra also occurs in Buddhist texts as a proponent of the Buddha's teachings (e.g. *Dīghanikāya* 19).

8 The grammarian Pāṇini explains the term 'Vāsudevaka' as meaning 'a bhakta [i.e. worshipper or devotee] of Vāsudeva', but as noted in Chapter 2, the dating of Pāṇini is far from certain.

9 For reproductions see Srinivasan 1997, plates 16.13 to 16.15 (Saṃkarṣaṇa/Balarāma), plates 18.10 and 18.11 (Vāsudeva/Kṛṣṇa), plate 16.5 and Couture and Schmid 2001 and p. 181, fig. 1 (Vṛṣṇi Triad).

representations of both Vāsudeva and Saṃkarṣaṇa in a numismatic context, on a coin of Agathocles dated to the first century BCE (Srinivasan 1997, plates 16.6 and 16.7), as well as some early sculptural representations (Srinivasan 1997, plates 16.13–16.15). These are clearly warrior deities, relatively crude figures holding conspicuous weapons. There are also a number of inscriptional references, of which the most famous is the Garuḍa pillar inscription of the Greek ambassador Heliodorus, who styles himself as a Bhāgavata, near Besnagar (Colas 2003: 230–2). The deity Nārāyaṇa, mentioned in some late Vedic texts (Brāhmaṇas and Āraṇyakas) is also associated with Vāsudeva and Saṃkarṣaṇa in some of these inscriptions, though the precise relationship is not clear.

These deities were in time to be brought together with the cult of Viṣṇu, another deity who appears in several hymns in the Ṛgveda, often in association with Indra, as well as in later Vedic texts. These deities came to form a scheme in which Vāsudeva (Kṛṣṇa), Saṃkarṣaṇa, and Kṛṣṇa's son and grandson. Pradyumna and Aniruddha, are all treated as emanations (*vyūha*) of Nārāyaṇa/Viṣṇu as supreme godhead. This is the basis of the later Pāñcarātra ritual tradition, as well as a precursor to the eventual concept of the multiple avatars or divine manifestations of Viṣṇu. As is well known, Kṛṣṇa is also treated as a manifestation of Viṣṇu in the *Bhagavadgītā*, which forms part of the Sanskrit *Mahābhārata*.

Dennis Hudson has suggested in a recent article that the Bhāgavata movement developed ritual procedures that legitimised the role of rulers who were technically *śūdra* or foreign (*mleccha*), and that much of the rise to prominence of Bhāgavata religion can be understood in relation to their association with such rulers (Hudson 2002: 135). Some of his argument depends on an assumption that we can read Pāñcarātra ritual into a considerably earlier period than is usually supposed. If we decide not to follow this part of Hudson's analysis, then his model of the Bhāgavatas as providing ritual services for upwardly-mobile dynasties of questionable origins might apply to later dynasties such as the Guptas and Pallavas rather than to the time of their initial growth. In any case, Brahmin theorists were doubtless working overtime on solutions for problems of this kind from quite an early date, and Viṣṇu was to become in later Indic tradition the deity most centrally associated with royal power and rule.

We find early Śiva images and early forms of the *liṅga*, the phallic representation of Śiva, at around the same time (von Mitterwallner 1984; Srinivasan 1984; N. Joshi 1984), and both Śiva (Oesho = Īśa, one of Śiva's titles) and the warrior-god Skanda figure on Kuṣāṇa coinage, in forms which may reflect some degree of syncretism with Iranian and Bactrian deities (first and second centuries CE).[10] Early depictions of Skanda present him as a warrior deity (e.g. Czuma 1985, pl.93); as noted above, he is mentioned in the *Chāndogya Upaniṣad* and was eventually identified as a son of Śiva.

As usual, the precise dates for these developments are unclear; the spectacular early *liṅga* at Guḍimallam in Andhra Pradesh has been variously dated from third century BCE to fourth century CE (von Mitterwallner 1984: 13 and pl.18; Srinivasan 1997: pl.17.9). However, Śiva had clearly become an important deity associated with royal power by the third and fourth centuries CE. He also became a central figure for the whole complex of ideas that we refer to as 'Tantra' (see Chapter 10). He is traced back to the god Rudra, who appears in the Ṛgveda as a marginal figure, 'the embodiment of wildness and unpredictable danger, he is addressed more with the hope of keeping him at bay than with the wish to bring him near' (O'Flaherty 1981: 219). Another fairly early Vedic text, the *Śatarudriya*, is a litany accompanying offerings to Rudra: Gonda describes it as representing Rudra-Śiva 'in his ambivalent character, both as a malevolent and as a benevolent deity' and notes that Rudra-Śiva in this text is 'unmistakeably on the way to become an All-God' (Gonda 1980: 82).

Perhaps understandably, Śiva is one of the deities in relation to which the conflict between 'orthogenetic' and more complex historical models has been most intense (see e.g. Srinivasan 1997; Bakker 1999, 2001). I do not have anything substantial to add to the controversy on this theme, though it is worth noting that while Śiva is a major figure in the *Mahābhārata*, *liṅga*-worship at any rate has a marginal role in Brahmanical texts until about the fifth and sixth centuries CE (Bakker 2001: 404). This might suggest that *liṅga*-worship was a more popular form of worship, and therefore that a model of multiple origins for Śiva may be more useful than an orthogenetic account. It is also perhaps significant that village gods and goddesses tend to be viewed as forms of Śiva and his consort (Durgā, Kālī, Umā, Pārvatī), rather than as forms of Viṣṇu and his consort (Lakṣmī). As in other areas, part of the genius of Brahmanical thought was to rework whatever it absorbed within its own vocabulary.

What is more relevant for my own argument is the relationship between Viṣṇu, as the deity who became identified with the appropriate and legitimate exercise of power, and Śiva, who maintained an edgier, more dangerous and potentially destructive *persona*. This is not so much a question of 'good' and 'bad' as of 'civilized' and 'uncivilized' forms of power. Viṣṇu, in part at

[10] Joe Cribb has, however, argued against the identification of the 'Oesho' figure with Śiva (1997).

least, represents the incorporation of the ideal of the just king or wisdom king into the Brahmanical model, as his association with Rāma suggests, although like all major Indian deities he is a complex figure who can take on a variety of roles, positive and negative. Śiva seems to have become a deity of royal power at a somewhat later stage, and this development is closely tied up with the development of dangerous and powerful forms of ritual to protect royalty and to support its less peaceful projects; in other words, with the early stages of Tantra. I return to this theme in Chapter 10.

To return to the pre-Kuṣāṇa and Kuṣāṇa context in which we first see these deities, it is worth noting that the distinction between the new deities and the *yakṣa* cults is not necessarily a sharp one. Gods such as Vāsudeva and Saṃkarṣaṇa presumably began as the focus of local cults and only gradually became upgraded and provided with Vedic pedigrees (or, if you prefer, assimilated to Vedic gods). However there is a marked difference in tone; these are clearly warrior gods, and in time gods of universal rule, rather than local protectors. The iconography contrasts too with the *yakṣa* protectors who tend to be presented as corpulent and benevolent, even when serving as 'generals' of *yakṣa* armies (Kubera, Pāñcika). The new deities tend to be young and muscular, with affinities perhaps to the cult of youthful virility that we have noted in the Brahmanical ascetic complex in Chapters 7 and 8.

We can perhaps distinguish between three general areas in the pre-Kuṣāṇa and Kuṣāṇa period, though the limited range of sculptural material from this period means that much may be a question of chance survivals. On the whole, the new deity cults seem to have been focused in the north and in parts of the Deccan.[11] In the Central Gangetic and Eastern region, the dominant deities at this period seem still to have been old-fashioned *yakṣa* deities such as Maṇibhadra (patron of travellers and traders; Thapan 1997) or Vajrapāṇi (protective deity of Rājagṛha, and now a major Buddhist protective deity; Lalou 1956, Lamotte 1966), along with Lakṣmī and her various equivalents (such as Ambikā, Manasā and Padmāvatī). Lakṣmī's cult seems to have been spreading into the northern area, with Chandraketugarh-like reliefs found extensively at Mathura, a major crossroads and point of confluence for different traditions.

Meanwhile, in the Gandhāra region, one finds confluences of Indic and Central Asian gods, such as the cult of Hāritī (with her consort Pāñcika) as deities of fertility and prosperity, overlapping with the cult of Ardoxsho

[11] For Śiva, see Srinivasan 1984 and fig. 1. If the Guḍimallam *liṅga* can really be dated as early as third or second century BCE, as Srinivasan and Mitterwallner 1984 propose, this would provide another site in the southern Deccan.

Figure 9.4. Anointing of Kumāra as Divine General (India, Gupta Period)

and Pharro (e.g. Lerner 1984: 186). There also appear to have been overlaps between Skanda or Kumāra (a young warrior god, who became identified as Śiva's son Kārttikeya) and the Iranian deity Sraoša (Pal 1986–88: vol. 1 no. S41; see also Czuma 1985: No. 93), between Śiva/Oesho, the Iranian wind god Oado and Greek Herakles, and between the Buddhist protective deity Vajrapāṇi, Indra and Herakles (e.g. Klimburg-Salter 1995: 122 & pl.xv). These mutual influences may have had a significant effect on later Indian conceptions of some of these deities, both in terms of the iconography which was only just beginning to develop at this period and the actual conception of the deity. Mathurā was closely connected to the Gandhāra region and the Hārītī/Pāñcika cult was important there as well (Lerner 1984; Czuma 1985; Harle and Topsfield 1987: 11 no. 13; Srinivasan 1989).[12]

[12] As noted in Chapter 5 the evidence for identifying the Gandhāran-Mathurān goddess with Hārītī is limited.

Deities such as Skanda, Śiva and the early Bhāgavata deities were clearly something other than benevolent city-protectors; what we are seeing here goes well beyond the confines of the *yakṣa* religion. For all of the philosophical depth and complexity of Śaivism and Vaiṣṇavism in later times, these deities can perhaps be best understood in this early period as divine patrons of aggressive rulers out to expand their kingdoms.[13] This probably holds for much of the early Gupta period as well.

This helps to explain why, unlike the *yakṣa* deities, these new – or at any rate newly-important – gods are much less tied to a specific local presence. They may and do have local cult centres, but their role is not that of a local deity. They are claimed to have supreme status among the gods. I do not think it is too crude or simplistic to link this with a new model of Brahmanical kingship in which the god is a divine reflection of the king. Indeed, the divine status of the king is a cliché of the Indian political theory of this time, and is clearly related to the supreme status of these new deities.

Thus we see a move from a polytheism, whether Kuru-Pañcāla or Central Gangetic, in which a variety of gods corresponds to a variety of coexisting powers, to a monotheistic or monistic universe in which the king is the god, and everybody and everything else is simply a projection or part of him. The Brahmanical law codes, in mandating the subordination of women, children and younger males to the male head of the household, replicated the same principle at the social level. This generates what the anthropologist McKim Marriott famously referred to as the model of people as 'dividuals' – subordinate parts of a greater whole, and sharing their substance with the wider whole – rather than individuals (Marriott 1979).

This emphasis on the social, and on the individual as subordinated to it, continued to be a strong ideological emphasis within Brahmanical religion into modern times. While one can exaggerate the extent to which it was internalised to produce a radically different personality structure – I think Marriott is taking the texts a little too seriously here – it was undoubtedly also very influential on how people saw themselves in relation to family and community.

THE SANSKRIT EPICS: *MAHĀBHĀRATA* AND *RĀMĀYAṆA*

The *Mahābhārata* and *Rāmāyaṇa*, our most substantial literary documents from the period, are an important source for these political and religious

[13] This is not to deny that, as Srinivasan has pointed out, the iconography and other aspects of the conception of these deities may have owed a considerable amount to the *yakṣa* deities (Srinivasan 1997).

developments. In Chapter 4 I considered some of the mythological material that presumably formed the basis for these two great epic poems, particularly the bodies of legends regarding the Lunar and Solar Dynasties. Here I consider the two epics as finished literary creations. Recent scholarship seems to confirm the picture of the Sanskrit text of the *Mahābhārata* in a form fairly close to the Critical Edition as a relatively integrated work (e.g. Hiltebeitel 2001; Fitzgerald 2004; Hiltebeitel 2004). As far as the *Rāmāyaṇa* is concerned, while there have been plausible attempts to identify earlier and later parts of the text, most notably in recent years by John Brockington (Brockington 1985), my present concern is with the Sanskrit text as a whole. There is no real agreement at this stage on either the absolute dates of these two completed works or on their relative dates. Fitzgerald suggests a shorter version of the *Mahābhārata* in pre-Gupta times, probably between c. 150 CE and 0 CE, followed by a rewriting during the Gupta Empire to produce a version close to the Critical Edition, whereas Hiltebeitel argues for a pre-Gupta (and pre-Common Era) composition for the entire work (Hiltebeitel 2004). There are arguments for placing the *Rāmāyaṇa* before the *Mahābhārata* and also for placing the *Rāmāyaṇa* after the *Mahābhārata*.

The *Rāmāyaṇa* appears to be the more straightforward of the two works. The central character, Rāma, in pre-*Rāmāyaṇa* legend perhaps an epic hero and ideal king of the old Central Gangetic variety, is transformed in the finished *Rāmāyaṇa* into a model for the new Brahmanical god-king. The opening and closing books, generally considered to be among the latest components for those who regard the work as incorporating earlier and later elements, are extensively concerned with articulating this model of kingship.

The *Rāmāyaṇa*'s position, however, though clearly Brahmanical, is a kind of compromise, of which the central marriage between Rāma and Sītā is a key image. Values of wisdom, renunciation and connection with the female powers of the earth are given considerable recognition here, despite the ambiguity created by Rāma's later treatment of Sītā. A similar message is conveyed in Book I of the *Rāmāyaṇa* (the 'Bālakāṇḍa') through the treatment of those old Vedic adversaries, Vāsiṣṭha and Viśvāmitra, who frequently serve as a proxy for opposing positions, particularly concerning relations between Brahmins and *kṣatriya*. Vāsiṣṭha is the court Brahmin of Rāma's father Daśaratha, but it is Viśvāmitra who arrives to request the young Rāma's assistance in dealing with some troublesome *rākṣasas*, so bringing about Rāma's marriage with Sītā and setting the story in motion (I, 17, vv.26ff.). Viśvāmitra, as we are told at length in a later section of

Book I of the *Rāmāyaṇa* (I, 60–4) is a *kṣatriya* who has attained the status of a Brahmin and a *ṛṣi* through his austerities and sacrifices. It hardly seems accidental that he acts, in effect, as matchmaker between Rāma and Sītā, daughter of the wisdom-king lineage of Mithila.[14]

The *Mahābhārata* is the more complex of the two epics. Deciphering its exact relationship to a political context regarding which we have only fairly vague ideas is not easy. The *Mahābhārata* incorporates elements of the 'wisdom king' model which is so central in the *Rāmāyaṇa* but the implicit relationship to Brahmanical authority is different and gives Brahmins a higher place. Yudhiṣṭhira, the main 'wisdom king' figure in the *Mahābhārata*, is a less central and more problematic figure than Rāma, and the renunciate king theme, though present, is also treated in a less positive way.[15] Fitzgerald has suggested that the five Pāṇḍavas can be seen as a divine raiding-party, sent to punish the Kṣatriyas for their rejection of Brahmanical authority.[16] Where the *Rāmāyaṇa* presents a compromise between the old Kuru-Pañcāla-style Brahmins and Central Gangetic wisdom-king values, the *Mahābhārata* has little room for conciliation. At a more general level again, however, both epics endorse a move from the old Vedic model towards a new model based on acceptance of a single supreme deity, and both also present a new conception of kingship, though this is more strongly articulated in the *Rāmāyaṇa*.

The new model incorporates elements of the old Vedic-Brahmanical model of kingship, such as the *aśvamedha* or horse-sacrifice, and there is an obvious concern to legitimise what is going on in terms of the older Brahmanical texts. In reality, though, the model of the tribal chieftain of a pastoralist people that underlay the old Vedic conception, even in its Kuru-Pañcāla recasting, has now been left drastically behind.[17] The Vedic chieftain hoped, through the proper performance of sacrificial rituals on his behalf, for the blessings and favour of Indra and a variety of other members

[14] See White 1991: 78–80 for more on Vāsiṣṭha and Viśvāmitra. Another interesting episode in Book I is Rāma's defeat of the archetypal Bhargava hero, Rāma Jāmadagnya (I, 73–5), which culminates in Rāma Jāmadagnya recognising Rāma as the god Viṣṇu (I, 75, vv 19–20)

[15] Yayāti, the renunciate king who is the subject of an extended episode in Book 1 of the *Mahābhārata*, is an ambivalent figure and hardly presented as a role-model. His renunciation follows on the excessive indulgence of his relationships with Devayānī and Śarmiṣṭhā and his thousand years of youthful pleasure at the expense of his son, Pūru, and he is subsequently thrown out of Indra's heaven for his excessive pride (cf. van Buitenen 1973: 175–210).

[16] See Hiltebeitel 2004: 212 and n. 31. Hiltebeitel appears to endorse this view of the *Mahābhārata* himself, though disagreeing with Fitzgerald in relation to the chronology of the text's composition among other matters.

[17] See also Gitomer 1992, which explores the character of Duryodhana as articulating old and new conceptions of masculinity and leadership.

of a divine pantheon. The new Brahmanical king was a god himself, in the image of a single supreme god of whom other deities were at most aspects or derivatives.

Elements of the Central Gangetic *dharmarāja* model are clearly also reflected in the new conception. The new Brahmanical king incorporated and enforced *dharma* and he, along with his divine patron and reflection, became its source. The newly devised law codes, such as the *Laws of Manu*, provided the basis for these developments.

Obviously, all this had to go along with a new version of religion for the masses of the population, at least those who lived in the towns and cities and the upper social levels of the rural population. The new forms of theism focused on the Vaiṣṇavite deities and on Śiva provided the basis of this new mass religion. They provided the successors of the innovative Brahmins discussed by Lubin (see Chapter 7), with new, more powerful and persuasive concepts and ritual techniques.

The classic statement is of course the *Bhagavadgītā*, often regarded as one of the later additions to the *Mahābhārata*. Here I would follow Norvin Hein, who suggests that the *Gītā* reflects the 'concerns and worries of the Indo-Aryan social leadership' who had become 'distressed . . . by secessions into non-brāhmanical religions and by the flight of disaffected householders from their civic duties into the monastic life' (Hein 1986b: 298). He describes the *Gītā* as

> essentially a great sermon calling the alienated young back to their duties in the brahmanical social order. In it Kṛṣṇa argues that the renunciation that brings salvation is not the repudiation of the world's work but the elimination of self-interest while remaining steadfast in one's earthly duties. (Hein 1986b: 298)

Certainly the *Gītā* is explicit that withdrawal from society is not the way to follow:

> He who does the work which he ought to do without seeking its fruit he is the saṃnyāsin, he is the yogin, not he who does not light the sacred fire, and performs no rites.
>
> What they call renunciation [*saṃnyāsa*], that know to be disciplined activity, O Pāṇḍava (Arjuna), for no one becomes a yogin who has not renounced his (selfish) purpose. (*Bhagavadgītā* 6,1–2, trans. Radhakrishnan 1963: 187)

While the concept of *bhakti* in the sense of devotion to a personal deity is very much part of this new picture, it did not yet carry the emotional content that it would bear at a later stage. This seems, as Fred Hardy has argued in his book *Virāha-Bhakti*, to be a primarily South Indian development, and to belong to a somewhat later period (Hardy 1983; see also Hart 1979). Its progressive adoption in the North can perhaps be linked, as Norvin Hein has argued, to the tensions associated with the enforcement of the new Brahmanical social order (Hein 1986b). Hein has a two-stage model here, with the Kṛṣṇa of the *Bhagavadgītā* and the later sections of the *Mahābhārata* being part of the Brahmanical rethinking which was to bear fruit in the Gupta state and other Hindu monarchies, while the later emphasis on Kṛṣṇa as child or as young lover was a response to the constraints of life after the new Brahmanical state model had been imposed.

The later development of these ideas can be seen in the Purāṇas, the great assemblages of mythology, history, ritual and other material that developed from about the fifth century CE onwards in various parts of South Asia. These texts also developed a new religious geography, prefigured in the *Mahābhārata* and *Rāmāyaṇa*, in which the sacred landscape of India was refigured in terms of the new versions of Brahmanical religion, centred on the new pantheon of great Brahmanical deities. The Purāṇic framework allowed for a great deal of absorption and reworking of local religious material, and the multiplicity of these texts also lead to a *de facto* acceptance of religious coexistence. Whether by choice or necessity, this was a model of religious pluralism, at least between different Brahmanical traditions, and implicitly in relation to the non-Brahmanical traditions, primarily the Buddhists and Jains. This certainly did not exclude local conflict, forced conversions, or worse, but the basic pattern appears to have been one of coexistence between a variety of religious traditions, with families and caste groups having traditional linkages with one or another priestly lineage or order, as indeed they still do in much of modern South Asia.

BUDDHIST DEVELOPMENTS

On the Buddhist side, the Mahāyāna Sūtras with their visions of cosmic Buddhas seem to belong to very much the same world. While Buddhism's fundamental stance in relation to the *samsāric* world of everyday life meant that many things which Brahmanical religion saw as its legitimate concern (such as marriage and the other *saṃskāra* or life cycle rituals, with the exception of death) fell outside the realm of operation of Buddhist clergy, one can see an increasing concern with matters of secular life, of politics and the state. Sūtras such as the *Suvarṇaprabhāsa* discuss the proper behaviour of kings (cf. Emmerick 1970); holy men such as Nāgārjuna wrote, or at least were held to have written, letters of advice to kings (the *Suhṛllekha*, see Kawamura 1975; Fynes 1995: 46). We will see more of these texts in Chapter 12, in relation to their adoption in East Asia. Alexander

Studholme has suggested that the *Kāraṇḍavyūha Sūtra*, dating perhaps from the late fourth or early fifth century, is written in conscious dialogue with contemporary Purāṇic material. This text proposes the Buddhist deity Avalokiteśvara as an appropriate figure for worship as a supreme deity and in particular propounds the teaching of his basic prayer-formula, the famous mantra *oṃ maṇipadme hūṃ* (Studholme 2002).

The Buddhist model of kingship seems to have remained for a long time however that of the *dharmarāja* – the king who rules according to the Buddhist *dharma*, so bringing prosperity to his country, and who patronises the Buddhist *saṅgha* with massive offerings. Deborah Klimburg-Salter has argued this in detail for the Kingdom of Bāmiyān in Afghanistan – the site of the colossal Buddhas destroyed recently by the Taliban (Klimburg-Salter 1989).

Precisely what was meant by the term 'Mahāyāna' is a complex issue, historically clouded by polemic on both the Mahāyāna and Theravāda sides (cf. R. Cohen 1995; Silk 2002; Skilling 2004; Hallisey 1995). The Mahāyāna was never a distinct organisational entity within Indian Buddhism; monks belonged to one or another of the Nikāyas or ordination lineages associated with the various early Buddhist schools. The Chinese pilgrim Yijing notes in his *Record of Buddhist Practices*, dating from 691, that 'Those who worship the Bodhisattvas and read the Mahāyāna Sūtras are called the Mahāyānists, while those who do not perform these are called the Hinayānists' (Silk 2002: 360). In reality, though, there is no single clear defining feature that enables us to distinguish Mahāyānists from others, and it seems likely that many monasteries in India continued through most of the history of Indian Buddhism to have both Mahāyānists, non-Mahāyānists and perhaps also others who would not have seen themselves as clearly within one of the two camps.

At the same time, the Theravāda, as we know it in later times, developed gradually as a conservative movement in Sri Lanka and South India. It appears to have added extra rules to the Vinaya and it undoubtedly edited its early texts in the light of its own developing position, as did all Buddhist schools (Prebish 1996; Collins 1990). As I noted in Chapter 2, there is no reason to regard the version of the early texts redacted in the Pali Canon as any more authoritative or representative of early Buddhism as the parallel texts from other, non-Theravādin Nikāyas. In addition, as Skilling has pointed out, Mahāyāna texts are not necessarily later than Theravāda texts: the earliest bodhisattva sūtras 'were probably composed in the second or first century BCE' (Skilling 2004: 147), and developed Mahāyāna sūtras were already being translated into Chinese in the second half of the second century CE. It is not unreasonable either to suppose that tendencies and modes of thinking that we now see as 'Mahāyāna' may have gone back to early days of the Buddhist tradition (cf. Lindtner 1991–93).

I focused in Chapter 6 on the emergence of monasteries in or near urban centres and it is clear that many of the major Buddhist centres were of this kind. Taxila (Takṣaśīlā), which was a major academic centre for Brahmanical scholarship (Pāṇini and Kauṭilya are both traditionally associated with it) was also a major Buddhist centre with numerous monasteries and *stūpas* (Dar 1993), and the important urban centre of Vidiśā had a large number of monastery and *stūpa* sites within relatively close proximity (Shaw 2000; Shaw and Sutcliffe 2001). As I noted at the start of the chapter, most of the archaeological material refers to sites of this kind; there is little evidence for the extensive presence of Buddhism at the village level, a development which perhaps never really took place in South Asia.[18]

At the same time we should take into account, as Reginald Ray has argued in his *Buddhist Saints in India* (1999), the importance of a tradition of forest-monk practitioners, perhaps centred mainly around the major pilgrimage sites. Certainly such practitioners have been important in more recent times in most Theravādin countries (Tambiah 1984; Carrithers 1983; Taylor 1993; Tiyaranich 1997, 2004; see also Keyes 1987; Lehman 1987; Tambiah 1987). Ray suggests that much of the initial growth of 'Mahāyāna' tendencies may have taken place in these circles, and that the 'Mahāyāna' might be seen as part of a forest response to the process of monasticisation. Thus Ray suggests that we need a threefold model of Buddhism in India, which incorporates urban monastics, forest renunciates and lay people.

Ray's model seems to me to be an important contribution to the debate and to make general sense, although it is difficult to be sure at this distance how clear-cut the distinction was between urban monastics and forest renunciates, and exactly how these divisions might have worked out 'on the ground'. The Chinese reports suggest that by the seventh century 'Mahāyāna' tendencies could be found in a wide variety of monasteries, many of which would presumably have been urban. However, given the apparent importance of visionary techniques and experiences in many 'Mahāyāna' sūtras one might imagine that they would have originated in contexts that were strongly committed to meditative practice, a situation unlikely to occur in a busy urban monastic centre with close links to lay

18 As noted earlier, it seems not to have taken place even in Southeast Asia until the thirteenth century onwards (Keyes 1987: 133). It may have developed earlier in Sri Lanka.

affairs (cf. Beyer 1977; Prebish 1995; McBride 2004). We will look in a little more detail at some of these techniques later in the chapter.

Ray suggests that what we see in the forest traditions is a continuation of a forest-bodhisattva ideal which is represented by the Buddha Śākyamuni himself and which existed among his immediate followers and contemporaries. In this sense, the 'Mahāyānist' forest-renunciates discussed by Ray, and the Mahāyāna itself as an attempt to recapture that early ideal, could be seen as deriving from 'the earliest and most authentic Buddhism' (Ray 1999: 417).

Leaving aside questions of authenticity, Ray's study points to a bifurcation in the Buddhist movement which undoubtedly goes back to early times. This bifurcation was between those parts of the tradition which engaged with urban centres, wealthy lay patrons and local rulers, and in effect developed a form of Buddhist practice which was part of the ongoing process of everyday social life, and those which maintained a renunciate ideal and saw themselves as essentially *outside* of society. In the later Buddhist texts, the figure of Devadatta, the Buddha's cousin and rival, stands for the extreme form of this position, in which only ascetic forest practice is seen as valid. Initially recognised as a saintly figure, Devadatta appears to have become progressively vilified until he becomes an embodiment of evil (Ray 1991: 162–73). However, forest asceticism was never completely prohibited, and the forest renunciate ideal continued to modern times.

Part of the point here can be seen in the association between forest practice, meditation and the acquisition of supernatural power. Some forest monks in more recent times have been charismatic figures whose image of purity, asceticism and magical ability can be channelled and accessed by the state and by the urban elite but which can also be seen as a threat to the state. I have suggested elsewhere that the constant concern with the 'purification of the *saṅgha*' in Theravāda Buddhist history can be seen as being largely about the need to keep charismatic figures under control, and that the gradual marginalisation and prohibition of Tantric approaches in societies dominated by Theravāda Buddhism reflects this need (Samuel 1993: 24–36, 2005: 52–71). In retrospect, I think that I understated in these analyses the extent to which supernatural power remained a major concern within 'Theravāda' societies even in modern times, but the overall argument here still seems to me to be valid. In Indian Buddhist history, as in other Indian renunciate traditions, we can see a continual dialectic between forms of Buddhism which have become more or less assimilated to the needs of the state and of 'respectable' society, and others which position themselves at the edges or outside society as a whole. It seems sense to me to see some of the early Mahāyāna material in these terms, although certainly later forms of the Mahāyāna developed into forms of religion fully compatible with the state and urban society. The same process occurs with the developments of 'Tantric' (Vajrayāna) forms of Buddhism, which initially position themselves in large part outside the world of the large monastic centres and of respectable society, but become progressively integrated within it.

The large monasteries in or near cities would doubtless have been more closely integrated with the political order, in those states where the ruling dynasty patronised Buddhism to a greater or lesser degree. It seems that at Bāmiyān, as in other Buddhist kingdoms of the time, the role of the king as patron of Buddhism was acted out annually through massive festivals in which huge presentations were made to the Buddhist *saṅgha* or monastic community. These were the so-called *pañcāvarṣika* rituals that have been documented widely in the Buddhist states of this period. At Bāmiyān, they were in fact depicted by paintings, which Klimburg-Salter reproduces. Klimburg-Salter suggests that this Buddhist ceremony may have evolved in part 'as a response to the revitalization of ancient Vedic state ceremonies by the Gupta kings' (Klimburg-Salter 1989: 125). In them, the king as a lay Buddhist 'legitimises his own authority as protector of society, including the *saṅgha*'.[19] This is a pattern which has continued into modern times with the Buddhist states of Southeast Asia, though the use of Brahmin priests in Southeast Asian kingdoms, and the popularity of the story of the *Rāmāyaṇa* (and to a lesser extent the *Mahābhārata*) in Southeast Asia indicates that the new Brahmanical model had considerable success even with Buddhist states. The Buddhist Kings of Thailand, after all, chose to name a later capital city, Ayutthaya, after Rāma's capital city of Ayodhyā, as did the rulers of Java (Jogja = Ayodhyā).[20]

As at Bāmiyān, one way to reinforce the message on the Buddhist side was through colossal Buddha statues that insisted visually on the majesty and supremacy of the Buddha. We find these in China too, where gigantic images of the cosmic Buddha were constructed at Yungang in the late fifth century (c. 460–7, during the Northern Wei period) and at Lungmen in the late sixth century, during the reign of the pro-Buddhist Empress Wu.

[19] Walter has discussed the evidence for alternative sets of state ritual procedures on the Buddhist side, such as the agricultural rituals, involving the *rāja* ploughing a furrow around the city, described in many Mahāyāna Sutras as well as in the *Dīpavaṃsa* and *Mahāvaṃsa* (Walter 2000). These are linked to the *pañcāvarṣika* rites, and to the idea of the king as a *cakravartin* (see also Aung-Thwin 1981 for Burma). But in practice even states which were in other respects committed to the support of Buddhism tended to accept much Brahmanical ritual in relation to the kingship, as in Thailand, Laos, Cambodia or Burma into modern times.

[20] In fact, Ayodhyā still forms part of the 'official' full name of the current Thai capital of Bangkok.

These statues are generally taken to represent the cosmic Buddha Vairocana, whom we will return to a little later. Amitābha in the *Saddharmapuṇḍarīka* ('Lotus Sūtra') has a similarly cosmic role, and became the basis of the major form of established state Buddhism in the Far East ('Pure Land' Buddhism).

PHILOSOPHICAL SCHOOLS

On the whole I have kept philosophy or theology in the background in this book. This is not because I think that it is unimportant, but because it has been so much at the centre of many other accounts that it helps to focus elsewhere for once. It is useful however to cast a very brief glance at the evolution of philosophical and theological conceptions throughout this period.[21]

Looking across the Brahmanical and non-Brahmanical traditions, there is an understandable similarity between what is happening in both areas at similar times. Brahmanical schools such as Sāṃkhya and Vaiśeṣika, like the various Buddhist Abhidharma traditions or Jain philosophy, work in terms of enumeration of the constituents of experience; essentially, a refined form of list-making. The Sāṃkhya school, said to have originated with the mysterious *asura*-sage Kapila,[22] was evidently particularly close to yogic circles.[23] All these approaches are based in analyses of experience into a discrete number of fundamental categories, which are regarded as providing the basis of a truer and more spiritually beneficial understanding of the world than is provided by our ordinary perception.

The similarities reinforce the impression we have gained from other material that everybody was operating within the same general climate of thought. There is also a strong impression in many of these systems that experience in the context of meditative practice is a primary element in the development of philosophical concepts, a point made many years ago by Edward Conze (1962: 17–19) and reinforced recently in the case of early Buddhist philosophy by Sue Hamilton (1996, 2000).

The significant resemblances between the two major later Buddhist philosophical schools or groups of schools, Mādhyamika and Yogācāra[24]

[21] On the whole, in India, it is hard to draw a rigid distinction between theology and philosophy, unless one restricts the term theology to philosophical understandings of the more theistic traditions.

[22] On Kapila, see e.g. Bronkhorst 1998a: 69–77. A chapter of the Jaina *Uttarādhyayana Sūtra* is attributed to him and consists on advice for renunciates (Jacobi 1985: 31–5).

[23] In the *Mahābhārata*, the goals of Sāṃkhya and Yoga are often said to be identical: 'that which the yogins see, is the same as is understood by the Sāṃkhyans' (Jacobsen 2005b: 9).

[24] The Yogācāra are also referred to as Cittamatrā ('mind only') and Vijñānavāda.

and the Brahmanical school of Advaita Vedanta have long been noted. Here we see a move away from enumeration towards the assertion of an underlying basis of unity. This move is undoubtedly prefigured in the early Upaniṣads, where *brahman* has already become a universal principle, but its rigorous working out in philosophical terms, whether negative or positive, is a new development and one which seems to have first taken place with Nāgārjuna's theoretical reworking of ideas from the Prajñāpāramitā Sūtras and with the development of alternative perspectives by subsequent Buddhist theoreticians. Nāgārjuna is traditionally dated to the second century CE and the first major Yogācāra scholar, Asaṅga, to the fourth century CE. Possibly the Yogācāra innovations can be linked to the new political situation, though they seem to be prefigured in a group of *sutras* from the third century, such as the *Avataṃsaka*, *Saṃdhinirmocana* and *Laṅkāvatāra* (Warder 1970: 423). Asaṅga himself is said to have been born in Gandhāra: Warder, who dates him from c. 290 to c. 360, suggests that he lived

> in a period of political instability before the new imperial system was completely established, though he may have lived to see the weak remnant of the Kuṣāṇa kingdom invaded by Samudra Gupta and attached to his empire by a rather tenuous form of vassalage. (Warder 1970: 436–7)

Thurman has suggested more recently that Asaṅga and his brother Vasubandhu 'presided over a sizeable expansion of the Buddhist movement in Gupta-dominated India of the fifth and sixth centuries CE' and that a key issue here was that the emphasis on consciousness in the new school made the *bodhisattva* vow, the vow to follow the Buddha's example and achieve enlightenment in order to relieve all beings of their suffering, seem a more meaningful and achievable ideal:

> How difficult it seems to make such a vow in the mind and heart if one is thinking of the 'universe of beings' as an infinite, substantial, external, dense, and heavy bunch of objects! [. . .] But, if the nature of all beings and things is mental, mind-constituted, and mind-created, then a radical transformation of the inner mind, in intersubjective interconnection with other minds, could very well be able to effect a total transformation of everything that exists with a semblance of greater ease. One could then take up the bodhisattva vow with a sense of possibility empowering the compassionate emotion and the messianic determination. (Thurman 2004: xliii)

Advaita Vedānta seems to be a much later development, with Gauḍapāda, the first major Vedāntic teacher, dating perhaps from the eighth century CE and referring back to a variety of Buddhist teachers. What is notable though is the similarity between these schools, all of which tend in one way or another to collapse phenomenal reality into a single substrate or underlying principle. T. R. V. Murti argued some years ago that the three groups of schools were saying essentially the same thing is different languages (Murti 1960). This was an oversimplification, but it points to a significant resemblance.

The shift in ideas from Sāṃkhya, Abhidharma and Jaina theory to these new kinds of approach can surely be correlated with a longer term social, political and religious process in which pluralism (the *mahājanapadas*, the numerous *yakṣa* cults associated with particular cities and places) has been replaced by an assertion of unity (the king claiming universal rule, the single supreme deity). A polytheistic universe, with a multiplicity of deities and powers with whom the individual must negotiate and deal, was being replaced by a monistic one, in which the individual increasingly became simply a separated part of the whole.

I am not suggesting here that we treat philosophy or theology as a simple derivative from politics. If this were the case, then we would have got to Rāmānuja's modified nondualism and Madhva's dualism much more quickly. In any case, it is clear that the philosophers had other things on their mind besides providing an ideology for the newly-emerging state. The Buddhists in particular had reason to avoid too strong a commitment to a supreme inclusive deity-figure. Arguably, they did not really reach this point until the Ādi-Buddha concept came in with the *Kālacakra Tantra* in the early eleventh century.

We can see another aspect of the same developments, however, in the realm of ritual and meditation. Here I turn to look at developments in Buddhist and Brahmanical meditation procedures, and also to consider one of the themes that would later be a central component of the Tantric synthesis: the *maṇḍala*.

MEDITATION IN THE BUDDHIST, BRAHMANICAL, AND JAINA TRADITIONS

The classic manual of the Theravāda tradition, the *Visuddhimagga* ('Path of Purification') of the early fifth-century scholar Buddhaghosa, presents a masterly synthesis of meditation as understood in his day in relation to the Pali Canon (Ñāṇamoli 1991). As for the Mahāyāna, there is a considerable amount of material on early Buddhist meditational procedures in the Mahāyāna sūtras, but it is often difficult to decipher; these texts were not necessarily meant as instructional manuals. They can be supplemented however by other material, such as the fragmentary Sarvāstivāda meditation manual found at Turfan (Schlingloff 1964; see also Karlsson 1999).

Theravāda meditation in the fifth century, if the *Visuddhimagga* can be taken as representative, placed considerable emphasis on the development of *samādhi* (concentration or trance, perhaps better described as a focusing of the body-mind). *Samādhi* here is treated mainly as equivalent to the four *jhānas*[25] and is developed through concentration on simple meditation subjects: a disk of clay (the earth-*kasiṇa*) or representations of the other elements; the foulness of corpses; recollections of the Buddha, Dharma and Sangha; the *brahmavihāras*, and so on (Ñāṇamoli 1991: 85–368). The earth-*kasiṇa* gets most extensive treatment (1991: 118–65); meditation on breathing, the most widespread technique among modern Theravādins along with its modern Burmese variation, awareness of abdominal movement, is also discussed though more briefly (1991: 259–85). The *kasiṇa* is used as a device to stimulate an internal visual image or *nimitta* that becomes the actual object of concentration (cf. Karlsson 1999: 80). A simple and ascetic lifestyle and quiet and peaceful surroundings are an important basis for the practice.

Outside the Theravāda, it seems that a wider range of visualisations developed, including visualisations of the presence of one or another of the Buddhas, with the intention of being in that Buddha's presence and listening to his teachings. These fall within the general category of *buddhānusmṛti* or 'recollection of the Buddha'. This kind of procedure can be seen in one of the first few Mahāyāna sūtras to be translated into Chinese (in the first century CE, perhaps a century or so after it was written), the *Pratyutpannabuddhasaṃmukhāvasthitasamādhi Sūtra* or '*Samādhi* of Direct Encounter with the Buddhas of the Present' (Harrison 1990, cf. also Karlsson 1999: 68–70), a text which is one of our earliest witnesses for the practice of meditation on the Buddha in front of images or paintings (Karlsson 1999: 69).[26] Texts such as the *Amitāyurdhyāna Sūtra* and *Sukhāvatīvyūha Sūtra*, which build up elaborate visualisations of the

[25] There is a second series of formless *jhānas* mentioned in the Sūtras, but it receives much less attention from Buddhaghosa, and one has the impression that these were not very real practices in his day.

[26] It is interesting to note that the *samādhi* which is the central theme of this text is defined not simply in terms of the five standard factors whose presence or absence are diacritic marks for the four *jhānas* (*vitakka, vicāra, pīti, sukha, ekaggatā*) but in terms of a long list of factors – Harrison counts 154 – which form an entire conspectus of the Buddhist path: desire to hear the dharma, unbroken faith in the Buddha's teaching, seeing one's sons and daughters as enemies and one's wife as a demonness (!), not causing schism in the Sangha, not boasting of one's high birth, and so on (Harrison 1990: 26–30). The implication may be that if one achieves this *samādhi*, these qualities and attributes will arise spontaneously.

presence of the Buddha in a heavenly realm, can also be seen as a witness to this kind of practice (cf. also Beyer 1977). Paul Williams and Robert Mayer have discussed how visionary procedures such as those found within the *Pratyutpannabuddhasaṃmukhāvasthitasamādhi Sūtra* may have provided the mechanism by which the Mahāyāna Sūtras in general were received and held to be the authentic word of the Buddhas (Williams 1989: 30; Mayer 1996: 74–5).

It is unclear how far there was an active meditation tradition in the urban monastic setting,[27] but it seems evident that there was a continuing meditation tradition in the 'forest' context and that this focused at least in part on the establishment of visionary contact with the Buddhas of the four directions (particularly Amitābha and Akṣobhya), with the future Buddha Maitreya, perhaps also increasingly with deceased masters of the past (e.g. Nāgārjuna) and with 'Vajrasattva' seen as the essence of all Buddhas. Legends such as that of the revelation of texts to Asaṅga suggest something of this kind of meditation, and indicate that it may also have been associated with long-term ascetic practice in solitude, doubtless conducive to the establishment of visionary contacts of this kind. In other words, this would have been part of Ray's forest monk component, not of the urban context. The recitation of *dhāraṇī* and *mantra* (ritual formulae) would probably also have played a significant role in such practices.

Whether we choose to call this kind of meditation 'Tantric' or 'proto-Tantric', or prefer to avoid the label altogether, is somewhat arbitrary. There is no reason to suppose the employment of sexual practices, let alone the 'transgressive' aspects of *kāpālika*-style practice (see Chapter 10). Nor are there indications of actual identification with the Buddha or other deity. The practice of visualising the presence of one or more Buddhas and receiving instruction in some form from them can be seen as a natural development from earlier forms of *buddhānusmṛti* meditation. To put this in other words, such visualisation and invocation practices formed a significant component to what would later become developed Buddhist Tantra, but they were only one component. (A second component, the *maṇḍala*, is discussed in a subsequent section of this chapter.) The *kriyā* and *caryā* classes of Buddhist Tantras can be seen as a later extension and formalisation of these practices in monastic ritual contexts.

[27] Edward Conze famously commented that the treatment of the path to enlightenment in the *Abhidharmakośa* was 'not a guide to action, but to the reverent contemplation of the achievements of others' (1962: 177). For all of his personal preference for the Mādhyamika, however, he was well aware of the extent to which the Yogācāra tradition derived from ongoing meditative practice (1962: 251–7).

Turning to Brahmanical forms of meditation in this period, the *Yogasūtra* of Patañjali, the classic meditational text of the Brahmanical meditational tradition, has generally been regarded as our chief witness. It has become clear in recent years that it needs to be supplemented by material in other texts such as the *Mahābhārata* and Saṃnyāsa Upaniṣads (Olivelle 1992; Bronkhorst 1993; Brockington 2003b; White 2006).

The references to yoga in the *Mahābhārata* are of particular interest and have been re-examined recently by White (2006) in relation to Upaniṣadic and early medical material. White argues against the frequent modern interpretation of yoga, based in large part on Vivekananda's selective reading of the *Yogasūtra*, as 'a meditative practice through which the absolute was to be found by turning the mind and senses inward, away from the world' (White 2006: 6). Yogic practices are about linkages between the microcosm and macrocosm, and they postulate an 'open' model of the human body, not a closed one.

In particular, White notes that the commonest use of the term 'yoga' in the narrative sections of the *Mahābhārata* is to refer to a dying warrior transferring himself at death to the sphere of the sun through yoga, a practice that links up with Upaniṣadic references to the channel to the crown of the head as the pathway by which one can travel through the solar orb to the World of Brahman (2006: 7). This channel is called *suṣumṇā* in the *Maitri Upaniṣad*, a term that recurs some centuries later in the Tantric context. So do the practices of transferring consciousness at the time of death, still a major concern within Tibetan Tantric practice, where a variety of techniques have been developed and are widely taught for this purpose (*'pho ba* in Tibetan; see e.g. Guenther 1963: 197–201; Brauen-Dolma 1985; Kapstein 1998).

Another theme in the *Mahābhārata* which recurs in later contexts, including both Tibet (Guenther 1963: 201–2) and a well-known Jain meditation manual, the *Yogaśāstra* of Hemacandra (Qvarnström 2002), is that of transferring one's consciousness temporarily or permanently into another human body (White 2006: 8–10).

The *Yogasūtra* of Patañjali in fact refers in passing to both these uses of yoga (White 2006: 10), though the central concerns of this text are more with yoga as a process of isolation from the world. The *Yogasūtra* has noticeable affinities to the *dhyāna* or *jhāna* meditations of the Buddhist tradition and has generally been regarded as strongly influenced by Buddhist meditational procedures, with *samādhi* seen, as in the Buddhist practices, as a state of withdrawal from external concerns and focusing of the body-mind. Rather than seeing this in terms of 'Buddhist influence', we should perhaps again see this more in terms of participation within a shared ascetic sub-culture.[28] Thus the *Yogasūtra* 1.17 defines an initial meditational state (*saṃprajñāta samādhi*) in terms close to the Buddhist definition of the first *dhyāna* state,[29] while 1.33 recommends the practice of the four states (friendliness, compassion, sympathetic joy, equanimity) known in Buddhist texts as the four *brahmavihāra* states (Satyananda 1980: 33, 57).

The dating of the *Yogasūtra* is problematic; Ian Whicher suggests around the second and third centuries CE, while Gavin Flood says 'sometime between 100 BCE and 500 CE' (Flood 1996: 96). Its author, Patañjali, may or may not be the same as the grammarian Patañjali (the general consensus at present appears to be that they are different) and in any case, as we saw in Chapter 2, the dating of the grammarian Patañjali is far from certain. A second to third century CE dating, or a little earlier, would, however, put it alongside the earlier Mahāyāna Sūtras, which makes some sense (see below).

In a series of recent writings (e.g. 1997, 1998, 2002, 2002–3), Ian Whicher has argued that the *Yogasūtra*'s overall position is not a rejection of the world but a 'responsible engagement' with it:

> Contrary to the arguments presented by many scholars, which associate Patañjali's Yoga exclusively with extreme asceticism, mortification, denial, and the renunciation and abandonment of 'material existence' (*prakṛti*) in favour of an elevated and isolated 'spiritual state' (*puruṣa*) or disembodied state of spiritual liberation, I suggest that Patañjali's Yoga can be seen as a responsible engagement, in various ways, of 'spirit' (*puruṣa* = intrinsic identity as Self, pure consciousness) and 'matter' (*prakṛti* = the source of psychophysical being, which includes mind, body, nature) resulting in a highly developed, transformed, and participatory human nature and identity, an integrated and embodied state of liberated selfhood (*jīvanmukti*). (Whicher 2002–3: 619)

As Whicher himself implies, this is somewhat at odds with how later Brahmanical tradition, particularly its modern variants, tends to view the *Yogasūtra*, and his reading has been criticised (e.g. Pflueger 2003). However, Whicher's position has some attractive aspects. For one thing, the third of the *Yogasūtra*'s four parts explains how to develop *samyama*, here a focused and exclusive identification with a specific object of concentration,

[28] Thus the list of six components (*ṣadaṅga*) of yoga, *praṇayāma, pratyāhāra, dhyāna, dharana, tarka*, and *samādhi*, first found in the *Maitrī Upaniṣad*, is adapted and used variously in Brahmanical, Buddhist and Jain contexts, eventually becoming a key component of the Buddhist *Guhyasamājatantra* (Zigmund-Cerbu 1963).

[29] *Saṃprajñāta samādhi* is characterised by the presence of *vitarka* (deliberation), *vicāra* (reflection), *ānanda* (joy) and *asmitā* (sense of individuality), while the first *dhyāna* state is characterised by *vitarka, vicāra, prīti* (joy) and *sukha* (bliss) (Bronkhorst 1993: 22–4, 71–2, 88).

and how to apply this state to a series of 'objects' (mental factors, the body, the *brahmavihāra* states, etc.) in order to develop various powers and knowledges. Many of these have obvious pragmatic utility; there seems little point in developing mind-reading (3.19), the strength of an elephant (3.25), knowledge of the position and movement of the stars (3.28–29) or knowledge of the internal structure of the body (3.30) if one is simply going to reject the world for a 'disembodied state of spiritual liberation'. It is here too that we find the ability to enter another body (3.38) and to travel upwards out of the body, implicitly at the time of death (3.39, cf. White 2006: 10). The achievement of the state of *kaivalya* in the fourth and final section of the *Yogasūtra* also seems to refer to an internal reversal rather than necessarily involving a cessation of existence in the world.

More significantly, perhaps, such a reading brings the *Yogasūtra* and its treatment of Sāṃkhya categories closer to Sue Hamilton's reinterpretation of Buddhist categories as primarily significant in relation to practice (see Chapter 6, and Hamilton 1996, 2000). The yogic practitioner is less concerned with the ontology of 'Spirit' (*puruṣa*) and 'matter' (*prakṛti*) than with the development of yogic states and the consequent inner transformation or reversal. A consistent emphasis on world-rejection is certainly found in major figures of later Indian philosophy such as Śaṅkara but does not need to be read into this earlier period.

The various psychic powers achieved by *samyama* on different objects in the third part of the *Yogasūtra* are reminiscent of the numerous different *samādhis* referred to in some of the Mahāyāna Sūtras dating perhaps from around the same period or slightly later, such as the *Saddharmapuṇḍarīka Sūtra* ('Lotus Sūtra'). The terminology is slightly different, since the *Yogasūtra* regards *samādhi* as one of three stages of *samyama*.[30] The process and result may be quite similar however; compare the practice of *samyama* to achieve a vision of the *siddhas* or masters of the yogic tradition (*Yogasūtra* 3,33) with the *Pratyutpannabuddhasaṃmukhāvasthitasamādhi Sūtra*'s development of the vision of the Buddhas (see above). More generally, the cultivation of these states suggest a pragmatic aspect to the yogic tradition, Brahmanical or Buddhist, in which renunciates, like modern Indian *sādhus*, are expected to have achieved special powers which enable them to help their lay followers and clients.

Little has been written on Jaina meditational practices in this period. As we saw in Chapter 6, the orientation of the Jaina traditions was towards the

[30] The others are *dhāraṇā* (concentration on the object) and *dhyāna* (exclusive focus on the object). *Samādhi*, defined as identity with the object of concentration, is the third and highest stage of the three.

cessation of all activity, above all that of the mind. A series of four meditational states (*śukladhyāna*) seems to have formed part of the path, at least in ideal terms, from early times (Qvarnström 2003: 131–2), although the Jaina appear to have emphasised external ascetic practice as their primary technique; Qvarnström notes that the theoretical requirements for undertaking the *śukladhyāna* are such as to exclude their employment (2003: 140 n. 10). Dundas comments that Jainism 'never fully developed a culture of true meditative contemplation' (Dundas 2002: 166) and that

> It is difficult to avoid the conclusion that later Jain writers discussed the subject only because participation in the pan-Indian socio-religious world made it necessary to do so. (Dundas 2002: 167)

This is perhaps unfair to Hemacandra, who claims in his great twelfth-century work on the Jain path, the *Yogaśāstra*, to be writing at least in part from his own experience. The techniques he describes, however, show signs of the Tantric approaches of Abhinavagupta and of the Nāth Siddha tradition, rather than deriving from earlier Jaina practices (Qvarnström 2002: 12–13, 2003: 134–8). I will return to the *Yogaśāstra* in Chapter 12.

THE *MAṆḌALA*

I turn now to what was eventually to become one of the most conspicuous elements of Tantric practice, the *maṇḍala*. The *maṇḍala* is mostly familiar to us now in the Tantric Buddhist form, particularly in the elaborate versions of the 'Anuttarayoga' practices,[31] culminating in the Kālacakra with its 722 deities (e.g. Bryant 1992; Leidy and Thurman 1997: 98–9). The *yantras* of Śaiva Tantra form a close parallel, and, as we will see, there were also Vaiṣṇava equivalents. However, as Stanley Tambiah, Ronald Davidson and others have pointed out (Tambiah 1985; Davidson 2002a), the *maṇḍala* is also a social model – it retains the meaning of administrative district in modern Indic-derived states such as Thailand (cf. Hanks 1975) – and its early versions were not 'Tantric' in any of the usual meanings of that term.

In fact, *maṇḍala*-type structures appear to go back to quite an early date in the history of Indic religions, and similar structures can be found in many other cultures. I noted this in my book *Mind, Body and Culture*, where I cited Australian Aboriginal examples among others (Samuel 1990: 90, 170

[31] As I explain in Chapter 10, the term 'Anuttarayoga' appears to be based on an incorrect re-translation from Tibetan back into Sanskrit. However, it has become so widely established in the Western-language literature that it would create more confusion not to use it.

n. 4). Nevertheless, there are differences between these various *maṇḍala*-type structures, and an examination of these will be of some significance. The most critical difference, it seems to me, is the extent to which the *maṇḍala*-type structure has a centre, and the degree to which the non-central components are treated as emanations of that centre and reducible to it. This sense of the outer elements as emanations or projections of an underlying unity is an essential component of the fully-developed *maṇḍala* scheme.

Thus, deities associated with the four directions can already be found in early Vedic material. In the *Bṛhadāraṇyaka Upaniṣad* however, we find something different: an underlying unity behind the deities of the directions. Interestingly, it seems to be signalled as new and unusual in the text: Yājnāvalkya explains that he is able to defeat the Brahmins of Kuru and Pañcāla because he knows 'the quarters together with their gods and foundations' (Olivelle 1998: 49 = *Bṛhadāraṇyaka Upaniṣad* 3.9.19). He explains that the Sun (Āditya) in the East is founded on sight, which is founded on visible appearances, and so on the heart (*hṛdaya*); Yama in the South is founded on the sacrifice (*yajña*), which is founded on the sacrificial gift (*dakṣina*), which is founded on faith (*śraddha*) which is again founded on the heart; Varuṇa God of the West is founded on water, semen and again on the heart; the Moon (Soma) in the North on the sacrificial consecration (*dīkṣā*), which is founded on truth (*satya*) and again on the heart. Finally Agni (Fire) at the zenith or centre is founded on speech (*vāc*), which is founded on the heart.

This proto-*maṇḍala*, if we can call it that, is from a Brahmanical context.[32] The earliest Buddhist proto-*maṇḍala* known to me, which is also the first reference to the Buddhist scheme of the four Buddhas of the four directions, is considerably later. It occurs in a well-known and important Mahāyāna sutra (not a specifically 'Tantric' text), the *Suvarṇaprabhāsa Sūtra* or 'Sutra of Golden Light'. This dates to some time before the beginning of the fifth century, since it was translated into Chinese between 414 and 421 CE. In the second chapter of this *sūtra*, the Bodhisattva Ruciraketu (or Śraddhāketu) is meditating on the Buddha – specifically, on why it was that the Buddha Śākyamuni only had an ordinary human life-span of eighty years.

As he does so, his house undergoes a visionary transformation into a vast building made of beryl and with divine jewels and celestial perfumes. Four

[32] For another early *maṇḍala* scheme from a Brahmanical context, of a rather different kind, see the discussion of the Atharvaveda's *Vrātyakāṇḍa* in Chapter 10.

lotus-seats appear in the four directions, with four Buddhas seated upon them: Akṣobhya in the East, Ratnaketu in the South, Amitāyus in the West and Dundubhiśvara in the North. They explain to him that the life-span of the Buddha Śākyamuni was not eighty years; its true limit is far beyond the understanding of any human or divine being. (J. Huntington 1987; also Emmerick 1970: 3–4.)

If this is a reflection of actual meditation practices, as seems likely, then these can be seen as a logical extension of the meditative procedure involving the summoning of the presence of the Buddha that we saw in the *Pratyutpannabuddhasaṃmukhāvasthitasamādhi Sūtra*. This text from the *Suvarṇaprabhāsasūtra* and another text translated into Chinese at around the same time (Matsunaga 1977a: 174) provide the earliest references so far known to a set of four Buddhas in the four directions, although Huntington suggests that we can see hints of such structures in iconography back to the second or first centuries BCE. This schema occurs in many more sūtras over the next couple of centuries. If we add a central Buddha, this yields the five-fold structure that later became familiar as the five-*tathāgata maṇḍala*, and forms a basic core for most later Buddhist *maṇḍalas* (Matsunaga 1977a: 174–5).

On the Vaiṣṇava side, the sculptural expressions of the *vyūha* scheme of the Pāñcarātra system, where deities in the four directions are seen as emanations from an underlying more complete divine nature, would seem to have much the same structure. Our earliest evidence for this scheme may be an image that Doris Meth Srinivasan dates to the first half of the second century BCE on stylistic grounds. As with Huntington, her interpretation may be optimistic, and Hans Bakker has cast some doubts on it (Srinivasan 1979 and 1997; Bakker 1999). The Pāñcarātra tradition did, however, develop a *maṇḍala*-type structure based around the *vyūhas*, with the four directional deities corresponding to four of the Bhāgavata deities, including Kṛṣṇa Vāsudeva himself, Saṃkarṣaṇa, Pradyumna and Aniruddha.

The Bhāgavata deities, as I mentioned earlier, are generally supposed to have begun as tribal deities of the Vṛṣṇis and were later patronised by the Kuṣāṇa kings. In this case one can again the see political point of the imagery as well as its philosophical meaning, particularly if we assume that the Bhāgavata deities started off as deities of different Vṛṣṇi groups and were only gradually incorporated into the *vyūha* scheme.

In any case, the idea of a *maṇḍala* in which the central figure represents a supreme deity, and the directional figures are subordinate aspects, seems a natural development in view of the political situation of the time. It closely reflects the idea of a supreme king at the centre in relation to whom lesser kings are expected to be local projections rather than independent rulers (cf. Davidson 2002a). We can see this at a somewhat later stage, I would suggest, in the imagery of Buddha Vairocana (sometimes replaced by Śākyamuni or Amitābha) at the centre of a *maṇḍala* of eight bodhisattvas, which rapidly became one of the commonest iconographical schemes in China and Tibet from the sixth century onwards (Heller 1994; Leidy 1997: 26–8). Vairocana's imperial imagery clearly proved tempting to rulers of the time.

This is perhaps enough to establish my line of argument. The fully-fledged Tantric *maṇḍala* is a model of a specific kind of state, what Stanley Tambiah has called a *galactic polity* (Tambiah 1985). In such a state, in principle, the centre is reduplicated at the various regional capitals, where local rulers imitate on a lesser scale the splendour of the royal court at the main centre. In reality, of course, the allegiance of the lesser rulers to the main centre may change quite rapidly if the centre is unable to maintain its role. Much of what one is seeing is a kind of theatrical performance, but it is a theatrical performance that suits the interests of both the central and lesser rulers.

One point is worth emphasising though. While these kinds of schemes have conventionally been called 'tantric', we are in a different world here from the kind of wild, aggressive, antinomian, and deliberately shocking imagery that is often associated with Tantra. The origins of this kind of Tantric material are the subject of Chapter 10. Tantra in the sense of the Pāñcarātra or of the Buddhist Tantric texts we are discussing here is about the ritual worship of divine beings who – at least once the new state has been established – are very much aligned with the respectable moral order.

On the Brahmanical side, this kind of imagery allowed for the creation of a whole series of new ritual procedures for the new deities associated with the Brahmanical states of this period. In the Buddhist context, things are not all that different in relation to the 'early' Tantras, those later allocated to the *kriyā* and *caryā* classes. Many of the Tantric texts of this class are not much different from the Mahāyāna Sūtras, except for a greater focus on ritual procedures, and in fact it is not that easy to draw the distinction between *sūtra* and *tantra* at this stage. Several texts that are classified as *tantra* in, for example, the Tibetan canonical collections, are in fact described as *sūtra* in their title, including the principal text for the Vairocana cult, the *Mahāvairocanābhisaṃbodhi Sūtra* (Yamamoto 1990; Wayman and Tajima 1992; Hodge 2003). The Mahāyāna Sūtras from quite an early date placed great emphasis on the cultivation of visionary modes of meditation, and themselves give the appearance of being the result of such modes, as suggested above. These *sūtras* also provided the basis for a whole series of new modes of ritual, in which Buddhist deities who partook directly in the power of the Buddha could be called on for assistance – rather than just *yakṣas* who acted under Buddhist auspices. In other words, one could access the power of the Buddha himself.

I am not suggesting that this was all some vast conspiracy on the part of self-interested Brahmin priests and Buddhist monks to ensure the patronage of the new rulers. One cannot dismiss such possibilities altogether, but as noted elsewhere I would go rather for a model based on what Max Weber called many years ago an 'elective affinity' (Weber 1976). He was talking about the relationship between the Protestant Ethic and the development of early capitalism, and saw these as developing a relationship on the basis of a kind of mutual sympathy. One can imagine something similar here: one can see a wide variety of religious models being elaborated at this time in both Brahmanical and non-Brahmanical contexts. Some of these would prove attractive to the new rulers, and would be supported. However, as rulers and wealthy patrons saw resources that they could use, or religious modes that appealed to their self-image, these resources and modes would gain new prominence, and become more and more part of people's consciousness, in a process of mutual reinforcement. Alternatively, one could regard it as a kind of resonance or mutual harmony, in which increasingly everybody ended up singing the same song, or finding themselves excluded.

These new religious modes allowed for a much closer fit between religion and the new social and political forms that were developing. Over time, the religious, political and social modes of the new Brahmanical state combined into a powerful and convincing mixture that enabled Indic cultural patterns to be widely exported and adopted, indeed to seem the natural way to run a state throughout much of South and Southeast Asia for many centuries.

The 'respectable' and positive aspects of kingship and the state that we have seen in this chapter were, however, only part of the picture. In Chapter 10 we turn to their dark complement, the forces of disorder and misfortune. These too were an important part of the evolving model of the Indic state.

CHAPTER 10

Tantra and the wild goddesses

If much of Chapter 9 dealt with the cult of respectable, high-status deities, linked with the new image of kingship in the new Brahmanical and Buddhist states of the post-Mauryan and the Gupta periods, on both *śramaṇa* (Buddhist) and Brahmanical sides, Chapter 10 introduces religious forms of a less respectable and more ambiguous kind. The practice of these forms of religion was for the most part, initially at least, the preserve of more marginal groups. It will become evident, however, that they were not unimportant for all that, and they were to become more important over the following centuries.

Tantric studies, and especially Tantric historiography, as Urban (1999), Wedemeyer (2001) and others have noted, has, like other fields of study, been historically dominated in various ways by Western fantasy (partly shared by Indian scholars under Western influence). The term itself is problematic, particularly in the Śaiva, Vaiṣṇava and Jaina contexts, though less so for the Buddhists where the Tibetans had an explicit category of works in the canon labelled 'Tantra' (*rgyud*). Many of the Śaiva works that are now customarily labelled 'Tantric' might have been called *kaula* or by other labels, particularly before the tenth and eleventh centuries; *Tantra* as a standard category of Śaiva texts emerged only at a fairly late period.

Defining Tantra remains a problematic business; the articles in Katherine Harper and Robert Brown's collection *The Roots of Tantra* (2002) spend quite a few pages on this topic without providing much enlightenment. Indigenous terminology is not necessarily very useful: *tantrika* in the Brahmanical context can mean not much more than 'non-Vedic', whereas the Tantra sections of the Tibetan Buddhist canon contain a very wide variety of material, varying from the invocation of peaceful deities by quite conventional ritual procedures to practices which, at least in a literal interpretation, are highly transgressive of any kind of conventional morality. It is primarily these transgressive styles of practice with which I am concerned in this chapter.

The first Western scholars to discuss Tantra had little doubt about what the category referred to, or about their attitude to it. The initial theme and one of the most dominant until modern times was outright rejection and condemnation. The oft-quoted comments of William Ward (writing in 1817) sets the tone:

> Many of the tantrus [*sic*] [...] contain directions respecting a most [...] shocking mode of worship. [...] These shastrus [*sic* = *śāstras*] direct that the person [...] must, in the night, choose a woman as the object of worship [...] Here things too abominable to enter the ears of man, and impossible to be revealed to a Christian public, are contained. [...] The priest [...] behaves towards this female in a manner which decency forbids to be mentioned. (Ward, cited in Urban 1999: 128)

What upset Ward above all was presumably the use of sexual practices in Tantric ritual. Ward was a Baptist minister, though from his other writings I suspect that he may not have been quite as prudish as this quote suggests. He may have felt some need though to be cautious in the face of the possible reactions of his 'Christian public'.

Horace Wilson, writing fifteen years later for a more scholarly readership perhaps, takes the other main line, which is polite distance. Certainly he deals with the subject much more calmly, though leaving most of the details safely in Sanskrit. He notes that Ward's account is based on hearsay, but observes that while such practices are 'certainly countenanced by the texts' they are in his opinion 'practised but seldom, and then in solitude and secrecy' (H. Wilson 1832: 225). He comments that

> although the *Chakra* [or Tantric ritual gathering] is said to be not uncommon [...] it is usually nothing more than a convivial party, consisting of the members of a single family, or at which men only are assembled, and the company are glad to eat flesh and drink spirits, under the pretence of a religious observance. (H. Wilson 1832: 225–7)

He also adds that

> In justice to the doctrines of the sect, it is to be observed, that these practices, if instituted merely for sensual gratification, are held to be as illicit and reprehensible, as in any other branch of the Hindu faith. (H. Wilson 1832: 227)

Wilson was right on this point, though whether Tantric *cakras* in the early nineteenth century were really no more than an excuse to indulge in meat and drink is hard to tell at this distance.

In more recent years, of course, the level of scholarship has increased significantly – though Horace Wilson's account as a whole is impressively knowledgeable for 1832, and reminds one that early colonial writers can provide valuable perspectives on the Indian religion of their times, which preceded the great reform movements of the nineteenth century. The main additional option in contemporary discourse however is that we now have a minority of Western yogic and Tantric followers, with affiliations to a variety of Asian traditions, often in forms that have been thoroughly repackaged and redigested for today's world – either in the Asian or Western context. This leads to another kind of rejection of Tantra as presented in the earlier Indian texts, by contemporary scholars who wish to present the tradition in forms more in accord with what they have learned from their lamas or gurus.

The issue of sexual practice remains a problem, both for those who find it objectionable and for those who find it attractive. The problem here is in part that sexuality undoubtedly has different meanings for a contemporary Western or Asian scholar, or a contemporary practitioner of Buddhist or Śaiva Tantra, from those that it had in the period when these practices developed. The physiology of sex is undoubtedly much the same now as it was then, but the meanings attached to the process are not. In particular, while our contemporary concerns tend to focus around immorality, a more important issue at the time was probably that of impurity and pollution. From this point of view, also, there are wide differences between various kinds of sexual practices, and we need to be careful about lumping them all together.

Arguably, while the early *kula* practices considered later in this chapter were regarded as transgressive in their own time, the sex itself was a relatively secondary consideration. What was really at issue was the impurity and pollution attached to sexual substances and the magical power that might in consequence be generated by using them in a transgressive fashion. Later Tantric sexual practices, in both Buddhist and Śaiva traditions, work differently, and sexual practice is used as a way of generating particular kinds of experience that are seen as conducive to the generation of liberating insight. These practices will be discussed in more detail in Chapter 11. Arguably, though, Tantra did not become primarily concerned with the spiritualisation of sex until it came to the West (Samuel 2005a: 345–66).

Modern Western Tantra, for all its dubious lineage and frequent commercialisation, is not necessarily a bad thing, and I have argued elsewhere that it deserves to be taken seriously as a cultural development within Western society (Samuel 2005a: 357–61). However, it is operating in a very different context to the Indic societies we are considering here, and it is at least as much a product of the West and of modernity as of Indic traditions.

We have quite a lot of material, one way or another, on 'transgressive' styles of Tantra. Historically, these transgressive styles of 'Tantra' developed in both Brahmanical (mainly Śaiva) and in Buddhist contexts. Modern Hindu scholars have often tended to blame Tantra on the Buddhists, while Buddhist scholars have either returned the compliment, or argued with varying degrees of plausibility that Buddhist Tantric practice (unlike that of the Hindus) was pure and compassionate, with only the most elevated of aims. In fact, it is easy to find both the elevated pursuit of enlightened consciousness, and the pragmatic exercise of power, on both sides of the Hindu-Buddhist Tantric divide. In any case, Śaivas and Buddhists borrowed extensively from each other, with varying degrees of acknowledgement (Sanderson 1994, 1995, 2001; Bühnemann 1996, 1999, 2000a; see also Davidson 2002a: 202–3, 206, 386 n. 105, 388 n. 120).[1] Vaiṣṇava and Jaina traditions were also involved with 'Tantric' material, although in a more selective way; neither appears to have adopted Tantric practices in transgressive and antinomian form as a pathway to spiritual realisation, although both incorporated elements associated with these practices in less controversial forms.[2]

I doubt that we will ever be able to trace the precise origins of the wild, transgressive, antinomian strain in Tantra in detail. However, we can follow a considerable part of the development of this religious style. The question, I think, is not just that of magical ritual for pragmatic ends. This has been a commonplace in virtually all human societies, and the Vedas, particularly the Atharvaveda, have plenty of examples, as do the Brāhmaṇas and even the Upaniṣads. What I want to understand is rather more specific.

While, as noted above, I have generally avoided the tricky question of defining Tantra, what I am interested in here can, however, be specified relatively easily. We have a body of ritual practices and traditions, in both Buddhist and Śaiva sources, that present themselves as sophisticated and elevated means for the attainment of exalted spiritual goals, yet contain constant reference to practices that seem deliberately transgressive and bizarre:

[1] For other examples of material apparently shared between Śaiva and Buddhist Tantra, see Benard 1994 (and Orofino 1998); Stablein 1976, which presents clearly Śaiva material in a Buddhist context; Schaeffer 2002; Walter 1992, 1996, 2003; White 1996: 72–3. See also White 2005: 9.

[2] For Pāñcarātra body practices, see Flood 2006: 99–119; for equivalent Jaina practices, see Qvarnström 2002, 2003. In later centuries, the Vaiṣṇava Sahajiyā tradition of Bengal employed sexual practices (e.g. Hayes 2003), as did the Bāuls, whose theology was part Vaiṣṇava, part Muslim (see e.g. Salomon 1991; Das 1992). The Jainas used a variety of fierce goddess rituals; for a survey see Cort 1987: 255. There were other traditions apart from those mentioned here that might be included within an extended definition of 'Tantra', for example the Gāṇapatyas, some of whom also engaged in 'transgressive' practices, but our knowledge of them is much more limited (see e.g. Courtright 1985: 218–20; Thapan 1997, esp. 176–97).

night-time orgies in charnel-grounds, involving the eating of human flesh, the use of ornaments, bowls and musical instruments made from human bones, sexual relations while seated on corpses, and the like.

There is little doubt that at least some contemporary practitioners of these traditions are what they claim to be: people whose lives are indeed dedicated to reaching high levels of spiritual attainment, and whose lives are guided by high moral principles. Having said this, there remains, in the Indian context at least, a divide between Tantric practitioners who are now respectable members of the wider society and those who are not. One can find South Indian or Orissan Brahmins who carry out rituals derivative of earlier 'transgressive' modes of practice in ways that are not in the least transgressive, but one can also find naked Aghoris, smeared with ash, eating and drinking from a human skull-cup and dwelling in cremation-grounds and other such unsavoury places. In Indian parlance, this is figured in terms of 'right-hand' and 'left-hand' styles of practice, terms which are rather more loaded in India than they are in the West, since the right hand is used for eating and pure functions, and the left for impure and polluted tasks.

This suggests that, in India, if one looks from *outside* the tradition, transgressive 'Tantric' practices were often viewed quite negatively. This is evident from the mostly negative depictions of early ritual practitioners in the *kāpālika* style as evil, horrifying or comic characters in Sanskrit drama and literature from the sixth or seventh centuries CE onwards.[3] The same cliché is alive and well in Bollywood movies (such as *Nagina*, made as recently as 1986).[4] This negative stereotyping does not, however, mean that people did not consult Tantric ritual practitioners in the past, or that they do not consult them today. Even in societies, like contemporary Tibet or Bali, where Tantric ritual practitioners are indeed highly respected by the lay population among whom they live, much of what they seem to do in practice, at least in relation to lay people, is the performance of pragmatic, this-worldly ritual for the health and well-being of their following.

All this may seem a contradictory situation, but it is perhaps not quite as anomalous as it might seem. At least one component of the mixture, the ambivalent status towards those who are believed to possess magical power, is familiar from recent studies of shamanic practitioners in many different societies. I give a couple of instances. The shamanic practitioners of the Peruvian Amazon, studied a few years ago by Michael Fobes Brown,

[3] With occasional exceptions, as in the sympathetic portrayal of Bhairavācārya in Bāṇa's *Harṣacarita* (Lorenzen 1991: 20).

[4] For a summary of the plot, see Kakar 1990.

are certainly thought of as possessing power, but those who consult them for healing are never sure if they can be trusted to use it on their behalf. Brown transcribes a consultation in which the tension between clients and shaman is palpable, with the husband of one of the women seeking healing threatening the shaman with violence if he does not heal his wife (Brown 1988).[5]

Again, there are tens of thousands of shamanic practitioners in modern Korea, but people consult them, according to a recent study by my former student Kim Chongho, with reluctance and distaste, and only when no other solution is available for their problems (C. Kim 2003). Nobody would admit in respectable company to visiting a shaman or to taking what she has to say (most Korean shamans are women) seriously. Shamanic practice is shameful, dirty and disreputable. To be compelled by the spirits to become a shaman is a real misfortune, and condemns one to the lowest level of Korean society.

Other anthropologists, working, perhaps significantly, for the most part with shamans rather than with their clients, have produced a more positive picture of shamanic ritual and its meanings, although presenting the same basic outlines of the situation (e.g. Kendall 1985, 1988 for Korea). There has been a recent tendency to celebrate shamanism as a Korean art form, and to emphasise the high level of accomplishment of shamanic drama, song and music, although it has had little impact on the situation of most Korean shamans, who continue to be regarded as disreputable and of low status. Nevertheless, the myths told in the songs of the shamans, such as that of Princess Pari, who is a kind of founding ancestor of the shaman tradition, emphasise their compassionate and altruistic nature, and their willingness to undergo suffering for the good of others (T. Kim 1988).

Readers should not be too concerned by the fact that the practitioners in both my examples were called 'shamans' by the anthropologists who studied them. It would be possible to find similar cases with a variety of other labels: *marabouts* in North Africa, perhaps, diviners or *nganga* in Southern Africa, *brujos* or *curanderos* in Latin America. The significant issue is that these are all, indeed, practitioners, with high levels of performative skills, who are carrying out pragmatic services for the surrounding population, yet are not really trusted by them. Also, there are suggestions in many of these cases that there is an 'internal' perspective, held by the practitioners themselves, in which what they do is seen as characterised by high levels of compassion.

[5] Yet Michael Harner, who worked with a closely-related group of shamans, also in the Peruvian Amazon, presents them simply as repositories of tribal wisdom and transmitters of a valuable body of knowledge (Harner 1982).

These people see what they are doing as spiritually rather than materially motivated.[6]

I think that for the earlier, transgressive stages of Tantra we are indeed dealing with magical practitioners who were both valued and feared. What is more surprising, perhaps, is that much Tantric practice, both in India and elsewhere, has become a respectable and valued mode of spiritual activity. I will try to explain how this came about in the course of the following chapters. As the above material suggests, and as I have commented earlier in the book, it is worth taking both 'internal' and 'external' perspectives. In other words, we need to understand why practitioners might see these forms of practice as worthwhile, and we have to understand why those who supported and paid for them thought they were worth supporting.

THE STATE AND THE POWERS OF DARKNESS

I start here with the 'external' perspective, more specifically with the question of why kings and rulers might see this involvement with the dark powers as appropriate and useful. George Hart's suggestions regarding the origins of caste in South India provide a convenient starting point (Hart 1987). I referred to Hart's work briefly in Chapter 4. Hart was dealing with hereditary practitioners, not people who have chosen to take on a renunciate lifestyle, but as we will see the boundaries here are not clearcut; Śaiva Tantric texts speak of *kula* traditions (hereditary or clan traditions) and *kaula* (traditions derived from hereditary or clan traditions), though the precise nature of the *kula* or clans in question is unclear (White 1998, 2003).[7] In fact, kula and kaula are more common labels for these traditions than 'Tantra' itself in the earlier Śaiva context, though I shall continue to use 'Tantra' below for convenience.[8]

Hart argued that the South Indian king was surrounded by a number of ritual specialists from low-status castes (drummers, bards, spirit-mediums, funeral priests, perhaps also priests of the Tamil deity Murugan)

[6] As do such devalued and underpaid secular practitioners as the *dāī* or traditional birth assistants in North India and Bangladesh (Rozario 2002, and Chapter 4 above).

[7] The *kula* in later times is a spiritual clan or lineage rather than one of hereditary practitioners, and it may be possible that this was also true of these early *kula*, though the shift from *kula* to *kaula* would seem to imply a move, as White suggests, from hereditary to spiritual lineage. The idea of a hereditary 'substance' passed down a genealogical lineage may also have existed and was certainly present in Tibet in later times (*gdung brgyud*, cf. Aziz 1978: 53; Samuel 1993: 279, 284). Cf. also Wayman 1961, who sees elements of 'totemic' clans in the Buddhist Tantras.

[8] White prefers to reserve the term for what he refers to as 'high Hindu Tantra', the result of the reforms of Abhinavagupta and others in the eleventh century (White 1998: 173).

who played a crucial role in relation to his power. The king was dependent on these people to maintain his power, and there was a kind of economy of power in which death and misfortune were continually processed into auspiciousness:

> The king can be seen as a sort of massive converter of power: he is supplied with disordered and dangerous power, and, with the proper ceremonies and institutions, he converts that dangerous power to its ordered and auspicious analogue, thus keeping his land in a flourishing condition. This explains one of the most common similes in the early war poems: the comparison of the process of war to agriculture. The enemy army is watered with showers of arrows, then cut down like grain; their bodies are heaped up like haystacks; then their bodies are scattered and trampled with elephants just as the grain is scattered and threshed by the tread of buffaloes. The most unimaginable scenes of death and horror are, like the process of sowing and harvest, the source of future fertility and prosperity. (Hart 1987: 473)

The king's royal battle-drum (*muracu*) was a critical element of his power, so much so that its possession was held actually to confer title to the kingdom. Hart notes that 'the most important element connected with the drum was the god – or spirit – who was supposed to inhabit it, and who had to be kept in the drum and made happy with blood and liquor sacrifice' (Hart 1987: 475).[9]

Thus Hart argues that

> [t]he role of groups 'of low birth' in ancient Tamilnad was to control, or order, dangerous power. [. . .] [they] had an inborn ability to deal with dangerous power, whether in the form of dead spirits or just dangerous power. [. . .] This is why the performers worked in symbiosis with the king: the king had need of the forces that the performers could summon; they fed his nature and made him a proper king, able to lead an army and kill in battle. But only the king could transmute those forces into the beneficial aura that kept disaster away from his kingdom. (Hart 1987: 476–7, 478)

Hart regards the Brahmins, when they arrived in the south in around the third and fourth centuries CE, as having provided a 'new and revolutionary' element; like the low castes, they could be sources of auspicious power, but their power was 'ordered and benevolent' and did not need transmuting and controlling by the king. In addition, it did not depend on the constant warfare that had been endemic in the South until that period; it offered the possibility of a more peaceful social order, resembling that established by the Guptas and other northern dynasties.

Hart's arguments are persuasive in relation to South Indian pre-Brahminical concepts of power and kingship. Where I might differ is in

9 It is worth comparing the hymns to the battle-drum in the Atharvaveda (5.20, 5.21). These provide no indication of ideas of this kind (Stutley 1980: 71–2; Griffith 1916: vol. 1, 220–3).

suggesting that such ideas of the necessity of channeling disordered and transgressive power for the good of society as a whole may already have been present elsewhere in South Asia at this period. In modern times, ritual drummers with clear parallels to those described by Hart are significant within Tibetan societies in Ladakh and Northern Nepal and again form a distinct low-status grouping (see Chapter 4).

In addition, there is plenty of evidence that such ideas were present in North India as well, at least from Gupta times. The *Arthaśāstra*, which was probably compiled between the mid-second and fourth century, clearly endorses the use of sorcery in support of political ends. This appears to have been in particular the role of the royal *purohita*, an Atharvavedan priest who was entrusted with protective rituals on behalf of the king and also with the employment of 'secret practices' in support of his political ends.[10] We will shortly see evidence for Brahmanical ritual of the Gupta period that employed transgressive and destructive powers for political and/or military purposes.

EXERCISING POWER: THE *VRĀTYAKĀṆḌA* OF THE ATHARVAVEDA

First, however, I return to the *vrātyas*, who seem to develop into a 'Vedic' equivalent of Hart's South Indian low castes. As I explained in Chapter 5, the *vrātya* tradition appears to have begun as the performance of a pragmatic and somewhat transgressive ritual by a sub-group of late Vedic society, perhaps an age-grade of young men. We might date this phase to the tenth to eighth centuries BCE on Witzel's chronology. By the time of the Laws of Manu (around first century CE), the *vrātyas* seem to have become a permanent outcaste group. If they still existed as a social reality rather than an abstract category, they presumably continued to make a living as ritual performers.

An Atharvavedic text relating to the *vrātyas* perhaps relates to a stage some way along this hypothetical development. This section of the Atharvaveda, the so-called *Vrātyakāṇḍa*, forms Book Fifteen of the Atharvaveda in the Śaunaka version[11] and consists of a single short text in prose, in a style resembling that of the Brāhmaṇas. It is generally regarded as a late part of the Atharvaveda, so might be dated between the sixth and third centuries BCE.

[10] Michael Willis (personal communication, 2004). I would like to thank Michael Willis for giving me access to some of his research work in this area, which is to be published shortly. On the date of the *Arthaśāstra*, see Willis 2004: 25 n. 114.

[11] The Atharvaveda has been transmitted in two rather different versions, the Śaunaka and Paippālada recensions. Only the first section of the *Vrātyakāṇḍa* is included in the Paippālada version.

The first part of the text describes a *vrātya* who 'rouses' Prajāpati and becomes Mahādeva (presumably meaning Śiva). After this, he is referred to as the Chief *vrātya* and the holder of Indra's bow. In the next section he is described as 'moving' in the four directions, and various occult connections or correspondences are described, much in the style of early Upaniṣads such as the *Bṛhadāraṇyaka* or *Chāndogya*. The *vrātya* then sits on his ritual seat, and further correspondences are stated in the subsequent sections to the components of his seat and to the six seasons of the year. He is provided with six gods as attendants in the four directions, zenith and nadir, and then 'moves' into a series of further directions, with further correspondences including the earth, gods, sacrificial fires and such.[12]

The remaining sections describe how a *vrātya* knowing this knowledge should be treated by kings and other people – in both cases, very respectfully – and provide some additional correspondences, including sets based on his various internal breaths (*prāṇa*) and on parts of his body.

Early Western translators of the Atharvaveda were rather dismissive of this text: Whitney (1905: vol. 2, 770) calls it 'puerile' while Griffith describes it as a 'unique and obscure Book' whose purpose is the 'idealization and hyperbolical glorification of the Vrātya' (Griffith 1916: vol. 2, 185). A more recent translation by Sampurṇānand[13] (1956) treats it essentially as a meditation on the nature of Śiva. I would suggest that it might be both 'glorification of the Vrātya' and 'a meditation on the nature of Śiva'; in other words that it is essentially, at least as far as the first five sections are concerned, a liturgy for the self-identification of a *vrātya* practitioner with Śiva. If read in this way, the resemblance with the much later deity yoga practices of Śaiva and Vajrayāna Tantra is quite striking. The remainder of the text sets up further correspondences that might be used in specific ritual contexts, and also prescribes the appropriate behaviour for kings and other people whom the travelling *vrātya* visits.

If this interpretation of *vrātya* ritual as involving the *vrātya's* self-identification as a deity is plausible,[14] then this is the first example known to me of this significant theme. We can perhaps also see in it an initial occurrence of an important structural relationship that will come up again in later chapters. This is the situation of the renunciate or outsider who is

[12] Thus the text provides another version of an early *maṇḍala* scheme, though of a rather different kind from those discussed in Chapter 9.

[13] I.e. the Hon. Sri Sampurṇānand, who was the Chief Minister of Uttar Pradesh at the time.

[14] Such an interpretation is made more plausible if one thinks of the process of incorporating animal spirits into the body for healing purposes in some South Asian folk healing ('shamanic') traditions (e.g. the Magar, de Sales 1991).

viewed ambivalently or negatively by the surrounding 'respectable' society, while at the same time valued or even viewed as necessary for their ritual services. The members of the outsider group themselves, however, have a different and more positive self-image focused on their possession of spiritual power, and the self-identification with Śiva that seems to be at the core of this text suggests how this might work.

This is a widespread cultural pattern both in South Asia and elsewhere, and it can be seen clearly in cases such as the Pāśupatas and the *kāpālika*-style ascetics (see below). In such contexts, the vocabulary of 'magical power' may be in part a question of conscious trickery, but it is unlikely that it is only this. The performance carries conviction because the members of the outsider group themselves take it seriously to at least some degree, and because they have acquired the genuine skills needed to carry it off.

So far, we have an opening for ritual practitioners, and we have hereditary groups (low caste groups in South India, *vrātya* in the North) filling the role. What is also significant is that we find renunciate ascetic groups taking over similar functions over the following centuries. This is perhaps not entirely surprising. As we have already seen, the renunciates have placed themselves outside society. I suggested in Chapter 6, in relation to the Buddhists and other early *śramaṇa* orders, that renunciate ascetics placed themselves outside ordinary society in formal terms, however closely they might in fact interact with it subsequently. In practice, there was an ongoing dialectic between forms of renunciate practice that became more or less assimilated to the needs of society, and others that positioned themselves at the edges or outside society.

For renunciates who felt it appropriate to operate in the latter, more marginal position, the status of a low-caste practitioner of sorcery and dubious magical practices made some sense as a new identity. It capitalised on the powers associated with ascetic practice, while positioning the renunciate firmly outside respectable society. The early willingness to take over the cult of dead spirits in marginal places outside the cities (see Chapter 6 and deCaroli 2004) suggests that Buddhists initially occupied a somewhat similar role.[15]

[15] This is reflected only to a limited degree in the early Buddhist and Jaina texts. One might explain this in a variety of ways, such as the fact that these aspects of the role were largely taken for granted, or the desire to offer a relatively 'respectable' account at a later point in time when monastic Buddhism was more fully integrated into society. One would not realise from a random sample of modern books on Buddhism that perhaps the most important role of Buddhist monks in many parts of the Buddhist world remains that of dealing with death. Arguments from silence are always risky, but in this case the texts do include at least some indications of such a role (see deCaroli 2004). We might also note that such a role would help to explain the possible derivation of the term *shaman* from

In the next section I look at some of the Śaivite ascetic groups that came to occupy this space.

ŚAIVA ASCETICS: PĀŚUPATAS AND *KĀPĀLIKA*-STYLE ASCETICS

Early ascetic practice in South Asia appears to have been mainly performed by devotees of Śiva and of various forms of the Goddess, all of whom would perhaps have identified generically as Śaivite. This is perhaps not surprising; Śiva, for all of his appropriation as a respectable state deity, has always retained a more transgressive side to his image, later on increasingly expressed through subsidiary gods such as the Bhairava deities, whom we will consider later in this chapter.

Ascetic practice in modern South Asia is still closely linked with Śaivite traditions, although Vaiṣṇava forms of asceticism have become more important in recent centuries. Modern Śaiva ascetics are generally linked to one or another branch of the so-called *Daśanāmī* tradition, which is regarded as going back to the time of Śaṅkara. In reality, the *Daśanāmī* order appears to have taken shape at a considerably more recent time, probably in the late sixteenth or seventeenth century (Clark 2004). Śaiva ascetics however go back to a much earlier period, well before the time of Śaṅkara, who probably lived in the eighth or ninth century CE.

Leaving aside the *vrātya* themselves, who might be regarded as Śaivite or proto-Śaivite ascetics, the earliest group of Śaivite ascetics known to us are the Pāśupatas. The Pāśupatas do not seem, initially at any rate, to have been involved with 'Tantric' religion as such, but they were practitioners of a style of spirituality that involves deliberately shocking behaviour and the conscious courting of disrepute, elements that we also find in the Tantric context.[16]

The Pāśupatas are first mentioned in the *Mahābhārata*[17] and are commonly referred to in the Purāṇas. By the seventh and eighth centuries, we find them being patronised by the rulers of Orissa, where a series of temples in Bhubaneswar have Pāśupata iconography, and also in Southeast

śramaṇa (cf. Harold Bailey, cited in Blacker 1986: 321–2; Menges 1989: 240–1), and the success of Buddhist and Jaina monks as 'middlemen' in relation to marginal territories (Bailey and Mabbett 2003).

16 For general introduction to the Pāśupatas see Lorenzen 1991: 173–92; Ingalls 1962; Donaldson 1987: 284–9; Dyczkowski 1989: 19–26. For more recent material, see Bisschop and Griffiths 2003; Bisschop 2005; Clark 2004: 137–8.

17 In the *Śānti Parvan*, 349.64, though this passage is generally regarded as a late addition, perhaps c. 300–500 CE (Clark 2004: 137).

Asia, where they served as court ritualists for the Khmer kings and, perhaps somewhat later, in Java.[18] Their somewhat legendary founder, Lakulīśa or Nakulīśa, who is regarded as an incarnation of Śiva, is generally placed in around 100 CE, mainly on the grounds of the number of generations required for the lineages of Pāśupata teachers cited in later dateable sources. If Lakulīśa is a legendary rather than historical figure, this becomes a weaker argument, and in any case orally-transmitted lineages can easily lose some early members. Thus the Pāśupatas might well have existed somewhat earlier.

In fact, Daniel Ingalls pointed some years ago to the intriguing resemblances between the Pāśupatas and the classical Greek cult known as the Cynics, who appeared in Athens at around the beginning of the fourth century BCE, though they continued well into the Roman Empire (Ingalls 1962: 281). Both Cynics and Pāśupatas adopted practices that were deliberately intended to attract rejection and dishonour and lead them to be regarded as crazy. These involved wandering from place to place and indulging in deliberately shocking and improper acts. Hercules, who was on earth 'the most trouble-ridden and wretched of men' (Ingalls 1962: 283) but eventually became a god, was regarded as the first teacher of the Cynic tradition: Ingalls notes the similarity in both name and iconography between Hercules (Heracles in Greek) and Lakulīśa. Both are typically depicted holding a club, an attribute that makes little sense for a renunciate ascetic, though it links to Lakulīśa's name (*lakula* = club) (Lorenzen 1991: 173).[19]

Ingalls avoids suggesting any direct connection between the Pāśupatas and the Cynics, but the idea does not seem inherently absurd. David White considers it as a possibility in his book *Myths of the Dog-Man*, noting that the Black Sea region from which the Greek Cynics traced their tradition had trading links to the port of Broach on the Arabian Sea in the first centuries of the common era (White 1991: 104; see also Lorenzen 1991: 178–9). One might also consider the Indo-Greek presence in India from the late fourth century BCE onwards, which could have provided a channel

[18] For the extensive Pāśupata/Lakulīśa iconography in Orissan temples from the seventh century onwards, see Mitra 1984; Donaldson 1987: 288–9; for references to Pāśupatas in Cambodia and Java, see Chapter 12 and Becker 1993.

[19] There are also intriguing overlaps between Hercules imagery and that of the Buddhist deity Vajrapāṇi (e.g. Klimburg-Salter 1995: 122, abb.XV) and between later Lakulīśa imagery and depictions of the Buddha Śākyamuni (Mitra 1984, plates 82, 8396, 106, 108, 110, 125 etc.). I do not have any explanation for these similarities, but they suggest that there were linkages between some of these apparently distant or separate groups of which we now know little or nothing.

at a somewhat earlier date. Clearly, though, if there was a common element to the Cynics and Pāśupatas, there was also a specifically Indic element, and whatever the *vrātya* had become by this time might well have contributed to this.

While we do not have much material directly from Pāśupata circles, there are enough references to give a reasonable picture of their practices, which are classified in terms of a series of stages (*avasthās*) in the practitioner's spiritual development (Lorenzen 1991: 185). The first or 'marked' (*vyakta*) stage involves bathing in ash, living in a temple and performing specified acts of worship, which include laughing, dancing and singing. It is at the second or 'unmarked' stage (*avyakta*) that he leaves the temple and deliberately courts criticism and censure from the public. Ingalls gives an example from Kauṇḍinya's commentary on the *Pāśupata Sūtra* (ch. 3):

> He should take up his stand by a group of women neither too close nor too far away but so that he falls within their sight. Turning his attention to one of them that is young and pretty he should stare at her and act as though he were setting his desire upon her and honouring her. When . . . she looks at him, he should act out the symptoms of love such as straightening his hair, etc. Then every one, women, men and eunuchs will say, 'This is no man of chastity; this is a lecher.' By this false accusation their merit comes to him and his bad karma goes to them . . . (Cited in Ingalls 1962: 290)

We can see the continuity here with practices such as the ox-*vrata* and dog-*vrata* discussed in Chapter 7. The point of this kind of behaviour is to court disrepute, and the logic is given in the last sentence; since the Pāśupata practitioner is not *really* a lecher, and is being falsely accused, he acquires the merit or good karma of the accusers and his own bad karma is transferred to them.

This 'unmarked' stage is transitional, and another way of viewing what is happening here is that the would-be Pāśupata practitioner is placing himself[20] firmly outside conventional society. At later stages, the Pāśupata practitioner is held to achieve the magical powers of a *siddha* or 'accomplished one' (cf. Bisschop 2005). *Siddha* is a term that we will meet again in its specifically Tantric context, but it is significant that the Pāśupata practitioner is expected to gain magical ritual powers that could support a career as an itinerant ritual practitioner or as part of a court ritual establishment. The powers achieved are essentially those of Śiva himself (Bisschop 2005: 542). Thus we seem to have, as with the *vrātya* passage in the Atharvaveda, a

[20] It is unclear whether there were significant numbers of female practitioners among the Pāśupatas, although, as we will see later, *kāpālika*-style practitioners include women as well as men.

ritual identification with Śiva that enables the practitioner to exert various kinds of magical power.

A variety of further Śaiva ascetic groups are described as existing over the next few centuries. In addition to the Pāśupatas and Lakulīśas,[21] we hear of Kāpālikas, Kālāmukhas, Bhairavas and other terms; it is not always clear how far these are distinct groups and how far they are labels applied to these ascetics by others (Lorenzen 1991). The term *kāpālika* in particular seems not to have referred to a distinct order of renunciates, and we should be wary of over-reifying it.[22] However, it was evidently used to refer to a distinct mode of practice and one that seems to have been closely associated with the growth of the more 'extreme' forms of Tantra. These '*kāpālikas*' were regarded as associated with the god Bhairava, a violent and criminal transform of Śiva who appears to continue the inauspicious and dangerous aspects of the late Vedic Rudra-Śiva. It is here too that we appear to find a growing involvement with fierce and dangerous female deities.

These *kāpālika*-style practitioners, as mentioned above, were worshippers of Bhairava. In the later Purāṇas at any rate he is described as an emanation or projection of Śiva, just as Bhairava's consort, the fierce goddess Kālī, is described in the probably eighth-century *Devīmāhātmya* as an emanation of Durgā (Coburn 1982, 1988, 1991; Yokochi 1999). Bhairava, like his followers, the *kāpālika*-style ascetics, is generally depicted as an explicitly transgressive figure, smeared in ashes, living in cremation-grounds, accompanied by dogs, and carrying a skull (*kapāla*), which is where the term *kāpālika* or 'skull-man' comes from. Bhairava does this because, like the *kāpālika*-style ascetics, he is performing the *mahāvrata*, the great *vrata*, vow or mode of behaviour, which is imposed as a penance according to the Brahmanical law codes on the most evil of criminals: the person who has murdered a Brahmin. In Bhairava's case, he is carrying the guilt for Śiva's having destroyed the fifth head of the god Brahmā.

In fact, there are three related sets of ideas here, which occur to some extent separately: We have the *mahāvrata* for Brahmin-killers in the law-codes, which involves wandering around wearing ashes, carrying a skull, living in cremation-grounds and the like. We have the *kāpālika*-style ascetic, who is performing this *mahāvrata* but presumably, in general, has not killed a Brahmin. Lastly, there is Bhairava, who is believed to have performed the

[21] For the later history of the Pāśupata/Lakulīśa grouping in India, see Lorenzen 1991: 107–9. They appear to have moved to the South after the Muslim conquests in the North of India.

[22] White has noted that there 'are no Hindu Tantric scriptures that contain the term kāpālika in their title, or whose authors call themselves Kāpālikas, and there is not a single inscription in all of South Asia that names the Kāpālikas in a way that would indicate an actual sectarian order' (2005: 9).

Figure 10.1. Bhairava. Vidisha Museum

mahāvrata because he cut off Brahmā's fifth head at Śiva's request and so 'killed a Brahmin'.

The law-code is the first of these three to be attested in the literature, but it would seem more natural to suppose that the practice of performing the *mahāvrata* for religious purposes already existed and that the law-code was, as in other cases such as the 'explanations' of various caste-groups as originating from improper marriages between various groups of persons, simply legitimating something that already existed. If Gombrich is right about Aṅgulimāla in the Pali Canon being intended as some kind of early version of the *kāpālika*-style ascetic (Gombrich 1996: 135–64), this is further evidence pointing in the same direction.[23] The Bhairava myth comes from relatively late Purāṇic sources but in a sense closes the circle: the *kāpālika*-style ascetics are approaching the deity Śiva by imitating his aspect Bhairava who is performing the penance.

What the whole complex of ideas does is to 'justify' a stance which is outside society and which involves a radical rejection of social norms. The *kāpālika* type of ascetic behaves like the most despised and contemptible of people in Brahmanical terms, the murderer of a Brahmin. In a sense, there is nowhere further that he can go, and nothing worse that he can do, so he is free to behave more or less outside all social constraints. In reality, *kāpālika*-style ascetics, like everyone else, developed their own modes of social behaviour, which we know mainly from the caricatures in the Brahmanical plays and stories of the times (see e.g. Lorenzen 1991), but also from sources such as the Buddhist *caryāgīti* songs where the Buddhist Tantric yogin takes on the *kāpālika* style of behaviour and consorts with a real or metaphorical low-caste woman (*ḍombī* or *caṇḍālī*):

> Outside the town, o Ḍombī, is your hut; the shaven-headed brahmin boy goes constantly touching you.
>
> Ho Ḍombī! I shall associate with you, I Kāṇha, a kāpāli-yogin, shameless and naked.
>
> One is the lotus, sixty-four its petals; having mounted on it, the poor Ḍombī dances.
>
> Ho Ḍombī! I ask you earnestly: in whose boat, o Ḍombī, do you come and go?
>
> Strings you sell, o Ḍombī, and also baskets; for your sake I have abandoned the actor's box.
>
> Ho! You are a Ḍombī, I a kāpāli. For your sake I have put on the garland of bones.

[23] I am not fully convinced, since, as Sanderson observes (cited in Gombrich 1996: 152 n. 7), we do not know of any later *kāpālika*-style ascetics, as distinct from Śākta devotees, who indulged in murder as part of their religious practice. Aṅgulimāla might conceivably have been intended as some sort of hostile parody of an extreme Śaivite ascetic.

Troubling the pond, the Ḍombī eats lotus-roots – I kill you, o Ḍombī, I take your life! (Kvaerne 1986: 113)

***

I dispelled the three worlds by means of amorous play, having fallen asleep in the sport of sexual union.

How, o Ḍombī, is your coquetry? The noble-born is outside, the kāpālika inside.

By you, o Ḍombī, everything has been disturbed; for no purpose the Moon has been agitated.

Some there are who speak ill of you; (but) those who discern do not remove you from their neck.

Kāṇha sings of the amorous Caṇḍālī; there is no greater harlot than the Ḍombī. (Kvaerne 1986: 150)

These songs, as the commentators point out, are coded descriptions of the practices of sexual Tantra (the lotus-roots are *bodhicitta*; killing the Ḍombī is purifying *avadhūti*, the central psychic channel), but, like the 'Bāul' songs of modern Bengal that are their lineal descendants, the imagery is realistic, and it presupposes a world in which there are *ḍombī* women living outside the town and selling petty goods, and *kāpālika*-style yogins consorting with them.

If our information can be taken at face value, these *kāpālika*-style yogins felt free to indulge in sex and alcohol as part of their spiritual path. What also comes through these accounts is that *kāpālika*-style practitioners were regarded as claiming or actually exercising magical powers, including flying through the air, and that their powers were linked to their relationships with the female spirits and/or human female practitioners known as *yoginīs*, *ḍākinīs* and by other names. These were frightening and dangerous spirits, and they form part of an 'alternative pantheon' of dark and scary female deities associated with Bhairava and his various transforms. We turn now to them. They include such deities as the skeletal witch-figure Cāmuṇḍā, and the goddess who was eventually to become the best known of them all, Kālī.

WILD GODDESSES AND DISEASE GODDESSES

In later contexts, these deities have been somewhat tamed and civilised. Kālī in modern Bengal is seen as a loving mother, though she retains an ambivalent side to her image (S. Gupta 2003; McDermott 1996; McDaniel 2004). In Tibet, the reversal has been more radical; the Tibetan word for *ḍākinī* (*khandroma*) is a highly positive term when applied to a woman, implying a high level of spiritual attainment. In most North Indian vernaculars, however, the term *ḍākinī* or its modern derivatives (such as *ḍāin* in Hindi) means 'witch', in the sense of 'woman who harms people through malevolent spiritual power'. Certainly, in the earlier material, as we will see, these goddesses were seen as both dangerous and malevolent.

I have argued elsewhere that a key element in the growth of 'Tantra' was the gradual transformation of local and regional deity cults through which fierce male and, particularly, female deities came to take a leading role in the place of the *yakṣa* deities (Samuel 2002d; see also Chapter 12). Much of this seems to have taken place between the fifth to eighth centuries CE.

While the new universal deities which I referred to in Chapter 9 became the object of state cults closely related to the role of their new royal patrons, texts such as the *Mahāmāyūrī* (Lévi 1915; Sircar 1971–72) or the various Purāṇic accounts suggest that the *yakṣa*-type deities remained important as patron deities of cities and regions well into the Gupta period. Increasingly, from around the sixth century onwards, we see the emergence of a new deity type, of whom the best-known example in the West is undoubtedly Kālī: fierce, violent deities, wearing flayed human skins, garlands of human heads and the like, surrounded by flames, often portrayed in cremation-grounds or similarly terrifying backgrounds. Not all these deities are shown in such extreme forms, and Kālī herself became a dominant figure at a somewhat later period, but the violent, transgressive nature of the imagery is characteristic.[24]

We can start by asking where these wild, dangerous goddesses came from. The goddess iconography that I referred to in Chapter 5 shows no real sign of a cult of wild or fierce goddesses. Early goddess iconography is relatively gentle. Even the early Kuṣāṇa-period images of what Doris Meth Srinivasan calls the 'Warrior Goddess' (mostly showing the theme later known as Mahiṣamardinī, Durgā killing the buffalo demon), are quite mild (Srinivasan 1997, plates 20.1–7, plates 20.16–19; Divakaran 1984, plate 251) and this continues throughout much of the first millennium CE (e.g. Divakaran 1984, plate 252–6; Harle and Topsfield 1987: 23–4, no.31). Later Durgā imagery is a little more forceful, but it is still a long way away from the violence and horror of some of the imagery of the new deities (e.g. Cāmuṇḍā; Dehejia 1979: 13, 24).

The textual record shows more indication of the fierceness of the new deities, and there have of course been plenty of references to female demons,

[24] Gombrich has pointed to possible early evidence for the goddess Kālī in the Pali Canon (1996: 158–62).

rakṣasīs, and to *yakṣinīs* who also seem quite demonic in their behaviour, in the Buddhist *sūtras* and *jātakas* and similar sources (Sutherland 1991). Some of these stories are of considerable interest, such as the well-known story of the goddess Hāritī, who has already been mentioned in Chapters 5 and 9. Hāritī in the Pali Canon and other Buddhist sources is a demoness who kills and eats small children. One day she loses one of her own five hundred children, and the Buddha brings her to a realisation of the suffering she has caused the mothers of the children she has killed. She becomes a protector of children, and is given regular offerings in the monasteries (e.g. Strong 1992: 36–7; Samuel 2002b: 1–2).

Hāritī's role as child-murderer may be in part Buddhist propaganda against the locally-important cult of a respected deity – Elinor Gadon and Janet Chawla have suggested something similar for Ṣaṣṭhī, who plays a parallel role in the Brahmanical context (Gadon 1997; Chawla 1994). If the large number of images of a mother goddess of fertility and prosperity from Gandhāra, Mathurā and elsewhere have been correctly identified as representations of Hāritī, she would seem to have been a respected deity; her iconography overlaps with both Lakṣmī and the Iranian goddess of prosperity, Ardoxsho, and it is not at all terrifying (see Chapter 5).

The death of young children, however, was a common enough occurrence in pre-modern societies, and there certainly were female demons linked to the illness and death of children at a slightly later date, since they are discussed in early medical texts. In fact, the dangerous new female deities seem closely related to these goddesses of illness who have retained an important role in Indian folk religion into modern times. Often these occur as a set of similar goddesses, described as mothers or sisters, and five, nine or, most often, seven in number (Kosambi 1960; Freed and Freed 1998: 122–36; Mayaram 2000). Some individual goddesses of this class have achieved independent status, the best known being Śītalā, the goddess of smallpox and cholera (e.g. Dimock 1982). Such diseases are seen as a sign of possession by the goddess, who may or may not be willing to let her victim go. In South India, Śītalā's equivalent, Mariamman, is one of a range of *amman* goddesses who are very important in village religion in Tamil areas of India and Sri Lanka. An *amman* goddess is often married to a male god who is the village protector and who also seems to be related to the buffalo killed in village sacrificial rituals to the goddess and in the well-known iconography of the goddess killing the buffalo demon (Biardeau 1989; Brubaker 1983).

Kosambi attempted to trace Brahmanical references in North India for a cult of these mother goddesses and came up with little that is substantial for an early Brahmanical cult (Kosambi 1960). They may well have been present in non-Brahmanical, village religion. The situation in South India, where goddesses with a strong local identity have clearly been assimilated to Durgā/Pārvatī, suggests this, though whether it can be generalised to the rest of South Asia is unclear. It is unclear too how far back the disease-demonesses in the medical literature can be traced back. In Book Three of the *Mahābhārata*, they occur in the context of a narrative about the god Skanda (here the son of Agni, not Śiva), and appear to be conflated with the Pleiades or Kṛttikā sisters, wives of the seven *ṛṣis* (3.214–17, 3.219; see van Buitenen 1975: 650–6; 656–9; White 2003: 35–49). The same narrative also discusses other *graha* ('graspers') who are both male and female and are emanated by Skanda himself (3.219 = 1975: 658–9). *Graha* is also the word for planet, and the planetary deities, who are all male in Brahmanical thought, are again seen as possible sources of illness. All in all, I do not think that it is possible at present to say when the idea of female disease-demons arose, though if it were significant in the Vedic period one would expect more reference to it in sources such as the Atharvaveda, which is very concerned with countering diseases of all kinds. If, as Richard Gombrich has suggested, the move to living in cities was associated with a substantial increase in the incidence of epidemic disease, this may have provided a context for such ideas to originate or become more significant.[25]

In any case, the disease-goddesses and demonesses seem to give us both a plausible source for the female deities of the proto-Tantric complex, and a sense of how they could be seen as powerful and dangerous, feared but also invoked as a protectress. The question of illness might also underlie the idea of the *ḍākinī*; if the human *ḍākinīs* were folk healers from low-status castes such as the modern birth attendants or *dāī*, constantly suspected also of being sorceresses, then their ambivalent role as partners for the male Tantric practitioners, and their elevation to high status in Tibet where this whole complex of ideas was more or less irrelevant, might make sense.[26]

BRAHMANICAL EQUIVALENTS

In fact, there are a couple of sets of Brahmanical goddesses that are worth some attention in relation to this question. These are the Pleiades or Kṛttikā sisters, mentioned above in relation to Skanda (hence his name

[25] The Nine Witch Sisters of the Magar shamans and neighbouring groups provide a 'tribal' equivalent but the presence of influence from literate and urban Tantric traditions here is evident and it would be inadvisable to take current Magar practices as reflecting early conceptions (see de Sales 1991; Oppitz 1978–80, 1981; Maskarinec 1995).

[26] On the concept of the *ḍākinī* see also Herrmann-Pfandt 1992.

Karttikeya), and the Saptamātṛkā ('Seven Little Mother') deities. The Kṛttikā sisters seem to be mainly significant in relatively early texts such as *Mahābhārata*. The Saptamātṛkā goddesses are another matter, and seem to represent a Brahmanical adaptation of a set of seven or nine fierce disease-causing goddesses who are found in different forms throughout South Asia from Tamil Nadu to Nepal (Coburn 1988; Meister 1986; K. Harper 2002). They occur extensively in both Śaivite and Buddhist Tantric contexts.

In these contexts, the Mātṛkā deities, often expanded to eight so as to form the eight members of a circle in the *maṇḍala*, are subordinated to the power of the male deity (or male-female couple) at the centre of the *maṇḍala*, a pattern that would appear to reflect the idea of a male Tantric magician, with or without a female partner, controlling the powers of these deities for magical ritual purposes. A Śaivite example is the *Kulacūḍāmaṇi Tantra* (Finn 1986). Finn dates this text to between the ninth to eleventh centuries CE, probably towards the earlier end, in part on the grounds that the cult of the Saptamātṛkās was at its height between the fifth to eighth centuries, though in the light of Harper's arguments (see below) it may well include earlier elements. The *Kulacūḍāmaṇi Tantra* deals at some length with both Mahiṣamardinī (Durgā as slayer of the buffalo-demon) and the Mātṛkā deities, and is strongly oriented towards this-worldly and pragmatic results. It requires that the female participants in the ritual be identified with specific members of the Mātṛkā deities, which suggests an 'acting out' of the *maṇḍala* similar to that found in the Tantric ritual dance traditions of Nepal and Tibet, which I shall discuss in Chapter 12.

For a Buddhist example, we could cite the *Vidyottama Mahātantra*, discussed by Davidson (2002a: 300–2). Here the Seven Mothers (*sapta mātaraḥ*) offer mantras to the Buddhist Tantric deity Vajrapāṇi, the former *yakṣa* protector of the Magadhan capital of Rājagṛha and of the Buddha who had become by this period a key representation of Tantric power (Snellgrove 1987: 134–41). They explain a series of rituals (*mātṛvidhi*) for protection, including 'overcoming Vināyaka demons and Graha spirits, ruining harvests, spoiling liquor, making an enemy ugly and diseased (but then turning him back again), discovering who one's enemies are, and expelling them' (Davidson 2002a: 302). The ritual includes the making of a painting showing Vajrapāṇi surrounded by the Seven Mothers, whose appearance should be ferocious (2002a: 301). The general structure of a male deity or male–female couple at the centre surrounded by a circle of eight female deities (some of whose names are in this case those of low caste women) is also the basis of the *maṇḍala* of the well-known *Hevajra Tantra* (Snellgrove 1959;

Farrow and Menon 1992; Willemen 1982; Huntingdon and Bangdel 2003: 454–67).[27]

The Saptamātṛkā deities vary somewhat from list to list. In the earliest versions known to us, from the early fifth century, they generally consisted of six *deva-śaktis*, female consorts of major Brahmanical deities, along with the fierce goddess Cāmuṇḍa, and are often, as in the three Saptamātṛkā reliefs at the important early Gupta site of Udayagiri, accompanied by the war-god Skanda (Harper 2002: 117). Katherine Harper has argued that the Saptamātṛkā deities first rose to importance in the context of state sorcery, more specifically the performance of military rituals to aid the Gupta kings in their campaign to expel foreign rulers from India (Harper 2002).

Her argument is based to a considerable degree on an interpretation of the material at Udayagiri. This site is associated in particular with Candragupta II, who visited there in 401–2 and was responsible for the building of a shrine to Śiva that incorporated a relief of the Saptamātṛkās holding a series of emblematic banners. Elsewhere at Udayagiri the banners, which Harper identifies as war-banners, occur twice as a separate set. Harper argues that the Gupta kings kept their usage of such ritual veiled in allusive and indirect language, since they did not want it to fall into hostile hands. If she is right about the meaning of the Saptamātṛkā reliefs, and the frequent occurrence of the Saptamātṛkā in later Tantric contexts suggests that she may be, then this is very early evidence for the aggressive and violent use of 'Tantric'-style ritual.[28] Whether the rituals were at this point conducted by explicitly 'Tantric' priests is perhaps another question. Michael Willis, who has studied this site in detail, has suggested, as noted earlier, that this kind of ritual work would have fallen within the domain of the Royal *purohita*, in origin and by training an Atharvavedic Brahmin priest.[29] We will see evidence in Chapter 12 for the role of the royal *purohita* being taken over at a later stage by explicitly Tantric priests (Sanderson 2004).

If a site such as Udayagiri is the initial context of the Saptamātṛkās as an explicit set of deities used for destructive ritual, how do these deities relate to the disease goddesses? The Saptamātṛkās themselves have respectable

[27] This maṇḍala consists of Hevajra and his consort Nairatmyā at the centre, surrounded by eight female deities: Gaurī (E), Śavarī (SE), Caurī (S), Caṇḍalī (SW), Vetālī (W), Ḍombī (NW), Ghasmarī (N) and Pukkasī (NE).

[28] There is a problem in relation to her argument about the dating of the *Devīmāhātmya*, which is probably much too early (cf. Harper 2002, Yokochi 1999), but this is not critical in relation to the point I am making here.

[29] Willis (personal communication, 2004). For Udayagiri see also Willis 2001, 2004; Dass and Willis 2002.

Brahmanical identities, as wives of the major Brahmanical gods, and only one of the set, Cāmuṇḍā, is particularly terrifying in her appearance, but if we assume that the disease-goddesses were around at or before this time, then it would make sense to see the Saptamātṛkās as a Brahmanical transform of these goddesses, whose purpose was to control disease and misfortune but also to release them on the enemies of the state. This would also fit with the defensive role of the set of eight Mātṛkā deities, who are an expansion of the set of seven Mātṛkās, in Nepalese state ritual, which I will discuss in Chapter 12.

ŚAIVA TANTRA AND THE YOGINĪ CULTS

These practices occur in both Śaiva and Buddhist contexts. I shall return to the specific situation of this borrowing later, but to begin with we might try to make sense of the Śaiva case.

I have suggested already that the Śaiva ascetics were consciously positioning themselves outside of respectable society and thus found themselves among the low-caste and marginal groups such as the performers of magical ritual. The Pāśupata rationalisation of this, as we have seen, was in terms of unloading bad *karma*.[30] The *kāpālika*-style ascetics saw themselves as identifying with Śiva through his negative aspect of Bhairava. We can assume however that a key element in both these cases and with other renunciates is the issue that we have already discussed in Chapter 6, that of the liberating insight. For the 'Tantric' traditions, the transmission of the liberating insight was the function of the guru or spiritual teacher, and a central step was the process of initiation, in which the guru passed on his insight to the initiate. As David Gordon White has pointed out, the initiation here took on a sexual form, in which the initiate consumed the sexual substances (semen and female sexual secretions) produced in ritual intercourse by the guru and his consort, and thus also ingested the essence of the clan or spiritual family (*kula*) (White 1998, 2003). This might, as in modern Tibetan practice, take place symbolically, but the question of 'joining the family' and thus of being in a specific lineage of practice is nevertheless a critical one.

These sexual substances, along with other polluting bodily substances, also provide the offerings needed by the *yoginīs* and other fierce female spirits (Sanderson 1988: 671; White 2003). In modern times, both the 'clan

[30] One might expect them to reject *karma* altogether, and it is a little surprising that the passage cited by Ingalls above speaks of taking on the good *karma* of those who reject them.

essence' and the offerings may be offered in symbolical form, although this is not necessarily always the case.[31]

What, though, was the nature of the 'liberating insight' as understood by these renunciate (and in some later cases also lay) practitioners? In a significant conspectus of the Śaiva systems of Kashmir in the early mediaeval period, Alexis Sanderson notes that Tantric Śaivites in Kashmir at that time were divided between those who adhered to the dualist theology of the Śaiva Siddhānta[32] and those who followed the non-dualist theology of the Trika system. Here one can see among other things the contrast between Tantric practitioners who accepted the validity of antinomian and transgressive practices (the non-dualists) and those who rejected such practices (the dualists, see Sanderson 1995: 17). According to Sanderson, the Trika

> adhered to a nondualistic theology according to which all phenomena are nothing but the spontaneous self-projection of an all-encompassing divine consciousness, so that the substance of the universe and its efficient cause are one and the same. This absolute idealism was formulated and defended by Somānanda (*fl. c.* AD 900–950), Utpaladeva (*fl. c.* AD 925–75), and the latter's commentator Abhinavagupta (*fl. c.* AD 975–1025). The principal works of this philosophical tradition came to be known as the Śāstra of Recognition (Pratyabhijñāśāstra) after their central concept, namely that liberation comes about as the recognition (*pratyabhijñā*) that the true identity of oneself and all phenomena is the Lord (*īśvaraḥ*) defined as this all-containing, autonomous consciousness. (Sanderson 1995: 16)

This is significant, in that it indicates that the identification with Śiva which was originally perhaps intended as a mode of access to magical power is here seen as in itself a liberating insight. What we have here, however, is a discursive and verbal presentation of the nature of the liberating insight, which could be paralleled to other such expressions in Śaiva and non-Śaiva traditions. What was significant for practitioners was not the words ('my true identity is *īśvaraḥ*', etc.) but the inner realisation which scholars in the tradition attempt to describe through those words. It is this inner realisation that the guru attempts to transmit, or rather attempts to provoke the student into achieving for himself or herself.

This is an important point both for the Śaiva tradition and for other traditions, including the Buddhists, and it links to the fact that these are lineages of practice, and that the texts throughout are held to be secondary to the practice lineage as conveyed through the teaching of the guru. A key element here is the secrecy and power of the teaching; not all gurus and

[31] See Hanssen 2002 for a recent account of the use of menstrual blood among Bāuls in Bengal.

[32] As Sanderson notes, Śaiva Siddhānta is nowadays generally used to refer to the South Indian traditions of which this Kashmiri tradition was a predecessor.

lineages are equal, and what we find is a succession of schools of practice, each of which defines itself as superior to the one before.

A related element is that of the *mantra*, which can perhaps be defined in this context as a ritual formula transmitted from guru to student through which the presence of the deity is invoked or compelled. This is linked in Śaiva tradition to a complex theology of the role of sound, seen as a constitutive and creative force through which the manifest universe takes place (e.g. Padoux 1990; Beck 1995).

For the nondualist Śaiva traditions the hierarchical succession of schools of practice has been described in some detail by several authors, including Sanderson himself (Sanderson 1988; see also Dyczkowski 1989; Dupuche 2003; Brooks 1992a). Thus the Śaiva tradition was divided by its textual exponents into the Atimārga, the Outer path, intended for ascetics alone, and the Mantramārga. The Atimārga consisted of the Pāśupata and Lākula division (Sanderson 1988: 664–7); the Lākula here includes the *kāpālika*-style and Kālāmukha ascetics. The Mantramārga is regarded as a higher teaching than that of the Atimārga. It can be practised by householders as well as renunciate ascetics and includes both the Śaiva Siddhānta texts and a series of yet 'higher' teachings, commencing with the Tantras of Bhairava, which are themselves hierarchically subdivided several times further, culminating with the Tantras of the Trika tradition and the highest group of all, the Tantras of the goddess Kālī (Sanderson 1988: 667–9).

The progression from Pāśupata to the Trika and Kālī Tantras involves a progressive shift from male deities to female deities. Thus the Bhairava Tantras are divided into the Mantrapīṭha, which is centred around the cult of the male deity Svacchandabhairava, and the Vidyāpīṭha, which involves the cult of the *yoginīs* or fierce female deities and culminates in the Trika and Kālī cults (Dupuche 2003: 13–14; Sanderson 1988: 672–8).[33] Thus the 'higher' teachings move increasingly into the area of the Śākta cults or Goddess cults and it is the Śākta *pīṭhas*, the sacred sites of the Goddess cults, which become the ideal sites for their performance (Sircar 1973; Banerji 1992: 308ff; Heilijgers-Seelen 1994: 152; Hartzell 1997: 1020–8, 1050–4; Pal 1988). There are strong suggestions of groups of travelling renunciates and lay practitioners meeting at these *pīṭhas* for ritual gatherings, but there are also practices in which the *pīṭhas* are relocated within the practitioner's body. As we will see, the same is true of the Buddhist Tantras.[34]

[33] For other classifications see Dyczkowski 1989.

[34] The role of the so-called *yoginī* temples, a group of open-air, mostly circular temples in central and east India (present-day Madhya Pradesh and Orissa) with images of sixty-four or eighty-one *yoginī* figures arranged in a circle facing towards the centre, within this development is unclear.

It should be noted that this is a logical progression, as viewed from within the tradition, and not necessarily a historical sequence, although to a considerable degree it probably does correspond to a historical succession in which each new school positioned itself as superior to preceding schools. In reality, however, at any given time there were a number of competing traditions, and schools that were of considerable importance at one stage (for example the traditions associated with the deity Tumburu, to which we will return in Chapter 12) might at a later stage be reduced to a marginal position (Sanderson 1988: 669).

In the course of this movement from 'lower' to 'higher' teachings, the role of the female deities also changes, from an entourage surrounding the male practitioner to being the primary objects of worship and identification in their own right. We will consider what this development might mean after looking at what was happening in the non-Śaiva traditions.

It is worth noting here though that one further important development takes place in these 'higher' Tantras. This is the introduction of a system of 'internal' yogic practices based on a subtle anatomy of internal channels (*nāḍī*) and meeting places (*cakra*). In the Śaiva context these practices are explained in terms of the ascension of the deity Kuṇḍalinī through the *cakras* and the consequent untying of knots in the *nāḍī* (e.g. Silburn 1988). These ideas are closely related to the practice of sexual yoga, and they enable a reconceptualisation of the sexual practices so that these are no longer primarily concerned with linking to the tradition or producing food for female spirits but are seen as a practice able to lead to liberating insight in its own right.

This important development also takes place in other Tantric traditions, and will be considered in some detail in Chapter 11.

For the present, though, we might consider what has been something of a point of contention in Tantric studies for many years: what was the original context of the fierce goddess practices? The two broad positions that have been taken are to consider them as part of a 'pan-Indian religious substrate' of some kind, as postulated by Ruegg (1964), an assumption that goes back to Paul Mus (e.g. 1975) and earlier scholars, or to regard them as an essentially 'orthogenetic' development out of the Vedic material. In this case, the first approach would seem to require some kind of pre-existing goddess cult, a Śākta or at least 'proto-Śākta' tradition, which was gradually incorporated into Śaiva and Buddhist practice.

They appear to represent a regional development promoted by ruling dynasties within this general area, presumably with the intention of accessing the power of the *yoginīs* for State political ends (cf. Dehejia 1986).

The disadvantage of this first approach, as Davidson, following Sanderson, notes, is that evidence for such a 'nonaffiliated religious system' is lacking; 'all the personalities, both human and divine, are associated with specific institutionalized lineages and not simply free-floating forms' (Davidson 2002a: 171–2). The problem with the second approach is that the Vedic material simply does not provide the basis for such developments. The Vedas undoubtedly include transgressive practices, sexual rituals and some material about female deities, but the continuity between these and later developments is limited, and easily explainable by the need for Brahmanical and Buddhist scholars to justify their practices in terms of their own previous traditions.

In fact, we seem to see the progressive introduction of Goddess cult material in texts such as the *Harivaṃśa* and the *Skanda Purāṇa*, with deities such as Ekānaṃśa, Koṭavī and Vindhyavāsinī (Couture and Schmid 2001; Couture 2003; Yokochi 2004) showing every sign of having a substantial local history before they enter the Brahmanical mainstream. Thus Yokochi, on the basis of the *Harivaṃśa* and the *Skandapurāṇa*, reconstructs a 'proto-myth' of Vindhyavāsinī, the goddess of the Vindhya mountains, which she regards as initially independent from either Bhāgavata-Vaiṣṇava or Śaiva myths (Yokochi 2004: 83–96). This proto-myth already includes Brahmanical elements in the form Yokochi reconstructs (the demons Sumbha and Nisumbha, an *abhiṣeka* by the Brahmanical gods, Indra's adoption of Vindhyavāsinī as his sister), but it would seem entirely plausible to suppose that it might derive from a pre-Brahmanical cult of a Vindhya mountain goddess.[35]

There are also clear indications, as we have seen above, of potentially malevolent female deities as agents of illness in the *Mahābharata* and in the medical treatises, as well as in the continuing popular religious tradition from all over South Asia. The existence of this popular religious tradition is worth emphasising as a general issue, as well as in the specific context of the cult of disease-goddesses. Its uniformity can be exaggerated, though I think that Paul Mus was by no means entirely mistaken in pointing to common themes throughout and beyond South Asia (Mus 1975, cf. also Samuel 2001a). Its existence though can scarcely be doubted. Even in the modern period, after more than two thousand years of Brahmanical and Sanskritic presence, much of the religion of Indian village society has a strongly local character and is clearly not a simple transform of Vedic and Brahmanical cults (see e.g. Marriott 1969b). This is particularly true in relation to Goddess cults, although a systematic process of assimilation to

[35] On the present-day cult of Vindhyavāsinī, see Humes 1996.

Brahmanical ideas, such as the widespread Durgā-Mahiṣamardinī mythology, is apparent (e.g. Biardeau 1989).

It is important here, as elsewhere, to disaggregate the category of 'Tantra' (and for that matter 'Śākta') since there are several different elements involved in each case. As I have said, local Goddess cults, however limited our direct sources of information, seem to me to be a near-certainty. What is perhaps a different question is the organised presence of pilgrimage sites associated with a widespread Goddess mythology, the so-called Śākta *pīṭhas*.

As is well-known, these are now associated on the Śaiva side with the myth of Dakṣa's sacrifice and the self-immolation of Śiva's consort Satī (=Pārvatī) (e.g. Sircar 1973). The Buddhist mythology associated with these locations is considered briefly later in this chapter. Each of the Śākta *pīṭhas* today consists of a goddess temple, associated with a named form of the goddess, regarded as deriving from a specific part of Satī's body that is held to have fallen to earth at that point, along with a temple of a named aspect of Śiva. Often the Goddess's body-part is associated with a specific natural feature, such as the 'tongue' of flame at Jwālamukhī in the Punjab.[36]

Today, these sites include many of South Asia's most celebrated pilgrimage sites, such as Jwālamukhī (Jālandhara), Hiṅglāj in Pakistan (Baluchistan), Kāmarūpa in Assam or Kalighat in Calcutta (White 1996: 121; Desani 1973; S. Gupta 2003; Morinis 1984). In the Śaiva and Buddhist Tantras from the eighth or ninth centuries onwards we find lists of twenty-four sites, of which four are regarded as of particular importance. The names mentioned vary from list to list, and are not always identifiable, although certain sites are common to most lists (e.g. Davidson 2002a: 206–11; Heilijgers-Seelen 1994: 152). Several cremation-ground locations are also included.

We do not have a clear picture of how this network of pilgrimage sites arose. As Davidson notes, they are not necessarily sites associated with *kāpālika*-style practice, nor are they generally sites with a previous history of Buddhist religious activity. At this stage, I think that we have to leave the question open of the milieu within which this network of sites came into being, and whether it can meaningfully be labelled 'Śākta' in some sense distinct from the general Śaiva milieu with which the sites later became associated. Assuming, however, that these sites had a material reality in the eighth and ninth centuries, it was probably within this general context that many of the specific features of *kaula* and *anuttarayoga* practice developed.

[36] In relation to Jwālamukhī, I am indebted to the unpublished research of Rosemarie Volkmann (personal communication, 2003).

Figure 10.2. Cakreśvarī. Mount Abu

It is possible that we are mistaken in any case in looking for a primarily Śaiva or Buddhist identity. These places may have been from an early stage location where practitioners from different traditions, Śaiva, Buddhist and perhaps also early Sufis, along with 'hereditary' low-caste *kula* specialists, might have gathered for ritual purposes.

BUDDHIST, JAIN AND VAIṢṆAVA TANTRA

In any case, the three major components we have seen, the identification with a fierce male deity, the cult of the fierce goddesses, and the internal 'subtle body' yoga practices, also developed in the Buddhist traditions, and within much the same chronological frame as within the Śaiva traditions. Here, again, there is a hierarchical arrangement of successively more and more profound or powerful styles of practice starting with the *kriyātantra* and *caryātantra* classes and moving on to *yogatantra*, *mahāyogatantra*, etc.[37] It is mainly in the later stages that the new elements enter, in the *mahāyogatantras* and *yoginītantras*.

[37] For the various schemes in which these revelations came to be arranged, cf. Snellgrove 1987, 1988; Orofino 2001; Dalton 2005.

As we saw in Chapters 6 and 9, the basic orientation of the practice of Buddha recollection (*buddhānusmṛti*) as it appears to have developed in 'Mahāyāna' circles was to summon up the Buddhas and communicate with them, but increasingly also to identify with them as a mode of obtaining insight.[38] This perhaps happens more naturally in Buddhism, which is non-dualistic, and where the Buddha is clearly an ideal which people sought to realise from early on.

The early phases of the Buddhist Tantras develop fairly smoothly out of the later Mahāyāna *sūtras* and as mentioned earlier the same text may in some cases be given either label. This is still true, for example, for the *Mahāvairocanābhisaṃbodhi Sūtra* or *Tantra* (Yamamoto 1990; Wayman and Tajima 1992; Hodge 2004), which, Stephen Hodge suggests, appeared in around 640 CE. This text was of major importance both in the Tibetan tradition, where it is the main text of the *caryātantra* class and in East Asia where it forms one of the two principal scriptures of the Shingon or Japanese Tantric tradition.[39]

From the perspective of the contemporary Tibetan tradition of the 'new' or 'reformed' traditions that grew up from the eleventh century onwards, the important subsequent developments are the *yogatantras*, for which the most significant text is the *Sarvatathāgatatattvasaṃgraha* (probably end of seventh century, Matsunaga 1977a: 177–8), and the so-called *anuttarayogatantras*, which are much the most important texts for contemporary Tibetan practitioners.

In fact, the reconstructed Sanskrit term *anuttarayogatantra* is not entirely appropriate, since it is apparently based on a Tibetan misunderstanding.[40] Initially these Tantras fell into two main groups. The first was known as *mahāyoga*, and included texts such as the *Guhyasamāja Tantra* (perhaps

[38] As Hartzell notes, the transition from the situation in the *Suvarṇaprabhāsa Sūtra* (translated into Chinese in the early fifth century CE so probably dating from the fourth century) where the meditator is surrounded by Buddhas in the four directions, and that in the *Mahāvairocanābhisaṃbodhi Sūtra*, where the deity Vairocana takes the central place, still needs to be traced and explained (Hartzell 1997: 278–9). The *Mahāvairocanābhisaṃbodhi* still feels a need to justify and explain the use of a visualised *mandala* of deities (Hodge 2003: 89) but clearly includes the self-identification of the practitioner with the deity (e.g. Hodge 2003: 100, where the Vajra-master transforms himself into Vajrasattva).

[39] The *Mahāvairocanābhisaṃbodhi Sūtra* is known as the *Dainichi-kyô* in Japanese and is one of the two fundamental sūtras of Shingon, the other being the *Kongôchô-gyô* (*Vajraśekhara*), a generic term for a number of texts of which the most important is the *Sarvatathāgatatattvasaṃgraha*, translated into Chinese by Amoghavajra in 753. This is regarded as the principal text of the *yogatantra* class. (Yamasaki 1988: 83–6; Linrothe 1999: 151–8).

[40] See e.g. Isaacson 1998: 28 n. 11. Isaacson suggests *yoganiruttara* as the original form; Orofino gives *yogānuttara* (Orofino 2001: 545). See also English 2002: 5, again citing Isaacson but suggesting the form *yogottara*.

seventh century, though both later and much earlier dates have been suggested)[41] and *Guhyagarbha Tantra* (perhaps early eighth century).[42] The second, probably slightly later, group was known variously as *yoginītantra*, *bhaginītantra* ('sister') or *prajñā* Tantras.[43] A variety of classificatory terms were used in India and Tibet over the next two centuries (cf. Isaacson 1998; Orofino 2001; Dalton 2005). These Yoginī Tantras include the *Hevajra Tantra* (perhaps late eighth or early ninth century), *Cakrasaṃvara Tantra* (sometimes referred to simply as *Saṃvara Tantra*, also probably from the late eighth or early ninth century) and *Kālacakra Tantra* (mid-eleventh century, see Chapter 12).[44] In most of these cases the Tantric cycle is named after the central deity.

We should be wary in all these cases about identifying a particular Tantra with its core text or 'root Tantra'; what is significant for the tradition is more the ongoing practice lineage. The core texts were not necessarily stable, with additional sections being added and earlier components modified for some time, and in some cases, as with the *Guhyasamāja Tantra*, divergent traditions of practice developed (Matsunaga 1977b; Wayman 1977; Wedemeyer 1999, 2002, in press).

The *Guhyasamāja Tantra* was classified as part of the *mahāyogatantra* group, as was another important work that has only survived in Tibetan translation, the *Guhyagarbha Tantra* (Dorje 1987). As mentioned, the dating of the *Guhyasamāja Tantra* is controversial. It gives the impression of being an early text. The central deities of the *Guhyasamāja Tantra* (Fig. 10.3) are relatively normal Buddha-forms with extra arms and attributes, unlike the innovative and clearly Śaiva-influenced deities of the later *yoginī* Tantras. The teachings in the *Guhyasamāja Tantra* seem to be presented in such a way as to maximise their transgressive and antinomian nature:

> [T]hose who take life, who take pleasure in lying, who always covet the wealth of others, who enjoy making love, who purposely consume faeces and urine, these are worthy ones for the practice. The yogin who makes love to his mother, sister or daughter achieves enormous success in the supreme truth *(dharmatā)* of the Mahāyāna. (Snellgrove 1987: 170–1)

[41] See discussion in Linrothe 1999: 241–3; Wedemeyer 2001.

[42] On the *Guhyagarbha*, which contains an early version of the *maṇḍalas* of the Peaceful and Fierce Deities familiar from the later Tibetan *bar-do* visualisations, see Dorje 1987; Blezer 1997: 39–56.

[43] *Bhaginī* means 'sister'. *Prajñā* means 'wisdom' or 'insight', but is probably also in this context a code term for the female partner.

[44] Complete or partial English translations are available of all of these texts. Fremantle 1971 for the *Guhyasamāja Tantra* (there is also a German translation, Gäng 1988); Snellgrove 1959, Farrow and Menon 1992 and Willemen 1982 for the *Hevajra Tantra*, Gray 2001 and 2007 for the *Cakrasaṃvara Tantra*; Newman 1987, Wallace 2004, Andresen 1997 and Hartzell 1997 for various sections of the *Kālacakra Tantra*.

Figure 10.3. Guhyasamāja. Vajrabhairava Temple, Tsaparang, Western Tibet

Perhaps not surprisingly, the audience of Bodhisattvas is terrified, falls into a swoon and has to be magically revived by the Buddha.

These references to apparently antinomian behaviour, however, do not appear to be meant literally; the *Guhyasamāja Tantra* certainly teaches practices of sexual yoga, which were perhaps already current in pre-Tantric lay Buddhist circles (see Chapter 11) but the references to taking life, lying, consuming faeces and urine, making love to one's mother, sister or daughter, etc., are undoubtedly meant metaphorically or symbolically. The *Guhyasamāja Tantra* root text was not interpreted in a radically antinomian sense by the later Indian or Tibetan tradition (Wedemeyer 2002).

In fact, we can see a series of developments that took place over the seventh to tenth centuries that led to the introduction of these new deities. The first of these was the idea of identification with a fierce male deity. Initially this was Vajrapāṇi (also known as Vajrasattva or 'Vajra being' although in later Tibetan tradition these are distinct deities), the one-time fierce *yakṣa* protector of the Buddha.

Linrothe's book *Ruthless Compassion* is a study of these fierce deities, on the basis of both iconographic and textual material. Linrothe refers to these deities as *krodha-vighnāntaka* or 'fierce destroyers of obstacles'. He sees the idea of identification with a wrathful deity at the centre of the *maṇḍala* as happening in three phases (Linrothe 1999). In the first phase, fierce protective deities (Hayagrīva, Yamāntaka) appear in secondary roles in iconography. In the second phase (around the seventh century CE?), they appear as independent figures: the basic five Tathāgata *maṇḍala* is generally expanded in the texts of this period to include the consorts of the deities and four *krodha-vighnāntaka* guardian deities, but the consorts or the fierce *krodha-vighnāntaka* can also substitute in secondary *maṇḍalas* for the principal deities (the Buddhas or Tathāgatas), and a *krodha-vighnāntaka* may occasionally be found at the centre of the *maṇḍala*. Phase Two texts include the *Mahāvairocanābhisaṃbodhi Sūtra* and the *Sarvatathāgatatattvasaṃgraha*.

In the third phase, appearing in iconography from the late tenth or early eleventh century, the *krodha-vighnāntaka* deity normally appears, with or without a female consort, at the centre of the *maṇḍala*, often surrounded by an entourage of eight or a multiple of eight goddesses (the pattern I referred to earlier in the chapter). The *Hevajra Tantra* (Fig. 10.4) and *Cakrasaṃvara Tantra* would be representative of this phase.

Thus the Buddhist *maṇḍala* model was progressively adapted by the incorporation of the wild goddesses and Bhairava-type deities, initially as guardians and protectors at the edges of the *maṇḍala* but increasingly as major figures, as we can see in the Hevajra *maṇḍala*. The circle of fierce goddesses comes in this last stage, as does the question of identifying directly with the goddess (rather than a god) at the centre of the *maṇḍala* (English 2002).

As implied by my earlier comments, the sexual practices also take on a new and different significance in the course of this development. I am not

Figure 10.4. Hevajra. Abu Cave, Piyang, Western Tibet

clear how far this is parallel to the Śaiva development. There, as we have seen, it seems that the initial point is that these practices are there to connect one to the family (in a suitably transgressive manner) and also to feed the female spirits. In the Buddhist context, as we will see in Chapter 11, there are suggestions of sexual yoga at an earlier stage, but they are not necessarily transgressive.

The Mahāyoga Tantras however include both the transgressive initiation rituals and the idea of a sexual yoga that is intended to produce a state of experience of enlightenment.[45] Dalton discusses this in some detail on the basis of Dunhuang meditation handbooks apparently linked with the *Guhyasamāja Tantra* and *Guhyagarbha Tantra* (see Chapter 11). The more complex subtle-body practices however develop at a somewhat later phase, and are first fully attested in the texts of the mid to late eighth century onwards (*Hevajra Tantra*, etc.; see Dalton 2004).

The sexual practices raise the question of how far practitioners were celibate. This is a complex issue, but it seems that in the Indian context these late Tantras with the associated sexual yogas were not regularly practised in the monastic context. Certainly the iconography is mostly small-scale and apparently considerably later than the surviving texts. This may suggest that the travelling *siddha* model that we find in the tradition was not entirely inaccurate, and that Tibetan descriptions of the great monasteries of northeast India as centres of Tantric teaching, if accurate, refer to a very late stage.[46] We might also imagine however that these were private interests of particular monks rather than being the basis of large-scale monastic ritual.[47]

If Sanderson is right in arguing that the Yoginī Tantras represent a Buddhist appropriation of Śaiva Tantra, how did this take place? In fact, as I have noted above, one can ask how far this really is an adaptation of 'Śaiva Tantra'. For both Buddhist and Śaiva Tantra the rise to primacy of female

45 Nāgārjuna, who is traditionally associated with the *Guhyasamāja Tantra* lineage, is regarded in later Indian thought as an alchemist and a specialist in sexual techniques. This however raises the problematic topic of whether there was more than one author using the name Nāgārjuna (Ray 1997; Mabbett 1998). As Wedemeyer notes, the historiographical issues are certainly not fully resolved (Wedemeyer 2001), but to assume that the Madhyamika philosopher Nāgārjuna was associated with the *Guhyasamāja Tantra* raises more problems than it solves. Wedemeyer has recently argued that the attribution to Nāgārjuna should be understood more in terms of visionary inspiration by Nāgārjuna and/or the assertion that the tradition represents a valid continuation of Nāgārjuna's teaching; this seems to me to make considerable sense (Wedemeyer 2006).

46 In Tibet, the Bengali monastic teacher Atiśa seems to have hedged his bets somewhat on the issue, saying that the sexual practices should not be undertaken by monastics, but inserting a proviso that they could be performed if the practitioner had knowledge of *śūnyatā* (Samuel 1993: 471). Davidson however translates this passage differently to imply that a celibate yogin can attain knowledge of *śūnyatā* without recourse to the sexual practices (Davidson 1995a: 301). The sexual practices already had great prestige, and even the school of the great fourteenth century lama Tsong-kha-pa, known for its emphasis on celibate practice and opposition to the sexual practices, accepted that they had to be performed in some form for the attainment of Buddhahood (Samuel 1993: 276, 511).

47 The rDzogs-chen tradition also avoided the sexual practices. This tradition developed mostly in Tibet, but seems to go back to India and perhaps to earlier origins outside the subcontinent. It presented an alternative path to the attainment of the central liberating insight of the tradition, with its own specific methodology, and initially at least rejected most of the Tantric techniques (Germano 1994, 2005).

divinities and the sexual yogas seem to have been a new development. These developments seem to have taken place more or less at the same time among Buddhists and among Śaivas, and borrowings have been traced in both directions.[48]

The female divinities may well best be understood in terms of a distinct Śākta milieu from which both Śaivas and Buddhists were borrowing; certainly the historical relationship between Śākta and Śaiva practices is far from clear. I shall discuss the sexual yogas in more detail in Chapter 11; in this case there are both suggestions of an earlier history in a Buddhist context and of borrowings from or connections with circles outside South Asia.

Other elements, such as the *kāpālika*-style practice, and perhaps also the use of sexual and other polluting substances in initiation and ritual magic, seems more clearly to have had a Śaiva prehistory before their Buddhist adoption. It is apparent, too, that these elements were seen as problematic in the Buddhist context, and as needing some kind of justification; we will see below how this was undertaken.

The *pīṭhas*, the Śākta cult centres associated with the new practices for the Śaivas were centres for the Buddhists as well. As mentioned above, we find more or less the same lists of sites in sources from both traditions, including four main sites and various subsidiary sites, yielding for both the Śaiva Kubjikā tradition and the Buddhist Cakrasaṃvara three circles of eight sites. Many of the sites are also common to both lists. It is not clear however how far we should accept the picture of a cultic underground presented by the texts, in which practitioners are meeting at the *pīṭhas*, recognising each other through special signs and coded language, and coming together for ritual gatherings. It is not intrinsically unlikely that such things happened. In fact, we have seen something like this with the shared early Buddhist-Jain-Ājīvika-Brahmanical renunciate scene, and at a later stage there were sharings between Sufis and Hindu yogis, still visible today in the dual identities of Nāth gurus (van Skyhawk 1993, Khan 2004) and in the Bengali Bāul traditions (Openshaw 1997, 2002; McDaniel 1989, 1992; Salomon 1991). However, there was also an alternative mode of practice in which practice was largely internalised. I turn further to this in Chapter 11.

The incorporation of all this material within the Buddhist tradition involved a certain amount of reconceptualisation of Tantric thought within the Buddhist frame. Some things could be taken over fairly directly.

[48] See references given at beginning of chapter.

The Buddhist equivalent of Bhairava, Mahākāla, has virtually the same iconography and became the protective deity of Buddhist Tantrics just as Bhairava was the protector of Śaiva Tantrics (see Stablein 1976; Snellgrove 1987: 150, 317; Linrothe 1999: 123–4).[49] However, it had to be made clear that the Buddhist path was pre-eminent, and that Tantra was not simply borrowed from the Śaivas. Sandy Macdonald (1990), Rob Mayer (1996), Toni Huber (1999), Ronald Davidson (1991, 1995b, 2002a) and others have helped to show how this was achieved, in particular through the Cakrasaṃvara myth, which legitimates the Buddhist takeover of Śaiva sacred sites. Mayer summarises this conversion myth as follows:

> A variety of evil non-human spirits occupy and rule over the 24 power places; they invite Śiva in extreme kāpālika form as Bhairava and his consort Kālarātri/Kālī to be their lord, and they rule the 24 power-places in Bhairava's name. Bhairava is too busy making love to Kālarātri/Kālī to visit the sites in person, so he sets up liṅgams to represent himself and receive worship in each of the 24 power places. In this way, Bhairava and his following establish control over all who move in the entire triple world (khecara, bhūcara and nāgaloka), and encourage transgressive Tantric practices that lead beings to hell. In response, Buddhist herukas emanate in forms identical to Bhairava, kill Bhairava, revive him, convert him to Buddhism, absorb all his wealth and power, and seize the power places and Bhairava's accoutrements, consorts and retinues and even mantras for their own Buddhist use. Bhairava and Kālarātri joyfully offer themselves in devotion as the Heruka's seats, as do all their following. (Mayer 1996: 119, referring to Kalff 1979: 67–76; Huber 1999: 40–41 and 236 n.5)

Mayer connects this sequence by which Śiva and other deities of his entourage are killed, liberated and converted into devotees of the Buddha to the well-known Indian pattern of 'demon devotees', a term introduced by Alf Hiltebeitel (Hiltebeitel 1989). Śiva becomes, in effect, the Buddha's 'demon devotee', the symbolic representation of the attachment to self which the Buddhist practitioner has to overcome (Mayer 1996: 109ff). He and related deities (e.g. Mahākāla) then take on the role of 'divine policemen', protectors and assistants of the peaceful and elevated Buddhist Tantric deities.

The conversion process also made it appropriate for Buddhist Tantric deities such as Vajrakīlaya or Vajrabhairava themselves to take on the fierce and aggressive nature of the Śaivite Tantric deities. Here the foremost and prototype figure was Vajrapāṇi, who was now upgraded from his status as

[49] Though Rhie says of Mahākāla only, 'Possibly there has been some relation to or assimilation of certain aspects of the Hindu god Shiva' (Rhie 2004: 44).

the Buddha's *yakṣa*-protector to be the key representative of the new kind of terrifying and aggressive deity who was nevertheless identical with the ultimate nature of the Buddha's enlightenment.[50]

This Buddhist adoption of Tantra also created the opportunity for the development of a new and powerful set of meditational techniques, in which negative emotions and behavioural modes such as anger could be transformed directly into the divine anger of the fierce Tantric deity and directed towards the destruction of negative forces within the practitioner. The visual and dramatic performance of these techniques, in the masked ritual dances which are still an important practice in most major Tibetan monasteries, maintained the dual orientation or dual interpretation towards the destruction of obstacles to the successful pursuit of the goals of everyday life, and the destruction of obstacles for the practitioner's progress to enlightenment.

The above discussion has focused on Buddhist (Vajrayāna) and nondualist Śaiva Tantric traditions. There were other Tantric traditions, both among Brahmanical and non-Brahmanical schools, but to the extent that these are known to us in any detail they have steered clear from the antinomian and transgressive elements conspicuous in the nondualist Śaiva and the later Vajrayāna traditions. They include Śaiva traditions (principally Śaiva Siddhānta) and the Vaiṣṇava Tantric school known as the Pāñcarātra Āgama, which was mentioned briefly in Chapter 8. These two traditions are major sources of later Indic ritual procedures, and indeed 'Tantric' in this context primarily implies that these are sources of non-Vedic ritual procedures (Colas 2003). They also share, however, much of the ritual structure, techniques and theoretical presuppositions of the nondualist Śaiva traditions (Sanderson 1995; S. Gupta 1972, 1989, 1992; Flood 2006: 99–145).

The Jaina tradition too shared some of these techniques and procedures, and developed a specialist class of ritualists performing Tantric-style ritual primarily to the various *yakṣa* and *yakṣī* deities associated with the *tīrthaṅkaras* (Jaini 1991: 196). These deities appear to have progressively developed as male and female 'protectors' of the *tīrthaṅkaras*. The earliest iconographic and textual evidence is from around the sixth century CE,

[50] The Śaivas, naturally, developed their own response to these myths of Buddhist supremacy. Sanderson narrates a 'well known Śaiva myth' according to which Bṛhaspati invented Vajrayāna Buddhism, complete with its images of Buddhist deities standing on the heads of Śaiva deities, as a ruse to distract the demons from their devotion to Śiva so that they could be destroyed (Sanderson 1994: 93).

and there appears to be a progressive development from an original male-female pair to separate male and female deities for each of the twenty-four *tīrthaṅkara*. These *yakṣa* and *yaksī* deities offered a context in which various existing deity-cults could be acknowledged within Jaina practice (Cort 1987; J. Sharma 1989). Some of these deities, for example the goddesses Padmāvatī and Jvālāmālinī, have elements in common with the fierce goddesses known from the Śaiva and Buddhist traditions, and would appear to derive from a similar context. The same would appear to be true of Vāgīśvarī, a fierce form of Sarasvatī whose worship was popular in the mediaeval period, and the so-called *vidyādevīs*, such as Cakreśvarī (Fig. 10.2), associated with magical powers attained through ascetic practice (Cort 1987: 237–40; cf. also Pal 1994, Cat.No.67). Rituals of Padmāvatī can be used to perform a set of six ritual actions (ṣāṭkarman) closely similar to sets of four and six ritual actions in Buddhist and Śaiva sources (pacification, subjugation, etc.) (Cort 1987 245–6; see also Jhavery 1944). The Digaṃbara and Śvetāṃbara Jains have somewhat different sets of *yakṣas*, *yaksīs* and *vidyādevīs* (Cort 1987: 253–4 nn. 30, 33).

None of these cults have a soteriological aim, however, and it appears that the Jains employed fierce goddess rituals only for pragmatic purposes. There does not seem to be any cult parallel to that of the major Buddhist or Śaiva Tantric deities, with whom the practitioner identifies as a way of accessing the central liberating insight of the tradition. However, as Olle Qvarnström has noted, much research still remains to be done before we have a clear picture of Jaina Tantra (Qvarnström 2000: 595).

Thus it seems to have been principally among the two groups I discussed above, the nondualist Śaivas and the Mahāyāna Buddhists, that the development of 'Tantra' as a transgressive spiritual path took place.

CONCLUSION

I began this chapter, after some preliminary discussion of Western attitudes to Tantra, with the low-caste ritual practitioners who supported the role of South Indian kings and perhaps had equivalents elsewhere outside the Vedic regions of early India. These people were specialists, in a sense, in death and misfortune, and their low and polluted status, however necessary to society, derived from this involvement.

I then suggested that early Indian renunciants, particularly the Pāśupata and those who had adopted a *kāpālika* style of practice, had in a sense made a choice to live in this world of death and misfortune rather than the everyday world of the householder. We then turned to the fierce goddesses of illness and disease and I suggested that the Saptamātṛkā deities used in state ritual by the Gupta kings represented a Brahmanical appropriation of these forces of misfortune. It is these dangerous goddesses who come to take a leading role in the more transgressive aspects of 'Tantra', and the *kula* or 'family' traditions by which they are initially approached may derive from earlier hereditary low-caste practitioners.

All this suggests a convergence of interests in the early stages of the transgressive styles of Tantra. This convergence is between low-caste, polluted ritualists from hereditary backgrounds, cult-groups of the Pāśupata and *kāpālika* kind who were already close to them, and a new style of ritual for which the script was perhaps written in large part by the court Brahmins of the Gupta kings and others of the new Brahmanical regimes of the fourth and fifth centuries onwards.

In this case, the significance of pollution and impurity, as David White has suggested (White 1998, 2003) was primarily to do with the power of the ritual. Thus the initial rationale for the ritual use of sexual substances was that they were extremely polluting, powerful and therefore effective when used transgressively, rather than because sex as such was seen as a source of spiritual fulfilment. Given the logic of Brahmanical thought, the more polluted, extreme and transgressive the ritual and its performers, the more powerful it might be. Thus *kāpālika*-type practitioners, to the extent that they made a living by selling ritual services to local rulers and other wealthy people, had some interest in both exaggerating their transgressive behaviour, and in developing a mythic justification for it.

From within the practice tradition, the perspective was quite different. For their employers, the important things about these early Tantric practitioners is that they were unsavoury, dangerous and *therefore* effective at bringing about the this-worldly ends which the employers wanted. For the practitioners themselves, however, this rejection of everyday life had a positive spiritual value; it was a path to a liberating insight.

This may already have been the case to some degree for the low-caste groups who took on this role in the South Indian state. Anthropologists have found that most low Indian castes today have, at the least, caste myths which justify a higher status than that assigned to them by the surrounding society (e.g. Lynch 1969). Many, too, have adopted religious perspectives, such as that of the low-caste saint Ravidas, which see the caste hierarchy and the value systems of respectable society as irrelevant to human worth (e.g. Khare 1984).

In any case, it makes sense both that the initiation by which renunciates took on this new identity was specifically centred around pollution (the ingestion of the sexual fluids of guru and consort) and was also seen as an occasion for the direct perception of the liberating insight.

The self-identification as a deity which is a key element of Tantric practice may have originated primarily as a way of accessing divine power for ritual purposes, for example by the ritualist seeking to control a circle of fierce goddesses, but this too could easily be read in spiritual terms. Certainly, as Paul Muller-Ortega has shown, 'becoming Bhairava' by the tenth century CE could be reinterpreted by Abhinavagupta in purely spiritual terms, as a mode of access to nondual consciousness. 'Here, Bhairava comes to mean the unencompassable and exquisitely blissful light of consciousness that is to be discovered as the practitioner's true inner identity' (Muller-Ortega 2002: 213).

The possibility for such interpretations, which may well go back to quite early stages, helps to explain why practices of this kind could appeal to Buddhists as well. It is generally assumed that these transgressive practices in Buddhism were initially carried out in non-monastic contexts and only at a fairly late stage – perhaps tenth or eleventh century – started to become a significant part of the monastic scene. By this stage there is evidence, particularly outside India proper, for the Pāśupatas and *kāpālika*-style practitioners having long taken on a role as court ritualists (see Chapter 12). This would have brought them into direct competition with the Buddhists, and one can see a double attraction of the new approaches for the Buddhists: they offered new, more powerful ritual techniques that would be competitive with those of their Śaivite competitors, and they also offered new, more effective and direct, modes of accessing the central goal of Buddhism itself, that of Buddhahood.

What we have not yet examined in any detail is how the sexual practices might have operated as a form of meditation to achieve liberating insight. This question is tied up with the emergence of the subtle body practices that form the main subject of Chapter 11.

CHAPTER II

Subtle bodies, longevity and internal alchemy

As we have seen, a striking innovation in both Śaiva and Buddhist traditions in the course of the eighth to tenth centuries was a new series of yogic practices and techniques based on a subtle anatomy of the practitioner's body. Specifically, these practices assume an internal 'subtle physiology' of the body (or rather of the body-mind complex) made up of channels (*nāḍī*) through which substances of some kind flow, and points of intersection (*cakra*) at which these channels come together. The practices typically involve moving these substances through the body, clearing 'knots' in the flow, and directing the substances into a central channel flowing along the spine (Fig. 11.1). I refer to these practices, as do a number of other authors, as 'subtle body' practices (Samuel 2005b; White 1996).[1] What I shall do in this chapter is to track this new pattern and explain how it developed.

A key element of the 'subtle body' practices is their close connection with sexual practices. Sexual intercourse, real or imagined, is used as a way to stimulate the flow of substances along and within the body, a process which is associated in various ways with meditative techniques for the attainment of health, long life and/or liberating insight. The subtle body practices thus provide a new and different purpose and significance for sexual practices within the Tantric context and increasingly take over from earlier views of sexual practice as being about initiation or feeding fierce female spirits.

SEXUAL PRACTICES IN THE GUPTA PERIOD

An obvious place to look for the development of sexual practices in early mediaeval India would seem to be the *kāmaśāstra* literature, the technical

[1] The term 'subtle body' is also used in English to translate *sūkṣma-śarīra*, which is a key concept in the Vedantic philosophy of Śaṇkara. This is the second of a series of three increasingly subtle 'bodies', the material or physical body (*sthūla-śarīra*), subtle body (*sūkṣma-śarīra*) and causal body (*kāraṇa-śarīra*), beyond which lies identity with the ultimate self, itself identical with Brahman (Samuel 2005b). It should be noted that I am using the term here in a wider sense.

Figure 11.1. Meditator with Cakras and Kuṇḍalinī

literature on erotics, of which the best-known text is of course the *Kāmasūtra* of Vātsyāyana (e.g. Upadhyaya 1961). Vātsyāyana is variously dated between the first and fourth centuries CE; Daud Ali suggests the early third century (Ali 1998: 164). Vātsyāyana represents himself as the latest in a sequence of authorities on *kāmaśāstra*, often referring back to the opinion of his predecessors. None of the works of these earlier authorities survive, but there are many later works on *kāmaśāstra*, mostly considerably shorter than Vātsyāyana and reflecting the changed social circumstances of later times (Archer 1964; Comfort 1964).

Anyone looking at the *Kāmasūtra*, or for that matter at later *kāmaśāstra* texts, for enlightenment on sexual yoga and the subtle body will, however, be disappointed. It is clear from Indian and Tibetan texts on sexual yoga that their authors had some familiarity with the *kāmaśāstra* literature (e.g. George 1974: 71–3; G. Dorje 1987: 900–7; Guenther 1963: 77–8), which was evidently seen as relevant knowledge by practitioners of these techniques. The influence, however, is all one way; there is nothing in the work of Vātsyāyana or his successors to suggest any knowledge of or concern with sexual yoga. The *kāmaśāstra* literature is about the pursuit of sexual pleasure (*kāma*), not the quest for liberation (*mokṣa*).[2]

At the same time, there are aspects of the *Kāmasūtra* that are worth our attention. As Daud Ali noted, the *Kāmasūtra* is part of what Foucault has called a 'technology of the self' (Foucault 1988a, 1988b).[3] In other words, this is a text that presents a 'code' or set of rules on how to live one's life. Only one of the seven sections of the *Kāmasūtra* deals with the actual physiology and technique of sex; most of the book is concerned with laying down the appropriate codes of behaviour for men and women within and outside marriage. Ali suggests that as a 'technology of the self', this courtly code of behaviour bears a notable resemblance to the monastic code as laid down in the Buddhist monastic Vinaya. He suggests that despite the different states of life at which these codes are directed, 'the technologies deployed for the achievement of these states share a common and novel conception of reality as a complex system of "signs", "marks", and "surfaces" to be engaged and disengaged with, manipulated and deconstructed' (Ali 1998: 159). This novel conception of reality was part of the classical pattern discussed in Chapter 9. Ali goes on to argue that 'the technology of Buddhist monastic discipline was [...] constituted in "complementary opposition" to the practices of the urban courts' (Ali 1998: 163).

Buddhist treatises, like those of other renunciate traditions, needed to bring about this reversal, to seek to transform the code of everyday life into

[2] While the *Kāmasūtra* begins with a homage to *dharma*, *artha* and *kāma*, the three classical aims of life (*puruṣārtha*) in Indian thought, excluding *mokṣa*, a later verse recognises *mokṣa* as an appropriate pursuit for the closing years of life (Rocher 1985).

[3] Technologies of the self according to Foucault 'permit individuals to effect by their own means or with the help of others a certain number of operations on their own bodies and souls, thoughts, conduct and way of being, so as to transform themselves in order to attain a certain state of happiness, purity, wisdom, perfection, or immortality' (1988a: 18). See also Samuel 2005a: 335–8, and Chapter 14.

that of the renunciate who has stepped outside the concerns of *saṃsāra*, whether or not he or she is still physically present within it. The passage in the *Mahāyānasūtrālaṃkāra* (IX, 41–7) of Asaṅga, a classic Buddhist treatise dating probably from the fifth century CE, which Snellgrove has pointed out as containing indications of sexual yoga can be understood in these terms (Snellgrove 1987: 126–8).[4] It forms part of a series of reversals of ordinary experience:

> Supreme self-control is achieved in the reversal of the five sense-organs with regard to the universal operation of all of them, associated wth the manifestation of twelve hundred good qualities.
>
> Supreme self-control is achieved in the reversal of mental activity with the consequent self-control with regard to knowledge which is free of discriminating thought and thus totally immaculate.
>
> Supreme self-control is achieved in the reversal of appearances and their (imagined) significance in a (Buddha-)realm that is thus purified for the blissful vision just as desired.
>
> Supreme self-control is achieved in the reversal of discriminating thought resulting in the nonobstruction at all times of all knowledge and acts.
>
> Supreme self-control is achieved in the reversal of substrata resulting in that imperturbable state of the Buddhas, *nirvāṇa* without any substratum.
>
> Supreme self-control is achieved in the reversal of sexual intercourse in the blissful Buddha-poise and the untrammelled vision of one's spouse.
>
> Supreme self-control is achieved in the reversal of spatial perceptions resulting in the supernatural production of thought-forms and in material manifestation in phenomenal spheres (*gati*). (Snellgrove 1987: 127–8)

Snellgrove suggests, plausibly, that the reference to the 'reversal of sexual intercourse' here indicates the deliberate avoidance of male ejaculation in a form of sexual yoga:

> It is by no means improbable that already by the fifth century when Asaṅga was writing, these techniques of sexual yoga were being used in reputable Buddhist circles, and that Asaṅga himself accepted such a practice as valid. The natural power of the breath, inhaling and exhaling, was certainly accepted as an essential force to be controlled in Buddhist as well as Hindu yoga. Why therefore not the natural power of the sexual force? [. . .] Once it is established that sexual yoga was already regarded by Asaṅga as an acceptable yogic practice, it becomes far easier to understand how Tantric treatises, despite their apparent contradiction of previous Buddhist teachings, were so readily canonized in the following centuries. (Snellgrove 1987: 127)

[4] On the interpretation of this controversial passage see also Thurman 2004: 89.

The point is well taken, but one should also note that there is nothing particularly transgressive in Asaṅga's text. The reference is explicitly to practices carried out in the context of a marital relationship, not by supposedly celibate Buddhist practitioners.[5] There is no suggestion here of a context such as that of the *kāpālika*-style practitioner, with its transgressive use of sexual substances in frightening and dangerous places to attract dangerous female spirits. We need to be careful here of the temptation to lump all sexual practices together.

At most we might note that sexuality is closely tied up with *saṃsāric* existence, so that its occurrence in this context seems somewhat paradoxical. However the *Mahāyānasūtrālaṃkāra* elsewhere notes (XIII.11, 13):

> There is no element (*dharma*) apart from the elemental sphere (*dharmadhātu*),
> So passion, etc. (viz., wrath and delusion) serve as their own extrication in the opinion of the Buddhas. [...] In that one has recourse to them, passion and the rest, at the source (*yoniśaḥ*) one is released by their means; thus they are their own extrication. (Snellgrove 1987: 126)[6]

This is essentially the same justification that was later to be offered by the Tantric texts themselves: through passion one becomes free from passion.

Here we might return to Ali's discussion of the *Kāmasūtra* and the wider courtly culture of the period, which regarded sexual pleasure both as an entirely legitimate object of pursuit for men and for women but also as a source of danger if one did not maintain an appropriate degree of self-discipline and self-mastery in one's approach to it (Ali 1998, 2004: 240–1). Over-attachment to sexual pleasure could lead to the 'royal disease', *rājayakṣman* (Ali 2004: 242–5), a weakening and wasting away of the body caused less, Ali suggests, by physical over-indulgence than by 'an excessive predisposition or inclination *of the mind* towards sexual desire' (2004: 243).[7] One could imagine a ready opening in a culture preoccupied with such matters for teachings that involved male seminal control and

[5] Snellgrove's 'spouse' translates *dāra*, 'wife', so it is clear that the partners are married. The lack of reference in the Chinese pilgrims' accounts suggests that such practices, and indeed any distinctively 'Tantric' observances, were absent from monastic contexts up to the early seventh century.

[6] Thurman translates: 'Since no thing is found outside of the ultimate realm, the buddhas consider that passions and so on constitute their own transcendence [...] Thus, one properly engages with the passions and so forth, and thereby becomes liberated from them; such is their transcendence' (Thurman 2004: 169–70). Snellgrove suggests that *yoṇiśaḥ* ('at the source') here may have an intentional double meaning (*yoṇi* = vagina) (Snellgrove 1987: 126).

[7] The disease of *rājayakṣman* is described in Caraka's medical treatise (Ali 2004: 242–3). See also David White, who points out the connections between ideas of *rājayakṣman* and the underlying logic of *rasāyana* (elixir or rejuvenation therapy) and *vājikaraṇa* (sexual rehabilitation therapy), major concerns for both the Āyurvedic tradition and the related discipline of medical alchemy (1996: 24–5).

self-mastery in the sexual context. Our evidence for such practices is, however, only indirect.

There is at least a possibility, then, that some kind of sexual yoga existed in the fourth or fifth centuries. Substantial evidence for such practices, however, dates from considerably later, from the seventh and eighth centuries, and derives from Śaiva and Buddhist Tantric circles. Here we see sexual yoga as part of a specific complex of practices. On the Śaiva side this is associated with a series of named teachers in South and North India, the Cittar (Siddha) teachers in the south, including Tirumūlar and Bogar, and the so-called Nāth teachers in the north, where the principal names are Matsyendra (Matsyendranāth) and Gorakh (Gorakhnāth). On the Buddhist side, it is associated with so-called *mahāyoga* Tantras. These developments appear to be happening at more or less the same time in all three areas, again suggesting a shared ascetic culture. We begin with the Śaiva developments.

THE TAMIL CITTARS AND THE NĀTH REFORMS

The Tamil Cittars in the South and Matsyendra(-nāth) and his companions in the North are all legendary figures in the form that we know them. Their names are however attached to a coherent body of approaches and techniques. The elements of the pattern include practices aimed at health, long life and immortality, sexual practices, internal 'subtle body' practices, and alchemical practices (*rasāyana*) associated with mercury-based elixirs.

Sanderson and White associate Matsyendra with the translation from the *kula* traditions, with their cremation ground associations and symbolism, to the reformed, domesticated, *kaula* traditions (Sanderson 1985: 214 n.110; White 1998: 173). This enabled the techniques developed among *kāpālika*-style ascetics to be adopted by the 'wider community of married householders' (Sanderson 1988: 679). In these cults sexual ritual has been 'aestheticised':

> The magical properties of the mingled sexual fluids are not forgotten: those seeking powers (*siddhis*) consumed it and even those who worshipped for salvation alone offered the products of orgasm to the deities. However the emphasis has now moved to orgasm itself. It is no longer principally a means of production. It is a privileged means of access to a blissful expansion of consciousness in which the deities of the Kula permeate and obliterate the ego of the worshipper. The consumption of meat and alcohol is interpreted along the same lines. Their purpose, like that of everything in the liturgy, is to intensify experience, to gratify the goddesses of the senses. (Sanderson 1988: 680)

Something else however can also be seen in the Cittar and Nāth teachings than the blissful expansion of consciousness, and this is the emphasis on the practices as giving rejuvenation and immortality. This is a major theme, for example, in the *Kaulajñānanirṇaya*, a text often ascribed to Matsyendranāth and apparently dating from the ninth or tenth century (White 1996: 73):

Devi said – O Grace Giver, Mahādeva, speak freely of the conquering of death. [. . .] Speak from Your inmost being, Mahādeva, (of that method by which) a person may roam on earth immortal! [. . .]

Dear One, listen one-pointedly to the details (of this knowledge) I speak of. (One should meditate) inwardly on a pure, white, cool, celestial, fragrant and vast effulgence, the heavenly cause of all lunar refreshment, like the centre of space, flowing within oneself, through all the many channels. Doing this one becomes long-lived and conquers death. (*Kaulajñānanirṇaya* 5, 1–6, Bagchi and Magee 1986: text, 13–14)

The remainder of this *paṭala* or chapter of the *Kaulajñānanirṇaya* gives further details, again focusing on the imagery of the inner moon and its cool moist white rays;[8] subsequent chapters give further methods for defeating old age and disease. Later chapters present another key element of the Nāth tradition, the sequence of *cakras* along the spinal column and the importance of the 'raising' of the goddess (*śakti*, Kuṇḍalinī) from the lowest *cakra* up through the *cakras*, so 'piercing' through the upper *cakras* and attaining the liberating insight of this tradition. This practice is closely associated with sexual yoga, and the earliest descriptions of it in Śaiva sources come from this text and the *Kubjikātantra*, a text belonging to a slightly later branch of the *kaula* reform movement (cf. Sanderson 1988: 686–8; Heilijgers-Seelen 1994; White 1996: 134–5).

The emphasis on defeating old age and disease extends beyond these inner yogic practices, since these Siddha traditions were also involved in physical alchemy with the aim of producing elixirs of immortality. These were mostly based on mercury, which shared the cool white lunar associations visible in the above quotation from the *Kaulajñānanirṇaya*. As White has pointed out, the imagery of elemental mercury also links up with *soma* (another name for the moon, as well as the sacrificial substance of Vedic ritual), and seminal fluid, whose preservation and use is a central issue for the sexual yogic practices. Mercury is identified with the seed of the god

[8] Variants of this cool white light practice are common in the Śaiva and Buddhist literature; a dateable example from a literary source comes from Ratnākara's *Haravijaya* (between 826 and 838; D. Smith 1985: 265). The Vajrasattva purification practices of present-day Tibetan Vajrayāna have a similar structure, involving visualisations of purifying white nectar pervading the practitioner's body (e.g. Beyer 1973: 434–5).

Śiva, caught in the mouth of Agni the fire god and scattered in deep wells in the earth, while the other principal substance of Indian alchemy, sulphur, is associated with the menstrual blood of the Goddess (White 1996: 191–3, 213). Outer or physical alchemy (*rasāyana*) was most fully developed by the *rasāyana* siddhas of Western India, but it was important in the Tamil Cittar tradition and appears in association with inner alchemy throughout these traditions.[9]

THE ORIGINS OF THE SEXUAL AND ALCHEMICAL PRACTICES

Where though did this new body of complexes come from? How did it originate? Here we can examine individual elements of the complex, and we can also look at the complex as a whole. If we take the second option, the similarities with Chinese alchemical practices and 'technologies of the self' are striking and have long been observed (Filliozat 1969; White 1996: 53–4, 61–5). These Chinese practices, closely associated with Daoism, have been described in detail by a number of scholars (for recent accounts see Schipper 1994; L. Kohn 2006a), and there is little doubt that they predate the Indic versions by several centuries. Early versions of these practices are found in the Mawangdui manuscripts, recovered from a burial dated to 168 BCE (D. Harper 1987, 1997). They include sexual practices based on the internal movement of 'subtle' bodily substances (*qi*), are aimed at long life, health and immortality, and are again linked to alchemical practices associated with mercury-based elixirs (e.g. Schipper 1994: 174–81).[10]

The similarities here are quite close; thus one can parallel the Daoist practise of 'living without grains' (*bigu*), involving extended fasts during which the practitioner eats only specially-prepared alchemical compounds (Shawn 2006, Jackowitz 2006, Schipper 1996: 167–70), with similar *rasāyana* practices, still carried out in the Tibetan tradition (*bcud len*).[11] One might also

[9] For Buddhist versions of these alchemical practices, see Fenner 1979; Walter 1980; Samuel 2006b.

[10] Mercury-based medicines are mentioned in the Āyurvedic treatise of Vāgbhaṭṭa, so it appears that they were already entering the Āyurvedic pharmacopoeia at around the same time. Apart from possible Chinese relationships, in this case there are also possible connections with Islamic alchemy, whose rather more historical founding figure Jabir ibn Hayyan also dates from the eighth century. There was certainly a developed alchemical tradition in Western India at a slightly later point.

[11] One also might note that the original *mise-en-scène* of the Chinese 'bedroom arts' is said to be the need of Chinese emperors to maintain the sexual abilities needed to deal with their large harems and produce enough descendants, as well as to attain longevity (Winn 2006: 153). Early Chinese texts on sexology, such as the *Sunü Jing*, are often presented in the form of a dialogue between a female sexual adept and the Yellow Emperor, the mythical founding-figure of the first Chinese imperial dynasty (see also Mussat 1978; Wile 1992). Here we might note the significance of *rājayakṣma* or 'royal consumption' as a disease in Indian medical and literary convention (White 1996: 24–6).

point to the similarity between the Chinese meditational practice of the 'microcosmic orbit', in which *qi* is directed along a circuit which moves up the spine from the perineum and returns down the front of the body and the Indian *kriyā* practices which utilise the same circuit. In both cases, a crucial link is made by contact between the tongue and the back of the upper palate (known as *khecarī mudrā* in Sanskrit).[12] In both cases, Chinese and Indian, physical exercises are also used to bring the body as a whole into a suitable condition to perform the internal practices. These are the exercises that later become known in various versions as *daoyin* or *qigong* in the Chinese context, as *haṭha yoga* in the Śaiva context, and as *'phrul 'khor* in the context of the Tibetan Vajrayāna.[13]

At the same time, there is no doubt that the Indian version of these practices is as thoroughly Indian in its vocabulary and conceptual structure as the Chinese version is Chinese. Compare the internal landscape of the Chinese practices according to the *Huangting Jing* ('Book of the Yellow Court'):

> In the Yellow Court sits someone dressed in scarlet.
> The door is locked, its two leaves tightly closed.
> The Dark Towers rise to vertiginous heights.
> In the Cinnabar Field, semen[14] and breath subtly mingle.
> Above, the clear water of the Jade Fountain flows abundantly,
> Making the Divine Root sturdy and hard; it will not ever weaken.
> In the Center lake a noble person, dressed in red.
> Below lies the Field, three inches away; that is where the god lives.
> Lock the passage between the Inner and Outer with a double lock.
> Always keep the Hut spotlessly clean.
> When suddenly you receive through the tunnel of the Mysterious Meridian the semen's signal,
> You should quickly retain semen and hold yourself together.
>
> (Schipper 1994: 140–1)

with that of the *Ṣatcakranirūpana* ('Description of the Six Cakras'):

However, *rājayakṣma* was already a matter of concern for Āyurvedic texts before the development of Chinese-style sexual yogic practices.

12 For modern versions of these practices, see Chia 1983 for China; Saraswati 1985 for India. On the importance of the *khecarī mudrā* in India, see White 1996: 252–4.

13 Of these, the *'phrul 'khor* exercises are the least known to Western scholars; the only substantial academic publication so far is Loseries-Leick 1997. On the Tantric origins of *haṭha yoga*, see Alter 2005. Kohn 2006b describes *daoyin* and compares them with yoga, but discounts the possibility of mutual influence because of yoga's 'strong otherworldly and theistic orientation' (2006b: 129). Here she is perhaps misled by popular Vedantic-influenced Western accounts of yoga. It is noticeable however that she sees *haṭha yoga* as developed by the Nāth yogis as being closest in orientation to *daoyin* (L. Kohn: 2006b: 141–2).

14 According to Schipper, the term used can also refer to female sexual secretions (Schipper 1994: 140).

Near the mouth of the Nāḍī called Vajrā, and in the pericarp (of the Ādhāra Lotus), there constantly shines the beautifully luminous and soft, lightning-like triangle which is Kāmarupa, and known as Traipura. There is always and everywhere the Vāyu called Kandarpa, who is of a deeper red than the Bandhujīva flower, and is the Lord of Beings and resplendent like ten million suns.

Inside it (the triangle) is Svayaṃbhu in His Liṅga-form, beautiful like molten gold, with His head downwards. He is revealed by Knowledge [*jñāna*] and Meditation [*dhyāna*], and is of the shape and colour of a new leaf. As the cool rays of lightning and of the full moon charm, so does His beauty. The Deva who resides happily here as in Kāśī is in forms like a whirlpool.

Over it shines the sleeping Kuṇḍalinī, fine as the fibre of the lotus-stalk. She is the world-bewilderer, gently covering the mouth of Brahma-dvāra by Her own. Like the spiral of the conch-shell, Her shining snake-like form goes three and a half times round Śiva, and Her lustre is as that of a strong flash of young strong lightning. Her sweet murmur is like the indistinct hum of swarms of love-mad bees. She produces melodious poetry and Bandha and all other compositions in prose or verse in sequence or otherwise in Saṃskṛta, Prākṛta and other languages. It is She who maintains all the beings of the world by means of inspiration and expiration, and shines in the cavity of the root (Mūla) Lotus like a chain of brilliant lights. (*Ṣatcakranirūpana* verses 8–11, trans. Woodroffe 1974: 340, 343, 346–7)

The Indian account represents the lowest of the series of *cakras* through thoroughly Indian imagery, including a homology with the Tantric *pīṭha* of Kāmarupa and a Śiva-liṅga that is compared to that at Kāśī. One might also refer to the way in which mercury, the prime alchemical substance, is treated in Indian alchemy in terms of a complex series of symbolic connections that identify it with the Moon, semen and with Vedic *soma*, also seen as a source of immortality.

It is not surprising that the question of orthogenetic explanation comes up again in this context. David Gordon White argues both sides in his *Alchemical Body*. He notes the likelihood of contacts via the sea route from South India to China (which was in fact the chief supply route for mercury, an import from China):

Since India's original fascination with alchemy most probably arose out of early contacts with a China [. . .] whose Taoist speculative alchemical tradition had been developing since the second century A.D.,[15] one might conclude that such traditions reached south India via a maritime route. (White 1996: 53)

Elsewhere, he points to the similarities between the South Indian Cittar tradition and the physiological alchemy (*neidan*) of Daoist traditions (1996: 55). However, he wants to deny that we are dealing with the import of the whole complex of ideas:

[15] The Mawangdui texts would now enable us to push this back to the second century BCE.

While Chinese (Taoist alchemy) and Persian (the Shi'a Jabirian school) traditions no doubt interacted with Tantric alchemy, the Indian material is so specifically Indian–as much in the subcontinental provenance of its *materiae primae* as in its nearly exclusive Hindu religious and metaphysical presuppositions – as to preclude any possibility of this being a matter of wholesale borrowing. (White 1996: 54–5)

What counts as 'wholesale borrowing' is perhaps arbitrary; it is partly a matter of how one defines 'the Indian material'. It is certainly possible to make a good case for individual components of Tantric ideas, including aspects of the subtle-body practices and even sexual rituals, going back to the 'Vedic' culture of Kuru-Pañcāla, or at least to the Upaniṣads. However, in the eighth-century material these elements have come to be combined in a pattern of behaviours, a cultural complex, that is recognisably not Vedic or even Upaniṣadic or Buddhist. The elaborate internal structure of the subtle body, with the series of *cakras* along the central channel, has no real precedent in Indian material, for all that the language in which it is described is entirely Indic.

It seems also that links between South India, probably the earliest Indian location for the complex of sexual practices, inner and outer alchemy, and China, where the same complex had taken form at a considerably earlier date, are plausible. The Cittar tradition has stories of teachers with Chinese connections, but our sources for these appear to be relatively late (White 1996: 61–3). They mostly centre around the figure of Bogar, described either as a Indian alchemist who studied in China or as a Chinese adept who came to India. He is connected with the famous Murugan shrine at Palani in South India, where he is credited with making the main shrine-image of Murugan from a compound of nine poisonous metals. The image is bathed with substances that are then regarded as medically potent and are sold off to visitors to the pilgrimage site. Bogar himself is supposed to have gained the *siddhi* of long life and still dwells somewhere inside the hill of Palani (White 1996: 61; Samuel 2001a). A realistic picture, as White suggests, might be of an ongoing exchange along the India-China route, though it seems that most of the innovations came from the Chinese end (White 1996: 63).[16]

In this connection, it is worth pointing out that the material we are looking at has a degree of conceptual unity in its early Chinese context that is less obvious in its later Indian versions. In the Mawangdui texts both medical and sexual prescriptions are essentially to do with maintaining the

[16] Other material suggestive of Chinese connections includes the story of Vasiṣṭha and the Cīnacāra practices (e.g. Bharati 1965: 65–79) and the Chinese associations of the rDzogs-chen teacher Śrī Siṅgha (Guenther 1974).

optimal health of the human organism. It has been argued persuasively that early concepts of *qi* also grew out of medical practice, and that the whole idea of learning sensitivity to *qi* derives from the doctor learning to be sensitive to the movement of sensation in a patient's body (Hsu 2005). In later forms of Chinese medicine this is best known in the context of the sophisticated techniques of pulse-reading. These are now a standard part of Āyurvedic practice, but they almost certainly spread from China to India, since they do not occur in the early Āyurvedic texts. They came to form part of the Siddha medical tradition in South India (Daniel 1984), and are also a principal means of diagnosis in Tibetan medicine (Samuel 2001c).

In the next section, however, I turn to look briefly at precedents for these practices in Indic traditions.

VEDIC AND INDIC COMPONENTS IN THE TANTRIC SYNTHESIS

Firstly, we should note that 'sexual practices' in a generic sense were present in the Vedic and Upaniṣadic material. I have already discussed some of these in relation to the 'transgressive' aspects of the horse-sacrifice (*aśvamedha*) and the Vrātyas, and considered the close relationship between sexual energy and ascetic practice in the Vedic material (see Chapter 7). As is well known, late Vedic texts treat sexual intercourse as symbolically equivalent to the Vedic sacrifice, and ejaculation of semen as the offering. This theme occurs in the *Jaiminīya Brāhmaṇa* (Hartzell 1997: 86–7) and the *Chandogya Upaniṣad* (5.8.1), as well as in the *Bṛhadāraṇyaka Upaniṣad*, which has a particularly elaborate version:

> Her vulva is the sacrificial ground; her pubic hair is the sacred grass; her labia majora are the Soma-press; and her labia minora are the fire blazing at the centre. A man who engages in sexual intercourse with this knowledge obtains as great a world as a man who performs a Soma sacrifice, and he appropriates to himself the merits of the women with whom he has sex. The women, on the other hand, appropriate to themselves the merits of a man who engages in sexual intercourse with them without this knowledge. (*Bṛhadāraṇyaka Upaniṣad* 6.4.3, trans. Olivelle 1998: 88)

The *Bṛhadāraṇyaka Upaniṣad* goes on to specify a series of sexual rituals and practices, mostly directed to obtaining a child of a particular kind, but also including rituals to be carried out before and after the birth of a child (6.4.9–28 = Olivelle 1998: 88–93). The concern in this text with male loss of virility and power is striking, and as is well known this has been a continuing theme in Indian thought up to modern times (e.g. Carstairs 1957; Alter 1997).

What we are dealing with in the new sexual rituals of the seventh and eighth centuries is different, although there is a certain relationship, in that avoidance of ejaculation fits into the logic of the need for seminal continence to preserve male vitality and virility (see Chapter 8; the same theme is found in Chinese material). Rather than sexual *intercourse* being homologised with the sacrifice, the process of sexual *excitation* is now homologised with the movement of internal substances or energies within the body.[17] As is well known, the most familiar Śaiva imagery here is of the arousal of the serpentine goddess Kuṇḍalinī, conceived of as dwelling in the lowest of the *cakras* within the human body, and her ascent through the higher *cakras* (e.g. Silburn 1988). Silburn's account is particularly useful because it is based on the earlier Trika texts, particularly the work of Abhinavagupta and his commentator Jayaratha, and so predates the development of the elaborate imagery of deities, multi-petalled lotuses and so on familiar from later material:

> During the rising of Kuṇḍalinī, since the yogin experiences a vigorous whirling at the level of the centres located along the central axis, the latter are called 'whirling wheels'. From there the divine energies spread out and become active in the body. Each wheel has a definite number of spokes; fifty in all have been listed for the whole body. [...] In ordinary persons these wheels neither revolve nor vibrate, they form inextricable tangles of coils, called accordingly 'knots' (*granthi*), because they 'knot' spirit and matter, thus strengthening the sense of ego. [...] Together they constitute the unconscious complexes (*saṃskāra*) woven by illusion, and the weight and rigidity of the past offers a strong opposition to the passage of the spiritual force. Each knot, being an obstruction, must be loosened so that the energy released by the centres can be absorbed by the Kuṇḍalinī and thus regain its universality. These wheels are by no means physiological and static centres of the gross body, but centres of power belonging to the subtle body, centres that the yogin alone, during the unfolding of Kuṇḍalinī, can locate with as much accuracy as if they belonged to the body. (Silburn 1988: 25–6)

Abhinavagupta's scheme employs five *cakras* rather than the seven more familiar from more modern accounts (Silburn 1988: 27–30):[18]

[17] It is worth noting that there are also statements in the Brāhmaṇas where orgasm is identified with divine bliss (*ānanda*), see Olivelle 1997. I would see these more as indicative of a theme that was taken up in the later sexual practices rather than as a direct precursor of those practices.

[18] Another early source, the *Kaulajñānanirṇaya*, discusses a number of different schemes, including one with eleven *cakras* (ch.5, vv.25–7) and one with eight (ch.10; cf. Bagchi and Magee 1986).

bhrūmadhya[19]	Between eyebrows
kaṇṭha	Base of neck or back of throat
hṛdayacakra	Heart
nābhicakra	Navel
mūlādhāra or *mūlabhūmi*	Base of spine

While there is no direct precedent for such a scheme in earlier Brahmanical sources, there are certainly suggestions of an internal 'subtle physiology'. These include the five-body structure of the *Taittiriya Upaniṣad* II.1–5.[20] These bodies were later developed by Vedantic writers into five 'sheaths' or *kośa* obscuring the inner self (e.g. in Śaṇkara's *Vivekacūḍāmaṇi*). The *Taittiriya Upaniṣad* is generally regarded as one of the earliest Upaniṣads; Olivelle dates it to the fourth or fifth century BCE, though the dating is far from certain (Olivelle 1996: xxxvii).[21]

Apart from the discussion of the five bodies, the *Taittiriya Upaniṣad* also includes a passage (I.6) suggestive of ideas regarding an internal anatomy of the subtle body, with a central channel through the body and the possibility of movement in different directions from that central channel. Similar ideas can be found in other probably early texts in the Upaniṣadic corpus, as well as in Greek thought at what was perhaps around the same time (McEvilley 2002).[22] The idea of five breaths or forms of *prāṇa* within the body is also found in the later Vedic material, and homologised in various ways with the sacrificial ritual (e.g. Hartzell 1987: 100–7). Connolly comments on the concept of *prāṇa* in the *Śatapatha Brāhmaṇa* that

> It exists in two principal modes, a unitary one, when it is the foundation of all existence and the inner controller of the individual, and diversified one, when it is the various cosmic forces and the breaths and faculties which exist in the body. [...] The unified *prāṇa* enters the body by way of the head and then spreads

19 The *bhrūmadhya* centre is also often known as *bindu* (point) 'because, when this centre is pierced, the pent-up energy that has accumulated there is realeased, and a dot of dazzling light appears, "a subtle fire flashing forth as a flame". This is the "*bindu*", a dimensionless point – free therefore from duality – in which a maximum of power is concentrated' (Silburn 1988: 29.) *Bindu* (*thig-le* in Tibetan) is a key term in the Buddhist versions of these practices as well, though it is there given a somewhat different meaning.

20 These start from the physical body formed by food (*anna-maya*) and proceed through a series of other, subtler bodies or selves, each one shaped like a human being and pervading the one before: the body or self made of vital breath (*prāṇa-maya*); the body or self made of mind (*mano-maya*); the body or self made of consciousness or intellect (*vijñāna-maya*), and finally the body or self made of bliss (*ananda-maya*).

21 I have moved Olivelle's dates in the main text forward a century in accordance with his note at 1996: xxxvi n.21, since I have assumed the 'later' chronology for the Buddha in this book.

22 McEvilley cites the *Chāndogya* and *Maitri Upaniṣads*, Plato's *Timaeus*, and the early Greek medical tradition (2002: 93–6). I should add that I do not endorse some of the later, more speculative sections of McEvilley's article.

throughout, infusing every limb. In doing so it nourishes and vitalizes the body. Those parts not reached by the *prāṇa* dry up and wither away. The distribution of *prāṇa* appears to be effected by means of definite pathways, though the text is not clear on this. (Connolly 1997: 24)

However, the idea of breath/ *prāṇa* as a substance to be moved consciously around the body does not appear to be present in any of the early sources discussed by Connolly. All of this material is suggestive in various ways of later developments, and it can hardly be denied that the language of the internal yogas as it was later formulated was influenced by these ideas, but there is nothing here which implies yogic practices in which *prāṇa* or other similar substances are consciously moved along internal channels. It is certainly not predictive of them.

We are unlikely ever to know precisely how the 'internal yogas' of Tantric Śaivism and Buddhism developed. All we can really say at this stage is (1) we have evidence for similar practices in China many centuries before our earliest Indian evidence, and we know that there had been several centuries of active interchange along the China-India trade routes by the time that these practices appeared in India, and (2) from their earliest appearance in India, these practices were conceptualised (or reconceptualised) within a specifically Indic vocabulary.[23]

BUDDHIST AND JAIN DEVELOPMENTS

The earliest explicit versions of these practices in North Indian Śaiva material (in the *Kaulajñānanirṇaya* and *Kubjikātantra*) probably date from the ninth and tenth centuries. If the *Tirumantiram*, ascribed to the Tamil saint Tirumūlar, can really be dated to the seventh century CE, it would seem to be the earliest Indic account of these practices (see Zvelebil 1973: 73–80, esp. 78–9; 1996: 121), but the dating of this work is by no means certain.[24] On the Buddhist side, the *Hevajra Tantra*, perhaps dating from the late ninth century in its present form, represents a stage similar to that discussed above by Silburn on the Śaiva side. Book One, Chapter 1 of the *Hevajra* describes thirty-two named *nāḍīs* (channels) of which the three principal ones are Lalanā, Rasanā and Avadhūti, and four *cakras* (the lowest *cakra* of the Śaiva scheme is omitted):

[23] It is worth mentioning that we have clear evidence for such radical reconceptualisation of Tantric yoga in at least one more recent context: in the songs of the nineteenth century Bengali saint Lalon Fakir and his fellow 'Bāuls' we find the internal practices rewritten in Islamic terms (Salomon 1991).

[24] Venkatraman argues for a tenth to eleventh century date on the grounds that the text refers to the Nine Nāths, the teachings of Matsyendranātha and Goraknāth, and the Kālacakra (1990: 42–8; see also N. Subrahmanian's comments in his foreword, 1990: xi–xiii).

mahāsukhacakra ('Centre of Great Bliss')	Head[25]
saṃbhogacakra ('Centre of Enjoyment')	Throat
dharmacakra ('Centre of Essential Nature')	Heart
nirmāṇacakra ('Centre of Creation')	[Navel]

As the names suggest, these *cakras* are named after the four bodies of the Buddha (an expansion of the more familiar set of three bodies, *nirmāṇakāya, saṃbhogakāya, dharmakāya*). They are then correlated with various further components of the Buddhist teachings (Farrow and Menon 1992: 16–21). The last verse of the chapter presents the equivalent to the arousal of Kuṇḍalinī in a highly condensed form:

Caṇḍalī blazes up in the navel. She burns the Five Buddhas. She burns Locanā and the others. Ahaṃ ['I'] is burnt and the Moon flows down. (Farrow and Menon 1992: 21)

Caṇḍalī, another fierce goddess, here occupies the place of Kuṇḍalinī in the Śaiva system.[26] The ninth century *Yogaratnamālā* commentary interprets the name in terms of Caṇḍa = 'fierce', but Caṇḍalī also means a woman of the Caṇḍala low-caste group, suggesting a connection with 'polluted' social groups. Caṇḍalī is also one of the eight goddesses of the Hevajra maṇḍala, discussed in Chapter 10; others bear names relating to other polluting occupational groups (Ḍombī) or tribal populations (Śavarī).

As I mentioned in Chapter 10, we can to some degree at least trace the adoption and development of these practices within the Buddhist tradition from the eighth century onwards. There appears to be a gradual evolution from the tantras classed by the later tradition as *kriyā* and *caryā*, which are primarily about 'external' ritual practices, to the *yogatantra* (c. 700–c. 750 CE) where the emphasis becomes much more on the achievement of inner purity, and we first find the identification of the practitioner with a Tantric deity, a form of the Buddha. From then on, as Dalton has noted, there is a progressive *interiorisation* of the ritual, leading eventually to the major Tantric cycles of the so-called *anuttarayoga* Tantra, the Hevajra, Cakrasaṃvara, etc., in the late ninth century.

The Tantric interiorization of Buddhist ritual was not a rejection of ritual. Nor was it a psychologization [. . .]. This shift took place in the physical realm. Its beginnings can be traced to the first half of the eighth century, and the ritual technologies it spawned continued to develop through the ninth century. By the

[25] The locations of the four *cakras* are not stated directly in the root text of the *Hevajra Tantra*. The upper three are specified in the ninth century *Yogaratnamālā* commentary (Farrow and Menon 1992: 14–16). Verse 32 makes it clear that the lowest centre is at the navel.

[26] The Tibetan for Caṇḍalī is *gtum-mo*, the term for the well-known 'psychic heat' or 'mystic heat' practices which derive from the yogic processes discussed here (e.g. Guenther 1963: 53–60; Huber 1999: 86–90).

end of these two crucial centuries, a new ritual discourse of the bodily interior was in place. The Tantric subject had become the site for the entire ritual performance; the body's interior provided the devotee, the altar, the oblations, and the buddha to be worshipped. (Dalton 2004: 2)

Dalton's recent study focuses on the period between the *yoga* Tantra and the *anuttarayoga* Tantra. The key category here, *mahāyoga* Tantra, has been elided from the dominant 'New Tantra' classification in Tibet, but was important in India and remains part of the 'Old Tantra' (rNying-ma-pa) classification. Dalton notes that it was the *mahāyoga* Tantras, such as the *Guhyasamāja* and *Guhyagarbha*, which introduced 'the ritualized sexual practices for which tantra has since become so notorious. They focused on the body's interior, on the anatomical details of the male and female sexual organs and the pleasure generated through sexual union' (2004: 3).

The development of the initiation ceremony, and specifically the introduction of the second initiation, the *guhyābhiṣeka* where the initiate consumed a drop of the combined sexual fluids of the Tantric master and his consort, was a particularly significant part of this development. As noted in Chapter 10, this was a key component of Śaiva tradition as well, where it was seen as ingesting the essence of the clan or lineage of practice.

While the sexual practices hinted at by Asaṅga in the *Mahāyānasūtrālaṃkāra* were not necessarily transgressive, there is little doubt that this initiation would have been a transgressive act for those taking part. What is also striking is that it was seen as an occasion for the direct experience of the central liberating insight of the tradition, and also as a model for later *sādhana* or ritual practice, in which the disciple would himself re-enact the rite with a female consort.

This is most explicit in ritual manuals from Dunhuang in Central Asia, which appear to present a picture of the *mahāyoga* Tantras as practised in the ninth and tenth centuries, than in the later Indian and Tibetan commentarial material, particularly that of the 'Ārya tradition', where the sexual aspects are often significantly downplayed (Dalton 2004: 9; cf. Wedemeyer 2002). In these Dunhuang meditation texts we find the identification of *bodhicitta*, the classic altruistic motivation to achieve Buddhahood in order to relieve all sentient beings of their suffering, with the seminal drop held at the tip of the penis in the Perfection Stage, the second of the two stages of the practice.[27] Dalton suggests that the symbolism here is of procreating

[27] In later Tibetan versions of the Perfection Stage, male and female sexual substances, both seen as internal to the body of either male or female practitioner, are directed into the central channel of the body (Huntingdon and Bangdel 2003: 240–51). As Beyer comments, however, the 'experiential dimensions of Great Bliss and Clear Light' were always balanced with the 'intellectual categories of Emptiness'; 'bliss or light without Emptiness was simple sensual indulgence' (Beyer 1973: 133).

the Buddha; in the first (generation) stage, the practitioner 'has imagined himself as a son of the Buddha, generated out of the buddha's seed syllable, [w]hereas in the second stage the Buddha is generated out of the practitioner's own seed, a syllable that arises at the tip of his penis inside the vagina of the female partner' (Dalton 2004: 9):

> The practitioner is then instructed to worship the maṇḍala, using the blissful sensations flowing through his body. Such instructions seem to reflect an early prototype of the subtle body systems that were articulated in more complex forms in later works. The later systems involved intricate arrangements of *cakras* and energy channels mapped across the body's interior. In the early Mahāyoga texts, however, the technologies are simpler, the descriptions limited to the energies associated with sexual pleasure which rushes through the practitioner's torso. (Dalton 2004: 10–11)

Dalton suggests that these more complex systems only appear in the Perfection Stage yogas in the late ninth and tenth centuries. At this earlier stage, the sexual energy is more 'a raw physical force that is used to worship and energise the buddhas' (2004: 12). The ritual ends with the consumption of a sacrament (*samaya*; the term also means 'vow' or 'commtment'), presumably the combined sexual fluids of the two participants, by both partners, taken from the female partner's vagina, thus re-enacting the initiation rite in the form of a self-consecration (2004: 15–16). Dalton argues that this practice was the 'defining characteristic' of *mahāyoga* practice at this period, although it later dropped out of the tradition.[28]

In fact, while *mahāyoga* practice (at least as interpreted by Dalton) includes the moderately transgressive and polluting element of the consumption of sexual fluids from the female partner's vagina,[29] it seems in other respects rather close to the kind of early sexual yoga implied by Asaṅga, with the seminal restraint being a key element during the 'Perfection Stage' of the practice.[30] The imagery becomes much more transgressive with the

[28] Dalton also suggests that the initial context of the term 'Great Perfection' (Tibetan *rdzogs chen*), also described in the *Guhyagarbha Tantra* as a *samaya* or sacrament, was the state of liberating insight associated with this self-consecration (2004: 8, 17–20 and n.56). Note here Isaacson's discussion of the various interpretations of the four consecrations associated with the initiation proper (1998: 32).

[29] Doubtless somewhat more transgressive if the male practitioner was high caste and the woman was from a low caste background. The *Guhyasamāja Tantra*, as noted in Chapter 10, presents itself as a shocking and radical new teaching, but the radically antinomian language for which it is known is not for the most part intended to be taken literally.

[30] If the sacrament is made up of the combined sexual fluids of the two partners, the male obviously does ejaculate before this stage; Dalton cites another Dunhuang text in which the fall of the *bodhicitta* (i.e. semen) is seen as an offering to the goddess (PT841, see Dalton 2004: 16). See also *Guhyasamāja Tantra* 7.33–4: 'What is that meditation on recollection of the pledge [*samaya*]? In accordance with the pledge, he who desires the fruit should pour out his seed and drink it according to the rite; he should

late ninth and early tenth century *anuttarayoga* or *yoginī* tantras such as the Hevajra and Cakrasaṃvara, with their cremation-ground symbolism, the central role of fierce goddesses, and similar *kāpālika* or Śākta material.

As far as the 'internal' yogic practices are concerned, there is a significant step from the kind of practice Dalton is suggesting, where sexual practice is used to energise the ritual and perhaps create the state of bliss and loss of personal identity which is homologised with liberating insight, to the *cakra* and *nāḍī* practices. One could read the development of the new system in either of two ways, as an indigenous inspiration suggested by continued yogic practice in *mahāyoga* style, or as a set of concepts and processes incorporated from another source into the more basic sexual yoga discussed here. To me, the second alternative seems more likely, especially given the presence of such ideas in the cognate Chinese practices. If Buddhist practitioners were already employing sexual yoga of the kind suggested here, the *cakra* system would provide both a structure to aid practitioners in directing their sensations, and a grid through which associations could be built up with other elements of the symbolic world within which the practice was taking place. There are no obvious grounds here for deciding whether the *cakra*-based sexual practices first arose in a Śaiva or Buddhist context, but it is evident that they were being actively developed in both by the tenth century.[31]

Some Jainas also appear to have adopted the internal yogic practices involving the circulation of *prāṇa*, but as far as I know there is no evidence for Jaina use of sexual yoga. Since the principal evidence for Jaina meditation practices derives from the writings of Hemacandra in the twelfth century I shall leave discussion of them to Chapter 13, where I shall be dealing with that period.

CONCLUSION

As we have seen, these new Tantric traditions are a confluence of a variety of different factors and components: *maṇḍala* and *mantra* practices going back to the late Mahāyāna sūtras and early Tantras, internal sexual yogic practices of the kind discussed in this chapter, with the incorporation of fierce male and female deities and cremation-ground symbolism apparently

kill the host of Tathāgatas and attain supreme perfection. What is that meditation on recollection of the pledge of transcendent wisdom? All are naturally luminous, unarisen, uninfluenced; there is no enlightenment, no realisation, no end and no origin' (Fremantle 1990: 109, 113).

[31] For a summary of the developed Tibetan approach to Guhyasamāja practice, see Thurman 1997: 135–43.

from *kāpālika* and other Śaiva contexts, all within a philosophical and conceptual frame which goes back to the early Mahāyāna and in some respects to the common Indian background of the early renouncer traditions. It is natural to wonder why Buddhist practitioners might choose to put together this particular complex of ideas and practices. But before we look further at this question, we should turn to look at the people who employed these practitioners, above all the rulers and states of the time.

CHAPTER 12

Tantra and the state

As we saw in Chapters 10 and 11, there were striking innovations in both Śaiva and Buddhist practices from the seventh and eighth centuries onwards.[1] While these innovations have been frequently lumped together under the label of 'Tantra', they include a variety of different components on both Śaiva and Buddhist sides.

To summarise, on the Śaiva side, a 'transgressive' tradition of rituals involving cremation grounds, polluting substances associated with sex and death, fierce gods and particularly goddesses appears to have been originally carried out as ritual sorcery by hereditary caste groups (*kula*). The initiation rituals for these traditions involved the consumption of the 'clan essence', the mixed sexual secretions of male guru and female consort.

These practices were adopted by renunciate practitioners in the so-called *kāpālika* style and gained increasing importance in the seventh to ninth centuries (the *kaula* lineages associated with the early Nāth siddhas). The more extreme elements were mostly dropped and the 'external' practices were progressively substituted by 'internal' yogic practices which have a marked sexual component and involve a subtle body physiology of *cakras* and internal flows and channels. Within these practices, sexual ritual became a mode of access to a state of the body-mind in which the liberating insight central to the tradition could be directly perceived.

On the Buddhist side, early 'Tantric' practices (sixth and seventh centuries) were mostly a further development of established deity-visualisation practices in the later Mahāyāna *sūtras*, with fierce, mostly male deities initially introduced as secondary figures in the *maṇḍala*. In the eighth to tenth centuries, fierce Śaiva-style male and female deities, and couples in sexual union, took over as primary figures at the centre of the *maṇḍala*, *kula*-style initiation rituals were adopted, and there was a progressive shift

[1] The Vaiṣṇava Tantric tradition of the Pāñcarātra seems by and large to have stayed clear of these developments, and Jaina involvement also appears to have been relatively limited.

to 'internal' yogic practices closely parallel to those which were developing at around the same time or a little later in the Śaiva tradition. Again, sexual ritual became a mode of access to a state of the body-mind in which the liberating insight central to the tradition could be directly perceived. Circles of fierce Śaiva-style deities were incorporated into the structure of Buddhist *maṇḍalas*. These new practices formed the basis of the Mahāyoga and Yoginī ('Anuttarayoga') Tantras.

It is not clear to what extent practices involving sexual intercourse were undertaken literally by supposedly celibate practitioners,[2] though there are certainly stories of formerly celibate Buddhist practitioners abandoning their vows to take on these new 'Siddha' practices. In the later Tibetan Buddhist context, where these Tantric lineages were performed by celibate practitioners, they were mostly undertaken in symbolic form. This is also true of much later Śaiva practice. In the eighth to tenth century Indian context, however, it would seem that they were mostly performed literally, by both Śaiva and Buddhist non-celibate practitioners, who might be renunciates or (particularly in the later stages) ordinary lay people.

I will consider some of the later history of these practices in Chapter 13. In the present chapter, I look at the initial development of these practices and attempt to relate it to the wider social and political context in which they took place. I begin with a brief introduction of political developments.

INDIC STATES IN THE EIGHTH TO TENTH CENTURIES

Gupta and Vākāṭaka rule came to an end in the early sixth century; the precipitating factor in the Gupta case may have been the invasions of the Huns (more properly, the Hephthalite Hūṇa peoples). Ronald Davidson has attempted to catalogue the numerous, often short-lived, dynasties and the political interplay of the succeeding centuries; the results understandably verge on the unreadable, but give some indication of the complex and chaotic politics of the period (Davidson 2002a: 30–62). States between the early sixth and mid eighth centuries were for the most part relatively short-lived and unable to maintain control of substantial areas for sustained

[2] Sanderson notes that '[t]he tradition of Abhayākaragupta and Darpaṇācārya remained true to the early tradition, insisting that any Buddhist, layperson or monk, may take the Tantric vows and receive all the consecrations, including the problematic consecrations involving sexual intercourse, provided he has achieved insight into the doctrine of emptiness' (1994: 97). This also appears to have been the position of the Indian guru Atīśa, who came to Tibet in the mid-eleventh century (Samuel 1993: 470–1). In the longer run, however, as Sanderson again notes, the rituals were generally modified to avoid transgressing vows of celibacy, as in Tibet, or practised only by non-celibates, as among the Newars (Sanderson 1994: 97).

periods of time. In the early seventh century, much of North India was temporarily unified under King Harṣa (c. 606–47 CE); we are particularly well informed about this period through the accounts both of Harṣa's court poet Bāṇa and the Chinese Buddhist visitor Xuanzang, who visited India between approximately 629 and 645 CE. However, Harṣa's empire fell apart at his death, and another century of rapidly changing short-lived regimes followed.

The mid-eighth century marked the emergence of a more stable situation, with three major empires, the Gurjara-Pratīhāra dynasty, based at Ujjain and extending over much of North-West India, the Pāla state, based in Bengal and Bihar, and the Rāṣṭrakūṭa kings, based in the southern Deccan. North India was contested territory between the Gurjara-Pratīhāra and Pāla states. In South India, the Cōḻa dynasty also established a stable and long-lasting state, centred at Tanjore in modern Tamilnadu (Fig. 12.1).

What is more significant than the details of dynastic conflicts and shift in territorial control from the sixth to eighth centuries are the new social and cultural patterns that emerged during this period. Davidson speaks of a culture of 'military adventurism', leading to 'decentralisation and the coalescence of fiefdoms'; military defence became a prime imperative, with a rapid increase of castles and other other fortifications (Davidson 2002: 67).

The key political concept of the new order was the feudal lord (*sāmanta*), with each major state ideally surrounded by a circle of lesser states whose rulers paid homage to the king at the centre and replicated his style at the local level. This political structure was referred to as a *maṇḍala*, and formed a conscious model for the Tantric Buddhist *maṇḍala*, with its central divinity surrounded by lesser deities in the four or eight directions. As Davidson notes, the 'sāmantisation' of Indian society was mirrored by the 'sāmantisation' of the deities, who increasingly came to be viewed on the model of feudal lords and ladies (Davidson 2002a: 71–2).

The 'wisdom king' ethic of the *Rāmāyaṇa* had been in part a literary fantasy, but it had also been an ideal to which rulers in the first few centuries CE paid at least lip-service. Davidson points to a new trend emerging from the late fifth century onwards: the 'divine erotization of kingship and, ultimately, of warfare' (2002a: 68). War was the domain of Śiva and of the fierce goddesses, and it is not surprising that rulers turned increasingly to these cults in both non-Tantric and Tantric forms.

The Pāla dynasty was pro-Buddhist, and was responsible for the creation of a major series of new monastic centres in the late eighth and early ninth centuries. The Gurjara-Pratīhāra, Rāṣṭrakūṭa and Cōḻa were pro-Brahmanical, as were most of the smaller powers of the period, and while

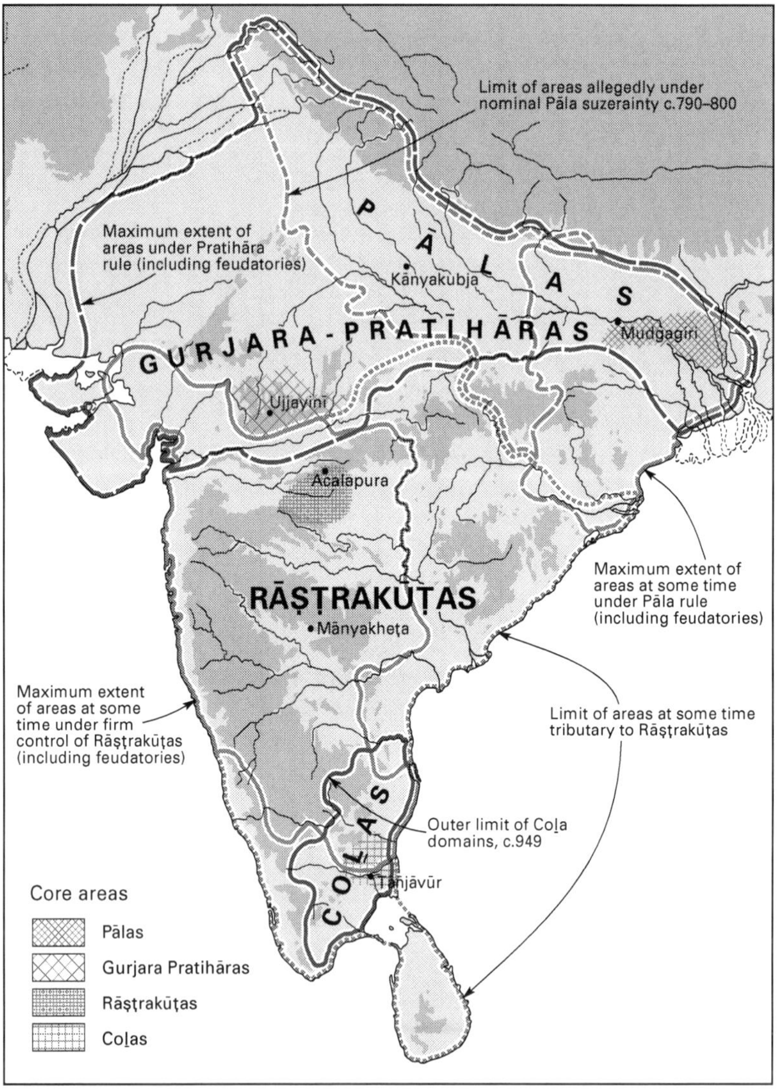

Figure 12.1. Map of South Asia, eighth to tenth centuries

a general pattern of religious pluralism continued, state support for the non-Brahmanical traditions was decreasing. Jainas were occasionally successful at gaining royal protection and support, as in Gujarat during the time of King Kumaragupta and the Jaina teacher Hemacandra (mid-twelfth century), but they too were increasingly marginalised during this period. The weakening of long-distance trade consequent on the Muslim expansion into Iran, Afghanistan, and the northwestern parts of South Asia, and the general disturbance of urban life due to the constant warfare of these centuries, may also have affected the economic base on which the Buddhists and Jainas, with their close links to merchant and artisan communities, depended.

Buddhism was by now becoming established in parts of Southeast Asia, but the *sāmanta* model and the accompanying religious cults were also increasingly exported from South Asia. By the eighth and ninth centuries, the major states in the region were Pagan in present-day Burma, the Khmer state (Kambuja), Champa in present-day Vietnam and Śrīvijaya in peninsular Malaysia, Sumatra and Western Java (Fig. 12.2). These regions were increasingly part of the wider Indic cultural orbit, and we find, for example, Buddhist scholars such as Atiśa travelling to Southeast Asia to study with local Vajrayāna Buddhist teachers (Chattopadhyaya 1967).

Northwest India and Central Asia were still important parts of the Indic cultural sphere up to the Muslim conquests, and there remained a scattering of significant Śākta and Tantric centres in the Northwest, including the important pilgrimage site of Hiṅglāj (White 1996: 66, 121–2) and the major Tantric centre of Oḍḍiyāna, which is now generally accepted as being located, as the Tibetan pilgrims believed, in the Swat Valley (Davidson 2002b: 160). By the ninth century, however, these regions were increasingly cut off from direct contact with the surviving Buddhist communities in India, and they were significant more as legendary locations for the origins of Tantric teachings than as real places (Davidson 2002b: 160–3). The culmination of these imaginings was the mythic realm of Śambhala, origin of the Kālacakra Tantra which arrived in northern India in the early eleventh century (Davidson 2002b: 166–8; Bernbaum 1980; Newman 1998). Those parts of Central Asia that remained Buddhist, such as the oasis state of Dunhuang, the Tangut (Xixia) kingdom at Karakhoto, or the Mongols, turned to the Tibetans and Chinese for continuing contact and renewal.[3]

3 As we saw in Chapter 11, Dunhuang includes a large body of Buddhist texts in Tibetan representing the latest developments in Tantric Buddhism in Tibet at the time. Shen Weirong has recently shown how the Buddhist scholars of Karakhoto in the eleventh and twelfth centuries were producing translations of works by sGam-po-pa and other Tibetan scholars within a few years of their composition (Shen 2006).

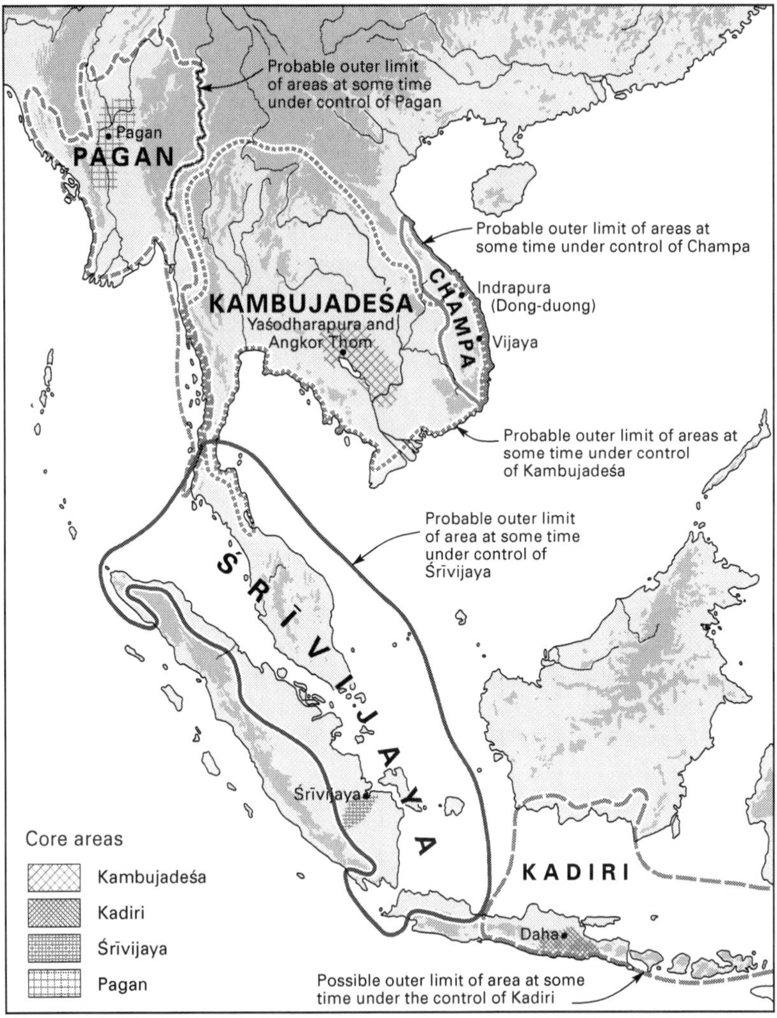

Figure 12.2. Map of Southeast Asia, eighth to tenth centuries

POLITICS AND TANTRA IN SOUTH ASIA

To return to South Asia proper, the process of 'sāmantisation' and military adventurism described by Davidson doubtless goes a long way to explain the increasing interest in fierce deity cults and Tantric ritual in general by the rulers of this period. We saw what was probably an early example of this in the relief carvings of the Saptamātṛkā deities at Udayagiri, patronised by Candragupta II in 401–2, which I discussed in Chapter 10. It is unclear whether Saptamātṛkā rituals at Udayagiri were carried out by an old-style royal *purohita* from an Atharvavedic Brahmin background, as suggested by Michael Willis, or by non-Vedic priests who specialised in these new rituals. If the director of the ritual was a Vedic Brahmin, then he was certainly employing techniques that go well beyond anything found in the Atharvaveda, and which we later see in specifically *kaula* and Tantric contexts. Within the next few centuries, at any rate, Tantric-type deity-cults employing fierce goddesses such as the Saptamātṛkā deities would seem to have progressively taken over in state ritual throughout South and Southeast Asia.

In this connection, Sanjukta Gupta and Richard Gombrich argued some years ago that

> for at least the last thousand years, perhaps longer, the concept of power in its political and social application has been intimately connected with Tantric theology – so intimately, one might suggest, that the one cannot be adequately understood apart from the other. (Gupta and Gombrich 1986: 123)

They noted that images of Durgā 'start to show many royal insignia from about 500 AD on' (1986: 132). Durgā is the most common exoteric representation of *śakti* or power in Tantric terms, and she is particularly associated with battle. Gupta and Gombrich imply that this shift in symbolism reflects the importance Durgā increasingly had for Hindu kingdoms from this time onwards. The king was symbolically married to Durgā when he ascended the *siṃhāsana* or 'lion throne', and the annual Durgā festival of *navarātrī* was a 'major political occasion' and an 'annual ceremony of reintegration' in Hindu kingdoms into modern times (1986: 133). Typically, kings were also symbolically married to other more local or esoteric Tantric goddesses; the king was regarded as an earthly representative of whichever male god was currently regarded as most important (typically a form of Viṣṇu or Śiva) and so as married to whichever local goddesses were treated as that deity's consort (Gupta and Gombrich 124–5; Vergati-Stahl 1979).

The Saptamātṛkā goddesses lost much of their importance after the eighth century, to be replaced by a variety of other female deities, including Durgā, Gaurī, Lakṣmī, Pārvatī and others. They were, however, absorbed into sets of eight or more goddesses who formed one of the circles of the *maṇḍala*. Ritual forms based on these goddesses have survived into modern times, and have been studied in relation to the Newar cities of Kathmandu Valley, primarily Bhaktapur, Patan or Kathmandu. Each of these Kathmandu Valley cities, formerly the capitals of small Newar kingdoms, is surrounded by a protective circle of eight Mātṛkā temples (Gutschow 1982, 1993; Levy 1987, 1992). These goddesses, accompanied by Bhairava and Gaṇeśa, and generally referred to now as Navadurgā (the 'Nine Durgās'), assume human form through masked low-caste trance-dancers in annual ritual dances throughout the valley (Gutschow and Bāsukala 1987; Iltis 1987, van der Hoek 2005; Korvald 2005; Sardar n.d.). We find masked-dance traditions of this kind in many parts of South Asia and there seems every reason to assume that they go back to the early mediaeval period that we are discussing here. I consider these practices in a little more detail later in this chapter.

First, however, we look at further evidence from Indian textual material. One of the most striking pieces of evidence is provided by the *Netra Tantra*, a text probably composed in Kashmir in the eighth or (more likely) early ninth century. In a recent article, Alexis Sanderson has argued that this text constitutes, in effect, a manual for a Tantric Śaivite priest to take over virtually the complete role of the royal *purohita* and *rājaguru*. This includes the entire cult of non-Tantric deities such as Viṣṇu, Sūrya, Brahmā, the Buddha and Gaṇeśa, along with deities from a wide variety of other Tantric cycles, all of whom are regarded by the *Neta Tantra* priest as transforms of his own central Tantric deities, Amṛteśvara (also known as Amṛteśabhairava) and Śrī (Amṛtalakṣmī) (Sanderson 2004: 245). It is no great surprise to find a set of eight mātṛkā goddesses in a circle around Amṛteśvara and Amṛtalakṣmī, though they are worshipped in this case in order to ward off ills rather than invoke them on one's enemies (2004: 245–6). Sanderson argues that

> [The Śaiva Mantramārga] succeeded in forging close links with the institution of kingship and thereby with the principal source of patronage. I see four main elements here: (1) the occupying by Śaiva officiants of the office of Royal Preceptor (*rājaguruḥ*) and in this position their giving Śaiva initiation (*dīkṣā*) to the monarch followed by a specially modified version of the Śaiva consecration ritual (*abhiṣekaḥ*) as an empowerment to rule beyond that conferred by the conventional brahmanical royal consecration (*rājyābhiṣekaḥ*); (2) the promoting by Śaiva officiants of the practice of displaying and legitimating a dynasty's power by their officiating in the founding of Śaiva temples in which the new Śivas that they enshrined bore as the individuating first half of their names that of the royal founder or, where complexes of royal Śiva temples were established, those of the founder and any kin that he might designate for this purpose; (3) the provision of a repertoire of protective, therapeutic and aggressive rites for the benefit of the monarch and his kingdom; and (4) the development of Śaiva rituals and their applications

to enable a specialized class of Śaiva officiants to encroach on the territory of the Rājapurohita, the brahmanical expert in the rites of the Atharvaveda who served as the personal priest of the king, warding off all manner of ills from him through apotropaic rites, using sorcery to attack his enemies, fulfilling the manifold duties of regular and occasional worship on his behalf, and performing the funerary and other postmortuary rites when he or other members of the royal family died. (Sanderson 2004: 232–3)

Apart from taking over the office of official royal chaplain and *purohita*, Tantric officiants might be independent practitioners called upon at times of need. Sanderson cites a twelfth-century example in a Coḷa inscription, where the ruler called on a Tantric specialist to destroy an invading Sri Lankan army (2004: 233–4), and also discusses the well-known Sdok kak Thom inscription from Cambodia, which I will consider later in this chapter (see also Sanderson 2003–4). We will see further examples in Buddhist contexts from East Asia.

From Sanderson's account, it seems that the Kashmiri kings adopted the new Tantric procedures. The popularity of *kaula* thought in Kashmir is also demonstrated by the extensive reference to *kaula* ideas in the *Haravijaya*, a Sanskrit court epic composed in Kashmir between 826 and 838 CE (D. Smith 1985: 262–5).

Elsewhere in South Asia, *kaula* ideas were also widely adopted (e.g. Gupta and Gombrich 1986; A. Cohen 1992, 1997). David Gordon White has noted that

In their seventh-to-eleventh century heyday, these forms of Kaula theory and practice were so compelling, as direct paths to gnosis, power, and godhead, that they won the adherence of some of the great royal houses of the period: the Somavaṃśis, Chandellas and Kalacuris, whose kingdoms stretched across the Vindhya range and beyond, from Rajasthan to Assam. It was these royal patrons who constructed many of the Yogini temples whose unusual architectural ruins dot this swathe of central India, who built the 'erotic' temple complexes at such sites as Bhubanesvara and Khajuraho, and who undoubtedly sought out Kula and Kaula specialists for their expertise in both the sacred and secular spheres. (White 1998: 198)

White's reference to the erotic temple complexes is significant, and this theme requires further discussion. We have seen something of the internal alchemical aspects of Tantra in Chapter 11, and of their close association with sexual rituals. It seems likely enough that the promise of health, long life and magical power through sexual practices was an appealing mixture for members of the ruling dynasties of these times.

I referred earlier to Davidson's comment on the eroticisation of warfare during this period; kingship was being made over in the image of a heroic male figure whose sexual powers were homologised with his military power and his very ability to fill the royal role. Thomas Donaldson notes the poetic use of double meanings at this time, in which a king may be eulogised at one and the same time 'as a lover and as a great warrior' (Donaldson 1986: 315). He cites as an example the Somavaṃśī king Yayāti II Chandīhara Mahaśivagupta III (c. 1015–40 CE) of Orissa, of whom one of his charters states that he,

> is a winking sensualist in (curing) the love-fever (the war-fever) of Karṇāta, Lāṭa and the lord of Gurjjara; [...] an expert voluptuary in removing the jingling girdles of women (in removing the warring Kāñcī, i.e. the Colas); [...] a fierce wind in opening and taking away the clothes of Gauḍa and Raḍhā ([...] a fierce wind in the sky of Gauḍa and Raḍhā for capturing and exposing) and [...] a full moon in the clean clothes of the love-afflicted body of Vaṅga ([...] a full moon in the bright sky of the peaceful Vaṅga). (Donaldson 1987: 315)

In this series of *double-entendres*, the king's wars against neighbouring countries are portrayed as a series of erotic encounters.

The hypereroticism of Indian temple architecture at this period is well known. The relatively restrained *mithuna* figures which we find as auspicious devices on earlier Buddhist shrines and temples (Agrawala 1983, e.g. plates 73–83; Stone 1994: plates 128–32, 168–71, 214–15) now became occasions for increasingly exaggerated erotic display, culminating in the well-known temples of Khajuraho (mid-tenth to mid-eleventh centuries) and Konarak (mid-thirteenth century); Rabe's analysis of the Khajuraho temples as a kind of celestial transform of the royal harem, focused around the king as their implicit male partner, seems entirely appropriate (Rabe 1996).[4] The earlier auspicious function of the *mithuna* images seems to have been buried under exuberant sexual display.

[4] A charter of an earlier Somavaṃśī ruler, Yayāti I Mahaśivagupta (c. 922–55 CE) provides an extraordinary description of the royal city, Yayātinagara, as a kind of sexual paradise, as 'Kāmadeva's pleasure garden' in Donaldson's phrase, 'where the enjoyment of love is being continually intensified and still more intensified by the close embraces (of lovers), by which fatigue is removed, in which hissing sound often appears and in which hairs stand on their ends, although such enjoyment suffers interruptions as the ardent young couple show their skill in the various processes of conjugal enjoyment with their eyes dilated (with excitement) and with their minds subdued and fascinated by amorous thoughts; where, even in the midst of quarrels arising from jealousy, lovers, beaten by lotuses from the ears of women who have cast the beauty of the celestial damsels into shade by the greatness of their endless and peculiar charms, have all their mental anguishes roused to action by the entrance of the sharp arrows of Cupid', and so on for several more lines (Donaldson 1987: 316; see also Dehejia 1979: 203 n. 4).

The poetry and the temple architecture I have referred to are for the most part erotic (and by implication martial) rather than Tantric, though explicit Tantric themes are occasionally found in temple imagery (e.g. White 2003: 97–9).[5] One can begin to see here though how Tantra provided both a ritual celebration of the new ideal and a set of techniques that promised to preserve and strengthen the sexual ability and personal power of the initiate, in part by giving him control over a pantheon of terrifying (but also enticing) female deities (see also White 2003: 123–59).

One can also imagine the vulnerability of rulers in such a climate to those who offered these techniques. A king who could not fulfil the conjoined military and sexual demands of his role, after all, would feel under considerable threat of being replaced by a younger and more virile man. Consider in this connection the description of the Kashmiri king Harṣa (reigned 1089–1101) in Kalhaṇa's *Rājataranginī*, in which the king is being ridiculed for his addiction to what were clearly Tantric sexual and alchemical practices aimed at health and long life:

> Others brought slave girls before him and said they were goddesses. He worshipped them, and abandoning his exalted position and wealth was laughed at by the people. These [slave girls], instructed by the parasites, who taught them [to give] counsels etc. [pretended to have obtained] from conversations with the gods, confused his mind. Some among these [slave girls] showed themselves eager for amorous intercourse at those occasions, and the king forsook his good fortune by touching them with his own body.
>
> As he was anxious to live for a very long time, they [the goddesses] granted him, when in his foolishness he asked for a long life, hundreds of years to live.
>
> When he desired to give magic perfection to his body (*piṇḍasiddhi*) some *ḍomba* [low-caste laundress] made him swallow a drink which he pretended was an elixir having that power. [. . .]
>
> What respectable man could relate the other even more shameful practices of his which he followed to obtain strength and beauty? (cited in Rabe 1996)

It is easy enough perhaps to make fun of king Harṣa. No doubt most sizeable Indian courts of the time had their quota of snake-oil merchants. However, Kalhaṇa's comments, or those of the twelfth-century Kashmiri satirist Kṣemendra (Gupta and Gombrich 1986: 132; see also Wojtilla 1984, 1990) would make little sense if the idea of kings seeking long life and bodily

[5] The small group of *yoginī* temples which have survived in Central and East India, which appear to have been explicitly designed as locations for *kaula*-style Tantric ritual (Dehejia 1986; White 2003 and see Chapter 10) are by contrast more restrained; the images here are more serious and central to the business at hand. They are figures of power, not of erotic display.

perfection through sexual practices was not in fact common currency at the time.[6]

Much of the imagery of Khajuraho and Konarak has rightly been valued as among the world's finest artistic achievements in the visual celebration of sexual love, but there is an uncomfortable undertow to the royal cult of Tantra that gave rise to it. For all of the exotic imagery of King Yayāti II's royal charter, its combination of martial violence and eroticism strikes a note that is both profoundly disturbing and all too familiar from our own time, in which the fantasy world of contemporary cinema constantly retails much the same story. Doubtless the association between sex and violence is grounded in some basic elements of human ethology, but a culture that allows itself to indulge too far in such fantasies runs the risk of distorting the basic relationships between men and women, and between men and men, in damaging ways.

Certainly, if perhaps ironically, as women were increasingly displayed as sexualised and spiritualised objects on the one hand, or invoked as powerful protective goddesses on the other, their role and autonomy in everyday life was progressively diminishing. Davidson has pointed to the striking decrease in female donors, especially autonomous female donors, at Buddhist sites (Davidson 2002a: 91–8). At Sāñcī, an early site, there are almost as many female donations as male, many of them from nuns. At Nālandā, founded in the sixth century, personal sealings and inscriptions attributable to women are a tiny minority. Inscriptions on Pāla and Sena period sculptures (late seventh to twelfth centuries) include only a small number of references to women. The few women who are mentioned are either members of the royal family, or otherwise defined by their relation to men (Davidson 2002a: 93–5).

Miranda Shaw has suggested that women took a central role in Tantric Buddhist practice but in reality there is little concrete evidence for this (M. Shaw 1994). There are indications of women acting as Tantric gurus in their own right, and as originating particular Tantric lineages, but they are relatively few in number. It is true that Vajrayāna Tantric vows required respectful behaviour towards women, in a society where they were clearly second-class citizens, and that the role of Tantric consort might legitimate a degree of independence which was increasingly difficult to find in the wider social context, but the evidence we have suggests that the Buddhist

[6] On other occasions, rather than imported slave girls, the members of the court might themselves take on the roles of Tantric deities. This is the situation envisaged, for example, in the doubtless legendary account of the physical enactment of the Vajradhātu maṇḍala at the court of King Indrabhūti of Zahor (Davidson 2002a: 243).

Tantric cults, and doubtless also the Śaivite *kaula* and Tantric cults, were male-directed and male-controlled.[7]

W. G. Archer suggested some years ago that the growth in mystical and symbolic interpretations of sexuality, and in sculptural representations of sexuality, was a kind of compensatory development in a society where morality was becoming ever more restrictive and women's position was increasingly subordinate (Archer 1964: 17–25): 'What is condemned in actual life is countenanced in sculpture and religion' (1964: 25). No doubt the increasingly patriarchal and Brahmanical influence associated with 'sāmantization' progressively brought to an end the relatively liberal gender climate I noted in the early period; purity and chastity become key themes. It is among the new martial elite groups, the Rajputs, that the cult of *satī* developed (Harlan 1992). Women's new situation, increasingly enclosed and controlled by their menfolk, mirrored that which was found in the Islamic states who were beginning to make inroads into South Asia at the start of this period (seventh to eighth centuries) and would control most of the subcontinent by its end (late twelfth and thirteenth centuries).[8]

It is unclear at this distance how far the sources of this increasingly restrictive situation for women were internal or external. India already had its own sources for notions of female purity, in texts such as the Laws of Manu or myths such as that of Kannaki (Pandian 1982), and the process of 'sāmantization' was driven as much by internal factors as by external attack. What one can say perhaps is that the conflict with Islam led to a polarisation and a militarisation on both sides. The early Rajputs, increasingly militantly Hindu and with Tantric overtones in many cases, were the classic Hindu form of leadership to evolve.

[7] Unfortunately, most of these indications, including the few female members in the Mahāsiddha lists, are difficult to pin down. The Shangs-pa bka'-brgyud tradition of Tibet claims to go back to a series of women teachers in India, including Sukhasiddhi, but their historicity is problematic (Kapstein 1980, 1997, 2005). Sukhasiddhi is however also named in a short text attributed to Tilopa, which survives in a Tibetan version as the source of *bar do* (intermediate state) and consciousness-transference practices associated with the 'Six Yogas of Nāropa' (Mullin 2006: 28–9). There are a number of other similar examples (Shaw 1994). In the modern South Asian context, Tantric sexual practices seem to vary from situations of relative equality (e.g. among the Bauls, McDaniel 1992) to those where women act as Tantric consorts on a commercial basis.

[8] Another sign of this change can be seen in the way in which, towards the end of this period, dress codes for women become much more confining. Neither men nor women in the first millennium routinely covered the upper part of the body; this remained the case in non-Muslim parts of rural Southeast Asia (Thailand, Laos, Bali, etc.) into modern times, as in parts of South Asia itself (Kerala, see Devika 2005). Court versions of women's clothing were often sexually revealing, as a vast body of evidence from Indian sculpture and literature makes clear. One can see a progressive change from the late first millennium onwards, although the near-total body cover of the modern *sari* is in fact a very late development (Fabri 1994).

TUMBURU AND HIS SISTERS IN CAMBODIA

While the pattern of Śaivite Tantric ritual for state purposes in South Asia is evident in many places, the textual documentation for such ritual is fairly limited. What is probably the best-known historical example of such documentation comes from Southeast Asia (Cambodia), in the form of an inscription at Sdok kak Thom, written in Sanskrit and Khmer and dated from 1052. This refers to the introduction of a new official cult by Jayavarman II, a Khmer king of the early ninth century.

We have evidence of a Pāśupata presence in the early years of the Khmer state, in seventh-century inscriptions (Wolters 1979: 431; Snellgrove 2000: 443) and Śaivite forms of religion were evidently established from quite early on. By the time of kings Indravarman (877–89) and Yaśovarman (889–900), extensive Śaivite temples and monasteries were being erected. There are signs of support for other Brahmanical communities and for Buddhists as well, but substantial signs of Buddhist support are mostly rather later and on a smaller scale; the only Khmer king to construct large-scale Buddhist monuments was Jayavarman VII (1181-?1219) (Snellgrove 2000: 458–87). The dominant elements of the Buddhist pantheon were the triad of the Buddha, Avalokiteśvara and the female deity Prajñāpāramitā (Felten and Lerner 1989: 237–8 and no. 38), suggesting *kriyā* or *caryā* Tantra practice, but there are also substantial indications of the presence of the Hevajra Tantra and other anuttarayoga material.[9]

The Sdok kak Thom inscription however is one our most substantial pieces of evidence for Śaiva state ritual. There have been a number of studies of this inscription, among the most recent being those of Ronald Davidson (2002a: 204–6) and Alexis Sanderson (2003–4, cf. also 2004: 234–5). It describes how a Brahmin named Hiraṇyadāma, an 'expert in the science of *siddhis*' (here meaning Tantric powers) revealed a unique *siddhi* to the king. At the king's invitation, he performed a ceremony intended to accomplish the total independence of Kambuja from Javā[10] and to establish Jayavarman's position as a *cakravartin*. The ceremony was performed according to the *Vīṇāśikha*, a Tantric text that corresponds to and is spoken by one of the four faces of the deity Tumburu. Again with the king's permission, Hiraṇyadāma taught the *siddhis* of the *Vīṇāśikha Tantra* and the other three Tantras corresponding to the other three faces, along with the methods of realising them, to Śivakaivalya, the king's own religious teacher.

[9] Cf. recent work by Peter Sharrock (personal communication, 2004).

[10] It is not clear what 'Javā' meant at this period, but the reference may be to the kingdom of Śrīvijaya in peninsular Malaysia and Sumatra (Sanderson 2004: 234 n. 8).

The inscription was actually put up in 1052 CE by a descendant of Śivakaivalya. Śivakaivalya's family claimed to have continued as court ritualists to the Khmer kings, and managers of the Tumburu cult, as well as of the *devarāja*, which was perhaps a moveable cult-image associated with the cult, in the intermediate two and a half centuries. In reality, as Davidson (2002a: 204–6) has pointed out, our evidence refers to the mid-eleventh century, not to the early ninth, but it still provides definite evidence for the use of the *Vīṇāśikha Tantra* and the cult of Tumburu at this later date.

In 1973, Teun Goudriaan summarised the then-available sources on Tumburu (Goudriaan 1973). In brief, Tumburu is known from three main contexts. He occurs in mainstream Brahmanical texts as a *gandharva* or minor celestial deity. He is described in several Śaivite and Tantric texts (*Yogavāsiṣṭha, Viṣṇudharmottara Purāṇa, Agni Purāṇa, Śāradātilaka, Ṣaṭkarmadīpika*, etc.) as a (usually) four-headed form of Śiva, always in association with four or seven Mātṛkā-type goddesses who are his consorts, and he occurs in one Buddhist Tantric text (the *Mañjuśrīmūlakalpa*), where he is accompanied by four goddesses described as his sisters. Goudriaan summarised this material as follows:

> From all these references a picture emerges of Tumburu as a healing god of sovereignty seated in the midst of four fierce goddesses with allegorical names expressive of various aspects of victory. The god commands these and occasionally counteracts their evil influence. (Goudriaan 1985: 23)

Some years later, a copy of the *Vīṇāśikha Tantra* itself turned up in the National Archives of Nepal, and Goudriaan subsequently edited and translated this text. It takes the usual form of a dialogue between Śiva and his consort, who are seated on Mount Kailās, 'surrounded by Ganas (headed by Mahākāla), Siddhas, sages and other supernatural beings' (Goudriaan 1985: 30).

The picture of the god that emerges in this text is much the same as that in the previously known sources: a royal manifestation of Śiva, particularly associated with healing, but clearly able to exercise more destructive powers. The Goddess, interestingly, says that the three other Tantras Śiva has spoken so far (which correspond to the texts associated with the three other faces of Śiva by the Sdok kak Thom inscription) are about the realisation of higher wisdom, whereas humankind needs techniques to deal with everyday problems. The text goes on to describe preparatory rituals, the construction of the *maṇḍala* and the worship of the deities, and the structure of *nāḍīs* and *cakras*, etc. The goddesses and four further attendant goddesses are described as fear-inspiring and the symbolism reinforces this in various ways (for example, one is seated on a corpse). These are still definitely wild and dangerous goddesses who Tumburu controls – and allows the *sādhaka* or practitioner to control and employ.

The Tantra goes on to explain how to use the Tumburu practice to achieve various magical results: to attract a woman or man, to destroy a person through sorcery, to subjugate someone, to eradicate or expel an enemy army, to cause dissension among friends, to restore a person to health and protect them from danger, and so on. A subsequent section provides a further series of rituals, many of them love magic of various kinds: to make someone impotent, to increase sexual potency, and the like. There are various additional instructions on meditation and ritual, including directions for performing a fire offering (*homa*).

These are all very typical contents and ritual purposes for both Śaivite and Buddhist Tantra. Many texts also give techniques for the attainment of higher knowledge, liberation or enlightenment. This particular Tantra, as the Goddess's opening request implies, is not concerned with such matters. The significant thing about the *Vīṇāśikha Tantra* however is that we have a dated historical reference stating that rituals according to this Tantra were performed over a period of two and a half centuries on behalf of Khmer royalty. While one can never be sure that a particular Tantric text which has survived to modern times is actually the same as that which is mentioned in an eleventh-century description, Goudriaan clearly felt that the similarities here were close enough that we were probably dealing with the same or a closely related text.

Tumburu's healing powers occupy a rather small part in this text, but in general healing and in particular the restoration of youth and sexual potency appear to have been an important component of what Tantric priests had to offer, often augmented by material medicines from the techniques of physical alchemy. We have already seen that much of the appeal of the possibly fraudulent Tantrics to King Harṣa was that they would provide him with long life and a perfect body.[11]

Certainly in East Asia, which we turn to next, the ability of Buddhist Tantra to provide healing seems to have been a major part of its appeal to Chinese and Japanese rulers, as the frequency of the iconography of the Healing Buddha, Bhaiṣajyaguru, shows. There are also reports of incidents where the successful performance of Bhaiṣajyaguru rituals for members of the ruling family led to state patronage of Bhaiṣajyaguru and of the

[11] Another Kashmiri text, Kṣemendra's *Samayamātṛkā*, provides a range of further examples of the use of Tantric ritual, again told in satirical style (Wojtilla 1984, 1990).

Tantric ritualists associated with his cult. However, it is worth noting that Bhaisjyaguru himself is not only a healing deity. He has his own *maṇḍala* of *yakṣa* generals who will protect those who reverence him (e.g. Kobayashi 1975: 119; Sugiyama 1982).

The conclusion of Goudriaan's introduction to the *Vīṇāśikha Tantra* is worth quoting:

> Just like his deity, the Sādhaka is ambivalent: he can protect and destroy. It can be imagined that such claims, if supported by a powerful and resourceful personality (his mental power enhanced by concentration on the internal deity), could be of interest to the South East Asian rulers who would be unable to find a similar competence among native practitioners. (Goudriaaan 1985: 61–2)

There is a nice balance in this quote. Goudriaan sees meditation on the deity as enhancing the mental power of the practitioner, but also gives full value to the pragmatic demands and credulity of the Khmer kings. Goudriaan goes on to say that 'It is in any case a remarkable fact that a tradition considered as inferior in India was able to strengthen its position in South East Asia by royal support' (1985: 62). There may well be some truth in this picture of Tantric ritual being most prevalent at the frontier areas, but in fact we would seem by now to have enough inscriptional, iconographical and textual evidence to suggest that kings in the Indian subcontinent were also calling on the services of Śaiva Tantric gurus.

As for Buddhist Tantra, our main evidence for mainland South Asia comes from the Pāla state and from the Tibetan chronicles, since the Tibetans acquired much of their own version of the Buddhist Tantric teachings from the great monastic universities of the Pālas in the eleventh and twelfth centuries. Our evidence here is supplemented in part by the remains of Buddhist monasteries and by surviving Buddhist images in South and Southeast Asia; the Khmer state is particularly rich in Hevajra iconography.

The prevalence of *maṇḍala* schemes in temple and monastery architecture is one significant indicator of the importance of Tantric practice for their builders. A particularly common temple form of the period, first found in the Pāla and Samataṭa states from the late eighth century onwards, consists of four ritual halls in the four directions, as at the great monastery of Paharpur in northern Bangladesh (Samuel 2002c). Here we are probably concerned with *yogatantra* and perhaps with the idea of four kinds of ritual action. Other monasteries excavated in Bangladesh and East India also seem to follow this pattern of a large *maṇḍala*-style temple in a courtyard. The central temple of the monastery of Samye (bSam yas) in Tibet is also built according to a *maṇḍala* scheme, and is said to have been modelled on another major Indian monastery, Odantapuri, the location of which has not yet been identified.

Paharpur is in the core area of the Pāla state, which along with Nepal and Kashmir was the main part of the subcontinent where Mahāyāna and Vajrayāna Buddhism continued to be patronised from the seventh century onwards. While this region was later to be the source of many of the Tantric teachers who brought Buddhism to Tibet and elsewhere, it seems that Buddhism here was relatively conservative in the early Pāla period, with a stress on the role of the historical Buddha Śakyamuni, and the sites associated with him.[12] It is only in the late ninth and tenth centuries that *anuttarayoga*-type material, with the cult of the fierce goddesses and Śaivite-derived male deities such as Hevajra and Cakrasamvara, begins to appear in the iconographic record at sites such as the monastery of Ratnagiri in Orissa (Hock 1987).

By this stage, the Pāla state was the only major Indian state where Buddhism was still flourishing; Susan Huntington has described it as 'an anomaly in the otherwise totally Hindu world of India at the time' (S. Huntington 1990: 70), though this perhaps understates the survival of Buddhist institutions elsewhere, particularly perhaps in South India, Nepal and Kashmir. Huntington is probably right however to argue that the expanding presence of Buddhism overseas was a major source of patronage which enabled the Buddhist institutions of the Pāla state to keep afloat:

> [R]ecent research has demonstrated that only a few of the the Pāla kings were exclusively Buddhist and that royal patronage constituted only one of the many sources of support for the religious institutions of the day. Instead, it may be posited that the survival of this island of Buddhism in India's Hindu world was in great measure due to the international activity of the period, which not only fostered the religious institutions but must have contributed greatly to the economy of the region. (S. Huntington 1990: 70–1)

Here, as earlier in its history, Buddhism was an internationalist religion, doubtless preserving its close association with the mercantile class but also as a consequence vulnerable to the disruption of long-distance trade and to the need for traders to keep on good terms with the local political elites. How far the eventual collapse of Buddhism in the region was a result of direct military activity, how far to the loss of state patronage, and how far to the fact that its traditional lay support base was no longer in a position to support it is difficult to decide at this distance. Probably all these factors

[12] Kinnard 1997 contrasts the conservatism of early Pāla Buddhism with Rāṣṭrakūṭa-patronised Buddhism in the Deccan, where the new *maṇḍala* schemes appear earlier.

played a part. International support was undoubtedly a factor, however, and it is noticeable that by the twelfth and thirteenth century there appears to be a shift away from Tantric *maṇḍala*-form temples, perhaps resulting from an increasing reliance for patronage on the territories of Arakan and Burma to the east, where Mahāyāna and Vajrayāna Buddhism was being increasingly replaced by Theravādin orthodoxy (Samuel 2002c). In time, what was left of Buddhism in East Bengal would be re-oriented towards Arakan and the Theravāda (Tinti 1998).

BUDDHIST TANTRIC RITUAL IN CHINA, JAPAN AND KOREA

In the eighth to tenth centuries, despite the progressive incursions of Islam in the West, the Buddhist support base continued to grow in East Asia. Further evidence for the state use of Buddhist ritual procedures comes from this region, where these procedures were at various times adopted by the Chinese, Korean and Japanese states. Here, with the aid of the dated Chinese translations and the generally better East Asian historical record, one can see the progressive development of Buddhist rituals for the state over several centuries.

Thus the *Suvarṇabhāsottama* or *Suvarṇaprabhāsa Sūtra*, the non-Tantric text that I referred to in Chapter 9 as providing the earliest evidence for Buddhist Tantric *maṇḍalas*, gives considerable importance to political issues. The *Suvarṇaprabhāsa Sūtra* was translated into Chinese between 414 and 421. It was in fact classified in Japan as one of three 'State Protecting Sūtras'. The other two were the *Saddharmapuṇḍarika* or 'Lotus Sūtra' and the so-called *Renwang Jing*, a text in the style of a Prajñāpāramitā Sūtra that is generally regarded as a Chinese production.[13]

Thus, in Chapter 6 of the *Suvarṇaprabhāsa Sūtra*, the Four Great Kings, the four *yakṣa*-style deities of the four directions whom we encountered in Chapter 5 of this book, approach the Buddha. They proclaim that should a king of men who has heard this *sūtra* protect and support monks who hold this and the other chief *sūtras*, they, the four Great Kings, along with their twenty eight *yakṣa* generals and numerous hundreds of thousands of *yakṣas*, will protect and assist that king and ensure him peace and welfare.

[13] In a recent book review, Whalen Lai has suggested that the *Suvarṇaprabhāsa* might have been used as the basis of 'a pact among early Buddhist kings dedicated to the propagation and protection of the Dharma, in early Mahāyāna Northwest India'. It was apparently used in this way in the Northern Dynasties in China. The *Renwang Jing* was used in a similar way. (H-Net book review of Wang Zhenping's *Ambassadors from the Islands of Immortals*, published by H-Buddhism@h-net.msu.edu, September 2006.)

Similarly, if he makes gifts to the monks, nuns, laymen and laywomen who hold the chief *sūtras*, the Four Kings will make his population prosperous. (Emmerick 1970: 24–5) They also promise to cause dissension and trouble for any neighbouring king who wants to invade his territory. Venerating and reciting the *sūtra* will itself strengthen the Four Great Kings, while if this is not done the region in question will suffer various kinds of trouble.

In subsequent chapters of the *Suvarṇaprabhāsa* the message is reinforced. The earth-goddess promises to make the earth stronger and more fertile where the *sutra* is preached and to produce more fragrant, moist, tasty and beautiful leaves, flowers, fruits and crops, so that people who eat them will be stronger, more beautiful and live longer. Chapter 12 is an 'Instruction concerning Divine Kings' stressing that kings should act justly and that disaster will follow should they fail to do so. A long series of *yakṣas* and other spirits promise protection to those who hear the *sūtra*.

I shall leave aside the *Saddharmapuṇḍarika*, though it was, of course, to assume immense importance in East Asian Buddhism in later times, and look briefly at the *Renwang Jing*. The *Renwang Jing*'s full title can be translated as *The Prajñāpāramitā Sūtra Which Explains How Benevolent Kings May protect Their Countries*. It is extant in two Chinese translations, the first by Kumārajīva, dating from 401, and the second by Amoghavajra, dating from 765. There were, however, doubts from early times about the existence of a Sanskrit original for this text: Stanley Weinstein in his *Buddhism under the T'ang* suggests that it originated in China, and that '[I]ts anonymous author was apparently attempting to dissuade Northern Wei rulers from interfering with the autonomy of the [Buddhist sangha]' (Weinstein 1987: 176 n. 6; see also De Visser 1928–35; Conze 1973, 1978; Orzech 1998).

Whatever the case, this text, which is described as being preached to the sixteen kings of the *mahājanapadas*, led by King Prasenajit of Śrāvastī, was to become an important text both in China, and also in Japan. Chapter 5 of this *sūtra* recommends that kings sponsor elaborate rituals, based around the reading of the *sutra*, for times when 'riots are imminent, calamities are descending, or robbers are coming to destroy'. Chapter 7 prescribes a further ceremony that can be performed to protect from other difficulties, and promises that the Five Bodhisattvas of Great Power and various other deities will protect the countries of kings who receive and keep the Buddha, *dharma* and *saṅgha*.

A variety of other *sūtras* including rituals for various pragmatic ends were translated into Chinese from the early fifth century onwards, but the two texts which were to form the basis of East Asian Tantra, the

Sarvatathāgatatattvasaṃgraha and the *Mahāvairocanābhisaṃbodhi Sūtra*, were not translated until 723 and 724 respectively. Both seem to have been written considerably before that time, with the *Mahāvairocana Sūtra* probably being the earlier (Matsunaga 1997a: 177–8; Hodge 2003). In fact, the Chinese Buddhist traveller Wuxing had already obtained a copy of the *Mahāvairocanābhisaṃbodhi Sūtra* in India in 685 CE. The delay in the Chinese translations was due to internal political factors in China.

Buddhism had reached China quite early and began to gain popularity among the Chinese from the first century CE. By the fourth century it had a widespread following among all levels of society, and the various rulers of the Northern and Southern Chinese dynasties at this period were all basically supportive of Buddhism. The Tang Dynasty was a different matter, and the establishment of the Tang state was immediately followed by a repressive edict against Buddhism, in 621 CE.

While Buddhism in South and Southeast Asia was primarily competing against Brahmanical religion, and in some areas also the Jain religion, in China the competition was from the Daoists. Gaozu, the first T'ang emperor, was pro-Daoist, declared Buddhism a foreign religion and moved to reduce the power of the Buddhist clergy. The second T'ang emperor, Taizong (620–49), was also by and large anti-Buddhist, and decreed, for example, that Daoist monks and nuns should take precedence over Buddhist monks and nuns, although he patronised the famous translator Xuanzang towards the end of his life (Weinstein 1987).

Xuanzang continued to be influential under the early years of the following emperor, Gaozong (649–83). Xuanzang was unsympathetic to Tantric traditions and apparently used his influence at court to block the introduction of Tantric teachings by an Indian *paṇḍita* who arrived in China in 655. It seems that some Tantric teachers continued to be active in China during this period, all the same, since the Korean monk Myongnang is said to have studied Tantric ritual in China at this time. After Myongnang's return to the Korean kingdom of Silla, he was responsible for the Silla state's ritual defence against attempted Tang invasions in 668 and 669. His rituals were successful, and on each occasion the Tang fleet heading for Silla was sunk at sea (Grayson 1989: 59).

After Xuanzang's death, the emperor Gaozong blocked further translation activities. However, the emperor had a stroke and his wife, the famous or notorious Empress Wu (Wu Zetian), who took over from him, was strongly pro-Buddhist. A reaction followed after Empress Wu's reign, and the next significant Emperor, Xuanzong (712–56) again moved to restrict the power of the Buddhist clergy. Xuanzong was, however, interested in Tantric

Buddhism, and it was during his reign and that of his two immediate successors, Suzong (756–62) and Daizong (762–79), that the main translations of Tantric texts were undertaken. These were made by the Indian Tantric masters Śubhakarasiṃha (arrived in China 716, died 735) and Vajrabodhi (arrived in China 719, d.741) and by Vajrabodhi's students Yixing (d.727) and Amoghavajra (also known as Bukong, d.774) (Weinstein 1987). This was a period of Tibetan and Uighur invasions and Chinese civil wars, and there was plenty of demand for Tantric defensive ritual at court. As I mentioned above, the *Mahāvairocanābhisaṃbodhi Sūtra* and the *Sarvatathāgatatattvasaṃgraha Sūtra* were translated in the 720s. These correspond to the earlier stages of Indian Buddhist Tantra, those which Tibetans nowadays classify as *kriyā*, *caryā*, and *yoga* Tantra, and the emphasis here is on peaceful deities, although some fierce and violent deities are included. These two texts were transmitted on to Japan within a few years and formed the basis of Japanese Tantric or esoteric Buddhism (Yamasaki 1988).

I have elsewhere narrated the famous story of the defeat of a Tibetan, Arab and Sogdian attack in 742 by Amoghavajra, using rituals derived from the *Renwang Jing* (Samuel 2002d). Weinstein (1987: 170 n.41) regards the story as suspect, since it is not in the early biographical sources on Xuanzong's reign, but there is little doubt that, as Lokesh Chandra has argued, the translations of Tantric texts at this time were carried out in large part 'for the security and stability of the State against the attacks of Tibetans and Arabs . . . Reverses on the battlefield were followed by renewed vigour in translating the Tantras' (Chandra 1992b: 266; see also Chandra 1992c).

Some more translation activity followed in China in the late eighth century, but the increasingly chaotic conditions of the later Tang were unfavourable to Buddhism. A massive purge of the Buddhist *saṅgha* took place in 835, followed by a period of brutal suppression under the emperor Wuzong (840–6), beginning in 842 and climaxing in 845 and 846 with the closing and destruction of almost all monasteries, the burning of scriptures and the forcible disrobing of the *saṅgha*. The Emperor's death brought this to an end but the extent of the destruction, followed by a devastating rebellion some thirty years later (875–84), effectively brought all schools of Buddhism in China except Chan and Pure Land to an end (Weinstein 1987). The later 'Anuttarayoga' Tantric material, in which the fierce Śaivite gods and goddesses move to the centre, thus did not reach China or Korea until it arrived with the Mongol court some four centuries later, and it was never really assimilated into Chinese Buddhist practice.

The Mahāyāna State Protecting Sūtras and the earlier phases of Tantric Buddhism continued to be influential in Korea and particularly Japan, and again I have narrated some of this story elsewhere (Samuel 2002d). In Japan, the *Renwang Jing*, or the *Ninno-kyō* as it is called in Japanese, was extensively used in state-protecting rituals. Marinus De Visser's *Ancient Buddhism in Japan* refers to many occasions on which such rituals were in fact performed in Japan, for example in 940 CE by the Tendai priest Jōzō, when the Japanese state was threatened by the rebellion of Taira no Masakado (de Visser 1928–35; Chandra 1992a).

The well-known Naritasan Shinshōji temple, in the small town of Narita close to Tokyo's main airport, owes its legendary origins to another set of rituals held to suppress this same rebellion. In this case, they involved a specifically Tantric deity, Fūdō (Acala), who is an important figure in the *Mahāvairocanābhisaṃbodhi Sūtra* (*Dainichi-kyō* in Japanese) (see Linrothe 1999: 151–3; Yamasaki 1988: 12, 83–4, 172–5). The Shingon priest Kanjo was directed by the Emperor to bring an image of Fūdō to Narita in order to defeat the rebellion. This image had been carved and consecrated by Kōbō Daishi (c. 774–835 CE), the founder of the Shingon tradition. After three weeks of continual fire offerings, the leader of the rebellion, Taira no Masakado, was killed by the Emperor's forces and peace was restored. At least some of the credit for this was given to the Fūdō rituals. The image itself refused to move back to Kyōtō (Acala means 'immoveable' in Sanskrit so it was just living up to its name), and Fūdō directed Kanjo in a vision to build a temple for the image at Narita. This was the origin of the Naritasan Shinshōji temple.

Perhaps this is enough to make the point: both *sūtras* and *tantras* were employed to defend the Chinese, Korean and Japanese states against attack, and it seems clear that the translation of these texts into Chinese and the establishment of monasteries to maintain the ritual traditions associated with them was motivated in large part by their believed usefulness to the state. We have little direct evidence to demonstrate that the same was true of Buddhist Tantras in South or Southeast Asia, but it seems likely that this was the case. We might consider, for example, the Buddhist and Śaiva establishments supported at a slightly later date by the Javanese court of Mataram (Becker 1993). The Javanese pattern of dual support for Śaiva and Buddhist Tantric ritualists continued into modern times in Bali, which still has both Śaiva and Buddhist hereditary Brahmin priests.

THE NEW PATTERN: KATHMANDU VALLEY AS EXEMPLAR

In Chapters 6 and 7 I gave the cities of Chiang Mai in Thailand and Madurai in Southern India as examples of the Theravada Buddhist and

Brahmanical Hindu patterns as they developed in later times. If the Tantric pattern represents a third option, the place that comes closest to representing it in modern times is probably the Kathmandu Valley. The valley today is nearly a thousand years distant from the period of which we are speaking, as are Chiang Mai and Madurai, and it has undergone two centuries of strongly pro-Hindu rule since the Gurkha conquest, but it is still suggestive in many ways of how a mediaeval Tantric polity might have operated.[14]

The Valley is a pluralistic society in both ethnic and religious terms, with major pilgrimage sites associated with both Buddhism (the two great *stūpas* at Svayambhū and Bauddha, along with many lesser sites) and the Śaiva-Śākta traditions (including Paśupatināth, Guhyeśvarī and a host of other temples). The main urban population, the Newars, have a strongly mercantile and artisan component[15] and have both Buddhist and Brahmanical groupings, with religious identity being mainly a question of whether one's family traditionally calls on a Buddhist or Brahmanical Tantric priest for family rituals (G. S. Nepali 1965; Gellner 1992; Toffin 1984; Gellner and Quigley 1995).

Buddhist Tantric priests have traditional associations with one or another 'monastery' (*bāhāḥ* or *bahī*, Locke 1985; Gellner 1992), but monasticism as such ceased to be practised some centuries ago in traditional Newar society. Boys of the appropriate high Buddhist castes spend a week as monks before formally renouncing the monastic life.[16] Tantric priests are initiated in the *anuttarayoga* Tantra traditions of Vajrayāna Buddhism. Vajrayāna Buddhism has explicitly exoteric and esoteric components, with separate shrines and also multiple layers of meaning and interpretation associated with individual shrines and images (Gellner 1992). The same would seem to be true on the Śaiva side, although there has been less work on this. Major valley cults such as that of the deity Buṃgadyaḥ (Lokeśvara) again have multiple meanings and multiple identities, in this and some other cases including both Buddhist and 'Hindu' identities (Locke 1980; Owens 1995; Tuladhar-Douglas 2005).

Another example here is the cult of the Buddhist deity Hārītī, whom we met in Chapter 5 as converted *yakṣa*, and possibly also as an important deity of Gandhāra and Mathurā. She remains a significant figure in the

[14] The Hindu-Buddhist society of Bali in Indonesia has many parallels to Newar society (Samuel 1982). While Vajrayāna Buddhism is also the principal religion of Tibetan societies, they have there become part of a quite different social structure, for reasons sketched in Samuel 1982 and discussed at length in Samuel 1993.

[15] See e.g. Lewis 2000: 50–4.

[16] In the early twentieth century, the Theravāda monastic tradition was imported into the Valley, and has now become quite significant.

Kathmandu Valley, where she is linked to a Tantric healing cult which is still of some importance in the valley (Iltis 2002; Merz 1996). The principal temple of Hāritī, on the hill at Svayambhū, nowadays has a second identity for Hindu worshippers as a temple of Śītalā, one of the principal disease-goddesses of the Brahmanical pantheon.

At the time of the Gurkha conquest, the Valley had been divided for some time into three small Newar kingdoms, each with a chief town (Kathmandu, Patan, Bhaktapur) and a palace complex centred on the temple of the royal deity, Taleju, a fierce goddess regarded as a form of Durgā (Vergati-Stahl 1979). Each of these cities is surrounded by circles of temples, including sets of the eight Mātṛkā deities (Slusser 1982; Gutschow 1982, 1993; Gutschow and Bāsukala 1987). As mentioned earlier, these deities are brought to life in annual cycles of ritual dances that form part of an extremely complex ritual 'choreography' that encompasses the whole Valley throughout the year (Levy 1987, 1992; Toffin 1996, 1999; Gutschow 1996; van den Hoek 2005; Korvald 2005). The dancers are collectively known as Navadurgā (the Nine Durgās). Alongside the various Goddesses (Fig. 12.3), they also include Gaṇeśa and Bhairava. These rituals are mostly sponsored by associations (*guthi*) linked to one or another religious institution, a pattern that goes back in some respects to the guild structure of mediaeval India and has largely disappeared elsewhere in the subcontinent (Vergati 1986).[17]

This is a highly simplified sketch of a complex and fortunately well-studied society, but it may serve to suggest some of the lines along which the mediaeval Tantric polity functioned, both in terms of the way it was instantiated in civic and royal ritual, and in regard to how sites maintained multiple meanings and interpretations for the various social, religious and ethnic groups within the Valley.

MASKED RITUAL DANCE TRADITIONS IN THE NEPAL VALLEY AND ELSEWHERE

I mentioned the masked ritual dances through which the Aṣṭamātṛkā deities are embodied in the Kathmandu Valley. Even today, these are not entirely safe folkloristic performances. The dancers are in a trance, they carry swords and burning torches that may be thrown at the audience, and they drink the blood of sacrificed animals. There are legends of human sacrifice associated

[17] For the rather different tradition of the Newar Buddhist town of Sankhu, in which the three dancers (Devī, Caṇḍī, Bhairava) are seen as representing the Buddhist goddess Vajrayoginī, see Shrestha 1999. The role of Vajrayoginī in Sankhu is discussed further in Zanen 1986.

Figure 12.3. (left to right) Indrayāṇī, Brahmayāṇī, Cāmuṇḍā

with the dances; Toffin notes that in Theco village, where the dancers are brought out for two village festivals each year, their emergence

> is much feared. Every year, it is believed that a person will die in the village or in the neighbourhood during these two festivals. The fierce goddesses, it is said, "eat" this ill-fated villager. Kumārī and Viṣṇudevī [. . .] are the most dangerous deities. They have to swing their faces continuously during the dance and the processions in the streets since if they fixed a devotee for a few seconds without moving their head he would die at once. (Toffin 1996: 233)

A major festival is held every twelve years when the masks are renewed, and there is a strong belief that human sacrifice formed part of this ritual in the past and occasionally still does so today.

> Even today, a feeling of insecurity and fear spreads around the village and the neighbouring localities during the twelfth year festival. The families do not walk out at night, and they watch over their children with special attention. (Toffin 1996: 245)

As this suggests, children are seen as particularly at risk, and the disappearance of small children in the recent past has been associated with genuine fears that they may have been killed as offerings to the dancers. This is acted out in a sequence in another set of these dances today in which a dancer, representing a form of Bhairava, chases and tries to catch the local children (Sardar n.d.).

Obviously there is an element of play here, but there is also an underlying presence of something else. I would suggest that the *dangerousness* or perhaps one should say rather the 'scaryness' of these deities – the stories of human sacrifice and of villagers who die during the annual dances, the frightening aspects of the dance performances – is an important part of how they operate now and an important indication of how they operated in the past.

A significant issue raised by practices such as this is what could be called the emotional and psychic force of divine forms in popular consciousness. Tantric ritual is about powerful and dangerous forces, which must be encountered and dealt with for the good of the community. These forces can only be manipulated by specialist priests and ritualists, and even then there is still a risk that things can 'go wrong'. The seven wild and dangerous goddesses who dance through the villages of the Kathmandu Valley in the company of Bhairava and Gaṇeśa are participants in one of a series of Tantric rituals that undergirded and maintained the Newar state and which were continued by the Nepali state that followed it. One can imagine that in a pre-modern society, without the corrosive presence of modernity or

Figure 12.4. ’Cham dancer at Zangs mdog dpal ri dgon pa, Kalimpong

the competing visual claims of the cinematic or television fantasies, such rituals would have some real purchase on the collective psyche.

We can see versions of these masked ritual dance traditions in many places throughout South and Southeast Asia, and it is worth referring to a few other examples. Of these traditions, the Tibetan masked ritual drama of the *'cham*, which has also received the most intensive study, is the most sophisticated and complex (Fig. 12.4). This is normally performed by monks, and in fact almost all large monasteries perform *'cham* annually. Most of the deities are male, including transforms of Mahākāla and forms of Padmasambhava as well as Tibetan local gods, though in some versions, such as the Bon-po *cham* of the goddess Srid pa'i rgyal mo (Schrempf 1999, 2001), there are important deities of the 'wild goddess' class. As I pointed out in *Civilized Shamans*, relying in large part on the work of Stephan Beyer (1973), the *'cham* is structurally a modification of a standard Tibetan ritual procedure of Indic origin, the *tshogs* or *gaṇapūja* ritual, in which the power of Tantra is directed to the destruction in symbolic form of 'obstacles' to the spiritual progress of the monks and the well-being of the associated village community (Samuel 1993: 265–7). The dancers represent in external physical form the deities of the *maṇḍala* who would otherwise simply be visualised internally by the performers of the ritual (see also R. Kohn 1988, 2001).

There is little sense here of possession by the deity or of the element of risk and danger which goes along with it. Perhaps at the other extreme are the *teyyam* rituals of Kerala and the *bhuta* rituals of southern Kannada. In both of these cases, ferocious deities, mostly of the 'wild goddess' type, are held to possess masked low-caste dancers. Normally in these cases one dancer appears at a time, wearing the elaborate costume of a specific named deity. He is expected to be possessed by the god or goddess. The deities here mostly have Sanskritic identities and include many familiar figures, such as Bhairava, Kālī and Cāmuṇḍā. Richard Freeman and Gavin Flood, who have studied the *teyyam* rituals in detail, note the overlap here between spirit-possession (or more accurately spirit-mediumship) and local Tantric traditions. The dance of the *teyyam* cannot be simply classed as a form of popular spirit-possession ritual, nor as a learned Tantric procedure (Freeman 1993, 1994, 1999; Flood 1997; Pallath 1995). As Flood makes clear, it needs to be analysed at several levels. However, it is undoubtedly an occasion of heightened emotion, deriving from the controlled violence at its heart: '[t]he emotion evoked in the crowd is [. . .] integral to the structure and process of the ritual' (Flood 1997: 177).

The *bhuta* dances of South Kanara (Tulunad, Fig. 12.5) seem close to *teyyam* (e.g. Claus 1973, 1979, 1984, 1993; Nichter 1977). One can see obvious resemblances too in the *yak tovil*, the Sri Lankan tradition of masked exorcistic dances, but there are notable differences here too – *yak tovil* is normally performed today as a healing and exorcistic ritual, in which specific malevolent deities are persuaded to stop afflicting a patient. There are, I think, important commonalities, but these rituals require more extensive treatment than I can give them in this context (Kapferer 1979, 1983; Vogt 1999).

Figure 12.5. Bhuta dancer, South Kanara District

Other dance traditions that appear to share some of the same fundamental assumptions can be found in Orissa (Emigh 1984) and elsewhere in South Asia.

We can also see significant resemblances with some of the Indonesian masked dance traditions, such as or the well-known Rangda-Barong dances of Bali (e.g. Belo 1949; Geertz 1975).[18] While there is a dramatic structure of sorts to the Rangda-Barong dances, they are essentially centred around

[18] Another Indonesian example is the *warok* tradition of Ponorogo in Eastern Java, where the association of male Tantric power remains quite strong (I. Wilson 1999). On the use of Tantric power in

a struggle between two contending powers, a male being who has the form of a lion and is, like Bhairava, explicitly identified as a transform of Śiva, and a female figure, Rangda, who takes the form of a terrifying witch, and is closely linked to the Balinese form of Durgā (see Stephen 2001 for these identifications). Leo Howe says of these dance-dramas:

> The drama is usually put on in times of trouble for the village or as part of the celebrations of the annual festival of the 'death' temple. It is often performed near the graveyard. It begins quietly with much joking and slapstick, but around midnight, when the anticipation and tension in the audience is high, Rangda erupts into the arena causing mayhem and fear. Rangda's acolytes possess the Barong's supporters, who try to stab themselves with daggers while the Barong tries to safeguard them. Sometimes Rangda shoots off into the crowd scattering it in all directions, and people are genuinely afraid. The performance ends in a stand-off between Rangda and Barong [...], but there is always the fear that the dangerous magical forces released may get out of control. (Howe 2000: 71–2)

As with the Newar and Keralan dances, when performed as a serious part of a temple festival, for all that everybody knows what is going to happen, this can be a genuinely scary occasion even today. There is also a transgressive element, both in Rangda's introduction of the unsavoury powers of night, death and sorcery, and in the risk of spectators losing control and being caught up in the possession-state that Rangda invokes on Barong's followers. One can sense on such occasions the ways in which Tantric styles of ritual generated the conviction necessary to perform their state- and society-supporting function.[19]

The reported use of human sacrifice in Tantric rituals of state in the past can also be read in this way. I have already mentioned the association of the Newari Navadurgā dancers with rumours of child-sacrifice. The use of human sacrifice in foundation rituals for cities and other major state enterprises in the past seems well-attested, though again one cannot be sure how much of this is rumour and how much reality. Examples include foundation sacrifices in Burma in the early nineteenth century, for the construction of the city of Mandalay (Houtman 1996; see also Jordaan

contemporary Bali by policemen, tax-collectors and others who wish to bolster their personal abilities with Tantric magic, see Connor 1995.

19 I have not attempted to speculate on when these masked dance practices may have arisen. There are indications of participants in ritual gatherings taking on the role of Tantric deities, for example with the Saptamātṛkās in the *Kulacūḍāmaṇi Tantra* (Finn 1986), and there are also indications in early South Indian material and elsewhere of spirit-possession cults and dance rituals (e.g. Hart 1975). The Tantric masked dances seem to integrate elements from both, and might be seen as a progressive development under the influence of court ritualists. For all we know, they could go back to the Gupta Saptamātṛkā cults. We do not however appear to have any iconographic record of early versions of such practices.

and Wessing 1999), routine foundation sacrifices of low-caste men in pre-modern Kerala (Uchiyamada 2000), and human sacrifice in nineteenth-century Bali to empower the local rāja's magical weapons (Wiener 1995).

CONCLUSION

One can portray a picture in which Tantric ritual dominates mediaeval South Asian society, but this would perhaps be exaggerated. This is in part a question of balance. The mass of the population were committed to the slowly 'Brahminising' village cults, while the official royal cults were for the most part Vaiṣṇnava or 'orthodox' Śaiva. Tantric practice, in the sense we are discussing here, was part of the ritual technology of the state, but probably a relatively minor part in most cases; most state ritual did not employ ferocious goddesses or transgressive imagery or inhabit this dangerous fringe territory between the respectable and ordered world of the social community and the realm of misfortune, terror and death. The use of Tantric practitioners for pragmatic purposes was doubtless widespread, but hardly everyday; most people would approach such ritualists, rather like the *mudang* of contemporary Korea (C. Kim 2003) unwillingly and only when other more straightforward solutions to their problems had failed.

There was also a continuing issue about whether these practices were legitimate and appropriate, which is perhaps hardly surprising because their position on or beyond the edge of the legitimate was intrinsic to their power. Śaṅkara, the great Indian Vedāntic philosopher, who probably lived in the early ninth century, is portrayed in his biography, the *Śaṅkaravijaya*, as condemning the approaches of various kinds of Tantric practitioners and defeating them through argument or spiritual power (e.g. Lorenzen 1991: 31–48; Courtright 1985: 218–19). He is also associated with the replacement of fierce goddess cults with those of benign female deities through the encouragement of the Śrīvidyā tradition, and thus with the 'establishment of a chaste Vedic (*vaidika*) goddess worship untainted by Tantric elements (*tāntrika*) and the elimination of "objectionable" practices such as oblations of blood, alcohol, human flesh and sexual rites' (Wilke 1996: 123–4). Whether the historical Śaṅkara actually campaigned against transgressive Tantric practices is far from certain, but he came to stand in later Indian tradition for the 'purification' of ritual and the removal of these practices.

Further north, we have already met Kalhaṇa and Kṣemendra's attacks on the Kashmiri kings who indulged in Tantric practices. In Buddhist Southeast Asia, King Aniruddha (Anawratha) of Burma is supposed to have disbanded the 'Tantric' *ari* monks (Ferguson and Mendelson 1981), and

Theravādin monarchs elsewhere similarly opposed Tantric-style practices (Tambiah 1984). These practices never completely disappeared, but they were increasingly marginalised. Much the same was true in large parts of South Asia.

In my earlier book, *Civilized Shamans*, I suggested that the anomalous character of the Tibetan religious and political system in comparison with the Buddhist societies of Southeast Asia was because, unlike those societies, it had never had an effective centralised state that was able to control and marginalise Tantric practices (Samuel 1993: 24–36). My argument did not imply that the state was incompatible with Tantra as such, and I had previously discussed the Newars and Balinese as examples of centralised states where Tantric practice had retained a relatively central position (Samuel 1982). It is clear though that Tantra was a double-edged sword when wielded by a king. It offered the possibility of strengthening his power, but might also constitute a threat to his legitimacy. As in Kashmir or Burma, a new ruler might justify his kingship in terms of the inappropriate use of Tantric power by his predecessors. Those states that maintained a transgressive Tantric element to their ritual life often tended to keep it relatively undercover, as with the 'secret' Tantric meanings of the *devadāsī* rituals of Puri (Marglin 1985b: 217–42).

In Chapter 13 I will discuss developments in Śaiva and Buddhist Tantra, at the end of our period, the tenth to twelfth centuries, and will also sketch the transformations undergone by these practices in subsequent centuries and in recent times.

CHAPTER 13

The later history of yoga and Tantra

Chapter 12 emphasised the ways in which the transgressive Tantra of the fierce goddesses, criminal gods and destructive magic, in both Brahmanical and Buddhist variants, was a part of state policy, adopted and supported by Indic and Indic-influenced states both in South Asia and overseas. In the Brahmanical states, as Gupta and Gombrich have noted, royal power and Tantric theology became closely intertwined, so much so that, as they note 'one cannot be adequately understood without the other' (Gupta and Gombrich 1986). The Buddhists provided similar services to the East Asian states, while in Southeast Asia we find elements from both Buddhist and Brahmanical sides.

It seems scarcely deniable that these pragmatic uses of Tantra provided a major context for the growth and development of Tantric religion. We can see early signs of this accommodation of state needs in Buddhist texts by the start of the fifth century, with the proto-Tantric *maṇḍala* and the state-supporting rituals of the *Suvarṇaprabhāsa Sūtra* and the *Renwang Jing*. We can see the development fully under way by the eighth and ninth century, with Buddhist Tantric rituals for state purposes being translated into Chinese and transmitted on to Japan, court patronage of Śaiva Tantra in Kashmir, and Śaivite rituals being used for state consecrations and state-protective rituals by the Khmer kings. Doubtless there was plenty of smaller-scale employment of Tantric religion, at any rate by those wealthy enough to employ Tantric ritualists.

One can imagine a situation similar to that in Bali in recent times, where Śaivite and Buddhist Brahmins officiate at important temple ceremonies and for high-status families, and other priests, often using rituals derivative from Śaiva or Buddhist Tantra, perform rituals in less important contexts or for lower status families (e.g. Hooykaas 1973a, 1973b). For that matter, one can see a relatively similar picture in Burma or Thailand, where the label 'Tantra' has disappeared, but pragmatic ritual procedures similar to those of Tantra are still part of religious life at all levels (e.g. Spiro 1967, 1971;

Mendelson 1961a, 1961b. 1963; Ferguson and Mendelson 1981 for Burma; Tambiah 1984; Terwiel 1975; Mulder 1992: 15–41 for Thailand).[1] In India itself, while much of the more dramatic and transgressive varieties of Tantric ritual, particularly at the state level, has disappeared along with the spread of *bhakti* religion and dramatic political transformations since the time I have been speaking of, it is not hard to find traces of pragmatic, results-oriented Tantric ritual in all kinds of context (e.g. Diehl 1956 for South India; McDaniel 2004 for Bengal).

All this is a very different picture of Tantra from that with which we are familiar today, particularly as taught by contemporary Tibetan lamas, but equally within the Śaivite ascetic traditions of India. Tantra, as we tend to experience it with contemporary Tantric teachers, is primarily about the individual quest for self-realisation: the performance of public ritual for rulers or lesser clients is a distraction from the true nature of the Tantric quest.

We can see the move to this view of Tantra as primarily a quest for individual liberation or self-realisation prefigured in the Śaivite *kaula* and the Buddhist *mahāyoga* traditions, with their progressive internalisation of ritual. There is undoubtedly still a concern here with state patronage, and in fact many of the examples of such patronage cited in Chapter 11 referred to Tantric traditions with 'internalised' ritual components (e.g. the *Netra Tantra* and the *Vīṇāśikha Tantra*). The progressive phasing out of the more 'transgressive' elements, such as the cremation-ground practices, prepared the ground, however, for a move to a Tantric cult that could be presented as primarily soteriological and which could be carried out on an individual basis by both lay and monastic practitioners. The 'privatisation of Tantra' in the title of this chapter refers to these developments.

Thus, on both the Śaiva side and the Buddhist side, we can see by the tenth and eleventh centuries a recasting of Tantric ideas in forms that are much less open to negative stereotyping and where the more transgressive elements are removed or practised only in secret. On the Śaiva side, this has been associated above all with the activity of the great Kashmiri Tantric master Abhinavagupta and his students and followers, and the Trika system of which Abhinavagupta was the most eminent exponent (Silburn 1988; Sanderson 1988, 1995; Dupuche 2003; Dyczkowski 1989; White 1998). On the Buddhist side, it can be linked with the gradual appropriation of Tantra by practitioners who were based or at least trained in a monastic milieu, and who were concerned to incorporate or justify Tantric procedures much

[1] See also Cousins 1997 on esoteric traditions within Southern ('Theravāda') Buddhism.

more explicitly within the general context of Mahāyāna Buddhism. I begin with the Śaiva developments.

THE TRANSFORMATION OF ŚAIVA TANTRA

David White, following in part from Sanderson's work, periodises Śaiva Tantra into three phases. The first of these is *kula* ('clan') practice: 'cremation-ground practice centred on the "terrible" worship of Śiva-Bhairava together with his consort, the Goddess . . . and clans of Yoginīs and/or the worship of the goddess Kālī, independent of a male consort but surrounded by circles of female deities' (White 1998: 173). This is where the *kāpālika*-style practice and the magical uses of sexual substances are first found.

Phase Two, the *kaula* ('clan-derived') phase, resulted from a reform in about the ninth century, associated with the semi-legendary figure of Matsyendranāth. Here we find more emphasis on the erotic element and less on the cremation-ground location, the skulls and bones and so forth, and a variety of cults associated with sexual initiation of the kind discussed in earlier chapters. These *kaula* practices formed the basis of the Nāth Siddha tradition (cf. Briggs 1989).

Phase Three results from a further reform which took place in Kashmir in the eleventh century, leading to the Trika and similar systems. The theoreticians of this school (above all Abhinavagupta) developed a sophisticated philosophical basis for *kaula* practice, based on reversing the process of divine manifestation through light and sound so that the practitioner could identify with its origins.

> Here, in the socioreligious context of eleventh-century Kashmir, these reformers of the Trika sought to win the hearts and minds of the populace by presenting a whitewashed version of *kaula* theory and practice for public consumption, while continuing to observe the authentic *kaula* practices in secret, among the initiated. This eleventh-century development was Tantra, a religion of dissimulation and of the progressive refinement of antinomian practice into a gnoseological system grounded in the aesthetics of vision and audition. (White 1998: 173)

This was the basis of the Śrīvidyā system, which was exported soon after to South India where it has remained an important tradition to modern times (Brooks 1990, 1992a, 1992b). White prefers to reserve the label 'Tantra' to this last phase, which he also refers to as 'high Hindu Tantra'.

While this periodisation is a good starting point in general terms, there are some problems with it. In particular, it should be noted that the *kula* period (Phase One) is largely conjectural; we have no direct textual material regarding this period, although there are certainly plausible reasons to associate it with the widespread *kāpālika* trope in Sanskrit literature of the time. Since the *kaula* phase (Phase Two) is already in part 'reformed', the question of whether the *kula* phase existed as a historical reality, and of what it might have consisted, remains somewhat open. On the whole, I am sympathetic to White's position here, given the early Tamil evidence for low-caste ritualists and the indications at Udayagiri and in textual sources of early destructive magical rituals on behalf of the state. Large gaps nevertheless remain in our account.

On White's analysis, the primary functions of sexual practice in Phase One were to do with initiation and with generating magically potent substances. In the context of initiation, transgressive sexual practice served to connect the practitioner with the origin of the lineage through the transmission of sexual fluids from male guru to student in conjunction with the sexual secretions of a female partner. Offerings of sexual and other polluted substances also served to gratify the fierce female deities and secure their assistance. The use of sexual and transgressive substances was an ongoing part of the ritual practice – the *Kulacūḍāmaṇi tantra* for example prescribes that the basic *yantra* for the ritual should be drawn with a mixture of menstrual blood, sexual substances and various red and yellow pigments – but Phase One was not concerned with the spiritualisation of erotic experience.[2] The key element was transgression and impurity as generating power.

The significant innovation in the *kaula* phase (Phase Two) was the internalisation of the practice through sexual yoga, perhaps, as I noted in Chapter 11, through contact with similar Chinese practices. This would have radically transformed the meanings associated with the whole system, as it did in the case of the Buddhist Tantras as well. However, the idea of transgression and impurity as generating power remained important. It continued to be so even in the work of Abhinavagupta, the key theorist of White's Phase Three. As Alexis Sanderson has put it, referring to Abhinavagupta, 'the Tantric's sense of power was inseparable from his sense of transgression' (Sanderson 1985: 211 n. 61).

However, the incorporation of the internal sexual yogas in the *kaula* practices meant that the transmutation of sexual experience was an increasingly central part of the process. This was particularly so as the third phase involved the progressive internalisation of the Tantric ritual scenario. The

[2] Nor, I think, was Tantra ever centrally about popular protest against religious orthodoxy, although this can be found as a secondary theme in some Tantric writings, and one or two modern scholars have been tempted to appropriate the Tantric *siddhas* for this purpose (e.g. Meenakshi 1996).

deities and the ritual locations were increasingly seen as entities and locations within the practitioner's body. With Kālī and Bhairava now seen less as cosmic powers that could be evoked and used for ritual purposes, and more as symbols of the practitioner's internal transcendence of the limits of ordinary consciousness, the role of sexuality and transgression within the system could also transform. Thus, Sanderson writes that 'The act of sexual union which produced the quintessences necessary to invocation, became in this inner idealism the vehicle of illumination itself; for it was in orgasm that the deity revealed itself as the transcendental core of the energies of cognition and action, the unity of light and emptiness' (Sanderson 1985: 202). This, Sanderson says, enables the tradition to 'colonise the mental life of the Kashmirian householder' and indeed to deeply penetrate the court and the intelligentsia (1985: 203).

BUDDHIST AND JAINA DEVELOPMENTS

The Buddhist context was rather different, since a key issue here was the relationship to the monastic context, although some level of adoption of Tantric practices among court circles and wealthy householders in Pāla-period Bengal is likely; late *siddhas* like Nāropā clearly built up a substantial following, and the local *rāja* felt it worthwhile calling to pay his respects (Davidson 2002a: 317). We have little direct information regarding developments among the laity, however, to put alongside such sources as the satires of Kṣemendra (Sanderson 1985: 203; Wojtilla 1984, 1990; Meyer 1903) and the history of Kalhaṇa (Stein 1900) for lay Śaivite practice in Kashmir. We have plenty of Buddhist ritual texts, and quite a lot of stories about the various Tantric masters, but these are for the most part legendary rather than historical.

However, it is clear enough that a similar transformation can be traced on the Buddhist side, and at around the same time. If Matsyendranāth and his close associates, such as Goraknāth and Cauraṅginăth, are the semi-historical originators of *kaula* practice on the Śaiva side, other figures among the so-called *mahāsiddhas*, or 'Great Perfected Ones', such as Sarāha, Kṛṣṇācārya (Kāṇha) and Nāgārjuna, played a similar role on the Buddhist side (see Linrothe 2006). Our accounts of these figures, dating from the late eleventh century or later, are, as noted above, more story than history, but they give a picture of the context within which the sexual practices and the fierce deities were progressively incorporated into Buddhist practice (J. Robinson 1979; Dowman 1985; Yuthok 1990). These Tantric masters are described as primarily concerned with the *Guhyasamāja*, *Cakrasaṃvara* and *Hevajra Tantra* cycles, in other words with the *mahāyoga* and *yoginī* (*anuttarayoga*) phase of Buddhist Tantra.

The material in Chapter 12 suggests that the critical transformation, corresponding to White's Phase Two,[3] took place with the *Guhyasamāja* and other Mahāyoga practitioners, and that it was already taken for granted in the *Cakrasaṃvara* and *Hevajra* systems which dominate Abhayadatta's late-eleventh or early-twelfth century hagiographic sketches of the eighty-four Mahāsiddhas (J. Robinson 1979: 285–8).[4]

A Buddhist equivalent to White's third Śaivite phase can be seen as commencing with some of the latest figures among the *mahāsiddhas*, figures such as Nāropā who lived in the late tenth and early eleventh century. It is fully developed in the *Kālacakra Tantra*, the last major Indian Buddhist Tantra, also from the early eleventh century, to which I shall turn shortly. By the late eleventh century and twelfth century we find a variety of figures such as Abhayākaragupta (Lee 2003) who are producing scholarly treatises and commentaries on the basis of the new Tantras, as well as indications of their adoption in the monastic context. As I have noted elsewhere, the surviving icons are mostly small, suggesting that we are dealing with individuals within the monastery who are specialists in the new practices, rather than full-scale adoption as the major ritual practices of the monastery as a whole (Samuel 1993: 412). We have textual material from this period, however, which provides rituals based on *mahāyoga*-type procedures for all kinds of major rituals, including the construction and consecration of monasteries and *stūpas* (e.g. the *Kriyāsaṃgraha*; Skorupski 1998).

It is primarily in Tibet, however, that we see the development of synthetic schemes in which the new Tantric procedures are included as part of a progressive scheme of teachings, commencing with the *sūtra* teachings. The Bengali teacher Atīśa, who came to Tibet in the early eleventh century, wrote a short text, the *Bodhipathapradīpa*, of this kind (Sherburne 1983; Snellgrove 1987: 481–4) and this became the basis of the *lam rim* or 'Gradual Path' teachings of the dGe-lugs-pa school in Tibet (Wayman 1978). In the developed Tibetan version of these teachings, Vajrayāna, particularly as presented in the *anuttarayoga* texts, was accepted as the central means to the attainment of Buddhist Enlightenment, but its full practice was seen

[3] Linrothe's three-phase periodisation of Buddhist Tantra (or rather Esoteric Buddhism), which I discussed in Chapter 10, is based on different principles (the evolution of the *krodha-vighnāntaka* theme) so does not correspond to White's three phases. The *Guhyasamāja* is an early text within Linrothe's third phase (1999: 226).

[4] For the forty-one cases where Abhayadatta identifies the Tantric cycle involved, eighteen refer to *Cakrasaṃvara*, sixteen refer to *Hevajra*, and seven to *Guhyasamāja* (J. Robinson 1979: 285–8).

as suitable only for an elite group of highly-qualified initiates.[5] Part of the problem here was how to reconcile a set of teachings in which sexual practices played a central role with a context in which practitioners were increasingly expected to be celibate monks. In the long term, the Tibetan version of Vajrayāna resolved this tension by reducing the significance of the sexual practices. While these practices were never entirely eliminated, they have a marginal position within contemporary Tibetan Buddhism (Samuel 1993: 206–7, 240–1, 275–8).

THE KĀLACAKRA TANTRA

The most complete expression of the 'third phase' on the Buddhist side was the last major Buddhist Tantra, the *Kālacakra Tantra*. This is dateable to the early eleventh century (Wallace 2001: 3; Newman 1998). The basic structure of the Kālacakra practices does not differ dramatically from the other *anuttarayoga* Tantras, though there are variations in matters of Tantric physiology; the Kālacakra's system of *nāḍīs* and *cakras*, internal channels and psychic centres, is somewhat different from those of the earlier Tantras. There is also a significant elaboration of the early and introductory stages, with an extensive series of preliminary empowerments (e.g. Sopa 1985: 95–6). The main text of the *Kālacakra Tantra*, which is held to have been compiled by Mañjuśrī Yaśas, the eighth king of Śambhala, presents itself as an abridged version of a full *Tantra*. The full *Tantra* is said to have been originally revealed in India, at the Dhānyakaṭaka stūpa at Amarāvatī in Andhra Pradesh but preserved in Śambhala, a probably mythical land to the West where it was transmitted onwards through the succession of kings of Śambhala (Bernbaum 1980; Sopa, Jackson and Newman 1985). This abridged *Kālacakra Tantra* text, along with the early *Vimalaprabhā* commentary attributed to a later Śambhala king, Puṇḍarīka, places the Tantric practices in a different and new kind of social and intellectual context.[6] While the root texts of Tantras such as the *Hevajra* are primarily ritual handbooks, and make little attempt to situate their teachings in a wider context, the *Kālacakra Tantra* is notable for its broad and synthetic

[5] The *lam 'bras* or 'Path and Result' cycle of teachings of the Sa-skya school (cf. Ngorchen 1987; Yuthok 1990, 1997) formed another such scheme. The Indian root text attributed to the *mahāsiddha* Virūpa, however, on which the *lam 'bras* is based, is almost entirely Tantric in content. The extensive non-Tantric teachings which are now presented as part of the *lam bras* are based on three lines of the original text (cf. Davidson 2005: 477 and Ngorchen 1987).

[6] The commentary and the text seem to have appeared together in India and may well have been composed together, despite being attributed to different (presumably both legendary or mythical) figures.

approach. It is not just a system for the advanced adept involved in Tantric practice, but provides a virtual encyclopaedia of knowledge on a wide range of topics.

Thus the first of the Kālacakra's five sections, the 'Outer Kālacakra' or description of the world-system, includes an extensive treatment of cosmological and astronomical topics (Newman 1987), while the second, the 'Inner Kālacakra' or description of the individual, includes a detailed description of embryology, an analysis of the person in terms of *abhidharma* categories, and a very elaborate account of the *cakras* and channels of the body. All of this is related back to the Kālacakra *maṇḍala*, which with its 722 deities is perhaps the most complex of all Tibetan *maṇḍalas* (Wallace 1995, 2001, 2004). The 'Inner Kālacakra' chapter also includes practices to lengthen life, and alchemical practices, along with an extensive critique of other systems of thought, Buddhist and non-Buddhist. The third and fourth chapters cover the more conventional topics of initiation and generation-stage processes respectively, while the fifth includes the completion-stage processes and the path to Buddhahood (Hartzell 1997).

Vesna Wallace, in a recent book on the second section of the *Kālacakra Tantra*, suggests that the author of the *Kālacakra* was openly aiming at the conversion of heterodox groups, Buddhist and non-Buddhist. The text refers extensively to non-Buddhist teachings, although it also disparages and criticises them (Wallace 2001: 38–9). At the same time, features of the system seem to have been deliberately designed to make it easier for non-Buddhists to approach *Kālacakra* practice (2001: 40–1). Wallace speculates that the author of the *Kālacakra Tantra* 'may well have sought to form a united front of heterodox groups and Buddhists' against the common foe of the Islamic invasions (2001: 42; see also Orofino 1997).

Another notable feature of the *Kālacakra* regards its attitude to the sexual practices, which have a much more central and explicit place here than in previous systems. The *Vimalaprabhā* comments that in previous Tantras, including the *Guhyasamāja Tantra* and the *Cakrasaṃvara Tantra*, the Buddha 'taught the blissful state that arises from sexual union, but concealed it out of his great compassion for the sake of the spiritual maturation of simple-minded people'. In the *Kālacakra*, the use of sexual practices as part of the spiritual path is quite explicit. Thus Wallace notes (2001: 11–12) that

> The generation of sexual bliss without emission of regenerative fluids is regarded in this *Tantra* as the most direct method of generating the mental bliss that refines the mind by diminishing conceptualisations and thus makes it fit for the realization of

the empty nature of phenomena. One who practices the generation of sexual bliss without emission, which is referred to as sublime, imperishable bliss, is considered to be like a young virgin. Such bliss is believed to empower one's mind, just as the mind of a young virgin, who has not experienced sexual bliss with emission, can be empowered by deities and *mantras* that enable her to see appearances in a prognostic mirror.

At the same time, the author of the *Kālacakra* was concerned to minimise the conflict that might be caused by antinomian and transgressive practices with the wider society. Thus '[t]he Tantric beginner is advised to eat, drink, and have sexual relations according to the customs of his own country' (Wallace 2001: 121) until he attains a suitably high level of realisation. The use of impure substances is not to be prescribed to beginners, but only to *yogīs* who 'by the power of their *mantras* and meditative concentration are able to transmute these poisons into ambrosias (*amṛta*)' (Wallace 2001: 121–2). Here one can see the move to a 'religion of dissimulation' similar to that described by Sanderson and White for the third phase of Śaiva Tantra. If the watchword of 'high Hindu Tantra' was 'privately a Śākta, outwardly a Śaiva, among people a Vaiṣṇava' (White 1998: 173, quoting the *Yoṇi Tantra*), the Buddhist equivalent was 'outwardly Hinayāna, inwardly Mahāyāna, secretly Vajrayāna'.[7]

JAINA PRACTICES IN THE TENTH AND ELEVENTH CENTURIES

We have less information on Jaina developments during this period. Briggs mentions two Nāth subgroups who are named for two 'sons' of Matsyendranāth, Nīmnāth and Pārasnāth, in his classic account of the Nāths (Briggs [1938] 1989: 72). These are the names of two of the Jaina *tīrthaṅkaras*, Nemi and Pārśva. It is not clear from Briggs' account whether the members of these subgroups were actually Jains.[8] There were certainly Jains involved in alchemy, however (White 1996: 114, 372 n.16), and several important Jain pilgrimage sites, including Girnar and Mount Abu, also have strong Nāth Siddha connections (White 1996: 114–20, 331–4). It seems likely that there were close relationships between Jain ascetics and Nāth Siddhas at these locations.

One of the most famous of all Jaina writers, however, the Śvetāṃbara scholar and ascetic Hemacandra (c. 1089–1172) gives extensive material on Tantric-type practices in his *Yogaśāstra* (Qvarnström 2000, 2002, 2003).

[7] A traditional Tibetan saying which I first heard from the late Geshe Ngawang Dhargyey (personal communication, 1972).
[8] White assumes so at 1996: 119, but Briggs may only be saying that Nīmnāth and Pārasnāth were Jains.

The *Yogaśāstra* is a kind of general handbook on Śvetāmbara Jainism and it was mostly known in later centuries for its first four chapters, which present a detailed account of the Jaina path. The remaining seven chapters deal with meditational and yogic practices. Chapters 5 and 6 cover such topics as breathing, including the internal circulation and control of *prāṇa* and the prediction of death from breathing and other signs, as well as a technique for taking over the body of another being (Chapter 6, 264–72). Chapters 8 to 10 include various forms of meditation (*dhyāna*) including elaborate internal *cakra* meditations closely paralleling those in the Śaiva Tantra traditions (e.g. Chapter 8, 1–28, 47–56) and including techniques to bring about the four kinds of ritual action (Chapter 8, 29–32), recollections of the qualities of the *jina* (Chapter 9, 1–15; Chapter 10, 1–6), and so on. Hemacandra is clearly concerned to justify the validity of the practices he describes, none of which strictly speaking would be forbidden by monastic vows. They are described as useful for converting and otherwise aiding other beings, as reducing attachment (e.g. Chapter 9, 13; Chapter 10, 18–24) and also, in some cases, as leading to liberation (e.g. Chapter 8, 40, 43, 59, 78).

Chapter 11 covers the canonical topic of 'pure meditation' (*śukladhyāna*) which as I noted earlier (in Chapter 9 of this book) was regarded as beyond the capacities of ordinary human beings, but Chapter 12 provides a somewhat abstract account of Hemacandra's own meditational experiences which according to Qvarnström shows clear signs of Nāth Siddha influence (e.g. 2002: 11, 191 n. 4; 2003).

The cautious tone in which Hemacandra discusses these practices doubtless reflects his own status as a celibate monastic and perhaps also the *Yogaśāstra*'s role as an official presentation of the Jaina teachings for the Caulukya king of Gujarat, Kumārapāla (Qvarnström 2002: 2–5). It is striking that Hemacandra is nevertheless familiar with, and feels it appropriate to expound, such a wide range of *kaula* and Nāth practices, suggesting that these practices were widespread among the Jaina community in his time. It is noticeable that he does not discuss any of the 'Tantric' *vidyādevī* practices that appear to have been current in both Śvetāmbara and Digambara circles at around the same time (Cort 1987). These were perhaps more specialist practices and less appropriate for inclusion in a general text of this kind. Many of the practices given by Hemacandra are relatively simple and straightforward and might be seen as suitable for a lay practitioner, though some, such as the practices for taking over the body of another person, or the various practices to predict the time of death, are hardly of this type.

LAY AND HOUSEHOLDER PRACTICE

The whole question of lay practice at this stage is worth considering in some more detail. The sexual practices clearly create problems for practice by celibate monastics, whether Buddhist or Jaina, though these might be justified in some way as not in fact breaking the rules,[9] or by-passed through symbolic performance. This aside, much of the clientele envisaged in the Tantric texts or referred to in Sanskrit literature of the time appears to consist of professional practitioners, whether from hereditary or renunciate ascetic backgrounds. The state sorcery rituals at Udayagiri would surely have been performed by professionals who were hired for the job, and the various ritual performers at the Kashmiri, Khmer and East Asian courts were clearly also full-time practitioners. Indeed, the sheer complexity of much Tantric ritual would make it difficult to undertake without at least one or more highly-trained experts. Tibetans such as Mar-pa who came south across the Himalayas to acquire Tantric teachings also appear to have taken it for granted that they were going back home afterwards to start a family business as ritual practitioners (or, perhaps, to revive one with the aid of some new techniques) (Samuel 1993: 459–60).

However, Tantric priests seem ready enough to initiate kings and members of royal courts into Tantric practice; apart from the examples of King Harṣa of Kashmir and the legendary King Indrabhūti of Zahor, which have been cited already, one could cite as distinguished a figure as Khubilai Khan, who received the *Kālacakra* empowerment from O-rgyan-pa and *Hevajra* empowerments from the Sa-skya hierarch 'Phags-pa (Shakabpa 1967: 64–71; Roerich 1976: 701). Twenty-five of his ministers are also said to have been initiated into the Hevajra cult.

In any case, the 'second' and particularly the 'third phase' Śaivite Tantric teachings, and the new 'internalised' Buddhist practices both seem to be oriented at least in part to the needs of lay (non-professional) followers. The laity here are seen not just as clients for ritual services but as participants within the ritual context. We could see this in instrumental terms, as part of a move into a new market area, and there is doubtless some truth in this. It would be a mistake, however, to reduce this to a purely instrumental business. This would imply that Śaivite and Buddhist ritualists were living in the same demythologised universe as most contemporary Western academics. This is unlikely; it makes much more sense to see Abhinavagupta's

[9] As in Atīśa's argument that the practices could be undertaken by celibates provided that they had a true understanding of *śūnyatā* (Samuel 1993: 471).

circle or the propagators of the *Kālacakra* as people who genuinely felt that they possessed something of great value that they wished to make available to others. We might also wonder how far the Kālacakra mythos fed into a general consciousness at the time of a society under threat from external forces.

TANTRIC PRACTICE IN LATER TIMES

It is unclear how widespread Tantric practice became at the householder level throughout Indian society in the twelfth and thirteenth centuries. Today it exists in a number of places, including the Śrīvidyā practitioners of South India (Brooks 1992a, 1992b), the householder Nāths of Rajasthan (D. Gold and A. Gold 1984; A. Gold 1993), and the so-called Bāuls and other lay Tantric practitioners of Bengal (McDaniel 1989, 2004; Openshaw 1997, 2002; R. Das 1992; Hanssen 2002).

Tantric or closely related practices also continued within the similar Sufi context, where traditions of dissimulation and transgressive behaviour had long had a role. In fact, contacts between Sufi or earlier Islamic mystical traditions and the Śaiva and Buddhist yogic contexts long pre-dated the Islamic takeover of most of North India in the twelfth and thirteenth centuries. The Bengali Bāuls present their teachings and practices in both Vaiṣṇava and Islamic forms, and are able to translate freely between the two (Salomon 1991). Similarly fluid identities can be found in Western India and the Deccan, especially among the Ismailis, though increasingly under threat from modern 'purist' religious forms on both the Hindu and Muslim sides (Khan 2005; Van Skyhawk 1993).

New devotional styles of Brahmanical Hinduism were, however, to take over as the dominant religious style of much of India over the succeeding centuries, including the urban upper and middle classes which would have constituted the natural target group for the Phase Three Tantric practices. These new devotional styles of religion, with their emphasis on emotional submission to a supreme saviour-deity, whether Śaivite or Vaiṣṇavite, were better adapted, perhaps, to the subaltern role of non-Muslim groups under Muslim rule (Hein 1982). It is difficult to know how widespread Tantric practice remained among the general population before the modernist movements of the nineteenth and twentieth centuries. White cites reports from Bihar in the early 1800s suggesting that over 40 per cent of the population were either Tantric or Śākta but his assumptions are optimistic and East India (Bihar, Bengal, Orissa, Assam) is an area where one might perhaps expect higher levels of support for Tantra than elsewhere in South Asia.[10]

Ascetic practice of Tantra among renunciates was more widespread; in fact most Śaivite ascetics appear to have adopted some version of Tantric practice, both as their personal *sādhana* or spiritual practice and as the basis for the ritual services they performed for their lay clientele. This is still the case today, although Vaiṣṇava ascetics now form a significant part of the Indian renunciate scene and are less likely to be primarily Tantric in their practice.

At a more exalted social level, Tantric ritualists continued to play a significant role at some Hindu courts. We can see them, for example, in Frédérique Marglin's excellent ethnography of the temple dancers at the Jagannāth Temple at Puri, which was closely associated with the Kings of Orissa until modern times (Marglin 1985b).

The development of modernist forms of Hinduism in the nineteenth and early twentieth centuries (e.g. Flood 1996: 250–73; King 1999) led to a revival of yoga but also a radical reframing of yogic practices away from the Tantric context. As Alter has noted, *haṭha yoga*, the basis of modern forms of health, medical and recreational yoga, originated as an adjunct to Nāth Tantric practice (Alter 2005). The principal *haṭha yoga* text, the *Haṭhayogapradīpikā*, is an explicitly Nāth text directed towards the classic Nāth internal yogic and sexual practices. Given the extremely negative views of Tantra and its sexual and magical practices which prevailed in middle-class India in the late nineteenth and twentieth centuries, and still largely prevail today, this was an embarrassing heritage. Much effort was given by people such as Swami Vivekananda into reconstructing yoga, generally in terms of a selective Vedāntic reading of Patañjali's *Yogasūtra* (de Michelis 2004). The effort was largely successful, and many modern Western practitioners of yoga for health and relaxation have little or no knowledge of its original function as a preparation for the internal sexual practices of the Nāth tradition.

[10] See White 2003: 5. Specifically, White assumes that when Francis Buchanan's *pandit* informants reported that 'one-fourth of the population's religion was "unworthy of the note of any sage"' this implied that 'they consisted of cults of (predominantly female) village deities whose worship was often conducted by the socially and culturally marginalized, in other words, Tantric cults' (2003:5). This sounds like a very broad definition of Tantra. To this he adds the one-quarter of the remaining three-quarters (i.e. 18.75 per cent) who are described as Śākta, but, even leaving aside the rather approximate numbers, Śākta covers a variety of folk religious forms (cf. McDaniel 2004), and assimilating them into a general Śākta-Tantra category may be misleading. What White's figures do however demonstrate is that 'orthodox' Śaiva and Vaiṣṇava cults were far from dominating village religious life. My limited impressions of village religion from the nearby Maithili region of Nepal in the 1990s suggests that this is still the case (Samuel 2001a).

Within Buddhism, Tantric practice survived in a number of somewhat marginal contexts: as an elite tradition of hereditary Tantric priests in the Kathmandu Valley (Gellner 1992; Stablein 1991) and in Bali, where the remains of the Tantric-oriented court culture of Java regrouped after the Muslim takeover of Java (Hooykaas 1973a, 1973b); as one of a variety of ritual traditions in Japan (Yamasaki 1988); and in a transformed version among the Tibetans and Mongolians, a story the Tibetan part of which I have told elsewhere at considerable length (Samuel 1993).

In the eleventh to fourteenth centuries, there was still a significant Tantric presence throughout much of Southeast Asia. In some ways, arguably, there still is, in that sophisticated traditions of quasi-Tantric practice of magical rituals have remained important in Thailand, Burma and Cambodia into modern times. Stanley Tambiah has argued that the Thai practitioners of this kind represent a 'Tantric' modality within Thailand (Tambiah 1984), and if one can use the term of the forest monks and other magical ritualists of Thailand, the occult masters of Burma would certainly deserve the title as well (Mendelson 1961a, 1961b, 1963; Ferguson and Mendelson 1981; Spiro 1967, 1971). These practitioners no longer call themselves Tantric, however, and while some, at least, of the specific Tantric initiation and teaching lineages associated with the major Buddhist Tantric cycles were still present in Southeast Asia as late as the fourteenth century, they appear to have vanished over the succeeding centuries.

In part, this was a product of a consistent theme within the puristic Theravāda-style Buddhism which became the norm in Southeast Asia and Sri Lanka: the need for a regular 'purification' of a corrupt *saṅgha* by Buddhist kings and rulers. One can see this as an ideological statement of the morality and strength of new rulers, often associated with a blackening of the reputation of their predecessors as dabblers in dubious occult arts and immoral practices. One can also see it, as Tambiah has noted, as an assertion of state control over the aspects of Buddhism that are most likely to lead to autonomous centres of power and resistance to royal authority. Either way, the periodic purifications of the Buddhist community left little space for the elaborate ritual structures and practices of the major Tantric lineages (Tambiah 1984; cf. Samuel 1993). Magical ritual for pragmatic ends never disappeared from Southeast Asia, and it remained linked to *dhyāna*-style meditation practices (Pali *samatha* = Skt. *śamatha*), associated in particular with the ascetic forest-monk tradition (Tambiah 1984; Tiyavanich 1997, 2004; Carrithers 1983), but the formal Tantric teaching lineages, with their explicit connection to Buddhist soteriological ends, gradually vanished.

The modernist forms of Theravāda Buddhism that developed from the late nineteenth century onwards (e.g. Gombrich and Obeyesekere 1990; King 1999) tend to present Buddhism as a rational, scientific tradition and to play down religious and magical aspects. *Samatha* meditation, which retains an association with the attainment of magical power, has been generally reduced to a brief introduction to *vipassanā* or 'insight meditation', with a focus on awareness of breathing and other bodily sensation rather than the systematic reshaping and transformation of experience involved in the older techniques (Cousins 1984, 1996b). However, the increasing global presence of Tibetan lamas in the aftermath of the takeover of Tibet by the People's Republic of China has meant that these techniques are now competing in the global marketplace against the much more elaborate and largely unreconstructed Tibetan practices, which have gained for at least one form of Tantra a global following its original creators could hardly have envisaged.

CHAPTER 14

Postlude

In this final chapter, I reflect back on some of the material in the book as a whole. I begin with the whole question of meditation, yoga and mind-body processes, which has been central to this book. What do we make today of these techniques, which are, as I noted in my introduction, rapidly becoming a significant part of contemporary global society, if often in much modified and adapted versions? Such techniques are of course not unknown in other societies, and can generally be classed, in Foucault's phrase, as 'technologies of the self'. Foucault introduced this term to refer to methods by which human beings act upon their minds and/or bodies (perhaps we should speak more generally of the mind-body complex) with the intention of bringing about transformations of some kind (Foucault 1988a, 1988b; cf. Samuel 2005a: 335–7). Indic societies appear to have been particularly rich in these techniques, at least as compared to other large-scale literate cultures, and to have seen them as bound up with the acquisition of some kind of liberating insight. I begin then by asking what we might make of the historical evolution of meditation, yoga and Tantra within Indic societies and religions.

If we look at the evolution of these techniques historically, we can see an overall development from simple to more complex approaches. The early (pre-Buddhist) *śramaṇa* traditions seem to have had a concept of liberating insight, but no systematic means for achieving it via training of the mind-body complex. Instead they relied on simple ascetic practices aimed at the forceful stopping of physical and mental activities. A critical step forward was that taken by, or at least attributed to, the Buddha, the systematic cultivation (*samādhi*) of a specific state or series of states (*dhyāna*) of the mind-body complex within which the liberating insight might arise. The Jainas may also have had and then lost an early version of these *dhyāna* practices.

Early Vedic procedures were centred more on the visionary revelation of sacred knowledge in the form of hymns and statements of sacred truth, which could then be used in ritual contexts. Initially, these were for the most part perhaps chemically induced (assuming that *soma* is interpreted as a psychedelic substance or entheogen of some kind) and appear to have had affinities to 'shamanic' procedures in many other societies, using 'shamanic' in a wide sense.[1] This tradition was lost, perhaps because of the non-availability of the original *soma*, and the Brahmanical ascetic tradition gradually developed a version of the Buddhist practices, as seen in the *Yogasūtra*.

Another central emphasis of the Vedic-Brahmanical tradition was on a right death and a proper transition to a heavenly afterlife; this was an important issue within the Upaniṣads, and, as we have seen in Chapter 9, was one of the primary contexts of the term *yoga* in the *Mahābhārata*, along with the idea of *yoga* as a technique for entering the body of another human being (White 2006). These were both seen as skills to be developed by warriors as well as by sages, a connection that perhaps makes more plausible the linkage postulated by Bollée and Dundas between the *vrātyas* and the early *śramaṇa* traditions.

In the later Indian Buddhist tradition, as represented by the Mahāyāna *sūtras*, from around the second or first century BCE onwards, the *dhyāna* techniques were combined with increasingly elaborate visionary procedures, based for the most part around the imaginative summoning of one or another Buddha-form. These techniques, described in terms of entry into various specific *samādhi* states, provided the basis for a cult of visionary communication with the Buddhas and perhaps also for the production of the Mahāyāna Sūtras themselves (Chapter 9). Early Buddhist *maṇḍala* structures such as those in the *Suvarṇaprabhāsa Sūtra* appear closely related to these procedures, as do the early stages of what are known in the Buddhist tradition as *kriyā*, *caryā* and *yoga* Tantras, which were developing by the sixth and seventh centuries CE. Later versions of these practices began to incorporate the self-identification of the practitioner with the main Buddha-form as a central feature, and a number of ferocious deities, mostly male to start with, as outer figures in the *maṇḍala* (cf. Linrothe 1999).

[1] Even Eliade, who was insistent on the distinction between shamanic 'ecstasy' and yogic 'entasy', seems prepared to concede a shamanic *origin* for yoga: 'As a developed spiritual technique (we are not discussing its possible "origins"), Yoga cannot possibly be confused with shamanism or classed among the techniques of ecstasy' (Eliade 1958: 339). I should note in this connection that, given the close links between yoga and Tantra, and the presence of both ecstatic procedures and concepts of magical flight in the latter (e.g. White 2003: 188–218), as indeed the vision-quest theme that runs throughout Buddhist practices, Eliade's distinction is difficult to maintain. Rather than insisting on the identity of shamanism(s) and yoga, however, I would like to see a more subtle and fine-grained understanding of the whole range of practices involved and of their underlying mechanisms.

Meanwhile, the transgressive techniques of ritual magic, White's *kula* practices, may have been related to similar techniques of visionary communication with deities. Here, however, the deities with whom communication was sought were the fierce goddesses of illness and misfortune, and the main purpose was, initially at least, sorcery and destructive magic. The early history of these practices is impossible to trace at present, though it may have been associated with a specifically Śākta milieu and with the Śākta *pīṭhas*, locations where the power of the fierce goddesses could be contacted and utilised. By the fourth or fifth centuries CE these practices were being adopted by transgressive *kāpālika*-style Śaiva ascetics, in combination with *maṇḍala* structures incorporating the fierce goddesses. In these contexts, they came to be seen as constituting a pathway to liberating insight in their own right.

While there are suggestions of (non-transgressive) sexual practices in Mahāyāna Buddhist contexts as early as Asaṅga (fifth century), a new set of techniques, closely related to and perhaps influenced by the Chinese *qi* cultivation and 'inner alchemy' practices, started to spread throughout South Asia in the seventh or early eighth century. The Indic versions of these internal practices involve the movement of *prāṇa* through the channels of the body and are closely linked to the conscious control of bodily processes during intercourse, and so to the practices of sexual yoga. While building on some old themes, in particular the idea of the movement of *prāṇa* through the channels of the body, they added both new understandings of the meaning of *prāṇa* and a much more elaborate internal structure for the body (or mind-body complex).

These new techniques allowed for an internalisation of the deity practices. They were adopted both by *kāpālika*-style Śaiva ascetics (the *kaula* practitioners) and by Buddhist practitioners of *mahāyoga* Tantra, who were beginning to incorporate increasingly transgressive elements within their own practices. With the *yoginī* Tantras, in the late ninth century or thereabouts, the fierce goddesses and the Śaivite male deity-forms through which they were controlled were adopted by Buddhist lay practitioners as well, leading to the ritual cycles of the *Hevajra* and *Cakrasaṃvara Tantras*.

In the eleventh and twelfth century, modified versions of these practices were developed in both Śaiva and Buddhist traditions (Abhinavagupta, *Kālacakra Tantra*), in which they became 'esoteric' practices for advanced practitioners, carried on in conjunction with non-transgressive practices for beginners and ordinary lay-people. The transgressive components were not entirely eliminated, but were largely internalised, and the sexual practices were increasingly now seen in terms of access to enlightened consciousness and liberating insight. This is White's 'high Hindu Tantra' and the *anuttarayoga* phase of Vajrayāna Buddhism. Elements of these practices were also adopted by some Jaina practitioners and there were also close contacts with Sufis and other Islamic traditions.

This body of techniques was also applied to the old questions of how to transfer consciousness at the time of death and how to enter the body of another human being. The procedures for consciousness-transfer at the time of death are still important in the modern Tibetan context (generically known in Tibetan as *'pho ba*).

I have attempted to trace as much as possible of the social and institutional basis for these developments in the course of the book. The transition to Muslim rule over most of India dramatically changed this institutional basis and led to the marginalisation of these practices throughout South Asia; other factors had a similar effect in much of Southeast and East Asia. Versions of these practices survived, however, in a variety of contexts throughout South, Southeast and East Asia.

I think that it is clear from the wide range of material that I have discussed in the book why it can often seem hard to get a clear line on just what yoga, meditation and Tantra are about. The connections back to the *vrātyas*, to low-caste ritualists and early Pāśupatas are speculative, if plausible, but there is certainly a clear sequence of historical development that includes most of the later Śaiva and Buddhist practices. However, the practices involved are very varied – from aggressive military ritual carried out by Gupta kings and Chinese emperors to householders belonging to secret cults in eleventh-century Kashmir and contemporary Tibetan monastics – and the extent to which people performing these practices necessarily saw themselves as *tantrikas*, or used the term at all, also varied. One can understand why it is not at all easy to define or specify precisely what Tantra is. Nor have I done so here: I think it is more useful to trace the genealogical connections of practices and ideas than to try to shoe-horn the variety of historical instances into a comprehensive definition. Yet we can ask what general conclusions might be drawn from the account sketched in this and the preceding chapters.

SOCIETY, POLITICS AND VALUE SYSTEMS

In looking at the social and political grounding of religious practice. I have tried as far as possible to make sense of why specific religious forms were practised and why they were patronised. As I have pointed out at intervals, this is not intended as a reductionist exercise, but as emphasising a central component of the understanding of Indic religious traditions which often gets marginalised or left to odd asides and comments, particularly in our more general accounts. I wanted to see how far one could follow through some of these themes on a larger scale to give an overall view of the development of Indic religions over a long period of time.

A related theme in the book has been the question of value systems within Indic society. I started off with the opposition between Hopkins' 'two worlds', the region of Kuru-Pañcāla on the one hand, which was the centre for the expansion of Vedic-Brahmanical culture, and the surrounding belt of evolving cities and states to its east (Central Gangetic region) and south (northern and western Deccan) on the other. Connections with other regions (Northwest India and Central Asia, the Bengal Delta, South India, Southeast Asia) were brought in as the story proceeded. It seems to me that an initial tension between the values of the Vedic society of Kuru-Pañcāla and those of the Central Gangetic region can be sensed through much of the early development of Indic religions, and in various ways continues into much later times.

Here one could characterise the Central Gangetic model as that of the agrarian society with rulers who are expected to have elements of the philosopher and the renunciate, as contrasted with the Kuru-Pañcāla model of the warrior-chieftain of a culture many of whose values derive from a pastoralist context. I emphasise here again, to avoid misunderstanding, that this is not a simple question of indigenous people and 'Āryan invaders'. We are talking about a cultural contrast that developed between populations who were already mostly speakers of Indo-Aryan languages and who were genetically doubtless quite mixed throughout both regions. There is, nevertheless, a sense in which the early Vedic material represents one pole, whatever its origins, and the Central Gangetic region another.

In terms of value systems, I have suggested in Chapter 8 that the ideal of the Vedic material, like that of many pastoralist societies, is the young male warrior, transformed in later Brahmanical reworking to the image of the *brahmacārin* or celibate young man. One can think, for example, of the later imagery of such religious heroes of the Hindu tradition as Śaṃkara, Rāmānuja, or, in a somewhat different vein, Caitanya and his associates, all of them characteristically depicted as young men in celibate garb. These men still have much of the young warrior in them, even if their warriorship takes place for the most part on the inner stage of the self, and it is not altogether surprising that the idea of the Hindu warrior-ascetic remained throughout Indian history (Bouillier 1993) and also surfaced in Buddhist contexts, particularly in East Asia (Mohan 2001; Victoria 2005).

The central ideal of the agrarian societies, by contrast, was that of the *mithuna* or marital couple, endlessly replicated as a decorative theme on Buddhist stūpa railings and Brahmanical temples. The virtuoso eroticism of Khajuraho or Konarak can, I think, best be read in terms of the royal appropriations of Tantra that we discussed in Chapter 12. The earlier versions, by contrast, I would read as cultural representations of good fortune, fertility and prosperity.

The Upaniṣadic, Buddhist and Jain material suggests that the tension between the two patterns was resolved initially by a cultural pattern in which the celibate young warrior ideal became adopted as the basis of the renunciate traditions, in the form of the Buddhist and Jain monastic orders and the Brahmanical renunciates. These ascetic orders also provided a context for the continuance of the wisdom traditions associated with the Eastern Gangetic states. They co-existed with an agrarian society whose values were essentially this-worldly, but they provided a counterbalancing emphasis which gradually came to pervade village society. In effect, this is the pattern that continued into modern times in the Theravādin societies of Southeast Asia and Sri Lanka. The Jaina tradition still shares many of the same assumptions, though since Jains in modern times have mostly lived in a Brahmanical Hindu context, as part of a society with a large majority of Hindus, Jains have adapted in various ways to this context.

The reassertion of the Brahmanical tradition provided an alternative pattern, doubtless strongest, as Lubin notes, in the rural context but also of increasing appeal to the royal courts and urban centres of South and Southeast Asia. The elite and urban forms of this tradition were associated both with the various sophisticated priestly ritual technologies of which Śaiva Tantra is one, and also with the devotional Hinduism of the developing *bhakti* movement. Within this tradition, the Brahmin as teacher and ritual performer could guide the spiritual life of the householder. This cultural pattern, which is the basis of modern Hinduism, dominates South Asia today, though it is still contested among lower castes, in particular by various heterodox movements, such as the *nirguṇi* devotional traditions.

Over the second half of the first millennium, one can see the two cultural patterns, the one built around the *śramaṇa* traditions, the other around the evolving Brahmanical religion, developing throughout South and Southeast Asia, in competition but also in constant interaction with each other. The ultimate weakness of the Buddhist pattern[2] in its Indian version was probably its reliance on state and urban support for Buddhist

[2] The Jain tradition survived somewhat better, through the ongoing patronage of the Jain merchant community, and has retained a presence within South Asia, if on a limited scale. There seems no obvious explanation beyond historical contingency for the different trajectories of the two *śramaṇa*

monasteries. The progressive loss of such support in Hindu and Muslim kingdoms, along with the large-scale destruction of monasteries that apparently accompanied the Muslim invasions in the early thirteenth century, meant that the major teaching centres where the Buddhist clergy at the local level were trained were no longer there. The Brahmanical variant was better adapted to survive in this situation, since the extensive land-grants made to Brahmins over the centuries had provided them with a secure base at the village level. Elsewhere, in Sri Lanka, Southeast Asia and Tibet, Buddhist monasticism would in time develop a solid base at the village level, but it appears that this never happened in mainland South Asia.

Within the developed Brahmanical pattern, the Brahmin-centred values of purity and pollution became a major axis around which the village structure was built, while the this-worldly and pragmatic values of everyday life continued as a parallel set of values and orientations, classed by anthropologists in recent years under the generic label of 'auspiciousness'. This is a theme I have discussed briefly in Chapters 7 and 8, and have also written on elsewhere (e.g. Samuel 1997; Rozario and Samuel 2002a).

The contrast between these patterns is, I think, an important key to understanding the differing structures of religion and of social life in South Asia and Southeast Asia today. It is important, though, to recognise that both of these variants, the Buddhist-Jaina pattern and the later Brahmanical pattern, are equally Indic, and contain many of the same components in differing arrangements. The Brahmanical solution, like the Buddhist, incorporated the ideal of the wise king, the *dharmarāja*, and of the ascetic teachings leading to transcendence, and it too allowed for the recognition and sacralisation of the processes of everyday life.

Beyond these more general questions of value systems, there is the more specific question of the role of 'technologies of the self' within society. In one sense, such technologies are a common feature of very many human societies (cf. Foucault 1988a: 18). Ideas of this kind are perhaps intrinsic in the rites of passage that small-scale societies employ to manage the transitions through life of their members, particularly where there is an element of initiation into secret or private knowledge in such processes, and of choice in how far one may progress through them. It is easy enough to point to the similarities between the systems of initiatory knowledge that can be found in widely

traditions, though the higher profile of Buddhism at the time of the Muslim conquests may have made it a more obvious target, and the existence of other Buddhist societies outside South Asia may have led to Buddhist monks and teachers choosing to migrate rather than to remain and adapt. Buddhism in South Asia today, leaving aside Sri Lanka and the newly-converted Ambedkar Buddhists, survived only in Nepal and in parts of East Bengal, where it developed links with Arakan and Burma (Tinti 1998).

different societies, but these similarities are also accompanied by radical differences deriving from the contrasting social context and meaning of initiation in, say, Melanesia and Bhutan (e.g. Barth 1990).

What we are dealing with in the Indic material has itself undergone radical transformations over the long historical period considered in this book. In the first half of the first millennium BCE we can perhaps see traces of two rather different kinds of system of initiatory knowledge, that of the Vedic priests and the *vrātyas* on the one hand, and that of the proto-*śramaṇa* cults of the Central Gangetic region on the other. These traditions undoubtedly interacted in all kinds of ways in many regions and places in what was an, at least partly, shared milieu of ascetic practice, but it seems worth exploring, as I have done in this book, the possibility that their origins were distinct, and tied up with different cultural contexts. The Vedic system was for the most part a system of hereditary ritual knowledge passed down in Brahmin families, but there are also suggestions, in the *vrātya* material, of a period of collective initiation for young men as a whole, based around ritual and military activity in the forest away from the settled community. If I am right in suggesting that the origins of the *śramaṇa* cults might be found in early initiatory cults in and beyond the Central Gangetic region,[3] with resemblances to the West African initiatory cults that played a significant role in the growth of wider social and political networks in that region in recent centuries, or perhaps to the early phases of the initiatory cults of the Hellenistic world, we can glimpse here the historical origins of these two different patterns and of their different emphases and approaches.

For the *śramaṇa* cults, initiation is an elective process undertaken by a limited sector of the population whose way of life or whose personal career has made such a choice meaningful and desirable. The often-suggested links between Buddhism and the trading communities of the newly-developing North Indian states of that time provide one way in which this may have worked, in that cult-initiation would have offered both a network of potential trading partners in distant places, an ethical code that provided a basis for such transactions, and a world-view in which members of distant communities shared with oneself a common human nature and common potentialities for spiritual advancement. The cultural pattern built around the *śramaṇa* orders presupposes a background of local deity cults, but not necessarily the development of large-scale Brahmanical religious cult-centres which, for much of North India, may not have taken place until a much later period, perhaps that of the Gupta kings.

[3] I say 'in and beyond' with reference to Williams' suggestions about Gujarat (R. Williams 1966).

All this, it must be said, is speculative, but it provides a context in which we can make sense of the teaching careers of the various semi-legendary predecessors of the Buddha and Mahāvīra and perhaps too of the legendary renunciate kings of Mithilā and elsewhere. It might also provide an interpretive background to the activities of the Buddhist and Jain founding figures themselves, and to the interest of the historical kings of the fifth and fourth century states and of the Mauryan Empire in their teachings.

In the court culture of the second and third centuries and particularly of the Gupta and Vākāṭaka kings, the idea of a consciously undertaken pattern of life, with formalised bodies of rules, had become institutionalised in a variety of contexts, including the legal handbooks (Dharma Sūtras), the *artha* and *kama śāstras*, and the various formalised rules for yogic and religious activity. Daud Ali is surely right to see the Buddhist Vinaya code as part of the same world and as sharing many of the same assumptions (Ali 1998). Some of these regulated modes of life were inherited, others were voluntarily undertaken, but in all cases there was an expectation of a controlled and disciplined way for the individual to follow. The various traditions of meditation and yoga at this period need to be seen as specific 'technologies of the self' within such a context. They offered a particular set of alternatives, both for lay followers who might be involved in yogic and meditational practices to various degrees of seriousness and for those who chose to commit themselves further and become full-time professional renunciates.

At the same time, we need to recall that most people in South Asia were not living in the courtly or urban middle-class milieu. Both in villages and urban centres, the cycle of collective seasonal rituals and of contact with the deities through spirit-mediums and shamanic-style practitioners continued, and the renunciate career involved an ongoing interaction with this milieu as well as with the courtly milieu.

The initial placing of the *śramaṇa* community and of the Brahmanical *sannyāsin* outside the ordered life of the city and village, in the social and physical spaces associated with death and misfortune, provided one basic reason why they needed to build a relationship with the wider community. As the increasing size and wealth of the Buddhist and Jain monastic communities demonstrated, they developed other modes of support, centred around their spiritual appeal to the new urban elites and doubtless also to the various pragmatic ways in which they became integrated into the social, political and economic life of the urban centres (cf. Heitzman 1984; O'Connor 1989; Bailey and Mabbett 2003). The ideal of the forest ascetic, on the edges or outside of the settled community, or living with other practitioners in remote locations, nevertheless persisted and, as Reginald Ray has suggested, formed the basis for a vital ongoing dialectic between the civilised and regulated urban monastics and a creative and visionary milieu (Ray 1999). A similar dialectic perhaps took place between the ordered and secure world of the settled Brahmins and the various renunciate practitioners, including the Pāśupatas and the *kāpālika*-style ascetics, though it is clear, as with the Buddhist forest-monks, that these groups developed their own institutional base and their own connections with the courts and cities. This dialectic between institutionalised and less regulated versions of the traditions probably provided a major source for innovation and change. It was doubtless also a key element in the growth of the various *kaula* and Tantric traditions which provided new 'technologies of the self' for the changing conditions of ninth and tenth century CE South and Southeast Asia, as well as a body of practices which could be used to take over the role of Atharvavedic purohits and other ritualists (cf. Sanderson 2004).

SEXUALITY AND GENDER RELATIONS IN TANTRA

This brings us to one of the most controversial issues about Tantra for many modern readers, its use of sexuality and of 'transgressive' elements in general. Why did Indian spiritual traditions develop in this particular direction in the ninth and tenth centuries?

To begin with, we might ask how Tantric sexuality fits into the picture of two cultural patterns that I drew up above, the *brahmacārin*-centred Vedic pattern and the *mithuna*-centred Central Gangetic pattern. As we have seen, the development of the *kaula* and *mahāyoga* practices took place at a time when South Asian societies were becoming increasingly dominated by feudal and military values (Davidson's 'sāmantisation' process, see Chapter 12). The Southeast Asian states that adopted Tantric models probably shared many of the same values and orientations. We have already noted the conflation of warfare and eroticism that appeared to go along with these values in parts of India in particular.

Whether the values of Tantric practice can be seen as a development of such problematic emphases or as a potential counter or response to them is a difficult question. It might have been some of each, at different times. A variety of different meanings can also be given to the sexual and transgressive elements within Tantra.

Viewed from the point of view of the modern Tibetan tradition in particular, it is tempting to stress the elements of asceticism and control within Tantra, and to marginalise the sexual and transgressive elements. This is true enough for contemporary Tibetan practice, where these elements are mostly a matter of visualisation or symbolic performance, but all the indications are that the sexual practices, at any rate, were seen as essential by both Buddhist and Śaiva Tantric practitioners in the ninth to twelfth century Indian context, and that *kāpālika*-style practice, with its transgressive and antinomian elements, also had some historical reality.

An alternative approach would be to focus on the use of Tantric ritual for pragmatic ends, and to see the transgression purely in terms of pragmatic power. As I have noted in earlier chapters, it seems clear that the use of sexual practices and fluids, initially at least, derived from the ritual effectiveness of impure and transgressive substances, both for creating the initiate's link to the lineage and for bringing about magically effective ritual, rather than from any kind of spiritualisation of sexual experience as such. This phase of Tantric practice adds little to a history of masculinity or sexuality in South Asia, except perhaps to illustrate the power associated with breaking the rules, and the need for religious practitioners to provide what their employers are looking for. By the ninth and tenth centuries, it is clear that both Buddhist and Śaiva practitioners were in the business of selling aggressive and destructive rituals (and also, one might add, healing rituals and rituals for prosperity) to their secular employers, and that there was a market for both Buddhist and Śaiva versions.

Yet, as a series of contemporary scholars have made clear in relation to the later, 'spiritualised', versions of Tantric practice associated with the great Kashmiri scholar Abhinavagupta and his followers,[4] and as is equally clear from the practice of Buddhist Tantra in the late Indian context and afterwards in Tibet, this is not all there is to the story.

These more spiritualised understandings of *kaula* and Tantric practice may go back some way before the reforms of the eight to tenth centuries. As I have commented elsewhere in this book, one needs to bear in mind an 'internal' understanding of what is going on in Tantric ritual as well as an external understanding. As we have seen in relation to the Pāśupatas and the *kāpālika*-style practitioners, the reasons why people undertook these apparently bizarre and transgressive practices may not bear much resemblance to the image which the society as a whole had of them. Whether, as in the case

4 E.g. Sanderson 1985, 1995; Silburn 1988; White 2003; Muller-Ortega 2002; Dupuche 2003.

of the low-caste hereditary practitioners, people were born to the career of a Tantric ritualist, or whether, as with the Pāśupatas and the *kāpālika*-style ascetics, they chose it voluntarily, the ritualists were likely to develop a perspective on their activities which allowed them a degree of self-respect.

It is here perhaps that we find the sources of *kaula* practice as a path to spiritual transcendence, along with the striking imagery that accompanies it, in which the transgressive behaviour, the cremation ground and the fierce deities become aids to achieving the breakthrough from ordinary worldly experience which had already long been the central goal of the Indian ascetic paths. In time, this provided the basis for a 'spiritualised' understanding of Tantra, and a morally elevated view of the relationship of male and female individuals that was at the base of its core practice.

Much the same would also be true on the Buddhist side, where these practices were adopted within a tradition that already had a very strong ethical orientation in the *bodhisattva* ideal, and where the sexual practices were connected directly with this ethical orientation through the identification of male and female sexual substances with *bodhicitta*, the empathetic desire to relieve the sufferings of other beings that is the central motive force of the Buddhist quest for the liberating insight (Samuel 1989).

As for the politics of gender in South Asian societies, Tantra by itself could scarcely have reversed the long-term processes by which the status of women in South Asia became increasingly confined and restricted, but it did at least enjoin and legitimate a more positive and equal relationship between the sexual partners who were involved in its practice at the time. Even this was a difficult and unstable position to uphold. Perhaps that is as much as we can reasonably ask of it.

In the longer term, the sexual practices were marginalised both in India and in Tibet, with the celibate practitioner, whether Hindu *sannyāsin* or Buddhist monk, being increasingly seen as the ideal. Whether contemporary Western versions of Tantric sexuality have the potential to aid in the all too necessary restructuring of sexual relationships within today's society is another question (Samuel 2005a: 357–61).

PHILOSOPHY, SPIRITUAL REALISATION AND SOCIAL PRACTICE

Philosophical understandings of Indic religions have played a fairly small part in this book.[5] My interest here has been more on the techniques used

[5] I apologise to those who would have liked it to have had a larger part, but there are plenty of good books on Hindu and Buddhist philosophy already.

to attain the 'liberating insight' within specific traditions, and on the wider social context within which seekers of that insight have operated.

Indian traditions of spiritual realisation tend to assume that spiritual practice is an ascetic process of one or another kind, and as we have seen the amount of specific guidance as to technique varies from little or nothing, in the early period, to extremely elaborate internal visualisations and mind-body transformations, in the later Tantric traditions. Indian spiritual traditions also assume that one understands or perceives something as a result of the successful accomplishment of spiritual practice, and that the understanding or perception cannot be separated from the inner transformation brought about as a result of the practice. The liberating insight is both understanding and inner transformation.

Even if the understanding could be understood as a logical proposition outside from the inner transformation, and Indian traditions have been far from united about whether this is possible, it is ineffective without the transformation: the point is not to assert the logical proposition that one is Śiva, or that all is Buddha-nature, but to directly experience the truth to which those words refer. The liberating insight is thus not a logical proposition but something intrinsic to a patterning or attunement of the mind-body system as a whole to the wider universe of which it forms an indissoluble part. This is one reason why the techniques employed to bring this inner transformation about are of at least as much interest as the logical propositions through which the resulting insight may be expressed.

Yogic and meditational procedures are taken more seriously now than they were in Western societies even half a century ago, but the question of how far we should regard these processes of inner transformation as having real effects remains open within many parts of Western and global society. In fact, this is a good question, though only partly answerable. There is enough solid research to show that Indian techniques of yoga and meditation, including the various internal yogas of Tantric practice, can indeed affect the functioning, and so the health and vitality, of the organism, and that the special awarenesses and sensitivities that are trained by these techniques do have real correlates accessible to modern scientific investigation. I have written a little elsewhere about these matters (Samuel 2006a, 2006c), and this is an area in which there is also beginning to be some serious research in the natural sciences.

If we can accept this much, then we can also perhaps accept that the complex set of techniques and approaches which was assembled by the Tantric practitioners of the ninth to twelfth centuries may be less arbitrary and less bizarre than it initially appears. The fundamental Tantric techniques deal with sexuality and our connection with other human beings, with the basic processes of life and vitality and with the ultimate breakdown of the human organism in death. These aspects of human existence are still part of our lives today. The encounters, real or visualised, with the ferocious Tantric deities and the horrific environment of the charnel-ground allow for a confrontation and resolution of deep-rooted conflicts within the human mind-body organism. The internal yogic practices valorise and operate with the fundamental affective bond between sexual partners, and treat it as a gateway to a liberating insight in which universal compassion is a key element. They also confront the practitioner with the process of the dissolution of personality in sleep and in death, and treat this too as an opening to spiritual realisation. From this point of view, Tantra seems less of a historical aberration, and more a set of techniques that might allow for a healing and productive encounter with the basic problems of the human condition.

With regard to the ultimate state or condition to which these practices aim, that associated with the liberating insight itself, it is less possible to speak in scientific terms. Persons who have achieved such conditions, if they exist, are generally not available for scientific investigation. Perhaps in the present context it is enough to say that these matters were clearly taken seriously over thousands of years by many highly intelligent people.

One should go on, however, to ask a further question. What are the consequences for contemporary society as a whole if it is choosing to take such states seriously and to commit substantial numbers of people to their pursuit? That question is in the background of much of what I have written in this book, but we are still some way from being able to answer it fully. Yet issues of this kind may be critical in relation to the future of our planet. We can no longer treat the question of human feeling, motivation and consciousness as something to be determined simply by the logic of commercial exploitation and by the patterns of desire, dissatisfaction and resentment that it inevitably creates. Nor do the various modernist forms of religion, the so-called fundamentalisms, help the situation. They are part of the same logic as the world of commerce. They operate with the same crude levels of consciousness and emotion and they lead into much the same resentments and destructive political directions. Only the enemies against which the resentment and anger is focused are different.

In such a world, a body of traditions and techniques that claims to detach the practitioner from excessive emotion, and to purify his or her consciousness, is worth taking with some seriousness. In addition, much of later Tantric practice, as we have seen, moved beyond this initial context to constitute a complex and subtle series of processes for transforming the mind-body totality of the practitioner.

If we regard the techniques of yoga, meditation and Tantra as tools that may still be worth investigating as of use in today's global society, then our ability to make sense of them and use them constructively can only be assisted by an understanding of the historical context within which these practices developed and out of which their imagery and language was born. I hope that this book will provide some of the elements for such an understanding.

References

Aasen, C. 1998. *Architecture of Siam: A Cultural History Interpretation.* Kuala Lumpur: Oxford University Press.

Adriaensen, R., Bakker, H. T. and Isaacson, H. 1994. 'Towards a Critical Edition of the *Skandapurāṇa*'. *Indo-Iranian Journal* 37: 325–31.

Adriaensen, R., Bakker, H. T. and Isaacson, H. 1998-. *The Skandapurāṇa.* Critically edited with Prolegomena and English synopsis by R. Adriaensen, H. T. Bakker, H. Isaacson. 2 vols. so far. Groningen: Egbert Forsten.

Agrawala, Prithvi K. 1983. *Mithuna: The Male-Female Symbol in Indian Art and Thought.* Delhi: Munshiram Manoharlal.

Agrawala, V. S. and Motichandra 1960. 'Yaksha Worship in Varanasi: Matsyapurāṇa (Ch. 180)'. *Purāṇa* 1: 198–201.

Ali, D. 1998. 'Technologies of the Self: Courtly Artifice and Monastic Discipline in Early India'. *Journal of Economic and Social History of the Orient* 41: 159–84.

Ali, D. 2004. *Courtly Culture and Political Life in Early Medieval India.* Cambridge and New York: Cambridge University Press.

Allchin, B. 1995. 'The Environmental Context', in Allchin 1995, pp. 10–25.

Allchin, B. and R., F. 1982. *The Rise of Civilization in India and Pakistan.* Cambridge, London and New York: Cambridge University Press.

Allchin, F. R. 1963. *Neolithic Cattle-Keepers of South India: A Study of the Deccan Ashmounds.* Cambridge: Cambridge University Press.

Allchin, F. R. (ed.) 1995a. *The Archaeology of Early Historic South Asia: The Emergence of Cities and States.* Cambridge and New York: Cambridge University Press.

Allchin, F. R. 1995b. 'Mauryan Architecture and Art', in F. R. Allchin 1995a, pp. 222–73.

Allchin, F. R. 1995c. 'Language, Culture and the Concept of Ethnicity', in F. R. Allchin 1995a, pp. 41–53.

Allen, M. R. 2005. *Anthropology of Nepal: Peoples, Problems, and Process.* Reprint. Kathmandu: Mandala.

Allen, N. J. 1987. 'The Ideology of the Indo-Europeans: Dumézil's Theory and the Idea of a Fourth Function.' *International Journal of Moral and Social Studies* 2(1): 23–39.

Allen, N. J. 1996. 'Romulus and the Fourth Function', in *Indo-European Religion after Dumézil*, Polomé (ed.), pp. 13–36. Washington: Institute for the Study of Man.

Allen, N. J. 1998. 'The Indo-European Prehistory of Yoga'. *International Journal of Hindu Studies* 2: 1–20.

Alter, J. S. 1997. 'Seminal Truth: A Modern Science of Male Celibacy in North India'. *Medical Anthropology Quarterly* 11: 275–98.

Alter, J. S. 2005. 'Modern Medical Yoga: Struggling with a History of Magic, Alchemy and Sex'. *Asian Medicine: Tradition and Modernity* 1: 119–46.

Ames, M. 1964. 'Magical Animism and Buddhism: a Structural Analysis of the Sinhalese Religious System', in *Religion in South Asia,* Harper (ed.), pp. 21–5. Seattle: University of Washington Press.

Ames, M. 1966. 'Ritual Prestations and the Structure of the Sinhalese Pantheon', in *Anthropological Studies in Theravada Buddhism*, Nash (ed.), pp. 27–50. New Haven, CT: Southeast Asia Studies, Yale University.

Andaya, B. Watson 1994. 'The Changing Religious Role of Women in Pre-Modern South East Asia'. *South East Asia Research* 2: 99–116.

Andresen, J. 1997. *Kālacakra: Textual and Ritual Perspectives.* PhD Dissertation, Harvard University. UMI AAT 9733170.

Archer, W. G. 1964. 'Preface', in Comfort 1964, pp. 7–38.

Archer, W. G. 1974. *The Hill of Flutes: Life, Love and Poetry in Tribal India: a Portrait of the Santals.* London: Allen and Unwin.

Atre, S. 1998. 'The High Priestess: Gender Signifiers and the Feminine in the Harappan Context'. *South Asian Studies* 14: 161–72.

Aung-Thwin, M. 1981. 'Jambudipa: Classical Burma's Camelot'. *Contributions to Asian Studies* 16: 38–61.

Aziz, B. N. 1978. *Tibetan Frontier Families: Reflections of Three Generations from D'ing-ri.* New Delhi: Vikas Publishing House.

Bagchi, P. C. and Magee, M. 1986. *Kaulajñānanirṇaya of the School of Matsyendranātha. Text Edited with an Exhaustive Introduction by P. C. Bagchi. Translated into English by Michael Magee.* Varanasi: Prachya Prakashan. (Tantra Granthamala, 12)

Bailey, G. and Mabbett, I. 2003. *The Sociology of Early Buddhism.* Cambridge and New York: Cambridge University Press.

Bakker, H. 1986. *Ayodhyā.* Groningen: Egbert Forsten.

Bakker, H. 1999. [Review of Srinivasan 1997.] *Artibus Asiae* 58: 339–43.

Bakker, H. 2001. 'Sources for Reconstructing Ancient Forms of Śiva Worship', in Grimal 2001, pp. 397–412.

Bakker, H. (ed.). 2004. *The Vākāṭaka Heritage: Indian Culture at the Crossroads.* Groningen: Egbert Forsten.

Balcerowicz, P. 2005. 'Monks, Monarchs and Materialists'. [Review essay of Bollée 2002.] *Journal of Indian Philosophy* 33: 571–82.

Banerji, S. C. 1992. *New Light on Tantra: Accounts of Some Tantras, Both Hindu and Buddhist, Alchemy in Tantra, Tantric Therapy, List of Unpublished Tantras, etc.* Calcutta: Punthi Pustak.

Barth, F. 1990. 'The Guru and the Conjurer: Transactions in Knowledge and the Shaping of Culture in Southeast Asia and Melanesia'. *Man* 25: 640–53.

Barua, B. 1934–37. *Barhut. Books I to III.* Calcutta.

Basham, A. L. 1951. *History and Doctrines of the Ājīvikas.* London: Luzac.

Bautze, J. K. 1995. *Early Indian Terracottas.* Leiden: E. J. Brill. (Iconography of Religions, XIII, 17.)

Bayly, S. 2001. *Caste, Society and Politics in India from the Eighteenth Century to the Modern Age.* Paperback edn. Cambridge: Cambridge University Press. (*New Cambridge History of India*, IV, 3.)

Bechert, H. (ed.) 1991–97. *The Dating of the Historical Buddha = Die Datierung des historischen Buddha.* 3 vols. Göttingen: Vandenhoeck & Ruprecht.

Beck, G. L. 1995. *Sonic Theology: Hinduism and Sacred Sound.* Delhi: Motilal Banarsidass.

Becker, J. 1993. *Gamelan Stories: Tantrism, Islam, and Aesthetics in Central Java.* Tempe, AZ: Arizona State University, Program for Southeast Asian Studies.

Bell, S. and Sobo, E. J. 2001. 'Celibacy in Cross-Cultural Perspective: An Overview', in Sobo and Bell 2001, pp. 11–12.

Bellwood, P. 1999. 'Southeast Asia Before History', in Tarling 1999, pp. 55–136.

Belo, J. 1949. *Bali: Rangda and Barong.* Seattle: University of Washington Press.

Benard, E. A. 1994. *Chinnamastā: The Aweful Buddhist and Hindu Tantric Goddess.* Delhi: Motilal Banarsidass.

Bentley, G. Carter 1986. 'Indigenous States in Southeast Asia'. *Annual Review of Anthropology* 15: 275–305.

Bernbaum, E. 1980. *The Way to Shambhala.* Garden City, NY: Anchor Press/Doubleday.

Berreman, G. D. 1971. 'The Brahmanical View of Caste'. *Contributions to Indian Sociology* (N.S.) 5: 16–23.

Beyer, S. 1977, 'Notes on the Vision Quest in Early Mahāyāna', in *Prajñāpāramitā and Related Systems: Studies in Honor of Edward Conze*, Lancaster (ed.), pp. 329–40. Berkeley: University of California Press. (Berkeley Buddhist Studies Series.)

Beyer, S. 1973. *The Cult of Tara. Magic and Ritual in Tibet.* Berkeley: University of California Press.

Bharadwaj, O. P. 1989. 'Yaksha-Worship in Kurukshetra', in *Prācī-prabhā: Perspectives in Indology: Essays in Honour of Professor B. N. Mukherjee,* Bhattacharyya and Handa (eds.), pp. 203–23. New Delhi: Harman.

Bharati, A. 1965. *The Tantric Tradition.* London: Rider.

Bhattacharyya, N. N. 1996. *Ancient Indian Rituals and Their Social Contexts.* Delhi: Manohar.

Bhawe, S. S. 1939. *Die Yajus' des Asvamedha. Versuch einer Rekonstruktion dieses Abschnittes des Yajurveda auf Grund der Überlieferung seiner fünf Schulen.* Stuttgart: W. Kohlhammer.

Biardeau, M. 1989. *Histoires de poteaux: variations védiques autour de la Déesse hindoue.* Paris: Ecole française d'Extrême Orient.

Bisschop, P. 2005. 'Pañcārthabhāṣya on Pāśupatasūtra 1.37–39 Recovered from a Newly Identified Manuscript'. *Journal of Indian Philosophy* 33: 529–51.

Bisschop, P. and Griffiths, A. 2003. 'The Pāśupata Observance (Atharvavedapariśiṣṭa 40)'. *Indo-Iranian Journal* 46: 315–48.

Blacker, C. 1986. *The Catalpa Bow: A Study of Shamanistic Practices in Japan*. Second edn. London and Boston: Mandala/Unwin Paperbacks.

Blench, R. and Spriggs, M. (eds.) 1998. *Archaeology and Language II: Correlating Archaeological and Linguistic Hypotheses*. London and New York: Routledge.

Blench, R. and Spriggs, M. (eds.) 1999. *Archaeology and Language III: Artefacts, Languages and Texts*. London and New York: Routledge.

Blezer, H. 1997. *Kar gliṅ Źi khro: A Tantric Buddhist Concept*. Leiden: Research School CNWS, School of Asian, African, and Amerindian Studies, Leiden University. (CNWS Publications, 56.)

Bollée, W. B. 1981. 'The Indo-European Sodalities in Ancient India'. *Zeitschrift der Deutschen Morgenlandischen Gesellschaft* 131: 172–91.

Bollée, W. B. 2002. *The Story of Paesi (Paesi-kahāṇayaṃ)*. Soul and Body in Ancient India: A Dialogue on Materialism. Text, Translation, Notes and Glossary. Wiesbaden: Harrassowitz. (Beitrage zur Kenntnis südasiatischer Sprachen und Literaturen 8.)

Bolon, C. Radcliffe 1992. *Forms of the Goddess Lajjā Gaurī in Indian Art*. University Park, PA: Pennsylvania State University Press.

Bouillier, V. 1993. 'La violence des non-violents, ou les ascètes au combat'. *Puruṣārtha* 16: 213–42.

Boyce, M. 1997. 'Origins of Zoroastrian Philosophy', in *Companion Encyclopedia of Asian Philosophy*, Carr and Mahalingam (eds.), pp. 5–23. London: Routledge.

Brauen-Dolma, M. 1985. 'Millenarianism in Tibetan Religion', in *Soundings in Tibetan Civilization*, Aziz and Kapstein (eds.), pp. 245–56. New Delhi: Manohar.

Brereton, J. P. 1981. *The Ṛgvedic Ādityas*. New Haven, CT: American Oriental Society. (American Oriental Series, 63.)

Briggs, G. Weston 1989. *Gorakhnāth and the Kānphaṭa Yogīs*. Reprint. Delhi: Motilal Banarsidass.

Brockington, J. L. 1985. *Righteous Rāma: The Evolution of an Epic*. Delhi: Oxford University Press.

Brockington, J. L. 1998. *The Sanskrit Epics*. Leiden: Brill. (Handbuch der Orientalistik. Zweite Abteilung, Indien; 12. Bd.)

Brockington, J. L. 2003a. 'The Sanskrit Epics', in Flood 2003, pp. 116–28.

Brockington, J. L. 2003b. 'Yoga in the *Mahābhārata*', in Whicher and Carpenter 2003, pp. 13–24.

Brohm, J. 1963. 'Buddhism and Animism in a Burmese Village'. *Journal of Asian Studies* 22: 155–67.

Bronkhorst, J. 1993. *The Two Traditions of Meditation in Ancient India*. Delhi: Motilal Banarsidass.

Bronkhorst, J. 1998a. *The Two Sources of Indian Asceticism*. Second edn. Delhi: Motilal Banarsidass.

Bronkhorst, J. 1998b. 'Did the Buddha Believe in Karma and Rebirth?', *Journal of International Association of Buddhist Studies* 21: 1–19.

Bronkhorst, J. 2000. 'The Riddle of the Jainas and Ājīvikas in Early Buddhist Literature'. *Journal of Indian Philosophy* 28: 511–29.

Bronson, B. and White, J. C. 1992. 'Radiocarbon and Chronology in Southeast Asia', in Ehrich 1992, I, pp. 491–503; II, pp. 475–515.

Brooks, D. Renfrew 1990. *The Secret of the Three Cities: An Introduction to Hindu Śākta Tantrism.* Chicago and London: University of Chicago Press.

Brooks, D. Renfrew 1992a. *Auspicious Wisdom: The Texts and Traditions of Śrīvidyā Śākta Tantrism in South India.* Albany, NY: State University of New York Press.

Brooks, D. Renfrew 1992b. 'Encountering the Hindu "Other": Tantrism and the Brahmans of South India'. *Journal of American Academy of Religion* 60(3): 405–36.

Brown, C. Henning 1996. 'Contested Meanings: Tantra and the Poetics of Mithila Art'. *American Ethnologist* 23: 717–37.

Brown, M. Fobes 1988. 'Shamanism and its Discontents'. *Medical Anthropology Quarterly* 2(2): 102–20.

Brown, R. L. 1990. 'A *Lajjā Gaurī* in a Buddhist Context at Aurangabad'. *Journal of International Association of Buddhist Studies* 13(2): 1–16.

Brubaker, R. L. 1979. 'Barbers, Washermen, and Other Priests: Servants of the South Indian Village and the Goddess'. *History of Religions* 19: 128–54.

Brubaker, R. L. 1983. 'The Untamed Goddesses of Village India', in *The Book of the Goddess: An Introduction to Her Religion*, Olson (ed.), pp. 145–60. New York: Crossroad.

Brückner, H., Lutze, L. and Malik, A. (eds.) 1993. *Flags of Fame: Studies in South Asian Folk Culture.* New Delhi: Manohar.

Bryant, B. 1992. *The Wheel of Time Sand Mandala: Visual Scripture of Tibetan Buddhism.* San Francisco: HarperSanFrancisco.

Bryant, E. F. and Patton, L. L. (eds.) 2005. *The Indo-Aryan Controversy: Evidence and Inference in Indian History.* London and New York: Routledge.

Bühnemann, G. 1996. 'The Goddess Mahācīnakrama-Tārā (Ugra-Tārā) in Buddhist and Hindu Tantrism'. *Bulletin of the School of Oriental and African Studies* 59: 472–93.

Bühnemann, G. 1999. 'Buddhist Deities and Mantras in the Hindu Tantras: I The *Tantrasārasaṃgraha* and the *Īśānaśivagurudevapaddhati*'. *Indo-Iranian Journal* 42: 303–34.

Bühnemann, G. 2000a. 'Buddhist Deities and Mantras in the Hindu Tantras: II The *Śrīvidyārṇavatantra and the Tantrasāra.*' *Indo-Iranian Journal* 43: 27–43.

Burghart, R. 1978. 'The Disappearance and Reappearance of Janakpur'. *Kailash* 6: 257–84.

Cardona, G. 1976. *Pāṇini: A Survey of Research.* The Hague: Mouton.

Carman, J. B. and Marglin, F. A. 1985. *Purity and Auspiciousness in Indian Society.* Leiden: E. J. Brill.

Carrithers, M. 1983. *The Forest Monks of Sri Lanka: An Anthropological and Historical Study*. Delhi: Oxford University Press.

Carrithers, M. and Humphrey, C. (eds.) 1991. *The Assembly of Listeners: Jains in Society*. Cambridge and New York: Cambridge University Press.

Carstairs, G. Morris 1957. *The Twice-born: a Study of a Community of High-Caste Hindus*. London: Hogarth Press, 1957.

Castells, M. 1997. *The Power of Identity (The Information Age: Economy, Society and Culture. Volume II)*. Malden, MA and Oxford: Blackwells.

Chakrabarti, D. K. 1995. *The Archaeology of Ancient Indian Cities*. Delhi: Oxford University Press.

Chakrabarti, D. K. 2001. *Ancient Bangladesh: A Study of the Archaeological Sources with an Update on Bangladesh Archaeology, 1990–2000*. Dhaka: The University Press Limited.

Chakrabarti, D. K. n.d. 'The Historical and Archaeological Context of Chandraketugarh'. Downloaded from www.historyofbengal.com/articles.html, 4 Oct 2006.

Chandra, L. 1992a. *Cultural Horizons of India*. Delhi: International Academy of Indian Culture. (Śata-Piṭaka, 366.)

Chandra, L. 1992b. 'Tantras and the Defence of T'ang China', in Chandra 1992a, vol. 2, pp. 257–66.

Chandra, L. 1992c. 'Emperor Hsüan-Tsung, Vajrayāna and Quarter of Vajras', in Chandra 1992a, vol. 2, pp. 267–76.

Chatterji, B. Chandra 1992. *Anandamath*. Translated and adapted from original Bengali by B. Koomar Roy. New Delhi and Bombay: Orient Paperbacks.

Chattopadhyaya, A. 1967. *Atisa and Tibet: Life and Works of Dipamkara Srijnana in Relation to the History and Religion of Tibet with Tibetan Sources*. Delhi: Motilal Banarsidass.

Chawla, J. 1994. *Child-bearing and Culture: Women-Centered Revisioning of the Traditional Midwife, the Dai as a Ritual Practitioner*. New Delhi: Indian Social Institute.

Chawla, J. 2006. 'Celebrating the Divine Female Principle'. Women's Feature Service. Downloaded from www.boloji.com/wfs/wfs082.htm, 23 September 2006.

Chia, M. 1983. *Awaken Healing Energy Through the Tao: The Taoist Secret of Circulating Internal Power*. Santa Fe, NM: Aurora Press.

Choong, M. 2005. 'The Importance of Pali-Chinese Comparison in the Study of Pali Suttas'. *Khthonios: A Journal for the Study of Religion* (Queensland Society for the Study of Religion) 2(2): 19–26.

Clark, M. J. 2004. *The Daśanāmī-Saṃnyāsīs: the Integration of Ascetic Lineages into an Order*. PhD dissertation, University of London. [Revised version published under same title by Brill, 2006.]

Claus, P. J. 1973. 'Possession, Protection, and Punishment as Attributes of the Deities in a South Indian Village'. *Man in India* 53: 231–42.

Claus, P. J. 1979. 'Spirit Possession and Mediumship from the Perspective of Tulu Oral Traditions'. *Culture, Medicine and Psychiatry* 3: 29–52.

Claus, P. J. 1984. 'Medical Anthropology and the Ethnography of Spirit Possession', in Daniel and Pugh 1984, pp. 60–72.

Claus, P. J. 1993. 'Text Variability and Authenticity in the Siri Cult', in Brückner, Lutze and Malik 1993, pp. 335–74.

Clothey, F. W. 1978. *The Many Faces of Murukan̲: The History and Meaning of a South Indian God*. The Hague: Mouton.

Coburn, T. B. 1982. 'Consort of None, *Śakti* of all: The Vision of the *Devī-Māhātmya*', in Hawley and Wulff 1982, pp. 153–65.

Coburn, T. B. 1988. *Devī-Māhātmya: The Crystallization of the Goddess Tradition*. Delhi: Motilal Banarsidass.

Coburn, T. B. 1991. *Encountering the Goddess: A Translation of the Devī-Māhātmya and a Study of its Interpretation*. Albany, NY: State University of New York Press.

Coedès, G. 1975. *The Indianized States of Southeast Asia*. Edited by W. F. Vella; translated by S. Brown Cowing. Canberra: Australian National University Press.

Cohen, A. L. 1992. 'The King and the Goddess: The Noḷamba Period Lakṣmaneśvara Temple at Avani'. *Artibus Asiae* 52: 7–24.

Cohen, A. L. 1997. 'Why a History of Monuments from Noḷambavāḍi?' *Artibus Asiae* 57: 17–29.

Cohen, R. S. 1995. 'Discontented Categories: Hinayana and Mahayana in Indian Buddhist History', *Journal of the American Academy of Religion* 63/1 (Spring 1995): 1–25.

Cohen, R. S. 1998. 'Nāga, Yakṣinī, Buddha: Local Deities and Local Buddhism at Ajanta'. *History of Religions* 37: 360–400.

Colas, G. 2003. 'History of Vaiṣṇava Traditions: An Esquisse', in Flood 2003, pp. 229–70.

Collins, S. 1990. 'On the Very Idea of the Pali Canon'. *Journal of Pali Text Society* 15: 89–126.

Comfort, A. 1964. *The Koka Shastra: Being the Ratirahasya of kokkoka, and Other Mediaeval Indian Writings on Love*. Translated by A. Comfort. London: Tandem Books.

Connolly, P. 1997. 'The Vitalistic Antecedents of the Ātman-Brahman Concept', in Connolly and Hamilton 1997, pp. 21–38.

Connolly, P. and Hamilton, S. (eds.) 1997. *Indian Insights: Buddhism, Brahmanism and Bhakti. Papers from the Annual Spalding Symposium on Indian Religions*. London: Luzac Oriental.

Connor, L. H. 1995. 'Acquiring Invisible Strength: A Balinese Discourse of Harm and Well-Being'. *Indonesia Circle* 66: 124–53.

Conze, E. 1962. *Buddhist Thought in India: Three Phases of Buddhist Philosophy*. London: George Allen and Unwin Ltd.

Conze, E. 1973. *The Short Prajñāpāramitā Texts*. London: Luzac & Co.

Conze, E. 1978. *The Prajñāpāramitā Literature*. Second rev. and enlarged edn. Tokyo: Reiyukai. (Bibliographia Philologica Buddhica. Series Maior; 1.)

Coomaraswamy, A. Kentish 1928–31. *Yakshas. Parts I and II.* Washington, DC: Smithsonian Institution.
Coomaraswamy, A. Kentish 1956. *La sculpture de Bharhut.* Translation J. Buhot. Paris: Vaneost. (Annales du Musée Guimet, Bibliotheque d'Art, nouvelle série, 6.)
Cort, J. E. 1987. 'Medieval Jaina Goddess Traditions'. *Numen* 34: 235–55.
Cort, J. E. 2001. *Jains in the World: Religious Values and Ideology in India.* New York: Oxford University Press.
Courtright, P. 1985. *Gaṇeśa: Lord of Obstacles, Lord of Beginnings.* New York and Oxford: Oxford University Press.
Cousins, L. S. 1973. 'Buddhist *Jhāna*: Its Nature and Attainment According to the Pali Sources'. *Religion* 3: 115–31.
Cousins, L. S. 1983. 'Pali Oral Literature', in *Buddhist Studies: Ancient and Modern*, Denwood and Piatigorsky (eds.), 1–11. London: Curzon.
Cousins, L. S. 1984. '*Samatha-yāna* and *Vipassanā-yāna*', in *Buddhist Studies in Honour of Hammalava Saddhātissa*, Dhammapāla, Gombrich and Norman (eds.), pp. 55–68. Nugegoda, Sri Lanka: Buddhist Research Library Trust.
Cousins, L. S. 1991. The 'Five Points' and the Origin of the Buddhist Schools', *The Buddhist Forum Vol. II*, Skorupski (ed.), pp. 27–60. London: School of Oriental and African Studies.
Cousins, L. S. 1992. 'Vitakka/Vitarka and Vicara: Stages of Samādhi in Buddhism and Yoga'. *Indo-Iranian Journal* 35: 137–57.
Cousins, L. S. 1996a. 'The Dating of the Historical Buddha: A Review Article'. *Journal Royal Asiatic Society* Series 3, 6: 57–63. Available as e-text from www.ucl.ac.uk/~ucgadkw/position/buddha/buddha.html (downloaded 3 Aug 2006).
Cousins, L. S. 1996b. 'The Origins of Insight Meditation', in *The Buddhist Forum Vol. IV: Seminar Papers 1994–1996*, Skorupski (ed.), pp. 35–58. London: School of Oriental and African Studies.
Cousins, L. S. 1997. 'Aspects of Esoteric Southern Buddhism', in Connolly and Hamilton 1997, pp. 185–207. London: Luzac Oriental.
Cousins, L. S. 2005. 'New Discoveries and Old Baskets: Perspectives on the Development of Pali and Sanskrit Buddhist Canons in the Light of the Recently Discovered Sanskrit Dīrghāgama'. Numata Lectures, School of Oriental and African Studies, University of London.
Couture, A. and Schmid, C. 2001. 'The Harivaṃśa, the Goddess Ekānaṃśa, and the Iconography of the Vṛṣṇi Triad'. *Journal American Oriental Society* 121: 173–92.
Couture, A. 2003. 'Kṛṣṇa's Victory Over Bāṇa and Goddess Koṭavī's Manifestation in the Harivaṃśa'. *Journal of Indian Philosophy* 31: 593–620.
Crangle, E. Fitzpatrick 1994. *The Origin and Development of Early Indian Contemplative Practices.* Wiesbaden: Otto Harrassowitz.

Cribb, J. 1985. 'Dating India's Earliest Coins', in *South Asian Archaeology 1983*, Schotsmans and Taddei (eds.), vol. 1, pp. 535–54. Naples: Istituto Universitario Orientale, Naples.

Cribb, J. 1997. 'Śiva images on Kushan and Kushano-Sassanian Coins', in *Studies in Silk Road Coins and Culture*, Tanabe, Cribb and Wang (eds.), pp. 11–66. (Special volume of Silk Road Art and Archaeology 1997)

Curtis, V. Sarkhosh and Stewart, S. (eds.) 2005. *Birth of the Persian Empire, Vol. I.* London and NY: I. B. Tauris.

Czuma, Stanislaw J. 1985. *Kushan Sculpture: Images from Early India.* With the assistance of Rekha Morris. Cleveland, Ohio: Cleveland Museum of Art in cooperation with Indiana University Press.

Dalton, J. 2004. 'The Development of Perfection: The Interiorization of Buddhist Ritual in the Eight and Ninth Centuries'. *Journal of Indian Philosophy* 32: 1–30.

Dalton, J. 2005. 'A Crisis of Doxography: How Tibetans Organized Tantra during the 8th–12th Centuries'. *Journal International Association of Buddhist Studies* 28: 115–81.

Daniel, E. Valentine 1984. 'Pulse as Icon in Siddha Medicine', in Daniel and Pugh 1984, pp. 115–26.

Daniel, E. Valentine and Pugh, J. F. (eds.) 1984 *South Asian Systems of Healing.* Leiden: E. J. Brill. (*Contributions to Asian Studies*, 18.)

Daniélou, A. 1964. *Hindu Polytheism.* London: Routledge and Kegan Paul.

Dar, Saifur Rahman 1993. 'Dating the Monuments of Taxila', Spodek and Srinivasan 1993, pp. 103–22.

Dass, M. I. and Willis, M. 2002. 'The Lion Capital from Udayagiri and the Antiquity of Sun Worship in Central India', *South Asian Studies* 18: 25–45.

Das, R. P. 1992. 'Problematic Aspects of the Sexual Rituals of the Bauls of Bengal'. *Journal American Oriental Society* 112: 388–432.

Das, V. 1987. *Structure and Cognition: Aspects of Hindu Caste and Ritual.* 2nd edn. Delhi: Oxford University Press.

Davidson, R. M. 1991. 'Reflections on the Maheśvara Subjugation Myth: Indic Materials, Sa-skya-pa Apologetics, and the Birth of Heruka'. *Journal of the International Association of Buddhist Studies* 14/2: 197–235.

Davidson, R. M. 1995a. 'Atiśa's *A Lamp For the Path to* Awakening', in *Buddhism in Practice*, Lopez, Jr. (ed.), pp. 290–301. Princeton, NJ: Princeton University Press.

Davidson, R. M. 1995b. 'The Bodhisattva Vajrapāṇi's Subjugation of Śiva', in *Religions of India in Practice*, in Lopez, Jr. 1995, pp. 547–55. Princeton, NJ: Princeton University Press.

Davidson, R. M. 2002a. *Indian Esoteric Buddhism: A Social History of the Tantric Movement.* New York: Columbia University Press. [References to Davidson 2002 are to this.]

Davidson, R. M. 2002b. 'Hidden Realms and Pure Abodes: Central Asian Buddhism as Frontier Religion in the Literature of India, Nepal, and Tibet'. *Pacific World* 3rd series, 4 (Fall 2002): 153–81.

Davis, R. 1984. *Muang Metaphysics*. Bangkok: Pandora Press.

de Michelis, E. 2004. *A History of Modern Yoga: Patañjali and Western Esotericism*. London and New York: Continuum.

de Sales, A. 1991. *Je suis né de vos jeux de tambours: La religion chamanique des Magar du nord*. Nanterre: Société d'Ethnologie.

de Silva, L. 1981. *Paritta: A Historical and Religious Study of the Buddhist Ceremony for Peace and Prosperity in Sri Lanka*. Columbo: National Museums of Sri Lanka. (= *Spolia Zeylanica. Bulletin of the National Museums of Sri Lanka*, vol. 36 part 1.)

de Visser, M. W. 1928–35. *Ancient Buddhism in Japan: Sutras and Ceremonies in Use in the Seventh and Eighth Centuries A.D. and their History in Later Times*. Paris: P. Geuthner. (Buddhica. Documents et travaux pour l'Étude du bouddhisme . . . 1. sér.: Mémoires, t. 3–4.)

DeCaroli, R. 2004. *Haunting the Buddha: Indian Popular Religions and the Formation of Buddhism*. Oxford and New York: Oxford University Press.

Deeg, M. 1993. 'Shamanism in the Veda: the *Keśin*-Hymn (10.136), the Journey to Heaven of *Vasiṣṭha* (ṚV.7.88) and the *Mahāvrata*-Ritual'. *Nagoya Studies in Indian Culture and Buddhism (Saṃbhāṣā)* 14: 95–144.

Deeg, M. 2006. 'Aryan National Religion(s) and the Criticism of Asceticism and Quietism in the Nineteenth and Twentieth Centuries', in *Asceticism and Its Critics: Historical Accounts and Comparative Perspectives*, Freiberger (ed.), pp. 61–87. Oxford and New York: Oxford University Press.

Dehejia, V. 1979. *Early Stone Temples of Orissa*. New Delhi: Vikas Publishing House.

Dehejia, V. 1986. *Yoginī Cult and Temples: A Tantric Tradition*. New Delhi: National Museum.

Desai, D. 1990. '12.6 Mother Goddess'. *Encyclopedia of Indian Archaeology*, ed. A. Ghosh, pp. 267–9. Leiden: E. J. Brill.

Desani, G. V. 1973. 'Mostly Concerning Kama and Her Immortal Lord'. *Indian Horizons* 32: 1–44.

Deshpande, M. M. and Hook, P. E. (eds.) 1979. *Aryan and Non-Aryan in India*. Ann Arbor, MI: University of Michigan, Center for South and Southeast Asian Studies.

Deshpande, M. M. 1995. 'Vedic Aryans, Non-Vedic Aryans, and Non-Aryans: Judging the Linguistic Evidence of the Veda', in Erdosy 1995a, pp. 67–84.

Devika, J. 2005. 'The Aesthetic Woman: Re-Forming Female Bodies and Minds in Early Twentieth-Century Keralam'. *Modern Asian Studies* 39: 461–87.

Dhyansky, Y. Y. 1987. 'The Indus Valley Origin of a Yoga Practice'. *Artibus Asiae* 48: 89–108.

Diehl, C. G. 1956. *Instrument and Purpose: Studies on Rites and Rituals in South India*. Lund: Gleerup.

Dimock, E. C., Jr. 1982. 'A Theology of the Repulsive: The Myth of the Goddess Śītalā', in Hawley and Wulff 1982, pp. 184–203.

Divakaran, O. 1984. 'Durgā the Great Goddess: Meanings and Forms in the Early Period', in Meister 1984, pp. 271–89.

Dollfus, P. 1989. *Lieu de neige et de genévriers: Organisation sociale et religieuse des communautés bouddhistes du Ladakh.* Paris, Éditions du CNRS.

Donaldson, T. 1987. *Kamadeva's Pleasure Garden: Orissa.* Delhi: B. R. Publishing Corporation.

Dorje, G. 1987. *The Guhyagarbhatantra and its XIVth Century Commentary Phyogs-bcu Mun-sel.* PhD Dissertation, School of Oriental and African Studies, University of London.

Dowman, K. 1985. *Masters of Mahamudra: Songs and Histories of the Eighty-Four Buddhist Siddhas.* Albany, NY: SUNY Press.

Dreyfus, G. 1998. 'The Shuk-Den Affair: History and Nature of a Quarrel. *Journal International Association of Buddhist Studies* 21: 227–70.

Dumont, L. 1960. 'World Renunciation in Indian Religions'. *Contributions to Indian Sociology* 9: 67–89. (Reprinted in Dumont 1970, pp. 33–60.)

Dumont, L. 1970. *Religion, Politics and History in India.* Paris and Leiden: Mouton.

Dumont, L. 1972. *Homo Hierarchicus: the Caste System and its Implications.* London: Granada.

Dumont, P. É. 1927. *L'asvamedha, description du sacrifice solennel du cheval dans le culte védique d'après les textes du Yajurveda blanc.* Paris: P. Geuthner.

Dundas, P. 1991. 'The Digambara Jain Warrior', in Carrithers and Humphrey 1991, pp. 169–86.

Dundas, P. 2002. *The Jains.* Second edn. London and New York: Routledge.

Dupuche, J. R. 2003. *Abhinavagupta: The Kula Ritual As Elaborated in Chapter 29 of the Tantrāloka.* Delhi: Motilal Banarsidass.

Durrenberger, E. P. and Tannenbaum, N. 1989. 'Continuities in Highland and Lowland Regions of Thailand'. *Journal of the Siam Society* 77: 83–90.

Dyczkowski, M. S. G. 1989. *The Canon of the Śaivāgama and the Kubjikā Tantras of the Western Kaula Tradition.* Delhi: Motilal Banarsidass.

Ehrich, R. W. (ed.) 1992. *Chronologies in Old World Archaeology.* Chicago: University of Chicago Press.

Eliade, M. 1958. *Yoga, Immortality and Freedom.* Translated from the French by W. R. Trask. New York: Pantheon Books. (Bollingen Series, 56.)

Elwin, V. 1947. *The Muria and their Ghotul.* London: Oxford University Press Indian Branch.

Emigh, J. 1984. 'Dealing with the Demonic: Strategies for Containment in Hindu Iconography and Performance'. *Asian Theatre Journal* 1: 21–39.

Emmerick, R. E. 1970. *The Sūtra of Golden Light.* London: Luzac and Co.

English, E. 2002. *Vajrayoginī: Her Visualizations, Rituals, and Forms: A Study of the Cult of Vajrayoginī in India.* Boston: Wisdom.

Erdosy, G. (ed.) 1995a. *The Indo-Aryans of Ancient South Asia: Language, Material Culture and Ethnicity.* Berlin and New York: Walter de Gruyter. (*Indian Philology and South Asian Studies*, ed. Albrecht Wezler and Michael Witzel, Vol. 1.)

Erdosy, G. 1995b. 'The Prelude to Urbanization: Ethnicity and the Rise of Late Vedic Chiefdoms', in F. R. Allchin 1995a, pp. 75–98.

Erdosy, G. 1995c. 'City States of North India and Pakistan at the Time of the Buddha', in F. R. Allchin 1995a, pp. 99–122.

Eschmann, A., Kulke, H. and Tripathi, G. Charan (eds.) 1986. *The Cult of Jagannath and the Regional Tradition of Orissa.* Second printing. Delhi: Manohar. (South Asia Institute. New Delhi Branch. Heidelberg University. South Asian Studies No. 8.)

Evans-Pritchard, E. E. 1940. *The Nuer: a Description of the Modes of Livelihood and Political Institutions of a Nilotic People.* Oxford: Clarendon Press.

Evans-Pritchard, E. E. 1956. *Nuer Religion.* Oxford: Clarendon Press.

Fabri, C. 1994. *Indian Dress: A Brief History.* New Delhi: Orient Longman (Disha Books.)

Falk, H. 1986. *Bruderschaft und Würfelspiel: Untersuchungen zur Entwicklungsgeschichte des Vedischen Opfers.* Freiburg: Hedwig Falk.

Farmer, S., Sproat, R., and Witzel, M. 2004. 'The Collapse of the Indus-Script Thesis: The Myth of a Literate Harappan Civilization'. *Electronic Journal Vedic Studies* 11(2) (13 Dec. 2004): 19–57. Downloaded from www1.shore.net/~india/ejvs/issues.html, 22 Sept. 2006.

Farrow, G. W. and Menon, I. 1992. *The Concealed Essence of the Hevajra Tantra With the Commentary,* Yogaratnamālā. Delhi: Motilal Banarsidass.

Felten, W. and Lerner, M. 1989. *Thai and Cambodian Sculpture from the 6th to the 14th Centuries.* London: P. Wilson Publishers.

Fenner, T. 1979. *Rasāyana Siddhi: Medicine and Alchemy in the Buddhist Tantras.* PhD Dissertation, University of Wisconsin, Madison. UMI 80–08814.

Ferguson, J. P. and E. M. Mendelson 1981. 'Masters of the Occult: The Burmese Weikzas'. *Contributions to Asian Studies* 16: 62–80.

Ferreira-Jardim, A. 2005. '"Separated from Desires . . .": New Light on the Historical Development of the Four Meditations [*dhyāna*] Pericope Amongst Śrāmaṇical Groups in Ancient India'. Paper given at the 14th Conference of the International Association of Buddhist Studies, School of Oriental and African Studies, University of London, 29 Aug.–3 Sept. 2005.

Ferreira-Jardim, A. 2006. 'Some Notes Towards a History of Early Buddhist and Jaina Meditation: *vitakka, viyāra/-i* and Terms Referring to Mental One-Pointedness (*egatta, egaggamaṇa,* etc.)'. Paper for the Australasian Association of Buddhist Studies conference, University of Sydney, 16–17 June 2006.

Filliozat, J. 1969. 'Taoisme et Yoga'. *Journal Asiatique* 257: 41–87.

Finn, L. M. 1986. *The Kulacūḍāmaṇi Tantra and The Vāmakeśvara Tantra with the Jayaratha Commentary introduced, translated and annotated by Louise M Finn.* Wiesbaden: Otto Harrassowitz.

Fitzgerald, J. L. 2001. 'Making Yudhiṣṭhira the King: the Dialectics and the Politics of Violence in the *Mahābhārata*'. *Rocznik Orientalistyczny* 54: 63–92.

Fitzgerald, J. L. 2002. 'The Rāma Jāmadagnya "Thread" of the *Mahābhārata*: A New Survey of Rāma Jāmadagnya in the Pune Text', in *Stages and Transitions: Temporal and Historical Frameworks in Epic and Purāṇic Literature. Proceedings of the Second Dubrovnik International Conference on the Sanskrit Epics*

and Purāṇas, August 1999, Brockington (ed.), pp. 89–132. Zagreb: Croatian Academy of Sciences and Arts.
Fitzgerald, J. L. 2004. 'The Many Voices of the *Mahābhārata*'. *Journal American Oriental Society* 123: 803–18.
Flood, G. 1996. *An Introduction to Hinduism*. Cambridge: Cambridge University Press.
Flood, G. 1997. 'Ritual Dance in Kerala: Performance, Possession, and the Formation of Culture', in Connolly and Hamilton 1997, pp. 169–83.
Flood, G. (ed.) 2003. *The Blackwell Companion to Hinduism*. Oxford: Blackwell.
Flood, G. 2006. *The Tantric Body: The Secret Tradition of Hindu Religion*. London and New York: I. B. Tauris.
Fluegel, P. 2005. 'The Invention of Jainism: A Short History of Jaina Studies'. *International Journal of Jain Studies* 1: 1–14.
Foucault, M. 1988a. 'Technologies of the Self'. In *Technologies of the Self: A Seminar with Michel Foucault*, ed. by L. H. Martin, H. Gutman and P. H. Hutton, pp. 16–49. Amherst, MA: University of Massachusetts Press.
Foucault, M. 1988b. *The Care of the Self: History of Sexuality vol. 3*. New York: Random House.
Fox, R. G. 1996. 'Communalism and Modernity', in *Making India Hindu: Religion, Community, and the Politics of Democracy in India*, Ludden (ed.), pp. 235–49. Delhi: Oxford University Press.
Freed, S. A. and Freed, R. S. 1998. *Hindu Festivals in a North Indian Village*. American Museum of Natural History, distributed by University of Washington Press, Seattle. (Anthropological Papers of the American Museum of Natural History, 81.)
Freeman, J. R. 1993. 'Performing Possession: Ritual and Consciousness in the Teyyam Complex of Northern Kerala', in Brückner, Lutze, and Malik (eds.), pp. 109–38.
Freeman, J. R. 1994. 'Possession Rites and the Tantric Temple: A Case-Study from Northern Kerala'. *Diskus* [Electronic journal of religious studies.] vol. 2 no. 2 (Autumn 1994).
Freeman, J. R. 1999. 'Gods, Groves and the Culture of Nature in Kerala'. *Modern Asian Studies* 33: 257–302.
Fremantle, F. 1971. *A Critical Study of the Guhyasamāja Tantra*. PhD Dissertation, School of Oriental and African Studies, University of London.
Fremantle, F. 1990. 'Chapter Seven of the *Guhyasamāja Tantra*', in Skorupski 1990, pp. 101–114.
Fruzzetti, L. M. 1990. *The Gift of a Virgin*. Delhi: Oxford University Press.
Fuller, C. J. 1992. *The Camphor Flame: Popular Hinduism and Society in India*. Princeton, NJ: Princeton University Press.
Fulton, R. M. 1972. 'The Political Structures and Functions of Poro in Kpelle Society'. *American Anthropologist* 74: 1218–33.
Fussman, G. 1993. 'Taxila: The Central Asian Connection', in *Urban Form and Meaning in South Asia: The Shaping of Cities from Prehistoric to Precolonial*

Times, Spodek and Meth Srinivasan (eds.), 83–100. Washington: National Gallery of Art.

Fynes, R. C. C. 1991. *Cultural Transmission between Roman Egypt and Western India.* D.Phil. dissertation, Oxford University.

Fynes, R. C. C. 1993. 'Isis and Pattinī: The Transmission of a Religious Idea from Roman Egypt to India'. *Journal Royal Asiatic Society, Series 3*, 3: 377–91.

Fynes. R. C. C. 1995. 'The Religious Patronage of the Sātavāhana Dynasty'. *South Asian Studies* 11: 43–50.

Gadon, E. W. 1997. 'The Hindu Goddess Shasthi, Protector of Children and Women', in *From the Realm of the Ancestors: An Anthology in Honor of Marija Gimbutas*, Marler (ed.), pp. 293–308. Manchester, CT: Knowledge, Ideas & Trends.

Galaty, J. G. 1979. 'Pollution and Pastoral Antipraxis: The Issue of Maasai Inequality'. *American Ethnologist* 6 (1979): 803–16.

Galvão, A. 1971. *A Treatise on the Moluccas (c. 1544), probably the Preliminary Version of Antonio Galvão's lost Historía das Molucas.* Trans. H. Jacobs, S. J. Rome: Jesuit Historical Institute.

Gäng, P. 1988. *Das Tantra der Verborgenen Vereinigung = Guhyasamāja-Tantra.* München: Diederichs.

Geertz, C. 1975. 'Religion as a Cultural System', in C. Geertz, *The Interpretation of Cultures*, pp. 87–125. London: Hutchinson.

Geiger, W. 1964. *The Mahāvaṃsa or the Great Chronicle of Ceylon.* Translated into English by Wilhelm Geiger. London: Published for the Pali Text Society by Luzac & Co.

Gell, A. 1982. 'The Market Wheel: Symbolic Aspects of an Indian Tribal Market'. *Man* 17: 470–91.

Gellner, D. N. 1992. *Monk, Householder, and Tantric Priest: Newar Buddhism and its Hierarchy of Ritual.* Cambridge: Cambridge University Press.

Gellner, D. N. and Quigley, D. (eds.) 1995. *Contested Hierarchies: a Collaborative Ethnography of Caste among the Newars of the Kathmandu Valley, Nepal.* Oxford: Clarendon Press; New York: Oxford University Press.

George, C. S. 1974. *The Candamahārosana Tantra. A Critical Edition and English Translation. Chapters I–VIII.* American Oriental Society, New Haven. (American Oriental Series, 56.)

Germano, D. 1994. 'Architecture and Absence in the Secret Tantric History of the Great Perfection (*rdzogs chen*)'. *Journal International Association of Buddhist Studies* 17: 203–335.

Germano, D. 2005. 'The Funerary Transformation of the Great Perfection (Rdzogs chen)'. *Journal International Association of Tibetan Studies* 1 (October 2005): 1–54. Downloaded from www.thdl.org, 19 Aug 2006.

Gibson, T. 1997. 'Inner Asian Contributions to the Vajrayāna'. *Indo-Iranian Journal* 40: 37–57.

Gitomer, D. 1992. 'King Duryodhana: The *Mahābhārata* Discourse of Sinning and Virtue in Epic and Drama'. *Journal American Oriental Society* 112: 222–32.

Gnoli, G. and Lanciotti, L. (eds.) 1988. *Orientalia Iosephi Tucci Memoriae Dicata*, Roma: IsMEO (Serie Orientale Roma, LVI, 3.)

Gold, A. Grodzins 1993. *A Carnival of Parting: The Tales of King Bharthari and King Gopi Chand as Sung and Told by Madhu Natisar Nath of Ghatiyali, Rajasthan*. Delhi: Munshiram Manoharlal.

Gold, D. and Gold, A. Grodzins Gold 1984. 'The Fate of the Householder Nath'. *History of Religions* 24: 113–32.

Goldman, R. P. 1977. *Gods, Priests and Warriors: the Bhṛgus of the Mahābhārata*. New York: Columbia University Press.

Goldman, R. P. 2005. *Rāmāyaṇa Book One: Boyhood, by Vālmīki*. Translated by R. P. Goldman. New York: New York University Press and JJC Foundation.

Gombrich, R. F. 1971. *Precept and Practice: Traditional Buddhism in the Rural Highlands of Sri Lanka*. Oxford: Clarendon Press.

Gombrich, R. F. 1988. *Theravāda Buddhism: A Social History from Ancient Benares to Modern Colombo*. London: Routledge.

Gombrich, R. F. 1990. 'Recovering the Buddha's Message', in *Earliest Buddhism and Madhyamaka*, Seyfort Ruegg and Schmithausen (eds.), 5–23. Leiden and New York: E. J. Brill.

Gombrich, R. F. 1992. 'The Buddha's Book of Genesis?' *Indo-Iranian Journal* 35: 159–78.

Gombrich, R. F. 1996. *How Buddhism Began: The Conditioned Genesis of the Early Teachings*. London: Athlone Press.

Gombrich, R. 1997. 'The Buddhist Attitude to Thaumaturgy', in *Bauddhavidyāsudhākaraḥ: Studies in Honour of Heinz Bechert on the Occasion of his 65th Birthday*, Kieffer-Puelz and Hartmann (eds.). Swisttal-Odendorf: Indica et Tibetica Verlag.

Gombrich, R. 2003. '"Obsession with Origins": Attitudes to Buddhist Studies in the Old World and the New', in *Approaching the Dhamma: Buddhist Texts and Practices in South and Southeast Asia*, Blackburn and Samuels (eds.). Onalaska, WA: Pariyatti.

Gombrich, R. and G. Obeyesekere 1990. *Buddhism Transformed: Religious Change in Sri Lanka*. Delhi: Motilal Banarsidass.

Gonda, J. 1961. 'Ascetics and Courtesans'. *Adyar Library Bulletin* 25: 78–102. Reprinted in Gonda 1975 vol. 4.

Gonda, J. 1963. *The Vision of the Vedic Poets*. The Hague: Mouton.

Gonda, J. 1975. *Selected Studies. Presented to the Author by the Staff of the Oriental Institute, Utrecht University, on the Occasion of his 70th Birthday*. Leiden: Brill.

Gonda, J. 1980. 'The Śatarudriya', in *Sanskrit and Indian Studies: Essays in Honour of Daniel H. H. Ingalls*, Nagatomi, Matilal, Masson and Dimock, Jr. (eds.), pp. 75–91. Dordrecht, Boston and London: D. Reidel.

Good, A. 1991. *The Female Bridegroom: A Comparative Study of Life-Crisis Rituals in South India and Sri Lanka*. Oxford: Clarendon Press.

Goodison, L. and Morris, C. (eds.) 1998. *Ancient Goddesses: The Myths and the Evidence*. London: British Museum Press.

Gottschalk, P. 2000. *Beyond Hindu and Muslim: Multiple Identities in Narratives from Village India*. Delhi and Oxford: Oxford University Press.
Goudriaan, T. 1973. 'Tumburu and His Sisters', *Wiener Zeitschrift für die Kunde Südasiens* 17: 49–95.
Goudriaan, T. 1985. *The Vīṇāśikha Tantra. A Śaiva Tantra of the Left Current Edited with an Introduction and a Translation*. Delhi: Motilal Banarsidass.
Goudriaan, T. (ed.) 1992. *Ritual and Speculation in Early Tantrism: Studies in Honor of André Padoux*. Albany, NY: State University of New York Press.
Gray, D. Barton 2001. *On Supreme Bliss: A Study of the History and Interpretation of the Cakrasaṃvara Tantra*. PhD Dissertation, Columbia University, New York. UMI AAT 9998161.
Gray, D. Barton 2007. *The Cakrasamvara Tantra: A Study and Annotated Translation*. New York: Columbia University Press for American Institute of Buddhist Studies.
Grayson, J. Huntley 1989. *Korea: a Religious History*. Oxford: Clarendon Press.
Grenet, F. 2005. 'An Archaeologist's Approach to Avestan Geography', in Curtis and Stewart 2005, pp. 29–51.
Griffith, R. T. H. 1916. *The Hymns of the Atharva-Veda Translated with a Popular Commentary*. 2 vols. Second edn. Benares: E. J. Lazarus & Co.
Griffiths, P. 1981. 'Concentration or Insight: The Problematic of Theravada Buddhist Meditation-Theory'. *Journal of the American Academy of Religion* 49: 605–24.
Grimal, F. (ed.) 2001. *Les sources et le temps/ Sources and Time: A Colloquium, Pondicherry, 11–13 January 1997*. Pondicherry: Institut Francais de Pondichery: École Français D'Extrême-Orient.
Guenther, H. V. 1963. *The Life and Teaching of Nāropa*. Oxford: Clarendon Press.
Guenther, H. V. 1969. *Yuganaddha: The Tantric View of Life*. Varanasi: The Chowkhamba Sanskrit Series Office. (Chowkhamba Sanskrit Series, 3.)
Guenther, H. V. 1974. 'Early Forms of Tibetan Buddhism'. *Crystal Mirror* 3: 80–92.
Guillon, E. 2001. *Cham Art: Treasures from the Da Nang Museum, Vietnam*. Bangkok: River Books.
Gupta, E. M. 1983. *Brata und Alpana in Bengalen*. Wiesbaden: Steiner. (Beiträge zur Südasienforschung 80.)
Gupta, S. 1972. *Lakṣmī Tantra: A Pāñcarātra Text. Translation and Notes*. Leiden: Brill.
Gupta, S. 1989. 'The Pāñcarātra Attitude to Mantra', in *Mantras*, Alper (ed.), pp. 224–48. Albany, NY: State University of New York Press.
Gupta, S. 1992. 'Yoga and *Antaryāga* in Pāñcarātra', in Goudriaan 1992, pp. 175–208.
Gupta, S. 1999. 'Hindu Woman, the Ritualist', in Tambs-Lyche 1999, pp. 88–99.
Gupta, S. 2003. 'The Domestication of a Goddess: *Caraṇa-tīrtha* Kālīghāṭ, the *Mahāpīṭha* of Kālī', in McDermott and Kripal 2003, pp. 60–79.
Gupta, S. and Gombrich, R. 1986. 'Kings, Power and the Goddess'. *South Asia Research* 6: 123–38.

Gutschow, N. 1982. *Stadtraum und Ritual der Newarischen Städte im Kāthmāndu-Tal: eine Architekturanthropologische Untersuchung*. Stuttgart: W. Kohlhammer.

Gutschow, N. 1993. 'Bhaktapur: Sacred Patterns of a Living Urban Tradition', in Spodek and Srinivasan 1993, pp. 163–83.

Gutschow, N. and Bāsukala, G. Mān 1987. 'The Navadurgā of Bhaktapur: Spatial Implications of an Urban Ritual'. In *Heritage of the Kathmandu Valley*, Gutschow and Michaels (eds.), pp. 135–66. Sankt Augustin: VGH Wissenschaftsverlag.

Gutschow, N. 1996. 'The Aṣṭamātṛkā and Navadurgā of Bhaktapur', in Michaels, Vogelsanger and Wilke 1996, pp. 191–216.

Haaland, G. and Haaland, R. 1995. 'Who Speaks the Goddess's Language? Imagination and Method in Archaeological Research', *Norwegian Archaeological Review* 28: 105–21.

Hall, K. R. 1999. 'Economic History of Early Southeast Asia', in Tarling 1999, pp. 183–275.

Hallisey, C. 1995. 'Roads Taken and Not Taken in the Study of Theravāda Buddhism', in *Curators of the Buddha: The Study of Buddhism under Colonialism*, Lopez (ed.), pp. 31–61.

Hamilton, S. 1996. *Identity and Experience: the Constitution of the Human Being in Early Buddhism.* London: Luzac Oriental.

Hamilton, S. 2000. 'The Centrality of Experience in the Teachings of Early Buddhism'. Oxford: Religious Experience Research Centre, Westminster Institute of Education. (2nd Series Occasional Paper 24.)

Hanks, L. M. 1975. 'The Thai Social Order as Entourage and Circle', in *Change and Persistence in Thai Society*, Skinner and Kirsch (eds.), pp. 197–218. Ithaca, NY: Cornell University Press.

Hanssen, K. 2002. 'Ingesting Menstrual Blood: Notions of Health and Bodily Fluids in Bengal'. *Ethnology* 41: 365–79.

Haque, E. 2001. *Chandraketugarh: A Treasure-House of Bengal Terracottas*. Dhaka: The International Centre for the Study of Bengal Art. (Studies in Bengal Art, 4.)

Hardy, F. 1983. *Virāha-Bhakti: the Early History of Kṛṣṇa Devotion in South India.* Delhi: Oxford University Press.

Harlan, L. 1992. *Religion and Rajput Women: the Ethic of Protection in Contemporary Narratives*. Berkeley and Oxford: University of California Press.

Harle, J. C. 1974. *Gupta Sculpture: Indian Sculpture of the Fourth to the Sixth centuries A.D.* Oxford: Clarendon Press.

Harle, J. C. and Topsfield, A. 1987. *Indian Art in the Ashmolean Museum.* Oxford: Ashmolean Museum.

Harman, W. P. 1992. *Sacred Marriage of a Hindu Goddess*. Delhi: Motilal Banarsidass.

Harner, M. 1982. *The Way of the Shaman*. New York: Bantam Books (Harper and Row).

Harper, D. 1987. 'The Sexual Arts of Ancient China as Described in a Manuscript of The Second Century B.C'. *Harvard Journal Asiatic Studies* 47: 539–92.

Harper, D. 1997. *Early Chinese Medical Literature: The Mawangdui Medical Manuscripts*. London: Kegan Paul International; New York: Columbia University Press.

Harper, K. A. 2002. 'The Warring Śaktis: A Paradigm for Gupta Conquests', in Harper and Brown 2002, pp. 115–31.

Harper, K. A. and Brown, R. L. (eds.) 2002. *The Roots of Tantra*. Albany, NY: State University of New York Press.

Harrison, P. 1987a. 'Who Gets to Ride in the Great Vehicle? Self-Image and Identity among the Followers of the Early Mahāyana'. *Journal International Association of Buddhist Studies* 10: 67–89.

Harrison, P. 1987b. 'Buddhism: A Religion of Revelation After All'. *Numen* 34: 256–64.

Harrison, P. 1990. *The* Samādhi *of Direct Encounter with the Buddhas of the Present. An Annotated English Translation of the Tibetan Version of the* Pratyutpanna-Buddha-Saṃmukhāvasthita-Samādhi-Sūtra. Tokyo: The International Institute for Buddhist Studies. (Studia Philologica Buddhica. Monograph Series, V.)

Harrison, P. 1993. 'The Earliest Chinese Translations of Mahāyāna Buddhist Sutras: Some Notes on the Works of Lokakṣema', *Buddhist Studies Review* 10(2): 135–77.

Hart, G. L. 1975. *The Poems of Ancient Tamil: Their Milieu and their Sanskrit Counterparts*. Berkeley, Los Angeles and London: University of California Press.

Hart, G. L. 1979. 'The Nature of Tamil Devotion', in Deshpande and Hook 1979, pp. 24–33.

Hart, G. L. 1987. 'Early Evidence for Caste in South India', in *Dimensions of Social Life: Essays in Honor of David G. Mandelbaum*, Hockings (ed.), pp. 467–91. Berlin: Mouton-de Gruyter.

Hartzell, J. F. 1997. *Tantric Yoga: A Study of the Vedic Precursors, Historical Evolution, Literatures, Cultures, Doctrines, and Practices of the 11th Century Kaśmīri Śaivite and Buddhist Unexcelled Tantric Yogas*. PhD Dissertation, Columbia University. UMI No. 9723798.

Hawley, J. S. and Wulff, D. M. (eds.) 1982. *The Divine Consort: Rādhā and the Goddesses of India*. Boston: Beacon Press.

Hawley, J. S. and Wulff, D. M. (eds.) 1996. *Devī: Goddesses of India*. Berkeley and Los Angeles: University of California Press.

Hayes, G. A. 2003. 'Metaphoric Worlds and Yoga in the Vaiṣṇava Sahajiyā Traditions of Medieval Bengal', in Whicher and Carpenter 2003, pp. 162–84.

Heesterman, J. C. 1962. '*Vrātya* and Sacrifice'. *Indo-Iranian Journal* 6: 1–37.

Heesterman, J. C. 1985. *The Inner Conflict of Tradition: Essays in Indian Ritual, Kingship, and Society*. Chicago: University of Chicago Press.

Heesterman, J. C. 1993. *The Broken World of Sacrifice: an Essay in Ancient Indian Ritual.* Chicago: University of Chicago Press.
Heilijgers-Seelen, D. 1994. *The System of Five Cakras in Kubjikāmatatantra 14–16.* Groningen: Egbert Forsten. (Groningen Oriental Studies, 9.)
Hein, N. 1982. 'Radha and Erotic Community', in Hawley and Wulff 1982, pp. 116–24. Delhi: Motilal Banarsidass.
Hein, N. 1986a. 'Epic *Sarvabhūtahite Rataḥ*: A Byword of Non-Bhārgava Editors'. *Annals of the Bhandarkar Oriental Research Institute* 67: 17–34.
Hein, N. 1986b. 'A Revolution in Kṛṣṇaism: The Cult of Gopāla'. *History of Religions* 25: 296–317.
Heitzman, J. 1984. 'Early Buddhism, Trade and Empire', in *Studies in the Archaeology and Paleaoanthropology of South Asia*, Kennedy and Possehl (eds.), pp. 121–37. New Delhi: Oxford and IBH.
Heller, A. 1994. 'Early Ninth Century Images of Vairochana from Eastern Tibet'. *Orientations* 25(6): 74–9.
Herrmann-Pfandt, A. 1992. *Ḍākinīs: zur Stellung und Symbolik des Weiblichen im tantrischen Buddhismus.* Bonn: Indica et Tibetica-Verlag.
Higham, C. F. W. 1999. 'Recent Advances in the Prehistory of South-East Asia', in *World Prehistory: Studies in Memory of Grahame Clark*, Coles, Bewley and Mellars (eds.), pp. 75–86. Oxford: Oxford University Press for British Academy. (*Proceedings of the British Academy*, 99.)
Hiltebeitel, A. 1978. 'The Indus Valley "Proto-Śiva" Reexamined through Reflections on the Goddess, the Buffalo, and the Symbolism of *Vāhanas*'. *Anthropos* 73: 767–97.
Hiltebeitel, A. (ed.) 1989. *Criminal Gods and Demon Devotees: Essays on the Guardians of Popular Hinduism.* Albany, NY: SUNY Press.
Hiltebeitel, A. 2001. *Rethinking the Mahābhārata: a Reader's Guide to the Education of the Dharma King.* Chicago and London: University of Chicago Press.
Hiltebeitel, A. 2004. 'More Rethinking the *Mahābhārata*: Toward a Politics of Bhakti'. *Indo-Iranian Journal* 47: 203–27.
Hinnells, J. R. 1985. *Persian Mythology.* Revised edn. London: Hamlyn.
Hock, N. 1987. *Buddhist Ideology and the Sculpture of Ratnagiri, Seventh through Thirteenth Centuries.* PhD thesis, University of California, Berkeley.
Hodge, S. 2003. *The Mahā-Vairocana-Abhisaṃbodhi Tantra with Buddhaguhya's Commentary.* London: RoutledgeCurzon.
Hoffman, E. 1992. *Visions of Innocence: Spiritual and Inspirational Experiences of Childhood.* Boston and London: Shambhala.
Holt, J. C. 2004. *The Buddhist Viṣṇu: Religious Transformation, Politics, and Culture.* New York: Columbia University Press.
Hooykaas, C. 1973a. *Religion in Bali.* Leiden: Brill.
Hooykaas, C. 1973b. *Balinese Bauddha Brahmans.* Amsterdam: N. V. Noord-Hollandsche Uitgevers Maatschappij (Verhandelingen der Koninklijke Nederlandse Akademie van Wetenschappen, Afd. Letterkunde. Niewe Reeks. Deel LXXX).
Hopkins, T. J. 1999. 'Some Reflections on Hinduism'. Unpublished typescript.

Horsch, P. 1968. 'Buddhismus und Upaniṣaden', in *Pratidānam: Indian, Iranian, and Indo-European Studies Presented to Franciscus Bernardus Jacobus Kuiper on his Sixtieth Birthday*, Heesterman, Schokker [and] Subramoniam (eds.), pp. 462–77. The Hague and Paris: Mouton.

Houben, J. E. M. (ed.) 2003a. Papers from workshop, The Soma/Haoma-Cult in Early Vedism and Zoroastrianism: Archaeology, Text, and Ritual, at Leiden University, 3–4 July 1999. Special Issue of the *Electronic Journal of Vedic Studies* 9, 1. E-text at www1.shore.net/~india/ejvs/issues.html, downloaded 6 Aug 06.

Houben, J. E. M. 2003b. 'The Soma-Haoma Problem: Introductory Overview and Observations on the Discussion', in Houben 2003a. E-text at www1.shore.net/~india/ejvs/ejvs0901/ejvs0901a.txt, downloaded 6 Aug 06.

Houtman, G. 1996. 'From Mandala to Mandalay: Vipassana Insight Contemplation as an Instrument for Aristocratic Enlightenment and Delineation of Domain in the Mindon Era'. Seminar at Lancaster University, 21 Oct 1996.

Houtman, G. 1999. *Mental Culture in Burmese Crisis Politics: Aung San Suu Kyi and the National League for Democracy*. Tokyo: Institute for the Study of Languages and Cultures of Asia and Africa, Tokyo University of Foreign Studies.

Howe, L. 2000. 'Risk, Ritual and Performance'. *Journal Royal Anthropological Institute* 6: 63–79.

Hsu, E. 2005. 'Tactility and the Body in Early Chinese Medicine'. *Science in Context* 18: 7–34.

Huber, T. 1999. *The Cult of Pure Crystal Mountain: Popular Pilgrimage and Visionary Landscape in Southeast Tibet*. New York: Oxford University Press.

Hudson, D. D. 1993. 'Madurai: The City as Goddess', in Spodek and Srinivasan 1993, pp. 125–44.

Hudson, D. 2002. 'Early Evidence of the *Pāñcarātra Āgama*', in Harper and Brown 2002, pp. 133–67.

Humes, C. A. 1996. 'Vindhyavāsinī: Local Goddess Yet Great Goddess'. In Hawley and Wulff 1996, pp. 49–76.

Huntingford, G. W. B. 1980. *The Periplus of the Erythraean Sea*. Translated and edited by G. W. B. Huntingford. London: The Hakluyt Society.

Huntington, J. C. 1987. 'Note on a Chinese Text Demonstrating the Earliness of Tantra'. *Journal of the International Association of Buddhist Studies* 10(2): 88–98.

Huntington, J. C. and Bangdel, D. 2003. *The Circle of Bliss: Buddhist Meditational Art*. Columbus, OH: Columbus Museum of Art; Chicago: Serindia Publications.

Huntington, S. L. 1990. 'Introduction', in Huntington and Huntington 1990, pp. 69–71.

Huntington, S. L. and Huntington, J. C. 1990. *Leaves from the Bodhi Tree: The Art of Pāla India (8th–12th Centuries) and Its International Legacy*. Seattle and London: University of Washington Press in Association with Dayton Art Institute.

Iltis, L. L. 1987. 'The Jala Pyākhā: A Classical Newar Dance Drama of Harissiddhi'. In *Heritage of the Kathmandu Valley*, Gutschow and Michaels (eds.), 199–214. Sankt Augustin: VGH Wissenschaftsverlag.
Iltis, L. 2002. 'Knowing All the Gods: Grandmothers, God Families and Women Healers in Nepal', in Rozario and Samuel 2002a, pp. 70–89.
Inden, R. 1992. *Imagining India*. Cambridge, MA and Oxford,UK: Blackwell.
Insler, S. 2004. *Ancient Indian and Iranian Religion: Common Ground and Divergence*. 2004 Jordan Lectures in Comparative Religion, School of Oriental and African Studies, University of London, 23–29 April 2004.
Ingalls, D. H. H. 1962. 'Cynics and Pasupatas: The Seeking of Dishonor', *Harvard Theological Review* 55: 281–98.
Isaacson, H. 1998. 'Tantric Buddhism in India', in *Buddhismus in Geschichte und Gegenwart: Weterbildendes Studium. Band II.* Hamburg: Universität Hamburg.
Jackowitz, S. 'Ingestion, Digestion, and Regestation: The Complexities of *Qi* Absorption', in Kohn 2006a, pp. 68–90.
Jacobi, H. 1895. *Gaina Sûtras. Part II. The Uttarâdhyayana Sûtra. The Sûtrakritâṅga Sûtra.* Oxford: Clarendon Press. (Sacred Books of the East, 45.)
Jacobsen, K. A. (ed.) 2005a. *Theory and Practice of Yoga: Essays in Honour of Gerald James Larson*. Leiden: Brill.
Jacobsen, K. A. 2005b. 'Introduction: Yoga Traditions', in Jacobsen 2005a, 1–27.
Jahan, S. H. 2004. 'Location of the Port of Tmāralipti and Condition of the Harbour'. *Journal Asiatic Society of Bangladesh (Humanities)* 49: 199–220.
Jaini, P. S. 1977. 'Jina Ṛṣabha as an *avatāra* of Viṣṇu'. *Bulletin of School of Oriental and African Studies* 40: 321–37.
Jaini, P. S. 1991. 'Is There a Popular Jainism', in Carrithers and Humphrey 1991, pp. 187–99.
Jairazbhoy, R. A. 1994. 'The First Goddess of South Asia, A New Theory', in Jairazbhoy, *The First Goddess of South Asian and Other Essays*, pp. 7–26. 2nd edn. Karachi: Menander Publications.
Jamison, S. W. and Witzel, M. 2003. 'Vedic Hinduism'. Pdf version downloaded from www.people.fas.harvard.edu/~witzel/vedica.pdf, 17 Sept 2006.
Jayakar, P. 1989. *The Earth Mother.* New Delhi: Penguin Books. [Revised and updated edn. of Jayakar 1980.]
Jest, C. 1976. *Dolpo: communautés de langue tibétaine du Népal.* Paris: Éditions du CNRS.
Jhavery, M. B. 1944. *Comparative and Critical Study of Mantrasastra, with Special Treatment of Jain Mantravada, being the Introduction to Sri Bhairava Padmavati Kalpa*. Ahmedabad: Sarabhai Manilal Nawab.
Jootla, S. Elbaum 1997. *Teacher of the Devas.* Kandy: Buddhist Publication Society. (The Wheel Publication No. 414/416.)
Jordaan, R. E. and Wessing, R. J. 1999. 'Construction Sacrifice in India, "Seen from the East"', in *Violence Denied: Violence, Non-Violence and the Rationalization of Violence in South Asian Cultural History*, Houben and Van Kooij (eds.), pp. 211–48. Leiden: Brill.

Joshi, M. S. 2002. 'Historical and Iconographic Aspects of Śākta Tantrism', in Harper and Brown 2002, pp. 39–55.
Joshi, N. P. 1984. 'Early Forms of Śiva'. In Meister 1984, pp. 47–61.
Jurewicz, J. 2000. 'Playing with Fire: The *Pratītyasamutpāda* from the Perspective of Vedic Thought'. *Journal Pali Text Society* 26: 77–103.
Kaelber, W. O. 1989. *Tapta Mārga: Asceticism and Initiation in Vedic India.* Albany, NY: SUNY Press.
Kakar, S. 1990. *Intimate Relations: Exploring Indian Sexuality.* New Delhi; Harmondsworth: Penguin Books.
Kakar, S. 1998. *The Ascetic of Desire: A Novel.* New Delhi: Penguin Books.
Kala, S. C. 1951. *Bharhut Vedikā.* Allahabad: Municipal Museum.
Kalff, M. M. 1979. *Selected Chapters from the Abhidānottaratantra: The Union of Male and Female Deities.* PhD. Dissertation, Columbia University, New York.
Kammerer, C. A. and Tannenbaum, N. (eds.) 1996. *Merit and Blessing in Mainland Southeast Asia in Comparative Perspective.* New Haven, CT: Yale University, Southeast Asia Studies. (Monograph series / Yale University. Southeast Asia studies; no. 45.)
Kapferer, B. 1979. 'Mind, Self and Other in Demonic Illness: The Negation and Reconstruction of Self'. *American Ethnologist* 6: 110–33.
Kapferer, B. 1983. *A Celebration of Demons: Exorcism and the Aesthetics of Healing in Sri Lanka.* Bloomington, IN: Indiana University Press.
Kaplanian, P. 1981. *Les Ladakhi du Cachemire: Montagnards du Tibet Occidental.* Hachette (L'Homme Vivant.)
Kapstein, M. 1980. 'The Shangs-pa bKa'-brgyud: An Unknown School of Tibetan Buddhism'. In *Studies in Honor of Hugh Richardson*, Aris and Kyi (eds.), pp. 138–44. Warminster: Aris and Phillips.
Kapstein, M. 1997. 'The Journey to the Golden Mountain', in *Religions of Tibet in Practice*, Lopez, Jr. (ed.), pp. 178–87. Princeton, NJ: Princeton University Press.
Kapstein, M. 1998. 'A Pilgrimage of Rebirth Reborn: The 1992 Celebration of the Drigung Powa Chenmo', in *Buddhism in Contemporary Tibet: Religious Revival and Cultural Identity*, Goldstein and Kapstein (eds.), pp. 95–119. Berkeley, Los Angeles and London: University of California Press.
Kapstein, M. T. 2005. Chronological Conundrums in the Life of Khyung po rnal 'byor: Hagiography and Historical Time'. *Journal International Association of Tibetan Studies* 1 (October 2005). Downloaded from www.thdl.org/collections/journal/jiats/index.php?doc=kapstein01.xml&s=d0e1526, 3 Oct 2006.
Karlsson, K. 1999. *Face to Face with the Absent Buddha: The Formation of Buddhist Aniconic Art.* Uppsala: Acta Universitatis Upsaliensis. (PhD dissertation, Uppsala, 2000.)
Kawamura, L. 1975. *Golden Zephyr.* Translated from the Tibetan and annotated by L. Kawamura. Emeryville, CA: Dharma Pub.
Kawanami, H. 2001. 'Can Women Be Celibate? Sexuality and Abstinence in Theravada Buddhism', in Sobo and Bell 2001, pp. 137–156.

Kendall, L. 1985. *Shamans, Housewives and Other Restless Spirits.* Honolulu: University of Hawaii Press.

Kendall, L. 1988. *The Life and Hard Times of a Korean Shaman: Of Tales and the Telling of Tales.* Honolulu: University of Hawaii Press.

Kenoyer, J. M. 1995. 'Interaction Systems, Specialised Crafts and Culture Change: The Indus Valley Tradition and the Indo-Gangetic Tradition in South Asia', in Erdosy 1995a, pp. 213–57.

Kenoyer, J. M. 1998. *Ancient Cities of the Indus Valley.* Karachi: Oxford University Press and American Institute of Pakistan Studies.

Keyes, C. F. 1984. 'Mother or Mistress But Never A Monk: Buddhist Notions Of Female Gender In Rural Thailand'. *American Ethnologist* 11: 223–41.

Keyes, C. F. 1986. 'Ambiguous Gender: Male Initiation in a Northern Thai Buddhist Society', in *Gender and Religion: On the Complexity of Symbols*, Bynum, Harrell and Richman (eds.), pp. 66–96. Boston: Beacon Press.

Keyes, C. F. 1987. 'Theravāda Buddhism and its Worldly Transformations in Thailand: Reflections on the Work of S. J. Tambiah'. *Contributions to Indian Sociology* N.S. 21: 123–45.

Khan, D.-S. 2004. *Crossing the Threshold: Understanding Religious Identities in South Asia.* London: I. B. Tauris in association with The Institute of Ismaili Studies.

Khandelwal, M. 2001. 'Sexual Fluids, Emotions, Morality: Notes on the Gendering of Brahmacharya', in Sobo and Bell 2001, pp. 157–79.

Khare, R. S. 1984. *The Untouchable as Himself: Ideology, Identity and Pragmatism Among the Lucknow Chamars.* Cambridge: Cambridge University Press.

Kilambi, J. S. 1985. 'Towards an Understanding of the *Muggu*: Threshold Drawings in Hyderabad'. *Res* 10: 71–102.

Kim, C. 2003. *Korean Shamanism: The Cultural Paradox.* London: Ashgate.

Kim, T. 1988. *The Relationship between Shamanic Ritual and the Korean Masked Dance-Drama.* PhD Dissertation, New York University.

King, R. 1999. *Orientalism and Religion: Postcolonial Theory, India and 'The Mystic East'.* London and New York: Routledge.

Kinnard, J. 1997. 'Reevaluating the Eighth-Ninth Century Pala Milieu: Icono-Conservatism and the Persistence of Sakyamuni'. *Journal International Association of Buddhist Studies* 20: 281–300.

Kirsch, A. T. 1973. *Feasting and Social Oscillation. A Working Paper on Religion and Society in Upland Southeast Asia.* Ithaca, NY: Cornell University Department of Asian Studies. (Southeast Asia Program, Data Paper No. 92.)

Kirsch, A. T. 1985. 'Text And Context: Buddhist Sex Roles/Culture Of Gender Revisited'. *American Ethnologist* 12: 302–20.

Klimburg-Salter, D. E. 1989. *The Kingdom of Bāmiyān: Buddhist Art and Culture of the Hindu Kush.* Napoli: Istituto universitario orientale, Dipartimento di studi asiatici; Roma: Istituto italiano per il Medio ed Estremo Oriente. (Series maior (Istituto universitario orientale (Naples, Italy). Dipartimento di studi asiatici); 5.)

Klimburg-Salter, D. E. 1995. *Buddha in Indien: Die frühindische Skulptur von König Aśoka bis zur Guptazeit.* Wien: Kunsthistorisches Museum Wien; Milano: Skira.

Kobayashi, T. 1975. *Nara Buddhist Art: Todai-ji.* Translated and adapted by R. L. Gage. New York and Tokyo: Weatherhill/Heibonsha.

Kohn, L. (ed.) 2006a. *Daoist Body Cultivation.* Magdalena, NM: Three Pines Press.

Kohn, L. 2006b. 'Yoga and Daoyin', in Kohn 2006a, pp. 123–50.

Kohn, R. J. 1988. *Mani Rimdu: Text and Tradition in a Tibetan Ritual.* PhD dissertation, University of Wisconsin, Madison.

Kohn, R. J. 2001. *Lord of the Dance: The Mani Rimdu Festival in Tibet and Nepal.* Albany, NY: State University of New York Press.

Korvald, T. 2005. 'The Dancing Gods of Bhaktapur and Their Audience', in Allen 2005, pp. 405–15.

Kosambi, D. D. 1960. 'At the Cross-Roads: Mother Goddess Cult Sites in Ancient India'. *Journal of the Royal Asiatic Society*: 17–31; 135–44.

Kosambi, D. D. 1965. *The Culture and Civilisation of Ancient India in Historical Outline.* London: Routledge & Kegan Paul.

Kosambi, D. D. 2002a. *Combined Methods in Indology and Other Essays.* Edited by B. Chattopadhyaya. New Delhi: Oxford University Press.

Kosambi, D. D. 2002b. 'The Vedic "Five Tribes"', in Kosambi 2002a, pp. 75–86.

Krasser, H., Much, M. T., Steinkellner, E. and Tauscher, H. (eds.). 1997. *Tibetan Studies: Proceedings of the 7th Seminar of the International Association for Tibetan Studies, Graz 1995.* 2 vols. Wien: Österreichische Akademie der Wissenschaften. (Österreichische Akademie der Wissenschaften. Philosophisch-Historische Klasse, Denkschriften, 256. Band. Beiträge zur Kultur- und Geistesgeschichte Asiens, Nr. 21.)

Kuan, T. 2005. 'Clarification on Feelings in Buddhist *Dhyāna/Jhāna* Meditation'. *Journal Indian Philosophy* 33: 285–319.

Kulke, H. and Rothermund, D. 1990. *A History of India.* Rev. updated edn. London: Routledge.

Kulke, H. 2004. 'Some Thoughts on State and State Formation under the Eastern Vākāṭakas', in Bakker 2004, pp. 1–9.

Kvaerne, P. 1986. *An Anthology of Buddhist Tantric Songs.* 2nd edn. Bangkok, White Orchid Press. (First edn. 1977, Oslo, Universitetsforlaget. (Det Norske Videnskaps-Akademi. II.Hist.-Filos. Klasse. Skrifter. Ny Serie, 14.)

Lalou, M. 1956. 'Four Notes on Vajrapāṇi'. *Adyar Library Bulletin* 20: 287–93

Lamotte, É. 1966. 'Vajrapāṇi en Inde', in *Mélanges de Sinologie offerts a Monsieur Paul Demiéville*, pp. 113–61. Paris. (Bibliotheque de l'Institute des Hautes Études Chinoises, 20.)

Landaw, J. and Weber, A. 1993. *Images of Enlightenment: Tibetan Art in Practice.* Ithaca, NY: Snow Lion.

Lariviere, R. W. 1997. 'Power and Authority: On the Interpretation of Indian Kingship from Sanskrit Sources', in *Lex et Litterae: Studies in Honour of*

Professor Oscar Botto, Lienhard and Piovano (eds.), pp. 313–27. Alessandria: Edizioni dell'Orso.

Lee, Y.-H. 2003. *Synthesizing a Liturgical Heritage: Abhayākaragupta's Vajrāvali and the Kālacakramaṇḍala*. PhD Dissertation, University of Wisconsin at Madison. AAT 3089732.

Lehman, F. K. (Chit Hlaing) 'Monasteries, Palaces and Ambiguities: Burmese Sacred and Secular Space'. *Contributions to Indian Sociology* N.S. 21: 169–86.

Leidy, D. P. 1997. 'Place and Process: Mandala Imagery in the Buddhist Art of Asia', in Leidy and Thurman 1997, pp. 17–47.

Leidy, D. P. and Thurman, R. A. F. 1997. *Mandala: The Architecture of Enlightenment*. Thames and Hudson in association with Asia Society Galleries and Tibet House.

Leopold, R. S. 1983. 'The Shaping of Men and the Making of Metaphors: The Meaning of White Clay in Poro and Sande Initiation Society Rituals'. *Anthropology* 8(2): 21–42.

Lerner, M. 1984. *The Flame and the Lotus: Indian and Southeast Asian Art from the Kronos Collection*. New York: Metropolitan Museum of Art and Harry N. Abrams.

Leslie, J. (ed.) 1992. *Roles and Rituals for Hindu Women*. Delhi: Motilal Banarsidass.

Leslie, J. (ed.) 1996a. *Myth and Mythmaking*. London: Curzon.

Leslie, J. 1996b. 'Menstruation Myths', in Leslie 1996a, pp. 87–105.

Levy, R. I. 1987. 'How the Navadurgā Protect Bhaktapur: The Effective Meanings of a Symbolic Enactment', in *Heritage of the Kathmandu Valley*, Gutschow and Michaels (eds.) 105–34. Sankt Augustin: VGH Wissenschaftsverlag.

Lévi, S. 1915. 'Le catalogue géographique des Yakṣa dans la *Mahāmāyūrī*'. *Journal Asiatique* 11: 19–138.

Levy, R. I. with Rājopādhyāya, K. R. 1992. *Mesocosm: Hinduism and the Organization of a Traditional Newar City in Nepal*. Delhi: Motilal Banarsidass.

Lewis, T. T. 2000. *Popular Buddhist Texts from Nepal: Narratives and Rituals of Newar Buddhism*. Translations in Collaboration with S. M. Tuladhar and L. R. Tuladhar. Albany, NY: State University of New Work Press.

Lincoln, B. 2003. 'À La Recherche du Paradis Perdu'. *History of Religions* 43: 139–54.

Lindtner, C. 1991–93. 'Nāgārjuna and the Problem of Precanonical Buddhism'. *Religious traditions* 15–17: 112–36.

Lindtner, C. 1999. 'From Brahmanism to Buddhism'. *Asian Philosophy* 9: 5–37.

Ling, T. 1973. *The Buddha: Buddhist Civilization in India and Ceylon*. London: Temple Smith.

Linrothe, R. 1999. *Ruthless Compassion: Wrathful Deities in Early Indo-Tibetan Esoteric Buddhist Art*. London: Serindia.

Linrothe, R. (ed.) 2006. *Holy Madness: Portraits of Tantric Siddhas*. New York: Rubin Museum of Art; Chicago: Serindia Publications.

Little, K. 1965. 'The Political Function of the Poro'. *Africa* 35: 349–65.

Little, K. 1966. 'The Political Function of the Poro. 2'. *Africa* 36: 62–72.

Littleton, C. Scott 1982. *The New Comparative Mythology: an Anthropological Assessment of the Theories of Georges Dumézil.* 3rd edn. Berkeley, CA and London: University of California Press.
Locke, J. K. 1980. *Karunamaya: the Cult of Avalokitesvara-Matsyendranath in the Valley of Nepal.* Kathmandu: Sahayogi Prakashan for Research centre for Nepal and Asian Studies, Tribhuvan University.
Locke, J. K. 1985. *Buddhist Monasteries of Nepal: a Survey of the Bāhās and Bahīs of the Kathmandu Valley.* Kathmandu: Sahayogi Press.
Lopez Jr., D. S. (ed.) 1995. *Curators of the Buddha: The Study of Buddhism under Colonialism.* Chicago: University of Chicago Press.
Lorenzen, D. N. 1991. *The Kāpālikas and Kālāmukhas: Two Lost Śaivite Sects.* 2nd rev. edn. Delhi: Motilal Banarsidass.
Loseries-Leick, A. 1997. 'Psychic Sports: A Living Tradition in Contemporary Tibet?', in Krasser *et al.* 1997, vol. II, pp. 583–93.
Lubin, T. 2001. '*Vratá* Divine and Human in the Early Veda'. *Journal American Oriental Society* 121: 565–79.
Lubin, T. 2005. 'The Transmission, Patronage and Prestige of Brahmanical Piety from the Mauryas to the Guptas', in *Boundaries, Dynamics and Construction of Traditions in South Asia,* Squarcini (ed.), pp. 77–103. Firenze: Firenze University Press.
Lynch, O. M. 1969. *The Politics of Untouchability: Social Mobility and Social Change in a City of India.* New York & London: Columbia University Press.
McAlpin, D. W. 1981. *Proto-Elamo-Dravidian: the Evidence and its Implications.* Philadelphia: American Philosophical Society. (Transactions of the American Philosophical Society, v. 71, part 3).
McBride, R. D., II. 2004. 'The Vision-Quest Motif in Narrative Literature on the Buddhist Traditions of Silla'. *Korean Studies* 27: 17–47.
McDaniel, J. 1989. *The Madness of the Saints: Ecstatic Religion in Bengal.* Chicago: University of Chicago Press.
McDaniel, J. 1992. 'The Embodiment of God Among the Bauls of Bengal'. *Journal of Feminist Studes in Religion* 8: 27–39.
McDaniel, J. 2004. *Offering Flowers, Feeding Skulls: Popular Goddess Worship in West Bengal.* Oxford and New York: Oxford University Press.
McDermott, R. F. 1996. 'Popular Attitudes Towards Kālī and Her Poetry Tradition: Interviewing Śāktas in Bengal', in Michaels, Vogelsanger and Wilke 1996, pp. 383–415.
McDermott, R. F. and Kripal, J. J. (eds.) 2003. *Encountering Kālī: In the Margins, At the Center, In the West.* Berkeley: University of California Press.
McEvilley, T. 2002. 'The Spinal Serpent', in Harper and Brown 2002, pp. 93–113.
McGee, M. 1992. 'Desired Fruits: Motive and Intention in the Votive Rites of Hindu Women', in Leslie 1996a, pp. 69–88.
McGee, T. G. 1967. *The Southeast Asian City.* London: G. Bell and Sons.
Mabbett, I. W. 1969. 'Devarāja'. *Journal Southeast Asian History* 10: 202–23.
Mabbett, I. W. 1977a. 'The "Indianization" of Southeast Asia: Reflections on the Prehistoric Sources'. *Journal Southeast Asian Studies* 8: 1–14.

Mabbett, I. W. 1977b. 'The "Indianization" of Southeast Asia: Reflections on the Historical Sources'. *Journal Southeast Asian Studies* 8: 143–61.
Mabbett, I. W. 1998. 'The Problem of the Historical Nāgārjuna Revisited'. *Journal American Oriental Society* 118: 332–46.
Macdonald, A. W. 1990. 'Hindu-isation, Buddha-isation, Then Lama-isation or: What Happened at La-phyi?', in Skorupski 1990, pp. 199–208.
Mackenzie, J. M. 1995. *Orientalism: History, Theory and the Arts*. Manchester: Manchester University Press.
Madan, T. N. 1985. 'Concerning the Categories *śubha* and *śuddha* in Hindu Culture: An Exploratory Essay'. In Carman and Marglin 1985, pp. 11–29. Revised version ("Auspiciousness and Purity") as ch. 2 of Madan 1987.
Madan, T. N. 1987. *Non-Renunciation: Themes and Interpretations of Hindu Culture*. Delhi: Oxford University Press.
Madan, T. N. 1988. *Ways of Life: King, Householder, Renouncer. (Essays in Honour of Louis Dumont.)* Delhi: Motilal Banarsidass.
Madan, T. N. 1991. 'Auspiciousness and Purity: Some Reconsiderations'. *Contributions to Indian Sociology* (N.S.) 25: 287–9.
Magee, P. 2004. 'Mind the Gap: The Chronology of Painted Gray Ware and the Prelude to Early Historic Urbanism in Northern South Asia'. *South Asian Studies* 20: 37–44.
Majupuria, T. C. 1993. *Erawan Shrine and Brahma Worship in Thailand: With Reference to India and Nepal*. Bangkok: Tecpress Service.
Malandra, G. H. 1997. *Unfolding a* Maṇḍala*: The Buddhist Cave Temples at Ellora*. Delhi: Sri Satguru Publications.
Marglin, F. A. 1985a. 'Introduction'. In Carman and Marglin 1985, pp. 1–10.
Marglin, F. A. 1985b. *Wives of the God-King: The Rituals of the Devadasis of Puri*. Delhi: Oxford University Press.
Marglin, F. A. 1994. 'The Sacred Groves: Menstruation Rituals in Rural Orissa'. *Manushi: A Journal about Women in Society* 82 (May–June 1994): 22–32.
Marglin, F. A. 1995. 'Gender and the Unitary Self: Looking for the Subaltern in Coastal Orissa'. *South Asia Research* 15: 78–130.
Marriott, M. (ed.) 1969a. *Village India*. Chicago: University of Chicago Press.
Marriott, M. 1969b. 'Little Communities in an Indigenous Civilization', in Marriott 1969a, pp. 171–223.
Marriott, M. 1979. 'Hindu Transactions: Diversity without Dualism', in *Transaction and Meaning: Directions in the Anthropology of Human Issues*, Kapferer (ed.), pp. 109–42. Philadelphia: Institute for the Study of Human Issues.
Marshall, Sir J. 1931. *Mohenjodaro and the Indus Civilization: Being an Official Account of Archaeological Excavations at Mohenjodaro Carried Out by the Government of India Between the Years 1922–27*. Delhi: Indological Book House.
Masefield, P. 1986. *Divine Revelation in Pali Buddhism*. Colombo: Sri Lanka Institute of Traditional Studies.
Maskarinec, G. G. 1995. *The Rulings of the Night: an Ethnography of Nepalese Shaman Oral Texts*. Madison, WI: University of Wisconsin Press.

Matsunaga, Y. 1977a. 'A History of Tantric Buddhism in India with Reference to the Chinese Translations', in *Buddhist Thought and Asian Civilization: Essays in Honor of Herbert V. Guenther on His Sixtieth Birthday*, Kawamura and Scott (eds.), pp. 167–81. Emeryville, CA: Dharma Publishing.

Matsunaga, Y. 1977b. 'Some Problems of the *Guhyasamāja-Tantra*', in *Studies in Indo-Asian Art and Culture*, Chandra and Ratnam (eds.), pp. 109–19. New Delhi: International Academy of Indian Culture.

Mayaram, S. 2000. *Resisting Regimes: Myth, Memory and the Shaping of a Muslim Identity*. Delhi: Oxford University Press.

Mayer, R. 1996. *A Scripture of the Ancient Tantra Collection: The Phur-pa bcu-gnyis*. Oxford: Kiscadale Publications.

Maxwell, M. and Tschudin, V. 1996. *Seeing the Invisible: Modern Religious and Other Transcendent Experiences*. Oxford: Religious Experience Research Centre, Westminster College.

Meenakshi, K. 1996. 'The Siddhas of Tamil Nadu: A Voice of Dissent', in *Tradition, Dissent and Ideology: Essays in Honour of Romila Thapar*, Champakalakshmi and Gopal (eds.), pp. 111–34. Delhi: Oxford University Press.

Meister, M. W. (ed.) 1984. *Discourses on Śiva: Proceedings of a Symposium on the Nature of Religious Imagery*. Philadelphia: University of Pennsylvania Press.

Meister, M. W. 1986. 'Regional Variations in Mātṛkā Conventions', *Artibus Asiae* 47: 233–62.

Mencher, J. 1974. 'The Caste System Upside Down'. *Current Anthropology* 15: 469–93.

Mendelson, E. M. 1961a. 'A Messianic Buddhist Association in Upper Burma'. *Bulletin of the School of Oriental and African Studies* 24: 560–80.

Mendelson, E. M. 1961b. 'The King of the Weaving Mountain'. *Journal Royal Central Asian Society* 48: 229–37.

Mendelson, E. M. 1963. 'Observations on a Tour in the Region of Mount Popa, Central Burma'. *France-Asie* 179 (Mai–Juin 1963): 786–807.

Menges, K. H. 1989. 'Aus dem animistisch-schamanistischen Wortschatz der Altajer', in *Gedanke und Wirkung: Festschrift zum 90. Geburtstag von Nikolaus Poppe*, Heissig and Sagaster (eds.), pp. 221–51. Wiesbaden: Otto Harrassowitz. (Asiatische Forschungen, 108.)

Merz, B. 1996. 'Wild Goddess and Mother of Us All', in Michaels, Vögelsanger and Wilke 1996, pp. 343–54.

Meyer, J. J. 1903. *Kṣemendra's* Samayamatrika *(Das Zauberbuch der Hetären.) Ins Deutsche übertragen*. Leipzig: Lotus-Verlag.

Michaels, A., C. Vogelsanger and A. Wilke (eds.) 1996. *Wild Goddesses in India and Nepal*. Proceedings of an International Symposium in Berne and Zurich, November 1994). Bern: Peter Lang (Studia Religiosa Helvetica; 2).

Miller, J. 1985. *The Vision of Cosmic Order in the Vedas*. London: Routledge and Kegan Paul.

Misra, R. N. 1981. *Yaksha Cult and Iconography*. Delhi: Munshiram Manoharlal.

Mitchell, G. 1989. *The Penguin Guide to the Monuments of India. Vol. 1: Buddhist, Jain, Hindu*. London: Viking.

Mitra, D. 1984. 'Lakulīśa and Early Śaiva Temples in Orissa'. In Meister 1984, pp. 103–18.

Mitterwallner, G. von 1984. 'Evolution of the *Liṅga*'. In Meister 1984, pp. 12–31.

Mitterwallner, G. von 1989. 'Yakṣa of Ancient Mathura'. In Srinivasan 1989, pp. 368–82.

Mohan, P. N. 2001. 'Maitreya Cult in Early Shilla: Focusing on Hwarang as Maitreya-incarnate'. *Seoul Journal of Korean Studies* 14: 149–73.

Morinis, E. A. 1984. *Pilgrimage in the Hindu Tradition: A Case Study of West Bengal.* Delhi and Oxford: Oxford University Press.

Morrison, B. M. 1970. *Political Centers and Cultural Regions in Early Bengal.* Tucson, AZ: University of Arizona Press. (Association for Asian Studies, Monographs and Papers, XXV.)

Movik, K. 2000. *Bruk av Cannabis i Shivaittisk Tradisjon.* Hovedfagsoppgave i religionshistorie. Universitetet i Oslo. Downloaded from http://www.normal.no/txt/shiva/info.html, Sept. 2006.

Mulder, N. 1992. *Inside Thai Society: An Interpretation of Everyday Life.* 3rd rev. edn. Bangkok: Duang Kamol.

Muller-Ortega, P. E. 2002. 'Becoming Bhairava: Meditative Vision in Abhinavagupta's *Parātrīśikā-Laghuvṛtti*', in Harper and Brown 2002, pp. 213–30.

Mullin, G. H. 2006. *The Practice of the Six Yogas of Naropa.* Ithaca, NY and Boulder, CO: Snow Lion.

Mumford, S. R. 1989. *Himalayan Dialogue: Tibetan Lamas and Gurung Shamans in Nepal.* Madison, WI: University of Wisconsin Press.

Murti, T. R. V. 1960. *The Central Philosophy of Buddhism: A Study of the Mādhyamika System.* London: George Allen and Unwin.

Mus, P. 1975. *India Seen from the East: Indian and Indigenous Cults in Champa.* Monash University, Melbourne: Centre for Southeast Asian Studies. (Monash Papers on Southeast Asia, 3.)

Mussat, M. 1978. *Sou Nü King: La sexualité taoïste de la Chine ancienne.* Translated by Leung Kwok Po. Paris: Seghers.

Nagarajan, V. R. 1997. 'Inviting the Goddess into the Household'. *Whole Earth* 90: 49–53.

Ñāṇamoli T. 1964. *Mindfulness of Breathing* (Ānāpānasati). *Buddhist Texts from the Pali Canon and from the Pali Commentaries.* 2nd edn. Kandy: Buddhist Publication Society.

Ñāṇamoli, B. 1991. *The Path of Purification (Visuddhimagga) by Bhadantācariya Buddhaghosa.* 5th edn. Kandy: Buddhist Publication Society.

Ñāṇamoli, B. and Bodhi, B. 1995. *The Middle Length Discourses of the Buddha: A New Translation of the Majjhima Nikāya.* Boston: Wisdom Publications.

Nanda, S. 1990. *Neither Man nor Woman: The Hijras of India.* Belmont, CA: Wadsworth.

Nattier, J. 1988. 'The Meanings of the Maitreya Myth', in *Maitreya, the Future Buddha*, Sponberg and Hardacre (eds.), pp. 23–50. Cambridge and New York: Cambridge University Press.

Nepali, G. S. 1965. *The Newars; An Ethno-Sociological Study of a Himalayan Community*. Bombay: United Asia Publications.

Newman, J. R. 1987. *The Outer Wheel of Time: Vajrayāna Buddhist Cosmology in the Kālacakra Tantra (India)*. PhD Dissertation, University of Wisconsin at Madison. UMI AAT 8723348.

Newman, J. 1998. 'The Epoch of the Kālacakra Tantra'. *Indo-Iranian Journal* 41: 319–49.

Ngorchen K. L. 1987. *The Beautiful Ornament of the Three Visions: An Exposition of the Preliminary Practices of the Path which Extensively Explains the Instructions of the "Path Including its Result" in Accordance with the Root Treatise of the Vajra Verses of Virūpa*. Singapore: Golden Vase Publications.

Nichter, M. 1977. 'The Joga and Maya of the Tuluva Buta'. *Eastern Anthropologist* 30 (2):139–55.

Nyanaponika, T. 1969. *The Heart of Buddhist Meditation*. London: Rider and Co.

Oberoi, H. 1994. *The Construction of Religious Boundaries: Culture, Identity and Diversity in the Sikh Tradition*. Delhi: Oxford University Press and Chicago: University of Chicago Press.

O'Connor, R. 1989. 'Cultural Notes on Trade and the Tai', in Russell 1989, pp. 27–65.

O'Flaherty, W. Doniger (=Doniger, W.) 1981. *The Rig Veda: An Anthology. One Hundred and Eight Hymns, Selected, Translated and Annotated*. London: Penguin Books.

Olivelle, P. 1992. *Saṃnyāsa Upaniṣads: Hindu Scriptures on Asceticism and Renunciation*. New York and Oxford: Oxford University Press.

Olivelle, P. 1993. *The Āśrama System: The History and Hermeneutics of A Religious Institution*. Oxford: Oxford University Press.

Olivelle, P. 1997. 'Orgasmic Rapture and Divine Ecstasy: The Semantic History of *Ānanda*'. *Journal Indian Philosophy* 25: 153–80.

Olivelle, P. 1998. *Upaniṣads*. Translated from the Original Sanskrit. Oxford and New York: Oxford University Press. (Oxford World's Classics.)

Olivelle, P. 2003. 'The Renouncer Tradition', in Flood 2003, pp. 271–87.

Openshaw, J. 1997. 'The Web of Deceit: Challenges to Hindu and Muslim "Orthodoxies" by "Bāuls" of Bengal'. *Religion* 27: 297–309.

Openshaw, J. 2002. *Seeking Bāuls of Bengal*. Cambridge and New York: Cambridge University Press.

Oppitz, M. 1978–80. *Schamanen im blinden Land (Shamans of the Blind Country)*. Documentary film. Wieland Schulz Keil Produktion/WDR.

Oppitz, M. 1981. *Schamanen im Blinden Land. Ein Bilderbuch aus dem Himalaya*. Frankfurt am Main: Syndikat Verlag.

Orofino, G. 1997. 'Apropos of Some Foreign Elements in the Kālacakratantra', in Krasser *et al.* 1997, Vol. II, pp. 717–24.

Orofino, G. 1998. [Review of Benard 1994.] *Tibet Journal* 23(3): 114–18.

Orofino, G. 2001. 'Notes on the Early Phases of Indo-Tibetan Buddhism', in *Le Parole e I Marmi: Studi in Onore di Raniero Gnoli nel suo 70° Compleanno*, Torella (ed.), pp. 541–64. Roma: Istituto Italiano per l'Africa e l'Oriente.

Orzech, C. D. 1998. *Politics and Transcendent Wisdom: the Scripture for Humane Kings in the Creation of Chinese Buddhism*. University Park, PA: Pennsylvania State University Press.
Owens, B. McCoy 1995. 'Human Agency and Divine Power: Transforming Images and Recreating Gods among the Newar'. *History of Religions* 34: 201–40.
Padoux, A. 1990. *Vāc: the Concept of the Word in Selected Hindu Tantras*. translated by Jacques Gontier. Albany, NY: State University of New York Press.
Pal, P. 1986–88. *Indian Sculpture: a Catalogue of the Los Angeles County Museum of Art Collection*. 2 vols. Los Angeles, CA: Los Angeles County Museum of Art in association with University of California Press, Berkeley.
Pal, P. 1988. 'The Fifty-one Śākta Pīṭhas', in Gnoli and Lanciotti 1988, pp. 1039–60.
Pal, P. 1994. *The Peaceful Liberators: Jain Art from India*. Los Angeles: Los Angeles County Museum of Art; London: Thames and Hudson.
Pallath, J. J. 1995. *Theyyam: An Analytical Study of the Folk Culture Wisdom and Personality*. New Delhi: Indian Social Institute.
Palmié, S. 2006. 'A View from Itia Ororó Kande'. *Social Anthropology* 14: 99–118.
Pandey, R. 1969. *Hindu Saṃskāras*. 2nd rev. edn. Delhi: Motilal Banarsidass.
Pandian, J. 1982. 'The Goddess Kannagi: A Dominant Symbol of South Indian Tamil Society', in *Mother Worship: Theme and Variations*, Preston (ed.), pp. 177–91. Chapel Hill: University of North Carolina Press.
Parpola, A. 1988. 'The Coming of the Aryans to Iran and India and the Cultural and Ethnic Identity of the Dāsas'. *Studia Orientalia* (Helsinki) 64: 195–302.
Parpola, A. 1994. *Deciphering the Indus Script*. Cambridge and New York: Cambridge University Press.
Parpola, A. 1995. 'The Problem of the Aryans and the Soma: Textual-Linguistic and Archaeological Evidence', in Erdosy 1995a, pp. 353–81.
Parpola, A. 1999a. 'The Formation of the Aryan Branch of Indo-European', in Blench and Spriggs 1999, pp. 180–207.
Parpola, A. 1999b. 'Sāvitrī and Resurrection: The Ideal of Devoted Wife, Her Forehead Mark, Satī, and Human Sacrifice in Epic-Purāṇic, Vedic, Harappan-Dravidian and Near Eastern Perspectives', in Parpola and Tenhunen 1999, pp. 167–312.
Parpola, A. 2002a. 'Pre-Proto-Iranians of Afghanistan as Initiators of Śākta Tantrism: On the Scythian/Saka Affliiation of the Dāsas, Nuristanis and Magadhans'. *Iranica Antiqua* 37: 233–324.
Parpola, A. 2002b. 'Πσνδαιη and Sītā: On the Historical Background of the Sanskrit Epics'. *Journal American Oriental Society* 122: 361–73.
Parpola, A. 2005. 'The Nāsatyas, the Chariot and Proto-Aryan Religion'. *Journal of Indological Studies (Kyoto)* 16–17: 1–63.
Parpola, A. and Christian 2005. 'The Cultural Counterparts to Proto-Indo-European, Proto-Uralic and Proto-Aryan: Matching the Dispersal and Contact Patterns in the Linguistic and Archaeological Record', in Bryant and Patton 2005, pp. 107–41.
Parpola, A. and Tenhunen, S. (eds.) 1999. *Changing Patterns of Family and Kinship in South Asia. Proceedings of an International Symposium on the Occasion of*

the 50th Anniversary of India's Independence Held at the University of Helsinki 6 May 1998. Helsinki: Finnish Oriental Society. (Studia Orientalia, 84.)

Parry, J. P. 1991. 'The Hindu Lexicographer? A Note on Auspiciousness and Purity'. *Contributions to Indian Sociology* (N.S.) 25: 267–86.

Parry, J. P. 1994. *Death in Banaras*. Cambridge: Cambridge University Press.

Pejros, I. and Shnirelman, V. 1998. 'Rice in Southeast Asia: A Regional Interdisciplinary Approach', in Blench and Spriggs 1998, pp. 379–89.

Pflueger, L. W. 2003. 'Dueling with Dualism: Revisioning the Paradox of *Puruṣa* and *Prakṛti*', in Whicher and Carpenter 2003, pp. 70–82.

Pirart, É. 1998. 'Historicité des forces du mal dans la Ṛgvedasaṃhitā'. *Journal Asiatique* 286: 521–69.

Pollock, S. 2007. *The Language of the Gods in the World of Men: Sanskrit, Culture, and Power in Premodern India*. Delhi: Permanent Black.

Possehl, G. L. and Rissman, P. C. 1992. 'The Chronology of Prehistoric India: From Earliest Times to the Iron Age', in Ehrich 1992, I, pp. 465–90; II, pp. 447–74.

Possehl, G. L. 1998. 'Sociocultural Complexity Without the State', in *Archaic States*, Feinman and Marcus (eds.), pp. 261–91. Santa Fe, School of American Research Press.

Poster, A. G. 1986. *From Indian Earth: 4,000 Years of Terracotta Art*. Brooklyn, New York: The Brooklyn Museum.

Potts, D. T. 2005. 'Cyrus the Great and the Kingdom of Anshan', in Curtis and Stewart 2005, pp. 7–28.

Prebish, C. A. 1995. 'Ideal Types in Indian Buddhism: A New Paradigm'. *Journal American Oriental Society* 115: 651–66.

Prebish, C. A. 1996. 'Śaikṣa-dharmas Revisited: Further Considerations of Mahāsāṃghika Origins'. *History of Religions* 35: 258–70.

Quigley, D. 1995. *The Interpretation of Caste*. Oxford: Clarendon Press. (Oxford India Paperback Edition.)

Quintanilla, S. R. 2000. 'Āyāgapaṭas: Characteristics, Symbolism, and Chronology'. *Artibus Asiae* 60: 79–137.

Qvarnström, O. 1998. 'Stability and Adaptability: A Jain Strategy for Survival and Growth'. *Indo-Iranian Journal* 41: 33–55.

Qvarnström, O. 2000. 'Jain Tantra: Divinatory and Meditative Practices in the Twelfth-Century *Yogaśāstra* of Hemacandra'. *Tantra in Practice*, White (ed.), pp. 595–604. Princeton, NJ: Princeton University Press.

Qvarnström, O. 2002. *The Yogaśāstra of Hemacandra: A Twelfth Century Handbook on Śvetāmbara Jainism*. Translated by O. Qvarnström. Cambridge, MA: Harvard University, Department of Sanskrit and Indian Studies. Distributed by Harvard University Press.

Qvarnström, O. 2003. 'Losing One's Mind and Becoming Enlightened: Some Remarks on the Concept of Yoga in Śvetāmbara Jainism and Its Relation to the Nāth Siddha Tradition', in Whicher and Carpenter 2003, pp. 130–42.

Rabe, M. D. 1996. 'Sexual Imagery on the Phantasmagorical Castles at Khajuraho'. *International Journal of Tantric Studies* 2(2) (Nov. 1996).

Rabe, M. D. 1999. '"Not-Self" Consciousness and the Aniconic in Early Buddhism'. In *Modeling Consciousness Across the Disciplines Symposium*, Jodan (ed.), pp. 269–80. Lanham, MD: University Press of America. On-line version downloaded from www.sxu.edu/~rabe/asia/bodhgaya/index.html, 25/12/2001.

Radhakrishnan, S. 1963. *The Bhagavadgītā: With an Introductory Essay, Sanskrit Text and Notes.* 2nd edn, 7th impression. London: George Allen and Unwin.

Rajaram, N. S. and Frawley, D. 1995. *Vedic 'Aryans' and the Origins of Civilization: A Literary and Scientific Perspective.* Quebec: WH Press.

Rao, S. R. 1973. *Lothal and the Indus Civilization.* Bombay: Asia Publishing House.

Rawson, P. 1981. *Oriental Erotic Art.* New York: Gallery Books.

Ray, R. A. 1997. 'Nāgārjuna's Longevity', in *Sacred Biography in the Buddhist Traditions of South and South Asia*, Schober and Woodward (eds.), pp. 129–59. Honolulu: University of Hawai'i Press.

Ray, R. A. 1999. *Buddhist Saints in India: A Study in Buddhist Values and Orientations.* New York: Oxford University Press.

Reid, A. 1988. 'Female Roles in Pre-Colonial Southeast Asia'. *Modern Asian Studies* 22: 629–45.

Rhie, M. M. 'Mahakala: Some Tangkas and Sculptures from the Rubin Museum of Art', in *Demonic Divine: Himalayan Art and Beyond*, Linrothe and Watt (eds.). pp. 44–98. Rubin Museum of Art; Chicago: Serindia Publications.

Rhum, M. R. 1987. 'The Cosmology of Power in Lanna', *Journal of Siam Society* 75: 91–107.

Rhum, M. R. 1994. *The Ancestral Lords: Gender, Descent, and Spirits in a Northern Thai Village.* DeKalb: IL: Northern Illinois University. (Center for Southeast Asian Studies. Monograph Series on Southeast Asia, Special Report 29.)

Robinson, E. 1996. *The Original Vision: A Study of the Religious Experience of Childhood.* Oxford: Religious Experience Research Centre, Westminster College.

Robinson, J. B. 1979. *Buddha's Lions: The Lives of the Eighty-Four Siddhas. Caturaśīti-siddha-pravṛtti* by Abhayadatta. Translated into Tibetan as *Grub tho brgyad cu rtsa bzhi'i lo rgyus* by sMon-grub Shes-rab. Translated into English by J. B. Robinson. Berkeley, CA: Dharma Publishing.

Robinson, S. P. 1985. 'Hindu Paradigms of Women: Images and Values', in *Women, Religion and Social Change*, Haddad and Findly (eds.), pp. 181–215. Albany, NY: SUNY Press.

Rocher, L. 1985. 'The Kāmasūtra: Vātsyāyana's Attitude Toward Dharma and Dharmaśāstra'. *Journal American Oriental Society* 105: 521–9.

Roerich, G. N. 1976. *The Blue Annals.* 2nd edn. Delhi: Motilal Banarsidass.

Rozario, S. 2002. 'The Healer on the Margins: The *Dai* in Rural Bangladesh', in Rozario and Samuel 2002a, pp. 130–46.

Rozario, S. and Samuel, G. (eds.) 2002a. *The Daughters of Hariti: Childbirth and Female Healers in South and Southeast Asia.* London and New York: Routledge.

Rozario, S. and Samuel, G. 2002b. 'Tibetan and Indian Ideas of Birth Pollution: Similarities and Contrasts', in Rozario and Samuel 2002a, pp. 182–208.

Ruegg, D. S. 1964. 'Sur les rapports entre le bouddhisme et le "substrat religioux" indien et tibétain'. *Journal Asiatique* 252: 77–95.

Russell, S. D. (ed.) 1989. *Ritual, Power, and Economy: Upland-Lowland Contrasts in Mainland Southeast Asia.* DeKalb, IL: Northern Illinois University Center for Southeast Asian Studies. (Monograph Series on Southeast Asia. Occasional Paper No. 14.)

Saheb, S. A. A. 1998. 'A "Festival of Flags": Hindu-Muslim Devotion and the Sacralising of Localism at the Shrine of Nagore-e-Sharif in Tamil Nadu', in *Embodying Charisma: Modernity, Locality and the Performance of Emotion in Sufi Cults*, Werbner and Basu (eds.), pp. 55–76. London and New York: Routledge.

Said, E. W. 1978. *Orientalism.* New York: Pantheon.

Salomon, C. 1991. 'The Cosmogonic Riddles of Lalan Fakir', in *Gender, Genre, and Power in South Asian Expressive Traditions*, Appadurai, Korom and Mills (eds.), pp. 267–304. Philadelphia: University of Pennsylvania Press.

Samanta, S. 1992. '*Maṅgalmayīmā, Sumaṅgalī, Maṅgal*: Bengali Perceptions Of The Divine Feminine, Motherhood and "Auspiciousness"'. *Contributions to Indian Sociology* (N.S.) 26: 51–75.

Sampurṇānand, Ś. 1956. *The Atharva Veda, Vrātyakāṇḍa With Srutiprabha commentary in English by Sri Sampurṇānand.* Madras: Ganesh.

Samuel, G. 1982. 'Tibet as a Stateless Society and Some Islamic Parallels'. *Journal of Asian Studies*, 41: 215–29. (Revised version in Samuel 2005, pp. 27–51.)

Samuel, G. 1989. 'The Body in Buddhist and Hindu Tantra: Some Notes'. *Religion* 19: 197–210.

Samuel, G. 1990. *Mind, Body and Culture: Anthropology and the Biological Interface.* Cambridge and New York: Cambridge University Press.

Samuel, G. 1992. 'Gesar of Ling: the Origins and Meaning of the East Tibetan Epic', in *Tibetan Studies: Proceedings of the 5th Seminar of the International Association for Tibetan Studies, Narita, 1989*, Ihara and Yamaguchi (eds.), pp. 711–22. Narita: Naritasan Shinshoji. (Reprinted in Samuel 2005a, pp. 165–91.)

Samuel, G. 1993. *Civilized Shamans: Buddhism in Tibetan Societies.* Washington and London: Smithsonian Institution Press.

Samuel, G. 1997. 'Women, Goddesses and Auspiciousness in South Asia'. *Journal of Interdisciplinary Gender Studies* 4: 1–23. (Reprinted in Samuel 2005a, pp. 256–87.)

Samuel, G. 2000. 'The Indus Valley Civilization and Early Tibet', in *New Horizons in Bon Studies*, Karmay and Nagano (eds.), pp. 651–70. Osaka: National Museum of Ethnology. (Bon Studies 2) (Reprinted in Samuel 2005a, pp. 138–64.)

Samuel, G. 2001a. 'The Religious Meaning of Space and Time: South and Southeast Asia and Modern Paganism'. *International Review of Sociology* vol. 11 no. 3 (Nov. 2001), pp. 395–418.

Samuel, G. 2001b. 'The Effectiveness of Goddesses, or, How Ritual Works'. *Anthropological Forum* 11: 73–91. (Reprinted in Samuel 2005, pp. 229–55.)

Samuel, G. 2001c. 'Tibetan Medicine in Contemporary India: Theory and Practice', in *Healing Powers and Modernity in Asian Societies*, Connor and Samuel (eds.), pp. 247–68. Westport, CT: Bergin and Garvey (Greenwood Publishing).

Samuel, G. 2002a. 'The Epic and Nationalism in Tibet', in *Religion and Biography in China and Tibet*, Benjamin Penny (ed.), pp. 178–88. Richmond, Surrey: Curzon Press.

Samuel, G. 2002b. 'Introduction', in Rozario and Samuel 2002a, pp. 1–33.

Samuel, G. 2002c. 'Ritual Technologies and the State: The *Mandala*-Form Buddhist Temples of Bangladesh'. *Journal Bengal Art* 7: 39–56.

Samuel, G. 2002d. 'Buddhism and the State in Eighth Century Tibet'. In *Religion and Secular Culture in Tibet: Tibetan Studies II (PIATS 2000: Tibetan Studies: Proceedings of the 9th Seminar of the International Association of Tibetan Studies*, Leiden 2000) ed. H. Blezer with the assistance of A. Zadoks, pp. 1–19. Leiden: Brill. (Reprinted in Samuel 2005a, pp. 94–116.)

Samuel, G. 2005a. *Tantric Revisionings.* New Delhi: Motilal Banarsidass; London: Ashgate.

Samuel, G. 2005b. 'Subtle Bodies in Indian and Tibetan Yoga: Scientific and Spiritual Meanings'. Paper for Second International Conference on Religions and Cultures in the Indic Civilisation, Delhi 17–20 December 2005.

Samuel, G. 2006a. 'Healing and the Mind-Body Complex: Childbirth and Medical Pluralism in South Asia', in *Multiple Medical Realities: Patients and Healers in Biomedical. Alternative and Traditional Medicine*, Johannessen and Lázár (eds.), pp. 121–35. New York and London: Berghahn Books.

Samuel, G. 2006b. 'A Short History of Indo-Tibetan Alchemy'. Paper for the Medicine, Religion and History Panel at the 11th Seminar of the International Association for Tibetan Studies, Königswinter, German, 27 August to 2 September 2006.

Samuel, G. 2006c. 'Tibetan Medicine and Biomedicine: Epistemological Conflicts, Practical Solutions'. *Asian Medicine* 2: 72–85.

Sanderson, A. 1985. 'Purity and Power among the Brahmans of Kashmir', in *Category of the Person,* Carrithers (ed.), pp. 190–216. Cambridge and New York: Cambridge University Press.

Sanderson, A. 1988. 'Śaivism and the Tantric Traditions', in *The World's Religions*, Sutherland, Houlden, Clarke and Hardy (eds.), 660–704. London: Routledge.

Sanderson, A. 1994. 'Vajrayāna: Origin and Function', in *Buddhism into the Year 2000: International Conference Proceedings*, Bhikkhu *et al.* (eds.), pp. 87–102. Bangkok and Los Angeles, CA: Dhammakaya Foundation.

Sanderson, A. 1995. 'Meaning in Tantric Ritual', in *Essais sur le rituel III: Colloque du centenaire de la section des sciences religieuses de l'école pratique des hautes etudes*, Blondeau and Schipper (eds.), pp. 15–95. Louvain and Paris: Peeters.

Sanderson, A. 2001. 'History through Textual Criticism in the Study of Śaivism, the Pañcarātra and the Buddhist Yoginītantras', in Grimal 2001, pp. 1–47.

Sanderson, A. 2003–4. 'The Śaiva Religion Among the Khmers'. *Bulletin de l'École Française d'Extrême-Orient*, 90–1: 349–462.

Sanderson, A. 2004. 'Religion and the State: Śaiva Officiants in the Territory of the King's Brahmanical Chaplain'. *Indo-Iranian Journal* 47: 229–300.

Saraswati, S. S. 1985. *Kundalini Tantra*. 1st Australian edn. Gosford, NSW: Satyananda Ashram.

Sardar, H. n.d. 'Trance-Dancers of the Goddess Durga'. Downloaded from www.asianart.com/articles/hamid/ on 10 Oct. 2001.

Satyananda P. (Swami Satyananda Saraswati) 1980. *Four Chapters on Freedom: Commentary on Yoga Sutras of Patanjali*. 2nd Australian edn. Mangrove Mountain, NSW: Satyananda Ashram.

Schaeffer, K. R. 2002. '*The Attainment of Immortality*: From Nāthas in India to Buddhists in Tibet'. *Journal Indian Philosophy* 30: 515–33.

Schalk, P. 1994. 'The Controversy about the Arrival of Buddhism in Tamilakam'. *Temenos* 30: 197–232.

Schipper, K. 1994. *The Taoist Body*. Translated by K. C. Duval. Taipei: SMC Publishing Inc. (First published in 1982 as *Le corps taoïste* by Librairie Arthème Fayard, Paris.)

Schlingloff, D. 1964. *Ein buddhistisches Yogalehrbuch*. Ed. and trans. Berlin: Akademie verlag. (Sanskrittexte aus den Turfanfunde, 7.)

Schmithausen, L. 1997. *Maitri and Magic: Aspects of the Buddhist Attitude Toward the Dangerous in Nature*. Wien: Verlag der Österreichischen Akademie der Wissenschaften.

Schopen, G. 1996. 'Immigrant Monks and the Proto-Historical Dead: The Buddhist Occupation of Early Burial Sites in India', in *Festschrift für Dieter Schlingloff*, Wilhelm (ed.), pp. 215–38. Munich: Reinbek.

Schopen, G. 1997a. *Bones, Stones, and Buddhist Monks: Collected Papers on the Archaeology, Epigraphy, and Texts of Monastic Buddhism in India*. Honolulu: University of Hawai'i Press.

Schopen, G. 1997b. 'Archeology and Protestant Presuppositions in the Study of Indian Buddhism', in Schopen 1997a, pp. 1–22.

Schrempf, M. 1999. 'Taming the Earth, Controlling the Cosmos: Transformation of space in Tibetan Buddhist and Bon-po Ritual Dances', in *Sacred Spaces and Powerful Places in Tibetan Culture: A Collection of Essays*, Huber (ed.). Dharamsala, The Library of Tibetan Works and Archives.

Schrempf, M. 2001. *Ethnisch-Religiöse Revitalisierung und rituelle Praxis einer osttibetischen Glaubensgemainschaft im heutigen China am beispiel ritueller Maskentanzenaufführungen der Bönpo-Klosterföderation von Gamel Gingka in Amdo Sharkhog in der Zeit von 1947 bis 1996*. Inaugural-Dissertation zur Erlangung des Doktorgrades am Fachbereich Politik- und Sozialwissenschaften der Freien Universität Berlin.

Schubring, W. 1942–52. *Isibhāsāiyam: Ein Jaina Text der Frühzeit*. Göttingen: Vandenhoeck & Ruprecht. (Nachrichten der Akademie der Wissenschaften in Göttingen. I, Philologisch-historische Klasse; Jahrg. 1942, Nr. 6, Jahrg. 1952, Nr. 2.)

Schwartzberg, J. 1992. *A Historical Atlas of South Asia*. 2nd impression, with additional material. New York: Oxford University Press.

Scott, D. 1993. 'Śiva and the East Iranians of Bactria: Hindu cross-cultural expansion – 1'. *International Journal of Indian Studies* 3: 87–106.
Searle-Chatterjee, M. and Sharma, U. (eds.) 1994. *Contextualising Caste: Post-Dumontian Approaches*. Oxford: Blackwell Publishers/The Sociological Review. (Sociological review monograph; 41.)
Sen, S. 1953. *Vipradāsa's* Manasā-Vijaya*: A Fifteenth Century Bengali Text* [...] Calcutta: Asiatic Society. (Bibliotheca Indica, 277.)
Seneviratne, H. L. 1978. *Rituals of the Kandyan State*. Cambridge and New York: Cambridge University Press.
Shaffer, J. G. 1992. 'The Indus Valley, Baluchistan, and Helmand Traditions: Neolithic through Bronze Age', in Ehrich 1992a, I, pp. 441–64; II, pp. 425–46.
Shaffer, J. G. and Lichtenstein, D. A. 1995. 'The Concepts of "Cultural Tradition" and "Palaeoethnicity" in South Asian Archaeology'. In Erdosy 1995a, pp. 126–54.
Shah, U. P. 1984. 'Lakulīśa: Śaivite Saint'. In Meister 1984, pp. 92–102.
Shahbazi, A. Shapur 2005. 'The History of the Idea of Iran', in Curtis and Stewart 2005, pp. 100–11.
Shakabpa, W. D. 1967. *Tibet: A Political History*. New Haven: Yale University Press.
Sharma, A. 1995. 'The Aryan Question: Some General Considerations', in Erdosy 1995a, pp. 177–91.
Sharma, J. P. 1968. *Republics in Ancient India, c. 1500B.C.–500B.C.* Leiden: Brill.
Sharma, J. P. 1989. *Jaina Yakshas*. Meerut: Kusumanjali Prakashan.
Shaw, J. 2000. 'Sanchi and its Archaeological Landscape: Buddhist Monasteries, Settlements and Irrigation Works in Central India'. *Antiquity* 74: 775–76.
Shaw, J. and Sutcliffe, J. V. 2001. 'Ancient Irrigation Works in the Sanchi Area: An Archaeological and Hydrological Investigation'. *South Asian Studies* 17: 55–75.
Shaw, M. 1994. *Passionate Enlightenment: Women in Tantric Buddhism*. Princeton, NJ: Princeton University Press.
Shawn, A. 2006. 'Life Without Grains: *Bigu* and the Daoist Body', in Kohn 2006a, 91–122.
Shen, W. 2006. 'Reconstructing the History of Buddhism in Central Eurasia (11–14 Cent.): An Interdisciplinary and Multilingual Approach to Khara Khoto Texts'. Paper for the 11th Seminar of the International Association of Tibetan Studies, August–September 2006, Königswinter, Germany.
Sherburne, R. 1983. *A Lamp for the Path and Commentary by Atīśa*. London: Allen and Unwin.
Shrestha, B. G. 1999. 'Visible and Invisible Aspects of the Devī Dances in Sankhu, Nepal', in Tambs-Lyche 1999, pp. 100–13.
Sick, D. H. 2004. 'Mit(h)ra(s) and the Myths of the Sun'. *Numen* 51: 432–67.
Silburn, L. 1988. *Kuṇḍalinī: The Energy of the Depths. A Comprehensive Study Based on the Scriptures of Nondualistic Kaśmir Śaivism*. Albany, NY: State University of New York Press.
Silk, J. 2002. 'What, if Anything, is Mahāyāna Buddhism? Problems of Definitions and Classifications'. *Numen* 49: 355–405.

Sims-Williams. N. and Cribb, J. 1996. 'A New Bactrian Inscription of Kanishka the Great'. *Silk Road Art and Archaeology* 4: 75–142.

Singh, U. 1993. *Kings, Brahmanas and Temples in Orissa. An Epigraphic Study AD 300–1147*. Delhi: Munshiram Manoharlal.

Sircar, D. C. 1971–72. 'Mahamayuri. List of Yaksas. Translation'. *Journal of Ancient Indian History* 5: 262–328.

Sircar, D. C. 1973. *The Śākta Pīṭhas*. 2nd rev. edn. Delhi: Motilal Banarsidass.

Sivaramamurti, C. 1976. *Śatarudrīya: Vibhūti of Śiva's Iconography*. New Delhi: Abhinav Publications.

Skilling, P. 2004. 'Mahayana and Bodhisattva: an Essay Towards Historical Understanding', in *Phothisatawa barami kap sangkhom thai nai sahatsawat mai [Bodhisattvaparami and Thai Society in the New Millennium]*, Proceedings of a Seminar in Celebration of the 4th Birth Cycle of HRH Princess Maha Chakri Sirindhorn, Limpanusorn and Iampakdee (eds.), pp. 141–56. Bangkok: Thammasat University Press. (Chinese Studies Centre, Institute of East Asia, Thammasat University.)

Skjærvø, P. O. 1995. 'The Avesta as Source for the Early History of the Iranians', in Erdosy 1995a, pp. 155–76.

Skjærvø, P. O. 1997. 'The State of Old-Avestan Scholarship'. *Journal American Oriental Society* 117(1): 103–14.

Skjærvø, P. O. 2005. 'The Achaemenids and the *Avesta*', in Curtis and Stewart 2005, pp. 52–84.

Skorupski, T. (ed.) 1990. *Indo-Tibetan Studies*. Tring: Institute of Tibetan Studies.

Skorupski, T. 1998. 'An Analysis of the *Kriyāsaṃgraha*', in *Sūryacandrāya: Essays in Honour of Akira Yuyama on the Occasion of his 65th Birthday*, Harrison and Schopen (eds.), pp. 181–96. Swisttal-Odendorf: Indica et Tibetica Verlag. (Indica et Tibetica, 35.)

Slusser, M. Shepherd 1982. *Nepal Mandala: a Cultural Study of the Kathmandu Valley*. 2 vols. Princeton: Princeton University Press.

Smith, B. K. 1989. *Reflections on Resemblance, Ritual, and Religion*. New York and Oxford: Oxford University Press.

Smith, B. K. 1994. *Classifiying the Universe: The Ancient Indian* Varṇa *System and the Origins of Caste*. New York and Oxford: Oxford University Press.

Smith, D. 1985. *Ratnākara's* Haravijaya: *An Introduction to the Sanskrit Court Epic*. Delhi: Oxford University Press.

Smith, D. 2003. 'Orientalism and Hinduism', in Flood 2003, pp. 45–63.

Smith, Relph B. and Watson, William (eds.) 1979. *Early South East Asia: Essays in Archaeology, History, and Historical Geography*. New York and Kuala Lumpur: Oxford University Press.

Snellgrove, D. L. 1959. *The Hevajra Tantra: A Critical Study*. 2 vols. London: Oxford University Press. (London Oriental Series, 6.)

Snellgrove, D. L. 1987. *Indo-Tibetan Buddhism: Indian Buddhists and Their Tibetan Successors*. London: Serindia.

Snellgrove, D. L. 1988. 'Categories of Buddhist Tantras', in Gnoli and Lanciotti 1988, pp. 1353–84.

Snellgrove, D. L. 2000. *Asian Commitment: Travels and Studies in the Indian Sub-Continent and South-East Asia*. Bangkok: Orchid Press.

Sobo, E. J. and Bell, S. (eds.) 2001. *Celibacy, Culture and Society: The Anthropology of Sexual Abstinence*. Madison, WI: University of Wisconsin Press.

Sopa, G. L. 1985. 'The Kalachakra Tantra Initiation', in Sopa, Jackson and Newman 1985, pp. 85–117.

Sopa, G. L., R. Jackson and J. Newman 1985. *The Wheel of Time: The Kalachakra in Context*. Madison, WI: Deer Park Books.

Southwold, M. 1979. 'Religious Belief'. *Man* 14: 628–44.

Southwold, M. 1983. *Buddhism in Life: the Anthropological Study of Religion and the Sinhalese Practice of Buddhism*. Manchester: Manchester University Press.

Spess, D. L. 2000. *Soma: The Divine Hallucinogen*. Rochester, VT: Park Street Press.

Spiro, M. E. 1967. *Burmese Supernaturalism: A Study in the Explanation and Reduction of Suffering*. Englewood Cliffs, NJ: Prentice-Hall.

Spiro, M. E. 1971. *Buddhism and Society: A Great Tradition and its Burmese Vicissitudes*. London: Allen and Unwin.

Spodek, H. and Srinivasan, D. M. (eds.) 1993. *Urban Form and Meaning in South Asia: The Shaping of Cities from Prehistoric to Precolonial Times*. National Gallery of Art, Washington; Hanover and London: University Press of New England.

Sponberg, A. 1992. 'Attitudes Towards Women and the Feminine in Early Buddhism', in *Buddhism, Sexuality, and Society*, Cabezón (ed.), pp. 3–36. Albany, NY: State University of New York Press.

Srinivas, M. N. 1952. *Religion and Society Among the Coorgs of South India*. Oxford: Clarendon Press.

Srinivasan, D. M. 1979. 'Early Vaiṣṇava Imagery: Caturvyūha and Variant Forms'. *Archives of Asian Art* 32: 39–54.

Srinivasan, D. M. 1984. 'Significance and Scope of Pre-Kuṣāṇa Śaivite Iconography'. In Meister 1984, pp. 32–46.

Srinivasan, D. M. (ed.) 1989. *Mathura: The Cultural Heritage*. New Delhi: AIAS.

Srinivasan, D. M. 1997. *Many Heads, Arms and Eyes: Origin, Meaning and Form of Multiplicity in Indian Art*. Leiden: Brill. (Studies in Asian Art and Archaeology, 20.)

Stablein, W. G. 1976. *The Mahākālatantra: A Theory of Ritual Blessings and Tantric Medicine*. PhD dissertation, Columbia University. (University Microfilms 76–29, 405.)

Stablein, W. 1991. *Healing Image: The Great Black One*. Berkeley and Hong Kong: SLG Books.

Stacul, G. 1992. 'Further Evidence for the "Inner Asia Complex" from Swat', in *South Asian Archaeology Studies*, Possehl (ed.), pp. 111–22. New Delhi: Oxford & IBH Publishing House.

Stargardt, J. 2000. *Tracing Thoughts Through Things: The Oldest Pali Texts and the Earliest Buddhist Archaeology of India and Burma*. Seventh Gonda Lecture.

Amsterdam, 12th November 1999. Amsterdam: Royal Netherlands Academy of Arts and Sciences.

Stein, B. 1994. *Peasant State and Society in Medieval South India*. Delhi: Oxford University Press.

Stein, M. A. 1900. *Kalhana's Rājatarangiṇī: A Chronicle of the Kings of Kasmīr*. Translated, with an introduction, commentary, and appendices by M. A. Stein. 2 vols. Westminster: A. Constable.

Stephen, M. 2001. 'Barong and Rangda in the Context of Balinese Religion'. *Review of Indonesian and Malaysian Affairs* 35: 137–94.

Stone, E. R. 1994. *The Buddhist Art of Nāgārjunakoṇḍa*. Delhi: Motilal Banarsidass.

Strong, J. S. 1992. *The Legend and Cult of Upagupta: Sanskrit Buddhism in North India and Southeast Asia*. Princeton, NJ: Princeton University Press.

Studholme, A. *The Origins of Oṃ Maṇipadme Hūṃ: A Study of the Kāraṇḍavyūha Sūtra*. Albany, NY: State University of New York Press.

Stutley, M. 1980. *Ancient Indian Magic and Folklore*. Boulder, CO: Great Eastern.

Sugiyama, J. 1982. *Classic Buddhist Sculpture: The Tempyō Period*. Translated and adapted by S. Crowell Morse. Tokyo, New York and San Francisco: Kodansha International Ltd and Shibundo.

Sukthankar, V. S. 1936. 'Epic Studies VI. The Bhṛgus and the Bhārata: A Text-Historical Study'. *Annals of the Bhandarkar Oriental Research Institute* 18(1): 1–76.

Sullivan, H. P. 1964. 'A Re-Examination of the Religion of the IndusCivilization'. *History of Religions* 4: 115–25.

Sullivan, H. P. 1971. 'The Prehistory of Indian Religion'. [Review of Allchin 1963.] *History of Religions* 11: 140–6.

Sutherland, G. H. 1991. *The Disguises of the Demon: The Development of the Yakṣa in Hinduism and Buddhism*. Albany, NY: State University of New York Press.

Svoboda, R. E. 1986. *Aghora: At the Left Hand of God*. New Delhi: Rupa & Co.

Svoboda, R. E. 1993. *Aghora II: Kundalini*. New Delhi: Rupa & Co.

Swearer, D. 1976. *Wat Haripuñjaya. A Study of the Royal Temple of the Buddha's Relic, Lamphun, Thailand*. Missoula, MT: University of Montana. (Published by Scholars Press for the American Academy of Religion.)

Tambiah, S. J. 1970. *Buddhism and the Spirit Cults in North-east Thailand*. Cambridge: Cambridge University Press.

Tambiah, S. J. 1973. 'From Varna to Caste through Mixed Unions', in *The Character of Kinship*, Goody (ed.), pp. 191–229. Cambridge: Cambridge University Press.

Tambiah, S. J. 1984. *The Buddhist Saints of the Forest and the Cult of Amulets: A Study in Charisma, Hagiography, Sectarianism and Millennial Buddhism*. Cambridge: Cambridge University Press.

Tambiah, S. J. 1985. 'The Galactic Polity in Southeast Asia', in *Culture, Thought, and Social Action: An Anthropological Perspective*, pp. 252–86. Cambridge, MA: Harvard University Press.

Tambiah, S. J. 1987. 'At the Confluence of Anthropology, History, and Indology'. *Contributions to Indian Sociology* N.S. 21: 187–216.

Tambs-Lyche, H. (ed.) 1999. *The Feminine Sacred in South Asia (Le sacré au feminine en Asie du Sud)*. Delhi: Manohar.

Tannenbaum, N. 1987. 'Tattoos, Invulnerability and Power in Shan Religion'. *American Ethnologist* 14: 693–71.

Tannenbaum, N. 1989. 'Power and its Shan Transformations', in Russell 1989, pp. 67–88.

Tarling, N. (ed.) 1999. *The Cambridge History of Southeast Asia: Volume One. From Early Times to c.1500*. Paperback edn. Cambridge: Cambridge University Press.

Tatelman, J. 2005. *The Heavenly Exploits: Buddhist Biographies from the Divyāvadāna. Vol. I.* New York: New York University Press (JJC Foundation). (Clay Sanskrit Library.)

Taylor, J. 1993. *Forest Monks and the Nation-State: An Anthropological and Historical Study in Northeastern Thailand.* Singapore: Institute of Southeast Asian Studies.

Taylor, K. W. 1999. 'The Early Kingdoms', in Tarling 1999, pp. 137–82.

Templeman, D. 1983. *Tāranātha's bKa'.babs.bdun.ldan. The Seven Instruction Lineages by Jo.nang Tāranātha.* Dharamsala, Library of Tibetan Works and Archives.

Templeman, D. 1989. *Tāranātha's Life of Kṛṣṇācārya/Kāṇha.* Dharamsala: Library of Tibetan Works and Archives.

Templeman, D. 1997. 'Buddhaguptanātha: A Late Indian Siddha in Tibet', in *Proceedings of the 7th Seminar of the International Association for Tibetan Studies, Graz 1995,* Eimer *et al.* (eds.), pp. 955–65. Wien: Verlag der Österreichischen Akademie der Wissenschaften.

Terwiel, B. J. 1975. *Monks and Magic: An Analysis of Religious Ceremonies in Central Thailand.* Studentlitteratur, Lund. (Scandinavian Institute of Asian Studies Monograph Series No. 24.

Thakur, U. n.d. *Madhubani Painting.* New Delhi: Abhinav Publications, c.1981 or 1982.

Thapan, A. R. 1997. *Understanding Gaṇapati: Insights into the Dynamics of a Cult.* New Delhi: Manohar.

Thapar, R. 2003. *The Penguin History of Early India: From the Origins to AD 1300.* New Delhi: Penguin Books.

Thieme, P. 1960. 'The "Aryan" Gods of the Mitanni Treatise'. *Journal American Oriental Society* 80: 301–17.

Thompson, G. 2003. 'Soma and Ecstasy in the Rgveda', in Houben 2003a. E-text at www1.shore.net/~india/ejvs/ejvs0901/ejvs0901e.txt, downloaded 6 Aug 2006.

Thurman, R. A. F. 1997. 'Mandala: The Architecture of Enlightenment', in Leoidy and Thurman 1997, pp. 127–45.

Thurman, R. A. F. 2004. *The Universal Vehicle Discourse Literature (Mahāyānasūtrālaṃkāra) by Maitreyanātha/Āryāsaṅga Together With Its Commentary (Bhāṣya) by Vasubandhu.* Translated from the Sanskrit, Tibetan, and Chinese by L. Jamspal, R. Clark, J. Wilson, L. Zwilling, M. Sweet, R. Thurman, editor-in-chief R. A. F. Thurman. *New York: American Institute of Buddhist*

Studies, co-published with Columbia University's Center for Buddhist Studies and Tibet House US.

Tinti, P. 1998. *Between Two Civilisations: History and Self-Representation of Bangladeshi Buddhism.* D.Phil. dissertation, University of Oxford.

Tiyavanich, K. 1997. *Forest Recollections: Wandering Monks in Twentieth-Century Thailand.* Honolulu: University of Hawaii Press.

Tiyavanich, K. 2004. *The Buddha in the Jungle.* Seattle: University of Washington Press.

Toffin, G. 1984. *Société et religion chez les Néwar du Népal.* Paris: Éditions du C.N.R.S.

Toffin, G. 1996. 'A Wild Goddess Cult in Nepal: The Navadurgā of Theco Village (Kathmandu Valley)', in Michaels, Vogelsanger and Wilke 1996, pp. 217–51.

Toffin, G. 1999. 'Possession, danses masquées et corps divin dans la vallée de Katmandou (Népal)'. *Puruṣārtha* 21: 237–61.

Trainor, K. 1997. *Relics, Ritual and Representation in Buddhism: Rematerialising the Sri Lankan Theravada Tradition.* Cambridge and New York: Cambridge University Press.

Trautmann, T. R. 1979. 'The Study of Dravidian Kinship', in Deshpande and Hook 1979, pp. 153–74.

Trungpa, C. 1982. *The Life of Marpa the Translator, by Tsang Nyön Heruka,* translated from the Tibetan by the N. Translation Committee under the direction of Chögyam Trungpa. Boulder, CO: Prajñā.

Tsuchida, R. 1991. 'Two Categories of Brahmins in the Early Buddhist Period'. *Memoirs of the Toyo Bunko* 49: 51–95.

Tucci, G. 1940. *Travels of Tibetan Pilgrims in the Swat Valley.* [Reprinted 1971 in Tucci, *Opera Minora,* 2 vols., Rome: G. Bardi.]

Tucci, G. 1980. *The Religions of Tibet,* translated by Geoffrey Samuel. London: Routledge and Kegan Paul; Berkeley, CA: University of California Press.

Tuladhar-Douglas, W. 2005. 'On Why it is Good to Have Many Names: the Many Identities of a Nepalese God'. *Contemporary South Asia,* 14: 55–74.

Turner, V. W. 1957. *Schism and Continuity in an African Society: A Study of Ndembu Village Life.* Manchester: Published on behalf of the Rhodes-Livingstone Institute by Manchester University Press.

Turner, V. W. 1968. *The Drums of Affliction: a Study of Religious Processes among the Ndembu of Zambia.* Oxford: Clarendon Press; London: International African Institute.

Turner, V. W. 1970. *The Forest of Symbols: Aspects of Ndembu Ritual.* Ithaca, London: Cornell University Press.

Uchiyamada, Y. 2000. 'Passions in the Landscape: Ancestor Spirits and Land Reforms in Kerala, India'. *South Asia Research* 20: 63–84.

Upadhyaya, S. C. 1961. *Kama Sutra of Vatsyayana: Complete Translation from the Original Sanskrit.* Bombay: Taraporevala's.

Urban, H. 1999. 'The Extreme Orient: The Construction of "Tantrism" as a Category in the Orientalist Imagination'. *Religion* 29: 123–46.

Urban, H. 2001. 'The Path of Power: Impurity, Kingship, and Sacrifice in Assamese Tantra'. *Journal of the American Academy of Religion* 69: 777–816.

van Buitenen, J. A. B. 1975. *The Mahābhārata. 2. The Book of the Assembly Hall; 3. The Book of the Forest.* Translated and edited by J. A. B. van Buitenen. Chicago and London: University of Chicago Press.

van Buitenen, J. A. B. 1983. *The Mahābhārata. 1. The Book of the Beginning.* Translated and edited by J. A. B. van Buitenen. Chicago and London: University of Chicago Press.

van den Hoek, A. W. (Bert) 2005. 'The Death of the Divine Dancers: The Conclusion of the Bhadrakali Pyakham in Kathmandu', in Allen 2005, pp. 374–404.

van Skyhawk, H. 1993. 'Nasīruddīn and Ādināth, Nizāmuddīn and Kāniphnāth: Hindu-Muslim Religious Syncretism in the Folk Literature of the Deccan', in Brückner, Lutze, and Malik 1993, pp. 445–67.

Venkatraman, R. 1990. *A History of the Tamil Siddha Cult.* Madurai: Ennes Publications.

Vergati-Stahl, A. 1979. 'Taleju, Sovereign Deity of Bhaktapur', in *Asie du Sud, Traditions et Changements:* [actes du VIe colloque européan sur les études modernes concernant l'Asie du Sud], Sèvres, 8–13 juillet 1978 / [organisé par M. Gaborieau et A. Thorner], pp. 163–7. Paris: Éditions du CNRS.

Vergati, A. 1986. 'Les associations religieuses (*guṭhi*) des temples de la vallée de Kathmandou'. *Puruṣārtha* 10: 97–123.

Vergati, A. 2000. *Gods and Masks of the Kāthmāṇḍu Valley.* New Delhi: D. K. Printworld.

Vetter, T. 1990. 'Some Remarks on Older Parts of the Suttanipāta', in *Earliest Buddhism and Madhyamaka*, Ruegg and Schmithausen (eds.), pp. 36–56. Leiden: E. J. Brill.

Victoria, B. 2005. *Zen at War.* New York and Tokyo: Weatherfield.

Viswanathan, G. 2003. 'Colonialism and the Construction of Hinduism', in Flood 2003, pp. 23–44.

Vogt, B. 1999. *Skill and Trust: The Tovil Healing Ritual of Sri Lanka as Cultur-Specific Psychotherapy.* Translated by M. H. Kohn. Amsterdam: VU University Press.

Volwahsen, A. 1969. *Living Architecture: Indian.* Calcutta: Oxford and IBH Publishing Company.

Walshe, M. 1995. *The Long Discourses of the Buddha. A Translation of the Dīgha Nikāya.* Boston: Wisdom Publications.

Wadley, S. S. 1980. 'Hindu Women's Family and Household Rites in a North Indian Village', in *Unspoken Worlds*, Falk and Gross (eds.), pp. 94–109. New York: Harper and Row.

Wallace, V. A. 1995. 'The Buddhist Tantric Medicine in the *Kālacakratantra*'. *Pacific World: J. of the Institute of Buddhist Studies* (N.S.) 10–11: 155–74.

Wallace, V. A. 2001. *The Inner Kālacakratantra: A Buddhist Tantric View of the Individual.* New York and Oxford: Oxford University Press.

Wallace, V. A. 2004. *The Kālacakratantra: The Chapter on the Individual Together with the Vimalaprabhā.* Translated from Sanskrit, Tbetan, and Mongolian by V. A. Wallace. New York: American Institute of Buddhist Studies at Columbia

University, New York. Co-Published with Columbia University's Center for Buddhist Studies and Tibet House US.

Walshe, M. 1995. *The Long Discourses of the Buddha: A Translation of the Dīgha Nikāya*. Boston: Wisdom Publications.

Walter, M. L. 1979. 'Preliminary Results from a Study of Two Rasayana Systems in Indo-Tibetan Esotericism', in *Tibetan Studies*, Aris and Kyi (eds.), pp. 319–24. Warminster: Aris and Phillips.

Walter, M. L. 1980. *The Role of Alchemy and Medicine in Indo-Tibetan Tantrism.* PhD Dissertation, Indiana University. UMI 8024583.

Walter, M. 1992. 'Jabir, The Buddhist Yogi. Part One'. *Journal Indian Philosophy* 20: 425–38.

Walter, M. 1996. 'Jabir, The Buddhist Yogi. Part Two: "Winds" and Immortality'. *Journal, Indian Philosophy* 24: 145–64.

Walter, M. L. 2000. 'Cakravartins in Tibet'. Paper for the 9th Seminar of the International Association for Tibetan Studies, 24–30 June 2000, Leiden University.

Walter, M. 2003. 'Jabir, The Buddhist Yogi, Part III: Considerations on an International Yoga of Transformation'. *Lungta* 16: 21–36.

Warder, A. K. 1970. *Indian Buddhism.* Delhi: Motilal Banarsidass.

Wayman, A. 1961. 'Totemic Beliefs in the Buddhist Tantras'. *History of Religions* 1(1): 81–94.

Wayman, A. 1977. *Yoga of the Guhyasamājatantra: The Arcane Lore of Forty Verses. A Buddhist Tantra Commentary.* Delhi: Motilal Banarsidass; New York: Samuel Weiser.

Wayman, A. 1978. *Calming the Mind and Discerning the Real.* New York: Columbia University Press.

Wayman, A. and Tajima, R. 1992. *The Enlightenment of Vairocana.* (Book I. Study of the *Vairocanābhisaṃbodhitantra* by Alex Wayman, Book II. Study of the *Mahāvairocana-Sūtra* by R.Tajima.) Delhi: Motilal Banarsidass.

Weber, M. 1976. *The Protestant Ethic and the Spirit of Capitalism.* Translated by Talcott Parsons. Introduction by A. Giddens. London: Allen and Unwin.

Wedemeyer, C. K. 1999. *Vajrayana and its Doubles: a Critical Historiography, Exposition, and Translation of the Tantric works of Āryadeva.* PhD dissertation, Columbia University.

Wedemeyer, C. K. 2001. 'Tropes, Typologies and Turnarounds: A Brief Genealogy of the Historiography of Tantric Buddhism'. *History of Religions* 40: 223–59.

Wedemeyer, C. K. 2002. 'Antinomianism and Gradualism: The Contextualization of the Practices of Sensual Enjoyment (*Caryā*) in the Guhyasamāja Arya Tradition'. *Indian International Journal of Buddhist Studies* 3: 181–95.

Wedemeyer, C. K. 2006. 'Visions and Treasures: Jo-nang Tāranātha and the Historiography of the Nāgārjunian Tantric Corpus'. Paper for the XIth Seminar of the International Association for Tibetan Studies, Königswinter, August 2006.

Wedemeyer, C. K. in press. *Āryadeva's Lamp that Integrates the Practices (Caryāmelāpakapradīpa): The Gradual Path of Vajrayāna Buddhism according to the Esoteric Communion Noble Tradition.* New York: Columbia University Press.

Weinstein, S. 1987. *Buddhism under the T'ang.* Cambridge University Press.

Werner, K. 1989. 'The Longhaired Sage of RV 10,136: A Shaman, a Mystic or a Yogi?', in *The Yogi and the Mystic. Studies in Indian and Comparative Mysticism*, Werner (ed.), pp. 33–53. London: Curzon Press.

Wheatley, P. 1979. 'Urban Genesis in Mainland South East Asia', in Smith and Watson 1979, pp. 288–303.

Wheatley, P. 1983. *Nāgara and Commandery: Origins of the Southeast Asian Urban Traditions.* Chicago, IL: University of Chicago, Dept. of Geography. (Research paper / University of Chicago, Department of Geography; nos. 207–8.)

Whicher, I. 1997. 'Nirodha, Yoga Praxis and the Transformation of the Mind'. *Journal Indian Philosophy* 25: 1–67.

Whicher, I. 1998. *The Integrity of the Yoga Darśana: A Reconsideration of Classical Yoga.* Albany, NY: State University of New York Press.

Whicher, I. 2002. 'The Integration of Spirit (*Puruṣa*) and Matter (*Prakṛti*) in the *Yoga Sūtra*', in Whicher and Carpenter 2002, pp. 51–69.

Whicher, I. 2002–3. 'The World-Affirming and Integrative Dimension of Classical Yoga'. *Cracow Indological Studies* 4–5: 619–36.

Whicher, I. and Carpenter, D. (eds.) 2003. *Yoga: The Indian Tradition.* London and New York: RoutledgeCurzon.

White, D. G. 1986. '*Dakkhiṇa* and *Agnicayana*: An Extended Application of Paul Mus's Typology'. *History of Religions* 26: 188–211.

White, D. G. 1991. *Myths of the Dog-Man.* Chicago and London: University of Chicago Press.

White, D. G. 1996. *The Alchemical Body: Siddha Traditions in Medieval India.* Chicago and London: University of Chicago Press.

White, D. G. 1998. 'Transformations in the Art of Love: Kāmakalā Practices in Hindu Tantric and Kaula Traditions'. *History of Religions* 38(4): 172–98.

White, D. G. 2003. *Kiss of the Yoginī: 'Tantric Sex' In Its South Asian Contexts.* University of Chicago Press.

White, D. G. 2005. 'Review of *Indian Esoteric Buddhism*, by R. M. Davidson'. *Journal International Association of Tibetan Studies* 1: 1–11.

White, D. G. 2006. '"Open" and "Closed" Models of the Human Body in Indian Medical and Yogic Traditions'. *Asian Medicine: Tradition and Modernity* 2: 1–13.

Whitney, W. D. 1905. *Atharva-Veda Saṃhitā Translated with a Critical and Extegetical Commentary.* Cambridge, MA: Harvard University Press.

Wiener, M. J. 1995. *Visible and Invisible Realms: Power, Magic, and Colonial Conquest in Bali.* Chicago and London: University of Chicago Press.

Wijeyewardene, G. 1986. *Place and Emotion in Northern Thai Ritual Behaviour.* Bangkok: Pandora.

Wile, D. 1992. *The Art of the Bed Chamber: Chinese Sexual Yoga.* Albany, NY: State University of New York Press.

Wilke, A. 1996. 'Śaṅkara and the Taming of Wild Goddesses', in Michaels, Vogelsanger and Wilke 1996, pp. 123–78.

Willemen, C. 1982. *The Chinese Hevajratantra.* Leuven: Uitgeverij Peeters. (Rijksuniversiteit te Gent, Orientalia Gandensia, VIII.)

Williams, P. 1989. *Mahāyāna Buddhism: The Doctrinal Foundations.* London and New York: Routledge.

Williams, R. 1966. 'Before Mahāvīra'. *Journal Royal Asiatic Society* 2–6.

Willis, M. 2001. 'Inscriptions from Udayagiri: Locating Dimensions of Devotion, Patronage and Power in the Eleventh Century'. *South Asian Studies* 17: 41–53.

Willis, M. 2004. 'The Archaeology and Politics of Time', in Bakker 2004, pp. 33–58.

Wilson, H. H. 1832. 'Sketch of the Religious Sects of the Hindus' 17: 169–313, *Asiatic Researches* (Calcutta).

Wilson, I. D. 1999. '*Reog* Ponorogo: Spirituality, Sexuality, and Power in a Javanese Performance Tradition'. *Intersections: Gender, History & Culture in the Asian Context* 2 (May 1999). Downloaded from www.sshe.murdoch.edu.au/intersections/issue2_contents.html, 10 Aug. 2001.

Wiltshire, M. 1990. *Ascetic Figures Before and in Early Buddhism.* Berlin and New York: Mouton de Gruyter.

Winn, M. 2006. 'Transforming Sexual Energy with Water-and-Fire Alchemy', in Kohn 2006a, pp. 151–78.

Witzel, M. 1989. 'Tracing the Vedic Dialects', in *Dialectes dans les littératures Indo-aryennes*, Caillat, (ed.), pp. 97–264. Paris: de Boccard.

Witzel, M. 1995a. 'Early Indian History: Linguistic and Textual Parametres [*sic*]', in Erdosy 1995a, pp. 85–125.

Witzel, M. 1995b. 'Ṛgvedic History: Poets, Chieftains and Politics', in Erdosy 1995a. pp. 307–52.

Witzel, M. 1995c. 'Early Sanskritization'. *Electronic Journal of Vedic Studies* 1(4), Dec. 1995, www1.shore.net/~india/ejvs.

Witzel, M. 1997. 'The Development of the Vedic Canon and its Schools: The Social and Political Milieu. (Materials on Vedic Sakhas 8)', in *Inside the Texts, Beyond the Texts: New Approaches to the Study of the Vedas,* Witzel (ed.), pp. 257–345. Cambridge, MA: Department of Sanskrit and Indian Studies, Harvard University. (Harvard Oriental Series. Opera Minora, vol. 2.)

Witzel, M. 2001. 'Autochthonous Aryans?: The Evidence from Old Indian and Iranian Texts'. *Electronic Journal of Vedic Studies* 7(3): 1–118.

Witzel, M. 2003. 'Vedas and Upaniṣads', in Flood 2003, pp. 68–101.

Witzel, M. 2005. 'Indocentrism: Autochthonous Visions of Ancient India'. In Bryant and Patton 2005, pp. 341–404.

Wojtilla, G. 1984. 'Notes on Popular Śaivism and Tantra in Eleventh Century Kashmir (A Study on Kṣemendra's *Samayamātṛkā*)', in *Tibetan and Buddhist Studies Commemorating the 200th Anniversary of the Birth of Alexander Csoma de Körös*, Ligeti (ed.), vol. 2, pp. 381–9. Budapest: Akadémiai Kiadó.

Wojtilla, G. 1990. 'Vaśīkaraṇa Texts in Sanskrit Kāmaśāstra Literature', in *The Sanskrit Tradition and Tantrism* (Panels of the 7th World Sanskrit Conference,

Kern Institute, Leiden: Augustus 23–29, 1987, vol. 1.), Goudriaan (ed.), pp. 109–16. Leiden: E. J. Brill.

Wolters, O. W. 1979. 'Khmer "Hinduism" in the Seventh Century', in Smith and Watson 1979, pp. 427–42.

Woodroffe, Sir J. 1974. *The Serpent Power: Being the Ṣat-Cakra-Nirūpana and Pādukā-Pañcaka. Two Works on Laya-Yoga, Translated from the Sanskrit, with Introduction and Commentary by Arthur Avalon (Sir John Woodroffe).* New York: Dover.

Wright, J. C. 1966. *Non-Classical Sanskrit Literature: An Inaugural Lecture Delivered on 24 Nov. 1965 by J. Clifford Wright, Professor of Sanskrit in the University of London.* London: University of London, School of Oriental and African Studies.

Wujastyk, D. 1997. 'Medical Demonology in the Kāśyapasaṃhitā'. Unpublished MS.

Wujastyk, D. 1999. 'Miscarriages of Justice: Demonic Vengeance in Classical Indian Medicine', in *Religion, Health and Suffering*, Hinnells and Porter (eds.), pp. 256–75. London and New York: Kegan Paul International.

Yamamoto, C. 1990. *Mahāvairocana-sūtra Translated into English from Ta-p'i-lu-che-na ch'eng-fo shen-pien chai-ch'ih ching, the Chinese version of Śubhākarasiṃha and I-hsing (A.D. 725).* New Delhi: International Academy of Indian Culture and Aditya Prakashan. (Śata-Piṭaka Series, 359.)

Yamasaki, T. 1988. *Shingon: Japanese Esoteric Buddhism.* Boston and London: Shambhala.

Yokochi, Y. 1999. 'The Warrior Goddess in the *Devīmāhātmya*', in *Living with* Śakti: *Gender, Sexuality and Religion in South Asia,* Tanaka and Tachikawa (eds.), pp. 71–113. Osaka: National Museum of Ethnology. (Senri Ethnological Studies, 50.)

Yokochi, Y. 2004. *The Rise of the Warrior Goddess in Ancient India: A Study of the Myth Cycle of Kauśikī-Vindhyavāsinī in the* Skandapurāṇa'. PhD dissertation, University of Groningen. Available on-line at dissertations.ub.rug.nl/faculties/theology/2005/y.yokochi/ (downloaded 2 October 2005).

Yuthok, L. Choedak Thubten 1990. *A Study on the Origin of Lam 'Bras Tradition in India between 630–940 A.D.* B.Litt. thesis, Faculty of Asian Studies, Australian National University.

Yuthok, L. Choedak Thubten 1997. *The Triple Tantra by Panchen Ngawang Choedak.* Translated and annotated by Lama Choedak Yuthok. Canberra: Gorum Publications.

Zanen, S. M. 1986. 'The Goddess Vajrayoginī and the Kingdom of Sankhu'. *Puruṣārtha* 10: 125–66. (*L'Espace du Temple II*, ed. J-C Galey).

Zigmund-Cerbu, A. 1963. 'The Ṣaḍaṅgayoga'. *History of Religions* 3: 128–34.

Zvelebil, K. V. 1973. *The Poets of the Powers.* London: Rider and Co.

Zvelebil, K. V. 1988. *The Irulas of the Blue Mountains.* Syracuse, NY: Maxwell School of Citizenship and Public Affairs, Syracuse University.

Zvelebil, K. V. 1991. *Tamil Traditions on Subrahmaṇya-Murugan*. Madras: Institute of Asian Studies.
Zvelebil, K. V. 1992. *Companion Studies to the History of Tamil Literature*. Leiden: Brill. (Handbuch der Orientalistik. 2. Abt., Indien. Ergänzungsband; 5.)
Zvelebil, K. V. 2001. *Hippalos*. Oxford: Mandrake.
Zvelebil, K. V. 1996. *The Siddha Quest for Immortality*. Oxford: Mandrake.
Zydenbos, R. J. 1992. 'The Jaina Goddess Padmavati', in *Contacts Between Cultures: South Asia vol. 2*, Koppedrayer (ed.), pp. 257–92. Lewiston, Queenston and Lampeter: Edwin Mellon Press.

Index

Printed in Great Britain
by Amazon

45925793R00258